FOODSERVICE PLANNING: LAYOUT AND EQUIPMENT

FOODSERVICE PLANNING:
layout and equipment 2nd Edition

Lendal H. Kotschevar

Professor, Hotel Administration,
University of Nevada, Las Vegas

Margaret E. Terrell

Professor Emeritus,
Institution Management,
University of Washington, Seattle

John Wiley & Sons, New York · Santa Barbara · London · Sydney · Toronto

Library of Congress Cataloging in Publication Data:

Kotschevar, Lendal Henry, 1908-
  Foodservice planning.

  Bibliography: p.
  Includes index.
  1. Food service management. 2. Food service—
Equipment and supplies. I. Terrell, Margaret E.,
joint author. II. Title.

TX943.K65   1977   647'.95   76-28763
ISBN 0-471-50491-2

Printed in the United States of America

10 9 8 7 6 5 4 3

Preface

Service of away-from-home meals constitutes one of America's major industries. Although the dollar volume for facilities and operations is large, the health and satisfaction factors make an even greater impact on life in the nation. Schools, hospitals, commerce, and industry make widely varied demands for foodservice. The production of palatable food, the provision of fast service, and the maintenance of a business operation that has satisfactory percentages for food, labor, and other operating expenses will be closely correlated with facilities provided for operation. The choice of equipment and its layout may be judged as satisfactory to the extent of the support of good standards and the promotion of approved methods of operation.

Planning foodservice facilities requires a familiarity with specific needs, a knowledge of standards acceptable to the clientele, and a keen awareness of suitable methods of operation and available resources. Persons responsible for planning must be well-informed and sharply analytical. The numerous aspects to be considered tend to cause confusion. These aspects include increased volume and specific demands of persons to be served, tight margins in utilization of available funds, multiplicity of food and equipment items on the market, and new modes of operation under experimentation. Planners must be wary of untried new schemes and equipment that does not give assurance of providing requisite values.

Several areas of expertness or specialized knowledge are needed in food facility planning. An administrator, who represents ownership, helps to establish goals and cost limitations. The architect guides design based on structural and engineering principles. He or the builder may be a source of information about building costs and standards to guide formulation of plans and specifications, and should see that approved plans are carried to completion. A food manager or a well-informed foodservice consultant is needed for essential information related to food needs and operational requirements. The individual who is to direct operations when the facility is completed should know and approve the plan of operation for which the facility is being specifically designed. Full, effective, and accurate communication between members of the planning committee is essential for success.

Careful studies should be made preliminary to planning. Early establishment of priorities will help to guide and unify the efforts of the planners. Market studies may be made to establish specific needs and locality helps and handicaps. Much value may be gained by observing experiences and procedures in similar food facilities. Modern science has brought many changes to the food field. Equipment changes are continually being made by manufacturers to meet user requirements. Scientific studies have been made to define elements of jobs, characteristics of workers, and requisite conditions for work efficiency. Skillful work planning can help to insure production of marketable products and meet concerns for utilization of labor time, which costs 5 to 15 cents per minute, and for the conservation of scarce fuel energy.

There are many varied systems for operating food establishments; they range from processing food from its raw state to completion of preparation for service to purchase and service of fully prepared meals. At some stage, food requires processing, whether in a commercial factory, a commissary kitchen, or in the specific service facility. Therefore, this book is directed toward full production requirements and discusses how to use the fully or partially prepared foods in service facilities of various types.

This book calls attention to certain significant points in planning. Selection of information was made with recognition of the fact that each topic treated merits an entire volume, and that the space in one book is too limited for complete discussion. The material chosen will be a guide to significant aspects and provide useful information for persons concerned with food facility planning. It will also stimulate further study in this field.

A foodservice unit, no matter how well planned, cannot be successful unless the organization of work done in the facility after it is constructed is related closely to plans on which the design was based. Little will be accomplished by the best efforts of the planning team unless those who operate the facility are aware of the aims and ideas on which planning was based and are sympathetic with them and competent to utilize them. This book is written, therefore, not only for those actively engaged in study or planning of food facility layouts, such as architects and students of architecture, educators, and students in foodservice management, equipment manufacturers and dealers, planners of food facilities and consultants, but also for dietitians and other food managers who will be responsible for operating facilities.

Lendal H. Kotschevar
Margaret E. Terrell

Contents

SECTION 3 SUPPORTING FACTORS AND PHYSICAL CONDITIONS

SECTION 4 EQUIPMENT SELECTION

List of Tables

List of Illustrations

Section   1
planning

Chapter 1

preparation for planning

Preliminary Decisions

A food facility is a complex organization performing highly specialized functions in the manufacture, sale, and service of food. The choice of equipment, the layout, and the physical factors supporting these functions directly influence the success with which the facility will operate. An orderly and logical study of essential functions and the development of facilities to promote their accomplishment with maximum efficiency and high standards forms the basis for layout engineering. The needs, resources, and characteristics of a specific situation govern functions to be performed. The essential functions, in turn, will influence the flow or sequence of operations, the equipment needed, and the space requirements. When the flow of work, the equipment, and space plus the physical factors are combined, the layout is largely determined.

The initial decisions, which serve as a basis for food facility planning, originate with ownership or a person representing authority. One of the first decisions is stimulated by awareness of the kind and extent of need for a food facility (as a desirable service and/or as a remunerative investment). Next, possibilities for financing are explored, both in terms of adequate funds for building and probable income sufficient to support a suitable budget of operation. Consideration then is given to the availability of adequate space and a desirable location. Information on such matters as these will indicate the advisability of going forward with plans.

Persons in authority are rarely informed in all the areas of specialization involved in designing, building, and operating a food facility. As soon as a decision has been reached to build, it is beneficial to choose a planning team of persons well informed in the specialized fields. It would be the function of each member of the team to submit information and recommendations for approval as needed from his or her respective field as planning progresses. Differences in background and viewpoint of the team members often call for certain tempering of ideas. A food manager, for example, may suggest an impractical idea judged from a construction standpoint, or a certain design by the architect may interfere with the best work flow or convenience. It is good to have more than one viewpoint presented.

Stages in Planning

A plan for a food facility usually develops in two stages. The first is conceptual. No *actual* plan results. Instead, the basic factors and data needed to develop the plan are identified. In this period estimates may be broad, and general rules of thumb may be used to estimate costs, space requirements, and other factors. For instance, there are standard cubic space requirements for refrigerator and freezer space per meal served. These are helpful in developing early concepts of needs but may lead to bad results if used for the actual plan. At this stage of the plan a feasibility or market study is needed. This involves gathering necessary data pertaining to site selection, consideration of codes and building regulations, financing, menus to be used, mode of operation, staff requirements, projected budget of operation, basic needs, and so forth. Contained in such a study should be all of the information needed to build a workable plan.

The second stage in planning develops from the first, growing naturally into an actual physical plan, with lists of equipment and specifications. The success of the plan is likely to depend upon how well the first part has been done. Requirements detailed in the first part will dictate what is to be done in the second part. The size and type of equipment, its placement, the flow of work, and actual physical requirements will be decided in this second part. While the first part developed broad concepts of needs, the second part must define needs based on precise and known requirements. For instance, while a broad estimate of refrigerator and freezer space needs was indicated in the conceptual planning, the actual amount required must now be calculated. The calculations are to be based on actual amounts of food to be stored in the units to meet menu and volume requirements for the numbers to be served. An allowance of 1.12 sq meters or 12 sq ft per person may be made in the dining area, and when tables and chairs are set into the plan, the estimate may or may not be found to be an acceptable allowance.

Basic Concepts

It is highly desirable to identify goals and determine policies at the outset of planning a food facility. These will guide planning activities, prevent errors and time loss, and help to ensure desired results. Goals are interpreted here to mean the general overall criteria set for proper performance of the required functions. For example, the goals for a specific hospital foodservice might be defined as suitable meals of safe, nutritious food of good quality served to patients, staff, and guests within specific schedule, manner, and cost constraints.

Policies govern modes, methods, and conditions for reaching specified goals. They are the road map that leads to goals and should point out acceptable standards and services to meet needs in a specific situation. Needs differ and standards vary. There are special expediencies that apply to a particular time, place, and situation that may deserve consideration. Statements of policy should be formulated to cover all aspects subject to variation, where significant choice of action or selection is to be made. Well-formulated and generally understood policies can do much toward unifying the efforts of a planning group.

Persons in authority are expected to enunciate and approve policies. This may or may not mean that those persons originate policies pertaining to every detail involved. Responsibility for policies rests with each individual who has accepted responsibility for a share in planning as it relates to that person's specific area of activity. This individual is in the position either to propose a policy for approval or to accept an approved policy to govern the action.

Goals should evolve from a clear and comprehensive analysis of needs and circumstances. Often it is necessary to search for basic motives behind stated views and ideas. A member of the medical staff views the role of the foodservice department much differently than does the food production manager. There should be an open-minded appreciation for different viewpoints as they relate to goals. The best plans frequently evolve through compromise. Goals should be realistic and pointed toward the highest standard of quality and performance possible in a given situation. Goals are usually expressed in general terms by those in authority and relate to four aspects of the operation. It is commonly desired that a food facility will do the following:

1. Meet the food needs of persons to be served with food that is adequate, appealing, safe, nutritious, and healthful.

2. Function with a consistently high standard of performance promoting efficient utilization of labor and equipment in clean, safe, attractive surroundings.

3. Function on a basis that is economically sound and within the design that can be created and function on the funds that will be available.

4. Cause a minimum of work and time expenditure on the part of persons who should not be directly involved in the operation, such as ownership or the administration, who should not be bothered by worker problems, supply shortages, or service complaints.

It is important to concentrate on the most significant goals and the selection of the best ways to satisfy them. It may mean devising new ways of doing work, utilizing equipment, or using new types of foods. The most important goal in one situation may be service of superior quality regardless of cost. In another, it may be preferable to serve food of acceptable, simple quality at a minimum price. Policies relating to such matters must be made for the specific organization according to its requirements.

In the early stage of planning, it is best to disregard minor obstacles and to review broadly several ways of producing desired standards. If adjustment of plans appears to be advisable due to factors having high priority, such as structural features or money limitations, careful analysis of other ways of securing desired results is recommended. Often, when an "ideal situation" can be shown to have significant value, a way to attain it is discovered. Finding a best method may mean changing a menu pattern instead of making an equipment investment. Another approach may call for the elimination of a wall to reduce steps, increase speed, or improve supervision. The Gilbreths said, "There's always a better way," and it is sometimes to be found in the little, easily overlooked areas or items that may be big time savers or quality protectors. Careful study may help to reveal these. It is wise to tabulate all alternatives and consider each. Otherwise a much better, but less obvious, way of accomplishing things may be overlooked. Goals are rarely reorganized, but policies are sometimes changed to accomplish goals in a slightly different way.

Statements of policy are needed before planning begins and as it proceeds in order to guide the planning activity adequately. Policies should indicate

1. Individuals who are to share in planning the facility, the contribution expected from each, and the extent of each one's authority.

2. A time schedule for presentation of various phases to be considered.

3. Nature and size of the facility to be planned in terms of
    a. service to be provided,
    b. number to be served,
    c. characteristics of persons to be served (age, health, activity, income, and so forth),
    d. type of service (cafeteria, table service, tray service, or other),
    e. method of operation (purchasing and storage system, amount of production, organization of service, and so on),
    f. working personnel characteristics required (men or women, large or small stature, young or more mature, skilled or unskilled, trained or untrained, and so forth),
    g. allowance for growth or eventual change, and
    h. cost restraints.

The Planning Team

Specialized knowledge is required for the successful planning of a food facility. It is rare, perhaps impossible, to find one person with all of the knowledge necessary. Normally, representatives of four areas of knowledge will be required: (1) ownership or administration, (2) operation, (3) architecture and engineering, and (4) building.

The first member of the team is the person in authority. He or she is likely to have a realistic view of the situation as applied to specific needs, desired benefits, and resources. This person's background may not be in foodservice, and his or her understanding of the requirements of a large food operation may be very limited. This important member may view the operation of food service as being as simple as preparing instant coffee in a home kitchen, or at the other extreme, he or she may overly fear it due to its normally complicated functions. Either viewpoint can prevent wise planning. It is to be remembered, however, that this person representing ownership has the authority for decision-making, and plans will not materialize without his or her approval. It is important that essential data be presented to the decision-maker accurately, completely, in an understandable form, and in time to guide judgment.

The need for the facility, its type, and its characteristics are usually stated by the owner or administrator. Thus a superintendent of a hospital or a board of governors may see the need for a new wing of a hospital and with it an enlargement of the food service facilities. Or a college president may see the need for a new dormitory. A hotel manager may become aware of the need for added banquet facilities to take care of convention trade. Means of financing the venture will be explored with other interested persons with whom he must act or by whom he is guided. Basic information such as that incorporated in a feasibility study may be compiled and analyzed. It is probable that the size and type of the operation will be fixed, and the location and general character of the facility will be determined.

Financial aspects confronted by ownership are many and varied. Members of the planning team can supply significant information from their special areas on which many of the decisions can be based. Factors relating to probable patronage, income, and operating costs need to be known early. A reasonable, workable budget should be projected for operation. If building funds are to be recovered through amortization, careful estimates will be required for obtainable rates of interest, probable income, and operating costs. Wise judgment is needed to identify significant services the facility should provide, important principles to be followed in the organization of work, and the facility's functioning as a business concern.

It is desirable that the person who is to direct food preparation and service when the facility is completed be a member of the planning team or be kept closely informed of decisions as planning proceeds. If the one who is to operate the facility is inexperienced, it may be wise to employ an experienced consultant who is well informed in food management. Many food service operators know how to operate a foodservice very well, but they may lack the ability to plan one. Participation of the food manager in planning discussions will give an opportunity for expression of personal views and the clarification of ideas. The success of the operation when the facility is completed will depend to a large degree on this person's understanding and acceptance of the intended organization of work and skill in carrying it out. It is frequently helpful to have the architect work closely with the operator after the facility is opened so that he can assist operation in utilizing the facility as it was planned.

The viewpoint of an architect obviously is important. It is the architect who interprets the views and ideas of management and of operation and translates these into a physical plan, even though other team members may assist in drawings and so forth whenever it can help to make their ideas clearer. The architect provides guidance on architectural and engineering principles, guides selection of designs and materials, prepares plans and specifications for structures, and supervises construction. Estimates of construction costs are made. After the plans have been completed, the architect will present them and the specifications for bidding and contracting following final approval by ownership. After the contracts are awarded, the architect supervises construction, issues certificates of insurance, and notarizes affidavits and waivers of lien. An architect often contributes valuable suggestions on financial arrangements, legal aspects, and operational points that have been gleaned from experience and knowledgeable observations.

The fourth member of the team is the builder. His part in planning may be very minor in many instances, but his viewpoint is helpful in indicating desirable building materials, construction features, timing of contract awards, and so forth. Normally, the job of the builder is to take the plan and specifications of the architect and put up the physical structure, which is not a part of planning but is the actual accomplishment of the plan. Nevertheless there is a bridge in this instance between the planning group and the fulfillment of the plan, and the builder frequently can play some small, but quite important, part in planning.

In the organization of any planning team, which will no doubt be established by ownership, ample consideration should be given to the use of all four viewpoints. The elimination of any of them is likely to be hazardous in terms of unnecessary costs and an unsatisfactory operation.

Communication

Varied background, experience, and points of interest tend to complicate communication between members of a planning team and those who are to share in the realization and operation of the food facility. Words tend to have different meanings for different members of the team and may have still other significance for other persons associated with the project. Forms of communication are needed that will convey ideas precisely. The two forms commonly used for expressing approved requirements are technical drawings and written specifications. Discussions and pictures are utilized to clarify ideas and to present arguments for or against them, while helping people to visualize the plans. It is important for technical drawings to have a high degree of accuracy in measurements and design. Specifications or word descriptions of materials, conditions, and/or procedures need to be sufficiently precise to prevent misunderstanding.

There are many vague phrases in common use that allow for wide interpretation. Familiar in the food industry are "good food," "adequate amount," and "fast service." The speaker is likely to have a definite picture in mind drawn from a specific experience. The listener will immediately picture the meaning in terms of his experience, which may be drawn from an entirely different background and set of standards. A little thoughtful effort in expressing thoughts precisely can help in pinpointing significant aspects. "Adequate amount" may vary widely depending upon the persons to be served, but it may become definite when stated in weight or volume per portion or for a given number of portions. "Fast service" is a more definite phrase when it is tied to an exact schedule or number served per minute or with limitation of the time lapse from pan to patron.

Good progress in planning springs from a keen awareness of need and a detailed analysis of ways to solve problems. Many standards, particularly those affected by layout designs and specifications, are mathematically measurable. Equipment and layout can be equated to needs and expressed in deck number and size, container capacity, and speed of output. Food goodness, in addition to materials utilized and techniques of preparation, calls for definite handling methods and limitation of time between preparation of the food and its presentation to the customer. Supplying volume requirements depends upon batch capacity and speed of output. Protection of palatability involves holding conditions and limits the size of delivery equipment so that the first plates or trays of food are not held and allowed to deteriorate while others are being prepared. Travel distance and mode of travel call for control to shorten time between preparation, dish-up, and presentation to the customer. The plan that evolves should meet these and other significant requirements.

It is the privilege and practice of the team member representing ownership to express goals in general terms. There may be requests for attractive surroundings, appropriate service, adequate portions, appealing food, and sound business practices. Specific policies in precise terms that will promote common understanding must evolve from these goals. They should be translated into precise terms by the team member most qualified to do it, and approval should be secured as the work of the planning team progresses and as the desirable aspects and hazards come to light. Precision of expression tends to be difficult for the novice, but it is an ability worth developing by those who must convey ideas accurately for understanding and action by others.

In seeking precision of expression one is forced to analyze characteristics that exactly identify an item or an idea. Such analysis helps to arouse awareness of characteristics essential for satisfaction. An analysis of "clean" will indicate the need to identify numerous factors pertaining not only to the product but also to the facilities. For example, all work surfaces will need to be smooth, easily cleaned, nonabsorbent, and free from lodging spots for soil. They will need to be sufficiently durable to permit frequent and vigorous cleaning. Thorough cleanliness will call for food machines that can be taken apart and reassembled easily and quickly. Hand-washing facilities must be convenient to work areas. Suitable cleaning arrangements will be required for the workshop and its equipment.

When writing specifications it is necessary to identify every significant characteristic or condition where choice is afforded. This will include such things as material, design, size, and special operating conditions such as water or power voltage and cycle. The complexity of specifications varies with the amount and type of identification required. Descriptions of manufactured items are simplified when a catalog description is available for reference. On manufactured items, information is needed as to size, model, source of power or heat, material, workmanship, and any other appurtenances or factors desired. Manufacturers usually supply specification sheets for fabricated items for equipment chosen from their company.

Equipment to be fabricated or custom built, where models are not available for examination, requires specifications made in greater detail. Construction details are needed as well as size, material, design, and function. Detail drawings are useful for specification as well as for shop drawings to guide construction. An architect's or engineer's assistance is likely to be required. The food manager or operator member of the team should work closely with the architect or engineer on the design and approve it when it is completed. Certain equipment fabricators provide detail drawings of equipment for use by buyers. They are drawn on plastic transparencies that will adhere to other drawings for printing. Where accepted, they can be readily made a part of the architect's drawings (see Figure 1.1).

The architect must have items identified and the size of the equipment given by the person who selects it, plus space relationships for a good flow of work. Satisfactory progress in planning calls for promptness as well as precision of communication. The team member representing operation should list all items of equipment to be used. It is best to separate the list into major equipment, which consists of all items to be shown on drawings, and minor equipment, needed but not shown on drawings, such as pots, pans, and small tools. Specifications that are sufficiently clear and adequate to ensure receipt of the desired item should be given for each listed item. The specifications will be needed not only by the architect but also for full and accurate understanding by bidders.

Communication among team members should be clear, dependable, and frequent enough to promote suitable speed in the progress of planning. Each should be able to understand customary modes of expression, such as those used in technical drawings and specifications. There are many symbols that have specific meaning, and all members of the team should understand their meaning. If a team member does not know this language and how to interpret scale, drawing perspective, details of construction, and how a series of plans fit together, such as the plumbing plan and electrical plan, reference should be made to sources of such information.[1] Designs of layouts, carefully drawn to scale, are useful in conveying ideas and for study of equipment placement for specific flow of work and space relationships. The operation team member should be able to try various schemes before reaching a decision as to the best one to recommend. A busy architect should not be expected to respond with a new drawing for each change of mind by an operator.

The operation team member's sketch should be accurate, neat, legible, and drawn to scale. Lack of accuracy can lead to allowing too much or too little space. Each square meter spells expense to build and maintain and for labor. Inadequate space will handicap work progress and good standards. The neatness of a sketch promotes respect for the ideas presented. It is customary for the architect to supply a blueprint of the proposed space in a specified scale, such as a $\frac{1}{4}$-in. or 6-millimeter scale, which means $\frac{1}{4}$ in. (6 mm) on the drawing equals 1 ft (305 mm) in the actual building, for use by the operation or other team members.

---

[1] For instance, consult a beginning draftsman's handbook. The three volumes of Elwyn E. Seelye, *Design*, 3rd ed., John Wiley, New York, 1960, will be helpful in explaining construction details.

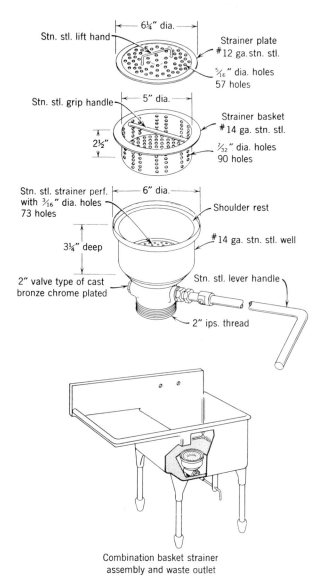

Stn. stl. lift hand

Strainer plate
#12 ga. stn. stl.

6¼" dia.

5⁄16" dia. holes
57 holes

Stn. stl. grip handle

5" dia.

Strainer basket
#14 ga. stn. stl.

2½"

7⁄32" dia. holes
90 holes

Stn. stl. strainer perf.
with 3⁄16" dia. holes
73 holes

6" dia.

Shoulder rest

3¼" deep

#14 ga. stn. stl. well

2" valve type of cast
bronze chrome plated

Stn. stl. lever handle

2" ips. thread

Combination basket strainer
assembly and waste outlet

Figure 1.1 Drawings such as these are made on plastic transparencies for transfer to sheet of drawings for blueprinting. (*Courtesy S. Blickman, Inc., Weehkawken. N. J.*)

The use of graph paper that has ¼-in. (6-mm) squares is sometimes convenient for preliminary sketches.

The operation team member with a limited knowledge of drafting will find the following equipment useful for promoting convenience and accuracy:

1. Drafting table or board that can be positioned for good posture and free, easy motion when drawing. The "working edge" must be true and straight.

2. T-square, preferably with a transparent edge.

3. 45° triangle with a 8-in. (203-mm) side and a 30° × 60° triangle with a 10-in. (254-mm) side. (Test for accuracy; these are subject to warping.)

4. Architect's scale rule. (A flat 6-in. (152-mm) rule is popular.)

5. Circle and lettering templets.

6. Drawing pencils: 4H for line drawings, 3H for sketching and lettering, and 2H for tracings to be blueprinted.

7. Sharpener and sandpaper pad for sharpening pencils.

8. Pencil eraser and art gum for cleaning and erasing.

9. Drawing paper that is tough, fine grained, and hard surfaced.

10. Draftsman's tape (preferably) or thumb tacks to fasten the drawing paper to the board.

Templets are available in various forms and sizes to assist in preparation of plans. Those who have difficulty in lettering neatly can obtain lettering templets in various sizes. Care should be taken to space letters and words so as to present a pleasing appearance and easy readability.

Equipment templets, made on lightweight cardboard and set to appropriate scale, are useful for moving about on a plan when trying out various arrangements. These templets may be made by a designer, or an individual can cut them from a discarded drawing in the same scale or draw them personally and cut them out. The small templets may be fastened to the plan with circular folds of tape. Some manufacturers of equipment have templets in quarter-inch or 6-mm scale for their equipment, as shown in Figures 1.2, 1.3, and 1.4.

It is advisable that some practice be gained in making drawings so that those made for presentation will be of a good standard. It is recommended that students studying food equipment planning be given instruction in identifying symbols and other features on drawings and in using the proper techniques in handling tools and making satisfactory drawings.

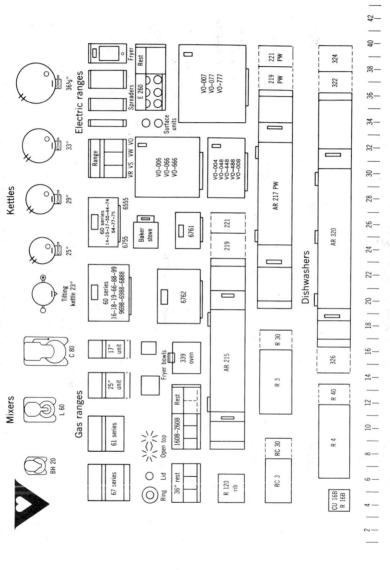

Figure 1.2 A manufacturer's equipment template printed on lightweight cardboard. (*Courtesy Vulcan-Hart Corp., Louisville, Ky.*)

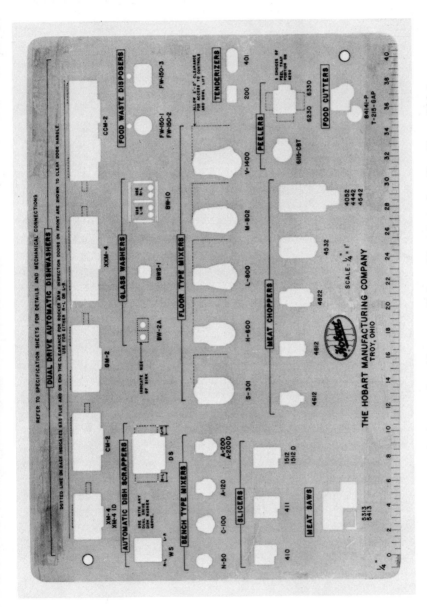

Figure 1.3 Perforated plastic templet. (*Courtesy Hobart Manufacturing Co., Troy, Ohio.*)

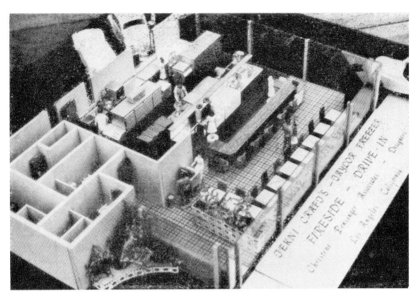

Figure 1.4 Three-dimensional model templets showing actual working conditions, in quarter-inch scale. (*Courtesy Christine Pensinger Associates, Los Angeles.*)

Metric measurements may cause some confusion for many years after the metric system has been generally adopted due to deeply entrenched habits of using the North American System of measurement. It is important to know terms, abbreviations, and rules of conversion to avoid errors. The four metric measurements that will be used most commonly in connection with foodservice planning are those which describe physical quantity, that is, length—expressed in meters instead of inches and feet; weight and mass—in grams instead of ounces and pounds; volume or capacity—in liters in place of pints, quarts, and gallons; and temperature—in degrees Celcius rather than Fahrenheit. The multiples and submultiples of meters, grams, and liters are indicated by prefixes (see Tables 1.1 and 1.2).

Research and Analysis

The importance of designing a facility that will function successfully and the expense involved emphasizes the need to explore sources of valuable information and to study, test, and evaluate ideas. Early investigation or market study should include a careful analysis of needs, tastes, and habits of individuals to be served, their probable number, plus

Table 1.1   Prefixes to Metric Measures*

Multiples and Submultiples	Prefixes	Symbols	Significance
10^6	mega	M	increase a million times
10^3	kilo	k	increase a thousand times
10^2	hecto	h	increase a hundred times
10	deka	da	ten
10^{-1}	deci	d	one tenth of
10^{-2}	centi	c	one hundredth of
10^{-3}	milli	m	one thousandth of
10^{-6}	micro	μ	one millionth of

* Adapted from Thomas Gilbert and Marilyn B. Gilbert, *Thinking Metric,* John Wiley, New York, 1973, and L. J. Chisholm, *Units of Weight and Measure, International (Metric) and U. S. Customary,* National Bureau of Standards, U. S. Government Printing Office, Washington, D. C. 20402.

amount and source of income. The likelihood of acceptance of a given type and amount of service and any promoting or detracting factors relevant to the success of the venture should be weighed.

When the decision has been reached to go forward in planning the facility, other well-informed persons may be asked for information by the planning team. The architect, who must give general estimates of space needs and probable costs, may seek outside advice. Both the architect's and operator's knowledge can be helpful in a feasibility study. It is important that the collection of data begin early. A suggested outline for one type of feasibility study appears in the Appendix. It is important to adapt any outline to meet the specific needs of the individual facility.

Selection of site is important even for nonprofit-oriented food facilities. It often is critical to the success of profit-oriented operations. Site selection can be computerized, and many restaurant and other operators collect specific data significant to selection and feed it into a computer programed to do site selection and evaluation. The Oklahoma Restaurant Association in Oklahoma City has found that its computer program on site selection has proven succeessful in indicating favorable sites. Other programs also are available.

Every source that can yield useful ideas for details in planning should be explored. Visits to other establishments may indicate how others per-

Table 1.2 Conversion Factors for Measurements Commonly Used in Food Facility Planning*

Physical Quantity	From	To	Multiply By
Length of area	inch	centimeter (cm)	2.54
	inch	meter (m)	0.025 4
	square inch	square centimeter (cm²)	6.451 6
	foot	centimeter (cm)	30.48
	foot	meter (m)	0.304 8
	square feet	square meters (m²)	0.092 903 04
	yards	meters (m)	0.914 4
	square yards	square meters (m²)	0.836 127 36
	miles	meters (m)	1 609.344
	miles	kilometers (km)	1.609 344
Weight and mass	ounce (avoirdupois)	grams (g)	28.349 523
	ounce (avoirdupois)	kilogram (kg)	0.028 349 523
	pounds (avoirdupois)	grams (g)	453.592 37
	pounds (troy)	grams (g)	373.241 721 6
Volume or capacity	cup (liquid)	milliliters (ml)	236.588 236 8
	pint (liquid)	liter (l)	0.473 176 473
	quart (liquid)	liter (l)	0.946 352 946
	pint (dry)	liter (l)	0.550 610 47
	quart (dry)	liter (l)	1.101 221
	quart (dry)	dekaliter (dal)	0.110 122 1
	gallons (liquid)	liters (l)	3.785 411 784

Temperature

Convert Fahrenheit to Celsius (centigrade) by subtracting 32, multiplying by 5, and dividing by 9. To change Celsius to Fahrenheit multiply by 9, divide by 5, and add 32.

* Adapted from Thomas Gilbert and Marilyn B. Gilbert, *Thinking Metric*, John Wiley, New York, 1973, and L. J. Chrisholm, *Units of Weight and Measure, International (Metric) and U. S. Customary*, National Bureau of Standards, U. S. Government Printing Office, Washington, D. C. 20402.

Figure 1.5 Some companies have models of equipment to help planners visualize and study equipment layout. (*Courtesy Market Forge, Everett, Mass.*)

form. Sometimes a single detail can prove valuable. Products and their quality and availability on the market should be studied to indicate how materials may be used differently. Trips to equipment dealers and/or manufacturers can also be helpful in indicating costs, items available, specifications, and the names of users of specific models. The opinions of those who have used various pieces of equipment, systems, or designs in layout are valuable. Brief, easy-to-fill-out questionnaires sent to food-service operators on significant points of operation or equipment can yield excellent information. Useful time can be spent in the library studying current institution foodservice books and magazines.

Reasonably complete notes should be taken on visits or during study. Keep the notes organized as to subject matter so that specific information can be readily found. Date and state source of information. Expect the information to fill a large-size notebook. Organize notes so that they can be filed in the notebook or file case according to the classification of the information. One section, for example, might be labeled "Planning Guides" and contain statements of policy and methods that specifically apply. The major part of the notebook might be divided into classifications relating to sections of the facility, such as receiving, storage, and cooking. Under each classification would be filed information relating to standards, space needs, flow of work, ideas for layout, and equipment. Equipment information might include specification sheets for different makes of items to be used.

Studies tend to be most fruitful when information is sought in answer to specific questions. For example, when a facility is being planned for a particular group of people, it is best to know facts about them that relate to the satisfaction of the purpose and success of the venture. What are their tastes, needs, buying power, and probable reaction to the proposed service? Are there social or psychological factors that will influence patronage? Current living conditions and changing social customs tend to affect eating habits, and these should be reviewed to ascertain if they are influential in the particular instance. Today Americans are restless, impatient, and mobile. A large percentage of women work outside the home, children eat lunch and sometimes breakfast at school, and many men and women dine in or near their industrial plant. Families often dine out as a group. Fast, informal, inexpensive service is popular. Prices paid for lunch are influenced by budgeted daily allowances. Adequate parking is required for the motor trade. The omission of one consideration or one detail may result in an inadequate plan.

The pleasure value of food makes mealtime ideal for entertaining. Many public restaurants plan entertainment quality into their menus and decor. Dramatic quality in food, surroundings, and service add enjoyment and reduce the humdrum aspect of everyday living. Culinary artsts win acclaim by making food not only delectably good but also artistically appealing. Many patrons who relish plain and simple food for daily fare want it to be more imaginative and dramatic for special occasions. Food is used to add drama and special significance to teas, weddings, receptions, professional meetings, and holiday celebrations. The ability to provide special service for a clientele can be facilitated through thoughtful and thorough initial planning.

When the type of establishment has been determined, a careful study should be made of institutions of comparable type. Every aspect, open to observation, that may influence success or failure should be noted. Organize data to preserve significant points and avoid confusion as to their relevancy and importance. Notes on visits are likely to be most accurate and complete if made "on the spot," if courtesy permits, or immediately

following the visit. The following is a suggested outline for gleaning
pertinent information:

Name and address of the operation
Type of operation (school, hospital, other)
General characteristics of patrons
Name and phone number of manager
Manager's education and experience
Type of service and menu pattern and prices
Number served and hours of service
Speed of service (average time from production to consumer)
Storage space and equipment—food, supplies, equipment, laundry
Kind of tableware—removal after meals, cleaning method, handling
    and storage
Specialty features—menu, service, decor, hospitality
Most popular menu items—volume sold, cost, selling price
Source of supplies and services
Buying—who does it, how often, nature of supplies, volume
Special service provided
Number of employees—production, service, cleanup
Labor sources and rates
Employee training—how much, by whom, for how long
Supervision, amount and type—production, service, cleanup
General plan of layout and approximate space allowances
Analysis of work flow and work timing
Equipment items—production, service, cleanup, office
Condition of equipment and length of service
Amount items are used and how used
Percentage allocation of costs—food, labor, operations, other
General condition and appeal of facility—decor, orderliness, cleanliness
Aspects that appeal most favorably
Aspects that detract most—how they could be avoided or remedied

When work requirements have been determined, various arrangements of equipment should be studied from the standpoint of flow of
work. There should be a minimum of time-consuming motions in accomplishing essential functions. Planners need to carefully calculate paths
for the logical movement of materials from receiving, to storage, through
preparation, service, and final cleanup. Utilization of man-hours and reduction of payroll costs are directly affected not only by the food purchased but also by the equipment selected and a layout that obstructs or
promotes efficient work. A job analysis should be made for every position

on which effort is regularly expended. Each motion deserves challenge as to whether it is necessary or done the right way, in the right place, at the proper time, and by the right person. Possibly it should be done by machine, combined with another task, or eliminated. One cannot hope to simplify work motions wisely without knowing what the motions are and how much each motion accomplishes. One needs to know also the order in which motions are made (see Chapter 3, Layout Analysis).

Preparation of a graphic picture or chart of work flow helps to clarify ideas and uncover blind spots. Accuracy of measurements is important to accuracy of information concerning distances covered and time required. It is necessary therefore at this point of study and research that some preliminary selection of equipment will have been made and measurements secured. Since the study is to explore the advisability of operational schemes, initial plans may be changed or abandoned as a result of the study. Frequently this part of the analysis is still in the conceptual phase, although some of the data and material obtained may begin to work into the actual physical plan or specifications. It is important for planners, especially novices, to remember that these studies are to promote eventual success of the facility, and they should not feel discouraged if ideas and carefully drawn schemes are later discarded. It is extremely desirable to isolate and identify all alternatives, weigh them and the data applying to them carefully, and then make the selection that seems best.

Useful research involves many careful calculations. Before one can evaluate a particular layout, one must determine precisely what work is to be accomplished. Food facilities are being planned today to do full meal preparation starting with basic materials and continuing to completed products, and others being planned are to do no production. The plan selected will determine work to be done and equipment needed. Before selecting one plan over the other, costs, consistency of quality, and dependability of supply need to be evaluated. The vagaries of the markets may present risks to standards and costs that are too great to accept with one type of operation. Good aspects of individuality and special skills developed in production of products in a particular institution may be lost. On the other hand, the quality of food fully produced commercially might be more consistent where labor is less qualified, and it may greatly reduce labor worries in procurement, training, supervision, and maintenance. The planner's calculations should help prevent shedding one set of worries only to assume others that are greater. It is best to evaluate change and look into the future to see what changes are likely to occur and should be considered in planning. Although a plan may satisfy immediate needs, a study of the trend may indicate that the

situation and needs are likely to change sufficiently to warrant preparations in the present plan to eventually meet them. It is always highly
desirable to obtain as firm a statement as possible from management
or ownership as to probability of expansion of plans in the future and
how soon the changes might occur.

Every labor minute counts in reducing costs. The 1976 wage for the
lowest-paid kitchen help is about 4 cents per minute. Most of the production labor receives at least 6 or 7 cents per minute. If one worker
wastes even 15 minutes per day at 5 cents per minute walking a needless
distance, coping with equipment that is in poor repair or hard to operate
or difficult to clean, and in hunting for items that are poorly stored, it
will mean a loss of 75 cents per day. This occurring 365 days per year
will amount to a loss of $275. In terms of 10 years, the depreciation
period for a kitchen machine, the loss would be $2,750. This multiplied
by the number of employees working in a kitchen, a 15-minute loss per
day for each would total a sizable amount.

Administrators need to have convincing proof of value before approving the purchase of costly equipment. A single item may cost as much as
a mink coat or two Cadillacs. It is not unusual for a large dishwashing
layout of equipment to cost as much as a very nice house and lot. Before
an administrator is willing to agree to the expenditure of such large
sums he needs to be convinced that there is a need, and that the expense
is justified through improvement and quality and/or saving in operational expenses.

The operation member of the planning team needs to make sure
which ideas have been accepted, understood, and approved by those in
authority. It can be hazardous to proceed on suppositions. It also is important to be sure that the architect understands recommendations that
have been approved and has incorporated them in the plans. The ideas
may be as major as a plan of operation or as small as the placement of a
power receptacle. There needs to be an established policy concerning the
extent of each team member's authority, and it should identify which
items require specific approval and by whom. This will give assurance
and help to save time for members of the planning team. It is unwise to
neglect viewpoints and to fail to do a thorough job of study and research
of all facets affecting a plan. It is said that one can tell how well a foodservice operation has been planned by the time lapse that occurs between
the time of its completion and the start of remodeling. Some facilities
operate for years without change or modification. Others begin to be
remodeled a few days after construction has been completed and
operation begun.

Sequence of Activities in Planning a Food Facility

There is a logical sequence in the planning of a food facility. Decisions on certain aspects tend to depend upon answers to related questions. Time spent in backtracking in the planning cycle is reduced if a logical procedure is followed. And by establishing such a procedure, serious omissions may be avoided. An order commonly used for considering the various aspects follows:

1. Analysis of needs and determination of kind and size of facility required.

2. Establishment of goals and policies relating to services, operations, standards, and activities of the planning committee.

3. Consideration of funds required, money available, and allocation of funds.

4. Selection of location, decision on space required, and allocation of space.

5. Determination of equipment needs, selection, specifications, and costs.

6. Presentation of tentative layout, based on studies, for team discussion.

7. Preparation of final layout for approval of ownership.

8. Preparation of equipment lists with specifications for use in bidding.

9. Letting of contracts.

10. Follow-up on construction and equipment.

11. Inspection and acceptance of building and equipment.

Suggested Student Assignments

Instructor: Bring to class a series of plans and show students how the plans are put together. Have examples of specifications and drawing equipment, including templets, available for examination and demonstration. Simulate a planning team meeting.

1. Identify symbols used and construction details on architectural plans.

2. Make a copy of a layout as assigned.

3. Prepare equipment templets using a scale of $\frac{1}{4}$ in. (6 mm) to equal 1 ft (305 mm).

4. Contribute ideas and evaluate contributions of other team members in a simulated planning committee meeting.

5. Visit a food facility and make a report following the outline suggested in the text.

Chapter 2

characteristics of food facilities

The type of food facility chosen to best serve the needs of a specific clientele will be influenced by many factors. Three of the major factors are (1) the food and service requirements of the group to be served, (2) the funds that will be available to meet expenses, and (3) the system of operation chosen. These factors are affected, in turn, by such influences as the available market supplies and services, company policies, time and place limitations, and the tastes, habits, and buying power of the patrons. The basic food and service needs of the specific clientele may be very simple and possible to supply at a minimal cost. The patrons' desires and ability to pay, on the other hand, might necessitate provision of a fuller menu selection, more elaboration of the food, larger portions, and/or a more refined service in order to interest sufficient patronage to support expenses. Public food service varies from the hasty, food-in-hand type of service of the snack bar or drive-in to the silver, napery, carpeting, and leisurely atmosphere of deluxe restaurants.

Gearing a kitchen for success calls for quality standards to be defined for the particular institution in terms of the level of acceptance by the specific patrons. The level of acceptance by patronage is strongly influenced by their physical needs, taste, income, time available, and convenience, as well as certain psychologic factors. A reasonably comprehensive knowledge of prospective clientele and wise judgment are needed in determining which standards need to be given precedence. Persons with cultivated taste, plenty of time, and a good income are willing to pay the price for highly palatable quality. Others will sacrifice palatability for conditions that, to them, appear more valuable.

Beef items appearing on menus in one form or another may be used to illustrate this point. The restauranteur who features superlative quality selects the tenderest cut of top quality meat. The menu price includes the cost of skilled labor and specialized equipment in preparing the meat for service as well as the cost of a generous portion. The beef will have been fully ripened in temperature- and humidity-controlled refrigeration. The roast will have been cut, trimmed, and tied shortly before roasting by a skilled butcher using meat-cutting equipment. It will have been cooked in a temperature-controlled oven to an exact degree of "doneness" and held at an unvarying temperature throughout hours of service. The tender, juicy meat, properly roasted and sliced to order, will glisten with freshness when served.

This quality is enjoyed by the majority of people. Money can be lost quickly, however, by supplying it to patrons who must give precedence to factors other than quality, for instance, price and time. A restaurant that offers fast service to a fluctuating patronage may have two or three orders of a menu item one day and fifty or sixty the next. Lengthy preparation, is out of the question. Service of items must be fast or not at all. Rapid reheating of fully prepared foods or short-order cooking must supply the answer. Equipment for individual portion handling or short-order cooking differs greatly from that required for mass preparation and long-period cooking.

A large number of individuals between the teens and middle age "eat and run" at breakfast and lunch. Many are snackers. These people are impatient for quick service, and they readily accept self-service. They are attracted by glamour and change, quickly tiring of "the same old thing." Economic aspects and coping with young children make the simpler types of food service popular for family dining. The number and success of coffee shops, hamburger stands, pancake houses, pizza parlors, and the fish and chip, fried chicken, and ice cream places attest to popular demand. Older people with requisite funds and leisure time, persons who are tired or tense, and those who entertain for business or social reasons desire the quieter atmosphere of service dining rooms.

SYSTEMS OF OPERATION

Characteristics of food operations differ as much in production sections as in service areas. High labor costs and shortage of trained personnel have caused managers to seek systems of operation that minimize labor to the greatest extent consistent with delivery of acceptable standards of products and services. System is a popular concept in modern planning. It may refer to total, partial, or no production connected with the foodservice facility. The term is used also to signify specialization in the kind of foods served, or it may be applied to the manner in which specific foods are handled. An important key to the systems approach is simplification. Development of a desirable system calls for thoughtful evaluation of all activities, products, and procedures in terms of desired results. A system of operation may be applied to any type of foodservice from the most simple to the most elaborate. Its goal is the improvement of operating efficiency in response to needs.

A system may involve the use of partially or fully prepared foods. Some foodservice organizations depend on commercially prepared food entirely and do not have a production department. Managers of these operations believe it possible to maintain more consistent quality and cost with the currently available personnel. Other operators, capable of training and controlling staff, recognize that in order to provide the degree of excellence and price acceptable to their patrons, the food must be produced largely within their organization.

The system of production strongly influences organization of the food facility and the equipment needs. Suitable, convenient storage facilities are more essential than mixers and choppers where prepared foods are delivered ready for service. Griddles and friers are more appropriate than oven and ranges for short-order preparation. Less equipment and more compact work areas are possible with specialization in limited menu items. Arguments favoring specialization also point to the possibility of higher-volume methods, to repetition and easier development of employee skills, to fewer errors in production, and to more speed. In situations where specialization can be utilized its value is worth considering.

The benefits of large volume handling have been obtained in some instances through the operation of a large central production kitchen with numerous satellite service stations. This has been popular in certain school districts and for retirement homes. The food may be fully prepared and sent in insulated containers for immediate service, or it may be frozen and require thawing and reheating. In other systems it is packaged in individual portion quantities, refrigerated, and shipped upon order with final cooking or refrigeration done at the point of service.

Diversity has been found to be the "surest route to long-term success" by large food corporations.[1] Obtaining adequate volume to support operating costs calls for satisfying a variety of conditions and tastes. No one food production and service program has been found to satisfy every situation. It is important, obviously, to choose a plan or system of operation at the outset of planning.

The component work units in a full-production kitchen include the following:

1. Ordering, receiving, and storage.

2. Preprocessing of raw materials such as meats, vegetables, and fruits.

3. Cooking—soups, vegetables, meats, sauces, and bakery products.

4. Pantry or set-up section—salads, sandwiches, beverages, and desserts.

5. Service areas.

6. Housekeeping or cleanup departments—pot washing, dishwashing, and janitor services (see Figure 2.1).

All food establishments require careful planning of Unit 1 of Figure 2.1, the facilities for ordering, receiving, and storage. The nature and volume to be stored will vary greatly as determined by the menu and system of operation as it affects the nature and volume of materials used.

[1] Institutions/Volume Feeding, Cahners Publishing Co., Inc., 5 South Wabash Ave., Chicago, July 15, 1974.

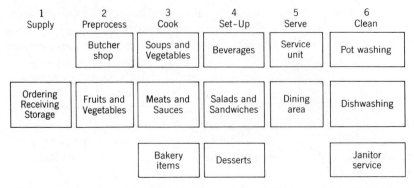

Figure 2.1 Component units of a full-production and service facility.

Many markets meet varied demands for supplies in forms and sizes ready for cooking or service. Unit 2 may be eliminated or greatly curtailed in new kitchens. Limited preprocessing, if needed, may be combined with cooking activities. Where specialization calls for short-order items only, such as grilled, broiled, and deep-fat fried foods, equipment for soup and vegetable cooking and a bake shop are not needed. Similarly, mass preparation of baked items, such as casserole dishes and steamed soup and vegetables, reduces the need for ranges, griddles, and deep friers. The serving station (1) may be combined with a short-order cooking section, (2) may be set up as a separate waitress supply unit, or (3) appear as a buffet or cafeteria that serves patrons directly.

SATISFACTION OF CHARACTERISTIC NEEDS

Colleges and Universities

The character of the campus food units is strongly affected by administrative policies and the school's financial limitations. Plans are usually geared to supplying "food at low cost." Recognition of and the social, health, and educational significance of good food habits and dining behavior differs greatly. The development of taste and well-ordered habits of daily living may be important adjuncts of a college education. The meals regularly consumed by college-age students have been shown to influence immediate health, growth, and mental capacity, and also the health of their offspring.

Plans for requisite facilities need to be preceded by a careful analysis of present and future enrollments and conditions. Funds available for building and policies or conditions that may effect the success of the operation should be considered. The source of funds, the program for repayment of funds, and the possibility for acceptable rates to meet operating costs and loan payments call for thoughtful calculation based on accurate information.

Rates for food service need to reflect all charges to be made against the account. Policies differ as to payment for space, heat, light, repairs, and special services supplied by other campus departments. The extent to which the facility is to be subsidized needs to be determined at the outset. The number of students, their needs and ability to pay given rates, administrative policies, and other sources of college funds will influence decisions.

Labor is a major cost and a worrisome problem on campuses as in food facilities elsewhere. The cost of labor may run from 25 to 40 percent, depending upon the type of service. Characteristics of student help necessitate special planning. Turnover is frequent, and workers are likely to be untrained and inexperienced. The job usually holds little interest for these workers. Their activities must be planned around class schedules that change each term. Simplicity must characterize schedules, work motions, and skills. Assembly line procedures may be used in processing or serving food during peak periods and for cleanup at the end of the meal periods. Major values lie in helping students earn an education and in having short-period help during peak periods of service.

Cafeterias. Cafeterias have met the common demand by students for speed, convenience, and low cost. Planners should consider effective methods of guiding the choice of balanced meals essential for good health. The use of plate combinations, meal-ticket grouping of foods when pricing, and attractive displays have a beneficial influence on choice. Counter arrangement and special equipment for merchandising may be effective.

Cafeterias providing a choice of food which are open to the general campus may serve both meals and snacks. The serving period may last throughout the day and have both peak and low periods of service. Self-service and self-bussing help to lower costs. Simplicity and convenience of procedures are important, such as having a deposit area for soiled dishes on the route out of the dining area. Easy cleanup should be planned. Unsightly litter may be common following service to a horde of students who dash off to class. Hard-surfaced floors and strategically placed soiled dish and paper receptacles make for a cleaner and more orderly appearance when a crowd is served.

Campus food facilities should be in convenient, attractive locations that are reasonably free from noise and distractions. On a large campus where distances are great, consideration should be given to dispersing food units. Near the entrance to the food area, there should be a place for depositing books and coats. The line-up area for the cafeteria should be located in a hall or entry rather than in a lounge where clutter and excessive wear will occur while students wait for meals.

College food services serve as social centers for students, and tables for four, six, and eight may predominate. Students tend to move tables to accommodate larger groups. Provision should be made for ease of movement. Floors and furniture chosen should be chosen for qualities that withstand wear.

Coffee Shops and Snack Bars. These are popular with students if a sociable atmosphere of fun and gaiety and fast service of popular foods are provided. Students respond readily to a friendly, informal atmosphere and enjoy the simplicity that characterizes this type of service. Menus permit freedom of choice, and individual pricing of items makes selection possible for those on the most limited allowance. Check averages tend to be low, but the continuous flow during a day results in an impressive total.

Coffee shop hours vary according to needs and may be scheduled according to the opening and closing hours of other campus food services. The menu offerings may need to supply full meals or snack-type foods not offered in other facilities. It is best to choose a system of operation that provides speed of service and a limited number of items that are the most popular. It should also permit flexible volume and the lowest cost. Menus are usually built around short-order and ready-to-serve foods, such as beverages, grilled foods, and bakery items.

Special Catering. Special catering may supply significant social needs on a campus and varies widely in nature (see Figure 2.2). Economy is best when it is performed through a regular foodservice department. The demands tend to be sporadic. A regular production staff, with some added assistance, usually has the equipment and time to handle the extra load without strain. Space and equipment to meet probable catering requirements need to be incorporated in the initial foodservice plans. This will include work and storage space for special foods, supplies, and equipment, plus dining space.

Time and effort will be saved by having chairs, tables, and cover items stored conveniently on mobile carriers. Speed of service can be promoted by short distances and fast means of transportation. Service may occupy more than one room on one floor or different floors. A direct, straight-line route will help to ensure speed and prevent accidents. Refrigerated

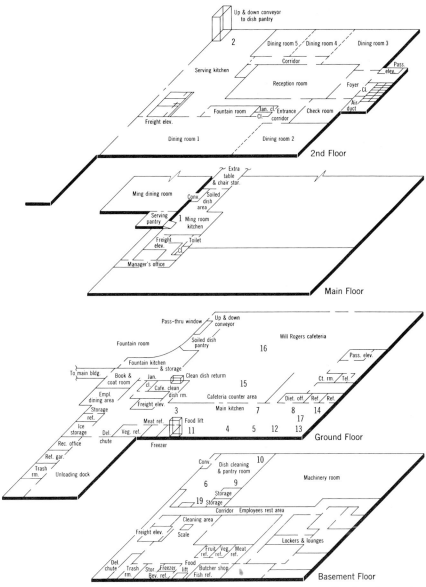

Figure 2.2 Food facility located on four floors, one immediately above the other, promotes well-organized catering at the University of Oklahoma. (*Courtesy Southern Equipment Company, St. Louis, Mo.*)

storage that will take mobile racks of predished cold foods, such as cock-tails, salads, and desserts, can save time and labor. In situations where a great many meals are catered, it has been found desirable to use a travel-ing belt for plate assembly. The belt carries plates at convenient speed to supply service. Workers place food on plates from both sides without touching the plates, except to place them on and remove them from the belt. Simple repetitive motion helps to develop speed and skill.

Programs are often a part of catered functions. Electrical outlets are required for a public address system, projector, recorder, spotlight, and other program equipment. A portable platform may be requested for a head table, particularly if the room is large. A projection screen, black-board, display panel, piano, and lectern may be desired.

Cloakroom and toilet facilities for men and for women should be pro-vided. Locate the cloakroom to promote good routing of guests. Rope and stanchions may be desirable for guiding traffic when groups are large. Directional and room signs large enough to be read easily are recommended if there are several dining rooms or a complicated route. Ticket takers or registration clerks may wish table space near the en-trance of the dining room.

Campus catering departments are sometimes asked to serve food in buildings other than the one where it was produced. Insulated handling equipment is needed to preserve palatability. If the heated or refriger-ated equipment requires electricity it is good to have a long, sturdy extension cord ready for use. Equipment that will ensure easy mobility in handling heavy, bulky food and dishes is highly desirable when catering.

Catering for a campus community may include requests for take-out foods. The foods may be used for teas, receptions, picnics, sack lunches, and home meals. The condition of the food may be ready for immediate service or frozen for later use. Attractive, convenient containers will facilitate handling. The use of disposable containers will avoid the need for keeping track of returnable equipment and making adjustments on costs.

Union Buildings. These are student centers that may incorporate all of the types of foodservice mentioned, or they may have only a small snack bar. This often depends upon whether the union building was built after other foodservices adequate to serve the campus had been provided. Since the building serves as a center for student recreation, meeting rooms, and offices, it is advisable for it to have some food facili-ties. There is usually a demand for refreshments for group meetings, food for banquets in the ballroom, punch for dances, and snacks for those enjoying recreation. The need for food service in this social center is such that planners are well advised to plan the requisite food facility and arrange the remainder of the building around it.

One kitchen may serve many areas in the building if relationships are planned wisely. Transporting food to several floors and to various rooms increases opportunities for accidents and theft. Control of labor and preservation of food quality are constant problems. A close, direct relationship between kitchen and serving stations should be maintained to the greatest extent possible. Mechanized means of delivery of food and return of soiled dishes should be considered. It is important that the layout permit adequate supervision of all production and service areas.

Faculty Club. This service can be an effective implement in creating good personnel relations on a campus. Faculty relationships benefit by having a place where members can meet on a friendly, informal basis and where they can entertain campus visitors. Understanding and respect developed through mutual acquaintance are effective morale builders. Recognition and support by the outside world for outstanding academic achievement are often stimulated through cordial hospitality.

Success of the faculty club requires careful and candid consideration of tastes, spending habits, and common characteristics, as well as specific needs for catering. Food, like the weather, is a common topic of conversation and frequently the proverbial whipping boy for relieving inner tensions. Heavy demands on modest faculty income, combined with a certain sense of insecurity, result in conservative spending habits. Faculty members admire an exclusive atmosphere and would like deluxe service but tend to feel that they should not support it.

Capable help for the short daily period required for noon table service is difficult to obtain, tends to be temporary, and needs constant training and supervision. The number usually served in faculty dining rooms is frequently too small to support labor for service without adding appreciably to meal rates. Higher rates tend to reduce patronage. Therefore plans that present an attractive dining area with self-service in an adjacent room have often been used successfully. The layout should also provide for quiet, inconspicuous removal of soiled dishes.

There are occasions when it is desirable for committees or special groups to be provided with served meals. If rooms are planned in convenient relationship to the kitchen or serving area, such catering can be handled at minimum cost. The possibility of regular or occasional teas, snacks, or coffee service, and the location where they are likely to be needed in the building should be considered and provision made for storage of certain materials, electric outlets, and water supply. If there are likely to be occasions when persons not connected with food management use the facilities, provision should be made for this separate from the main kitchen. Freedom in the use of the main kitchen frequently leads to misuse of supplies and equipment or, when refused, may arouse irritation. The planner's challenge is to reach the best point of balance between what a faculty wants, restrictions it will accept, and costs that members are prepared to pay.

Residence Hall.   This foodservice is usually designed for fullest utilization of labor, materials, and equipment in order to minimize costs to students. Cafeteria service is common for at least a part of the meals in order to promote speed of service and economy. The speed of the cafeteria line serving prepaid, limited-choice meals can almost be measured in terms of normal walking pace. Providing check points, for those eligible to enter, at the door rather than at the end of the line helps to speed the line.

Table service varies in residences from all meals to occasional party meals. In some halls it is used for dinner daily and in others for Sunday dinner only. Cafeterias are frequently criticized for encouraging poor social habits in students. The compromise of using cafeteria service for breakfast and lunch when time is most limited and table service for dinner has been used with success. Dining room size is important. Very large dining rooms tend to be cold and impersonal and create less of a sense of belonging. Units of one hundred or less tend to increase sociability.

Colleges and universities, through their food and residence facilities, may perform more than the obvious functions of meeting student needs for food and housing. The educational and health benefits to be gained through wise planning of facilities are important. Learning to live well and to get along with others are valuable adjuncts of a college education. Many students may be employed part-time and not only gain means offsetting some of their educational expenses, but under able supervision may learn some of the discipline of employment and the accomplishment of productive tasks.

An advisory committee is sometimes recommended to assist with residence planning. The members may represent financial planning, management, and student welfare and life in the halls. A fairly intricate job of coordinating will be required. The facilities must be extremely durable to withstand youthful exuberance and lack of concern for public buildings. Simplicity is usually desirable and forced by economic necessity. The amount of the school's subsidy of heat, light, services, and loan payment need to be known when planning.

Commercial Organizations

The profit motive is a major reason behind establishing a commercial food enterprise. Experience has shown that patronage is likely to be greatest and the profit most satisfactory where there is a strong demand for the material and services offered. Excellence of food and service, cordiality of atmosphere, good appearance, convenient location, and acceptable prices all have an influence on attracting and holding a profitable clientele. Very few restaurants please all patrons or satisfy many patrons for all meals. Both tastes and fashions in food service change. Unless there is a captive clientele, effective advertising of services and location is advisable.

Analysis of patronage potential is an important aspect of planning. It is best to know the number of people who will be in the vicinity at mealtime and the extent to which the proposed service will appeal to them. High volume for short periods calls for different plans than leisurely service over a longer time. Low check average calls for high volume and rapid turnover in order for volume to support costs. The patrons who desire leisurely service need to be willing and able to pay a larger margin in excess of food cost.

Urban service attracts the leisure diner and should be located near residence areas of sufficient population concentration and income to support it. Industrial and office workers want rapid service at low cost. Meal expense is likely to be budgeted. Glamour and cordiality are appreciated, but time and economy tend to be the strongest attraction factors. Snack shops are popular in school, amusement, and shopping areas. Drive-ins combined with coffee shops are favored by the motor trade. Distinctiveness of character is an advertising asset regardless of the type of operation. The considerable success of the many specialty dining operations may be attributed partly to this asset and also to economy resulting from greater simplicity in the system of operation. Space allowed for the facility is significant as it relates to labor saving and adequacy for profitable patronage.

Airlines. This food service consists of beverages, sandwiches or snacks, box lunches, and full meals served on trays. Some of the largest airlines own and operate their own kitchens. Others contract with outside food corporations to supply the food needed. In a few instances one airline may contract with another airline for the flight foods.

Satisfaction with food service is generally recognized for its influence on contentment with a company's overall service. One line says that "food sells seats." Another advises employees to give customers what they want. In-flight wine tasting, regional foods, gourmet foods, and special tidbits and liquors are culinary features used to make patrons content. Costs of operation are such that some companies are seeking means of gaining supportive income through on-ground operations, such as coffee shops, airport dining services, and hotels.

Cafeterias. Cafeterias find favor in serving large numbers quickly and in eliminating extra service expense. Characteristics that promote success are good food, popular selections, low cost, fast service, and smooth flow of patronage in and out of the line. Showmanship in displaying foods attractively helps to stimulate sales. Line, color, and effective lighting help to direct attention to the counter. Orderliness and clear labeling of items aid in making selections and help to speed movement of the line. Menus and prices should be well placed so that patrons can choose items according to their taste and pocketbook. The entrance and approach to the counter where individuals line up will influence patience at delay. Minutes drag when people are hungry or in a hurry.

Speed of service can be guarded through eliminating slowdown factors, such as complicated choices, preparation to order, service to order, self-service, and bottlenecks caused by too few servers, foods that are difficult to handle, and menu items that are not ready for service. Speed, personal meal selection, and seeing foods before purchase are significant values in cafeteria service and extra care should be taken to ensure them.

Coffee Shops. This is a classification used here to include dining rooms that serve a fairly limited selective menu and such specialty shops as those featuring pancakes, pizza, hot dogs, and hamburgers. The service and atmosphere are informal, cheerful, and friendly. The menu selection, service, and decor is likely to be free of nonessentials. A fresh, clean appearance is an asset. Prompt service is important. Short-order cooking, such as grilled or deep-fat fried foods, makes excellent ventilation a necessity. Fat odors and a smoky, cluttered appearance will turn hungry patrons away from the door. Good lighting throughout is desirable. Well-lighted display cases can be used to promote sales of salads and desserts.

Seating may be largely at counters and booths. Counter patrons enjoy watching the preparation of food. Skillful filling of orders can be as fascinating as a floor show. Observation of good sanitary procedures can stimulate patron confidence in the service. Furniture and finishes should be chosen that are durable and easy to clean. Step-saving compactness in arrangement is valuable. Specialization on a few menu items tends to

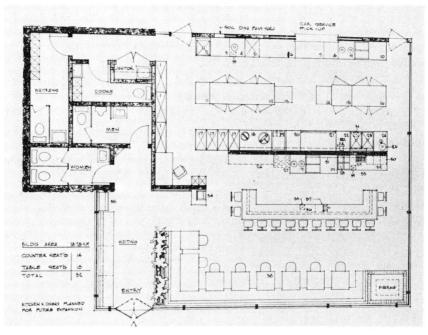

Figure 2.3 A plan designed for both coffee shop and car service. The Fireside, Los Angeles. (*Courtesy Christine Pensinger, Associates, Los Angeles.*)

promote speed and economy in production and service. Those items that are overly complicated to prepare or serve are likely to be eliminated.

A high percentage of coffee shops featuring specialty items such as hamburgers, pancakes, pizza, fish and chips, and fried chicken are operated by large organizations. Many function in a franchise program. Some operate on a fee basis for management, and others are company owned. Economic benefits are realized by the chains through management expertize, group advertising, large quantity buying and handling, and employee procurement and training. Although many of the large companies are best known for their operation of coffee shops or specialty food service, they are likely to be engaged in diversified food operations, such as hotels, hospitals, and schools.

Delivered Foods. This includes foods delivered on order to a specified location and varies from single items, such as sandwiches, pizza, and ice cream, to such full meals as those requested in hotels and clubs as room service and meals-on-wheels provided for shut-ins. Room service and the motorized "Good Humor man" are widely familiar because they have been in existence for many years. The program of meals-on-wheels, which provides a valuable service, has been slow in becoming established, and its potential has barely been realized. It can be expected, with fuller development, that profitable volume will result not only with the sick and shut-ins but also for the well and working individuals. The program needs to be better equipped and organized.

Equipment needs to be designed and programs of service developed that will make meals-on-wheels flexible and practical. Meal routes, like milk routes, may become common in the future to serve office workers and some factory groups. Certain desirable aspects now employed in packaged meals for school lunches may be used. Tableware is needed that is disposable, attractive, and impervious to absorption, and that will eliminate a second trip for pickup. Proper holding equipment that will preserve food safety and palatability is needed. The cost for extra labor time and special equipment expense must be supported by sufficient volume to bring prices in line with rates patrons feel able to afford and are willing to pay.

Drive-ins. Drive-ins are similar to coffee shops in terms of featuring limited menu items that are easy and quick to prepare and serve. Some provide car service, and others require placement of orders and pickup at a counter. Catering to the motor trade calls for fast service and tasty food. A safe, easy-to-follow traffic plan and ample, well-organized parking space are essential. Layout and organization should provide for safety and reduce travel in taking and filling orders in order to ensure speedy service. Menus should be posted where they can be easily seen and read by everyone in a car, so that the server will not have to present a printed menu and wait for a choice to be made. Menu terms and descriptions must be complete and understandable to reduce questions. Delays in ordering that keep servers waiting decrease the number who can be served.

Service Restaurants. Table service operations include those in hotels and clubs as well as in separate establishments. The service provided may vary from extremely simple to formal and elaborate. An appealing atmosphere is a significant aspect of this type of catering. Emphasis on decor reflects the difference between having a "bite" in the kitchen at home to having a meal in the dining room. More time is usually required for service than required in restaurants featuring fast and more limited service. Professional men and women who entertain or confer with business associates at mealtime like the service to be quick, quiet, and efficient. They wish the atmosphere, food, and service to be suitably impressive. Party diners choose a place that has an atmosphere that fits their mood.

The types of service offered by commercial restaurants may be divided into three general groups, according to services required:

1. Essential meal service. The style and quality of the foodservice are usually in keeping with the general standards of the organization. A hotel with low-priced rooms, for example, is likely to offer an economical type of service.

2. Food for or with entertainment. The pleasure value of good food, even if it is not particularly elaborate, is considerable for a normal, healthy, hungry person. When it is the heart or accompaniment of entertainment, artistry is used in its production and/or presentation to make it appeal both to the senses and the imagination. Prices in this type of service include costs for skilled labor, special foods, and expensive decor, plus leisurely service yielding low turnover. Extra space may be required for dancing, orchestra, stage, dressing rooms, and general spaciousness. Clever showmanship is the essence of this entertainment.

3. Catering for special needs or functions. Catering for group meals can add profitable volume. Space needs to be planned for flexibility of use in terms of size and type of meetings. Maximum room capacity must be considered in relation to frequency of demand and probable yearly income from use of space. A large area may be partitioned if the partitions are sufficiently soundproof to provide privacy. A speaker in one room competing with a dance band and gaiety in an adjacent room will not lead to satisfaction. The location and equipment for serving pantries and storage areas should be carefully planned in relation to probable use. Cloakrooms or checkrooms, toilet facilities, and traffic lanes should be considered in relation to catering areas and other public areas of the hotel, restaurant, or club. A layout that permits large groups to reach service areas without tying up elevators or traffic lanes in general use is desirable.

Labor in service restaurants is a significant expense. The operation should be of sufficient size to schedule labor for full utilization and allow for low and high patronage peaks. Layout and equipment that facilitate service have much economic value. Signal systems that save steps, mechanical devices for moving dishes and supplies, and strategically placed service stations may readily pay for their expense.

The amount of speed required in service may influence the type of preparation. Where heavy peak loads occur, advanced preparation may be necessary. The use of certain preprocessed foods and rapid reheating methods may prove advantageous. Facilities need to be geared to patron demand for specific menu items and the type of preparation required. Where the load is steady, short-order foods may be served that are slower in service. Proper timing requires care in planning. Palatability of short-order foods is as fragile as the seared crispness of a steak surface and the dry mealiness of a French-fried potato. Good holding equipment helps in the preservation of quality, but none will preserve that certain bloom food possesses at that instant when preparation is completed.

Smooth, rapid service is desirable but without giving the patron the impression of being hurried. Service stations should be close at hand to expedite removal of used covers and resetting of fresh ones. Table appointments chosen to harmonize with the restaurant decor should be appropriate for the service and sturdy enough to withstand normal wear. Plans should provide for suitable storage of all items needed in connection with service in order to save time and to ensure convenience and good appearance.

Take-out Foods.   Foods ready to cook or serve immediately are a great convenience for working homemakers and those who entertain without domestic help. Attractive mail-out menus and encouragement of telephone ordering help in building sales. The production equipment and traffic facilities of drive-in restaurants make them especially suitable for handling this business, but downtown locations can profitably utilize this sales potential also because of their nearness to large groups of employed persons. Refrigerated counters displaying these foods near the cashier promote sales. Packaging of items should afford protection in handling and may be used effectively for advertising items, prices, and ordering instructions. Directions for the proper method of reheating are helpful. Foil containers are durable and disposable and can be reheated in an oven. For microwave units sturdy paper or plastic containers may be used.

Hospital Foodservice

The functions of the dietary department of a hospital may be grouped into three categories.

1.   Chief of these is the preparation and service of adequate and appetizing food to patients and personnel.

2.   Calculation, preparation, and service of therapeutic diets and provision of dietary consultation.

3.   Instruction in nutrition and diet to nurses, patients, and interns. The amount of teaching required will depend upon the policies and the nature of the specific hospital. In hospitals where nurses and interns in medicine and dietetics are educated, members of the dietary department share in the instruction. Facility needs will be in terms of conference space, equipment for visual aids, and storage for classroom supplies.

Space that should be allowed for offices, therapeutic diets, and research varies according to the size and type of hospital and the organization of the dietary functions. There may be one centrally located office for the chief dietitian and assistant dietitians, or there may be separate locations for those concerned with the food management, therapetuic diets, dietary consultation, and service. Overseeing production calls for a location close to the main kitchen. Convenience of consultation with doctors and patients will help determine the location most suitable for the therapeutic dietitian's office. The kind of hospital and the type and number of special diets may govern the need for a special diet kitchen. In many hospitals food for modified diets is prepared in the main kitchen with a very limited area set aside for storage and preparation of special diet foods. Many handle modified diets on the regular tray line.

Metabolic diets and special dietary research require accuracy not only in the preparation of food but also in determining food consumed. It is desirable that the kitchen and serving unit be entirely separate from other food units as an insurance against error. The number served is likely to be small, and the equipment often can be of household size.

Funds for operating a hospital dietary department vary as to source and amount. Highly personalized service to patients imposes problems and costs not commonly experienced in other types of institution food service. Food is an essential need and has therapeutic value. This fact has sometimes been stressed to the neglect of operating factors important to economy and efficiency. The significant values of food in the care of patients should cause special stress to be placed on careful budgeting and planning of facilities.

The needs in the main kitchen of a hospital are approximately the same as those in any kitchen preparing food for a comparable number of meals. The greatest point of difference lies in the highly individualized service to patients and the hazards to quality imposed by such service. Delay in the transfer and presentation of food to patients tends to damage fragile food quality. Means and methods that help to speed service and delivery of patients' trays are of special value.

Careful scheduling is essential. The work of several departments needs to be synchronized with the meal service. The treatment of the patient, preparation of the patient for his meal, housekeeping, engineering care of the building, visiting hours for guests, as well as the food production call for integration with the schedule for patient feeding. The exact time acceptable will be affected by specific policies and conditions in the particular hospital. The serving of breakfast usually takes from 45 minutes to an hour, beginning as early as 7:00 A.M. in some places and lasting as late as 9:00 A.M. in others. The noon meal may be the heavy meal of the day or a light lunch. Service of the heavy meal at noon is thought by some to allow for better utilization of help and to be more satisfactory for patients. Others believe that because of the common habit of having dinner at night, it is better to serve it then.

Midmeal nourishment may be served from the main kitchen and presented by dietary personnel or delivered to floor pantries and presented by nurses. Refrigeration is needed for holding cold foods, and a heating device is needed for hot foods and beverages. Food for personnel, ambulatory patients, and hospital visitors is usually provided in a coffee shop or cafeteria. Food for the night staff presents a special problem. Various plans are used. Some large hospitals provide a regular cafeteria, and others provide short-order service. Many issue sandwiches, salads, desserts, and beverages to be served by a night nurse. Pilfering and quality deterioration are problems calling for solution.

The influence of the method of distributing patient trays on food quality and cost has caused continued search for a "better way." The general plan of the hospital in terms of multifloors or one-floor expanse will have some influence on the type of service used. Service may be decentralized, centralized bulk, or centralized service. These are discussed further under hospital service in Chapter 9, Serving Facilities. A reliable communication system between the main kitchen and the serving stations or points of delivery is essential. Information must often be given concerning special needs, omissions, and directions.

Nursing and Retirement Homes.   These have many services and problems similar to those in hospitals. Nursing homes are extended care facilities that provide convalescent care for a period longer than 24 consecutive hours for three or more patients not related by blood or by marriage to the operator.[2] Residents in retirement homes may be in good health, and any major impairment is due chiefly to age. The majority are ambulatory and enjoy the sociability of a common dining room. Many retirement homes have an infirmary where the residents are provided with hospital care.

Proper diet is a major contributing factor to the total welfare of the residents in either nursing or retirement homes. Dietary supervision is

[2] State of Washington Department of Health, *Directory of Licensed Nursing Homes,* Olympia, Washington, 1969.

specified in the licensing of nursing homes and must be provided in order to obtain certain financial benefits from the government. Food service for the aged presents many problems. Among these are their firmly established food likes and dislikes, certain physical impairment due to age, and the several restrictive diets required due to specific physical conditions. Calorie content of meals must be held at a no-gain level and at the same time provide all of the nutrients essential to health and well-being.

When planning for food service for the elderly it is important that psychological aspects be understood. Meals assume a very important role in the life of those whose life patterns have changed from home to institution living and whose emotional satisfactions and securities are limited. Friendliness and conviviality connected with food service can help to offset some of the stresses and frustrations characteristic of aging. Group conversation in family style service has been found to stimulate appetite. The offering of some menu selection encourages decision-making, and the residents are helped to retain a sense of personal identity and a feeling that their personal likes and dislikes are being considered.

Attractive table appointments have a beneficial influence. There has been a tendency in some homes to choose extremely durable, unattractive tableware to lessen breakage expense. Durability may be an important economic factor where fumbling grasp tends to result in more dropping of dishes. Bright, shining, colorful, attractive food containers create values, on the other hand, that should not be ignored.

Industrial Foodservice

Food service for employees may be required by any organization with a large personnel group. It is generally regarded as an effective implement in an industry's personnel relations program. Worker contentment, well-being, and good will are the goals. Employees do not rest when they rush several blocks to a lunchroom or perch on top of equipment or squat on the floor during their lunch break. It is important to production on the job for them to be seated comfortably at a table in an orderly, pleasant dining room. A close location; low-cost, good, nourishing food; and an attractive atmosphere are desirable.

There is a considerable range in the amount of subsidy afforded by different organizations. Some furnish space, heat, light, equipment, and janitor services. There are those that charge for the food cost only. A few serve meals free of charge. The management of the foodservice may be by the company, which employs and directs a food manager. The company may employ an outside person or agency to whom they turn over the responsibility of the operation on a fee or profit-and-loss basis.

Several factors influence probable patronage of an industrial lunch-room. Estimates may be based on a percentage of persons on the payroll, company policies in relation to costs and schedules, convenience of the location, wage scales, time allowance, proposed prices, type of menu, and quality of food and service. A lunchroom rarely serves as many as 85 to 90 percent of the payroll. The common range is from 50 to 75 percent of those employed. Cordiality, good food, convenient location, and price have a strong influence on promoting patronage.

Planning must consider arrival rate and speed of turnover. It is highly desirable that workers' lunch periods be on a staggered schedule, and the likelihood of this being possible should be ascertained from company management before planning. Assembly-line workers must leave and return to the line all at one time, and staggering is not possible. Where staggering of time is possible, arrival periods of 20 minutes for lunch and 30 minutes for dinner are satisfactory.

Probable growth of the firm and possible changes in policy have an important bearing on lunchroom planning. It is wise to determine whether the kitchen might have to produce food for service elsewhere and whether plant expansion is likely. The length of the lunch break and the distance to be traveled to the lunchroom will influence speed of service required. Determine whether more than one type of service will be required, such as an executive dining room, a cafeteria, and mobile service for coffee breaks or meals throughout the plant.

Executive Dining Room. Policies differ among companies concerning the desirability of having an executive dining room. Some feel that it is more democrat to dine with their workers. Surveys indicate, however, that an increasing number of executives favor separate facilities, which permit discussions of business matters at the lunch table and promote better acquaintance and fellowship in the group. Features may include a special menu, waitress service, special decor, carpeting, and air conditioning. Some are served from the main kitchen and serving area. Others have a separate kitchen. Patronage by executives was found to be about 82 percent where there was a separate dining room and 78 percent where executives patronized the general cafeteria.

Seated Service. Service dining areas may be provided for workers as well as for executives. These may be of the snack bar, counter and booth, or dining room type. The type of facility dictates the type of service offered. Factory workers with a short lunch hour will not favor this more leisurely type of service.

Cafeteria. Cafeterias that furnish appealing food and fast service are popular in industry. Speed and cordiality of service are very important to impatient workers. They like to see what they are buying and make selections within a definitely budgeted amount of money. Changes tend to be resisted and should have advance announcement. Choice in menu selections increases the satisfaction of varied tastes, needs, and buying power. Variety, on the other hand, delays choice and tends to increase production cost. Small to medium size cafeterias usually offer a choice of two entrees, three vegetables, two or three sandwiches, two or three salads, a salad plate, varied breads and beverages, and three or four desserts. Large cafeterias may departmentalize service to hot or cold foods, sandwich and limited short-order, beverages, and so forth, affording greater selection. A modified scramble-plan of service has been used effectively.

Mobile and Vending Service. Mobile service within an operation ranges from beverage and snack foods to complete meals. The mobile units may be complete in providing the service given or may be auxiliary to satellite serving stations. The food preparation may take place completely or largely in the central kitchen, with only limited or no preparation occurring in the outlying area. Vending may also be used to serve this need. The vending equipment includes such refrigeration and heating devices as needed for specific foods.

Chain organizations sometimes provide off-premise production. The preparation may be complete or to the point of final processing. The in-plant unit serves as a satellite serving station. Careful evaluation of the quality and selection of food obtainable should be made before deciding upon such a program. Equipment for holding and service and schedules for service need to be designed that will ensure protection of food quality and safety and speed of service.

School Foodservice

School foodservice is the largest segment of the public foodservice industry and, in terms of national health, the one that may provide the most pronounced and lasting benefit. Nutrition education is slowly arousing the general public and legislators to an awareness of its tremendous importance. Despite tight school budgets, major changes can be expected to develop in school food programs in the future.

Adequate, appealing, and economical meals that meet the nutritional requirements of children should be provided. Meals for the aged are being served in school lunchrooms in many areas. The lunchrooms can be used also for outstanding educational benefit. Food appreciation, eating habits, and social behavior can be taught that will have a lasting and beneficial influence. Research indicates that children have more vitality and alertness when they are properly fed and that there is a close connection between adequate food and learning ability.

Federal, state, and local funds are drawn upon to finance school foodservice. The funds available are modest in relation to the size of the undertaking. Plans are needed that will help to ensure the most economical operation in supplying good and adequate food at the lowest price possible. Success in the undertaking is considerably tempered by pupils' reaction to the food, to the manner in which it is served, and to personnel with whom students come in contact. Participation by students in the lunchroom service tends to reflect their reactions.

The larger the group, the greater the difficulty in discipline and the smaller the chance for effective instruction at mealtime. The students tend to look upon the lunch period as a recess from classroom and discipline. The amount of instruction and students' response vary with age and are strongly influenced by overall discipline policies and general teacher attitude toward the importance of such instruction. The relationship of food to health, sanitary practices, orderliness, and good manners should be taught at an early age. It is necessary to provide hand washing facilities in convenient relationship to the foodservice. Nutrition instruction should be given in the classroom as well as in the lunchroom.

The nutritional pattern for school meals is promoted by the federal Type A lunch program. Regardless of the foods offered, students' acceptance and enjoyment are vital to proper nourishment. Many children are guided by poor food habits in their homes and reject foods that they have not experienced before and have not learned to accept. This often causes waste of excellent foods, which are left on trays and are thrown into the garbage.

There is a variety of systems being used to supply school meals. A common one, which perhaps has been in existence the longest, has a complete food production and service in each school. The service is usually cafeteria style. An outgrowth of this is the satellite system that is being used where new schools are built or old ones exist that do not have enough space for full food production but do have enough space for service. The food for these is prepared in central kitchens and sent to the schools in insulated containers or in mobile, heated tables and served cafeteria style.

Other service plans have developed from the central kitchen plan. Among these are the hot sack lunches, in which one foil-wrapped hot food is placed in each cold sack lunch. A system that originated in

Bremerton, Washington, provides hot foods (entree, vegetable, and perhaps a hot roll) packaged in foil and cold foods and plastic tableware packed in clear plastic. The foods prepared and packaged in a central kitchen are refrigerated until ordered in specified numbers by schools. The food is sent to the schools in time for final cooking of the "hot" foods in an oven. Service of the meals may be in a general dining room or in a classroom. Each diner receives a cold package, a hot food package, and a container of milk. When the meal is over each pupil is responsible for clearing and disposing of the refuse.

Most schools providing lunch facilities have cafeterias that are used in common by all pupils. Those for lower grades usually have a set menu, but many junior and senior high schools offer a selective menu. The dining area may be utilized as a multipurpose room that may serve as an auditorium, gymnasium, study hall, and community meeting place. Whatever the plan, two significant qualities are strongly recommended: it should be designed and operated as an important part of the health and education program, and an efficient and economical operation should be made possible to provide adequate, appealing meals at low cost to pupils.

Miscellaneous Foodservices

Planners are often asked to devise food facilities that differ from those in a home or a commercial establishment. Camps and resorts have specific facility requirements in terms of size, location, and patron requirements. Fraternities or sororities on a college campus, dude ranches, lumbering camps, fishing boats, road camps, and facilities for forest fighters each have specific needs. Some operations are temporary, some seasonal, and others fairly permanent. Each type of plan calls for careful study of needs and available resources.

Churches, clubs, and other community organizations have kitchens to provide special meals. Members often share in preparing and serving the food. The friendship time of working together may be a significant part of the program. The task of the planner is to produce a facility in which a few may perform functions efficiently or where many may share in work without getting in each other's way. It is important to recognize and provide necessary sanitation protection. Each organization will have a pattern as to size, frequency of use, and type of functions to be served.

Suggested Student Assignments

1. Identify six plans of operation used in six different local institutions.
2. List the foods and services that each of the organizations provide and the prices charged.

3. State type of service provided by each of the organizations and list the special features that cause the food service to be patronized.

4. Evaluate the food in relation to:
    a. Acceptability to group served.
    b. Completeness of meals nutritionally.
    c. Appearance, quality, and temperature.
    d. Portion size in relation to hunger satisfaction.
    e. Portion value in relation to price charged.

5. Evaluate service in relation to:
    a. Acceptibility of type to group served.
    b. Speed (time from guest seating or ordering to time served).
    c. Attractiveness and cultural values.
    d. Outstanding characteristics, good and poor.
    e. Requirement in labor time per person served.

6. Evaluate general appearance and appeal. Identify aspects that are the result of:
    a. Layout and equipment planning.
    b. Essential economy.
    c. Managerial abilities.

7. Identify characteristics that make the food and service:
    a. Appropriate for the group served.
    b. Not suitable for the group served.

Chapter 3

layout analysis

Man-hours of work in a foodservice operation can be made most productive and easy through the use of scientific analysis in developing the layout of the facility. The goals of such analysis are various. It is largely directed toward improving efficiency, reducing labor, improving quality of products and services, making work easier, improving the morale of workers, and/or creating a more smoothly operating facility.

The techniques used by industrial engineers, system designers, and layout specialists are useful in making such analyses. Studies usually revolve around three basic areas:

1. Layout design and the selection and placement of equipment.
2. Work methods and factors that improve worker effort.
3. Utilization of equipment and materials to reduce labor required to produce and serve foods.

The first point is of major interest in planning since it directly affects the design, the type and size of equipment, and its location. The other two factors influence the layout plan and need to be understood also.

Layout Design

A layout design is a plan that indicates spatial allowances, physical facilities, construction features, and work areas with equipment located therein. In such a design, work sections should be joined together so that all necessary functions in the facility can be performed efficiently. Many significant factors will influence the design, such as quality and quantity of output, cost of operation, time scheduling, character of materials produced, and system of operation.

BASIC UNITS IN PLAN DESIGN

There are three distinct parts in a layout: (1) work centers, (2) sections, and (3) the layout made up of work centers joined into sections. The best plan results when work centers are planned first, then sections, and the sections are put together to form the total layout.

Work Centers

A work center is the basic component or unit in a layout. The relationship of work centers to the layout is similar to that of atoms to matter. There is nothing smaller. Work centers are areas where a group of closely related tasks is done by an individual or individuals, such as one might find in a bakeshop in a mixing center, a panning center, and

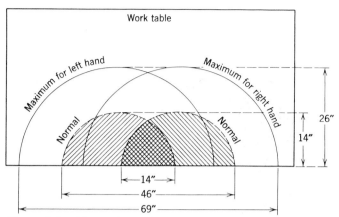

Figure 3.1 Chart of maximum and normal work areas for a sitting man of medium size (10 percent less for a woman of medium size.)[1]

a baking center. The number of functions to be performed and the volume of material handled determine the number of centers required. In some sections, numerous work centers are needed because the jobs are highly specialized. In a smaller facility fewer work centers may be required, and they may be used repeatedly for the changing tasks done in them.

The space allotted to a work center should be approximately 15 sq ft (1.39 m²) measuring about 2½ ft deep (76 cm) by 6 ft long (182 cm) for a worker of medium size (about 5½ ft or 1.68 m). A worker should be able to do all of the related tasks in the work center without moving from it. This is not always achieved in practice (see Figures 3.1 and 3.2).

Work center size is fairly standard, but it may be adjusted to specific production needs. Workers should not be required to reach or travel farther than the outer area of reach called the *maximum reach*. Most work motions should be within the normal reach areas. If heavy objects are lifted or difficult tasks done, these should be within the normal reach areas also. Less frequently made motions may occur in the maximum reach area (see Figure 3.3).

Useful studies of the placement of tools and materials for quick, convenient work in each work center may be made in various ways. It is very helpful to follow the preparation of recipes for representative menu items according to the sequence of activities required noting use of tools, equipment, and materials. Sometimes a simulation may be made in the

[1] To convert inches to centimeters multiply inches by 2.5; to convert feet to centimeters multiply by 30.

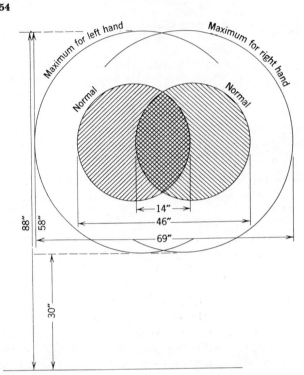

Figure 3.2 Chart of maximum and normal work areas for a standing man of medium size (10 percent less for a woman of medium size).[1]

form of a chalk drawing on the floor that allows the planner to see where the equipment may be placed for best use. Chairs, tables, or other furniture may be used to represent the equipment in the simulation to study the suitability of the location. Observation of work done in a center helps in discovering ways in which time may be saved. Usually observation in a work center for several days is sufficient to find the information needed. It is possible also to obtain good information from knowledgeable workers by having them indicate their estimate of the best equipment location in a work center for convenient work. Rating may start with 0 for little or no relationship between items of equipment in usual work procedures.

Figure 3.4 shows a worker's rating of the relationship of seven pieces of equipment in a bakeshop work center. The highest possible relationship is indicated by 4, whereas the lowest is given a rating of 0. Thus at

[1] To convert inches to centimeters multiply inches by 2.5; to convert feet to centimeters multiply by 30.

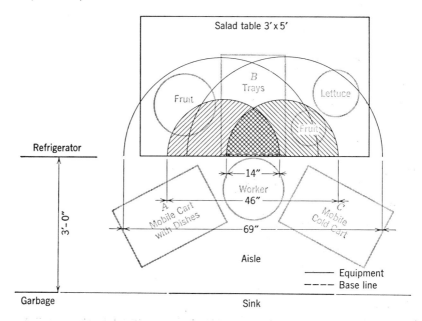

A Reach for plates at left.
B Construct salads.
C Store completed salads at right.

Figure 3.3 Chart of maximum and normal reach superimposed over a work area. This procedure is helpful in designing work centers.

point a on Figure 3.4 a high relationship of 4 is indicated between the mixer and workbench. At point b, where the lines for the workbench and refrigerator converge, another high relationship is shown. At point c, however, a low relationship valued at 0 is shown between the oven and mixer. Figure 3.5 shows the relationship based on the opinion of four workers. The values of the four workers' opinions are given on top where the lines between equipment converge, and the average of these opinions appears immediately below. Planners will find such opinions helpful in showing the relationship between equipment and its placement. Later it is pointed out that a similar technique used to indicate the relationship of work centers or even sections can be helpful in indicating to planners where to locate the respective work centers or sections.

Each unit of work done in a center should be challenged with questions of what, where, how, when, who, and why. Work motions should be considered carefully to see if they can be changed, rearranged, or eliminated to improve the work done. The frequency of movements

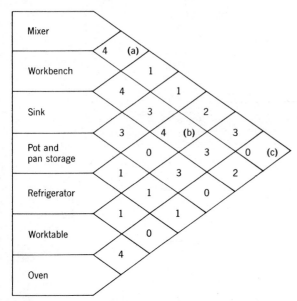

Figure 3.4 One worker's rating of the relationship of seven pieces of equipment in a bakeshop work center. Ratings from 0 to 4 are based on comparative-convenience value of close equipment location and shown in the diamond intercepted between specific equipment items.

between various pieces of equipment or units in a work center indicates the best arrangement of equipment. Distances of reach and keeping work in proper sequence are to be considered. Space allowance should provide for landing areas for food, adequate storage, and temporary holding of foods. Every use of space should be challenged. Flexibility is desirable to accommodate changes in procedures as they occur.

Compactness in a work center reduces travel and conserves time and energy. Mobile equipment, when not in use, can be moved aside to allow space for other equipment. Such an arrangement of the work center promotes both compactness and flexibility. Cross-charting is helpful in determining normal relationships of equipment. In a work center where a variety of related tasks are done, special study may be required to ensure smooth progress and prevent confusion in doing work. For example, if one has a sandwich preparation center and wishes to change it to a salad preparation center, the task is more complex than in planning a center for one set of tasks only.

Each work center should be developed by itself. It should be completely self-sufficient where possible for work done in it. Attention needs

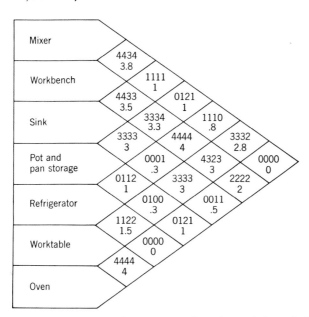

Figure 3.5 Rating by a group of workers of the relationship of equipment in the bakeshop work center. (See caption of Figure 3.4).

to be given, however, to other work centers with which it will be closely related or joined. The interrelationships of work centers and the dual use of equipment, especially in small facilities, may influence the location of the equipment. If a baker is to use steam equipment in a cook's section, the location of such equipment should be convenient for both workers. Sinks, tables, ovens, and power equipment, such as mixers and slicers, may be used by workers in more than one work center and therefore require special location. Mobility of equipment aids in duality of use when it can be moved from one work center to another.

Every job has three parts: "get ready," "do," and "put away and clean up." Man-hours are most productive when spent on the second part. Work planning can do much to see that the most "do" is obtained for the amount of "get ready" and "put away and clean up." Planning the work center to encourage this by sizing equipment properly and planning to have tasks done in quantity when possible is important also. For instance, instead of making cinnamon rolls every morning, it may be better to make them up once a week in a big batch and freeze a six-day supply, thus in one "get ready" and one "put away and clean up" accomplish the entire job. High labor rates emphasize the value of reducing time and motion and increasing efficiency in work centers.

Sections

A section is a group of related work centers in which one type of production occurs. The section is planned after all of the work center plans for the section have been completed and can be joined together. In the layout for a food facility there may be many sections, such as a baking section, a cooking section, a dishwashing section, a storage section, and a service section. The union or joining of work centers should be logical and scientific, and where work centers have a large number of interrelationships, they should be close together. In a section where a variety of functions is performed, special study may be required to promote smooth progress of work and prevent confusion between centers. In putting a section together, it is helpful to think of work centers as atoms being joined together to make up molecules of matter. Thus the smallest units in a plan are joined together with other small units to make up a larger particle of a plan.

A high amount of interrelationships, dual use of equipment, and compactness are to be considered in locating work centers in a section, just as these principles apply in work center planning. Setting up simulated systems can help one to see some of the interrelationships. Work center templets can be moved about on a layout much as templets of equipment are moved around in work center planning to find the most satisfactory arrangement. Supporting work centers, such as storage and distribution, should be located close to work centers where a high amount of interrelationships exists.

In work center planning, the opinion of workers was found to be helpful in locating equipment. Similarly, the opinion of workers can be helpful in locating work centers within a section. Workers can rate what they think are high, medium, low, or practically no relationships between work centers. The data can be compiled in a manner similar to that shown in Figures 3.4 and 3.5, using work centers instead of items of equipment. Individual opinions can be charted as shown in Figure 3.4 and a composite opinion as shown in Figure 3.5.

The sequence of work is important in locating work centers. If foods require preprocessing, such as vegetable washing or meat cutting, the sink or other equipment needed should be in or near the work center where the foods are to be cooked. Eliminating storage and transportation by bringing work centers close together so that direct delivery is possible helps to reduce travel and motion and promotes efficiency. Often mobile equipment can help to reduce spreading out work centers. Mobile equipment in a work center can be changed to turn it into another work center. For example, a cook's center in a small facility can readily be changed into a dish-up center by moving in a mobile steam table and other required units after removing work tables.

The Layout.

Sections are joined together to make up the complete plan or layout. Work sections should be joined that have a high amount of relationships, and supporting sections should be located close to the sections that they supply. For instance, if a large quantity of pots and pans come from the steam table section, the cooking section, and the bake shop, then the pot and pan section should be located in close proximity to these three sections. The analogy of the make-up of matter is applicable here. As atoms are joined to make up molecules and molecules are joined to make up matter, so in layout planning work centers are combined into sections and sections into layouts.

Striving for compactness of space, locating sections together that have a high amount of interrelationships, and seeking flexibility is as desirable, if not more so, in locating sections as it is in locating equipment in work centers or work centers in sections. Workers' rating of interrelationships between sections may be as helpful as their rating of interrelationships of work centers. Individual and composite opinions concerning interrelationships of sections in a layout may be charted in the same manner as the charting of equipment in a work center (see Figures 3.4 and 3.5).

FLOW OF WORK

The sequence of operations in the processing of materials or the performing of essential functions is called the flow of work. In a food facility it will include work accomplishment and the movement of materials from receiving, through preparation, service, and cleanup. The joining of work centers into sections and sections into a layout should follow certain rules relating to flow of work. Such flow is frequently defined as a natural and logical sequence of operations in the processing of materials or doing of work. Normally, the flow of materials is from receiving to storage, to preparation, to preparation (baking, cooking, and so forth), to finish holding, to service, to dishwashing and pot washing and other cleanup, to garbage disposal, and so on. This is sometimes changed to increase efficiency.

A basic flow pattern for a facility may be diagramed on a plan by using arrows to indicate direction of flow. Colored lines may be used to indicate flow of different materials. At the outset the diagram may be a rough sketch on a squared-paper plan indicating relationships between sections only. Later these sections may be allocated a specific amount of space with thought given to structural features that may aid or interfere with desirable flow.

There are eight basic rules that should be remembered in establishing flow in work centers, sections, and the entire layout.

1. Functions should proceed in proper sequence directly, with a minimum of criss-crossing and backtracking.

2. Smooth, rapid production and service should be sought, with minimum expenditure of worker time and energy.

3. Delay and storage of materials in processing and serving should be eliminated as much as possible.

4. Workers and materials should travel minimum distances.

5. Materials and tools should receive minimum handling, and equipment should receive minimum worker attention.

6. Maximum utilization of space and equipment should be achieved.

7. Quality control must be sought at all critical points.

8. Minimum cost of production should be sought.

The flow most suitable for one operation will differ from others according to the manner in which it meets the individual needs of the facility. Change and adjustment are often necessary in adapting a good flow to the specific structural requirements and building shape. A plan is seldom achieved without compromise. The need to make choices may stimulate extra care and thought that will lead to finding a better plan. The flow pattern should follow the functional relationship of work as indicated in Figure 3.6.

Types of Flow

The *straight-line* flow plan is frequently used by industries making a standardized product in large quantities. It may be called the unital, or assembly line, flow also. Materials in manufacture move steadily in a direct line from one process to another. The term straight-line may be misleading. The layout may actually be in the shape of a circle, parallel, U-shape, L-shape, or other form. Straight-line means that the flow of material being processed is continuous or direct in progress. Raw material in such a layout may start at the top floor and progress through various stages of assembly on successive floors until processing is com-

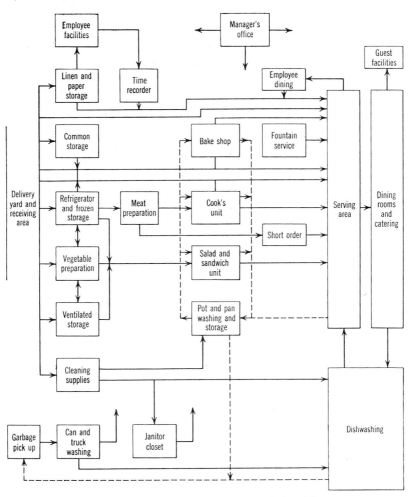

Figure 3.6 Flow diagram showing functional relationships.

pleted at the ground level, with storing and shipping occurring at the lower level. Straight-line flow is used on assembly lines.

The *functional* flow plan is often called the *process,* or one-shop, plan. It is adaptable to manufacturing where a number of specialty type products are made. Departmentalization of processing is characteristic. Frequently items are processed to a semifinished point and allowed to accumulate, with storage occurring until a sufficient quantity is obtained for transfer to another processing department. This layout tends to be less expensive to install, but the cost of manufacturing per unit may be higher.

There are advantages and disadvantages to each type. Factors that will influence the type best suited are nature of the product, sequence required for processing, and the quantity to be manufactured. The small quantities and the wide variety of products made in food facilities make the functional type of layout advisable. Products made in the various sections, such as pantry, cooking, and baking, are quite different in nature and usually cannot be processed on an assembly line. Often food is cooked to order and preparation must await demand. This is best done in functional type layouts. Straight-line layouts are most efficient with continuous production of a large number of products similar in nature.

Planning Flow of Work

Plans for the flow of work should begin with a study of the frequency of movement within the work center or the number of interrelationships among equipment. These indicate the best arrangement of tools, equipment, and the movement of supplies and materials. The aim should be eliminating excess travel and time- and energy-consuming criss-crossing and backtraffic and obtaining as direct line flow as possible. Flow may be improved by reducing distances of reach, inconvenient storage of tools and supplies, and inadequacies in equipment.

The location and amount of landing space, the size and location of sinks, and the size, location, and amount of equipment should be calculated on the basis of the type of work and the amount of food processed in the center. Compactness reduces travel, thus saving time and effort. Flexibility is necessary to allow for changes in flow necessitated by change of activities. Mobile equipment increases flexibility. Mobile equipment, where used, should easily move in and out and permit sufficient space to work around it. In work centers where a variety of related tasks are done, special study is required to promote smooth progress of work and to prevent confusion.

Attention must be directed not only to work flow within a center but also to the flow between it and related centers. It is desirable in a bakeshop, for example, for the landing area from the oven to be next to the make-up center where cakes are frosted or desserts are dished. The flow in the frosting or dish-up area starts where the flow from the baking and landing area ends. This shows application of the eight rules previously cited.

When related work centers are put together, a section is formed. Just as the flow of work needs to follow a logical sequence in a work center, it also has to follow a logical sequence of movement in the section. Many of the same principles apply in determining flow within a section as within a work center. A flow pattern may be drawn indicating flow in a section and then work centers arranged in logical sequence in the line of flow. Templets representing work centers may be moved around to test various arrangements in the same manner that equipment templets are used. When the most desirable arrangement of work centers within a section is accomplished, the other sections required for the plan can be arranged in similar fashion.

A flow plan for the entire facility is to be determined and sections located according to the best flow within it (see Figures 3.6 and 3.7). The relationship of activities of one section with another is to be kept in mind. For example, where the work in one section ends, the work flow in the related section should start. Templets of sections may be utilized in a similar manner as templets for work centers or equipment. They may be moved about until a best arrangement, considering aspects of work in the various sections, can be found. Structural elements often demand consideration in establishing flow. One cannot remove a supporting wall to favor a desirable flow that has minor importance.

The use of worker opinions in indicating the importance of relationships among equipment has been pointed out in Figures 3.4 and 3.5. Avery[2] used another technique, as illustrated in Table 3.1 and Figures 3.8 and 3.9. This requires that the number of interactions among equipment or work centers or sections is tabulated. Thus in Table 3.1 such a study indicated that there were 3,633 interrelationships between tray service and production (cooking), 1,309 between production and pot washing, and so on. Anything above 854 interactions (production and refrigeration) was classified as of the highest importance with a value "A." Interactions from 381 to 509 were given a value of "B" and below 381 interactions had a value of "C."

The values given in Table 3.1 are now used to indicate relationships between sections as shown in Figure 3.8. "A" values are shown by four lines between the circles indicating sections, as indicated by four lines between "11" (production) and "13" (tray service), which has 3,633 interactions. "B" values are indicated by three lines and "C" by two. (Arrows could be used to indicate the direction of flow).

[2] R. B. Pedderson, A. C. Avery, R. D. Richard, J. R. Osenton and H. H. Pope, *Increasing Productivity in Foodservice,* Cahners Books, Inc., Boston, 1973. (This is a series of monographs in the field of industrial engineering in the food service industry and a valuable tool for use in planning food facilities.)

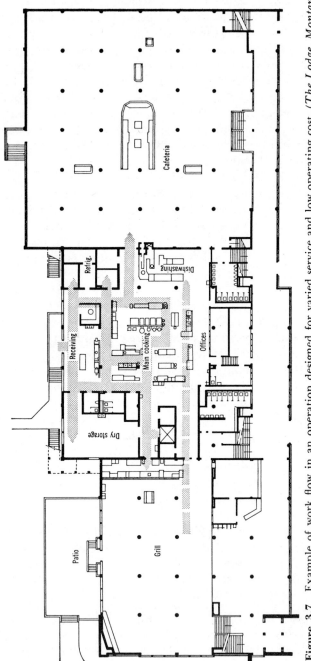

Figure 3.7 Example of work flow in an operation designed for varied service and low operating cost. (*The Lodge, Montana State University, Missoula, Mont.*) ·

Table 3.1 Breakdown of Interaction Totals into Important Categories*

Work Center Pairs	Total Interactions	Importance Category
Tray service—production (cooking)	3,633	A
Production—pot washing	1,309	A
Tray service—refrigeration	1,255	A
Tray service—tray cart storage	1,068	A
Production—meat preparation	936	A
Production—refrigeration	854	A
	Breakpoint	
Tray service—vegetable preparation	509	B
Meat preparation—pot washing	388	B
Dishwashing—tray service	386	B
Tray service—pot washing	381	B
	Breakpoint	
Dishwashing—dumbwaiter and elevator	307	C
Meat preparation—refrigeration	301	C
Bakery—pot washing	292	C
Bakery—production	291	C
Production—dry storage (unrefrigerated)	280	C
Vegetable preparation—pot washing	250	C
Pot washing—dry storage (unrefrigerated)	222	C
Bakery—dry storage (unrefrigerated)	220	C
Vegetable preparation—refrigerated	190	C
Receiving—refrigeration	177	C
	Breakpoint	

* A. C. Avery, *Increasing Productivity in Foodservice*, Cahners Books, Inc., Boston, 1973.

After Figure 3.8 is prepared, a further refinement can be made as shown in Figure 3.9, which shows a plan now emerging. Four, three, two, and no lines again indicate relationship importance. It is highly desirable to avoid crossing four or three relationship lines and, if possible, crossing two relationship lines should be avoided.

Planners who use methods outlined here in Figures 3.4, 3.5, Table 3.1, and Figures 3.8 and 3.9 will find that improved layouts result and,

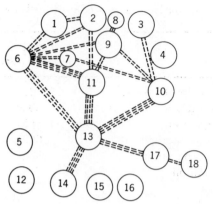

1. Storeroom	7. Meat preparation	13. Tray service
2. Bakery	8. Tray service (branch)	14. Tray cart storage
3. Receiving	9. Vegetable preparation	15. Diet kitchen office
4. Freezer	10. Refrigeration	16. Storeroom (branch)
5. Serving line	11. Production (cooking)	17. Dishwashing
6. Pot washer	12. Dietitian's office	18. Dumbwaiter–elevator

Figure 3.8 Work center activity relationship diagram. (A. C. Avery, *Increasing Productivity in Foodservice,* Cahners Books, Inc., Boston, 1973.)

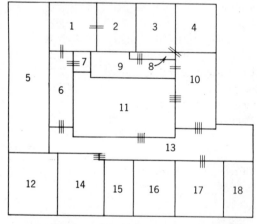

1. Storeroom	7. Meat preparation	13. Tray service
2. Bakery	8. Tray service (branch)	14. Tray cart storage
3. Receiving	9. Vegetable preparation	15. Diet kitchen office
4. Freezer	10. Refrigeration	16. Storeroom (branch)
5. Serving line	11. Production (cooking)	17. Dishwashing
6. Pot washer	12. Dietitian's office	18. Dumbwaiter–elevator

Figure 3.9 Work center area activity relationship diagram (assembled). (A. C. Avery, *Increasing Productivity in Foodservice,* Cahners Books, Inc., Boston, 1973.)

while the original compilation may be time-consuming, the effort pays off.

Revision, change, and perhaps compromise may be necessary before a plan evolves. It may be after sections are located along a desirable line of flow that one needs to go back and rework work centers, relocate work centers within sections, or do other adjusting. Once the sections are finalized along the line of flow, the basic form of the layout begins to appear. It is then necessary to allow adequate space in work areas and aisles. Thus the final plan takes shape.

MATERIAL HANDLING

The flow of materials is to be considered in establishing the overall flow patterns. Normally, the movement of materials and supplies follows the flow of work, and for this reason the flow patterns for each may coincide. However, at times this may not be true, and in instances where quality and efficiency may be affected suitable modification should be made.

A large percentage of time in food facilities may be claimed by the necessary handling of materials. Raw materials, tools, and utensils should be placed where they will require as little handling as possible. In transfers and movement the following points should be considered.

1. Store at point of first use. The point of first use will depend upon the organization of work in the specific facility. One plan may call for food supplies to be delivered directly to a central storage area that has an adjacent ingredient room. Here the supplies will be opened, checked, and measured into specific recipe quantities to be sent to individual production sections. Control of supplies, care in measurements, and compactness in work areas are counted as advantages of this system. Volume of material handled, variety of menu items produced, and type of food served will influence the desirability of this system. In some establishments it may mean extra handling, extra personnel, and larger space.

Where first use calls for measuring and utilizing materials in specific work centers, it is best to separate supplies into local storage. The utensils and materials will not be in a central area but where they are first needed for work. A pot to be filled with water, for example, will be stored near the sink; yeast, extracts, and other pantry supplies in the bakeshop; and crackers, breads, dairy products, and beverages in the serving section. Central or bulk storage will be used for large market packages that, for economical use of space, are to be divided later for storage in work areas. Frozen foods may be requisitioned in small lots from centralized low-temperature storage and held in a small freezer or ice

cream cabinet near the point of preparation. Reach-in refrigerators conveniently located in cooks', bakers', and pantry sections can be time-
and step-savers. Where storage is to supply more than one area, the location is usually best where it will be in closest proximity to the area
where the greatest number of trips will be made to it. The meat walk-in
refrigerator should be close to the cooks' unit, with material moving
from storage to butcher shop to cooks' unit in a straight line.

2. Allow for economy of motion.   Store according to frequency of
use, with most used items within normal grasp and less used items more
remote. Items should be arranged or positioned for easy pickup. A heavy
pot or package may have to be where it can be easily lifted in and out.
Items should be so placed that others will not have to be moved to reach
the one desired. This will influence stacking or placing dissimilar items
in front of others on a shelf. The therblig "search" (see page 71) will
be reduced if items are placed in plain view and in definite locations.
Items for transfer or movement should be even with the height of work
areas or mobile equipment used for movement.

3. Use space economically by providing for specific sizes.   Distances
between shelves as well as depth of shelves should be considered, with
only enough excess space to allow for ease of movement of items into
and out of position. Adjustable shelving permits varied spacing where
space requirements are likely to change.

4. Minimize handling and storage.   Handling is reduced if storage is
located and deliveries timed so that items can be placed when and where
required by the person who delivers them, such as milk to the serving
section or fruit and vegetables to the preparation area. Trucks or pallets
provided for weigh-in materials, movement into storage, and from thence
on the same unit to the processing area make for savings in handling.
Conveyors or mobile storage units reduce dish handling.

5. Systemize.   If storage is organized, search and handling will be reduced. If the most frequently used and largest volume products are most
convenient to reach or utensils and equipment are selected for modular
size thus eliminating transfer by making it possible to use in storage,
processing, or display and service, the number of handlings will be reduced. Grouping materials for common use and, where desirable, making
them mobile increases efficiency. Portable table organizers for waitresses
make it possible to refill table supplies quickly and lay fresh covers.
Mobile carriers for cleaning materials and equipment will save many
steps for workers.

6. Use good handling procedures.   Incorporation of safety, sanitation, and security in planning will reduce work. Lift trucks and other

mechanized devices should be provided to reduce lifting heavy items and for handling large volumes of goods. Loads should be limited to 35 lb for women and 50 lb for men. Clear aisles and good traffic flow are essential in a layout to reduce materials handling.

7. Coordinate. Communication is very significant in assuring complete and fast relay of information. A satisfactory system will save a great deal of time and effort in a large organization. It is important to select the type that will meet the needs of the specific establishment. Signal lights, buzzers, intercommunicating phones, and electric devices for transmitting writings from a pad in one place to another have been used with success.

STUDY AND CHARTING OF WORK METHODS

The organization of work and the manner in which it is done has much to do with the efficiency of a specific layout. A well-planned kitchen may not prove efficient if the work done in it is poorly organized and poorly done. Sometimes skillful organization and adaptation to shortcomings can make a poorly planned facility function with a surprising degree of efficiency.

Those who plan kitchens should be familiar with approved methods for doing work and know how to improve methods through planning. In addition, it is helpful in planning to know how workers can be taught to work efficiently so as to maximize the results of planning. Scientific analysis of work can provide a basis for locating equipment, which promotes time and motion economy. Useful methods of analysis have been devised by industrial engineers, and they vary according to the information desired. Some supply information as to the best motions to use in doing work. Others study the flow of materials through processing and indicate degree of efficiency of movement. Certain methods emphasize human characteristics and limitations in doing work and point out the easiest and quickest way to accomplish work with a minimum of fatigue, accident, or error. Such information can make a significant contribution in layout planning.

This scientific approach of obtaining facts and then proceeding to action may be time-consuming at the outset, but it is likely to compensate well in the long run. Results gained may mean time and money saved, better products produced, and happier workers. Scientific analysis may be summarized as including:

1. Recognition of a problem with analysis and definition.
2. Collection and analysis of data, eliminating unnecessary material.

3. Development of various aspects of the problem.

4. Evaluation of goals, materials, and methods.

5. Testing.

6. Taking action or putting results of analysis and development to work.

7. Evaluation and correction.

8. Formulation of final principles or action.

In analysis no phase should be blindly accepted or taken for granted. Every function or factor is to be challenged in terms of

What is to be done, and why it is to be done.

Who is to do it, and why that person is to do it.

Where it is to be done, and why it is to be done there.

How it is to be done, and why it is to be done by that method.

When it is to be done, and why that is the best time to do it.

The goal is to find the best way to do work. Analysis will supply information for the planner on which to base placement of equipment for achieving standard results with the least expenditure of time and effort.

Various methods are used to study work. Some go into considerable detail studying minute and basic motions, as is done in detailing therbligs, and then analyzing them through the use of simo charts or slow-motion film. Others may be done in less detail showing gross work motions such as might be used in work sampling or flow process charts. Some methods emphasize increasing productivity by improving work motions, whereas others may seek to improve jobs by rearranging equipment or improving flow. Each method must be suited to the information required and the practicalities of the situation. The following are some of the more commonly used methods in foodservice.

Therbling and Simo Chart Study

There are situations in which it is desirable to study work in detail. This occurs when a large number of similar motions are made doing a large amount of work. The saving of only a few seconds in doing a task that is repeated many times makes a substantial saving in time required to do all the work necessary.

Frank R. Gilbreth, an industrial engineer, was the first to define the most basic work motions and to identify them as therbligs (Gilbreth spelled backwards). He noted that all work, regardless of its nature, consists of approximately seventeen basic motions, which cannot be broken down into smaller units. The time it takes to make each of these is closely the same (about 1/2000th of a minute), regardless of the type of work done. He called this time lapse a "wink." Often a chronometer divided into 2,000 units as a hand swept around in a complete circle each minute was placed behind the worker so the number of winks could be recorded. The seventeen therbligs developed by Gilbreth are

Therblig	Symbol	Definition
Search	Sh	The eyes or the hands hunt the object
Select	St	A decision ending with choice of the object
Inspect	I	Examining and evaluating according to standard
Transport	TE	The hand moving toward an object
Grasp	G	Taking hold of an object
Hold	H	A delay in grasp with no movement of the object
Transport loaded	TL	The object being moved
Release load	RL	Releasing the object
Position	P	The object set into proper position for use
Preposition	PP	Setting into position for future operations
Assemble	A	Joining two or more objects together
Disassemble	DA	Separating two or more objects that are joined
Use	U	Manipulating a tool or device to perform work
Avoidable Delay	AD	Stopping the operation
Unavoidable Delay	UD	Stopping the work unavoidably
Plan	PL	Mental decision on procedure for action
Rest	R	Cessation of work to overcome fatigue

A job may be studied by an observer making a chart of a worker's motions indicating the therbligs used in sequence or by film taken at high speed and played back at normal speed, making it easy to record the motions. The therbligs taken in either manner are then transferred to a simo (simultaneous) chart. The chart is so named because it charts for a short term the simultaneous motions made by both hands or other parts of the body in doing work. After the motions are recorded, the work is analyzed to see if improvement can be made.

A *simo chart* is valuable in disclosing inefficient motion patterns, idle time, and waste motions. It may lead to improving motion sequence; to improving the placement of foods, tools, or equipment; or reducing the number of motions made. A reduction of motion, lessening of time, shortening of distance, and the development of a smooth, steady, rhythmic motion tend to increase production and make work easier. The construction of a simo chart from a film is shown in Figure 3.10 a,b,c.

The use of films in work analysis is known as *micromotion* study. The therbligs with an explanation of the work motion and time intervals are frequently transferred first to a *record of film analysis* and from there to a simo chart. Time may be recorded by means of a time device, such as a microchronometer, located to appear in the picture, or in terms of camera speed of so many frames per minute. In charting, the motions of one hand are recorded, the film is rerun, and the motions are recorded for the other hand. Idle time is indicated by a heavy black line in the column for the hand that is idle, directing attention to a place for possible improvement.

Gross Charting Techniques

There are a number of methods of studying work motions or improvement of equipment location that are done in less detail than studies done with therbligs. A number of therbligs may be grouped into one larger motion and instead of recording therbligs, only the larger motion is recorded.

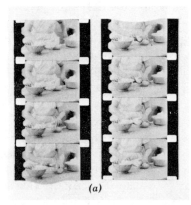

(a)

Figure 3.10 Use of film in motion analysis. (a) Film strip of worker trimming lettuce for salad. (b) Record of the film analysis. (c) The next step of recording motions of the simultaneous chart. This vividly portrays idle time for either hand.

RECORD OF FILM ANALYSIS

Film Number 52
Date Filmed July 15, 1956
Analysis by LHK
Date July 28, 1956

Operation Trimming lettuce
Operator Hefner
Part Name
Part No.

1 Sheet of 1
Dept. H. Economics
16 frames/sec.

Therblig Symbol	Clock Reading Subtracted Time (winks)	Left Hand Description	Right Hand Description	Therblig Symbol	Clock Reading Subtracted Time (winks)	Body Member	Therblig Symbol	Clock Reading	Subtracted Time	Notes
TE	16	To bowl of lettuce	Holds knife	H	16					Frame 1
S	19	Selects lettuce leaf	Holds knife	H	19					not shown
TL	18	Carries lettuce leaf	Holds knife	H	18					Frame 2
P	27	Positions leaf for cutting	Holds knife	H	27					Frame 3
H	29	Holds leaf for cutting	Moves knife to cutting position	TL	29					Frame 4
H	210	Holds leaf for cutting	Trims off lettuce cups	U	210					Frames 5-12
G	17	Picks up waste lettuce	Holds knife	H	17					Frame 13
TL	21	Waste to garbage can	Holds knife	H	21					Frame 14
RL	8	Drops waste lettuce	Holds knife	H	8					Frame 15
TE	16	Returns to pick up lettuce cups to deposit in bowl on left	Holds knife	H	16					Frame 16

(b)

Figure 3.10 Continued.

SIMO - CHART

Method _____   Film No. _52_____
Operation _Trimming lettuce_____   Operation No. _____
                                             Part No. _____
Part Name _____   Charted by _LHK_____
Operator _Hefner_____   Date charted _July 28, 1956_

Left hand description	Symbol	Time	Total time in sec	Time	Symbol	Right hand description	Clock
To bowl of lettuce	TE	.50	.50	.50	H	Holds knife	
Selects lettuce leaf	S	.60	1.10	.60	H	Holds knife	
Carries lettuce leaf	TL	.60	1.70	.60	H	Holds knife	
Positions leaf for cutting	P	.90	2.60	.90	H	Holds knife	
Holds leaf for cutting	H	.90	3.50	.90	TL	Moves knife to cutting position	
Holds leaf for cutting	H	2.10	5.60	2.10	U	Trims off lettuce cups	
(continued)						(continued)	

(c)

Figure 3.10 *Continued.*

Process Charts. A *process chart* can be made of a person at work, of materials being processed, of equipment in use, or any combination of these. It is a graphic presentation of work covering one function and not a series of functions. Fewer details are shown than on a simo chart (see Figure 3.11 *a* and *b*).

Motion Symbols. Certain symbols have been devised to represent work processes graphically. These group therbligs into a larger work function.

Although symbols may be individually designed, more general comprehension of charts and diagrams is promoted through the use of those that are standard. Five symbols have been established as standard by the American Society of Mechanical Engineers:

○ Operation
⇨ Transportation
☐ Inspection
◗ Delay
▽ Storage

Other industrial engineers have simplified the symbols by substituting the small circle for the arrow representing transportation and a triangle for a combination of storage and delay. Some retain the arrow and use it pointed right for forward movement and left for backtracking transportation. A letter may be used inside the symbol for added significance, such as Ⓗ for hand truck or T for temporary storage. The symbols may be combined when two components of work occur at the same time. The process chart may have a column for recording distance traveled and another for time required for an operation.

Symbol	Action	Definition	Example
○	Operation	Action that creates changes or adds to product.	Baker rolls pie crust.
☐	Inspection	Check or inspect quality. No change occurs.	Examines thickness of crust.
○	Transportation	Movement of product by any means.	Place in pan.
▽	Storage	Product awaits work or movement.	Sets aside for finishing.
▽	Delay	Cessation of productive action. Idle but not stored.	Filling boils over and requires attention.
◖	Combined Activity	Work components occuring at one time.	Stirs and examines filling for pie.

BASIC CHART FORM					
FLOW PROCESS ___ Type of chart			FOOD SERVICE ___ Department		
ORIGINAL OR PRESENT ___ Original or proposed			LHK ___ Charted by		
MATERIALS INTO PIE CRUST ___ Subject charted			May 26, 1956 ___ Date charted		

Details	Division of Work	Steps	Feet	Time*	
1. Get mixing bowl	⟶	6	9	0:35	
2. Weigh flour	◯	0	0	1:43	
3. Secure shortening from storeroom	⟶	28	49	3:03	
4. Weigh shortening	◯	0	0	2:22	
5. Weigh salt	◯	0	0	1:11	
6. Dump ingredients into bowl	◯	0	0	0:18	
7. Set bowl on mixer	⟶	2	3½	0:18	
8. Get mixing paddle	⟶	6	9	0:17	
9. Put paddle on machine	◯	0	0	0:08	
10. Start machine; blend ingredients	◯	0	0	3:12	
11. Stop machine	◯	0	0	0:02	
12. Get cold water at sink	⟶	4	7	0:29	
13. Add water; start machine	◯	0	0	0:07	
14. Blend ingredients	◯	0	0	0:40	
15. Stop machine	◯	0	0	0:02	
16. Remove paddle	◯	0	0	0:07	
17. Take paddle to sink	⟶	4	7	0:14	
18. Remove bowl and roll to table	◯ ⟶	7	13	0:18	
19. Store scales and water measure	◯	7	13	0:20	
Totals	13 ◯ 7 ⟶	64	110½	13:26	

(a)

Figure 3.11 Process chart. (a) Original operations in making pie crust, as shown on a process chart. (b) Revised operations in making pie crust. The summary at the bottom of the process chart shows the savings made in using the proposed method.

BASIC CHART FORM

FLOW PROCESS	Type of chart	FOOD SERVICE Department
PROPOSED	Original or proposed	LHK Charted by
MATERIALS INTO PIE CRUST	Subject charted	May 26, 1956 Date charted

Details	Division of Work	Steps	Feet	Time*	
1. Get mixing bowl and paddle	→	6	9	0:39	
2. Dump shortening, flour, and salt which has been delivered preweighed by storeroom man	○	0	0	0:19	
3. Put mixing bowl on mixer	→	2	3½	0:18	
4. Start machine; blend ingredients; while blending get water at sink	○ →	4	7	3:16	
5. Stop machine	○	0	0	0:02	
6. Add water	○	0	0	0:07	
7. Start machine; blend ingredients	○	0	0	0:40	
8. Stop machine	○	0	0	0:03	
9. Detach paddle and bowl	○	4	7	0:24	
10. Roll bowl to table	→	7	13	0:14	
11. Paddle to sink	→	4	7	0:05	
12. Scales and water measure stored	○	7	13	0:20	
Totals	8 ○ 5 →	34	59½	6:08	

SUMMARY

Item	Present	Proposed	Difference			
Operations	13	8	5			
Transportations	7	5	2			
Steps	64	34	30			
Distance (feet)	110½	59½	51			
Time (minutes)	13:26	6:08	7:18			

*Minutes and seconds

(b)

Figure 3.11 *Continued.*

Mundel[3] has used similar symbols to indicate flow of products through equipment. At times he uses only two to show:

Symbol	Action	Definition
◯	Operation	Productive work occurs; may include study or planning.
☐	Inspection	Study to ascertain if product conforms to standard.

These are about 3/8 in. across. Other symbols used by him indicate the following additional procedures:

Symbol	Action	Definition
◯	Operation	A modification of a product that takes place essentially at one location.
○	Movement	A change in location of a product from one place to another, not changing the product's characteristics.
▽	Controlled storage	Storage of a product under control such that a requisition or receipting is needed to withdraw it.
▽	Temporary storage	Storage of a product under such conditions that it may be moved or withdrawn without a requisition; for example, material banked on skids at a machine.
◇	Quality inspection	The verification of quality of product against a standard.
☐	Quantity inspection	The verification of quantity of a product against a standard.

After basic work components have been recorded on a chart (see Figure 3.11a and b), an analysis can be made and a new method of doing a job planned.

A *man and machine chart* is a type of process chart showing the working cycle of a worker and a piece of equipment. The time consumed by each in going through the cycle of work is indicated by a scale in inches. The shorter the time cycle of the operation being charted, the shorter the distance will be per decimal minute of time shown on the process chart. The analyst will chart both the worker and the machine, record-

[3] Marvin E. Mundel, *Systematic Motion and Time Study*, Prentice-Hall, Englewood Cliffs, N. J., 1955.

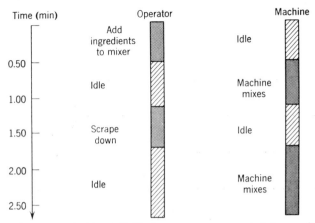

Figure 3.12 Man-machine chart showing a partial operation recorded in using a mixer. See page 78 for explanation of chart use.

ing time and operation. Productive time is indicated by a heavy straight line. Idle time is shown by a break in the line. Unloading or loading of a machine is shown by a dotted line. The information obtained may indicate how the work done by man and machine may be better co-ordinated for maximum achievement (see Figure 3.12).

A *sequence chart* is useful in the operational analysis of the complete layout. It is sometimes called a *master process* chart because it is fre-quently made up of a number of process charts of individual functions. These, when put together, give the complete operation in chronological order. The sequence chart shows when materials are introduced into the process in terms of time, location, and processing sequence, except those involved in material handling. Horizontal lines are used in the chart to show material being introduced into the manufacturing process. Vertical lines are used to indicate processing flow. Where lines intersect and no combination occurs, the symbol used is a small semicircle in the hori-zontal line at the point where the vertical line crosses it. The symbol is much the same as the one used in electrical drawings to show that no juncture of wires occurs. The motion symbols chosen by Mundel are useful in this type of charting.

The chart prepared by Thomas[4] to indicate the flow of products through equipment serves as an excellent example of this type of chart-ing (see Figure 3.13).

[4] Orpha Mae Huffman Thomas, *A Scientific Basis of the Design of Institution Kitchens*, 1947. Doctoral thesis on file at Purdue University Library.

Department: Range

Product type: Braised Meat   Product: Lamb Stew

Quantity: 75 quarts   300–1 cup portions

Equipment	Time	Explanation
		Storage
Table	3 hr.	To table
		Trimmed and cubed
		To refrigerator
Refrigerator shelf 2' x 5'		Stored overnight
		To table
Table 3' x 6'	10 min.	Floured
		To ovens
Ovens 3 range	90 min.	Browned
		To steam-jacketed kettle
Steam-jacketed kettle 25 gallons	60 min.	Simmered slowly
Range top	28 min.	

Ingredients: Lamb, Flour, Onions, Carrots, Potatoes, Flour, Water, Salt, Frozen peas

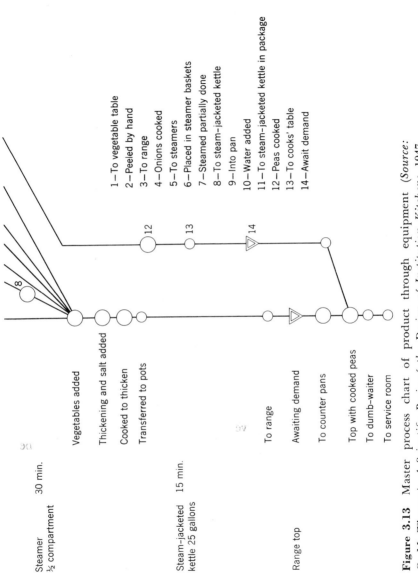

1 – To vegetable table
2 – Peeled by hand
3 – To range
4 – Onions cooked
5 – To steamers
6 – Placed in steamer baskets
7 – Steamed partially done
8 – To steam-jacketed kettle
9 – Into pan
10 – Water added
11 – To steam-jacketed kettle in package
12 – Peas cooked
13 – To cooks' table
14 – Await demand

Steamer   30 min.
½ compartment

Vegetables added

Thickening and salt added

Cooked to thicken

Transferred to pots

Steam-jacketed   15 min.
kettle 25 gallons

To range

Awaiting demand

To counter pans

Top with cooked peas

To dumb-waiter

To service room

Range top

Figure 3.13 Master process chart of product through equipment (*Source:* O. M. Thomas). *A Scientific Basis of the Design of Institution Kitchens*, 1947. Doctoral thesis on file at Purdue University. See page 79 for chart explanation.

A *distance chart* portrays the distance a worker or material travels in an operation. A scale drawing of the area to be covered by the worker or material travel is required for this. Movements of more than one worker or material, or of worker and material, may be imposed on the same plan by the use of different colors of string. It is well for the drawing to be made or mounted on cardboard so as to provide satisfactory firmness. A paper staple should be fastened through the plan at each point to which the worker or material will move. Fasten the string at that point where processing begins. Move the string along the path the worker or material moves and over the staple at each point of call. At the end of the process remove the string and measure it. If the drawing is scaled to $1/4$ in. $= 1$ ft, then each inch of string will represent 4 ft traveled in the process observed (see Figure 3.14).

Cross Charting. Cross charting can indicate the efficiency of equipment placement. This method of study is especially useful where diverse movements occur and a variety of items are processed in a work center. Movements for more than one product can be charted. Like other types of analysis, an improved method can be compared with an original one, and the relative efficiency of the change estimated.

A cross chart may be prepared as follows:

1. Prepare a list of equipment in order of its location. "Issue" or "pickup" is always counted as the first equipment item or location point on this list.

2. Prepare another list of movements made in doing work.

3. Number the movements in the order in which they occur. (Recipes listing order of procedures may be used in preparing list of movements.)

4. Draw a square and divide it equally into blocks, with one block more horizontally and one more vertically than the number of items of equipment used. (If there are six items of equipment, there should be seven vertical and seven horizontal squares or blocks.)

5. Draw a diagonal line from the upper left-hand corner to the lower right-hand corner.

6. List items of equipment on the left side of the square and from left to right across the top in the same order, using one block for each item of equipment.

7. Leave one empty space on the right side and at the bottom. These empty blocks are to be used for totaling movements.

8. Transfer work movements to the chart by the number of movements on the list. Placement should be guided by three factors: (*a*) equipment

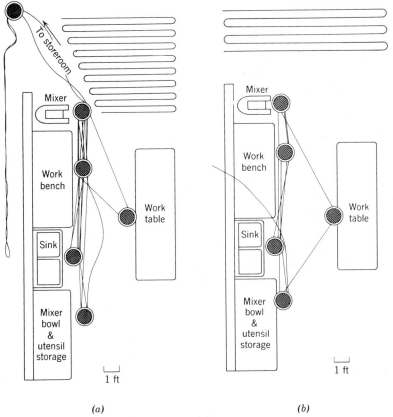

Figure 3.14 Distance or string chart. (*a*) Original work area. (*b*) Revised work area.

between which movement occurs, (*b*) number of pieces of equipment by-passed in making the movement, and (*c*) the type of movement. The first factor (*a*) shows travel occurring between two pieces of equipment by placing the movement number in the block where the horizontal and vertical blocks between two pieces of equipment meet. When cross charting is completed, frequency of movements between equipment can be determined by counting the numbers in the respective blocks. The second factor (*b*) indicates the number of pieces by-passed in making the movement. The number of the movement is placed in that space above or below the diagonal line according to the number of pieces of equipment by-passed. The third factor (*c*) is used to show two types of movements: (1) a movement that does not move a product forward (backtracks), called a *from* movement, and (2) a movement that moves a product forward, called a *to* movement. All *from* movements are placed above the diagonal line and all *to* movements below it.

If equipment is not in line but stands across from each other, the movement number cannot be shown as indicated by factors (*a*) and (*b*). When this conflict occurs, the number should be placed in the proper square as required by (*b*) and circled. An "x" should then be placed in the proper block for step (*a*) above, the first factor guiding placement of numbers. In counting the number of movements between equipment, the circled number is omitted from the count and the "x" is counted instead.

Figure 3.15a and b shows cross charts for an original and improved placement of equipment in a vegetable unit. The work done is peeling and chopping carrots. In the improved placement of equipment in Figure 3.15b, the chopper is mobile and the colander used to hold the carrots is moved under the drainboard on the left side of the sink. The list of equipment set into line for cross chart Figure 3.15a is issue, peeler, drainboard, sink, colander, table, and chopper. In cross chart Figure

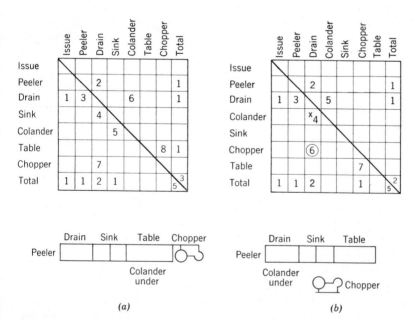

Figure 3.15 Cross charts. (*a*) Record for original arrangement. (*b*) Record for revised arrangement.

3.15b this is changed to issue, peeler, drainboard, colander, sink, chopper, and table. The chopper is opposite the sink, and this will necessitate the use of the "x" because the equipment is not in a linear position but across from others. The use of the "x" has been described.

The movements in doing the work are

(a)	(b)
1. Issue to drainboard	1. Issue to drainboard
2. To peeler	2. To peeler
3. To drainboard	3. To drainboard
4. Wash carrots in sink	4. Wash carrots in sink
5. Get colander	5. Place colander from under to top of sink
6. Colander to drain	
7. Carrots in colander to chopper	6. Carrots in colander to chopper
8. To table for use in salads	7. To table for use in salads

In Figure 3.15a the motions are recorded as follows:

1. The carrots are brought from issue to the drainboard. This is a *to* motion in that the flow is forward between pieces of equipment. The peeler is by-passed and 1 is placed as shown.

2. The motion is between the drainboard and the peeler, and it is a *from* motion. No equipment is by-passed and the 2 appears in the proper space indicating the movement as shown.

3. The carrots now move from the peeler to the drainboard and 3 indicates by its placement it is a *to* motion in which no equipment is by-passed. It is therefore next to the diagonal line in an under position.

4. The carrots move from the drainboard to the sink for washing. Another *to* movement is recorded in which no equipment is by-passed.

5. The worker goes to the table for the colander, which is underneath on a shelf. The movement is between the sink and colander. The number 5 is placed in the *to* area below the diagonal line in the square where the horizontal line from the colander meets the vertical line of the sink. No by-passing occurs.

6. Next, the colander is taken to the drainboard to allow the carrots to drain, by-passing the sink, and this and the fact that it is a backward or *from* motion dictates it be a square away from the diagonal line above it.

7. From the drainboard the colander and carrots move to the chopper. This is a *to* movement and the locations of sink, colander, and table are by-passed. Note that it is three squares from the diagonal line and under the line.

8. The carrots are then moved to the table where they are used for salad. This is a *from* movement with no equipment by-passed.

In Figure 3.15b the first four motions are recorded the same as for Figure 3.15a. Motions 5 and 6 in Figure 3.15a are combined into motion 5. It is a *from* movement from drain to colander where carrots are placed into the colander. Motion 6 is the movement of carrots in the colander to the chopper, which is now opposite the sink. While the chart must show this as a *to* motion by-passing two pieces of equipment—the colander and sink—there is no by-passing actually. Thus number 6 is shown where it should be showing the by-passing, but a circle is placed around it and the placement of the "x" where number 4 is shows the actual situation. In tabulating, the 6 is disregarded and the "x" is used instead. The carrots in motion 7 are moved to the table for use in salads, a *to* motion with no by-passing.

The *to* movements in each column are then totaled and the sum written on the bottom space intended for this. Similarly, the total *from* movements are written on the space on the right intended for this.

Whenever equipment is placed efficiently, the cross chart shows a large number of movement numbers close to and below the diagonal line. Inefficient location is indicated by numbers distant from the line and/or above the line. A computation can be made, as shown in Figure 3.16, to obtain a value rating for *to* and *from* movements. The various *to* movements are multiplied by the number of blocks away they stand from the diagonal line, and a sum of these results is obtained. This is done similarly for the *from* movements. The sum for the *from* movements is divided into the sum for the *to* movements, giving a value rating. The larger the rating, the more efficient is the placement of equipment. A weighted value rating can be obtained. To do this, the sum of *from* movements is doubled in value and divided into the *to* movements. (Multiplying by one half does this.) Figure 3.16 also shows how an efficiency rating is obtained. The number of *to* and *from* are added, and this is divided into the number of *to* movements. Perhaps this is the most meaningful figure obtained from these three ratings.

If the cross chart shows the number of movements between two pieces of equipment is high, the interpretation should be that these pieces of equipment need to be located adjoining or close together. Direction of flow of work as shown by movements also indicate recommended placement of equipment.

Cross charting has been shown to be adaptable to computer programming.

Analysis by Means of Pictures. If it is desirable to note travel and wasted motion in a specific work area, pictures may be recorded of fewer

1. Rating for Original Arrangement

Blocks from Diagonal Line		Number of Movements		Value
	To			
1	×	3	=	3
2	×	1	=	2
3	×	0	=	0
4	×	1	=	4
		5		9
	From			
1	×	2	=	2
2	×	1	=	2
3	×	0	=	0
4	×	0	=	0
		3		4

Value rating = 9/4 or 2¼.
(*Note:* Weighted value rating would be 9/4 × ½ or 1⅛).
% Efficiency = ⅝ or 62½%.

2. Rating for Revised Arrangement

Blocks from Diagonal Line		Number of Movements		Value
	To			
1	×	4	=	4
2	×	1	=	2
3	×	0	=	0
4	×	0	=	0
		5		6
	From			
1	×	2	=	2
2	×	0	=	0
3	×	0	=	0
4	×	0	=	0
		2		2

Value rating = 6/2 or 3.
(*Note:* Weighted value rating would be 6/2 × ½ or 1½).
% Efficiency = 5/7 or 71%.

Figure 3.16 Value and efficiency ratings of cross charts.

Figure 3.17 A stroboscopic picture. The salad worker is surrounded by portable equipment and prepositioned food supplies. Three basic positions are shown: (1) reaching for salad plates at worker's right, (2) constructing salads (center of picture), and (3) storing salads in portable cart (left).

motions over a longer period of time with a motion camera set for 1 time frame per second instead of 16 frames per second. When the film is projected, 8 hours of work can be viewed in 30 minutes. This is called *menomotion* study.

One negative may be used to record more than one motion so that movement is shown by one motion being imposed on top of another. This will produce a *stroboscopic* picture showing motion variation (see Figure 3.17).

Still camera pictures may be made to show motions of a small light attached to a body member, such as a hand. With the room in semidarkness, the camera is opened for the period that the motion is made. This picture is called a *cyclegraph* (see Figure 3.18).

Time Studies. One of the first techniques used to study work methods was to stand by a worker and record the time taken to make motions or to do a job. It is reliable if done by a keen observer, but it is very time-

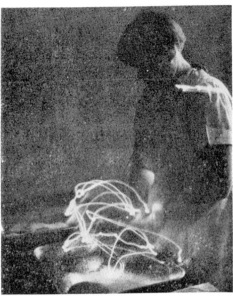

Figure 3.18 An example of a cyclegraph. The paths of light made by a worker's hands as she arranges cheese and sliced meat for a cold plate are studied.

consuming. In certain cases it is the only way to obtain the necessary information.

The technique of making time and motion studies is relatively simple. The observer should prepare for timing by first observing the whole operation of the job. In this initial observation an estimate should be made of the worker's skill, effort, technique, and results. Are proper work methods used and are products of good quality? The estimate of these factors, summarized on the timing sheet, will later be required for establishing a present rating factor. The description of the situation should be stated as to product prepared, recipe used, section where work is done, worker observed, and the name of the observer. Standard record sheets usually have space provided for this information (see Figure 3.19). A sketch of the work area with equipment placement is helpful. Starting and stopping period for each element timed should be established before timing is begun. The time for each element usually runs from 0.05 to 0.10 of a minute if therbligs are recorded and longer if an activity or more gross motions are being timed. If time periods are too short, they will be difficult to record accurately; if too long, they will include too much. The elements of the job are written down in units to be timed.

TIME STUDY OBSERVATION AND COMPUTATION

Job _____ Assembling cold plate _____   Section _____ Pantry _____

Date _____ 7/29/59 _____   Operator_____ J. B. _____

Observer _____ K _____   Recipe used _____ None _____

ELEMENT	OBSERVATIONS (MINUTES)								Average	% Rating Factor	Allowance Percent	Standard Time
	1	2	3	4	5	6	7	8				
1. Reach for 6 plates and space on pre-positioned tray	.12						.14		.13	90	112	.131
2. Lettuce to plate, left hand; scoop of potato salad to plate, rt hand	.21					.29						
	.09	.08	.10	(.12)	.07	.08	.08	.08	.083	90	112	.084
3. Slice ham left hand; cheese with right hand	.27	.16	.16	.19	.13	.14	.36	.14				
	.06	.08	.06	.07	.06	.06	.07	.06	.067	90	112	.068
4. Pickle and olive to plate, alternate hands	.32	.21	.21	.23	.18	.19	.41	.19				
	.05	.05	.05	.04	.05	.05	.05	.05	.050	95	112	.052
5. Store tray in cart at right	.48	.32	.33	.36	.30	.30	.52	.30				
	(.16)	.11	.12	.13	.12	.11	.11	.11	.116	90	112	.117

Notes _____

_____   Total standard

_____   per __plate__   .321

_____   tray   2.057

Note: Minutes shown above dotted line are cumulative figures, while those below are
time for the specific element obtained by subtraction of cumulative figures.
Thus, the time .16 for the fifth element "store tray in cart at right" is
derived by subtracting .32 from .48. Circled times indicate they were not
used in obtaining the average.

Figure 3.19 Cumulative time study of a worker setting up cold plates.

Then the job is timed. The watch for timing should record in decimals
of a minute. Timing may be done by one of three methods. One is a
snap-back method in which the stopwatch hands are started at zero for
each element and snapped back to zero at the end. The second is called
continuous method and is done by recording the time for each element
without snapping the watch back. A record is made at the end of each
element without stopping the watch. In the third method, two stop-
watches are used. They are mounted close together on the observation
board and are alternately activated and stopped at the beginning and at
the end of elements. This is an *accumulative* method that permits obser-

vation of a longer operation. Readings can be made more easily and accurately when the watch hands are not in motion.

Obtaining an accurate picture of a job requires timing it a sufficient number of times to arrive at a good average. When computing, those values that are too high or too low are circled and disregarded in making up the average. A *standard time* is the average time multiplied by the percent rating factor multiplied by the allowances made for personal time, delay, or fatigue time loss. A rating factor of 5 percent is often used for personal needs and 5 to 10 percent for fatigue slowdown and rest periods. This is called the performance *allowance percentage* and when used, 100 percent is added to this allowance. Thus if the personal percentage is established at 12 percent, 112 percent is recorded. A larger personal allowance percentage is usually required in heavy or difficult jobs. The standard time is shown in the proper column. Standard hourly production is obtained by dividing 60 minutes by the standard time.

Methods Time Measurement. A technique recently used by Freshwater and others to study work methods has been called MTM or Methods Time Measurement. This is a method in which pictures are taken at normal speed (16 frames per second). The picture is then played back at normal speed and the work methods studied. It is considered a better method than work sampling because it is more accurate in terms of what is happening, and it covers the actual period rather than a set of random observations. It also is considered better at times than time studies because the work is performed in a less formal situation. Workers tend to tighten up when under observation in time studies. This is why the allowance percentage is given. Furthermore, with Methods Time Measurement it is possible to replay the same task a number of times. In some respects this method resembles simo study except the film is made at normal speed rather than for slow-speed showing.

Work Sampling. Casual, random observations made to see what workers are doing and then charting these observations are called work sampling. The observations can be quite detailed or merely indicate on the chart that a worker is or is not busy. The advantage of random sampling is that a large number of different situations can be observed and charted, the theory being that if the observations are random over a period of time almost as good information will be obtained as by standing and observing for a much longer period. One must therefore be sure to take an adequate number of observations to be sure of having an accurate picture of what is occurring. By adding the percentages for times workers are busy and dividing by the number of employees observed, a percentage of efficiency can be estimated. A percentage of 80 percent or more is usually satisfactory. Figure 3.20 is a sample of random checks made of employees at random periods. To check productivity, write employees' names on a check sheet and go through your operation at different times to determine who is actually doing productive work.

Evaluating Work Methods Study

After obtaining the necessary data on how work is done, analysis is necessary to indicate how to improve work. All factors should be challenged and all alternatives considered. Most work study is directed toward changing work patterns in five ways that were first compiled by the industrial engineer Mundel.[5] He called these ways the Five Classes of Change, which are as follows:

Class of Change	*Example*
1. Motions—number, type; body or position	An arrangement for a baker to sit and scoop portions of muffin batter into pans will change the number and kind of motions from those required when standing.
2. Equipment—tools, workplace	Labor is saved by using a scoop for muffins instead of two spoons or by having a timer to stop the mixer when mixing is completed.
3. Production sequence—rearrange, simplify, combine, eliminate, or change sequence	Baking muffins in sheet pans will save scooping into individual pans.
4. Finished products—simple or elaborate	Garnish, such as nuts, may be used on top of each muffin or folded into the mixture.
5. Raw materials—require extra processing or simplify processing	Muffins made with fresh eggs to be broken, frozen eggs ready to measure, or powdered eggs that may be blended with dry ingredients. Ingredients to be assembled, measured, and blended, or a prepared mix used.

[5] Ibid.

Name	Observations										Total	Percent Efficiency
Mary	√	√	0	0	√	0	0	√	√	0	5	50
John	0	√	0	√	0	0	√	√	0	√	5	50
Sue	0	0	√	0	√	0	√	0	√	0	4	40
Tom	√	0	√	√	0	√	0	0	√	√	6	60
Ann	√	√	√	0	√	0	√	√	0	0	6	60
Kate	0	√	0	√	0	0	√	0	0	√	4	40

Figure 3.20 This chart shows how the sampling method may be used to estimate worker productivity. At different times observations have been made to determine who is doing productive work. A circle indicates no productive work; a check indicates productive work is being done.

In addition to considering whether classes of change can be made, many of the principles of motion economy and others cited in this chapter should be considered. It is not always possible to arrive at the best method of doing a job, but study will usually indicate a better way. As noted earlier, the Gilbreths were first to state a theory in motion study that has become a byword in the art: "There's always a better way." Even though a job has just been improved, one should always think: "There's always a better way." Usually in analyzing jobs, "before" and "after" situations are shown and a comparison made of any savings incorporated in the "after" way of doing the job. Some of these methods have been shown here in the examples used to illustrate the various methods of studying work.

Suggested Student Assignments

1. Choose a production kitchen, list all of the sections in it, and identify the work centers in each of the sections.
2. Evaluate the arrangement of the work centers in the sections in terms of interrelationships.
3. Prepare a diagram of the flow, using squares to represent sections and arrows to indicate direction of flow.

4. *Evaluate* the flow in light of the eight basic rules, and state the type of flow it represents.

5. *Redesign* the flow in light of the eight basic rules, and state the type of flow it represents.

6. Indicate, by a colored line on the section plan, the route taken by materials used, showing place where they originate, route followed in processing, and destination.

7. Make a man and machine chart in which a piece of power equipment is used to facilitate the work.

8. Draw one section to scale (representing the equipment in keeping with the designs commonly used by architects), and use it for preparing a distance chart.

9. Make a cross chart of the section that has been redesigned and prepare ratings of the original and the revised arrangement.

10. Observe a task that is being performed, making note of the materials, motions, and equipment used, the sequence of work, and the character of the finished products. Recommend changes that might be made based on the five classes of change.

Chapter 4

operational aspects
in layout planning

Food operations provide services by people for people. The human factors in such operations, therefore, merit special attention on the part of facility planners. Due to the nature of the work and the services provided, employee welfare, comfort, safety, and efficiency, plus the comfort, welfare, and safety of clientele are involved. The physical facilities within which the work is done can do much to ensure satisfactory conditions.

Each food operation in adapting to situations that are peculiar to its particular size, type of operation, location, advantages, and disadvantages has significant needs to be met by its system of operation. A system of operation that may be advantageous for one facility may be unsatisfactory and unprofitable for another, even of the same type. Clear identification of specific needs and possibilities must be made. A system of operation can then be chosen and layout plus equipment selected that will best implement the chosen system.

Experience has shown that a well-designed facility will not prove successful unless the person who later operates the facility fully understands and is capable of directing the work according to the plan for which it was equipped. The ability to function well according to a particular system is sometimes negated by a lack of enthusiasm or acceptance of the plan. Enthusiastic involvement in the planning and/or full understanding and approval of the plan by the operator can be beneficial in fitting the system to specific needs and in carrying out the work according to the plan for which the facility was designed and equipped.

HUMAN FACTORS IN WORK ACCOMPLISHMENT

Suitable utilization of man-hours involves consideration of human factors when planning work areas. It is important that workers be satisfied and able to produce good work in the allotted time with minimum fatigue. Conditions to be sought are those that promote a feeling of well-being and a desire to work, and which minimize causes of fatigue. There are two types of fatigue. The first is a tiredness brought on by physical effort and discomfort, and the second by psychological factors, such as monotony, frustration, dislike of the job, the supervisor, or fellow workers, and low regard for the value of the job. If a worker likes the work, feels that it is important, and has pride in doing it and wants to do it well, a certain buoyancy will be felt that will help to lessen fatigue. The fatigue that is brought on by physical effort and discomfort may be due to one or more of four causes:

1. Physical effort and strain involved in doing the job.

2. Length of time engaged in continuous effort, such as length of shift, length of working day, and hours per week.

3. Length of time and amount of comfort during rest breaks, plus schedule of breaks during shifts.

4. Working conditions in terms of temperature, humidity, light, ventilation, and sounds.

The physical effort and strain in doing tasks that require fast, continuous action, as in mixing ingredients or in chopping vegetables, can be relieved by power equipment. Awkward positions during work can be tiring. Work levels need to be appropriate for the work to be done and for the stature of persons who do it. A height generally accepted as standard for worktables and ranges used by women is 34 in. (86 cm). This is not always satisfactory. When a worker does hand work, such as rolling pie crust, the work surface should be 2 to 4 in. (5 to 10 cm) below the elbow. A short worker may need a lower surface and a tall worker a higher one. When tools are required for manipulation, such as long beaters or spoons, the height should be such that the worker can stand erect at the work surface with hands flat on the surface with arms straight but not stretched. In this case, a good work level can be 37 in. Workers who are tall and have a long reach can usually utilize a higher and deeper work area than those of shorter stature. Height and reach distances will vary, and it is good to know when plannning whether men or women are to be employed or Puerto Ricans who are generally short, versus Germanic people, who are tall. Adjustable levels help in overcoming the problem of providing comfortable heights for all workers.

Strain occurs when a worker is required to work at a faster than normal pace and continue for an extended time without a break. Loads greater than one's strength to handle, lifting in a manner that employs weaker muscles, and standing and walking on floors that have little or no resilience tend to induce strain and fatigue (see Fig. 4.1). Short-cycle

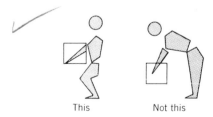

This   Not this

Figure 4.1 When lifting heavy objects, for minimum strain use the force of the legs and not the back. Grasp the object with fingers underneath and keep the weight close to the body.

jobs having repetitive motions tend to bore workers who have high mentality. Pace and rhythm are important and must be adapted to the worker's ability. Pace and rhythm in work can be stimulated mechanically with music or even by a conveyor operating at suitable speed.

Methods of Counteracting Fatigue

Satisfaction in quality of work and value of the job gives impetus for work. Recognition by management of the individual worker as a valuable person may not be possible to build into the facility, but it is an important factor in promoting satisfactory work in terms of quality and amount of accomplishment. Personal pride and social values are important. The social quality of working with others relieves boredom and imparts enjoyment to work. Social aspects can be promoted by rest breaks and meal periods together in a pleasant atmosphere.

Rest periods improve output through recuperation of physical and nervous energy. Relaxation is most effective when rest periods are management-approved and taken in a comfortable place at suitable intervals. Suitable length of periods and frequency will depend upon the nature of the work. For the majority of food facility workers, a 10-minute break near the middle of a 4-hour shift has been considered satisfactory. Studies indicate that less time is taken for personal needs when suitable rest periods are given (see Figure 4.2).

Plans made for proper body mechanics tend to reduce fatigue. The rate of breathing, heartbeat, blood pressure, and other body functions are increased by unnatural posture. The spine and hips of the body form a structure similar to a T that supports the body weight. The smallest amount of muscle pull results when the weight is in balance or evenly distributed on the T (see Figure 4.3). Workers who must bend over, squat down, stretch up, and lift while working experience a pull on muscles that is fatiguing.

The majority of work in a food facility calls for workers to change position and location repeatedly, and being seated at work would interfere considerably with quantity of work done. There are other situations where repetitive action in one location is necessary and where a worker can be seated while working. A suitable chair will help to reduce fatigue. One that is adjustable in height and sturdily built, with a back support for the spine just below the shoulder blade, allows the worker to hold a good position. The position should be one in which the body is straight from the hips to the neck without bending at the waist (see Figure 4.4).

Sounds Can Influence Work. Workers vary in their reaction to sound. Noise from outside the work area tends to be more annoying than that

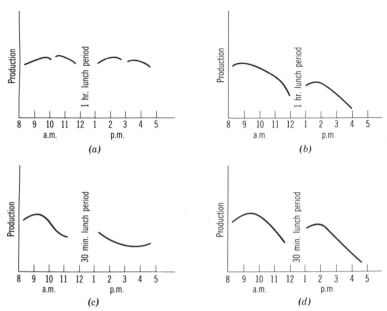

Figure 4.2 Production curves under various conditions. (*a*) Production curve of kitchen worker working at a normal rate with two 10-minute coffee breaks during a shift. (*b*) Production curve of a worker doing heavy work but not at a fast pace drops toward end of shift when worker is tired. (*c*) Production curve of a bored worker. Note how when worker sees end of shift approaching, work production increases. (*d*) Production curve of a worker doing heavy work at a fairly rapid pace.

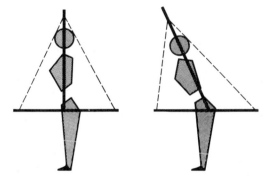

Figure 4.3 Body in balanced and unbalanced positions. The head, chest, and trunk of the body rest on an inverted "T" formed by the hips and spine. Correct posture insures that the weight will be evenly distributed over this "T" Poor posture will impose a heavier work load on some muscles, causing strain and fatigue.

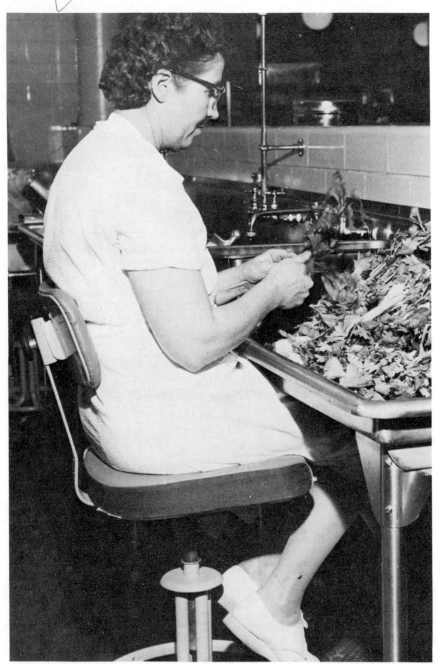

Figure 4.4 A good work chair. Note back rest, full sized seat, and foot rest 16 in. (406 mm) below worker.

in the worker's area. A study made to ascertain the effect of noise on workers indicated that, in a factory having an output of 80 units per worker per day, 60 were made when working near a noisy boiler factory and 110 were made when the workers were moved to a quiet work area. In the latter situation errors were also reduced. Noise interferes with attention, annoying workers and affecting their output. Verbal communications are apt to be misunderstood where noise is high.

The Environmental Protection Agency claims scientific evidence supports the recommendation that industrial noise be reduced to 85 decibels. The Occupational Safety and Health Administration ruling, which went into effect in 1971, stated noise limits to be 90 decibels averaged over an eight-hour day. This is a noise level approximately comparable to that made by a subway train or a 20-ton truck.

In controlling sounds, it is important to understand two physical characteristics of noise, that is, intensity and frequency. Intensity is measured in decibels (db). One decibel is the lowest sound intensity the average person can hear close to the ear, and 150 decibels is the threshold of pain. The ordinary factory areas may have sound intensities varying from 70 to 110 db. Noisy restaurants have registered sound intensity of 70 db. This is comparable to the noise of a vacuum sweeper. Through the use of appropriate controls, noise levels have been reduced by as much as 20 to 30 db. (See Chapter 16 for further information on Sound Control.)

High sound frequencies are more annoying than low sound frequencies. Low frequencies characterize such sounds as hums, thuds, and rumbles; middle frequencies those of roars and clangs; and high frequencies those of shrill ringing, hissing, or clicks. High-frequency sounds are easier to control than low-frequency sounds. Noises of the impact type of low frequency are annoying if rhythmic. Continuous and meaningful noises are less disturbing.

Noise may be reduced by training workers to work quietly, by choosing or designing equipment to operate quietly, through use of sound-deadening or absorbing materials, and by isolating or closing off noisy areas. Trucks with rubber tires and machines with smooth running parts and freedom from vibration are important in maintaining a quiet workshop. Screens or walls may be placed to deflect sound, and acoustic materials may be used to absorb it. A dropped ceiling helps to capture sound. The suspended ceilings are effective sound absorbers because of the dead air space above them. Space absorbers, sometimes called "functional" absorbers, may be used. Proper spacing is necessary to capture sound and absorb it when these are used. Grouping has not been found to be most effective. They should be hung in such a way that they will not throw shadows or oscillate in drafts.

Music helps in masking sound and in developing rhythms in work. It tends to reduce fatigue. In one instance, it was found to increase productivity 4.7 to 11.4 percent. It should not be played, however, more than 2½ hours a day in periods of 12 to 20 minutes. Light, fast music is preferable to slow, somber types.

Good Light Is Needed for Good Work. Good light helps workers to do a satisfactory job and enjoy their work with a minimum of eye strain. About five of every eight workers lack good vision. Few realize that this may be the cause of fatigue and dislike for the job. The cost of proper lighting will be readily offset by better workmanship, increased productivity, fewer accidents, and less waste due to errors. When planning for light in the work area consider (1) the direction from which it comes, (2) color, (3) diffusion, (4) steadiness, and (5) intensity. (See Chapter 13, Lighting.)

Light should be located to eliminate shadows on the work or glare and excessive brightness in the field of vision. The variation of brightness between the working area and field surrounding the working area should not be greater than 3 to 1, with the working area the brighter. In nonworking areas the contrast can be greater, but the ratio should never be greater than 10 to 1. Reflectances recommended by a committee studying lighting for kitchens were for ceilings to have a ratio of 80, walls 60, equipment 30 to 35, and floors not less than 15.

When selecting fluorescent lights choose those that will permit colors to appear natural. Color plays an important role in food enjoyment, and some lights can rob or change the color of food. Fluorescent lights listed in order of satisfactory color quality are cool fluorescent, warm white, and cool white fluorescent. Flickering light or stroboscopic effect may be caused by improper functioning of lighting or by fluorescent lights. It can be eliminated in the latter by the use of 60-cycle current and by the use of two-lamp auxiliaries.

The proper intensity of light will be dependent upon the kind of work to be done. Measured in foot-candles, the following recommendations are made: loading and transporting areas, 10 to 20; rough work, 15 to 35; general work, 35 to 70; and fine assembly, 70 to 150. The committee cited previously that studied kitchen lighting for food facilities recommended general areas, 30, and fine work or inspection, 50 foot-candles. We may need to evaluate our standards to meet limitations in energy expenditure. Excess in lighting should be avoided.

The absorption or reflection of light by colors selected for surroundings, as well as the psychological effect of colors on workers, should be considered. If color contrast between product and work place is great, eye fatigue may result. Walls of gray or green are restful for workers in bright work areas. Surroundings with proper color selection have been found to reduce absenteeism.

Temperature and Relative Humidity Influence Production Rates.

The feeling of pressure or strain experienced in relation to production rate may be measured in terms of increased rate of heartbeat. Studies made of workers performing in a temperature of 81°F (27.2° C) and relative humidity of 56 percent showed only a slight increase in heartrate. When temperature was raised to 99°F (37.2° C) and a relative humidity of 75 percent, the rate increased as the day progressed, and fatigue set in. A temperature that is satisfactory for a moderately active worker is 65°F (18.3° C). Stiffness of arms and legs develops at temperatures below 50°F (10° C), and fatigue increases with those above 75°F (29.4° C).

Fresh, clean air is invigorating. Good ventilation, with air conditioning where essential, and well-insulated equipment to prevent unnecessary heat loss is helpful in maintaining desirable temperatures. In the average kitchen an air change every 2 to 5 minutes is desirable. Hoods over cooking equipment help to eliminate cooking odors as well as heat. Draft is a requisite condition for removal of smoke, heat, and steam. Unless it is properly controlled a drafty condition results that is unpleasant for the workers. Hoods are somewhat similar to a vacuum sweeper in that their effectiveness increases in relation to their closeness in proximity to objects to be picked up or removed. Hoods located high above cooking equipment may have their effectiveness nullified by cross currents of air in the room or the draft made so strong as to cause workers the distinct discomfort of working in a draft. Chapter 15 discusses the planning for proper environmental conditions to meet these needs.

MATERIAL AND EQUIPMENT KEYED TO SYSTEM OF OPERATION

Specific conditions and purposes of the food operation will determine in large degree the system of operation that will be most advantageous. The possibility for suitable control of food and service type, quality, and cost will need to be evaluated in light of availability and adequacy of supplies, labor, and management. Probable acceptance of standards by consumers and the financial aspects of the operation are likely to have a determining influence on selection of a system of operation. The system may vary as follows:

1. All foods are processed from "scratch" within the facility.

2. The majority of foods are processed with the exception of convenience foods that offer the most significant advantage.

3. The majority of foods are purchased fully prepared and only limited preparation made of a few dishes.

4. All foods are purchased fully prepared and require final conditioning only for service.

Realistic calculation in detail, not suppositions, is needed in determining the most desirable system to adopt for a specific operation. The calculations need to explore and compare costs in preparing all, some, or none of the food served. Acceptability of standards for food and service and the dependability of food and labor supplies are to be considered. Unless the most careful evaluation, supported by reliable evidence, is done before planning and building the facility, the operation is likely to be tied to an impractical system. Detailed study at this point can have long-term benefits. The system of operation will determine the kind and amount of equipment needed and the best layout for efficient work.

There is a wide variation in facilities designed to prepare everything from basic raw materials and those that do no food preparation and are service stations only. Space allowance, storage requirements, and specific equipment needs will vary. The type of cooking, such as bulk preparation or individual short orders, as well as the extent of cooking need to be known. A different system may be required for each type of variation, and the planner needs to be thoroughly familiar with requirements for the specific system before designing the facility to accommodate it.

One of the first considerations to be made in choosing a system of operation is the menu or foods required to satisfy a particular clientele. Question whether the majority of foods commonly appearing on the specific menus are better in quality prepared by one system or another. Some foods can be prepared in factory quantities, frozen, thawed, and reheated with minimum damage to palatability. Others, with comparable menu classification, would be seriously robbed of appealing qualities. A potted steak, for example, might well survive such treatment, but roast beef could be expected to loose its "pink of perfection."

Preparation of food from "scratch" must be done at some point, and the information in this book is largely based on this premise. How much and what type is done in the individual kitchen depends upon the policy and planning of the particular organization or owner. Many factors influence the advisability of one system over another. Although menu demands are a first consideration, economics of operation are a close second and involve availability, reliability, and cost of supplies, labor, and management.

Modern markets offer foods at varying stages of preparation. High production costs, especially those for labor, have stimulated attention on foods requiring a minimum of time and skill in conditioning them for service. Such convenience foods as biscuit and cake mixes, dehydrated potatoes, oven-ready meats, and many other items have labor-saving advantages. Fully prepared menu items have helped to meet problems of labor shortage and lack of training and have given certain uniformity in quality standards. Management needs to be alert in adjusting labor schedules when introducing prepared food in order to offset the higher material cost of the menu items. Practical planners, where there is available food bank capacity, have doubled volume as items were produced of foods that could be frozen, thawed, and reheated without greatly affecting quality, for next use in the menu cycle.

Systems of operation may be distinct, mixed, or combined. Preparation of food from basic raw materials may be done in (a) a food facility kitchen that prepares food for one specific operation only, (b) a commissary kitchen that serves satellite serving units, or (c) a large commercial unit or food factory. All conditions that influence cost of output, such as volume, utilization of labor, variety of items, and amount of elaboration of products, will affect the ultimate cost. It is highly advisable for specific operators to evaluate which system will yield the quality, quantity, and variety of items that will best meet their specific needs. A food factory type production is finding favor where a large quantity of similar menu items are required within a specific operation, such as a corporation with many units, or within an organization of food operations that have similar meal requirements, such as hospitals, nursing homes, and schools. In the factory system meal schedules can be ignored.[1] Food may be produced in batches appropriate to quality requirements for specific dishes repetitively and in a manner to best utilize labor time and production costs. The food is then packaged, fast frozen, and held in a low-temperature food bank to await orders or appearance on the cycle menu.

The more meticulous the calculations the more significant will be the comparison of costs and desirability between private food facility produced food and factory produced items. The comparisons should be based on comparable quality, quantity, and choice of items to meet spe-

---

[1] B. J. Williamson, "*Tomorrow's System—The Food Factory—Today,*" *Journal of The American Dietetic Association,* May, 1975.

cific menu requirements, and in amounts customarily needed. Cost figures on the part of private production should include costs for: (1) raw
materials to produce specific quantities of items used daily, (2) daily
payroll cost for production, (3) production space needed in excess of that
required for final conditioning and service, and (4) production equipment needed in excess of that required for final conditioning and service.
The figures for space and equipment should include initial cost plus
interest and depreciation, or initial cost and interest for the period of
years of life expectancy; such as 30 or 40 years for space and 10 years for
equipment. The total cost for each should be divided by the number of
years of life expectancy and added together to get the cost per year for
space and equipment. This figure divided by the number of days per
year that the facility will operate will give the daily cost. The resulting
figure divided by the total number of portions produced daily will yield
the per portion cost for space and equipment. This added to the portion
cost for food, production operating expenses, and labor will give the
cost of private facility produced items. The differences under certain
circumstances may appear large, as when serving small numbers. When
serving larger numbers, or serving very simply prepared foods, the differences may be negligible or definitely on the side of privately produced
foods.

SAFETY AND SANITATION PROTECTION

The safety and sanitation hazards and need for protection is multiplied in relation to the number of food handlers and food consumers
involved daily in public food service. Food provides an excellent medium
for rapid growth of bacteria and molds. Requisite handling in its preparation, display, and service makes it readily subject to contamination. It
is essential to the health and well-being of the public served that proper
safety and sanitary practices be consistently observed. There are many
characteristics of layout and equipment which wise selection can promote safety and sanitation.

Sanitation

All food equipment, walls, floors, and work surfaces should permit
easy, thorough, and frequently repeated cleaning. To be cleanable, the
equipment and work surfaces, such as cutting boards, should be non-
absorbent and free from cracks or other lodging spots for soil. The surfaces should be smooth and the design such as to permit sanitizing all
areas. Machines should be designed for complete dismantling for thor-

ough cleaning. Self-cleaning equipment such as ovens and ventilators, is especially desirable.

Equipment should be installed in such a manner as to permit easy access around and under it for cleaning and inspection. Mobility that permits moving items away from the wall or other equipment is desirable. Ranges, fryers, and three-deck ovens are presently designed for sufficient moving to facilitate cleaning. Wall mounting of permanent fixtures eliminates legs, which interfere with cleaning. Where equipment is fitted to the wall, the fitting should be tight and sealed to exclude vermin or set out sufficiently from the wall that vermin cannot lodge behind it. Splash backs should be on equipment where required. Stationary equipment, such as sinks and ranges, when located in the center of the floor, facilitate cleaning and permit workers to work from both sides. When equipment is set on a base or raised platform, the base should be 4 to 6 in. (10 to 15 cm) high depending on height desired. The base should be recessed to allow for a 4-in. (10 cm) toe space and coved at the floor juncture on a ¾-in. (2 cm) radius. Flat surfaces that must rest directly on the floor or upon a base should be scribed to the surface with a mastic or cement to seal against the entrance of vermin.

Traps, drains, pipes, shelves, and bottom surfaces of equipment that are exposed should be at least 6 in. (15 cm) and preferably 8 in. (20 cm) above the floor to permit cleaning under. Grease traps need to be placed so as to be readily cleanable. They may be mounted on slightly raised bases coved at the floor. Spacers should be placed between equipment to seal in areas that may become soil catchers.

Fastenings on equipment should be designed to eliminate projections and ledges. Surfaces should be smooth. Wiring and pipes should be concealed. Hot steam and water pipes are especially difficult to clean and are a hazard to persons working around them. Pipes that must be visible should be of a design and material that will not mar the beauty of the installation. Service lines and utilities can sometimes be hidden by bringing them through the legs of the equipment.

Provisions for Cleaning. A firmly established policy pertaining to the responsibility for the care and cleaning of tools and equipment in each work center will greatly help toward promoting good housekeeping practices. It has been generally observed that workers tend to be more careless when an outside person or agency is brought in to do the cleanup. Unless pride and a responsible attitude is developed, only surfaces required for immediate use and equipment that can be sent to the pot washer may be cleaned regularly. Ample hot water, proper sanitizing materials, and suitable equipment should be provided and accessible to

all sections of work. Figure 4.5 gives some critical food temperatures that
should be known by workers.

Two-temperature hot water is required for dish and pot washing. A
booster heater may be used to ensure proper temperatures. Although
high temperature water is required for purposes of sanitizing, it is not
needed or desirable for general kitchen purposes. Planning should pro-

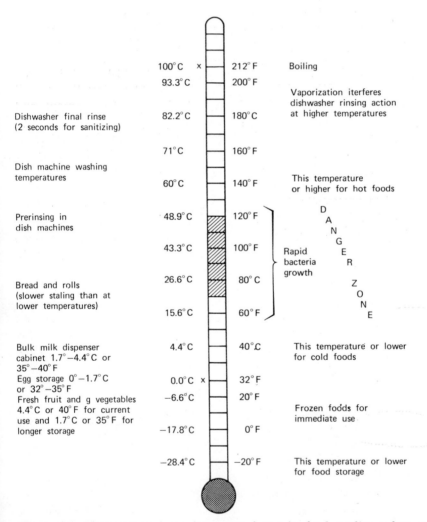

Figure 4.5 Temperature is an important factor in food quality, safety, and
sanitation.

vide water at proper temperatures at points where required. 1 ...be connections are needed for rinsing floors, flushing a soiled dish table, cleaning mobile equipment, and washing garbage cans. Drains to carry off the scrub water should be provided at locations where needed to remove the water quickly. All floors should be waterproofed and sloped gradually toward the drains, with about $\frac{1}{2}$ in. ($1\frac{1}{4}$ cm) drop at the drain plate to ensure satisfactory drainage. Floor drains should be provided with flushout valves and should be so located that workers will not have to walk or stand on them.

Utility connections coming from the floor should be minimized and made from the wall where possible. Pipe chases should be put on all vertical lines for gas, steam, electricity, and plumbing leads and designed so as not to harbor vermin. Openings for pipes should be sealed against entry of vermin. Watertight metal ferrules should be installed for all piping and other leads coming through the bottom of equipment, and these ferrules should extend 1 in. above the surface entry area. Drains should be placed in or close to all refrigerated areas and the drainage piped outside. Dripping and leakage from pipes and back-siphonage from drains into the fresh water supply, sinks, and the water bath of steam tables should be prevented. Cooling coils around food should be mounted to protect the food and insulated against condensate. Outlets to sinks should be a minimum of two times the diameter of the water inlet and never less than 1 in. ($2\frac{1}{2}$ cm) above the flood level rim.

Standards of the National Sanitation Foundation should be closely followed.

Safety

Safety is the state of being free from hazards. Common hazards existing in food facilties include cutting, burning, falling, colliding, and being hit. Carelessness, fatigue, excessive hurrying, inattention, and poor visibility are common conditions conducive to the occurrence of accidents. The unexpected or "surprise factors" account for the largest percentage of accidents. Among the hazardous surprise elements in food service facilities are blind corners, cross traffic, irregular surfaces, slick spots on floors, bumping by swinging doors, slipping of a knife, equipment out of place, sticking and wrong-way doors, and unexpectedly hot surfaces. Fire may be caused by faulty equipment, poor installation, and employee carelessness. Accident rates increase when workers become tired, lack interest, have poor work habits, have their attention diverted, lack understanding of their work, or cannot see their work clearly. Note in Figure 4.6 the relationship of the time of day to accident rates.

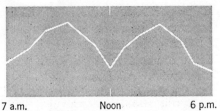

7 a.m.   Noon   6 p.m.

Figure 4.6 Accident record in relation to work day. Data compiled by the National Safety Council indicate that there is a sharp rise in accident probability 3 hours after starting time and 3 hours after the noonday break. This substantiates the author's statement that tired workers are accident-prone workers. Monotony and fatigue can be alleviated by work breaks.

Plan Suitable Protection Against Fire.   This will include not only the use of fire-resistant materials, but also detection and extinguishing facilities. Dangerous grease fires can be avoided by eliminating all grease accumulation. Elevators, shafts, and ventilating ducts should be sealed off in case of fire. Investigate extinguishing systems in selecting one that will be most effective and in keeping with local fire ordinances. Portable extinguishers may be installed, preferably those using carbon dioxide rather than carbon tetrachloride. Steam, carbon dioxide, or water may be piped into ducts for fire prevention. Self-closing louvres may be installed so that ducts close on reaching excessive temperatures. Many new pieces of equipment using steam or gas have instant disconnect systems. In times of emergency they may be crucial to safety.

Automatic and manual fire alarms may be installed. Where desirable they may be connected to fire department alarms so that automatic notification occurs. Place alarms near exits. Include the alarm system as a part of the electrical contract. Have an alarm that is readily distinguished from other sounds. It can be of a general type or coded. In coded type, the area of the fire is indicated. Certain fire ordinances require sprinkler systems and a coded alarm system. Some sprinkling systems give alarm when the water starts to flow. Signals can be sent to predetermined key locations, such as a telephone switchboard, office, or nurses' stations. The system used should prevent undue alarm to building occupants. The National Fire Protection Association and representatives of fire equipment manufacturers can assist in setting up good fire protection facilities.

Plan Safety Protection.   Have sturdy, smooth handrails, 30 in. high (76 cm), firmly installed on stairs. Stair treads, risers, and landings should be standard proportions. Provide adequate protection around floor openings and platforms. Windows and lighting fixtures should be constructed so that their cleaning and maintenance will not be hazardous, particularly from falls. Electrical wiring must not produce fire or shock hazards. Elevators must be equipped with interlocks to prevent operation with the doors open. Floors, ramps, stairs, and all walking surfaces must be rendered adequately nonslip. Provide good lighting.

Moving parts of equipment should be enclosed by guards or castings. Heavy objects should not be stored overhead but placed low enough for convenient use or transfer. Employees should be instructed in body mechanics in relation to proper ways of lifting heavy objects. Employees should not be required to lift loads that will cause excess strain. Provide structure strength for shelves, floors, and other areas sufficient for the greatest load they will bear. Arrange for storage of all toxic materials, such as cleaning compounds, away from areas used for storage of foods and where they will not have to be selected from storage in the dark or in inadequate light for seeing labels.

Avoid Toxic Materials in Tools and Equipment. Zinc, which is used for galvanizing, is a soft metal that is readily attacked by acids. It should not come in contact with foods. Its use in galvaneal should be restricted to areas where this is not possible. Copper and brass are soft metals that can form toxic substances, and these should be well plated with harder metals so that any possibility of reaction with food is eliminated. Antimony, used in gray enamelware, cadmium in plating, and lead, which is a common ingredient of solder, are also toxic.

Comply Strictly With Safety Codes. Consult codes and suggested standards of the National Bureau of Fire Underwriters, The National Fire Protection Association, American Standards Association, the United States Department of Commerce, The American Society of Mechanical Engineers, National Bureau of Standards, National Sanitation Foundation, United States Bureau of Health, and local ordinances. The requirements of the Occupational Safety and Health Act (OSHA) or, as it sometimes is called, "The Williams-Steiger Safety and Health Act of 1970" should be met in all plannning. This act establishes many safety requirements in the planning of foodservices, covering in detail electrical grounding and other electrical requirements, guarding dangerous equipment, the installation and maintenance of fire equipment, and the construction of stairways, rails, and so on. In the first five months of enforcement of this act, the national Restaurant Association reports, "OSHA inspectors conducted 10,668 inspections, found 26,771 violations,

Safety Check List   The Following Checklist Covers Both Physical Properties and Work Practices.*

Area	Yes	No	Comments
I. Receiving Area:			
A. Are floors in safe condition? (Are they free from broken tile and defective floor boards? Are they covered with nonskid material?)			
B. Are employees instructed in correct handling methods for various containers, etc., that are received?			
C. Are garbage cans washed daily in hot water?			
D. Are garbage cans always covered?			
E. Are trash cans leakproof and adequate in number and size?			
F. If garbage disposal area is adjacent to or part of the general receiving area, is there a program that keeps floors and/or dock areas clear of refuse?			
G. Is there a proper rack for holding garbage containers? Are garbage containers on dollies or other wheel units to eliminate lifting by employees?			
H. Are adequate tools available for opening crates, barrels, cartons, etc. (hammer, wire cutter, cardboard carton openers and pliers?			
I. Is crate, carton, and barrel opening done away from open containers of food?			
II. Storage Area:			
A. Are shelves, adequate to bear weight of items stored?			
B. Are employees instructed to store heavy items on lower shelves and lighter materials above?			
C. Is a safe ladder provided for reaching high storage?			
D. Are cartons or other flammable materials stored at least two feet from light bulbs?			

* By Raymond C. Ellis, Senior Engineer, National Safety Council, 425 North Michigan Ave., Chicago, II.

Safety Check List (*Continued*)

Area	Yes	No	Comments
E. Are light bulbs provided with a screen guard?			
F. Is a fire extinguisher located at the door?			
III. Pots and Pans Room or Area:			
A. Are duckboards or floor boards in safe condition (free from broken slats and worn areas that could cause tripping)?			
B. Are employees properly instructed in use of correct amounts of detergent and or other cleaning agents?			
C. Are adequate rubber gloves provided?			
D. Is there an adequate drainboard or other drying area so that employees do not have to pile pots and pans on the floor before and after washing them?			
E. Do drain plugs permit draining without the employee placing hands in hot water?			
IV. Walk-in Coolers and Freezers— (Refrigerators):			
A. Are floors in the units in good condition and covered with slip proof material? Are they mopped at least once a week?			
B. If floor boards are used, are they in safe conditions (free from broken slats and worn areas that could cause tripping)?			
C. Are portable storage racks and stationary racks in safe condition (free from broken or bent shelves and set on solid legs)?			
D. Are blower fans properly guarded?			
E. Is there a by-pass device on the door to permit exit if an employee is locked in?			
F. Or, is there an alarm bell?			
G. Is adequate aisle space provided?			
H. Are employees properly instructed on placement of hands for movement of portable racks to avoid hand injuries?			
I. Are heavy items stored on lower shelves and lighter items on higher shelves?			
J. Are shelves adequately spaced to prevent pinched hands?			

Safety Check List (*Continued*)

Area	Yes	No	Comments
K. Is the refrigerant in the refrigerator non-toxic? (Check with your refrigerator service man.)			
V. Food Preparation Area:			
A. Is electrical equipment properly grounded?			
B. Is electrical equipment inspected regularly by an electrician?			
C. Are electrical switches located so that they can be reached readily in the event of an emergency?			
D. Are the switches located so that employees do not have to lean on or against metal equipment when reaching for them?			
E. Are floors regularly and adequately maintained (mopped at least three times weekly and waxed with nonskid wax when necessary; are defective floor boards and tile replaced when necessary)?			
F. Are employees instructed to immediately pick or clean up all dropped items and spillage?			
G. Are employees properly instructed in the operation of machines?			
H. Are employees forbidden to use equipment unless specifically trained in its use?			
I. Are machines properly guarded? (Check with the manufacturer if there is a question.)			
J. Are guards always used by all employees?			
K. Is a pusher or tamp provided for use with the grinder?			
L. Are mixers in safe operating condition?			
M. Are the mixer beaters properly maintained to avoid injury from broken metal parts and foreign particles in food?			
VI. Serving Area:			
A. Are steam tables cleaned daily and regularly maintained (gas or electric units checked regularly by a competent service man)?			

Safety Check List (*Continued*)

Area	Yes	No	Comments
B. Is safety value equipment operative?			
C. Are serving counters and tables free of broken parts and wooden or metal slivers and burrs?			
D. Do you have regular inspection of: Glassware?			
China?			
Silverware?			
Plastic equipment?			
E. If anything breaks near the food service area, do you remove all food from service adjacent to breakage?			
F. Are tray rails adequate and set to prevent trays from slipping or falling off at the end or corners?			
G. Are floors and/or ramps in good condition (covered with nonskid material, free from broken tile and defective floor boards)?			
H. Are these areas mopped at least three times weekly and waxed with nonskid wax when necessary?			
I. Is the traffic flow set so that patrons or workers do not collide while carrying trays or obtaining foods?			
VII. Dining Areas:			
A. Are floors free from broken tile and defective floor boards? Are they covered with nonskid wax?			
B. Are pictures securely fastened to walls?			
C. Are drapes, blinds, or curtains securely fastened?			
D. Are chairs free from splinters, metal burrs, broken or loose parts?			
E. Are floors "policed" for cleaning up spillage and other materials?			
F. Is special attention given to the floor adjacent to water, ice cream, or milk station?			
G. Are vending machines properly grounded?			

Safety Check List (*Continued*)

Area	Yes	No	Comments
H. If patrons clear their own trays prior to return to dishwashing area, are the floors kept clean of garbage, dropped silver, and/or broken glass and china?			
I. If trays with used dishes are placed on conveyor units, are the edges guarded to keep students from catching fingers or clothing?			
J. If dishes are removed on portable racks or bus trucks, are these units in safe operating conditions (all wheels or castors working, all shelves firm)?			
VIII. Soiled Dish Processing Area:			
A. Are floors reasonably free of excessive water and spillage?			
B. Are floor boards properly maintained and in safe condition (free from broken slats and worn areas that cause tripping)?			
C. Are all electrical units properly grounded?			
D. Are switches located to permit rapid shutdown in the event of emergency?			
E. Can employees easily reach switches without touching or leaning against such metal units as tables and counters?			
F. Are switches readily accessible?			
G. Are employees carefully instructed in the use of detergents to prevent agitation of dermatitis, etc.?			
H. Do you have a program for disposition of broken glass and china?			
I. If a dishwashing machine is used, is the take-off board set to prevent fingers or hands from being caught?			
J. Where controls are in passageway, are they recessed or guarded to prevent breakage or accidental starting?			
K. Are dish racks in safe condition (if wooden, free from broken slats and smoothly finished to eliminate splinter-			

Safety Check List (*Continued*)

Area	Yes	No	Comments
K. *Continued* ing; if metal, free of sharp corners that could cause cuts)? Are these racks kept off the floor to prevent tripping?			
IX. Don't Overlook:			
A. Lighting, is it adequate in the Receiving Area?			
Storage Area?			
Pots and Pans Area?			
Walk-in Coolers and Freezers?			
Food Preparation Area?			
Cooking Area?			
Serving Area?			
Dining Area?			
Soild Dish Processing Area?			
B. Doors—do they open into passageways where they could cause an accident? (List any such locations).			
Are fire exits clearly marked and the passage kept clear of equipment and materials? (List any violations).			
C. Stairways and ramps: Are they adequately lighted?			
Are the angles of ramps set to provide maximum safety?			
If stairs are metal, wood, composition, or marble, have abrasive materials been used to provide protection against slips and falls?			
Are pieces broken out of the nosing, or front edge, of the steps?			
Are clean and securely fastened handrails available?			
If the stairs are wide, has a center rail been provided?			
D. Ventilation, is it adequate in the Receiving Area?			
Storage Area?			
Pots and Pans Area?			
Walk-in Coolers and Freezers?			

Safety Check List (*Continued*)

Area	Yes	No	Comments
D. Ventilation, is it adequate in the (*Continued*)			
Food Preparation Area?			
Cooking Area?			
Serving Area?			
Dining Area?			
Soiled Dish Processing Area?			
E. Shoes:			
Do employees wear good shoes to protect their feet against injury from articles that are dropped or pushed against their feet?			
F. Clothing:			
Is their clothing free of parts that could get caught in mixers, cutters or grinders?			
G. Is the extinguisher guarded so that it will not be knocked from the wall?			
H. If the door is provided with a lock, is there an emergency bell or a by-pass device that will permit exit from the room should the door be accidentally locked while an employee is in the room?			

issued 2,141 citations, and assessed penalties totaling $512,067."[2] Most were because of operational deficiencies but a large number were because of planning failures.

Suggested Student Assignments

1. Choose an employee for observation and note working conditions, manner in which the employee does work, and environmental and any other factors that may be identified as fatigue factors. List these, and recommend ways in which each may be overcome.

2. List ways by which the noise level in the kitchen which has been chosen for observation may be lowered. What provision has been made for control?

[2] National Restaurant Association, "OSHA Affects You—Disregard Will Bring Penalties," *NRA News*, reprint, n.d.

3. Evaluate the lighting in terms of adequacy, freedom from glare, sharp contrasts, and good color.

4. Use a thermometer for checking temperature in different section of a kitchen. (Permit the thermometer to remain for 10 minutes in each of the areas checked. Note the temperature in each of the areas, and evaluate from the standpoint of worker comfort).

5. Identify factors in the work situation that are hazardous to sanitation and/or safety. Recommend ways to eliminate the hazards.

6. Observe, if possible, food prepared (a) from raw materials to completed products, (b) in a satellite system in which food is prepared centrally and sent to service units, and (c) commercially and merely conditioned for service. Discover, if possible, the comparative costs of food and labor and note acceptability of food quality.

7. What provisions have been made for fire protection in kitchens in which observations have been made?

Chapter 5

space allocation

The challenge when allotting space for a food facility is to allow enough for functional efficiency without excess space to add to building, operating, and maintenance costs. The dining area, for example, needs to be large enough to provide for the number of persons who will require service during a given period of time. If larger than needed, not only will there be excess building expense measured in cost per square foot or meter, but also operating expense measured in labor time for extra steps in service and maintenance. When the area is too small, on the other hand, it is likely to be inadequate for the service load required of it and/or to provide for the volume of patronage needed to support the operation. Production, storage, and other areas must be similarly allocated.

Adequacy of space is contingent upon many factors. Typical of the questions that will call for answers are the following:

1. How many are to be served, and what are their particular food needs?

2. What is the largest number needing service at one time?

3. What foods are to be offered, and what kind of preparation is necessary?

4. What system of buying, storage, and preparation will be used?

5. What kind of service will be provided and on what schedule?

6. What type and amount of storage will be needed?

7. What are the space needs for maintenance, management office, employee facilities, and patron service?

Answers to the questions call for careful analysis of the current situation plus consideration of probable future changes occasioned by growth, market conditions, competitive influences, and organizational changes. Availability of space and investment funds is likely to temper decisions. Space allowance in relation to investment should be balanced in terms of (1) proposed permanence of the facility; (2) acuteness of need for the specific operation; (3) essentials for operating efficiency; (4) desirable standards in terms of appearance, sanitation, and good quality of production and service; and (5) immediate and future costs, depreciation, upkeep, and maintenance.

Choice of a system of operation has major influence on space requirements and probable success of the operation. It needs to be determined in relation to needs of the specific operation and the availability of acceptable supplies and services. It is important to be aware of systems being followed by similar institutions and the degree of their success.

Before adopting any system of operation, evaluate it carefully in relation to meeting demands in the specific situation. The characteristics of permanence of a building and the equipment make adjustment to change fairly inflexible after the choice of an operational system has become concrete. After a facility has been built according to a plan for the food needed, space and preparation equipment for a change of system is not likely to be readily available.

Future needs, as well as those that are immediate, call for study. If enlargement is probable, studies made before the building is planned as to how space may be added and how the initial plan should be designed to minimize ultimate cost will be helpful. Market trends and labor supplies are important. Thought should be given to any conditions that may influence patronage volume and/or service demands. Certain neighborhood changes may influence volume.

It is good to block out space allowances according to functions that the facility is to perform. Calculate area requirements in terms of (1) volume and type of service, (2) amount and size of equipment to be used, (3) number of workers required, (4) space needed for supplies, and (5) suitable traffic area. The dining area location and space allowance are usually determined first, the production areas next in terms of specific relationship to the dining area, and other sections as required to these. Planners should be careful in accepting general space recommendations. There are many variations from which to choose in meeting needs for a specific situation.

DINING AREAS

Space for dining areas is usually based on the number of square feet or meters per person seated multiplied by the number of persons seated at one time.

Space Requirements

Consider patron's size, comfort, and the type and quality of service. Small children may need only 8 sq ft (.74 m^2) for dining room seating, where an adult for comfort would require 12 sq ft (1.11 m^2). Banquet seating allowance might be as little as 10 sq ft (.93 m^2) per seat and a deluxe restaurant as much as 20 sq ft (1.86 m^2). The amount of serving equipment in the dining area and line-up space will influence footage allowance per seat. Space used for other than seating is included in the dining area square footage requirement.

Adequate space for comfort is important. Crowding is distasteful to many people. It is likely to be tolerated more readily by youngsters than

Figure 5.1 Dining room chairs located back to back tend to obstruct traffic and make unobstructed, free-flowing traffice lanes essential.

by adults. It is more acceptable in low-cost quick-service units than in those featuring leisurely dining. Both young and old enjoy having sufficient elbow room and enough space so that dishes of food and beverage are not crowded. Place settings for adults usually allow 24 in. (9.45 cm) and for children 18 to 20 in. (7.09 to 1.87 cm).

Table 5.1 Space Allowance per Seat for Various Types of Food Operations

	Allowance per Seat	
Type of Operation	**m²**	**sq ft**
Cafeteria, commerical	1.49–1.67	16–18
Cafeteria, college and industrial	1.11–1.39	12–15
Cafeteria, school lunchroom	.84–1.11	9–12
College residence, table service	1.11–1.39	12–15
Counter service	1.67–1.86	18–20
Table service, hotel, club, restaurant	1.39–1.67	15–18
Table service, minimum	1.02–1.30	11–14
Banquet, minimum	.93–1.02	10–11

All of the areas in a dining room used for purposes other than seating are a part of the square footage (or square meter) allowance for seating. This does not include waiting areas, guest facilities, cloakrooms, and similar areas. Excessive loss or use of space for other than seating in the dining area will, however, increase needs. Width and length of the room, table and chair sizes, and seating arrangements affect capacity.

Service stations may be estimated in the proportion of one small one for every twenty seats or a large central one for every fifty or sixty seats. The advisability of having a central serving station will be influenced by the distance of the dining area from the serving area. It is of special value if production and dining areas are on different floors. Plumbing and wiring, and whether supplies are delivered mechanically, will influence location of the stations. Small substations for silver, dishes, napery, beverages, ice, butter, and condiments may measure 20 to 24 in. (50 to 61 cm) square and 36 to 38 in. (91 to 97 cm) high. The size of central stations varies from that for a small enclosed room to that of a screened section measuring approximately 8 to 10 ft (2.44 to 3.05 m) long by 27 to 30 in. (.69 to .76 m) wide by 6 to 7 ft (1.83 to 2.13 m) high.

Table size will influence patron comfort and efficient utilization of space. In a cafeteria, for example, where patrons may dine on the trays, it is important that the table be of adequate size to accommodate the number of trays likely to be used. Four trays 14 × 18 in. (36 × 46 cm) fit better on a table 48 in. (122 cm) square than on a table 36 or 42 in. (91 or 107 cm) square. Small tables, such as 24 or 30 in. (61 or 76 cm) square, are economical for seating but are uncomfortable for large people. They are only suitable in crowded areas for fast turnover and light meals. Tables having a common width and height allowing them to be fitted together will give flexibility in seating arrangements (see Fig. 5.2). These are particularly good for banquette or cocktail bench seating along a wall. Tables in booths are difficult for waitresses to serve if they are longer than 4 ft (122 cm). The width of the booths including seats and table is commonly 5½ ft (155 cm). A lunch counter will have a minimum width of 16 in. (41 cm) and a maximum width of 24 to 30 in. (61 to 76 cm). The linear measurement is calculated on the basis of 20 to 24 in. (51 to 61 cm) per seat. The maximum area best served by one waitress is generally 16 ft (4.88 m) of counter. This will allow for eight to ten seats. U-shaped counters make maximum use of space and reduce travel. Space in depth of 8½ to 11 ft (2.59 to 3.35 m) will be required for every linear foot of counter. This will provide 3 to 4 ft (91 to 122 cm) of public aisle, 2½ ft (76 cm) for counter width, and 3 to 4½ ft (91 to 137 cm) for aisle space for employees. A width of 4½ ft (137 cm) is desirable

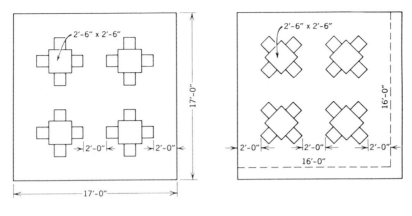

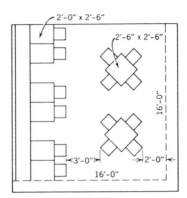

Figure 5.2 Variations in the utilization of space, using different table and seating arrangements. Table size 30 in. (0.76 m) square in a room 17 ft (5.18 m) square and in one 16 ft (4.88 m) square.

where employees must pass other workers. Figures 5.3 through 5.5 show various spatial relationships in seating.

Calculate aisle space between tables and chairs to include passage area and that occupied by the person seated at the table. A minimum passage area is 18 in. (46 cm) between chairs and, including chair area, tables should be placed 4 to 5 ft (122 to 152 cm) apart. Aisles on which bus carts or other mobile equipment are to be moved should be sized according to the width of such equipment.

The best utilization of space can often be arrived at through a study using templets or scaled models. Diagonal arrangement of square tables utilizes space better than square arrangement and yields more trouble-

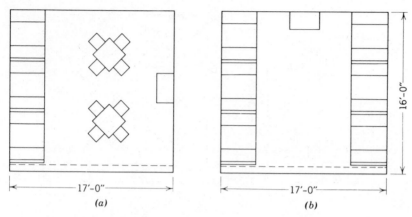

Figure 5.3 Seating arrangements affect capacity. (*a*) Use of booths and tables with serving station has capacity for 20. (*b*) Booth seating with serving station has capacity for 24.

free traffic lanes. Lanes that pass between backs of chairs are likely to be blocked when guests arise or are being seated.

Choose table height in terms of comfort of the diners. This is especially important in schools. In lunchrooms patronized by several grades a compromise height will be needed between 30 in. (76 cm) normally used for adults and 24 in. (61 cm) suitable for children, or two sizes used in

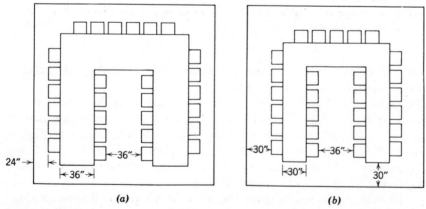

Figure 5.4 Table width and aisle space affect capacity. (*a*) A 36 in. (0.91 m) table in room 19 ft (5.79 m) square. Capacity—28. (*b*) A 30-in. (0.76 m) table in a room 19 ft square. Capacity—27.

different sections of the room. A table to seat 4, 6, or 8 is preferable to longer ones.

Number of Persons Allowance

The number of persons to be seated at one time is the second point of information needed for calculation of the dining room size. The total number of seats required at one time multiplied by the space required for each seat will give the total number of square feet or meters needed in the dining area. The number of times a seat is occupied during a given period is commonly referred to as "turnover." The turnover per hour multiplied by the number of seats available gives the total number of patrons that can be served in an hour. If peak loads, or the largest number to be served at one time, are known, the number of seats required can be estimated.

Turnover rates tend to vary. They are influenced by such factors as the amount of food eaten, the elaborateness of service, and the diner's time allowance. A breakfast meal of few foods may be eaten more quickly than dinner, and a simple fare faster than a many-course meal. Turnover can be quickest where food has been prepared in advance and where patrons serve themselves and bus their soiled dishes. The turnover time is speeded up 10 percent by patrons removing their soiled dishes so tables are available for other guests. Deluxe service for leisure dining, involving removal and placement of several courses, takes the longest time. Although specific turnover may vary from 10 minutes to 2 hours, actual eating time is normally 10 to 15 minutes for breakfast, 15 to 20 minutes for lunch, and 30 to 40 minutes for dinner.

The calculation of occupancy of seats in a dining room must take into consideration a certain percentage of vacancy, except where a given number are seated at one time according to assignment. In table service this has been estimated as 20 percent of total capacity, in cafeterias from 12 to 18 percent, and for counter operations 10 to 12 percent. Many factors influence this percentage, such as patrons arriving at different times, irregular rate of turnover, and reluctance to share a table with strangers.

The table sizes used in the dining room affect occupancy. It is often desirable to provide for groups varying from two to eight, with a predominance in most dining rooms of two persons. The "deuces" may be of a size and shape that can be put together to form tables for larger groups. In metropolitan areas where many tend to dine alone, wall bench-type seating and tables for two with a center ridge or line denoting space for one have been used successfully. Chairs with "tablet-arms" that will hold a tray have been used for fast turnover in crowded areas.

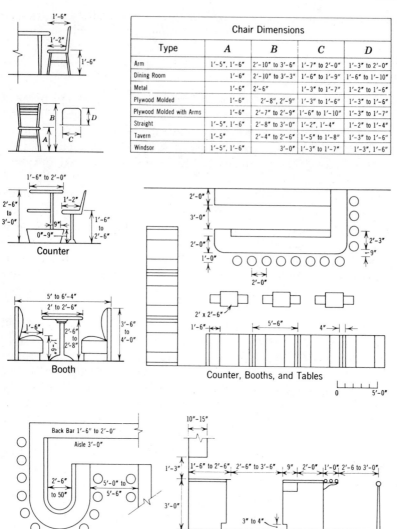

Chair Dimensions				
Type	*A*	*B*	*C*	*D*
Arm	1'-5", 1'-6"	2'-10" to 3'-6"	1'-7" to 2'-0"	1'-3" to 2'-0"
Dining Room	1'-6"	2'-10" to 3'-3"	1'-6" to 1'-9"	1'-6" to 1'-10"
Metal	1'-6"	2'-6"	1'-3" to 1'-7"	1'-2" to 1'-6"
Plywood Molded	1'-6"	2'-8", 2'-9"	1'-3" to 1'-6"	1'-3" to 1'-6"
Plywood Molded with Arms	1'-6"	2'-7" to 2'-9"	1'-6" to 1'-10"	1'-3" to 1'-7"
Straight	1'-5", 1'-6"	2'-8" to 3'-0"	1'-2", 1'-4"	1'-2" to 1'-4"
Tavern	1'-5"	2'-4" to 2'-6"	1'-5" to 1'-8"	1'-3" to 1'-6"
Windsor	1'-5", 1'-6"	3'-0"	1'-3" to 1'-7"	1'-3", 1'-6"

Counter

Booth

Counter, Booths, and Tables

Multiple Bay Counter

Cafeteria Backbar and Counter

Figure 5.5 Dining and service area dimensions.

Table 5.2 indicates the percentage of tables accommodating given numbers that are sometimes suggested for eating establishments of different types.

The utilization of seating capacity tends to be greater for cafeterias than for table service. While the patron may spend 25 to 50 percent of the time seated at the table waiting for service, the cafeteria diner may begin eating as soon as he is seated. One cafeteria line can serve 4 to 8 patrons per minute depending upon (1) the speed of the servers, (2) promptness of selection, influenced by amount of selection and clarity of information, (3) the convenience of layout, and (4) the type patrons. At these rates, 240 to 480 patrons will need to be seated within an hour. If the turnover rate is 2 per hour, then from 120 to 240 seats will be used. However, if 15 percent of the total capacity at the peak period remains unfilled, then between 140 and 280 seats will be required. An additional 14 to 28 seats, or 10 percent, would be needed if patrons do not bus their soiled dishes. All factors are important.

Patronage estimates for facilities of different types may be guided by the number of persons in residence, enrollments in a school, an in-

Metric Conversion for Feet and Inches Given

ft and in.	meters	ft and in.	meters
9″	.23	2′4″	.71
10″	.25	2′6″	.76
12″	.30	2′7″	.79
1′2″	.36	2′8″	.81
1′3″	.38	2′9″	.83
1′4″	.41	2′10″	.86
1′5″	.43	3′	.91
1′6″	.46	3′6″	1.07
1′7″	.48	4′	1.22
1′8″	.51	4′2″	1.27
1′9″	.53	5′	1.52
1′10″	.56	5′6″	1.68
1′11″	.58	6′	1.83
2′	.61	6′4″	1.93
2′3″	.69		

Figure 5.5 (*Continued*)

Table 5.2 The Percentage of Tables of Different Sizes Suggested for Food
Facilities of Different Types

Type of Dining Room	Tables for Two, Percent	Tables for Three or More, Percent
Campus commons	30	70
Industrial or business restaurant	60	40
Family restaurant	25	75
Hotel dining room	60	40
Shoppers' tearoom	80	20

dustry's payroll, the membership in a club, or the volume of meal-time
traffic in an office or shopping area. In each case a certain percentage
may normally be expected to dine in the facility. The percentage will
be influenced by such factors as its location in relation to other facilities,
the patrons' buying power, the prices (as based on subsidy or profit),
patrons' time allowance related to speed of service, and the convenience
of location.

The patronage estimate for a college cafeteria involves consideration
of total enrollment; the number of students who live at home, in organized houses, or residence halls; and competing food facilities on or near
the campus. A college residence providing table service may have to
allow a seating capacity that is 110 percent of occupancy if a policy
exists of having "special guest" occasions and seating all at one time.

An industrial lunchroom may serve as few as 25 percent and as many
as 90 percent of the payroll. Clues to probable patronage may be drawn
from such factors as nearness to other eating facilities, wage rates, type
of work, prices to be charged, policy of permitting or refusing patronage
by outsiders, and appeal qualities such as food goodness and attractive,
hospitable atmosphere. The attitude of management toward the lunchroom is likely to influence patronage. Pride in providing good food
and appealing service for the industrial family as opposed to a take-it-
or-leave-it attitude tends to influence patrons' response.

The size of the hospital dining room should be gauged by the size and
the number of the groups who may be served in it, such as employees,
patients, and/or guests. The size and type of a hospital will influence the
number of personnel likely to be employed and the number of ambulatory patients who may be served in the dining room. The ratio of personnel to patients will vary from 1 to 3, depending upon the amount of

special care required and the amount of teaching and research done. Food quality, price schedule, and appeal factors will influence the percentage of patronage by those eligible to eat in the facility.

School lunch participation has varied from 25 to 75 percent. It is strongly influenced by the amount of subsidy provided and the prices charged. The national average has been between 40 and 45 percent of enrollment. Where prices are low, the food good, meal selection appealing, and the food service program carefully integrated with the educational program, the percentage can be expected to be high. An acceptable schedule for staggering lunch periods is to be considered when determining seating capacity of the lunchroom.

Capacity for banquet seating needs to be flexible in order to satisfy different types of patrons, kinds of functions, and number of people to be served. Folding tables 30 in. (76 cm) wide are popular. These are obtainable in varying lengths, but 72 and 96 in. (183 and 244 cm) are commonly used. The spacing for the legs should permit comfortable seating when the tables are joined end to end and place settings are laid on 24-in. (61-cm) centers.

Restaurant operators anticipating establishing a business for profit need to determine requisite seating capacity on the basis of the amount of income essential to cover operating costs and provide a suitable profit. Labor, food, and operating costs must be met and a profit realized that covers risk-bearing, effort expended, and return on investment. Essential income is weighed in the light of probable patronage and probable average check. The number of seats provided must be sufficient for the volume of patronage that will yield the income required and which is reasonable to expect.

Flexibility in seating capacity is desirable. People do not like to be crowded nor do they enjoy the lonely experience of being seated in a huge area occupied by only a few people. Sparse patronage creates the impression of low popularity. Separate rooms, folding doors, screens, or other attractive devices can be used to reduce the size of an area during slack periods. Sections left open should be those easiest to serve. Balconies, backrooms, or other less desirable space can often be used for overflow numbers that occasionally require service.

Dining room operations often need a larger seating capacity at one meal than at others. This may be due either to increased numbers or different turnover rates. A residence cafeteria with a main dining room capacity of 600 has an adjoining room to seat 100 The adjoining room is used at dinner time only when a larger number appears for service at one time and the turnover because of the fuller meal is slower. The room is available at breakfast and lunch times for special groups.

Commercial restaurants located in shopping or office areas usually have a heavier demand at noon than at the dinner hour. Rooms used for general patronage at noon may be closed at night or used for private dinner parties. Entrances to these rooms should not require passage through the main dining area. Convenience for serving the special functions is important.

PRODUCTION AREAS

Many factors influence space requirements for production, and consideration of them when planning is essential for ultimate satisfaction A frequently quoted rule suggests allotting one-third to one-half of the total area for the dining room as the area size for the production facilities. It can be understood readily that the type and system of production quickly upsets this ratio. It is necessary to make a detailed study of the specific needs. Major points to be considered are

1. Type of preparation and service.
2. Amount of total production done in the facility.
3. Volume in terms of the number of meals served.
4. Varied of food offered in the menu.
5. Elaborateness of preparation and service.
6. Amount of individual service given, as in a hospital tray service.
7. Seating and service plan, whether on one floor or many.

Careful calculation of the best type of operation is needed to plan space. The cost of providing space, equipment, and labor for production is considerable. The value of providing food that is dependably good, adequate, and reliable in supply and suitably individual in character may be vital to the success of the operation and require production in the facility. New products on the market, new cooking methods, and new equipment available deserve evaluation. The use of preprocessed products in many metropolitan areas has made a pronounced change in the amount of space allotted for bake shop, meat cutting, and vegetable preparation areas. Where portion-cut meats are readily available, it is questionable whether even a large establishment can afford to equip and provide skilled labor for a butcher shop. The use of a large quantity of prepared and refrigerated or frozen foods affects storage needs. The cost and quality of market products, their availability, and the frequency of deliveries are all to be considered.

Variety in menu selection and elaboration of foods tend to increase space needs in work areas and storage. Small amounts of numerous items do not permit stacking and bulk packaging. Elaboration of food often involves individual portion treatment, with individual casseroles, for example, as compared to bulk steam table pans. A hospital food service requiring many special diets serves as a common example of menu variety and individual portion treatment imposing special space requirement.

Procedures and equipment used will affect space needs. Bulk garbage and refuse, for example, may require a sizable area for collection and storage awaiting pickup. Disposal units for food garbage, an incinerator for burnable refuse, and a crusher for tin cans will greatly reduce space requirements. Frequency of garbage collection will influence space needs also.

Structural features of the building may influence the utilization of space. Allotting kitchen space for efficient operation is sometimes forgotten when planning the location of ventilation and elevator shafts, support columns, and other floor to ceiling structures. It is important to consider whether the resulting space promotes or defeats forming a layout for efficient work. The location of entrances and exits for a good flow of traffic, window placement for good light and ventilation, and space relationships of sections need to be considered. Eliminate partitions whenever possible; this will reduce space needs and costs and also permit easier supervision of production areas.

Kitchens serving a small number of patrons require a larger square footage per meal than those serving large numbers. The following data used for industrial cafeteria kitchens show how space needs per meal tend to decrease as the number served increases:

Table 5.3 Variation in Space Needs in Relation to Numbers Served

Meal Load	Area per Meal		Variation in Total Area	
	m²	**sq ft**	**m²**	**sq ft**
100–100	.465	5.00	46–93	500–1,000
200–400	.372	4.00	74–149	800–1,600
400–800	.325	3.50	130–260	1,400–2,800
800–1,300	.279	3.00	223–362	2,400–3,900
1,300–2,000	.232	2.50	302–465	3,250–5,000
2,000–3,000	.186	2.00	372–557	4,000–6,000
3,000–5,000	.170	1.85	511–859	5,500–9,250

Planners are frequently asked to make estimates of space needs before having an opportunity to ascertain policies or make detailed plans for operation. Figures that will be found useful in making such estimates are given in Table 5.3. These figures pertain to average full-production kitchen areas found in food facilities of different types. Their use is to be regarded as tentative and to be measured carefully in terms of specific needs. The square footage or meters given is to be multiplied by the maximum number of meals estimated per hour of service in order to find the total space requirement.

After production policies have been established, work areas may be blocked out according to equipment needs and the number of workers required to do the work in sections. Linear space, depths, and heights for work centers should be controlled in terms of average human measurements. This must include distance to reach and grasp material or equipment used in working. The length and width of the worktable is adjusted in terms of the amount and size of equipment that will rest on it during the progress of work. The linear measurement will vary in terms of the number of workers using it at one time.

The width of the table may be 24 to 30 in. (61 to 76 cm) unless dishes or food containers are to rest at the back of the table. Tables 36 in. (91 cm) wide are preferable when the back of the area is used for such storage. Where two workers work opposite each other, a table 42 in. (107 cm) wide may be used. A work area 4 to 6 ft (1.22 to 1.83 m) long is within convenient reach of the average person. Tables 8 to 10 ft (2.44 to 3.05 m) long are used if two people are working side by side. A height of 34 in. (86 cm) is commonly used as a working height but should be evaluated in terms of specific work done and equipment used.

Aisle space should permit free, easy movement of essential traffic. The minimum width for a lane between equipment where one person works alone is 36 to 42 in. (91 and 107 cm). Where more than one is employed and where workers must pass each other in the progress of work, and mobile equipment is used, 48 to 54 in. (122 to 137 cm) are recommended. At least 60 in. (152 cm) are needed for main traffic lanes where workers regularly pass each other with mobile equipment. If workers or equipment must stand in the lane while working, appropriate space should be allowed for this. Thought must be given to space for a door opening into an aisle and for handling large pieces of equipment, such as roasting pans, baking sheets, and stock pots.

Main thoroughfares should not pass through work centers. Compactness is essential for step-saving. It is well for the work center to be in close proximity to main traffic lanes, with easy access to them. It is im-

Table 5.4 Kitchen Area Allowance per Meal for Food Facilities of Different Type and Size

Type of Facility		Estimated Maximum Meals per Hour				
		200 or less	200–400	400–800	800–1,300	1,300–7,500
Cafeterias	sq ft	7.5–5.0	5.0–4.0	4.0–3.5	3.5–3.0	3.0–1.8
	m²	.697–.465	.465–.372	.372–.325	.325–.279	.279–.177
Hospitals	sq ft	18.0–4.5	12.0–4.5	11.0–4.5	10.0–4.0	8.0–4.0
	m²	1.67–.418	1.11–.418	1.02–.418	.929–.372	.743–.372
Hotels	sq ft	18.0–4.0	7.5–3.0	6.0–3.0	4.0–3.0	4.0–3.0
	m²	1.67–.372	.697–.279	.557–.279	.372–.279	.372–.279
Industrial lunchrooms	sq ft	7.5–5.0	4.0–3.2	3.5–2.0	3.0–2.0	2.5–1.7
	m²	.697–.465	.372–.279	.325–.186	.279–.186	.232–.158
Lunch counters	sq ft	7.5–2.0	2.0–1.5			
	m²	.697–.186	.186–.139			
Railroad dining car	sq ft	1.6				
	m²	.149				
Restaurants (service)	sq ft	1.0–4.0	5.0–3.6	5.0–3.6	5.0–3.0	5.0–3.0
	m²	.092–.372	.465–.334	.465–.334	.465–.279	.465–.279
School lunchrooms	sq ft	4.0–3.3	3.3–2.2	3.0–2.0	2.5–1.6	2.0–1.6
	m²	.372–.306	.306–.204	.279–.186	.232–.149	.186–.149

portant both to avoid distraction from outsiders passing through work centers and to conserve space. Work centers at right angles to traffic lanes are efficient.

The percentage of floor area covered by equipment varies according to production needs and the type of equipment used. A satisfactory layout may claim less than 30 percent of total space for equipment, whereas work areas, traffic lanes, and space around equipment for easy operation and cleaning may require 70 percent or more.

Plans for space-saving compactness require use of actual equipment measurements when planning. Manufacturers' specifications for the food equipment chosen should be secured for this use. Templets made to exact scale for both fixed and mobile equipment are helpful to use in arriving at a suitable arrangement.

The allowance of 20 to 30 sq ft (1.86 to 2.88 m²) per bed is suggested in planning for hospital production and service areas, where full production is done. The need is reduced as the number of beds increases, for example, about 30 sq ft (2.88 m²) per bed for a 50-bed and 20 sq ft (1.86 m²) for a 200-bed hospital will be needed.[1] This allowance does not include major storage areas, dining rooms, employee facilities, or floor pantries. Some planners find data given in Table 5.5 helpful in making rough, preliminary estimates.

Space Needs Based on Equipment Requirements

After the menu plan, probable volume, system of operation, type of service, and time schedule have been determined, an analysis can be made of equipment needs and space requirements for the production area. The condition of the food as procured may require (1) refining, mixing, shaping, and processing, commonly described as "preparation from scratch"; (2) partial processing, as in mixing and whipping dehydrated potatoes or thawing and French frying cut and frozen potatoes; or (3) heating or chilling to palatable temperature fully prepared food, which may be packaged and delivered hot, refrigerated, or frozen in bulk or individual portions.

Space for equipment and work accomplishment will be affected by (1) the activities to be performed, (2) kind and variety of menu items, (3) volume of food required, and (4) type and time schedule of service. Tables 5.6, 5.7, and 5.8 illustrate an example of calculations made for an industrial cafeteria in determining space requirements for equipment.

[1] "Ordinance and Code Regulating Eating and Drinking Establishments," *Public Health Bulletin No. 280,* U. S. Public Health Service, Washington, D. C.

Table 5.5 General Space Needs in Hospital Dietary Department*

Section	Area Allowance per Bed			
	m²		sq ft	
Receiving		.0642		0.68
Food storage				
Refrigeration		.1412		1.52
Meat	(.0557)		(0.60)	
Fruit and vegetables	(.0557)		(0.60)	
Dairy	(.0297)		(0.32)	
Low temperature		.0595		0.64
Dry bulk storage		.2230		2.40
Total storage		.4237		4.56
Kitchen				
Meat preparation		.0372		0.40
Vegetable and salad				
preparation		.0743		0.80
Cooking		.1858		2.00
Bakery		.0743		0.80
Ice cream (if required)		.0372		0.40
Scullery		.0557		0.60
Janitors' facilities		.0111		0.12
Total kitchen		.4756		5.12
Staff dining				
Cafeteria		.1300		1.40
Auxiliary space (if				
required)		.0372		0.40
Dining room		.6735		7.25
Private dining room		.0650		0.70
		.9057		9.75
Dishwashing		.2044		2.20
Tray set up		.2044		2.20
Tray truck storage		.1672		1.80
Offices		.1858		2.00
Total for Dietary Department		2.6310		28.31

* Data adapted from materials compiled by Gladys Knight, Tourist and Resort Section, School of Hotel, Restaurant and Institution Management, Michigan State University.

Table 5.6 Analysis of Processing Equipment for Cafeteria Based on Menu

| Menu Item | Portion | | Total Amount | Batch | |
	Size	No.		Size	Rotation
*Soup	1 c (237 ml)	320	20 gal (76 l)	20 gal (76 l)	—
Roast meat or poultry or	4 oz (114 g)	120	30 lb (13.6 kg)	15 lb (6.81 kg)	30 min apart
boiled meat	4 oz (114 g)	120	30 lb (13.6 kg)	30 lb (13.6 kg)	—
Baked portions of meat, fish, poultry	3 to 6 oz (85 to 170 g)	120	24 to 48 lb (11 to 22 kg)	40 portions	30 min apart
Casserole entrees or	4 to 6 oz (114 to 170 g)	240	8 to 12 pans	2 to 3 pans	20 min apart
stews	1 c (237 ml)	240	15 gal (57 l)	15 gal (57 l)	—
*Gravies, sauces	3¼ c (59 ml)	480	7½ gal (29 l)	7½ gal (29 l)	—
Baked potatoes	6 to 8 oz (170 to 227 g)	240	240 potatoes	1 or 2 sheet pans	15 min apart
*Mashed potatoes	1½ c (118 ml)	240	8 gal (30 l)	2⅔ gal (10 l)	30 min apart
Frozen broccoli	4 to 6 oz (114 to 170 g)	200	8 to 12 pans	2 pans	15–20 min apart
Frozen peas	2½ oz (71 g)	360	60 lb (27 kg)	10 lb (4.55 kg)	15 min apart
Fresh carrots	2½ oz (71 g)	180	30 lb (14 kg)	10 lb (4.5 kg)	30 min apart
Canned vegetable	2½ oz (70 g)	180	30 lb (14 kg)	6 lb (2.7 kg)	20 min apart
*Sandwich, grilled	4 oz (114 g)	160	40 lb (18 kg)	on order	on order
Sliced foods	2 oz (57 g)	104	13 lb (5.89 kg)	all	—

and Volume Serving Period 11:30 A.M. to 1:00 P.M.

Equipment		Process Time	Reserve for Use	Comments
Item	Capacity			
Steam kettle	114 l (30 gal)	1–4 hr	9:00–1:00	Batch schedule depends on cream or broth soup
Oven 116°C (240°F)	2-pan deck	2–4 hr	7:00–11:30	Pan—305 × 508 mm (12 × 20 in.)
Steam kettle	114 l (30 gal)	2–4 hr	7:00–11:30	May be boiled and held in steam cooker
Slicer			11:00–12:30	Sliced as needed
Oven 163°C (325°F)	2 or 3 2-pan decks	½–2 hr	9:30–12:30	Pan size 305 × 508 mm (12 × 20 in.)
Oven 177°C (350°F)	4 or 6 2-pan decks	½–2 hr	9:30–12:40	Pan size 305 × 508 mm (12 × 20 in.)
Steam kettle	76 l (20 gal)	1–3 hr	8:00–12:30	May be prepared, placed in S.S. pans, held in oven
Steam kettle	38 l (10 gal)	½–1 hr	10:30–12:30	
Oven 205°C (400°F)	4 decks	¾–1 hr	10:30–12:30	Sheet pan size 457 × 660 mm (18 × 26 in.)
Mixer	19 l (20 qt)	¼ hr	11:15–12:45	
5 psi cooker	2-pan deck	15–20 min	11:00–12:40	
Steam kettle	14 kg (10 qt)	10–12	11:15–12:45	
5 psi cooker	2-pan deck	15–20 min	11:00–12:30	
5 psi cooker	2-pan deck	5–10 min	11:15–12:40	
Griddle	.61 × .91 mm (2 × 3 ft)	10 min	11:15–1:00	
Slicer				

(Continued)

Table 5.6 (*Continued*)

| Menu Item | Portion | | Total Amount | Batch | |
	Size	No.		Size	Rotation
Cream pudding	½ c (118 ml)	240	8 gal (30 l)	8 gal (30 l)	–
*Cake	2½ oz (71 g)	96	2 sheets	2 sheets	–
Frosting		96			
*Cookies	2 oz (57 g)	190	4 sheets	1 to 4 sheets	
*Breads	2 oz (57 g)	240	4 sheets	1 to 4 sheets	30 min apart
*Beverages	6 oz (170 g)	600	28 gal (106 l)	5 gal (19 l)	15 min apart

* Items served daily. Other items adaptable according to equipment needs.

SERVING AREAS

Space allowance for serving areas should be adapted to the needs of the specific facility. The menu, organization of work, and number served will influence size. The type of service will also be influential in dictating space needs.

In cafeterias the counter length should be regulated by the variety of foods served and the volume of patronage. Excess space partially filled is unattractive, but crowding is also undesirable. An estimate that may be used for allotting width is 14 ft (4.27 m). This allows for 4 ft (1.22 m) as patron lane space, 1 ft (30 cm) tray slide, 2 ft (61 cm) counter width, 4½ ft (1.37 m) for workers, and 2½ ft (1.07 m) for back bar. The size of the tray should dictate the width of the tray slide. The average length of counters in college residence halls and hospitals is about 30 to 32 ft (9.14 to 9.75 m), whereas those in school lunchrooms average around 15 to 20 ft (4.57 to 6.10 m). Some commercial cafeteria counters may have an overall length of 70 to 80 ft (21 to 24 m), but counters over 50 ft

Equipment		Process Time	Reserve for Use	Comments
Item	Capacity			
Steam kettle	38 l	½–1 hr	9:00–10:00	
Oven	2 decks	½–1 hr	8:00–9:00	Temp. 177°C (350°F)
Mixer	11.4 l (12 qt)	30 min	9:00–9:45	
Oven Mixer	1–4 decks	10–20 min	9:00– 8:00–9:00	Temp. 1770°C (350°F)
Oven 177°C (350°F)	1–4 decks	20–25 min	10:45–12:15	Retard to bake as needed
Mixer Proof	29 l (30 qt) 4 sheets	2 hr	8:45–10:45	
Urns	23–46–23 1 comb. (6–12–6 gal)	10–15 min	11:45–1:00	Brew as needed

(15.24 m) are often considered inefficient. Twenty feet (6.10 m) is usually thought to be a minimum, but under special conditions and where a limited menu is served, 6 to 8 ft (1.83 to 2.44 m) may be sufficient. In order to achieve smoother service and greater speed various plans have been adopted that influence overall counter length. Some use the continuous counter plan; others separate units into a shopping plan. Many have found shortening the counter and utilizing mobile units for dishes and serving equipment desirable. Counter height needs to be set at comfortable levels for workers and patrons. Schools may have lower counters so that children may see the food and move their trays along a slide as they are served. For little folks, 28 to 30 in. (71 to 76 cm) is desirable, with counters narrow enough to permit servers to reach across and assist children. A solid tray slide tends to result in fewer accidents than those made of bars or tubing. Plastic trays measuring 9 × 12 in. (23 × 30 cm), compartmented, and of pastel colors are popular. Slides for these may be on the server's side of the counter for ease of service and to eliminate

Table 5.7 Equipment Needs Based on Use Time Schedule

Time columns: 7:00 | 7:20 | 7:40 | 8:00 | 8:20 | 8:40 | 9:00 | 9:20 | 9:40 | 10:00 | 10:20 | 10:40 | 11:00 | 11:20 | 11:40 | 12:00 | 12:20 | 12:40 | 1:00 | 1:20

Steam kettles
  30 gal (114 l) Soup
  30 gal (114 l) Stew
1. 10 gal (38 l) Gravy and sauces
2. 2½ gal (9 l) Peas

Steam cooker
  Deck 1. Vegetables
    or entree ingredients
  Deck 2. Vegetables

Range top—Roux, etc.

Griddle

Ovens—Convection
  Shelf 1 Casseroles   Pans 1 and 2*
                        Pans 7 and 8
  Shelf 2 Casseroles   Pans 3 and 4
  Shelf 3 Casseroles   Pans 5 and 6
  Shelf 4 Ind. portions   Sheet 1
  Shelf 5 Ind. portions   Sheet 2
  Shelf 6 Ind. portions   Sheet 3
  Shelf 7 Potatoes   Sheets 1 and 5†
  Shelf 8 Potatoes   Sheets 2 and 6
  Shelf 9 Potatoes   Sheet 3
  Shelf 10 Potatoes   Sheet 4

Ovens—Conventional
  Deck 1 Cake   Sheet 1
  Deck 2 Cake   Sheet 2
  Deck 1 Cookies   Sheets 1 and 2
  Deck 2 Cookies   Sheets 3 and 4
  Deck 1 Bread   Sheets 1 and 2
  Deck 2 Bread   Sheets 3 and 4
  Deck 3 Roasts

Mixer 12 qt (11 l)
  Frosting, pudding, etc.
    30 qt Bread (28 l)
  Entrees, Dressing, etc.
    20 qt (19 l)
  Potatoes

Proof box

Slicer—entrees
  Sandwich fillings

* Pan size—12 × 20 in. (305 × 508 mm).
† Sheet pan size—18 × 26 in. (457 × 660 mm).

Figure 5.6 A short counter for small children with the tray slide on the server's side and space at the end for the filled tray to be picked up. (*Courtesy Shoreline Schools, Seattle.*)

spillage or accidents. The child picks up the completed service at the end of the line (see Figure 5.6).

When determining the number of serving lines needed, one must consider the time allowance of the patrons, the serving speed in terms of persons served per minute, and the total number to be served within a given time period. Some planners use, as a rough guide, one counter or line for every 250 to 300 patrons served. Arrival rate, speed of service, and turnover are factors that will strongly influence the number of lines required. Queing theory calculation may simplify such determinations.

Hospital service space will depend upon whether central or floor service is used, trays are set up in serving pantries, and modified diets are set up in serving line or in a diet kitchen. Space must be allowed for bulk food trucks, tray trucks, small tray carts, or special dispensing units.

Short-order units where food moves directly from production to the consumer require the least service space. The need for an intermediate

Table 5.8 Equipment Summary with Approximate Dimensions for Floor
Plans

Equipment Items			Dimensions	
No.	Type	Size	mm	In.

Processing Equipment

Steam kettles

1	stationary	30 gal (114 l)	914 × 838	36 w × 33 d
1	trunnion	30 gal (151 l)	914 × 838	36 w × 33 d
1	trunnion	10 gal (38 l)	600 × 836	24 w × 33 d
1 or 2 trunnions		2½ gal (9.5 l)	381 × 432	15 w × 17 d

(2 allow more time for heating and change between batches for rotation)

Steam cooker

1 Cooker   3 compartments 2-pan
                      wide   914 × 838   36 w × 33 d
(3 compartments allow for flexibility)

Range top

1 section   914 × 838   36 w × 38 d
(oven a desirable addition for roasting meat or holding food for service)

Ovens

2 convection compartments (stacked)   965 × 1118   38 w × 44 d
(if single-mounted double floor dimensions)
1 conventional   3 deck   1384 × 914   54½ w × 36 d
(1 roasting deck and 2 baking decks)

Griddle   914 × 610   36 w × 24 d

Mixers

1 bench		12/20 qt (11/19 l)	610 × 914	24 w × 36 d
1 floor		30/60 qt (28/57 l)	610 × 914	24 w × 36 d

(can operate with 1, but 2 gives desirable flexibility)

Proof box   1371 × 610   54 w × 24 d

This table summarizes equipment needs indicated in Table 5.6 of Processing
Requirements and Table 5.7 Schedule of Use.   *(Continued)*

Table 5.8 (*Continued*)

Equipment Items			Dimensions	
No.	**Type**	**Size**	**mm**	**In.**
		Auxiliary Equipment		
Refrigerators				
1 box (cook's)			1676 × 914	66 w × 36 d
1 box (salad and sandwiches)			1676 × 914	66 w × 36 d
1 box (baker's)			1676 × 914	66 w × 36 d
1 walk-in with low-temperature compartment			2.4400 × 4.27	96 w × 188 d
Tables				
1 cook's (high shelf, utensil drawer, roll bins)			2438 × 762	96 l × 30 w
2 salad and sandwich high shelf, utensil drawer, dish bins)			1829 × 762	72 l × 30 w
1 baker's (high shelf, utensil drawer, roll bins) (including sink)			2438 × 762	96 l × 30 w
1 baker's finishing (with dish storage bins)			1829 × 762	72 l × 30 w
Sinks				
1 cook's (2 compartments and 2 drainboards)			2032 × 610	80 w × 24 d
1 salad and sandwich (2 compartments and 2 drainboards)			2235 × 610	88 w × 24 d
1 baker's (single compartment in table)				
1 (3 compartments, pot and pan, 2 drainboards)			2235 × 610	150 w × 24 d
Pot rack			1829 × 610	72 w × 24 d
Food racks				
2 bakery			508 × 762	20 w × 30 d
Kitchen carts				
2 2-shelf, table height			610 × 914	24 w × 30 l
1 2-shelf, utility			508 × 762	20 w × 20 l
Slicer stand			610 × 914	24 w × 36 l

station is eliminated. Step-saving compactness saves space. The units requiring the most space are those furnishing elaborate or highly individualized service.

RECEIVING AND STORAGE AREAS

Space allocation for receiving and storage should be based on specific needs. Calculation of needs is to be based on the menu to be served; the temperature and humidity requirements of the items to be stored; availability, reliability, frequency, and cost of deliveries and/or the obtaining of supplies; and the largest volume for which provision must be made. Systems that have been recently introduced in the purchasing, processing, and handling of foods have changed storage needs. Short period holding of processed foods has increased space requirements for refrigerated storage and reduced the space needs for common storage.

Suitable and adequate space is needed for the receiving and checking in of supplies as they are delivered. Truck-bed height for delivery platforms and roll-in level for refrigerator floors help greatly in the movement of supplies. Cases of 6/10 cans stacked 6 cases high on flat trucks will have a bearing weight approximately 250 lb (113 kg) to 300 lb (136 kg) per sq ft. Where heavy items, such as 10-gal (38-liter) cans of milk, are stored, bearing weights may be increased. One case of 6/No. 10s, 24/No. 2½s, or 24/No. 2s weigh approximately 51 lb (23 kg) and occupy 1 cu ft (.028 m^3).

The storage area should be organized to promote quick location of items and convenience in handling. Where possible, items should be stored at points of first use and in a manner that facilitates inventory taking and prevents theft. Material handling is minimized when delivery personnel can put deliveries where they are to be checked in and stored. Convenience is the key for promoting this. Deliveries often arrive during busy hours of production. It is important that areas be so planned that delivery men and their loads will not get in the way of kitchen workers.

Common Storage

Items to be held in common storage are characterized by variety in size, use, and character. Major supplies usually include canned and bottled goods, cereals, pastes, sugars, flours, condiments and fats, soaps, paper supplies, and laundry. It is desirable for safety that soaps and other cleaning materials that may be injurious to health be stored in a separate area from food. Heavy items should be positioned to reduce lifting and facilitate dispensing. Drums of oil and vinegar should have spigots and be equipped with pumps or located on cradles. Table surface and scales should be located for convenient issuing of dry stores. Plan to have all products 8 in. (20 cm) above the floor or movable to facilitate cleaning. Limit the height of top shelves for easy reach without the aid of stool or stepladder. The average vertical reach of men is 84½ in. (2.15 m) and of women 81 in. (2.06 m). Use of the top shelf for light, bulky packages, such as cereal, is recommended.

The maximum stack height for cases that are handled without the aid of a motorized lift is 72 in. (1.83 m). Accessibility of items that differ in shape as well as volume will govern the number of stacks needed. A total of 3 cu ft (0.85 m³) per stack is estimated to include floor space covered by the case of canned food, plus a share of aisle space. One thousand cases piled 8 high in 125 stacks will require 375 sq ft (34.9 m²) or a storage area approximately 20 × 20 ft (6.1 by 6.1 m). Storage room aisles may be as narrow as 36 in. (91 m), but 42 to 48 in. (1 or 1.2 m) are preferred. Wider aisles may be required if motorized equipment is used. A 36-in. (.91-m) skid on a hydraulic jack needs maneuvering room. If rolling bins or garbage cans on dollies are used for storage, plan the location for these. If cans or bins are under shelves, adjust the height of the bottom shelf to clear and allow for space for easy removal of food from the containers. Fixed shelving needs to be planned to accommodate sizes of items to be stored. Consider both interspace and depth suitable. Condiment bottles, cereal packages, and canned goods differ in package size and stacking quality. The depth of a shelf should accommodate either the width or length of the case, and the interspace should be adequate for the number to be stacked one on top of another. Allow 1½ to 2 in. (3.8 to 5 cm) as free space for ease of positioning. Add thickness of shelving to interspace when stating measurements between centers.

Ventilated Storage

Root vegetables need cool, dark storage at 50 to 60° F (10 to 15° C) and a relative humidity of 85 to 90 percent. Allow for good ventilation by cross-stacking sacks on a floor pallet. A 100-lb (45-kg) bag of potatoes takes approximately 3 cu ft (.085 m³) of space, including aisle space. The bags should not be stacked higher than 6 ft (1.83 m). The method for ensuring good air circulation and the means of maintaining desired temperature in areas where there is likely to be injurious extremes in temperature are to be considered. Length of holding time for products held in ventilated storage should be considered also,

Table 5.9   Measurements of Representative Storage Items
(For use in determining interspace, width and linear space of shelving)

Product	Package	Approximate Capacity		Height		Width or Diameter		Length	
		lb	kg	in.	cm	in.	cm	in.	cm
Refrigerated									
butter	box	64	29	12	30	12	30	14	36
cheese	wheel	20–23	9–10	7½	23	13½	34	26	66
eggs	case	45	20	13	33	12	30		
milk, 10 gal	can	80	36	25	64	13½	34		
½ pt	case	24/8 oz	227 gr	10½	27	13	33	13	33
½ pt	case	24/8 oz	227 gr	7	15	13	33	19	45
margarine	box	60	27	10	25	14	36	17½	44
meat, portions	tray	40	18	3	7.6	18	46	26	66
cuts	box	140	63.5	6	15	18	46	28	71
cuts	box	50	23	10	25.4	10	25.4	28	71
apples	box	35–40	16–18	10½	27	11½	29	18	46
apples	carton	40–45	18–20	12	30	12½	32	20	51
berries	crate	36	16.3	11	28	11	28	22	56
cherries, grapes	lug	25–30	11–14	6	15	13½	34	16	41
citrus	crate	65–80	29–36	12	30	12	30	26	66
citrus	carton	45–65	18–29	11	28	11½	29	17	43
cabbage	crate	50–80	23–36	13	35	18	46	22	56
cauliflower	crate	40	18	9	23	18	46	22	56
celery	crate	55	25	11	28	21	53	24	61
lettuce	crate	40–50	18–23	14	36	19	48	20	51
lettuce	carton	40	18	10	25.4	14	36	22	56
tomatoes	box	30	13–14	7	18	13½	34	16	41

Frozen food									
eggs or fruit	can	30	13	12½	32	10	25.4		
fruit	carton	5	2.3	3	7.6	8¼	22	12	30
fruit juice	case	12/30 oz	850 gr	6	15	12	30	16½	42
ice cream, 2½ gal	carton	20	9	10	25.4	9	23		
meat	carton	10	4½	2½	6.4	9½	24	13½	49
vegetables	carton	2½	1.13	2½	6.4	5	12.7	10	25
	case	12/2½ lb	1.14	10	25.4	10	25.4	16½	41
Dry stores									
fruit and vegetable	No. 10 can	104 oz	3	7	15	6¼	15.9		
juice cans	No. 3 cyl	46–52 oz.	1.3–1.5	7	15	4¼	10.8		
fruit can	No. 2½	28 oz	.79	4 11/16	11.9	4 1/16	10.3		
fruit and vegetable	No. 2 can	20 oz	.57	4 9/16	11.5	3 7/16	8.7		
fruit, vegetable soup	No. 303 can	16 oz	.45	6 6/16	11.1	3 3/16	8.1		
juice, pork and bacon	No. 1 tall	12 oz	.34	4 11/16	11.9	3 1/16	7.8		
fruit, soup, vegetable	No. 1 picnic	10 oz	.28	4	10.2	2 11/16	6.8		
fruit, vegetable, and specials	No. 8Z tall	8 oz	.23	3¼	8.3	2 11/16	6.8		
canned foods	case 12/No. 3 cyl	46 oz	1.3	7½	19	12½	32	19	48
canned foods	case 6/10	104 oz	2.9	7½	19	12½	32	19	48
canned foods	case 24/No. 2	20 oz	.57	9½	24	12	30	16½	42
canned foods	case 24/No. 2½	28½ oz	.80	9½	24	12	30	16½	42
macaroni	box	20	9.07	6	15	9	23	21½	55
lard	can	50	22.7	15	38	12½	32		
oil, vinegar	glass jar	8	3.63	8½–12	22–30	8½	16.5		
oil	5 gal can	40	18	14	36	9½	24	9½	24
shortening	carton	50	22.7	13	33	12½	32	12½	32
storage	garbage can	33 gal	125 l	26	66	20⅜	52		
	garbage can	20 gal	75.7 l	26	66	16	41		
sugar, flour, potatoes	sack	100	45.4	8–11	20–28	18	46	33	84

(Continued)

Table 5.9 (*Continued*)

Product	Package	Approximate Capacity		Height		Width or Diameter		Length	
		lb	kg	in.	cm	in.	cm	in.	cm
Dry stores (*Continued*)									
soap, or other	bbl or drum	50 gal	189 l	34¾	88	22¾	56		
straws	carton	500		6	15	7	18	9½	23
paper towels	case	25 pkgs/110		15	38	18	46	21¾	55
fixture napkins	case	20 pkgs/500		15	38	19½	51	28	71
paper cups	carton	50 cups/16 oz		3¾	9.5	3¾	9.5	22	56
	carton	50 cups/5½ oz		3½	8.9	3½	8.9	21	53
	carton	50 cups/4 oz		3	7.6	3	7.6	19	48
portion cups	carton	250 cups/1 oz		1¾	4.4	3⅜	8.2	14¾	37
tumblers, glass	case 6 dz	9 oz	255 g.	9¼	24.7	12½	32	13½	34
Linen									
aprons	laundry fold 4 only			1	2.5	9	23	14	36
tablecloths	laundry fold 4 yds			1	2.5	12½	32	18	46
table pads	laundry fold 4 yds			4	10	14	36	18	46
uniforms	laundry fold 1 only			1	2.5	11	28	18	46
waiter coat	laundry fold 1 only			1	2.5	10	25.4	15	38

Refrigerated and Low-Temperature Storage

Many factors affect space needs for refrigerated and low-temperature foods. Specific menu offerings, volume, and required holding time are significant factors. The economics of deliveries in terms of frequency and cost may influence total amount to be stored. Small volume operations are often required to receive supplies for a longer period for volume to offset the delivery costs. This tends to be true also when the operation is remote from the supply center. Financial aspects in preserving food quality and in avoiding unnecessary cost in construction and maintenance point to the wisdom of making careful calculation of needs for the specific operation. Across-the-board figures should be used for early estimates only.

Allocations used for convenience in preliminary planning may be as follows: 20 to 35 percent for meat (portion-ready meats require ½ to ⅓ less space than carcass or wholesale cuts); 30 to 35 percent for fruits and vegetables; 20 to 25 percent for dairy products, including those in serving areas; 10 to 25 percent for frozen foods; and 5 to 10 percent for carry-over foods, salads, sandwich materials, and bakery products. A requirement of 15 to 20 cu ft (.42 to .57 m³) of refrigeration per 100 complete meals has been used also by some planners. Others state that 1 to 1½ cu ft (.03 to .04 m³) of usable refrigerator space should be provided for every three meals served. Analysis of several successful installations showed approximately 0.25 to 0.50 cu ft (.007 to .009 m³) per meal served. Additional low-temperature or refrigerated space in reach-ins was not calculated. In some climates, refrigerated space must be provided for dried fruits, nuts, cereals, and other foods to prevent weevil and insect infestation. It can be readily understood that the major use of frozen prepared meals will strongly affect requirements.

A walk-in refrigerator is feasible for an operation serving 300 to 400 meals per day, and refrigerated pass-throughs can be added when from 400 to 500 meals are served per day. A walk-in 5 to 6 ft (1.5 to 1.8 m) wide does not permit storage on both sides with adequate aisle space. Storage space of 1½ to 2 ft (.46 to .61 m) should be allowed on either side of the aisle. If crates or cases are stored, this may have to be wider. Walk-ins that are 8 to 9 ft (2.44 to 2.74 m) wide and 10 ft (3.05 m) long are minimum size. This allows for a storage area on each side 30 in. (.76 m) wide and an aisle 3 to 4 ft (.91 to 1.22 m) wide. If added width is desired for storage space in the center, allowance for storage area of 3 ft (.91 m) and 42 in. (1.60 m) minimum aisle width may be provided. Large walk-ins may be designed for lift truck operation, with doors opening from the receiving dock on one side and into the kitchen opposite. If this is done and lift trucks are used, space must be allowed in storage aisles for their working and turning. Doors should be a minimum of 42 in. (1.06 m) wide to permit large crates and containers or be sized to accommodate measurements of mobile equipment. Doors to low-temperature areas usually are planned to open into refrigerated areas to lessen temperature change. If this is not done a heating device may be needed on the door opening to prevent its freezing tight from condensation. About 12 to 15 sq ft (1.1 to 1.4 m²) must be kept free for every door opening. About 45 lb (20 kg) of frozen food, if stacked in cases, can be stored per cubic foot. About 30 to 35 lb (14 to 16 kg) of refrigerated food can be stored per cubic foot (or meter).

SANITATION AREAS

Dishwashing Area

Space needs in the dishwashing area will be affected by the volume of dishes arriving at one time, holding requirements, methods, and personnel for the operation and the equipment used. In all instances there should be adequate space to receive the volume of soiled dishes likely to arrive at one time without hazardous pile-up, plus space for scraping, stacking, and placing in baskets or on a conveyor of a machine or into a prerinsing operation. The dimensions may be only 30 to 36 in. (.76 to .91 m) for a single tank machine, 60 to 72 in. (1.52 to 1.83 m) for sinks, or 7 to 30 ft (2.13 to 9.14 m) for a conveyor-type machine. The clean dish space, whether a part of the machine or the table, should be sufficient for dishes to stand and air dry before stacking. The space for basket-type machines must be sufficient for at least three baskets, a stack of trays, and three or four racks of dishes. In calculating total space, it is usually recommended that the clean dish area occupy 60 percent and the soiled dish table area 40 percent of the total space.

Answers to the following questions will help guide space allocation: Will dishes be washed by hand or by machine? Will prerinsing be done by hand or by machine? If manually, will an overhead spray be used to rinse dishes in loaded baskets, or will a flush of water be used for scraping individual pieces? Will refuse be removed through a disposal unit? Will a soak-sink be used for dishes and silver? Are glass and silver washers to be used? What type of equipment will be used for moving and storing clean tableware? What storage will be provided for detergents, special cleaning equipment, and extra tableware?

Where mobile equipment is used more dish room space is needed than where one cart is used for transporting and is repeatedly loaded and

Figure 5.7 Dishes returned by conveyor to dishroom, clearing area at both sides of belt with high shelves for glass and cup racks and a space for stacked dishes in good relationhip to belt-conveyor machine. (*Courtesy St. Frances Hospital, Milwaukee, Wis.*)

unloaded. A table surface is desirable for sorting, treating, or inspecting silver and other tableware. Installation of a washer and drier for kitchen towels may need to be included in the space allowance.

POT AND PAN SECTION

Provide a soiled utensil collection area adequate for the largest number that normally arrives in the section at one time. The busiest periods are likely to occur when preparation containers are emptied for service and immediately following service when service equipment is brought from the serving area. Equipment for scraping refuse from equipment will be needed. A disposal unit or a removable strainer over a drain and an overhead spray for rinsing may be used.

When allowing space for the pot and pan section 40 sq ft (3.74 m²) is generally regarded as a minimum for the smallest unit. The free work aisle between sinks and other equipment should be 4 ft (1.22 m) wide. The space allowance above the minimum will vary widely according to equipment used and the volume of pots and pans handled. Less space will be needed in relation to the maximum load where a mechanical washer is used, and fewer labor hours will be spent in handling a large volume per unit handled.

Miscellaneous Sanitation Areas

Proper sanitation calls for the thorough washing of mobile equipment used in the preparation and service of food. The area should be one where splashing can be confined and where satisfactory drainage is provided. A hose supplying a flood of water with suitable force, a steam hose, and adequate ventilation will be needed. The size and type of equipment to be handled will govern space needs. Garbage cans washed in this area should have a rack for draining and storage.

A storage area for emergency cleanup equipment is needed in convenient relationship to dining area work sections. Spillage and breakage create unsightliness and are accident hazards. Immediate care usually does not require heavy or large equipment but may be handled by a small broom, dust pan, mop, and bucket not used for major cleaning. Thoughtful planning will help in locating small, inconspicuous cleanup closets near various areas for quick emergency cleanup.

Major cleaning equipment will depend on the floors, finishes, and furniture to be cleaned. Determine whether a power sweeper, scrubber, and waxer are to be used. Space may be required for storage of janitor supply carts and for miscellaneous replacement items, such as light bulbs. Provision will be needed for storing, emptying, cleaning, and filling mop trucks and for cleaning and air drying wet mops.

EMPLOYEE FACILITIES

Facilities for employees may include locker and lounge area, toilets, showers, time-recording equipment, handbasins near work areas, and dining room. An employee entrance should be so located that the employees may go directly to the dressing rooms without passing through dining or production areas.

Locker and Lounge Area

Employee possessions should be protected in a suitably safe and sanitary condition while employees are at work. Whether individual lockers or common cupboard, sufficient space should be provided for personal clothing to hang without crowding and wrinkling. If cupboards are used for clothing, a separate space should be afforded for street clothing and for uniforms and individual parcel lockers provided for storage of purses and other valuables. The height of the space for clothing should permit the longest garments to hang straight without wrinkling. The depth from front to back should be a minimum of 20 in. (.51 m).

Suitable size for an employee lounge depends largely on scheduling of workers, location, and rest period policies of individual establishments. Many operators discourage lounging in dressing rooms and recommend that the employees' dining area be used for rest breaks. Others having broken shifts in employee schedules favor an extra room for lounging. In all cases benches or chairs are to be provided upon which workers may sit when changing clothes or shoes. A cot or daybed 36 × 6½ ft (.91 × 1.98 m) should be provided in the women's room.

Toilets and Showers

The location of toilet facilities near work areas is preferable to a remote location in order to promote good health habits, lessen loss of labor time, and permit closer employee supervision. Separate facilities should be provided for men and women. They should be separated from food areas by a hallway or a double entrance. Supply one washbowl for every eight or ten workers, one toilet for every twelve to fifteen women, and one urinal and one toilet stool for every fifteen men. Toilet compartments measure approximately 3 × 4½ to 5 ft (.91 × 1.37 m to 1.52 m).

The type of employees, the climate, kind of work, and conditions of work will influence the need for shower facilities. Showers are appreciated and used by employees working in hot, humid kitchens. Food managers have regarded showers as essential in areas where there are likely to be inadequate bath facilities in the homes. Experience has demonstrated that they are little used in localities where the weather is cool most of the year, the work areas well ventilated, and workers drawn from an income group that has good facilities in their homes.

Time-Recording Equipment

Provide space for a recorder near and within view of the office. Wall-hung card racks of sufficient capacity to accommodate the total number of workers, both full- and part-time, who are likely to be employed during an accounting period will be needed. Space estimates may be based on a clock recorder approximately 18 in. wide × 12½ in. deep × 18 in. high (45.7 × 32 × 45.7 cm) and a rack for 50 cards approximately 1½ × 2½ × 34½ in. (3.8 × 6.4 × 88 cm).

Employee Dining Area

Ascertain the largest number to be accommodated at one time and allow 12 sq ft (1.12 m²) per person. The comfort and appearance of the

Table 5.10 Approximate Space Allocation Suggested for Preliminary Planning*

	Cafeteria			Lunch Counter			Restaurant			Hospital		
	Percent	sq ft	m²	Percent	sq ft	m²	Percent	sq ft	m²	Percent	sq ft	m²
Total space	100	5700	529	100	2400	223	100	4800	446	100	5250	488
Dining area	40	2280	212	50	1200	111	50	2400	223	18	945	88
Service and guest facilities	21	1197	111	18	432	40	7.5	360	33	9	472	44†
Production	18	1026	95	12	288	27	21	1008	94	20	1050	96**
Meat preparation and cooking		200	19					200	19	22	1156	107
Bake shop		200	19					200	19		220	20
Cold foods		106	10					120	11		200	19
Vegetable preparation		120	11					108	10		132	12
Traffic lanes and other		400	37					380	35		472	44

8	*456*	*42*	5	120	11	*384*	*36*	8	11.5	*604*	*56*
	56	5				48	5			56	5
	240	22				192	18			316	29
	160	15				144	13			232	22
7	*399*	*37*	8	192	18	*360*	*33*	7.5	10	*525*	*49*
	230	21				216	20			315	29
	60	6				60	5			80	7
	109	10				84	8			130	12
4	*228*	*27*	5	120	11	*192*	*18*	4	4.5	*236*	*22*
	108	10				84	8			116	11
	120	11				108	10			120	11
8	*114*	*17*	2	48‡	5	*96*	*9*	2	5	*262*	*24*

Row labels (top to bottom): Storage areas; Receiving; Common-dry; Refrigerated; Cleaning areas; Dish and truck wash; Pot washing; Trash, can wash and other; Employee areas; Toilets, lockers; Dining room; Office.

*Maximum meals per hour: cafeteria, 450; lunch counter, 250; restaurant, 320; hospital (175 beds central service).   Seats in dining room: cafeteria, 200; lunch counter, 100; restaurant, 200; hospital—for staff.   Note that totals are italicized.

†Personnel.

**Patients; the combined personnel and patient needs will give total space needs.

‡A portion of another area may be used and not enclosed.

employees' dining area may be an important rest and employee-satisfaction factor.

General Considerations

The size of employee facilities has been found to vary widely. Small operations may not supply lockers and may have only a toilet and lavoratory for workers. Some do not provide a separate dining room. Expediency in allowing ample space may be tempered by cost of space, available room, and acuteness of need. Total space may be increased where main toilet and locker rooms are remotely located and additional facilities are provided near work areas. It may be decreased where the food facility is a part of a larger organization providing facilities for other workers, as in a hospital or a hotel.

OFFICE SPACE

Space needs for an office depend largely upon the number and type of activities that are to be performed there, the number and type of equipment items to be used, and the number of people who are likely to be there at one time. Will it be used for employee or purchasing conferences while another person is doing accounting? Will table space be needed for assembling material or holding typewriters, calculators, or phones? The smallest office inside an enclosure, to be occupied by one person only, should measure 6 × 8 ft (1.83 × 2.44 m). Ventilation will be of special concern in an area this small. If enclosed by glass on at least two sides, it will give an impression of greater spaciousness. A space 96 sq ft (8.99 m^2) or, preferably, 108 sq ft (10 m^2) may be sufficient to accommodate two people.

The location of the office should be in close proximity to the production and dining areas for continuous supervision. It should have easy access to patron areas where outsiders may approach the office without going though work sections.

GUEST FACILITIES

Comfort and cordiality should characterize the entrance and waiting area for guests. The size of the area should be based on probable need for waiting, type of service, and number of persons likely to congregate at one time. If there is a lounge or hallway adjacent to the dining room, this may provide some waiting space.

Locate the public telephone, coat rack, and toilet facilities in convenient relationship to the waiting area. In college dining rooms provide ample space for books as well as coats. In residences, a hallway approaching the dining room will lessen wear on the lounge. Attractive benches òr seats are recommended.

Suggested Student Assignments

1. Select three food facilities of different types (school, industrial, commercial, hospital, other) and find out for each:
   a. The number served (including personnel).
   b. Serving hours or schedule.
   c. Total seated or served at peak periods.
   d. Seating capacity of the dining area.
2. Find out for each of the facilities the number of square feet or meters in:
   a. Dining area.
   b. Kitchen areas.
   c. Storage, both common and refrigerated.
   d. Employee areas.
   e. Guest areas.
   f. Office.
3. Evaluate adequacy of each (a) in conference with the manager and (b) from personal observation.
4. Make recommendations of possible means for better utilization of present space allocations.
5. Prepare an analysis of equipment needs based on a given system of operation, a time table for equipment use, and a summary with equipment dimensions for floor plans.

Section 2
functional areas
of food facilities

Chapter 6

functional outline
and check list

All layouts in food services are made up of sections joined together either by an overall processing plan or related tasks. Detailed consideration of work done in each section is necessary. Planning of these sections should begin with the general functions to be performed. Similarity exists as to functions in establishments producing and serving food, although the manner in which they may be satisfied may differ. This similarity of functions furnishes a basis for group study and planning the food facility. The general functions and certain of their significant elements and equipment include:

1. Preliminary Analysis
    a. Facility needed—type, patronage potential, probable income, and extent of need.
    b. Probable permanence and possible growth.
    c. Source of funds, amount available, probable financing expense, and total to be allowed.
    d. Selection of site, conditions of procurement, and legal or other restrictions.
    e. Availability of labor, materials, and utilities for operation.
    f. Selection of planning committee, ownership, management, and designer.
    g. Trends that may influence success of operation—population, competition, traffic flow, patronage, income, or other.

2. General Planning
    a. Character of the facility, number to be served, type of service, menu, serving hours, seating capacity, and prices.
    b. Policies relating to standards—quality of material and construction, safety, sanitation, lighting, food selection, portion sizes, prices, special purposes to be served (physical, social, educational, economic).
    c. Budget allowances for building, plumbing, lighting, equipment, designing.
    d. Schedule of construction and completion—labor supply or bidding advantages, season influence, specific need.
    e. Bidding and contracting procedures.
    f. Code requirements—zoning, fire, sanitation, plumbing, electrical, structural, and other.
    g. Building design and materials:
        permanence and ease of alteration for future expansion;
        type and harmony with structures nearby;
        original cost and upkeep;

relations to functions—weight stresses, space allotment, work flow;

advantages—patron appeal, ease of maintenance, durability.

h. Traffic needs—entrance and exit, parking, delivery, and trash removal.

i. Landscaping.

3. Physical Plant and Utilities

a. Gas—safety pilot, drainage, ventilation, venting, proper pipe size, open cock for singeing in butcher shop.

b. Electricity—proper voltage, proper grounding, adequate and convenient outlets, well-located and adequate panel.

c. Water—safe, right temperature and pressure, convenient supply in sections, adequate amount.

d. Steam—right pressure, right places in dishwashing, cooking, and cleaning sections, in hoods for fire prevention.

e. Plumbing—adequate waste lines, prevention of back siphonage, sufficient drop in lines from disposals that by-pass grease traps, provisions for cleanout of grease traps, proper venting, well-placed drains.

f. Ventilation—exhaust hoods over dishwashers, pot washers, coffee urns, cooking equipment, and steam tables; filters removable and of a size to pass through dishwasher; air change every 2 to 5 minutes in kitchen; air conditioning protected from excessive loss from ventilation; cleanout ducts and access panels provided.

g. Lighting—right kind and amount for specific area needs, freedom from glare and sharp contrast, easy-to-change, clean lights and fixtures.

h. Refrigeration—compressors, evaporative condensers, cooling tower.

4. Receiving and Storage

a. Ventilated storage for temporary holding of perishable foods.

b. Ventilated root storage.

c. Proper sizing and facilities at receiving dock.

d. Storage with proper temperature and humidity for refrigerated (meat, dairy, fruits, and vegetables) and frozen foods.

e. Common or dry storage for staple supplies.

f. Areas for cleaning supplies and equipment conveniently located.

g. Space for equipment replacement and paper supplies appropriate in size and location.

h. Linen supply storage.

i. Valued storage separately locked off.

Items, facilities, and equipment to be checked:

Covered dock and receiving area properly sized to handle deliveries.
Garbage storage area.
Scales—mobile, floor level, table.
Conveyors—(convenient access) elevator, dumbwaiter, belt or gravity, chute.
Mobile equipment—hand truck, dollies, platform truck, hydraulic lift.
Storage equipment—pallets, barrel cradles, platforms or tables for sacks, bins or mobile containers, cans on dollies, shelving that is adjustable, fixed, or mobile.
Temperature and humidity indicators and controls in refrigerated areas.
Refrigerators with hard-surfaced floors and walls, self-defrosting, adequate drains, flush floors for walk-ins, escape provision for anyone locked in, easy opening of door for low-temperature compartment, well-lighted interiors, adequate insulation, rail tracks, wire baskets.
Adequate storage provided in sections for supplies and equipment, (service, banquet, or processing sections).

5. Food Preparation
   a. Vegetable cleaning and preparation.
   b. Meat preparation.
   c. Cooking section.
   d. Bake shop and dessert section.
   e. Salad and sandwich making or pantry section.
   f. Short-order and breakfast section.
   g. Catering unit supplying take-out foods, special diets, and party service.
   h. Fountain item preparation.

Items, facilities, and equipment to be checked:

Flow of processing in logical sequence.
Adequate aisle space.
Minimum of—distance traveled, outside traffic in work areas, material handling, fixed space for little-used equipment, backtracking and cross traffic, accident hazards.
Maximum utilization of equipment, space, labor time and motion.
Use of transportation devices—vertical and other as required.
Adequate equipment in section to meet work requirements.

Vegetable Preparation

Rack for root vegetables
Platform truck
Peeler
Cleaning sink and drainboards
Waste disposal
Knife rack

Vegetable cutter and attachment rack
Mobile storage containers, racks
Mobile mixing bowls
Work table with storage for small utensils
Wire baskets

Meat Preparation

Meat block
Butcher's bench
Chopper and grinder with tamper
Overhead conveyor
Twine holder
Knife rack, tool rack
Chicken singer and tendon puller
Molder or patty machine

Slicer
Tenderizer
Saw
Sink and drainboard
Work table with drawer
Utility cart
Breading equipment
Mobile tables

Cooking Section

Ranges, griddle, broiler, salamander
Deep fat fryer
Roast ovens
Steam kettles—water faucet and drains
Steam cookers and drains
Hood—lights and removable filters
Utility carts
Mixer
Pot rack and attachment storage
Slicer
Can opener
Scale
Fat filter
Knife rack

Cooks table with spice bins and small equipment drawer
Mobile or fixed bins
Sink and drainboard
Worktables
Electrical outlets for equipment
Fire extinguisher
Garbage cans on dollies
Utensil shelves
Hot food table, bain marie, or mobile hot food cabinet
Mobile dish storage, heated
Refrigeration and low-temperature storage

Short-Order, Fountain, and Breakfast Preparation

Griddle
Broiler
Egg cooker
Dish storage, regular, refrigerated, and heated

Waffle irons
Coffee maker
Cream dispenser
Ice tea dispenser
Toaster

Refrigerator
Sink and drainboard
Work table with cutting board
Frozen dessert cabinet
Ice cream storage
Oyster stewer
Waste disposal
Table mixer
Roll warmer
Slicer
Pastry cabinet
Hot plate
Hood shelf type with removable filters
Soup warmer
Serving or pick-up counter

Butter dispenser
Beverage mixer
Carbonator and CO_2 tanks
Soft ice cream mixer
Ice bin
Equipment and tool storage and racks
Storage for glass and paper service
Dipper well with running water
Juice extractor
Malt dispenser
Fudge warmer
Glass washer
Cold pan
Mobile tables and carts

Garde Manger and Seafood

Serving counter
Cold pan
Ice bin
Slicer
Cold plate refrigerator
Dish storage

Sinks and drainboard
Waste disposal
Reach-in refrigerator
Utensil and tool storage
Seafood bar
Table and mobile carts

Banquet Kitchen

(Add facilities and equipment from Cooking Section, Salad and Sandwich Making, and Sanitizing Section as required. *See* Waiter and Bus Boy Facilities also.)

Service bar
Refrigerator salad storage
Tray storage, mobile or fixed
Hot food trucks
Hot food storage
Set-up counters
Dish and glass storage
Roll warmer
Waste disposal or garbage facilities

Dumbwaiter or elevators
Linen storage
Mobile equipment
Ice cream storage and fountain supplies
Dessert storage
Banquet equipment storage
Can opener

Salad and Sandwich Making

Refrigerated storage with tray slides
Mobile storage containers

Work table with utensil drawer and tray shelves

Mobile dish storage
Spice and dressing containers
Mixing bowls
Cutting boards
Food cutter
Mobile racks

Toaster
Electrical outlets for slicer, toaster, juicer, etc.
Can opener
Bread cabinet

Bakery

Baker's bench with spice bins and utensil drawer
Mobile bins
Work tables as required
Wooden tables for cutting and make-up
Scale
Mixers and storage for bowls and attachments
Bowl dollie
Mobile mixing bowls
Tilting steam kettle, water faucet, drain
Oven lighted inside
Hood with lights and easily removable filters
Electrical outlets for mixer, roller, proof box, scale, warmers, etc.
Marble-top table

Batch warmer
Can opener
Dough divider and rounder
Molder
Dough roller
Dough trough
Proof box with humidifier
Sinks and drainboard
Refrigerator and low-temperature storage
Dough retarder
Mobile racks and storage shelves
Power sifter
Doughnut machine and fryer
Mobile dish storage
Utility carts
Landing racks, mobile
Pastry stove
Bread slicer

If ice cream is made:

Ice cream freezer
Hardening cabinet
Storage cabinet
Worktable
Sinks and drainboard
Mixer

Scale
Refrigerator
Supply cabinet
Stove
Steam kettle
Special equipment and its storage

6. Housekeeping and Sanitation
    a. Soiled dish collection, transportation, and washing.
    b. Dish, glass, and silver handling, storage and dispensing.
    c. Pot and pan washing and storage.
    d. Garbage disposal, can washing, and storage.
    e. Mop truck filling, emptying, cleaning, and storage.
    f. Mop cleaning and drying.

g. Storage space for catering equipment, such as folding chairs, flower containers, and special tables.

Items, facilities, and equipment to be checked:

Quiet, inconspicuous soiled dish disposal.
Clean, neat, attractive uniforms and linens.
Provision made for sanitary cleansing and handling of facilities and equipment.
Design and materials—easily cleanable, durable, and proof against insects and vermin.
Food and equipment protected from contamination.
Adequate, well-kept equipment and facilities.

Dishwashing

Collection area, bussing port or conveyor for soiled dishes

Soiled dish table with scrap block, waste disposal, sorting space, and storage space for cups, glasses, silver

Dishwasher with detergent dispenser and rinse injector, water softener, booster heater, hood, hose for cleaning, and rack return

Silver washer and dryer, dip sink, burnisher

Locked storage for valuable silver

Clean dish table or machine extension

Sink for glass washing or glass washer and tables

Adequate light

Mobile storage, glasses, cups, etc.

Cart space

Storage for detergents and other cleaning materials

Splash guards on rack-type machines

Detarnishing sink

Pot and Pan Washing

Pot washer or pot sink (3 compartment) tables, overhead spray

Waste disposal

Pot storage, fixed or mobile

Pot scrubber

Mobile soiled and clean pot table

Garbage Disposal and General Cleaning

Garbage cans or waste disposal

Garbage disposal area, refrigerated

Waste paper disposal, cans, or incinerator

Janitor's closet

Hot water and steam hose

Detergent and supply storage

Kitchen laboratories, waste container, soap and towel dispenser

Can washer

Garbage can storage

Well-placed floor drains

Mop truck and facility for filling, emptying, cleaning, and storage

Mop sink

Drying rack for mops

Linens

Towel washer and drier
Soiled linen hampers and bags
Sorting table

Linen storage, uniforms, aprons, towels, table linens

Banquet and Catering Equipment

(Storage facilities for banquet equipment, tables, chairs, serving equipment, etc.)

7. Display and Service of Food
    a. Dining area with adequate, comfortable seating.
    b. Storage facilities with appropriate temperature control and sanitation protection with provision for display as needed.
    c. Provision for necessary beverage and water supply.
    d. Storage for dishes and serving equipment and supplies.
    e. Properly placed checker's and cashier's stations.
    f. Menus or menu boards.

Items, facilities, and equipment to be checked:

Inviting, attractive, and comfortable dining and service areas.
Facilities to preserve quality and sanitation of food.
Provisions for quick, quiet, appealing service.
Adequate lobby or waiting area.
Good intercommunicating system.

Dining Areas

Tables, chairs, booths, settees, benches
Waitress service stands, counters, wagons
Bus stands or tray stands
Dish conveyors to soiled dish area, carts, dollies, belt conveyors, subveyors
Counters, service, cafeteria, cashier, retail sales, cigar, candy, gift

Cash register
Rugs
Adequate lighting
Clean, comfortable air
Water and ice supplies
Condiment and linen supplies
Silver, glasses, dishes available

Coffee Shop or Fountain Luncheonette

Counter, stools, benches, booths
Cream dispenser
Soft drink dispenser
Carbonator and CO_2 tanks
Refrigeration

Toast and bread unit
Hot food table
Sandwich unit
Coffee maker and warmer
Water station

Back counters

Milk dispenser

Juice dispenser and extractor

Ice tea dispenser

Butter dispenser

Soup warmer

Syrup heater

Malt dispenser

Ice bin

Drink mixer

Sinks and work areas

Waste disposal

Counter dish and glass washer

Fudge warmer

Toaster

Broiler

Griddle

Grill

Deep fryer

Hot plate

Hood

Egg boiler

Waffle baker

Roll warmer

Pastry and salad display cases

Ice cream cabinet

Disher well

Dish conveyor, cart, belt, etc.

Soft ice cream machine

Hot chocolate dispenser

Cafeteria, Canteen, or Buffet

Serving counter

Coffee-making equipment

Cream, milk, ice tea dispensers

Ice bin

Mobile dish storage equipment

Ice cream cabinet

Disher well

Water cooler and fountains

Canteen carts

Napkin, silver dispensers

Roll warmer

Guard rail

Back counters

Short order counter

Grill and griddle

Broiler

Hot plate

Menus and menu board

Vending machines

Juice extractor and dispenser

Hot chocolate dispenser

Tray slide and guard rail **or call** window

Bar, Service or Public

Workboards

Sinks

Ice bins

Bottle cooler

Beer dispenser

Glass and dish storage

Stools, booths, tables, and chairs

Linen storage

Supply storage

Drink mixer

Blender

Refrigerator

Back or center bar

Portable bars

Room Service

Portable tables

Portable heaters

Toasters

Supply cabinet

Refrigerator	Water and ice
Set-up area	Phone
Linen and other storage area	Desk
Dish, covers, and other storage	File

Waiter and Bus Boy Facilities

Tray stands	Set-up tables
Water stations	Serving wagons
Ice bins	Pastry cart
Water bottle storage	Garnish sink
Waitress stations	Linen, silver, and other storage

8. Guest Facilities
    a. Entrance inviting and convenient.
    b. Comfortable waiting area, attractive chairs or benches, ash trays, cigarette vending, phone.
    c. Coat and hat racks or checkrooms, parcel and umbrella storage.
    d. Toilet facilities, conveniently located, clean, attractive, adequate.
    e. Dining room, good traffic flow, cheerful, attractive, well-lighted, comfortable.
    f. Telephone affording reasonable privacy.

9. Employee Facilities
    a. Convenient entrance
    b. Toilet, locker, and dressing room space equipped with:

coat cabinets	lavatories	mirror
lockers	soap dispenser	cot (for women)
toilets	towel dispenser	chair or bench.
urinals	waste container	

    c. Kitchen lavatories, soap dispensers, towel dispensers, paper cup dispensers, fountains, waste containers.
    d. Time clock and card rack.
    e. Bulletin board.
    f. Dining room.
    g. Clock.
    h. First-aid supplies.

10. Management and Supervisory Facilties
    a. Privacy for conferences and business.
    b. Freedom from unnecessary distraction.
    c. Safety fo money, files, and records.
    d. View for supervision of operations, control of supplies, food processing, and service.

e. Suitably equipped for work.

f. Control panel for lights and utilities.

g. Sound equipment control.

Items, facilities, and equipment to be checked:

Desk, table, and chairs.

Files—recipe, inventory, letter.

Machines—typewriter, calculator, adding machine, telephone.

Books—accounting, recipe.

Cabinets for coats and supplies.

Safe.

Private toilet and dressing room.

Waste baskets.

Suggested Student Assignments

1. Identify materials used for:
   a. Hood over cooking equipment.
   b. Floor and walls.
   c. Worktables and bins.
   d. Refrigerator shelving, storeroom shelving, dish bins or shelving.
   e. Pots, pans, and tableware.

2. List locations of the following:
   a. Electrical outlets for equipment.
   b. Water sources for work sections.
   c. Scales, state model and use.
   d. Bins for food, state whether mobile or stationary.

3. List all items of equipment in:
   a. Serving area.
   b. Dishwashing area.
   c. Office.
   d. Personnel facilities.

4. Trace path of food from receiving to service in terms of sanitary handling methods. List points where there is:
   a. Satisfactory protection.
   b. Possibility of contamination.

5. What methods used or conditions exist that:
   a. Promote good standards.
   b. Cause poor results.

Chapter 7

receiving and storage

Materials for a food facility are numerous, varied, often bulky, and subject to deterioration and misappropriation. Several people normally are involved with placing, taking, and filling orders and with the delivery and receiving of goods. Errors are possible at many points. Accurate, adequate, and timely communication is needed to ascertain that materials ordered are actually delivered. The system for protection of goods should extend from the time that the material is received until it has been used, and it includes orderly examination of deliveries, proper placement and protection in storage, and record of issues for use.

RECEIVING

The receiving area needs to be planned to receive the volume and type of merchandise that will normally be delivered and required to occupy the area until examined. The kind of examination of many of the bulky shipments of packaged goods allows them to be placed directly in storage under the supervision of the receiving clerk. Many items require minimal inspection and merely call for package, label, and count. Others, such as meat cuts, may call for opening of packages to inspect quality, sizing of cuts, count, and weight. Save time and money by providing facilities that will require a minimum of rehandling and permit direct transfer to points of use or storage. Many deliveries are heavy and bulky and should call for a minimum of movement. The material flow from receiving to storage and to processing should be as short as possible and cause a minimum of interruption of work in sections.

Locate the receiving area and the entrance to storage for easy supervision by the person in charge. In large facilities a desk or office may be located at this point. In smaller operations it may be in view of the manager's office and close enough for checking and acknowledging deliveries. The location of the receiving area must be where it is convenient for delivery trucks and other delivery equipment, and where arriving material is close to storage or points of use. Figures 7.1 through 7.4 show work-saving examples for receiving areas.

The size of the receiving area for a specific food facility is influenced by the nature and volume of materials received and going out at any one time. Some may be measured in terms of a hand truck and others in terms of a carload of merchandise. Satellite units receiving hot food in heated trucks or serving carts need space for the carts and perhaps electrical outlets for maintaining desired temperatures. Pallet delivery of quantities requiring the use of a fork truck need space for essential maneuvering of the truck. A stairway from the ground to the receiving

Figure 7.1 An unloading dock at proper height for truck deliveries. Note antipest fans over receiving doors, portable platform scales conveniently placed, and reflector-type lights providing good illumination. (*Courtesy Sky Chef, Los Angeles.*)

dock level should be provided. Immediate removal of supplies from the delivery carton calls for space for refuse.

Floor bearing weight should be studied and given adequate support to hold heavy loads. In addition to the weight of the merchandise, it is necessary to include the stress of carts, fork trucks, and other transportation equipment. Provide a floor that can be easily scrubbed and rinsed, and have adequate drains. A hose connection will be needed, and it is best to provide storage for cleaning supplies near this area.

Movement of shipments from truck to receiving dock calls for the dock to be close to the same height as the truck body. A problem is presented by heavy van trucks having a higher body than the smaller light delivery trucks. In order that both may use the same dock, the dock can be built for the heavier units and a movable platform provided that can be put in place before the lighter unit backs up, thus raising it to the proper height. Where deliveries are substantial, adding an adjustable platform that raises or lowers to meet the proper level of the truck is possible. Ordinarily, facilities will find that a dock 2½ to 3 ft (.76 to .91 m) and 8 ft (2.44 m) deep is adequate, with the length varying as needed. Door

Figure 7.2 Two illustrations of pallet handling of supplies showing: (*a*) Weighing on floor scales. (*b*) Movement to storage. (*Courtesy Norwalk-La Mirada City School District, Norwalk, Calif.*)

openings should be large enough to allow free passage of supplies and equipment; 3½ and 5 ft (1.07 and 1.2 m), respectively, are usually considered standard for single and double doors, but this may vary according to needs. Supplies may be moved into the facility by means of gravity slides, conveyors, elevators, motor-moved skids or platforms, platform trucks, dollies, hand trucks, and various carts.

Equipment in the receiving area should include an inspection table, scales, and container-opening tools, such as a crow bar, claw hammer, short-bladed sharp knife, and can opener. There must be space, place, and equipment also for record keeping. Accurate scales of appropriate size are essential. Freight scales level with the floor are recommended for large operations and smaller portable scales for small quantities and for weighing individual packages. New scales are available that can stamp the weight, date, and time and thus provide a useful record. Locate scales in proper lines of flow from receiving to storage or direct delivery.

(b)

Figure 7.2   (*Continued*)

STORAGE

Storage of supplies at the point of first use helps to minimize material handling. Full use of such a plan will be tempered by various factors, such as volume and nature of material, size and economics of the establishment, and the frequency of deliveries. Maintaining compactness in work sections may mean limiting the volume stored. In large organizations this may mean splitting shipments received. In small units, the money for space and equipment may prohibit proliferation of refrigerators or other storage compartments. Big institutions using a large volume are often able through frequent deliveries to lessen amounts carried in stock. Small operations and those located far away from supply sources often find it necessary to buy in sufficient quantity to support delivery costs. Man-hours and time saved through the convenience of having supplies at hand for work, however, have sufficient economic value to merit following the practice to the fullest extent possible.

When planning storage, differentiate between local (unit) and central (distant) storage needs. If space is provided at the local work unit, many

Figure 7.3 Direct delivery of milk to mobile dispenser by the delivery man reduces labor and the lifting frequently done by women workers. Ottawa High School, Grand Rapids, Mich. (*Courtesy Lincoln Manufacturing Co., Fort Wayne, Ind.*)

supplies may be delivered and held directly there, saving time and labor. Central storage should be provided for items to be held for longer periods or that are in sizable bulk. The policies of management should be ascertained before allowing larger holding areas in local units than those required for a day's use or short time use. It may not be desirable to have a lot of items stored in units in terms of safety and compactness of the work center. Management may prefer to have items stored in a central unit where there is better accountability and control.

Storage needs vary according to the nature of supplies and their specific holding requirements. Storage requirements differ, for example, for field potatoes in sacks, cartons of processed potatoes ready for cooking, and frozen precooked items that are to be thawed, reheated, and served. Short-order houses offering limited fare will have different storage needs than an establishment providing a complete menu and several choices. The service of vegetables has been eliminated from many menus in specialty restaurants, except for the simplest salads, such as sliced tomatoes, cole slaw, and tossed lettuce. School, college, military, and industrial

Figure 7.4 Shelving may be stationary or mobile and should have adjustable shelves. (*Courtesy Market Forge, Everett, Mass.*)

food units responsible for full nutrition of the diners use large quantities of fresh, frozen, and canned fruit and vegetables. Operators of large establishments sometimes find it financially advantageous to purchase in large amounts at "harvest" prices and warehouse the merchandise until needed.

Convenient compactness of work sections should be protected when locating storage areas. The storage space in work areas should be provided in a quantity and manner that will not interfere with efficient work. It is sometimes necessary to work out a compromise between unit and central storage, with only daily supply provision in the work section. When this is done, handling is facilitated if space is allowed for moving the supplies from one location to the other in a cart. This calls for level floors plus door size and compartment space to admit the carts. A similar storage requirement exists where large quantities of convenience foods or precooked meals are held for final processing. Moving and storage in cart quantities will lessen handling time and costs.

Figure 7.5 Storage equipment installed in the wall between production and service provides step-saving convenience.

Equip all storage areas with an inside safety release and/or signal system. Install thermometers at points where they will be easy to check. Design areas for easy, thorough cleaning and sufficient air circulation to prevent stagnant off-odors and to allow for uniform ventilation and even refrigeration in the refrigerated areas.

Types of Storage

The location of storage areas should be determined in relation to the sections depending upon them for space or supplies. Different types of storage and the workers who make the most frequent trips to the areas are as follows:

1. Dry, ventilated storage
   a. Staple food supplies—cook, baker, pantry, and counter workers.
   b. Fresh fruits and vegetables—fruit and vegetable processors, cook, and salad maker.
   c. Cleaning supplies and equipment—dishwashers, pot washer, and janitor.
   d. Linen—all workers for issue and return of uniforms and aprons, plus kitchen towels, and dining room linens to the respective workers.

e. Paper—dining room workers, baker, and cook.

f. Baker's supplies—a pantry adjacent to the work section or a convenient area in the stockroom is needed for numerous small, currently used items, such as spices, pie pans, fat, custard cups, and paper supplies. Although many of the items may be used frequently, but are not required daily, their number and character should not be allowed to interfere with suitable compactness in the work section—bakery workers.

g. Trash and garbage—janitor, garbage men, and perhaps those who unpack supplies.

h. Equipment storage, such as dining room tables, chairs, program equipment, flower holders, tableware, equipment supplies, and light bulbs—janitor.

2. Refrigerated and low-temperature storage
   a. Dairy—cook, baker, and service workers serving milk.
   b. Meat, fish, and poultry—cook, salad and sandwich workers.
   c. Fruits and vegetables—vegetable processor, cook, and salad maker.
   d. Frozen foods—cook, baker, salad and dessert makers, and counter workers.
   e. Garbage in certain institutions and in some areas—janitor, garbage men.

The plan and system of operation will influence storage needs. This point may be illustrated by produced versus ready-made bakery products, short-order versus full menu offerings, and production kitchen versus precooked, frozen meals. The organization of work will influence storage space requirements also. Where stores are all issued from a central area, weighed correctly for use in recipes, and supplies allotted for daily needs, space and facilities will need to be provided in the storage area for this. Where this is done the storage space may be reduced in the work areas.

Dry Storage

A room temperature of 70°F (21° C) is generally considered acceptable for common storage. A somewhat lower temperature—60°F (15.6°C)—is preferable for many foods held in storage. The lower temperature often can be assured through locating the area where it will not get heat from areas heated by the sun or heating equipment and transmission of heat from hot areas. Insulation of hot pipes that must pass through the area will help hold down the temperature. Protect the storage areas from moisture, such as sweating walls, dripping pipes, and subsoil dampness. Screen against insects and vermin. Use extermination means immediately if vermin are discovered. Even areas subject to the best housekeeping practices can become infested by pests riding in on food and laundry packages.

Satisfactory housekeeping calls for all materials to be stored off the floor at least 8 in. (20 cm) in or on mobile containers or on floor racks. Hydraulic packs may be provided to move bulky supplies on skids or slatted racks 8 to 12 in. (20 to 30 cm) high. Clearly labeled metal containers on wheels or dollies provide useful storage for loose bulk items, such as rice, beans, milk solids, and sugars. Rolling bins, interchangeable with those used in work sections, such as those for the cook and baker, save extra handling.

Provide suitable clearance for movement of materials and utilization of space. Shelving over mobile bins must provide for overall bin height and sufficient space for lifting the lid and removal of products. The space allowance may be least when the bin can be moved forward and the lid slid back. Having a place for the lid (as with a garbage can type of lid) presents a problem when it is removed for getting material from the container.

Adjustable shelving is desirable to allow for spacing and because it is vermin proof. It should be sturdy enough to support loads without sagging or collapsing. Locate shelving at least 2 in. (5 cm) from walls. If the size and shape of the room will permit, arrange so that shelving is accessible from both sides. Consider both interspace and depth suitable for a given number and types and sizes of packages likely to be stored on either the fixed or movable shelves. Condiment bottles, cereal packages, and canned goods due to difference in size and shape call for different allowances. Store in standard lots, such as number in a case, to facilitate inventorying. The shelf width should fit either the width or length of the case and the interspace adequate for the number of cans or cases to be stacked on top of one another. Allow $1\frac{1}{2}$ to 2 in. (3 to 5 cm) excess in an interspace for ease in positioning and removing packages. (Note dimensions given in Table 5.9, Measurements of Representative Storage Items.)

Safety and sanitation call for cleanable surfaces, prevention of tumbling of heavy stacks and collapsing of shelves, plus elimination of hazardous climbing on ladders, stools, or boxes, and excess lifting. Position heavy items so as to reduce lifting and facilitate dispensing. Drums of oil and vinegar or cleaning supplies should be equipped with pumps or located on cradles and have spigots. Limit the height of top shelves to 6 ft (1.8 m) for easy reach without the aid of a stool or stepladder. The average vertical reach of men is $84\frac{1}{2}$ in. (21.5 cm) and of women 81 in. (20.6 cm). Use the top shelf for light, bulky packages, such as cereals, or items used infrequently. Issuing of many bulk items, such as beans and rice, requires weighing. A table and scales should be positioned conveniently for this purpose.

Ventilated Common Storage

Satisfactory use of a ventilated common storage area, which does not have mechanical means of heating or refrigeration, depends upon current weather conditions. Extremes in temperature for several months of the year will limit this type of storage to the short period between delivery and preparation for other storage. Foods that may be held for two or three days at temperatures ranging from 50 to 60°F (10 to 15.6°C) include under-ripe avocados, bananas, grapefruit, lemons, limes, melons, cucumbers, eggplant, potatoes, squash, and firm tomatoes. A temperature of 65 to 75°F (18.3 to 24°C) is suitable for ripening rooms for bananas, avocados, tomatoes, pears, apples, and similar items. Potatoes should be stored at 50°F (10°C) if they are to be used soon, otherwise at 40°F (4.4°C) or below, and removed three weeks before use into 50°F (10°C) storage to allow sugars to develop into starch.

Refrigerated and Low-Temperature Storage

Modern food facilities show marked changes from a decade ago in their use of refrigerated and low-temperature storage. Many of the changes have been occasioned by the processing and/or use of precooked meal items (convenience foods). Commissary or central kitchen units are more common where foods are processed and sent to satellite units for service. These foods may be refrigerated for a short interim holding or frozen for longer holding or farther shipment. Fast feezing means are needed by processing kitchens where initial freezing is done.

Good quality in frozen foods calls for (a) understanding the characteristics of the specific food item, (b) fast freezing and storage at low temperature, (c) packaging to shut out air and protect the product, and (d) maintenance of uniform temperature. Quality loss speeds up approximately five times for every 5 to 10° rise in temperature from 0 to 30°F (−18 to −1°C). Very few products are improved by freezing. Quantity needs should be carefully calculated in order that frozen foods have a rapid turnover while their quality is at its best. This will help also in preventing excessive installation expense for larger space and heavier refrigeration equipment.

Refrigerators, in the average kitchen, must respond to repeated variations in temperature due to the continual opening and closing of doors. Such holding is unsatisfactory for long period holding of refrigerated items. Commercial warehouses are likely to be better equipped for the longer period holding of fruits and vegetables. The commodities held at temperatures just above freezing and with 80 percent relative humidity show less loss of flavor and dehydration than those at higher temperatures and lower humidity. Certain fruits and vegetables, such as avocados, some of the citrus fruits, pineapple, green beans, cucumbers, peppers, potatoes, sweet potatoes, and tomatoes, are preserved better when held at 50° F (10° C) with 85 percent relative humidity.

Compartments in refrigerators and low-temperature storage should be sized for the volume and method normally used for handling loads, whether by mobile cart or portable tray. Variations between requirements in the processing unit and the serving area are to be kept in mind by the planner. Where both activities are performed in the same establishment, pass-through refrigerators may serve as a highly desirable convenience even though the double entrance lessens insulation values and increases possibilities for temperature changes, plus there is a dehydrating effect on foods brought about by the temperature changes.

Cleanability that promotes sanitation is a significant need in these areas. Hard-surfaced, easily cleaned floors, walls, and fixtures are needed. The use of smooth, nonabsorbent materials is desirable. Drains should be provided for removal of scrubbing water and condensate. These may be located in or immediately outside the door opening to the compartment if they may freeze up inside. Care should be used to avoid a floor irregularity that might be hazardous to footing or cause the jarring of rolling carts carrying fluid foods. Satisfactory refrigeration requires uniform ventilation in all areas of the compartments. Provide lighting that will illuminate all areas adequately. In walk-in refrigerators equipped with locks provide an inside lock release and alarm system.

General Storage

General storage for linens, paper supplies, cleaning equipment, equipment parts, and replacement supplies may be located together or separately, according to use, volume handled, and flow of traffic. Some storage may be provided in work sections. The bulkiness of paper supplies requires auxiliary storage to protect compactness in the serving area. There must be sufficient space in the work section to provide supplies through the peak periods or until a break in service permits replenishing.

Multipurpose use of rooms, such as school lunchrooms or hotel banquet areas, requires the repeated moving of tables and chairs. Dual equipment, such as tables and benches that can be made into seats with backs, saves moving in school lunchrooms. Labor saving and the protec-

Figure 7.6 Under-stage storage for chairs in a multipurpose room. (*Courtesy Haywood Union High School District, Hayward, Calif.*)

tion of these furnishings will depend upon suitable methods of handling and storage. Stackable units and appropriate trucks or dollies for moving can save both labor and equipment. Adjacent cabinets or storerooms lessen moving time and should be included in the original planning. Under-stage storage may be used for folding chairs on low dollies (see Figure 7.6).

Linen and laundry room space needs will be influenced by policies related to owning, laundering, or using services of a supply laundry. If the institution owns and launders the linens, it will require laundry, mending, and pressing equipment, and space for the entire stock needed. Rotation of supplies with a supply laundry tends to reduce the total stock stored at one time. Some institutions find it desirable to have a domestic washer and drier for kitchen towels. The unit may be installed in the dishwashing area or near linen storage.

Linen storage should include shelving for linens, rods for hanging uniforms, and a counter for sorting and counting material to be sent out or received. Allow sufficient shelf space for storing uniforms according to size and other material according to size, type, and use. The type of fold given linens will govern size needed. If napkins are stored flat and not folded, the space would be wide and deep enough to hold them. The size of tablecloths and their fold will affect space requirements. Provide metal tab holders for listing item and size. A shelf, table height, and projecting 12 to 18 in. (30.5 to 45.7 cm) beyond the other shelves, may be used for packages while shelves are being filled. A cart or mobile table may be used instead, if space permits. Aisle space between shelving should be 42 to 48 in. (109 to 122 cm) wide. Have a table area where packages of clean linens may be opened and checked and where soiled linens may be sorted and counted.

Provide for collection of soiled linens. Mobile carts on which open bags or hampers can be hung are useful for soiled linen collection. Waitress stations may have bins for soiled table linen or hampers may be placed near the deposit area for soiled dishes or in passageways through which waitresses pass. Good ventilation is required, and frequent removal of these linens is desirable. Wet linen may sour or mildew quickly, and it is well to provide a drying rack for it.

Store cleaning materials and equipment separately from foods. Keep them close to the cleaning areas. The fact that certain cleaning materials are toxic and corrosive is to be considered in planning storage. Temporary and work center storage as well as central storage areas for these supplies should be planned. Janitor areas should have racks or wall pegs for hanging brooms and mops. Mops used where there is greasy soil should not be used in other areas. Shelves are needed for sundry supplies and inverted buckets. Good light and ventilation are necessary. Janitor's closets should have hard-surfaced walls and nonslip floors.

The garbage collection area should be located for easy garbage pickup. Refrigeration is sometimes required. Good ventilation is important. Allow adequate space for trash and empty crates, plus boxes or other containers that are to be returned. The garbage can cleaning area should be close to the collection and holding area. Provide a steam hose and/or can washer and a rack for can drainage and storage. A pipe platform over which cans can be inverted has been found to be satisfactory for this purpose. Provide sufficient space for the full complement of cans and for carts that are to be washed in the area. Provide hard-surfaced, moisture-proof strong walls and floors. Truck movement of heavy containers calls for steel jambs on doors and shields or bumpers on doors and walls.

Equipment storage is needed for new, surplus, or replacement equipment, and that which is infrequently used but required for special purposes. This storage may be centrally located or separated into use areas. Where it is kept together, it is well to locate it near the point of most frequent use, such as catering. Folding tables and chairs represent the largest volume generally found in such storage. Platform trucks or special dollies greatly facilitate movement and handling of these. It is customary for establishments to have a reserve supply of china, glassware, flatware, and other table appointments regularly used in quantities equal to approximately 10 to 20 percent of that required for current use. It is suggested that establishments with a limited need for flower arranging provide for this in the vegetable preparation section where sinks, knives, and carts are available for such work. Storage of vases, frogs, tools, and decorations may be located where they will be convenient to the area where used. In large facilities using many flowers, a separate area may be provided with storage, sink, and work area.

Special, lockable storage is required in facilities that handle costly items and those highly susceptible to theft, such as candy, cigarettes, and alcoholic beverages. Wine storage needs special shelving to keep corks moist.

Suggested Student Assignments

Select a specific food facility for the following study:

1. State foods on menus, type of preparation done in the unit, and volume served.
2. Classify foods in terms of storage needs and volume and time to be stored.
3. Chart movement of materials from receiving, to storage, to points of use.
4. List and evaluate storage equipment (shelving, carts, bins, other) in terms of:
   a. Convenience and adequacy for use.
   b. Safety for supporting load limits.
   c. Cleanability and sanitation.
   d. Appropriateness of cost on the basis of suitability, convenience, and durability.
5. Describe provisions made for storage of:
   a. Linen and laundry supplies.
   b. Paper supplies.
   c. Cleaning equipment and supplies.
   d. Reserve equipment and housekeeping supplies.
6. Recommend ways in which storage facilities might be improved, giving reasons for your recommendations and an estimate of probable costs.

Chapter 8

food processing

There are varying extents of food processing performed in public food facilities. Complete processing from raw materials to finished products may be done, or food may be procured in a condition ready for immediate service. There are currently public food facilities designed for:

1. Complete production of foods for variety menus.

2. Specialization in "fast foods" (such as broiled or grilled items) with utilization of certain ready-prepared dishes.

3. Use of frozen precooked foods for the full meal.

4. Use of prepared foods for specific parts of the menu, such as vegetables or desserts.

5. A satellite service of fully prepared, ready-to-serve food.

Planning requires that the system by which the kitchen is to operate be determined before proceeding with plans. Advanced calculation of best values for a specific operation is called for. There are many new products and procedures now current from which to choose. Few restaurants use frozen prepared food exclusively, but it is estimated by a National Restaurant Association spokesman that 25 percent of all restaurants use such foods in main courses.[1] Consumer advocates who wish to be assured of food freshly prepared on the premises are pushing for legislation to require identification on menus of items that are "frozen, prepared, off-the-premises." Even though the quality may be almost as good or good enough that its treatment is not readily discernible, it is felt that the consumer has a right to know what he is getting. Many large chains find it to be a desirable means of controlling quality as well as economizing on operational expenses. Many school systems have centralized production with a variety of means of packaging, transporting, holding, conditioning, and service. Modern economy tends to force consideration of new methods of operation.

Advanced calculation and formulation of policies are needed to prevent a facility being tied to a system that will not be the most advantageous. It is easy to be overly enthusiastic about certain values and miss having greater values in a specific situation. Those who try to eliminate labor problems by using ready-prepared food may be equally harassed by food selection and supply problems and standards control. Those who believe the ready-prepared foods to be a sure route to fairly uniform quality may eliminate opportunities for variety and quality freshness desired by a specific clientele or fail to gain a versatility needed to meet changing conditions. The most practical and thorough calculations and

[1] Ward Morehouse, III, *The Christian Science Monitor*, July 16, 1975.

research are called for in arriving at the basic decision as to the system to use. In addition, whatever system is chosen should be examined for possible flexibility if a desirable change may need to be made later.

In this text, information is given relating to complete food processing, but from time to time notations will be made as they relate to different systems. The basic functions of food production must occur even though they may not be done in the facility where the food is served. Specific systems are simplified by eliminating one or more of the basic functions performed in the unit. It is essential, since all of them must be performed somewhere, that all steps be covered in a basic text of this kind and then decisions may be made as to which ones to include in the specific plan.

Three general steps make up the full processing procedure: (1) preliminary preparation, (2) cooking of foods and manipulating of materials for salads, sandwiches, and desserts, and (3) finishing and portioning for service. In a small kitchen, one cook or department may perform all functions. In large establishments, each step may have subdivisions. The work in well-organized sections will be performed by definite persons on a specified time schedule according to established standards and procedures.

Planners of production units with the goal of efficient work will be mindful of time, place, persons, and method in relation to essential functions. Usually most of the full-time and highest-salaried workers are employed in the processing sections. The questions of who, where, when, and how call for answers that will maximize their production abilities. It is important that standards of quality be defined and quantity needs be determined so that proper equipment, convenient arrangement, and adequate space will be provided. A flow of work that produces the quality standards and the quantity requirements on schedule, with the fewest workers and the least amount of effort, should be developed regardless of the production plan.

PRELIMINARY PREPARATION SECTIONS

Fruit and vegetable preparation plus meat cutting make up the major part of preliminary preparation. The fairly simple, routine nature of fruit and vegetable preparation makes it possible for workers having limited knowledge and experience to perform the work satisfactorily. They are paid less than those doing meat cutting, which calls for special skill and knowledge. Some of the duties in these sections may be filled by workers from other areas. It is important for planners to know local conditions, wages, and the management's buying policies before allotting space or designing a layout for these areas. This is especially significant if certain units are to be eliminated and processed items obtained. Local market conditions are likely to influence this. The advisability of allowing for a given amount of flexibility in the preliminary preparation sections will be influenced also by future trends, changes in methods of processing and marketing, grading variations, different products on the market, and different needs in the facility.

A computer can be useful in studying the advisability of including space and equipment for preliminary preparation sections. Most of the value aspects, such as levels of quality and market dependability, can be coded. Costs of labor, space, equipment, and supplies can be weighed most easily if changed to a common denominator, such as time period, cost per minute, hour, or day. Availability and skill of labor (few cooks are proficient in meat cutting) require consideration. Some factors may be coded as absolute restrictions, such as space limitations and time restrictions and others with varying levels of acceptability.

The volume used will have considerable influence on the economic advantage of one system of purchasing over another. Cost of labor, space, and equipment in vegetable preparation, for example, is likely to be less per given volume per week when the volume used is large than when it is small, since there are more units to share costs and compete with purchase prices.

Vegetable and Fruit Preparation Sections

Characteristics of fruits and vegetables emphasize the relationship of this section with others. The bulk, weight, and soil typical of much of the merchandise make a minimum of movement desirable in getting it into the initial processing area. Its liability to spoilage calls for limiting time in getting it into suitable storage or use. Empty crates and bulky refuse require disposal quickly to clear space. After preliminary processing is done and materials stored, items move to the cooking and pantry sections. Economy in handling, insurance of sanitation, and protection of quality stress the importance of good flow of this material. Convenient relationships are to be maintained between (1) receiving of supplies, (2) work area or storage adjacent to the work area, (3) trash or garbage space, and (4) refrigeration adjacent to section where processing will be continued (that is, cooking, salad or sandwich making, and serving area).

Where heavy or bulky loads are handled, time and labor will be saved by moving on wheels or other labor-reducing means. Many types of platform and hand trucks, kitchen carts, and storage bins are available to fit various uses from receiving through the several stages of processing.

When selecting transportation equipment and planning storage, thought should be given to minimizing rehandling. Placing vegetables for cooking in steamer baskets and/or steam table pans as prepared can save rehandling time. Receiving and initial preparation may be performed on one floor level and the refrigerator and production section may be on another. Any flow that increases distance adds to the importance of study to reduce transportation of materials.

The work in the fruit and vegetable preparation section usually forms into three work centers, that is (1) cleaning, (2) paring, and (3) trimming, shaping, and chopping. Where the volume handled is small, all of the activities may be performed in one work center. When the quantity is very large, an assembly line production may be used, and one center completely separated from the others. Simplified and repeated motion in such activities makes it possible to develop rhythm of work and increases speed of accomplishment. Worker qualifications and essential instruction may also be simplified for work that does not require constantly changing motion and decision-making.

Potato paring has been eliminated where there is a dependable, reasonably priced supply of potatoes available in popular forms ready for cooking. Large volume operations and those where supplies are less readily available find it expedient to perform this function within their own establishment. In addition to the sacked field potatoes needed for baking or boiling, the market has a wide range of dried, dehydrated, frozen, or chilled products available. About 60 percent of the potatoes used currently in institutions are preprocessed potatoes.

Pared potatoes and root vegetables should be stored close to the peeling area. In multiple-function centers, it is often desirable to have mobile peelers that can be rolled out of the way when not required for use. In very large kitchens using a huge volume of pared potatoes and vegetables, it is useful to have a mechanical lift for gravity feeding to the peeler, and a moving belt under the peeler outlet for carrying the potatoes under a rinse spray to the worktable where eyes and spots are removed. They are next dropped into a water bath or an antioxidant solution. The sink for this final bath may be shallow and located at the end of the belt or eyeing table. In some operations the peeler is adjacent to a sink or empties over an inspection table leading to a sink that is a part of another work center. Plan small tool storage in a drawer or rack in a table and space for pans and mobile equipment under the table or adjacent to this work area.

The work done in the cleaning center requires a two-compartment sink. Size will depend upon the quantity of bulky vegetables and fruits to be cleaned. The work in this center bears a close relationship to the

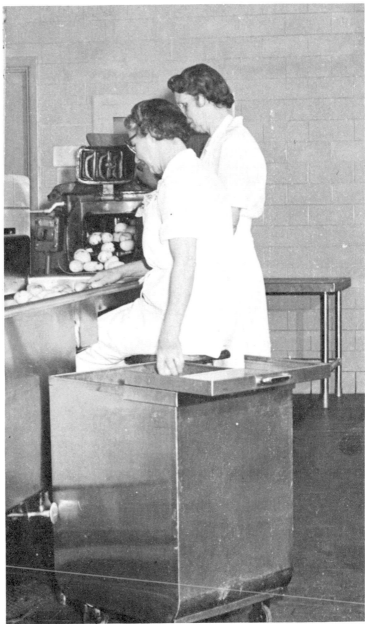

Figure 8.1 The potato peeler unloads onto the inspection and eyeing table. After final hand trimming, potatoes are placed in mobile bin to be wheeled to storage.

third center where trimming, shaping, and chopping are done. It may be combined with it for short, convenient movement of supplies. If possible, the entire length should be limited to 8 ft (2.5 m) for step-saving compactness. Limiting sink depths to 12 to 14 in. (30½ to 35½ cm) makes for convenient reach. A drain basket, made to fit between and be suspended from the sides of a sink compartment, is useful when washing fruits and vegetables by using an overhead spray. The basket may be perforated steel or heavy wire mesh. The weight and size should be suitable for women workers to lift when filled. A basket 18 in. (46 cm) wide may be fitted into a mobile cart designed for 18-in. (46 cm) modular pans and moved into storage. The pans may be placed on the table during work and require less stooping or reaching than cans on dollies (see Fig. 8.2). Choose storage containers to minimize handling as fruits and vegetables move to the next processing sections, such as pantry or cooking. Cooking is frequently done in steam table pans or containers. These may be placed on trucks and moved into storage until needed.

Motor-driven equipment, such as choppers, grinders, and shredders, is used in the third center. The hazards common to the use of this equipment makes an arrangement desirable in which the operator will not be liable to bumping or distraction of attention. The equipment is likely to have several loose parts and attachments requiring storage. A wall rack close to the machine may provide both convenience and protection of cutting edges. Certain machines may be needed in more than one center for only a limited time, and, if mounted on wheels, these could be used without duplication and pushed out of the way when not needed. Mobile carriers for such equipment should be equipped for storage of blades and attachments to provide for rapid change of work center arrangement.

Equipment shared by workers in two or more areas should be central to the respective areas for convenience. Equipment storage is an example. Cooking and storage pans, mixing bowls, and cutting tools are needed in more than one center. Various items on mobile equipment, such as bowls on mobile racks and storage carts, require space that should be provided nearby. A disposal unit or garbage container will be needed for refuse from trimming, cleaning, and sorting. The kitchen areas having a major need for garbage disposal include (1) the fruit and vegetable preparation section, (2) the scraping area in the dishwashing section, and (3) the pot washing section. Small operations that can afford only one power disposal may find it desirable to organize work and arrangement so that refuse from more than one section can utilize a disposal unit located in the center where it is most needed, such as dishwashing.

Figure 8.2 Two types of mobile vegetable storage units. The one requires excess stooping, and the other has pans that may be placed on a table at a convenient height.

Meat Handling

The cost and popularity of meat on menus, in addition to its nutritive values, give meat handling outstanding importance. Usually the most skilled and highest-salaried employees are given responsibility for its handling or preparation. Meat quality is highly perishable, being subject to absorption of off-flavors, dehydration, and spoilage. The cost of labor and perishability of the product highlight the importance of proper equipment, strict sanitation, and a layout for efficient work.

Very few facilities currently have fully equipped meat sections. Large commissary installations and those established for many years may have them. Satisfactory economics will also call for them to have skillful meat cutters and suitable outlets for all the meat processed from carcass and other wholesale cuts. A modified amount of meat cutting occurs in many restaurants featuring steaks, chops, and roasts. This tends to be suffi-

Figure 8.3 A wall rack for attachments located near food cutter. (*Men's Residence Halls, University of Washington, Seattle, Wash.*)

ciently repetitious to require somewhat less skill and less costly and extensive equipment. Instead of buying full carcasses, wholesale cuts or lesser units are bought. The meat may be aged in restaurant storage, and for this reason special space and facilities may be required. When needed for use it is processed ready for cooking. If freshly cut, it will have best quality.

Cuts of meat made to exacting specifications are available from packing houses and butcher shops in metropolitan areas. The majority of food operators rely on this service. Although the price of the fabricated meat appears high in comparison with the price per pound of carcass meat, it is usually found to compare well on a cost per portion basis. Part of the advantage lies in having uniform portion size, in freedom from having to utilize all of the various cuts in a carcass for specific types of menus, and in having exact, immediate knowledge of portion costs. Full realization of values is likely to depend in considerable degree upon the knowledge and skill of the buyer in making specifications and of the receiving clerk in recognizing and checking the extent to which the merchandise meets specifications when it is delivered.

The majority of cooks currently have little knowledge and skill in or time for meat cutting. There is a limited amount required in general preparation of meals for which appropriate equipment is needed, even with the purchase of fabricated meats. The cook's sink should be of adequate size for poultry cleaning or occasional thawing of frozen items that may be required. A heavy cutting board on the table may substitute for a butcher's block. A utility table, perhaps mobile, in the cook's section may be used for the meat grinder and possibly a cuber, scales for roasts and portions, and a slicer. If the slicer is mounted on a separate mobile table, it may be used by pantry workers as well.

Keep meat refrigerated. Use extra care in locating storage for meat as it is received, processed for cooking, and for supplies during a cooking process such as grilling or broiling. The nearer to freezing temperature that fresh meat is held the less the exchange of flavors. Temperatures from 34 to 38° F (1.1 to 3.3° C) are recommended as suitable for holding fresh meat. Repeated opening of a refrigerated compartment changes the temperature and has a drying effect on the meat. This point is good to remember when sizing the compartment and considering the door size. Location and convenient level of reach are significant to work efficiency where frequent reference is made for supplies. Space shelves appropriate to package size and/or trays of meat prepared for cooking. If carcass meat is handled, have an overhead track extending from the receiving area into the refrigerated holding area adjacent to the cutting or work center. Prevention of objectionable exchange of flavors calls for fish to be held in a separate compartment from fresh meat. A covering of cracked ice helps to prevent drying of fish and the escape of odors.

In a butcher shop the work is usually divided into three work centers: (1) carcasses are broken into "wholesale" cuts; (2) which are shaped into cooking portions, such as roasts, chops, steaks, or patties; and (3) will be grouped around sinks at which poultry may be dressed or fish cleaned. Where carcass meats are broken down, a meat hook will be needed near the block where a carcass can hang and from which cuts may be placed on the block. The block should be far enough from other equipment to allow the butcher to work around it and for large cuts to project beyond

Figure 8.4 Mobile equipment, such as the table mounted meat slicer, permits flexible use in a large kitchen.

the edge. A conveniently located hand or power saw will be needed. A rack should be on or near the block for the cutting and boning knives. A twine holder for tying roasts should be within easy reach above the block.

A power saw is used for breaking up carcasses and for making portion cuts. It should be located so that a cart with meat may stand on one side and a table or cart for pans of portions on the others. Avoid placing a power saw where the butcher is likely to be interrupted or have his attention diverted, as in areas where others may push past him.

The activity of the second center may be done at the meat block or saw. Depending upon menu requirements, this center may need a food chopper and pattie shaper, cuber, cutting block, and knives and scales for shaping portions. Pans should be stored within reach and mobile equipment supplied for moving the portioned material to the cooking section and refrigeration. A table drawer is needed for miscellaneous equipment and such supplies as larding needle, knife sharpener, parchment, and wax paper. Linear space requirements may be reduced through the use of mobile tables or carts that can be moved through processing from table to machine and back to table. A thick wooden cutting block on the table will lessen need to travel to the main block for small trimming and cutting.

Figure 8.5 A small meat cutting section meets requirements in the modern kitchen. Note the readily cleanable surfaces designed to promote good sanitation. (*Courtesy Hobart Manufacturing Co.*)

The flow of work in fish and poultry preparation is likely to proceed from cart to sink to table. When dressing poultry, a gas line overhead or from the wall may be desirable for singeing poultry. A tendon puller is needed for dressing turkeys. Position the knife racks for convenient reach and handling. The cutting board for work with fish and poultry should be absorption proof and thoroughly cleanable, such as plastic or compressed wood that is impregnated with chemicals. Thorough cleaning calls for scalding and use of detergents. The table on which portioning and panning are done may be a separate one or the same one used for the final preparation of food.

Arrangement of meat cutting sections vary according to need and organization of work. In many facilities the block is placed opposite the sink and against a table. This allows freedom for working on three sides and movement of items to the table within the maximum reach area. Figure 8.5 shows a small meat cutting area located conveniently between refrigerator and production area. Ample space needs to be allowed for a cart to stand beside the saw and block or to move along the table while work is proceeding. Note that the block has been placed on a sturdy, easily cleanable base, and table drawers have been provided for knives and other cutting equipment.

Provide good light in this section, at least 50 to 60 foot-candles. Place light sources so as to avoid glare or shadows on the work. Floors should be hard-surfaced and nonskid type. Place drains and slope floor toward them for proper cleaning and where drain depression will not be in a frequently used passage or be a footing hazard. Walls should be hard-surfaced and washable. Cantilevered tables and equipment permit easy cleaning and mobile cart storage.

COOKING SECTIONS

The cooking section is generally regarded as the heart of the kitchen. The materials used in this department are likely to be the most expensive; the work is usually done by workers who are paid the highest rates; and the quality of the products tends to be more fragile and requires more rapid service to ensure excellence than do the products from other sections. Therefore when a kitchen is designed, this department is likely to be shown preference as to location in relation to service, supervision, and flow of work. Where choice is made between the proximity of this section and other sections, the close relationship between cooking and serving is given precedence to ensure fast service and protection of fragile food qualities.

Material Flow

The flow of raw materials will come from three main sources: (1) the meat and vegetable preparation sections, (2) dry or common, refrigerated and low-temperature storage areas, and (3) direct delivery. Unless processed foods are refrigerated or frozen for delayed cooking, they will flow from the cooking section to points of service. Intermediate holding between preparation and service may occur in hot serving table, bain marie, hot cart, pass-through refrigerated cart, or other type of unit. Various means are used to shorten the distance between final preparation and service. One consists of locating a part of the cooking equipment, such as a grill for filling short orders, in a cafeteria lunch counter, or by using a pass-through to service in cafeterias and less formal table-service dining rooms. Food partially processed in a main kitchen may be sent to a service kitchen for final cooking, as in a decentralized service hospital.

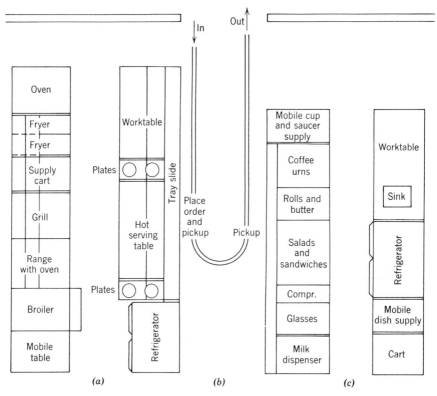

Figure 8.6 Plan for a service restaurant showing A—cooking section, B—waiters' route, and C—pantry section.

Some hotels send prepared foods to a grill or coffee shop to supplement the grill items prepared locally and to provide a more adequate menu selection. In order to ensure palatable food temperature for patients' meals, some hospitals utilize mobile microwave units and food on carts and do the final cooking close to the patient's room.

Cooking Functions

The functions in the cooking sections may be grouped according to treatment required and type of cooking done. Treatment will involve seasoning, mixing, shaping, breading, and panning. Cooking is by steam in cookers and kettles; by dry heat in ovens, ranges, grills, and broilers; by deep-fat frying; and in limited degree by microwave. Layouts for step-saving should provide not only for flow of materials in processing but also minimize backtracking in inspection, processing, and procurement of supplies. The variety and volume of items to be prepared will influence equipment needs and the forming of work centers. Work centers are often formed around a particular type of preparation, such as vegetable cooking, soup and sauce making, and meat cooking. In small establishments the various functions will be consolidated into one or two work centers. Simplification of menus to eliminate functions often helps to simplify equipment needs and increase production efficiency.

Detailed consideration should be given to individual work centers, the close coordination of the centers with others in the section, and the section with other sections of the facility. This includes planning for:

1. Good supervision. Make sections easy to supervise by avoiding unnecessary obstructions, such as posts, walls, and tall equipment to a view of areas.

2. Freedom from interruption of work. Avoid through-traffic in sections. Workers from other sections should not have to pass through to get supplies or to use equipment. Waiters and waitresses should not be permitted to enter work sections. Their area and traffic flow should be located so that they will move smoothly in a definite direction.

3. Good equipment-use relationship with others who require periodic use of certain items of equipment. The baker and the cook may need to share ovens, tilt kettles, and steam cookers. In small kitchens, one mixer may serve both sections. The pantry worker may need to steam potatoes, cook eggs, or prepare dressing using equipment in the cooking section. Where equipment is used by workers from more than one center, it should be mobile or so placed that it can be used with the least interference in a given center. If mobile, it may be moved to other work centers. The way it is used and the condition in which it is left may give rise to arguments that good planning can help to prevent. The prerogatives of ownership are less definite when equipment has no fixed location.

4. Step-saving calls for close proximity to pot and pan storage and washing.

The minimum width for a work center should be 9 ft (2.74 m) and the maximum length recommended is 6 ft (1.83 m) to confine work within a maximum work area for a normal person. The simplest section consists of one work center having a range top with oven below and a table parallel. Roasting, baking, and oven broiling may be done in the oven, and stewing, soup making, and other cooking on the range top. From this simplest center, gradual extension may be made until a section is formed of many highly specialized centers. Traffic flow and suitable supervision become more difficult as the section size is increased. The specialized work centers tend to be less complex, however, than the work center that incorporates all of the cooking functions. Ranges with ovens require extra stooping and lifting, but they are used where space limitations or other factors make them the most desirable.

The size of the cooking sections and the number of work centers required are affected by a number of factors. The most important is the volume of food to be processed, plus amount and type of processing required. As quantity increases, the labor required is likely to increase also. There is a point when it is economical to break down functions between two or more workers rather than allow each to begin and complete entire functions. In this instance a product·may be partially processed in one center and delivered for completion to another adjoining it. Such a plan may result in shorter and more repetitive motion that lessens production time. Coordination of work must be carefully planned where workers share in processing. Where centers process entirely different products, less coordination is required.

The type of service and the type of menu will influence the make-up of the section. A drive-in may require only a grill and a French-fryer, whereas a drug store counter may have to add a waffle iron, toaster, and hot soup cup besides. In certain facilities, cooking functions may be divided into separate sections. A hospital diet kitchen may process certain foods. A special kitchen may prepare food for hotel banquets. A breakfast unit may prepare eggs, waffles, hot cakes, and French toast in a pantry or serving area separate from the cooking section. A cooking section where waiters and waitresses come in and pick up their orders differs from that of a cafeteria. Short-order and complete meal preparation functions differ, and meeting their needs may cause basic differences in plans for the cooking section. A facility specializing in prime beef ribs and baked or French-fried potatoes will not need the extensive equipment required by a large facility offering a wide menu choice. The work and equipment needs are also simple in cooking sections assigned to thawing and completing the preparation of preprocessed foods. The trend is toward simplified menus and a reduction of functions performed by cooks. More quality control is possible and less supervision, labor, equipment, and space are required.

Specific methods of preparation, schedule of service, and organization of staff will influence the make-up of the cooking section. An operation open 24 hours a day and serving drop-in trade has different needs from one preparing three meals daily at scheduled times. A kitchen organized under an executive chef, a pastry chef, and a steward will differ in many details from one where a dietitian directs preparation. Procedures will vary. Where it may be necessary to oven-prepare hamburgers for a school lunch, a lunch counter may grill them to order and another restaurant may broil them. More steam-jacketed kettles and cookers are used in certain operations than in others where range-type cooking is greater. The amount and specific type of preprocessed foods used will affect equipment needs and organization of work. A thorough analysis of the requirements is necessary before planning this important section.

Layout Design

Take time to detail all functions that are to be regularly performed in the cooking section. List in order of performance each activity and the equipment required for doing it. Separate activities according to the number of employees required to do them and the number of work centers needed. A satisfactory section for one food facility may be unsuitable for another. For best performance the section must be custom fitted to specific needs, even though certain basic patterns may be helpful in planning new sections.

The arrangement of equipment and work centers may be linear, parallel, square, L- or U-shaped. The minimum width of 9 to 19 ft (2.74 m to 3.05 m) includes a work table $2\frac{1}{2}$ to 3 ft (0.76 to 0.91 m) wide, an aisle $3\frac{1}{2}$ ft (1.07 m), and a range top 3 ft (0.91 m) deep. Have work aisles $3\frac{1}{2}$ to 4 ft (1.07 to 1.22 m) wide. Where doors of equipment open or mobile equipment is rolled in, the latter measurement is usually required. Linear placement violates many principles of good work center arrangement. If linear arrangement must be used, breaks in frontal equipment every 12 ft (3.66 m) permit entry into the section. If four or more centers are planned in a linear section, the distance will be around 24 ft (7.32 m). This is a considerable travel distance. Linear placement works best in small facilities. If a linear section is placed at right angles to a service area, it is usually best to place hot top or grill, fryer, and broilers closest to service, and ovens last. Steam equipment may be in the center.

Face-to-face parallel arrangement may be used in areas where servers enter the kitchen and a traffic lane is required. Such an arrangement makes it possible to pick up soup, meat, or entrees from respective work centers. Parallel, face-to-face centers at right angles to a service area are often efficient. The volume of food processed must be sufficient to sustain the breakdown into several work centers. Traffic may become a problem along the parallel aisle into the service area.

The efficiency of face-to-face and back-to-back parallel sections is lessened by traffic through them, and this may be hard to prevent or supervise. It may be awkward for the sauce and vegetable cooks to work behind cooking units and coordinate production. Removal of walls between back-to-back arrangements improves communication. A chief advantage of this design is the minimizing of hood expanse over cooking equipment. The need for such grouping under one hood may be lessened by use of individual ventilators or hoods.

Arrangement of equipment in a square, or L- or U-shaped plan is often difficult. The square section tends to invite traffic through it, and care must be taken to provide good aisle space at the back or front to avoid conflict with traffic in the section. The angle in the L-shaped plan tends to discourage traffic. This type section is best divided at the angle juncture between range, oven, broiler, and steam equipment. This will isolate respective work centers and allow for a more orderly procedure of work. U-shaped sections are efficient if not too large. With 4 ft (1.22 m) aisle space between equipment, the workers can easily work from one area to another. U-shaped plans discourage traffic going through them.

Equipment Needs

The essential equipment for a production kitchen will be a worktable, sink, and cooking equipment. Depending on size and type of food facility, cooking equipment may include a hot top, such as a range or griddle, ovens, deep-fry kettle, steam kettles and cooker, and a broiler. Table 8.1 indicates how needs may vary.

Cooking Functions and Equipment Arrangement

What are the typical menu and volume requirements? Before planning the work centers, study menus for typical treatment required in preparation and the kind of cooking equipment needed. Most cooking activities can be grouped into patterns that will serve as a basis for work center planning. Consider volume and transportation required, in addition to work.

Common functions in cooking include:

1. Preparation of mixtures, such as quick breads and casseroles, that require a mixing center. Continued manipulation is required. Tables, scales, mixer, sink, utensil storage, and a supply cart will be needed.

2. Special treatment in chopping, mixing, shaping, breading, and panning may be done at the cook's table or on other working surface.

Table 8.1 Survey of Equipment Used in Hotels Serving 300, and 1,500 to 3,000 per Day

Type of Equipment	Meals Served per Day	
	300	1,500–3,000
Range top, 12 × 24 in. (30 × 61 cm)	3 to 6	9
Ovens, sq ft or m area	9 sq ft (.84 m²)	18–27 sq ft (1.67–2.51 m²)
Sinks, 2-compartment	1	1 to 3
Mixer	1*	1†
Steamer sections	1	2 to 6
Steam kettles, 30–40 gal (114-115 l)	1	3 to 5
Trunnion steam kettles 20 qt (19 l)	1	3**
Broiler	0	0 to 2
Fryer	0 to 1	1 to 2

Note: Modern kitchens that utilize new fast means of cooking, have reduced menu variety, and/or use some partially or fully prepared items will vary considerably from these figures, especially for range top or griddle space.

* 20 qt (19 l) table model.

† 60- to 80-qt (57 to 76 l) pedestal model with 30- and 40-qt (28 and 38 l) adapters.

** One to be 30 or 40 gal (114 or 151 l).

3. Browning may be done in a skillet on the range top, on a griddle, in a broiler, in a fry kettle, or in an oven.

4. Preparation of roux, sauces, soups, and gravy for which range top or steam kettles are required. Work will alternate between table and cooking equipment.

5. Roasting and baking in an oven may be timed and require little attention. Loading and unloading will be to table or cart. Slicing may be done.

6. Vegetable cooking by steaming or boiling may be in steam kettles, steam cooker, or on the range.

7. Broiling or deep frying may be required.

The cook's table is generally the core of the cooking section, for it provides a major working surface and is usually a storage place for ingredients for seasoning, thickening, and mixtures. Study work relationships from this area to points requiring repeated inspection or continuous manipulation.

Fryers should be arranged with work space nearby. End-of-line location to which a cart can be drawn is often used. Free movement is hampered when they are located between a tall oven and other cooking equipment, such as a broiler. A landing area at least 2 ft (61 cm) wide should be provided next to the fryer for supplies awaiting frying and for foods removed from the fryer. A cart may be used also to bring materials to grilling stations. A table opposite roast ovens is a convenient place on which roasts or other baked items can rest for filling or removal from the ovens. In large sections, space in front of ovens should be sufficient for carts or rolling tables to be brought to ovens for loading and unloading. Roasts may be moved to the meat slicer for slicing and panning. A slicer on a mobile table possessing wheel locks may be used conveniently in more than one section or location and rolled out of the way when not needed.

Water should be piped to equipment where it is needed for the cooking procedures, such as over steam kettles, ranges, and mixing centers. A utility sink may be placed where it is accessible to several work centers. Steamers are best located at the end of an equipment line because of plumbing needs, escaping steam, and for working from a cart. Ranges for large facilities are best without ovens and space below for storage. In small units, compactness may require ovens in ranges. Where space is limited, ovens are sometimes located with the steam equipment, and the ranges and grills are banked together. In some school lunch units with little need for range top cooking, it has been found desirable to have a small range top or hot plates placed in the steam section.

Some operators limit cooking functions to grill, bar, or counter production of a short-order type. Bulk cooking may be done in another area and transported to this section to supplement the foods prepared there. Toasters, waffle irons, French-fryers, and other light equipment are grouped around the grill. A highly efficient center can be planned with proper arrangement. Maximum utilization of space vertically as well as horizontally is desirable. A small steam table may be used for soaps, sauces, and other cooked foods.

Dry ingredients for use in the cooking center are usually stored in the cook's table, which is used as a mixing or treatment center. Herbs, spices, and other seasonings are stored in small quantities on a shelf or in tilt bins above the table, and tilt or rolling bins below the table are used for flour, salt, sugar, and milk solids. Wet ingredients, such as eggs, milk, and fat, are brought from storage on a cart. Space must be allowed for

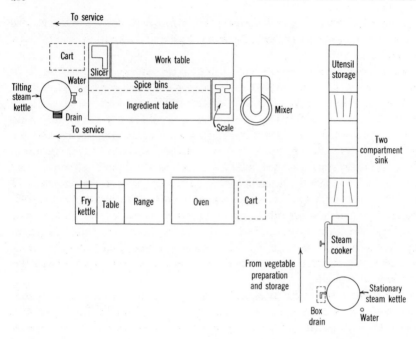

Figure 8.7 A suggested arrangement of equipment in a cooking section. Equipment is placed for interdepartmental use with a minimum of interference. The steam cookers and kettles may be arranged back-to-back with oven and range to permit use of a common hood.

foods arriving from storage or the ingredient room. Drawers directly under the table top and a rack above the spice bins are used for small equipment needed for manipulations.

In a cooking center, scales for ingredient measurement and a mixer are needed and should be in close proximity. Sink and utensil storage should be near the mixer. The work motions in mixing move from ingredient bins and cart onto the scale, then into the mixer. When mixing is finished, material is scaled into pans from the mixer and moved onto the table or a cart that transports the food to the oven. Where there is only one mixer in the cooking section, it should be placed where it is convenient to the steam cooker for mashing potatoes, unless dehydrated potatoes only are used. Rice and farinaceous products are often steamed and brought to the mixing center for the preparation of casserole dishes. The steam cookers are likely to be used by workers from more than one section and it is well to locate them with this in mind. Carts are commonly used for transporting loads to and from the cookers. Adequate

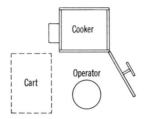

Figure 8.8   Equipment arrangement at the steam cooker.

space is to be allowed for the maneuvering of the carts and the swing
of the steam cooker door.

Steam kettles may be used for the preparation of bulky materials, such
as cooking vegetables or meats for stock. This type of preparation requires little manipulation and requires a large amount of water. The
average worker can easily cope with contents in a fairly large capacity
kettle. Smaller kettles should be used for contents that require stirring
or handling in a manner that may crush tender foods and which call for
an excess of energy. The preparation of puddings, sauces, and casserole
dishes requires weighing of ingredients as well as stirring. Stationary
kettles are satisfactory for fluid materials or materials from which it is
desirable to draw off liquid. Trunnion or tilt kettles are preferable for
thicker materials that are not to be drained and need to be poured from
the container. Large quantity kettles may have power stirrers and may
be emptied or filled mechanically.

Specialization in preparation and the fuller use of steam equipment
reduces the need for range top space. In some kitchens the hot top is
divided and one unit approximately 12 × 24 in. (30 × 61 cm) may be
located near the steam equipment and another near the cook's table
and oven. In residences, griddles may be located in or behind the serving
line for hot cakes, breakfast eggs, and hamburgers. The griddles may be
in fixed location or mobile.

Foods removed from the oven are likely to be hot and heavy. They
will be moved to a table for cutting into portions. Movement of the food
may be by hand or on a cart and the table may be the cook's table, a
slicing table, or other worktable. An oven located near a griddle, broiler,
or fry kettle provides a good holding place for serving plates and foods
that are ready for service.

Economical utilization of time is important in all areas of food production, but nowhere more than in final conditioning of precooked foods
and in short-order preparation and service. Extreme freshness and sharp
temperature essential to goodness, combined with time limitations make

Figure 8.9 Large kettle with power-operated stirrer. (*Courtesy Groen Manufacturing Co.*)

speed, for many diners, especially valuable. Menu plans and equipment arrangement should be evaluated for reduction of time and motion. If the volume of business requires only one worker to satisfy orders, the menu should be confined to equipment that can be located within easy reach of the worker and call for enough repetition of motion for the development of speed. Where the volume is large enough to employ several to prepare and set up orders, extra equipment and an assembly line with each worker performing specialized tasks can be used to advantage.

The equipment arrangement must permit two-handed work and free the right hand for performing those acts requiring greatest skill. The average worker will pick up and hold with the left hand and manipulate with the right. Deliveries of orders may be over a shelf-type hood over the grill and broiler or a shelf over a sandwich table. If china service is used, service to the plate will be most convenient with the plate located between the fryer and grill. If paper service is used, the fryer and grill may be adjacent and the paper supplies stored in the corner. Small plates should be located to the right of the sandwich table where they will be within reach of the grill for small orders. The sandwich maker, after cutting a sandwich, is likely to transfer it to a plate from the cutting board with both hands, so it is less significant to have the plate storage at the left hand rather than at the right.

Where counter service occurs in a dining area, the arrangement may have the cooking equipment located in the back counter and the sandwich preparation parallel with plate storage under the serving counter. Where plate levelers are situated between the fryer and griddle, it is advisable to have them mobile not only for easy transporting of plates from the dishwashing section, but also for thorough cleaning of the space. Fryers may be mobile also. The space below the supply table is usually blocked by other equipment and is therefore not usable, but the convenience of arrangement more than offsets this loss. Cantilevering tables permits movement in and out of mobile equipment under such tables. Utilization of the vertical space above is very important. Where paper supplies are necessary, the area above the supply table may be used for such supplies and for bread. Bread storage and a sink should be located near this section.

Pantry Section

Production requirements of this section dictate equipment needs and layout for efficiency. Wide diversity is common. In some facilities the

requirements are relatively simple, dealing chiefly with salad preparation. In others, beverages, salads, sandwiches, relishes, fruit, fruit juices,
cold plates, dessert dishing, tea and cocktail sandwiches, hot breads, ice,
and breakfasts may be prepared and dispensed. Pantry responsibility for
breakfasts will extend the load on its short-order section and reduce the
early production load in the cooking section. Some food facilities have
enlarged activities to encompass final conditioning of preprocessed foods
so that pantry-type preparation constitutes the total food preparation
done. The diversity emphasizes the need to identify activities to be performed and the order of their performance, plus indication of the number of workers required during peak hours of service and during slack
periods. Equipment requirements will correspond with functions to be
performed, and its layout should be one that will conserve motion,
ensure speed, and reduce travel and prevent criss-crossing of service
personnel.

The flow of raw materials will be from (1) central dry and refrigerated
storage, (2) direct delivery, and (3) vegetable preparation. Some flow may
be from the cooking section, where roast meat, poultry, and other foods
may be prepared. It is often desirable to have access to steam equipment
for cooking eggs, potatoes, and other foods for salads and salad dressings.
A table-type mixer will be needed for such preparations as salad dressings and whipped cream. The mixer in the bakery or cooking sections is
sometimes used. If desserts prepared in the bakery are to be dished in the
pantry, this flow should be considered.

A characteristic of pantry foods delivered for service is their bulkiness.
Individual salads, dessert portions, cold plates, and similar foods require
considerable surface area. Plates will vary from 5½ to 8 in. (17 to 20 cm)
in width and the clearance of 4½ in. (12 cm) between shelves is usually
adequate for lettuce cups or sherbert glasses. If portioned and arranged
on 18 × 26 in. (46 × 66 cm) trays and placed in mobile racks, they may
be moved into refrigerated pass-through storage areas or other sections
with a minimum of handling. Insulated carts with inserted chillers provide as efficient means of handling to distant points for service, as for
special service dining rooms. Where vertical transportation is needed,
attention should be given to easy access. The location of the pantry will
be governed by best relationships to sources of supplies, production flow,
and the intersectional operations. Production needs and flow of service
will influence interrelationships of work centers within the section.

Multiplicity and repetition of motions characteristic of this section
increase in terms of the variety of items required. Work centers can be
planned to resemble closely a well-designed work center in a factory,
using tier or vertical space. Assembly line preparation is possible where

the volume is large. A moving belt can often be used to advantage for supplies and/or carrying the finished products to service. Table heights are important. Plans should include the possibility of workers sitting to do certain tasks.

Convenient storage is needed for a wide variety of food and equipment. Food will be in large bulk, as lettuce, bread, and ingredients for salads and sandwiches, and in small quantities for special garnishes. Large and small food containers and mixing bowls will be needed, and diverse sizes and shapes of plates and glasses may be used for service. Good vertical use of space and well-planned storage is needed to reduce linear space. The vertical space may be in shelves above the table or in carts or mobile racks beside or under the table. A wide variety of serving dishes can be stored in bins under the table. Selection and reaching of items from the mobile bins is much easier than from low shelves. Prepositioning of many of the small tools and equipment used, gravity drops, and the elimination of search helps to promote fast work and is to be considered in designing these work centers. Pressure for speed is strong during peak periods when demands on this section is heavy.

The salad and sandwich-making sections have two work centers. The first includes assembling and such processing as slicing, chopping, dicing, and mixing of materials. The second division is the portioning or display arrangement after which the food will be sent to the serving station. In small operations, salad materials and other items may be cleaned and given preliminary handling here, especially if this section handles all of the preparation done. In the full production facilities, all washing, trimming, and even chopping of salad greens occur in the vegetable preparation section. Fruits and vegetables may be cut there also.

Salad operations call for use of a sink, table, can opener, slicer, chopper, juice extractor, shredder, dicer, mixer, hot plate or steam equipment, and local storage. The equipment may be shared with other sections or located in the pantry. A garbage grinder or garbage cans will be needed. The disposal unit is especially desirable where the vegetables are cleaned in the pantry. Refrigerators should be planned to hold a variety of shapes and sizes of food containers. High humidity to discourage drying is needed in the refrigerators. Floor-level doors are desirable to accommodate mobile bins or carts of salad greens or carts loaded with gelatin preparations to be cooled. This will help to reduce spillage and excess handling.

If lettuce and other salad greens are to be washed and trimmed here, provide sufficient drainage space at the sink and sinks of suitable size for the volume to be handled. The flow of work in this preliminary center should move from a sink placed at one end of the center to a drain

SANDWICH WORK CENTER

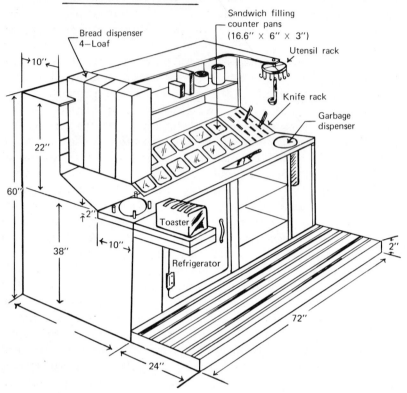

Figure 8.10 A compact sandwich unit with supplies and equipment within convenient reach. (*Courtesy of H. Eppel, HRI student, Michigan State University.*)

table, to a table for preparation, and thence into refrigerated storage, or by-pass preparation temporarily and go to storage and thence to preparation. In small units, the refrigerator may be used both for storage of raw materials and for completed products. In larger sections where two or more workers may be working, it may be desirable to have a double-compartment sink in the center of the work area. This will give access to workers from both sides without their criss-crossing. Dry storage will be needed for gelatin, spices, oils, vinegars, and other ingredients.

The second center should be in close relationship to the first for the final make-up of the salads and sandwiches. Calculate carefully space needs in terms of the number of workers, amount of materials, and the number of items that must be within reach while the workers are working. If a person is to place the serving dish on a tray and arrange the food on the dish, the tray will be on the table in front of the worker while food is arranged. Trays commonly used measure 14 × 18 in. (36 × 46 cm) or 18 × 26 in. (46 × 66 cm). Plan convenient storage for the trays. If mobile racks are used, storage may be on the racks or from mobile dispensers. The trays may be on a shelf under the table or in a mobile dispenser at the end of the table. When arranging salads, lettuce may be at the left of worker and ingredients that require manipulation of scoop, fork, or tongs at the right. Dishes are convenient immediately in front of the tray or toward the back of the table or in bins immediately below the table top in front of the worker. A sufficient number of dishes should be exposed at one time to enable the worker to pick up several at a time for placing on the tray. Placing dished products on trays and then into mobile carts to be rolled into refrigerators having floor-level doors provides for rapid, easy delivery of bulky items with a minimum of handling.

The arrangement area for sandwiches tends to differ from that for salads due to the volume and variety of fillings that are continually available to complete orders. The high perishability of the ingredients make it necessary to keep fillings refrigerated. Bread should be kept enclosed, so that it will not be subjected to air currents or hot dry air that has a staling effect. Studies show that bread tends to stale more rapidly when refrigerated (not frozen) than when held at room temperature. If hot, toasted, or grilled sandwiches are featured, the appropriate equipment should be located in or adjacent to the sandwich section.

The salad and sandwich making may be done in a dual center or in separate centers. Fruits, fruit juices, and seafood cocktails may be prepared here also. In a continental-type operation, where a garde manger work center is planned, the pantry section may not make up salad dressings, relishes, and other appetizers, cold plates, and meat dishes; or the pantry section may come under the supervision of the garde manger or cold-meat chef. In that case, the two should be located close together.

Where the make-up center for salads and sandwiches is placed in the service section, local refrigeration in or under the counter should be planned. Bulk preparation for this frequently occurs in the preliminary work center and materials are sent to this area for final make-up.

If breakfasts are prepared in the pantry, a grill work area similar to that planned for snack bars or in-line counter operations should be planned. This would include a griddle, waffle irons, toasters, burners for egg preparation, egg boiler, and a small steam table for holding hot cereals, cooked meats, and other breakfast items. This steam table can be used later for hot sauces and hot desserts for lunch or dinner desserts.

Figure 8.11 Ample space is required when making sandwiches in large quantity. (*Courtesy Bremerton School District, Bremerton, Wash.*)

Since this work center may be closed part of the day, its location should not interfere with the flow of work in other work centers during the remainder of the day. If designed as a mobile unit, the equipment could be removed when not needed and the space used for other purposes.

Ready-prepared or convenience foods sent to pantries for finishing differ in portion quantities and treatment required. Some are packaged with one portion of a single item, some with one portion of the main course hot foods, and others in multiple portions per package. The method of handling and equipment needed depends upon treatment required and the volume handled. The food may arrive from an adjacent commissary kitchen and require no other treatment than to be kept at palatable temperature and served. Frequently the food is frozen and requires low-temperature storage until needed, and may need refrigrated space for thawing plus completion of cooking before serving. The best equipment for this cooking depends upon the foods and the volume to be handled at one time. The cooking equipment currently used includes deep fryers, convection ovens, steam equipment, and microwave ovens.

The speed of microwave is often favored for units that can be prepared in one-portion quantities and the convection oven where large amounts must be prepared at one time. Deep fryers are often best suited to the requirements in a short-order facility that features deep-fried chicken, shrimp, and potatoes and other vegetables. The flow of work will move from storage area to table for panning or any other treatment required, thence to cooking equnipment, and then to the serving table.

A beverage unit in the pantry area should be planned close to a place where a worker can supervise it and remake a supply as needed. In large facilities, beverages are often the responsibility of one person. The beverage unit should be close to the service exits. Roll warmers, ice cream storage, dessert storage units, and any other items needed for service should be installed here, if service is to be from this section. Storage for ice should be provided if it is to be dispensed here. Fountain installations are sometimes combined with the pantry section.

It is likely that several pieces of power equipment may be used, such as toasters, shake makers, and coffee servers, and an adequate number of sufficiently ampered service outlets should be provided. Arrange for a convenient location of small-tool or equipment storage, cutting boards, numerous containers for small quantities of fruits, vegetables, and various mixtures to be used, and for refrigerated drawers and hot roll warmers under or near the work areas. The floor should be hard, moisture-proof, nonslip type. Light that reaches from 50 to 75 footcandles is desirable on work surfaces.

Bakery Section

The control of quality and cost of desserts and breads served by a food facility is very important to its successful operation. For short-order operations with limited kitchen equipment this is often a matter of careful purchasing of commercial products, but other establishments may prepare all or a part of their bakery items. There are economic advantages in many instances of having a suitably equipped bake shop as a part of a food service facility. In small operations, the baking may be done in a small appendage of the cooking section. Where the demand is heavy, the bakery may be a separate, fully equipped department.

When locating this section, it is well to consider the relationships with other sections for use of equipment and flow of work. It may bear close relationship with the cooking section for shared use of ovens, mixers, sink, and certain other items. The flow of raw materials will be from dry storage, refrigerators, and frozen food storage. A refrigerator and frozen food cabinet may be located in the bake shop, and dry stores for temporary supply stored in the table or a day-storage panty. Prepared products will move to set-up stations and service. The independent nature of the work in this section and the ease of transporting supplies and products make it possible for the bakery section to be remotely located in a large facility. There is sometimes a tendency to separate it from the main kitchen by walls that interfere with supervision and the sharing of equipment with other sections. The variety, complexity, and volume of items produced will influence space requirements and, to a certain extent, the most suitable location.

Production needs should be studied and the activities charted before planning the layout. Considerable traffic will occur to and from the section. Traffic aisles within the section should be planned with work aisles at right angles to them. Allow sufficient space for movement of mobile equipment to facilitate flexibility in work centers. The dough roller on a mobile table can be rolled out of the way when not in use. A mobile proof box can be moved from table to oven for easy transfer of items for baking. Arrange equipment so that it does not project into traffic lanes or work aisles, and so that workers will not have to cross main traffic aisles to reach commonly used equipment. At least 4 ft (1.22 m) should be provided in front of ovens so that workers will not be crowded when doors are open and hot items removed. If a peel is required, this distance should be proportionately increased for ease in handling and transporting items on the peel. (A peel is a long-handled, paddle-shaped implement for moving items in a deep oven.)

Work centers develop in relation to the items to be prepared and the common functions to be performed. Typical sections include: (1) formula weighing and mixing; (2) cooking of puddings, sauces, fillings, and frostings; (3) frying of doughnuts or other desserts; (4) folding, rolling, cutting, or shaping of Danish and French pastry; (5) pie and dough rolling, cutting, and panning; (6) proofing, baking, and removal to racks; (7) freezing of desserts; (8) landing, removal from pans, finishing, and dishing; and (9) pan washing and storage. Where a variety of spices, fats, extracts, garnishes, and other food items, and special tools and equipment are required, it is well to have a pantry storage area adjacent to the bake shop.

The flow of work in the formula weighing and mixing center and for cooking of puddings and fillings is much the same as that described for the cooking section. A steam-jacketed kettle is desirable for this. Placement of ingredients, scale, and mixer is important for a motion-saving flow of work. Raw materials in the pantry or refrigerator should be near this area. Pans for scaling cakes or other mixed products for baking should be conveniently located. Materials from the mixing center may

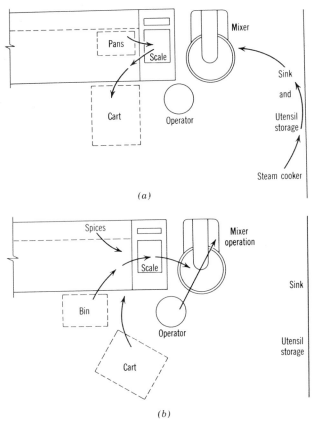

Figure 8.12 Equipment placement, with arrows showing work flow (a) for mixing, and (b) for panning foods.

move to each of the other centers. Convenient refrigeration will be needed for work with pastries, and material from bread dough rolling and shaping will move to proofing equipment. If retarded yeast doughs are used, extra refrigeration must be provided. The largest number of pans will be needed at the mixing and dough rolling centers in the average bake shop. The largest quantity of soiled equipment will come from mixing and finishing.

Plan facilities to minimize criss-crossing and backtracking in the flow of work. If ovens and baked storage units are located near the outer perimeter of the section, traffic into the section will be reduced. Linear travel should be eliminated as much as possible through effective utiliza-

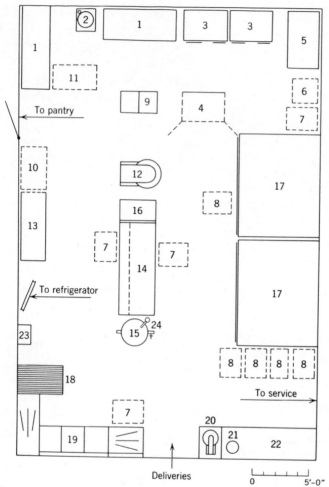

Figure 8.13 Suggested equipment arrangement for a bake shop.

tion of vertical space. If premixes are used, water should be available at the mixer, measures within reach, or automatic measuring devices provided. Plan under-table space for mobile bins and frequently used equipment. In planning space utilization, it is important to check for adequacy because cramping will lower productive efficiency. Adjust table heights in terms of work to be done. For example, where hand rolling of doughs is done, it is desirable to have the table slightly lower in height than that which is standard for other tables (approximately 2 in. (5 cm) lower).

A great deal of the work in a bake shop may consist of rolling, shaping, and cutting, especially if Danish pastries, puff paste, and rolls are made that require a good bit of hand work. The table space or bench may be limited to the convenient reach of workers if tiered, mobile storage units are provided. If breads, rolls, and sweet dough are produced, the bench requirements will differ from that needed if yeast products are made. Hand rolling may be done either on wood or stainless steel tables or rolling may be done by machine, but where a great deal of cutting is to be done the wood-topped tables are favored. The tables should be 6 to 8 ft (1.83 to 2.44 m) in legnth and 2½ to 3 ft (75 to 91 m) wide. Raised curbs of 6 in. (.15 m) may be used around three sides to prevent flour and dough from dropping to the floor. Tables are best centrally located away from the wall. When this is done, curbs may be omitted so that the table may be approached from all sides. Baking pans should be stored at this table.

Provide adequate landing space for products as they come from the oven. A tiered cooling rack is usually best. Mobility is desirable so that products may be moved out of the way and taken later to the finishing or dish-up stations.

The oven selected may affect space requirements and work efficiency. Deep ovens in which a peel must be used for movement of items to the expanse of the deck and for inspection or adjustment during baking use extra time, motion, and space for handling over that required by reel ovens with shelves the depth of one-bun pan 18 × 26 in. (46 × 66 cm) or cabinet ovens that have decks of two-bun pan capacity. Transportation time and oven space are saved by convection ovens into which a mobile rack of items for baking may be rolled from preparation table to oven and from oven to finishing table.

Variety in temperatures needed at one time is important. A reel or revolving oven may have small or large capacity. The shelves move within a single compartment and are therefore subject to one temperature. This works well where large quantities of a single item are prepared at one time or several items having a common temperature requirement. In facilties requiring two or more temperatures simultaneously, smaller reel ovens or deck ovens may be desirable to operate separately. Steam should be provided in ovens where hard-surfaced breads are baked.

The finishing center is combined with the dish-up center in many bake shops. In large operations, the finishing center may be separated into several work centers for the various functions. Cookies and cakes to be iced and decorated may constitute one center. A marble top table, a batch warmer, and other specialized equipment may be needed. A small-tool storage and a hand sink will be necessary and also, in convenient proximity, a baker's stove for sugar syrups, fondants, and icings.

The dish-up center may or may not be a part of the bake shop. In any case, portion sizes are a concern of the bake shop. The arrangement for dish-up should be similar to that described for salad making, with trays on which dishes are arranged and materials for arrangement in a semi-circle around the tray. A mobile rack at a convenient location is desirable to receive the trays of portioned desserts. Dishes may be stored (1) at the back of the table, if the table is 36 in. (91 cm) wide; (2) under the front edge of the table on a shelf; (3) in plate levelers; or (4) in mobile bins under the table, depending on the type and variety of items needed. Refrigerated mobile racks for cold desserts or enclosed carts that provide tiered storage will give maximum utilization of space. The vertical height of desserts seldom exceed 6 in. (15 cm) and when portioned will usually be from 3 to 4½ in. (8 to 12 cm). The dish-up center may require a refrigerated storage space and this may be combined with that of the preparation center. If this occurs, proximity of the two centers is a factor to remember in layout planning.

A variety of storage conditions are required for bakery items. Breads, rolls, and sweet goods tend to be best at room temperature with some ventilation. Cakes and pies may be stored at room temperature unless they have custard fillings. Custard-filled desserts, puddings, whipped cream desserts, and similar perishable products should be refrigerated. Dishing and loading into mobile units that may be taken to various points where needed add greatly to efficiency. Storage areas may be pass-through cabinets between bake shop and service area. Freezer space for frozen desserts and for holding items longer than normal periods is often needed.

Volume produced and variety of products to be made will govern equipment needs. Ice cream making calls for mixing equipment, a freezing unit, and a hardening unit. Where bread and rolls to be produced in large quantity, power sifters, dough mixers, dough rollers or sheeters, cutters and rounders, overhead proofers, pan greasers, dough troughs, and other special equipment need to be evaluated for inclusion. Cookies in quantity may require special mixers, pan greasers, and machines to drop cookies automatically onto pans. An efficient operation will depend upon suitable provision for the specific needs.

Miscellaneous Food Processing Facilities

Wherever groups live for a period of time or regularly meet at meal-time, there is need for a group-feeding facility. They vary considerably

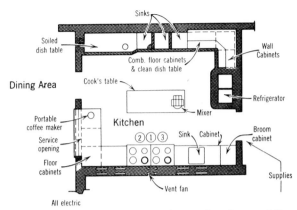

Figure 8.14 A small kitchen for community or church, providing for complete cooking and limited baking. Dish-up may be onto plates on a table or from cafeteria plan with hot food dispensed from containers arranged on the serving counters. (*Courtesy Hotpoint Co., Chicago.*)

in size, type, and foodservice requirements. Included in this classification are camps and resorts, community kitchens, kitchens for small clubs and such organizations as fraternities and sororities, and nursing and retirement homes. Inexperienced hands often work in some of them. Sanitation needs special emphasis, for workers may be unfamiliar with sanitation codes in public food service and possess questionable work habits. Equipment appropriate to work requirements and volume needs to be provided. Adequate storage and refrigeration facilities are likely to be important. A study of the specific requirements and conditions will reveal the individual situation pecularities and needs.

Camps and Resorts

Camps and resorts have certain characteristics in common. Seasonality and remoteness from markets, and perhaps limited utilities and services, may create problems with which plans must cope. Equipment selection will be affected by these factors and by the type of personnel available to operate it. Wide variation in facilities may be demanded. A boy scout camp, a lumbering camp, and a fine resort hotel obviously require different plans. Figures 8.14 and 8.15 show several plans for kitchens in such facilities.

If the resort is operated as a business to provide food, standards for services will be established on the basis of cost and quality to appeal to

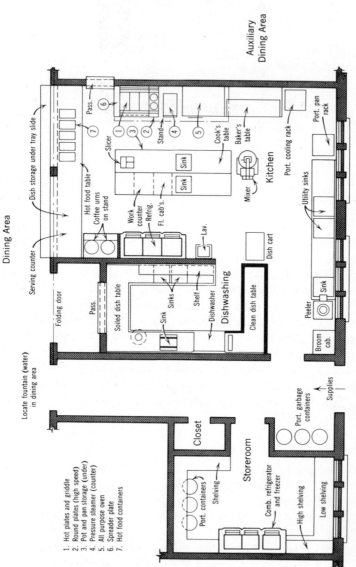

Figure 8.15 Community kitchen to serve maximum meal load of 600. (*Courtesy Hotpoint Co., Chicago.*)

1. Hot plates and griddle
2. Round plates (high speed)
3. Pot and pan storage (under)
4. Pressure steamer (counter)
5. All purpose oven
6. Spreader plate
7. Hot food containers

a certain class of patronage. Some resorts operate throughout the year and resemble hotels. Those that are seasonal may have different needs that will dictate specific facility and equipment needs. Water supply may be a problem for facilities located remotely from city systems. An adequate quantity of pure water is essential for drinking, cooking, and dishwashing. Delivery of supplies may be infrequent to food operations that are remotely located. Suitable and adequate storage may call for careful planning and considerable space. Low-temperature storage may be important for extending storage life when supply is infrequent. Use of power equipment may be curtailed by the amount and type of power available. Dishwashing in camps may be affected by both the power and water supply available. An incinerator is desirable for garbage and trash disposal, especially where bears or other wild animals may invade the area seeking food. Protect foods too from contamination by pests, vermin, or other dangers.

In camps a range area should be provided in terms of preparation of breakfast items, simmering of soup stocks, and cooking of vegetables and sauces. Cabinet ovens are recommended for the preparation of entrees, roasts, and desserts. Work tables are frequently of wood or galvanized iron in the more cost-limited facilities. A washable canvas stretched tightly over a wood tabletop is satisfactory for pastry work. Tin-coated steel bowls on mobile racks are desirable for mixing. Mobile racks can save many steps in the preparation and service of meals.

Community Kitchens

Community organizations, such as churches and clubs, may require a kitchen and dining area. The dining room may be utilized for additional purposes than food service. Efficiency may be promoted by planning work space so that either a few can do the work on occasion or many can share in it without confusion or getting in each other's way. Each organization will have specific needs for size, frequency of use, and type of functions for which it will cater.

The equipment requirements and layout will be influenced by the plan for the food preparation and service. Plans in common practice include: (1) work done by employed personnel, (2) preparation and service by members appointed by the organization as a committee. (3) contributed food prepared by members and brought in for service, and (4) prepared food brought in by a catering company for service. Plans for (1) and (2) necessitate a completely equipped kitchen; those for (3) and (4) require space for holding, reheating, beverage making, meal set-up, and service.

Attitudes toward the food program and the amount of money to be spent will differ greatly. Concern for the food service will be strongly influenced by the funds available and the amount of use anticipated. The common tendency is to seek simple adequacy for minimum cost. Due to irregular use, the rust-free, easy-to-care-for advantages and good appearance of stainless steel equipment should not be overlooked.

In community food units where the food is to be both prepared and served, equipment requirements will be similar to those in school lunchroom kitchens of comparable size. Where prepared food is to be brought in, either by members or a catering firm, adequate space for storing it for final processing will be needed. Mobile racks with baking sheets that may be used for shelves or serving trays will be convenient. Individual portion salads and desserts may be arranged on the baking sheets and moved to the dining room for service.

The need for providing adequate pot and pan and dishwashing facilities should be stressed. Many pots and pans and large quantities of soiled dishes may accumulate before workers are free to do them. Adequate facilities should be provided for this type of scheduled work.

Small clubs and organizations where members live in require facilities for three meals a day and occasional catering. These and boarding houses and small retirement homes usually serve a set menu to a given number. Many of the needs are similar to those of a small residence hall. The equipment selection and layout should be based on commercial rather than on domestic requirements.

Suggested Student Assignments

1. Observe procedures, equipment used, and labor required in:
   a. A full production kitchen.
   b. A food facility that uses all or a major portion of food served that is brought in fully prepared but requiring final treatment for service.

2. State for each of these food facilities:
   a. A list of the equipment required.
   b. Per portion costs based on purchase prices and recipe costs.
   c. Per portion labor costs for processing or conditioning food for service.
   d. Calculate margin of difference per portion when served of food processed and ready-food.

3. Evaluate in terms of adequacy, extra needs, or surplus:
   a. Equipment.
   b. Labor.

4. Compare storage requirements of the two systems, in terms of amount and kind.

5. Chart the flow of materials in a full-production kitchen from receiving to service.

6. Redesign the layout for the vegetable preparation section.

7. Evaluate the cooking section from the standpoint of:
   a. Supervision.
   b. Interrelationships with other sections.
   c. Freedom from interruptions by outsiders.
   d. Step-saving.

8. State length of time food is held after preparation until served, and means used for preserving quality of:
   a. Entrees (state kind).
   b. Vegetables.
   c. Salads and sandwiches.
   d. Desserts (state kind).

Chapter 9

serving facilities

Service occurs during the span of time between completion of production and presentation of food to the consumers. Its quality is likely to be at its most fragile point of excellence. Methods of service and facilities used have special significance in protecting important values. The dishing up and presentation of food varies. It may be done in the kitchen at the production center, in a separate serving section to service personnel who present it, to patrons as they go through a cafeteria, to those who eat in their cars, at a snack bar, or from a vending machine. The food when served may be transported by a waiter, nurse, car hop, or by the patron himself.

Regardless of the place of service and the method of transportation used, there are specific requirements to be met through planning. These include: (1) facilities that will help to preserve palatable quality; (2) fast, efficient service; (3) an atmosphere of hospitality and attractiveness; and (4) the protection of health through sanitation and accident prevention. The effective functioning of the service area will depend upon selection of equipment to meet specific needs, and a good flow of travel from customer order to service of food.

Figure 9.1 A serving area adjacent to preparation area.

The protection of quality calls for limiting holding time. Equipment capacity needs to be planned on the basis of speed of quality deterioration of different foods. Meats are best when served at the completion of their preparation. Coffee, on the other hand, can be held almost an hour. Mashed potatoes will have a short life of not over 20 minutes holding time. Vegetables under prolonged holding lose flavor, color, texture, and important nutrients. Flexibility in capacity is desirable since the same item may not be held in the serving unit each time. Another food with different quantity and holding time may be used. This is usually accommodated best by multiple pans sized to a basic 12 × 20 in. (30 × 50 cm) steam table pan.

Palatable quality requires proper temperature. A rare rib roast should not be held over 140° F (59° C) and soup should reach the consumer at a temperature of 180° F (81° C). Too high a temperature quickly destroys egg quality. Various means may be needed to supply the desired temperatures. Infrared heaters may be used for rare roasts, whereas soup may require a heating unit that will maintain a higher temperature. Temperatures commonly recommended for holding foods for service are:

Entrees, meats, roasts (except rare meats)	140 to 160° F (59 to 64° C)
Soups, coffee, and other thin liquids	185 to 190° F (85 to 88° C)
Sauces, gravies, etc. (except hollandaise or other products high in egg or cheese and fat)	160 to 180° F (64 to 81° C)
Salads and other sold foods	40 to 45° F (4½ to 7° C)
Frozen foods	8 to 15° F (−13° to −9° C)

It should be noted that these temperatures are given at the time the food is served, but some public health authorities are beginning to interpret such temperatures as those existing at the time of service to the patron, patient, or other consumer. This may cause some problems since the holding temperature must be considerably higher to allow for the cooling that will take place during dishing, transporting, and service. The proper temperature of dishes on which food is served will be significant for ensuring proper temperature for service.

Food appeal calls for a fresh, good appearance. This requires sufficient humidity in serving equipment to prevent dehydration and to reduce discoloration. Meat slices should glisten from fresh slicing. Vegetables should have a bright, natural color. Equipment is needed for some items that will supply air moisture, and for other foods, such as French fried potatoes, the air must be dry because they loose their quality quickly if moist. Dry heat from an infrared lamp is best for these.

Enjoyment of food involves appealing texture. Production treatment as well as service will have an influence. Eggs are toughened by high temperature. Salads are wilted by improper temperature and a lack of humidity in the air. Ice cream that is dished between 8 to 15°F (−13° to −90°C) will not only lack texture, either being too hard or too soft, but will also lack bright flavor. Overcooking of many vegetables and other foods in the serving unit is one of the greatest hazards. The relationship of time to quality should not be missed, and speed of service is important to quality standards as well as to customer satisfaction.

Fast, efficient service is gained by planning good work centers in the serving section. To ensure fast service, every element influencing speed deserves analysis. Some of the most common causes of slowdown are (a) excess travel distance in supplying the section from production, and in serving and reaching the customer; (b) confusion of arrangement in the serving section that does not follow a logical order of pick-up and provide a clear view of items available; (c) excess motion in serving because of the layout and menu selections; (d) delays caused by preparation-to-order; (e) numerous food choices that tend to delay judgment; (f) patrons serving themselves; (g) improper or inadequate equipment, such as wrong ladle sizes and ineffective serving tools or inadequate storage space; (h) information requests about choices, sizes, prices, and ingredients; and (i) accident hazards, such as obstructions in lines of travel, dangerously hot surfaces, blind corners, and sharp turns.

Planning a cafeteria counter that helps to speed decisions on where to go or what to select will do much to reduce costs and please customers. Customers should not be confused by the nature of the service. Thus in areas where customers are not familiar with the shopping center type of cafeteria service, considerable confusion may occur because customers do not know where to go to get their food. This does not happen when customers are frequent patrons and know the flow pattern.

In a hospital the speed of service may be influenced by comprehension of menu instructions on the dish-up line, the number and skill of serving personnel, the serving facilities, the speed of the tray line, the transfer to a cart, the waiting of a cart due to the number of trays placed on it or other reasons, the speed of the elevator or delivery service, speed of movement of the cart to the floor or ward, the distance of travel, and the promptness and method of presentation. Each facet needs to be followed and analyzed for speed-up. It is important to keep systems simple. Certain excellent plans have failed in drive-ins because they were too complex for the young carhops who worked in them.

There are certain essentials for a serving section regardless of the simplicity or elaborateness of the menu and service. Included in them are ready access to foods to be served, the dish-up tools, dishes on which foods are to be placed, and a landing area for convenient placement and pick-up. Eliminate any points of delay and provide for specific needs. Some serving sections prepare foods such as pancakes, hamburgers, French fries, waffles, and toast. Adequate storage and proper tool and equipment arrangement can speed such production and service. Some operations may restrict menus to fast foods, whereas others may utilize a hot serving table for additional foods or depend upon a hot table with occasional use of mobile short-order equipment. Close relationship of the serving section with the production section is a step-saving aid toward freshly prepared food.

Application of rules for good work center planning will help to speed service. Locate dishes to be used with consideration for quick, logical, or natural hand motions in picking up a dish and placing food on it. It is natural for a right-handed person to hold with the left hand and manipulate with the right. Thus the server will grasp a serving tool with the right hand, and lift and place food on a plate held in the left hand. The more that motions, through practice, become automatic the more quickly they can be made. Whenever judgments must be made as to size, pattern, condition, or location of the plate or the food, there is an instant slowdown. Search is a frequent slowdown factor. Length of reach causes delay in proportion to its length. Where far-reach is made frequently it may amount to an appreciable time and effort loss. Following the rules for storage cited previously, such as storing tools at point of use, will do much to speed work. Tools that reduce motion and aid skillful handling, such as dippers and ladles of full-portion capacity; pointed, offset spatulas for pie; slotted spoons for foods requiring draining; and many other tools that have specific use will be of benefit. Preproportioning may be used also to speed service.

Choose the dish storage location that best fits into the serving system. One server may find a mobile, self-leveling storage unit beside the table to be best, and another may prefer plates on a ledge immediately under the counter top or in a heated compartment at the back of the serving counter with a landing ledge above for served plates. Various factors may cause the choice of one over another, such as space allowance, type of menu and service, and the volume. Waiters in the restaurant sketched in Figure 9.3 serve the soup and beverages. The soup containers are set in line with heated cabinets for bowls and liners on the waiters' side of the serving counter, with a landing shelf for served plates on top. This arrangement makes the hot fluids available for easy, rapid service without rehandling. The coffee shop plan in Figure 9.2 permits waitresses to place and pick up orders from a window above the cooking section

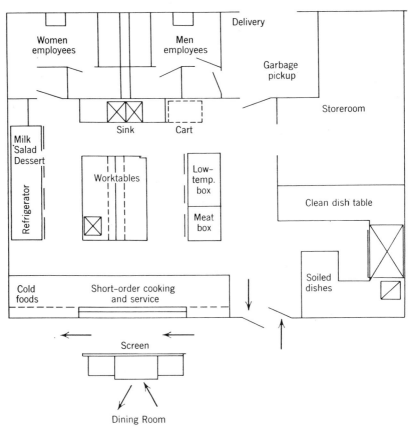

Figure 9.2 A simply arranged short-order facility showing close relationship between production, dish-up, and service to the dining room.

without going into the kitchen. This not only eliminates extra steps but also the slowdown hazard of going through swinging doors. The beverages, poured by waitresses, are conveniently located in the dining room with the serving containers beside them.

Effective food merchandising calls for serving sections that are orderly, attractive, and possess patron appeal. This requirement has special importance for cafeterias, snack bars, lunch counters, drive-in service windows, and for service carts and mobile catering units. Organization and neatness should be emphasized. The equipment and special units should fit well into the general decor. Colors and lighting should be pleasing. Food must be well displayed. The appearance should be planned to appeal to the taste of the specific group to be served. Students in a col-

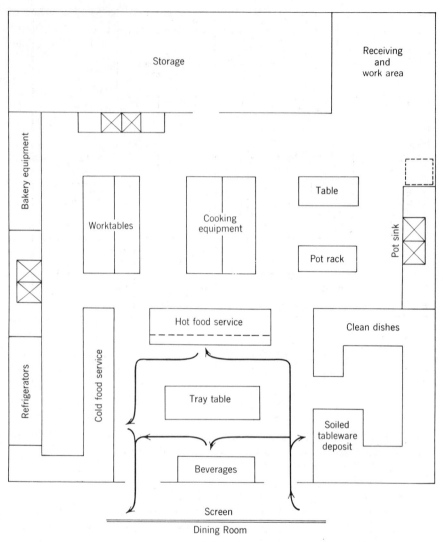

Figure 9.3 A kitchen plan showing serving section adjacent to production and the waiters' route of travel in picking up selective meals.

lege union coffee shop may want far less in special decor than members of a club who may have to wait in a buffet line.

Opportunities for contamination of food and equipment during serving are many. Speed is too often granted precedence over meticulousness. Chances of contamination are increased in proportion to the number of food handlers, amount of time food is exposed for service, amount of hand contact with food and food handling equipment, and use of temperatures that favor the growth of bacteria. Every possible protection should be afforded that is reasonable and in keeping with good practice. Workers grouped and talking back of a cafeteria counter may contaminate food more than customers moving in front, where food is protected by a sneeze-guard. The strong possibilities for accidents in dining areas, due to handling hot foods, food spillage on slick floors, hurrying workers, and patrons strange to surroundings plus minds that are elsewhere, such as on making food selections or searching for a place to sit, are common and call for awareness and careful planning.

DINING ROOMS

The appearance of and the atmosphere in the area where a consumer dines has much to do with his attitude of approval or disapproval of the food service. Even though hordes may be fed, the diner wants to feel that the service is personal. For a period of time, that spot takes the place of a home. An attractive surrounding will help to create a sense of well-being. In a home there are times when one is happy to snatch a bite at the kitchen table and other times when more leisurely dining in a well-ordered dining room is preferred. The locality in which the food facility is located will in large degree determine the type of dining room and service that will be most successful. There are times when satisfying hunger and nutritional needs is the major and perhaps the sole concern. At other times, sociability, entertainment, restfulness, sense of identity, change, and many other psychological factors may have an influence on selection and enjoyment of an eating place.

Size

Determine dining room size in light of preferences of the specific group. Diners in commercial establishments have shown preference for a certain amount of seclusion by gravitating to booths, wall locations, or other secluded areas of the rooms. In large operations managers have used various devices to divide rooms and to create the desired effect. One device is to center the serving sections and place the dining areas around it. Dividers, such as partitions, screens, furniture placement, planters, and other decorative arrangements, are used to create the desired feeling of intimacy.

Gregariousness will make people want to go where they believe the crowd goes. Those who possess this trait to a high degree, such as college students, would rather be crowded than patronize an excellent place that is sparsely filled. Sparsely filled dining areas spell lack of popularity to the average person and immediately raise a question of their desirability. This fact, in addition to limited investment, emphasizes the importance of choosing the probable capacity needs based on a close calculation of number to be served and speed of turnover.

Certain groups require control, and the dining room size may need to be adjusted to the amount and type of supervision required and available. Size adjustment may be desirable also for resident groups in order to promote acquaintanceship and a group spirit. There are fewer close acquaintances formed and a feeling of identity created when dining in a large, ever-changing group. Mealtime sociability has special significance in college residences and in retirement homes. Noise control and discipline are a frequent concern with young patrons and can best be handled with small groups. Banquet rooms where programs are presented may need to be large and have excellent acoustics.

Mealtime is a rest time for industrial workers. A change of pace and a change of atmosphere are helpful. If a person has been working somewhat alone the activity in a large room, with many individuals coming and going, will add interest. If the person has been with many people and perhaps supplying their wants, a smaller area and a quiet atmosphere may be more restful. Those who have been employed in a bleak, drab plant are given a lift by a dining room that is bright and cheerful.

Traffic Flow

Plans should be made for a logical patronage flow to and from the various areas of the room. This will mean having main aisles and side aisles according to the size and shape of the room. Diners are not comfortable and find it confusing when they must thread their way through a maze of tables, dodging elbows of diners and servers carrying food or dishes. Aisles should be wide enough for the number of people who are likely to be moving along them at one time (approximately 3 to 4 ft or .91 to 1.22 m). Provide adequate waiting areas to avoid clogging of aisles with people waiting.

Plan according to the normal movement cycle of patrons and workers in the dining room. Those points of call likely to be made should be included on the path of the respective person. If self-bussing is to be done by patrons, for example, the deposit point for the soiled dishes should be located on the patron's path to the door. If candy and cigarette vending machines are to be used, the patron should not have to cross a server's path in getting to them. All of the points of pick-up for a

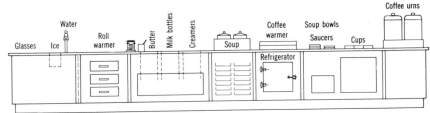

Figure 9.4 A central supply station can fill many service needs in dining area.

server should be in orderly location according to need on the server's path. Distances of travel for both groups should be as short as possible, giving preference to routes in terms of frequency of travel.

Well-equipped service islands help to reduce travel by service personnel. Communication or signal systems, with lights, phone, or other means of communication, between production and serving sections are valuable, especially when distances are great and traffic heavy. The use of conveyors for delivering food and removing soiled dishes will assist in speeding service and reducing labor. Ideas for reducing travel by using central supply stations are shown in Figures 9.4 and 9.5.

Figure 9.5 Waiter pick-up station with service window from production area.

Safety and Sanitation

Safety and sanitation codes pertaining to dining areas should be carefully checked and followed. The number of entrances and exits to rooms must comply with fire ordinances. Toilet facilities for guests and employees should comply with codes as to location, entrances, and sanitary facilities. Floors and floor treatment should be reasonably nonslip and free from "surprise factors," such as half-steps or obstructions, that might cause accidents. Follow a method of service and food handling that protects food sanitation and the sanitation of food service equipment.

COUNTERS

Counter service is commonly considered one of the quickest types. The menu, the size, and the arrangement will to a large degree determine how well it competes for speed with other types of service. A simplified menu, short travel distances, and minimized motion help to ensure speed. Each station should be approximately 16 to 20 linear ft (5 to 6 linear m). When determining the height and width of counters, consider (1) the average height and reach of servers, (2) the best utilization of space for supply storage, and (3) the comfort of patrons. Counter heights usually vary from 30 to 42 in. (0.76 to 1.07 m) and widths vary from 18 to 30 in. (0.46 to 0.76 m).

The high, wide counter allows for a ledge approximately 27 in. (68 cm) deep at the back of supplies, short-order equipment, dishes, and bus boxes. Table-height counters must depend upon the backbar for supplies and equipment. The wide counter is more generally favored for convenience and for hiding some of the normal clutter of service. It also allows more storage space. The seating at counters is usually on a pedestaled stool or chair. The seats should be 14 to 15 in. (36 to 38 cm) in diameter, a footrest 9 to 12 in. (23 to 30 cm) deep, knee space 8 to 10 in. (20 to 25 cm) from the edge of the seat to the counter pedestal, and 12 in. (30 cm) from the seat to the counter top. When stools are placed on step-ups, as required at high counters, accidents sometimes occur due to patrons forgetting to step down. This is one of the arguments for the table-height counter.

Plan this work center to have everything convenient, neat, and adequately equipped. In some operations food preparation may occur. Hot beverage making equipment may be located at the counter or on the backbar. Cups and saucers should be within easy reach and a source for refrigerated dairy products provided for those who wish them. Bread dispensing will need to be considered in relation to the types served.

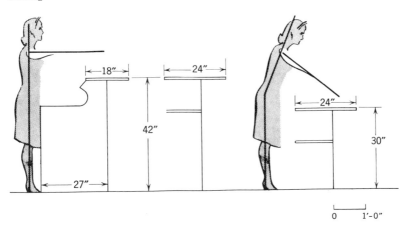

Figure 9.6 A waitress of average height and reach at counters of different height and width.

Hamburger and hot dog buns to be reheated on the griddle need storage to retain freshness. If sandwiches with bread slices are to be made to order, a self-leveling dispenser is convenient. Hot rolls are better stored in a roll warmer that can be used also for made-ahead hamburgers prepared for peak periods. These keep satisfactorily if wrapped and held at a satisfactory temperature. The barely appreciable quality change tends to be more acceptable to the average patron than having to wait for service. A refrigerated water supply with a push faucet and storage for glasses is needed in this area.

Refrigerated display cases are sometimes located on the counter or in a central area partly for convenience and partly to promote impulse buying. They may contain salads, sandwiches, and desserts. A cabinet for ice cream and a refrigerated table for sandwich making should be considered in terms of menu requirements. A fountain may be advantageous if there is a strong demand for fountain items. It should be recalled that reduced variety will reduce space that must be allowed and will aid in reducing time and energy output. Sales potential should be very carefully calculated for each menu addition.

Arrange place setting equipment to save motion. When serving across a counter a waitress places the service in a reverse position to her own. Forks and napkins will be placed with the right hand, and knives, spoons, glasses, and cups with the left. Blades and tines will be pointed toward her and away from the patron. Plates, cups, glasses, and bowls should be at the left, if possible, of the items to be served in them. Salt,

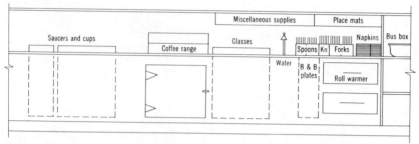

Figure 9.7   Counter serving station.

pepper, and sugar should be kept in a frame on the counter within reach of patrons.

The chief advantage of counter service—speed—is in a degree defeated by any factor that causes delay and handicaps the fast rate at which patrons receive service. When in operation, it is often beneficial to time service to ascertain whether speed is in keeping with the standard set, such as 1 or 2 minutes from the time the patron was seated until served. If the standard is not being met search for the reason. Common faults include menus that slow down choice or are complicated to serve, travel distance and excess motion, preparation-of-food delays, equipment inadequate and tools not available, awkward arrangement and overcrowding of space, and the nearest location to service not given to the most frequently served item, such as beverages. Compactness in a serving station may call for limitation of supplies to that required for a meal. Automatic handling can be used to relieve waitress time, such as conveyors extending under the counter top to remove bus boxes or to deliver supplies. Convenience may be served through the use of mobile dispensing units rolled into position so that bulk storage is at hand behind the scenes.

DRIVE-INS

The requirements for food preparation and service in drive-ins closely resemble those for short-order counter service. Menu offerings can be prepared with limited equipment. Paper service is customarily used. Patrons may pick up their food at a counter or may be served in their cars by waitresses or waiters. Fast service is essential for satisfaction. In a low-cost, self-service plan, the patron gives his order at a window and picks up the order when his number is called. Car service is speeded up when orders are called in by intercom. A special switchboard operator or the cook may take orders, answer questions, and make suggestions.

Figure 9.8 An intercom relays orders from parking area and booths to preparation and service sections. Carson Pirie Scott and Co., Chicago. (*Courtesy* Food Service Magazine, *Madison, Wis.*)

Menu boards with instructions for placing orders must be placed where they can be readily seen by patrons when they are parked. This will relieve the necessity of presenting menus and waiting for decisions on orders. The long walks with heavy loads, exposure to inclement weather, and continual honking of horns result in heavy turnover of carhops.

Parking should be as close as possible to production and service areas. The spaces should be carefully identified to ensure orders reaching the right person promptly. Attractive parking areas, like pleasant dining rooms, add appeal to the service. In some localities, a park or garden area with tables and benches is provided for warm or sunny weather. A certain amount of dropping of paper refuse is common during service. It is well therefore to have a parking place that is easy to clean and topped with blacktop, cement, or good gravel. In order for the drive-in to be seen in time to stop and also to avoid cause for accidents, drive-ins should not be located on curves or on top of a hill where they cannot be readily seen from a distance.

CAFETERIA SERVICE

Cafeteria-style service facilitates serving large groups quickly with limited personnel. Patrons are able to see the food before making a selection and may limit purchases according to the size of their appetites and money they wish to spend. Cafeteria service in public schools permits promoting nutritionally adequate lunches and in commercial operations foods may be displayed in a manner that aids merchandising. The service may be adapted to serving a large number within a limited time period, as in mealtime breaks in industrial organizations and between class schedules in colleges and universities.

Food quality protection and traffic control are major considerations when locating the cafeteria counter. It should be as close to the production of hot food, salads, and sandwiches as possible and convenient to patron traffic. The entrance hall should be spacious enough to accommodate persons who will be waiting. Toilet facilities and a cloakroom should be conveniently located near the waiting area. It is well to post the menu with prices and any special information to guide selection in the waiting area. The plan should invite an orderly line-up that will minimize confusion and slowdown in service. Long lines of children in public schools are often less disturbing when the line-up is in a hallway rather than in a part of the dining room. It is desirable for the line-up area and the serving section to be screened from the dining room so as to lessen noise and confusion.

Factors that affect the size and shape of the serving line are: (1) the volume of sales, (2) the complexity of the menu, (3) the size and shape of the available space, and (4) the flow of traffic. Simple, limited choice menus are common where there are few patrons to support costs, and where food costs must be kept low and the serving time short. The limited-choice menus may be served from a permanently installed, continuous line of cafeteria or one made up of mobile units. Where a large number are to be served and will support wide variety to satisfy the many food preferences, there may be multiple counter lines or a shopping center plan of service.

The shopping center or hollow square plan speeds service by reducing time spent standing in line (see Figure 9.9). Patrons may pass others to reach the station where their choice of food is obtainable. It is a scatter approach in service that is especially useful in serving large groups that arrive at one time. During the peak periods short lines may form at the most popular points. Space allowance for this and for movement of persons passing each other with trays must be made. Thought should be given to ease of supplying the various stations with foods and tableware during the serving time. When the traffic area is crowded it is difficult to supply centrally located stations. A shopping center plan may offer grilled items that are cooked to order, hot prepared foods served at a counter, and a variety of cold foods and hot and cold beverages that

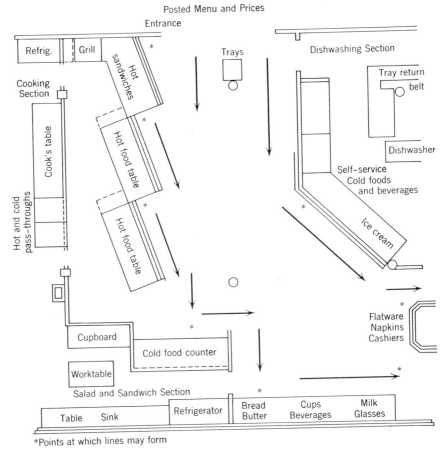

Figure 9.9 A shopping center plan in an industrial cafeteria.

patrons can serve for themselves. Trays are picked up at the entrance and the tableware, napkins, and condiments near the cashier. It is well to have tableware items convenient to the dining area where patrons may return for items missed or forgotten.

The quantity of food displayed will influence the length of the counters. Adequate space without crowding is desirable but should be sufficiently filled throughout service to give an impression of plenty. Step-saving compactness is desirable and the display space should not require so much to fill that there are too many leftovers at the end of service. The length of the counter can be reduced by setting food- or dish-dispensing units at right angles to the counter. The worker in an L or U work center works from left to right. It will be convenient for the worker and shorten distance for the patron. The speed of service in a cafeteria line is approximately five to eight customers per minute. The variation may be due to amount of selection, promptness of service, and clarity of instructions pertaining to menu offerings, prices, and procedures. Some linear counters serving a set meal and shopping center type cafeterias may achieve a record of twelve per minute with items ready for immediate patron pick-up.

Some of the major points which merit consideration when planning a cafeteria service layout pertain to (1) features that appeal to patrons, (2) food quality protection, (3) ease and speed in food and dish supply, (4) foods to be promoted, (5) selection habits of patrons, (6) handling of delay points in serving lines, (7) traffic flow, (8) minimizing accident hazards, (9) items for which customers return to serving area, (10) labor economies, (11) menu offerings, and (12) time limitations. Achieving a

Figure 9.10 Salads precede hot foods, curved sneeze-guard gives good view of display, and menu prices are clearly indicated in this cafeteria. Putsch's Cafeteria, Kansas City, Mo. (*Courtesy of Southern Equipment, St. Louis, Mo.*)

steady, even flow is a matter of knowing the items required, setting them up in proper sequence to balance serving rate, and providing facilities so that patrons use a minimum of selection time in making choices.

When patrons enter a cafeteria its various aspects should make a pleasant appeal to the senses. The freshly prepared foods should emit aromas that arouse appetite. The colors, design, orderliness, and most importantly the cleanliness should be attractive. Patrons touch trays, plates, and flatware and react quickly to smooth, clean surfaces as opposed to those that are gritty, greasy, or wet. Where action is, noise cannot be entirely muffled. Care should be used to eliminate any excesses such as strident voices and clattering pans and dishes. Heavy vitrified tableware, commonly used, is noisy to handle due to its ringing belllike tone when hit. Careful and minimum handling, plus use of acoustical treatments, will help to lessen noise.

Appearance of delectable quality promotes food sales, and ensuing experience that is gratifying to the taste encourages patrons to return. Cafeteria counters should provide attractive display of food and effective means of preserving good quality. The food needs to be seen in the best light, both literally and figuratively. Clear visibility helps to speed selection and enhances appearance. A counter display should appear suitably bountiful to the last customer. This calls for container sizes appropriate for the amount of contents. Rotation cooking is far better than use of oversize steam table containers that will be either slack-filled or full of food that will become overcooked and unpalatable by the end of the serving time. Counter openings for pans should permit variation in sizes interchangeably, thus permitting variation according to quantity, sales, and many other factors.

Sanitation is a quality aspect that requires alert vigilance. Careful equipment planning can help in its promotion. Limit possible exposure to contamination, and promote sanitary food- and equipment-handling practices. Provide protective sneeze-guards where foods are openly displayed, and appropriate tools to eliminate hand contact with foods, plus sanitary means of storing and dispensing dishes, flatware, and napkins. Provide holding temperatures that will discourage the growth of bacteria. Minimize food and equipment handling to the greatest extent possible and in keeping with fast, convenient operation.

In addition to sanitary aspects, methods of food storage will influence qualities of palatability. Temperature, humidity, and length of holding time are significant. Food arriving directly from production usually has the most palatable quality. When quality changes are slight with proper holding, the quality loss is balanced frequently against advantages in utilization of staff time and speed of service. The necessity of having to

Figure 9.11 A server removing a tray of portioned desserts from a food rack in a refrigerated cabinet behind the serving counter.

order and wait for supplies is relieved if foods are at hand when needed. Storage facilities set into the wall between production and service may be an answer. If the hot food requirement is small, a pass-through cabinet may be located opposite the oven and at the end of the cook's worktable. Where supply requirements are large the cabinets may be of a size to accommodate rolling racks of food that have been moved directly from roll-in ovens to heated compartments at the point of service. Short distance and mobility help to lessen transfer time.

The colorful beauty of fresh fruit and vegetable salads have led many operators to place the salad section at the beginning of the cafeteria line. They are splendid foods to promote nutritionally and a well-arranged display is enticing. This arrangement also has the advantage of hot foods being last so that they lose a minimum of heat. Many patrons, however, prefer to select hot foods first and then choose a salad to go with them. Both arrangements have merit and are subject to individual preference.

It is well to arrange foods together that go together or are normally chosen together, such as meat and vegetables. Sales can often be encouraged through locating such foods as soup near salads and sandwiches or ice cream near cake and pie. Balance the workload of employees in terms of motions required for service and item popularity.

Freshly grilled foods and made-to-order sandwiches are among the popular foods that cause traffic delay. This may be solved by placing such items in a separate station that can be by-passed by patrons who are not interested. Some employees alert to usual demands can anticipate orders with enough accuracy to have grilled items ready for almost immediate pick-up. Some cafeterias have a signal or communicating system for customers to use for placing orders as soon as they enter the cafeteria line so that they can pick up the orders when they reach that point where they are prepared. In other places, peak loads are supplied by preparing grilled foods ahead and holding them for a short period in a roll warmer. Short delays can often be lessened by preportioning accompaniments, such as lettuce, tomatoes, and slices of ice cream rather than scooping to order.

Planning for accident prevention includes such things as nonslip floors, freedom from obstructions in traffic lanes and blind corners, and protection from burns resulting from food or equipment. Some accident hazards are difficult to avoid due to inattentiveness and resulting spillage by patrons. Alertness in preventing accidents and provision for quick clean-up when they occur are important. It is advisable to have clean-up equipment stored so that it is convenient to the serving area. Accidents cause a disturbing interruption in traffic flow and claim employee attention during a busy period, in addition to discomfort or injury to guests.

When estimating probable traffic flow consider time required for patrons to determine and express choices and for servers to comprehend and fill orders. What information is required, and what is readily available? Question extent to which items may be offered for immediate pick-up or self-service in terms of customer satisfaction and sanitary protection. Is the layout for traffic flow sufficiently logical or directions clear enough that strangers to the cafeteria will know how to proceed?

Certain items are often forgotten by patrons when picking up meals. These include drinking water, pieces of flatware, and napkins. Many individuals like to return to the line also for beverages, condiments, and other items. Location of such items near the end of the line where they are convenient to the dining area will help to prevent interruption of the traffic flow moving to the cashier. One or more small islands might be placed in the dining area where patrons might select these items. Many of the aspects relating to labor supply, menu offerings, and time restrictions that influence plans will be affected by specific conditions and regulations.

Speed and economy are two major reasons for choosing a cafeteria type of service. The conditions and facilities for the service deserve challenge in detail in order to promote these qualities. Consider whether essential supplies and conditions are readily available, such as convenient storage of tools for service; ice bin for ice to use in iced tea, lemonade, or other drinks; items adequately labeled, such as milk, nonfat milk, buttermilk, and chocolate milk; supply storage for uncut pies, cakes, and other foods; a milk dispenser on a turntable so that when one unit is empty another may be turned around for immediate dispensing; adequate display space in proportion to speed of service (to accommodate individual portions or trays of from 6 to 12 portions); wells with drains for ice cream scoops; and a menu board, placed early in line, that is easily read and easily set up. Avoid bottlenecks and provide for easy by-passing areas where delays may occur, such as those offering numerous choices or which require dishing up, as with soups, hot plates, and some desserts. Estimate about 2 ft (61 m) linear measurement for each person standing in line.

Speed-up facilities, such as extra serving sections, are valuable if there is sufficient demand. Counter shape and length affect speed of service. Right angles slow traffic, whereas straight lines or long curves allow it to move more quickly. Sudden stops or turns are hazards that increase accidents. Limit selection if speed has greater value. Include foods in the menu that are quickly dispensed. Carefully evaluate inclusion of any that hold up movement of the line. Allow sufficient space for a guest to step out of line when waiting for a special order or service.

Providing smooth flow design aids in speeding customers through the line. Tray slides should be sufficiently wide to provide a good base for the trays used. A rail 12 to 14 in. (30 to 36 cm) is desirable for 14 in. (36 cm) wide trays. Solid construction leads to fewer accidents than rail construction but is less convenient for cleaning. Locating the slide lower than the top of the counter will make it easier to reach over and will lessen the danger of pushing the tray onto the counter. Reduce turns or bends and irregularities to eliminate bumping and spillage hazards. Angles of turn should not be abrupt but curve gradually. A guide on curves helps to prevent accidents.

Dispense tableware in a sanitary fashion. Patrons should be able to pick up items by the handles and not by the end that touches food, or silver may be wrapped in the napkins. This latter method tends to induce taking more items than required. Coffee urns sometimes boil over and may scald patrons unless equipped with a gooseneck to carry steam

Figure 9.12 A counter designed to promote a smooth flow of traffic has an outboard protector bar to keep trays from sliding off at curves. (*Courtesy S. Blickman, Inc., Wehawken, N. J.*)

and allow hot water to run over on back of urn close to the drain. Rough edges of metal or glass should be eliminated. Avoid accidents by having traffic lanes clearly lighted, and the path straight, clear, and unencumbered.

Provide an orderly approach to the checker and cashier. Less waiting is required when an unrestricted view of the tray is given for a suitable distance ahead of the checker's stand to permit calculation and quick presentation of the check. Allow for delay space where patrons can search for purse and change without holding up the line. Place for trays during such search and during selection of tableware is necessary.

Self-bussing has numerous advantages. When patrons remove soiled dishes to a bussing station as soon as they have finished, the table is cleared for use by others. The immediate clearing helps to eliminate a cluttered appearance in the room, especially when patrons during a peak period are leaving the area faster than personnel can handle clearing. It is a labor saver that can benefit price schedules.

ASSEMBLED MEAL SERVICE

Meals are assembled in various ways to meet specific needs in hospitals, satellite school foodservices, catering, room service, flight meals, and vending. Delay between completion of the food preparation and consumption of the meals is characteristic due to the necessity for meal assembly, food transportation, and dispatch or service to consumers. Each has its peculiar needs and the variety of activities must be suited to these.

Hospitals

The source of the food for hospital service may be from an on-premise kitchen, a separate commissary, or a commercial company. The food may be ready for immediate service, refrigerated and require further conditioning, frozen in bulk or portions and require thawing and reheating, or reheated from the frozen state. Regardless of the food source and initial state, service usually includes assembly of individual meals or its parts and distribution to patients. Some meals may come so assembled that the entire main course can be conditioned hot from a cold or frozen state.

Hospital food must meet many rather strict requirements. Ill people must be served foods at times that have dietary restrictions. Even if this were not the case, an individual when ill has less appreciation for food than when vigorous and healthy. Therefore food must be served which, as much as possible, meets each patient's personal tastes, diet requirements, and current state of health. The food quality must be above ordinary. Careful planning is required to produce a facility to satisfy such requirements.

Many systems have been tried to overcome quality hazards. Those who thought temperature to be the most important quality factor set up systems to hold meals hot only to find that overcooking and loss of palatability exceeded the value of satisfactory temperature. Regardless of the source of food and method of service, certain reasonable, obtainable, quality-protection standards need to be established in relation to service. The standards pertain to time allowance in five of the stages of dispatch and presentation of meals and are as follows:

1. Continuous supply of freshly prepared food. For many foods this means a rotation of preparation, timed in terms of the quality depreciation for specific foods.

2. Fast assembly. Search and correct slowdown factors, such as excess motions, not enough servers, inadequate space and equipment, slowdowns in the line, and so forth.

3. Short period for meal dispatch. This may mean limiting the size of the carts so meals are not kept waiting after assembly.

4. Shorten distances of travel. Suitable distance both vertical and horizontal should be measured in terms of time.

5. Immediate presentation. Involved at this point is the synchronizing with routine patient care and identification of personnel responsible for presentation of the meals.

The three methods of service commonly used in hospitals are *decentralized* with serving stations on floors or wards where food is sent for essential treatment and service; *centralized-bulk* in which food is sent in trucks for dispensing in corridors near patients' rooms or from a floor pantry; and *centralized* service in which all of the individual meals are produced, served, and dispatched. Satisfactory means of communication and food transportation in each one are needed between the supply source, serving stations, and the patient area. Information concerning supplies, special needs, omissions, and directions is frequently needed. Best satisfaction results when the means of food transport, such as conveyors, elevators, and carts, are used by the food department only. Where general elevators are used, delay of food service may be caused by other traffic.

Decentralized service is favored by those who believe that locating final treatment and service in pantries close to patients' rooms yields best quality. Some of these pantries receive hot food ready for immediate

Figure 9.13   Assembly center for service from trucks. (*Courtesy Tampa General Hospital, Tampa, Fla.*)

service and other foods are sent for portioning ahead of serving time. Other dietary departments send food to pantries in bulk and expect the preparation of major foods, such as baking of entrees, broiling of chops and steaks, and boiling of vegetables, to be done there. The development of convenience foods and fast methods of conditioning has promoted another plan for final preparation and service. Foods for this are individually portioned and stored for holding according to their specific requirements. Main course foods that have been purchased ready-prepared and frozen or prepared in a commissary kitchen and frozen have been processed to a point at which all may have a common period of time for final cooking. Items for the meal service are selected according to patient needs, arranged on baking sheets, and placed in a convection oven or other heating unit. The cooking of the items is rotated in step with the serving speed.[1]

Dishwashing in decentralized service may be done in the pantries or in a central dishroom. If disposable units are used, these move to the

---

[1] R_x Plan in Minimal Food Handling," *Institutions Magazine*, July, 1972.

Figure 9.14 View of tray assembly and equipment. (*Courtesy St. Francis Hospital, Evanston, Ill.*)

disposer and only those requiring washing and sanitizing are sent to the dishwashing area. In any case, the dishes and tableware are stored in the pantry. Storage facilities are needed for all items used in setting up trays, such as covers, tray cards, and holders, and other means of indicating diet needs, silver and dishes, salt, pepper, sugar, and condiments. Mobile racks are used for preassembly of trays. The amount and type of storage facilities, cooking equipment, tableware dispensers, and serving counters depends on the preparation and service plans used.

Centralized-bulk serving stations is from trucks or units stocked in the main kitchen and sent to individual pantries. Service also can be from trucks moved near patients' rooms. Advance set-up in the pantries occurs for the trays. Some hospitals have microwave ovens on trucks for rapid cooking of hot foods immediately prior to service. Dishes are usually washed in a central dishroom. The chief advantage of this system is the short time between service and the patient's receiving the food. Disadvantages include extra kitchen trips for omitted items, cumbersome

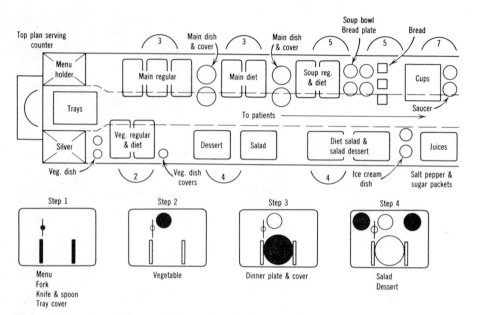

Figure 9.15 Steps in assembling a hospital tray. (*Courtesy Southern Equipment Co., St. Louis, Mo.*)

weight and size of trucks, traffic problems in halls and elevators, and where service is being performed simultaneously in a number of places supervision may be inadequate.

Centralized tray service has many advantages, which has led to its being widely used. In it, the patient trays are assembled in or adjacent to the main kitchen and the foods on them is sent by various transportation methods to the floors and then to the patients. Soiled dishes and trays are collected and sent to a central dishwashing room. Floor pantries are used for nourishments and trays held until they can be delivered to patients. Some dietary departments when trays cannot be delivered due to patient care, medical treatment, and so forth have the trays returned to the main serving area to be broken down and reassembled as needed.

Tray delivery may be (1) placing by hand on a dumbwaiter, moving to the floor, removing and placing by hand on carts where it moves to the patient's room; (2) placing by hand on a truck that is wheeled to an elevator, moved to the floor, and then to the point of delivery; (3) placing by hand on a small cart and moving via dumbwaiter to the floor, rolling off, and delivering to patients; and (4) moving mechanically from the assembly line on a conveyor to the floor or ward, there removing by

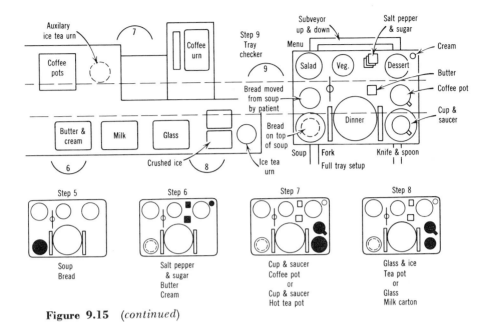

Figure 9.15 *(continued)*

hand, placing on a cart, and wheeling to the patient. Service by personnel at one point has been eliminated in the last two methods.

Speed and smoothness of movement of any transport system are desirable. The time lapse between food service and presentation to the patient requires means for retaining sharp temperatures. Large trucks that move slowly and are difficult to maneuver are delay factors. This raises the question of their desirability. Small carts for 6 or 8 trays can be utilized smoothly when plans are synchronized. With food quality depreciation in mind, a standard for the time span between service and patient presentation of the tray should be set. It should include (1) a reasonable rate for trays to come off the assembly line, (2) be loaded onto a cart and/or conveyor and discharged, (3) move to the point of delivery, and (4) be presented to the patient. If food is not protected by some device such as a heated pellet, insulated server, truck that keeps foods hot or cold, or other means, the time limit may be 5 minutes. Time schedules will involve distance and movement speed and equipment supply to have carts or other conveyance immediately ready for transporting.

The main virtue of cooked, frozen, and reheated foods is their convenience. If properly handled, the quality may be quite acceptable. The

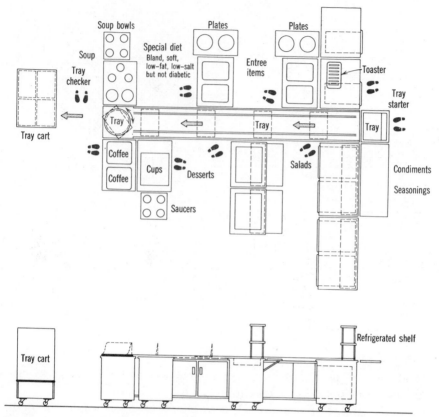

Figure 9.16 Floor plan of tray assembly line using conveyor belt and mobile equipment. (*Courtesy St. Francis Hospital, Milwaukee, Wis.*)

centralized system provides for the service of freshly prepared food, the value of which must be preserved through close control in getting the food to patients promptly and in satisfactory condition. The time required for a tray to move from the assembly line to the patient can be mathematically calculated. It is possible also to figure how many units of equipment are required to keep deliveries moving on schedule, how many serving lines and dumbwaiters (conveyors, elevators, and so forth) are required to serve a given number within the desired length of time, and how many employees are needed at each service point. A sample schedule might call for 4 trays per minute coming from the tray line, 2 minutes to check and load 8 trays into a cart, 1 minute for the cart to travel to the floor or ward, 1 minute to be received and rolled to the farthest point, and 1 minute to unload and present trays to patients.

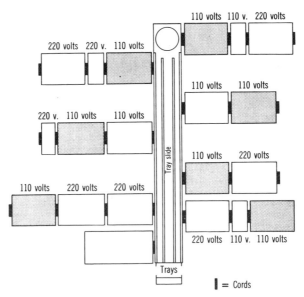

Figure 9.17 Electrical requirements for operating the mobile serving equipment. (*Courtesy* Institutions Magazine, *Chicago, Ill.*)

Planning must include arrangements for coding trays, giving complete information on a patient's needs in service, and so on. Foods for the trays should also be on hand for immediate placement as soon as the trays reach the servers. Trays may be pushed or moved mechanically on a belt. Trays are pushed by hand only in small operations where the assembly line is later used as a cafeteria for personnel. It is usually augmented by advance assembly of cold items on the trays. Mobile equipment may be moved into position at right angles to the assembly line. Reach should be planned for 14 in. (36 cm) to the front and sides. Least used items may be stored farther away or below on shelves. Slanting, overhead shelves, approximately 14 to 18 in. (36 to 46 cm) above the tray, give maximum use of vertical space.

The shortest travel distance for freshly cooked food can be ensured by having the assembly lines located in close proximity to the cooking section. Heated and refrigerated holding cabinets may be needed to hold food close to the serving counter. Mechanical means of moving the trays and a layout that permits servers to work simultaneously from both sides expedite tray assembly.

Dishwashing for the various types of service is usually done centrally, as this makes for best use of labor, equipment, and supplies. Some clearing and stacking may be done as dishes are collected or all of this activity may be confined to the dishroom to lessen noise in patient areas and utilize labor to the best advantage. Soiled units may be moved to the dishroom by cart or conveyor. Large hospitals may install two dishwashers, one for patients' dishes and the other for personnel dishes. Where a second is installed, it is well for the layout to permit use of either machine to handle the entire load in the event one breaks down. Some sanitary codes require complete separation, with partition between the soiled dish area and the clean dish section of the dishwashing area.

Metabolic diets and special research usually require a small food unit separate from the main food preparation, service, and dishwashing areas. Household size equipment is usually adequate. The facility needs include: shelves for storage of supplies, refrigerator and low-temperature storage, small range with oven, steamer, blenders (1 to 5 liters), dishwashing unit, work counter and tables, cabinets for dishes and equipment, two small carts, utility baskets, pitchers (2 to 5 liters), utensils for cooking and serving, wide-mouth screwtop bottles (100 to 500 ml), graduates (10 to 1000 ml), trays, glasses, dishes, flatware, and pots and pans.

School Foodservice Satellite Systems

Convincing needs combined with severe limitation of funds have caused school districts to search for economically satisfactory means of providing hot lunches to school children. Various types of satellite programs are used. The food is prepared in a central commissary kitchen and sent to satellite units for service. Three forms of packaging and service are in common use. In one the food is sent hot in bulk steam table containers ready for immediate service. The food in transit may be kept hot in a mobile hot table, rolled to the serving line, or in insulated carrier cases to be moved to the hot table at the point of service. The service at this point proceeds after the fashion of regular cafeteria service.

Two types have the hot food individually packaged in the production kitchen. One type is known as the hot sack lunch. For this, one hot item heated at the point of service is added after heating just prior to service to a sack containing the cold foods, napkin, fork and spoon or fork. The sack, cartons for milk and hot food, and the fork or spoon are disposable at the end of the meal. The paper container helps to insulate against rapid temperature change. The hot sack lunch can be planned to meet Type A specifications with raw relish, such as carrot and celery sticks, bread and butter, fruit or other simple dessert, milk, and a hot, protein-rich entree. The second type of individually packaged meals has foods also packaged in the production kitchen. Each meal consists of three units in separate containers; hot foods in foil for final cooking; cold foods, napkin, fork, and/or spoon in a plastic wrap; and a carton of milk. They are stored in the central commissary awaiting school orders. The foil-wrapped foods in wire baskets are heated or given final period of cooking at the school where served. The advance preparation of foods to be packaged together is brought to a point of completion that a common temperature and cooking time will complete preparation for service. The wire baskets separate the individual packages so that refrigerator cold or cooking heat circulates freely around them.

Refrigerators for food packages need to be located in convenient relationship to the assembly or serving lines and to loading platforms for

Figure 9.18 Hot food is dispensed into individual foil packages by machinery. (*Courtesy ABC Unified School District, Cerritos, Calif.*)

shipments. Service may be in a central dining area in the school or adjacent hall. Some schools may serve in classrooms; the food is served from carts. Cold food packaged with the napkin on top is sufficiently insulated to permit placement of hot food on top for short periods of handling. At the table or desk, the plastic cover of the cold food may be used as a placemat and the milk and other foods arranged on it. All service materials are disposable, which simplifies cleanup and eliminates dishwashing at the service point. However, thought needs to be given to problems of disposal and the availability of disposable materials.

The packaged meals have the advantage of economy, sanitation in food handling, easy assembly, supply to daily orders, and ease of service. Strong disadvantages argue for a cafeteria service. Students are loath to accept foods "sight unseen." Good food helps to sell itself, and buyers like to see what they are getting. There is less opportunity to teach

Figure 9.19 Cold food is packaged in clear plastic by machinery. (*Courtesy ABC Unified School District, Cerritos, Calif.*)

Figure 9.20 Each child receives a package of cold food, one of hot food, and a container of milk for lunch. (*Courtesy of ABC Unified School District, Cerritos, Calif.*)

children to chose foods wisely and to develop good habits in using normal tableware.

Catering

Many foodservices are asked to cater food and beverages for special occasions. Provisions of the catering service are usually in addition to normal daily food operation. The regular kitchen and other units may suffice for these supplementary needs, but for some facilities separate catering production units may be required. This may go as far as setting up a unit similar to a central commissary that transports food outside the premises and serves them. The requirements will dictate what will be needed in planning. Answers to the following questions will help guide planning:

1. What groups will request special service?

2. What are the sizes and nature of the groups? For instance, are they faculty, PTA, community meeting or party groups, convention delegates, an athletic team or sporting event crowd, alumni, stag, or other group?

3. What space can be made available for special functions and where is it to be located in relation to regular food production or specialized food production and service areas that support it only? Will off-premise service be required?

Figure 9.21 The plastic cover of the cold food serves as a placemat when the meal is opened. (*Courtesy Bremerton School District, Bremerton, Wash.*)

4. At what meal or time of day are these special functions likely to occur? What type of meal or food will be required and what types of service? Will alcoholic beverage service be required that may limit types of service personnel and require special equipment?

5. What facilities will be required for service—tables and chairs, serving equipment, water, refrigeration, electrical outlets, and so forth?

6. What special facilities will be needed by groups—cloakroom, toilets, program equipment such as speaker's podium, sound equipment, screen and projection equipment, blackboard, dance floor, dressing room, orchestra space, special lighting, other?

7. How frequently will space and equipment be used? What extra costs are involved?

8. Where will catering equipment be stored when it is not in use?

9. To what extent are catered events optional? Are they an essential service or will provision of them be based on balancing returns and costs?

Success calls for solving many characteristic problems. Food goodness, interest, and temperature plus service speed are usual rating values. Typical hazards in meeting these values include quality changes due to transportation of foods from production areas to service and the time lost waiting for guest arrival or cocktail enjoyment; plus supply inadequacies due to more or fewer patrons than specified, service slowdowns occasioned by overcrowding of space, inefficiencies of temporary help and insufficiencies in planning and advanced preparation. When special catering is well done, there is no part of the food service more liable to flattering acclaim.

In certain organizations, service of a catering nature may be frequent—even a daily part of the food operation. These include transported coffeebreak service in industrial organizations and faculty or medical luncheons. Some functions may be monthly or weekly such as church, PTA, or other organizational dinners. A hotel may have a wide variety of catering services going every day. The number and type of meals may be reasonably constant and require a minimum of special planning. Service may be in a remote location from production or adjacent and may be at the same hour as the regular service or at a later hour. Heterogenous functions that vary in nature and size from simple lunches to large elaborate buffets and banquets are often requested from commercial establishments and union buildings.

It is well to utilize but not overload regular staff and equipment for special catering unless the nature and volume is such that special facilities are required to take care of it. Time and effort load for employees and space and volume capacity for equipment tied into regular production units need to be closely calculated. A certain amount of flexibility is normally built into both staff and equipment that can cope with the occasional small increase. Special provisions should be made where catering is expected to be a regular part of the food operation. Such plans should include production, transportation, service, clean-up, space allowances, and equipment storage.

A pantry kitchen equipped to do some final cooking if located close to the point of service is most likely to serve food of the best quality. Modern, fast-heating equipment makes possible quick final cooking or heating of refrigerated or frozen foods. The pantry cooking would relieve some of the necessity of mealtime transportation and allow for rotation cooking and a more flexible time of service. Many foods can withstand treatment that is usually required of a convenience food with a reasonable degree of excellence. Menus for special meals handled in this fashion should be chosen from such foods. If very large groups are to be served preprepared, frozen, transported, stored, and finished foods, the equipment should be chosen to facilitate such handling. Appropriate size carts should be chosen on which the foods can remain through each of the steps of freezing, transporting, storing and baking or that will accommodate trays for handling food even to placement on the hot serving table. The cooking equipment might consist of a convection oven only, or in addition may have steam equipment for vegetables and deep fat fryer.

Remote service pantries should be compactly planned and provide for storage of all necessary dishes, flatware, linen, serving tools and other equipment. Facilities should be conveniently placed for water, ice, refrigerated milk, coffee, and hot water for tea plus the containers for the beverage service. Bars for liquor service are frequently necessary in hotels, clubs, and commercial restaurants. If the bar is mobile and the pantry attractive, the pantry may be used as a cocktail bar for direct service and the bar moved aside for mobile dish-up equipment. Provide locked storage on the mobile bar. Hot plates, mixers, and other electrical equipment may be required and provision should be made for sufficient and adequate electrical outlets.

An assembly line system similar to hospital tray assembly with the use of a travelling belt may be used for rapid banquet service, or the plates may be served at a hot table assembly line and pushed or handed from one server to the next. Advance preparation and portioning of cold menu items should be done and foods refrigerated ahead of time for service. Mobile rack storage will add convenience in transporting the items to the dining area for placement. Trays may be used for plate service or small, attractive, easily maneuverable carts. The carts with plate collars that permit stacking can handle a sizable load repeatedly with less fatigue, especially for women servers. Sufficient landing space for served plates and the filling of carts or trays should be allowed at the end of the serving line. Heated mobile dish storage units should be provided in the serving line, and sufficient space for backup storage.

Banquet or special service areas may be on other floors or in another building from the food production section. Means of transportation calls for consideration. For those located on another floor it is desirable that direct elevator service be provided. Thoughtlessness in relation to catering needs when designing the building can cost many dollars in labor time and sacrifice food quality and prompt service.

The demands connected with catered service are many and varied, and although many of them may have little connection with food service, provision to meet them is a part of satisfactory catering. The group may want special entertainment or dancing during the meal. Orchestra space, stage, dressing rooms, special lighting, sound effects, and other theatrical devices may be needed. A dining area may be used for a morning business meeting and coffee break, a style-show luncheon, and later in the evening, a dinner dance. Rugs should be removable and a hard floor provided for dancing. Sound equipment may be required for speakers and for transmission of orchestra music. Telephone plug-ins, speaker podiums, projection screens, blackboards, display panels, piano, and other equipment may be required. The kind of establishment doing the catering and the amount of use various equipment will be given will guide planning for its procurement.

It is usually desirable to provide directional signs to the special service rooms in order to guide traffic and save answering repeated questions. A cloakroom and toilet facilities should be provided. Electrical outlets should be suitably located for equipment to be used, either by the servers or the guests. The decor should provide a reasonably neutral background that can easily be varied with decorative features or items provided by groups in carrying out special themes. Provide well-finished tables and chairs of good design that are substantial and snag-proof. Folding equipment or stackables may be used to be readily storable, and easily transported. Provide platform trucks or other mechanical equipment for moving them and have adequate storage areas conveniently located.

Flight Meals

Airline companies recognize foodservice as an expensive but requisite service that influences customer satisfaction and flight sales. Many of the companies own and operate their own kitchens. Some of them sell meals to other lines, and some of the large lines buy meals from catering companies, airport restaurants or hotels. Hot meals are provided on the majority of mealtime flights and on some a cold box lunch and hot beverage is served. Certain lines have discontinued foodservice on economy flights.

Flight schedules and the number of passengers requiring meals vary. Food must be prepared, specially packed, and ready when needed for transport on schedule to the planes. Intercommunicating radio systems make it possible to transmit sudden changes in count or plane delay quickly. Ease of assembly on the plane, popular foods, and those that will withstand the quality hazards of long storage and customary handling are required. The packages for transporting and hold must be light, sturdy, insulated to protect temperature, easy to handle, and compact. Paper, plastic, or china service may be used.

The central production area of the airline kitchen closely resembles that of any other kitchen. The greatest difference exists in the scheduling of production and the assembly of meals. Time for shipping out orders, instead of meal times, control production time. The layout for the assembly center should provide for quick easy assembly of foods, tableware, paper supplies, meal accessaries, such as cream, sugar, salt, and pepper, relishes, and containers. A lone worker may work in a semicircle to assemble meals or three or four employees may work assembly line fashion as with hospital meals.

The storage place for completed meals should be convenient to the loading platform. Each airline will use its own special equipment and will require a special storage space where its equipment only is placed. Special storage will be required for liquor. Provision will be needed also for ice and other things used in connection with food and beverage service. Handling is facilitated when carts containing meals can be stored, rolled onto trucks, and moved to the planes.

The service of inflight meals requires special planning. Planes arrive loaded with soiled equipment. A large mass of soiled equipment must be processed through at one time and in a "turn-around-time" for the equipment being about $1\frac{1}{2}$ hours or under special circumstances even less. Thus the entire lot must be processed, filled with new meals and ready for loading on another outgoing plane within a very short time. Many items are also not cleaned easily since casserole dishes and other units may have food baked on them that is difficult to remove. Space is needed around the dishwashing and sanitizing area to hold "dead headed" equipment. Every plane must carry a full load of dishes and other serving equipment even though only a partial load of prepared meals is required. This is done because at the next airport a full meal

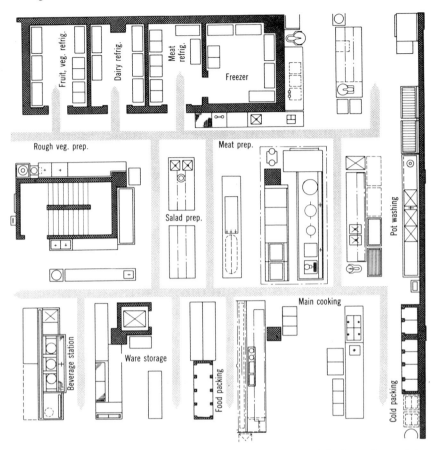

Figure 9.22 A layout showing a smooth flow of material through receiving, preparation and packing of flight meals. (*Courtesy* Institutions Magazine, *Chicago, Ill.*)

load will be required and the facility will have no equipment unless each plane is fully loaded. Space must be left also for carry-over items. While no opened food can be reused, canned pop and other unopened, sealed units may be.

Careful planning must occur to see that flow is facilitated. Incoming and outgoing materials must be kept separate, for reasons of sanitation. Loading docks must frequently receive both. Normally a U-shaped plan is best, where incoming materials come in on the left side of the receiving dock, go into washing and sanitizing, thence to storage, then to assembly, to production, to loading, and out to the loading dock to be taken away. If a separate receiving and loading docks are planned, the flow can be straight-line as is the case in the Los Angeles Airport central commissary. Since many tasks are repetitive in preparing trays, dishing up, and so forth assembly line flow with well-planned work centers function well.

Room Service

The majority of hotels and resident clubs provide room service. Breakfast usually is in heaviest demand with as many as a fourth of the breakfasts eaten being provided by room service. In this service as in other types of assembled and transported meals, quality is dependent upon protection of the food during assembly and transit. Depending upon the preparation required, an order should be delivered within 4 to 15 minutes of the time it was placed. Time stamps that indicate the time the order was received, time it was ready, time it was picked up for transport to the rooms is helpful in promoting promptness. One of the latest innovations in room service is a specially designed elevator that is equipped to prepare breakfast and other orders for the rooms. Thus, the order can be taken and prepared while the elevator is enroute. Some supplemental assistance will usually be required from the main or supplemental kitchen. It is wise to assure that room service has its own elevator service or has ready access to service elevators.

The number of tables required, the amount of equipment, and other room service needs will depend upon the volume and type of service carried. Many hotels and motels now try to restrict room service and have it available only a part of the day. Where the volume warrants a separate facility apart from the main production area, but supported by it. Kosher breakfasts are traditionally dairy and for this reason must be prepared in a separate kitchen.

With sufficient volume it is advisable to have a separate room for meal assembly. One of the most common faults in planning room service areas is the failure to provide enough space for tables that must be opened and preset awaiting demand. Such space needs should be calculated and provided. Otherwise there is likely to be a large number of preset tables in halls or work aisles. This usually is a violation of fire codes and constantly a point of inconvenience and friction.

Bottled goods, beverages, and other required items should be stored in the area. All items required, with the exception of prepared foods, should be readily available. It is desirable to have a counter space for work with storage over or below. Adequate space for orderly storage of supplies and for setting up some parts of orders ahead will help to speed

Figure 9.23 A tractor can quickly distribute dispensing units to many points in a large plant. Whirlpool Corp., Evansville, Ind. (*Courtesy Lincoln Manufacturing Company, Incorporated, Fort Wayne, Ind.*)

service. If volume is sufficient, a service bar may be provided. A desk with phones will be needed for handling calls. The room service section should be located close to elevators and where the route will permit the shortest, most direct path with a minimum of delays.

Vending Service

The vending service may be mobile or in a fixed location equipped with appropriate equipment for storing and dispensing foods. In mobile service the products are assembled in a central area and may be dispensed some distance away from the production area. Provision is required in this type of vending for suitable temperature holding equipment for foods, appropriate means for transporting it, and seating arrangements for patrons. Successful vending in fixed locations also depends upon proper protection of foods to and in the location and some plans for patrons' comfort while consuming it.

Box lunches are easy to assemble and transport for mobile service and can readily be augmented with hot soup and beverages in vacuum containers. The service can be speedy and require few employees to serve a large number. Meals for plant employees may be handled also in the manner described under satellite school foodservice in which hot foods are given final cooking or heating at the point of service. It is now common practice where vending machines are in a fixed location to provide a fast means of heating, such as microwave, for heating single portions of hot foods.

Vending machines dispensing snack foods or a complete meal are available. Either hot or cold foods may be dispensed. The foods are assembled and packaged in a central commissary kitchen and brought to the machine for loading. A coin activates dispensing and, where hot foods are required, may activate heating unless the foods are already hot or to be heated outside the equipment. Some vending machines have automatic cycles of heating for service and cooling down to refrigerated temperatures for holding.

The vending equipment may be owned by the organization requiring the service, the company supplying the food, or a vending equipment firm. If owned by the company served or providing the food, they can prevent many problems through careful selection of the vending equipment. Sanitation standards must be high and it is therefore important to carefully investigate both the record of the equipment and the organization supplying the food. Significant points to consider in relation to the equipment are simplicity of operation, freedom from mechanical failure, servicing record and servicing available by the company, accuracy in dispensing and change making (if this is included), ability to reach parts likely to require servicing, sanitation and ease of filling. Choose equipment that will provide the specific services required. It is advisable to investigate the record of the equipment and/or the company supplying food before a purchase or contract is made.

Vending may not provide an ideal meal service, but there are situations where making food available in this manner is greatly appreciated. Organizations where the number of personnel to purchase food is inadequate to support a more complete and expensive food operation and those with very irregular patronage over a long span of the day and/or night, may be served best by a vending operation. Some organizations which provide a well operated foodservice find vending of certain items a satisfactory answer for snackers, gripers and out-of-schedule diners.

Vending equipment for various foods and beverage items show considerable variety in size and appearance. Plan, for satisfactory appearance, to overcome the heterogeneous aspects. Where the equipment is owned by the company providing the service, it may be possible to set the equipment into a wall and provide a facing that will give a uniform appearance. An attractive decorative scheme may be used to harmonize the whole. Clearly posted menu items available with prices will help to guide choices. Machines should be located away from heavily populated traffic areas and in a manner that will help to guide traffic flow in front of them.

Suggested Student Assigments

1. Observe three different dining areas and evaluate means used and degree of success in providing:
   a. Preservation of quality (explain measures used for your judgment of freshness, temperature, and appearance).
   b. Fast service, (How much time elapsed from time of entrance until guests were served?)
   c. Hospitality and attractiveness. (Are guests made to feel welcome? What group of people would be especially attracted to the decor?)
   d. Sanitary food and service. (What protection is given and what chances exist for contamination?)
   e. Safety from accidents. (List points where special provision for safety has been made or where hazards exist.)

2. Chart traffic flow in a cafeteria or commercial restaurant showing lines followed by food facility personnel and customers.

3. List small equipment and state use in service for:
   a. Counter service.
   b. Cafeteria.
   c. Catering Service.
   d. Room service.

4. Plan layout for service in a specified type of food facility. Explain arrangement and reasons for choice.

Chapter 10

housekeeping sections

Attractive decor, though valuable in a food facility, has less patron appeal value than does order and cleanliness. A good, clean appearance in an eating place makes an immediate impression on the senses. Beauty, order, cleanliness, and appealing aromas help to create a desirable atmosphere. People are repulsed by musty, stale, smoky, greasy odors, messiness and haphazard appearances. Happy, mellow sounds of activity and pleasure are enjoyed. Orderliness and good repair not only tend to promote safety, but also lend the impression of carefulness. Maintaining these agreeable qualities and protecting the well-being of personnel and clientele is within the province of housekeeping.

Ease and insurance of satisfactory maintenance can be promoted through the selection of durable materials and finishes, avoidance of difficult to-clean areas and items, and provision for adequate care and cleaning. The type and amount of use give indication of probable wear and cleaning needs. The likelihood of excessive wear, breakage, spillage, accumulation of clutter and soil, and accident hazards is greater in some areas of kitchens and dining rooms than in others. Special provision needs to be made for prevention and/or quick repair and cleanup in such areas.

Many of the protective measures for safety, sanitation, and good housekeeping can be provided through alert planning of the facility. Typical of such planning is the allowance of sufficient space around and beneath equipment for cleaning. Even large ovens and ranges are now designed so that they may be raised by lever or moved to facilitate cleaning behind and underneath. Drains should be placed in areas where there is likely to be spillage and distributed in sufficient number for satisfactory drainage when scrubbing. Place storage for cleaning equipment where it can be readily reached for incidental cleanup as needed.

Plan dining room cleanup equipment according to the care that will be required. A vacuum cleaner and attachments will be needed for rugs, draperies, and certain acoustic equipment. Many floor finishes require the use of waxers and polishers. Carts for handling pails, mops, brushes, and cleaning supplies help to save steps. A closet for these and also a location for small items needed in dining areas for quick cleanup should be a part of dining room plans.

Housekeeping requirements, in keeping with reasonable expense and effort, call for consideration when selecting and installing the various parts of a food facility. It is desirable to have food machines that can be readily dismantled and reassembled, surfaces that will retain a bright, new appearance after scrubbing, and surfaces that can be fully sanitized. There are numerous aspects for which planners need to make provision for promoting safety, sanitation, and good housekeeping. Every area deserves questioning on this basis. The following is a suggested list of questions to stimulate thoughtful evaluation of housekeeping potential when making selections.

HOUSEKEEPING EVALUATION LIST

1. All items of major equipment. Will materials and finishes withstand necessary cleaning? Does the design or ease of disassembling permit thorough cleaning?

2. Acoustical treatment. Will the material and/or design permit adequate cleaning and periodic refinishing if necessary for good appearance?

3. Chairs, tables, stools, counters, tray rails, and other furniture. Is the structure sturdy, the surfaces smooth, and the materials cleanable?

4. China and glassware. Are they of a design and material that will withstand reasonable wear? Is there adequate stock for replacement? Are suitable facilities provided for handling and storage?

5. Conveyors. Is the operation smooth and reasonably hazard-free? Are all parts readily cleanable?

6. Drains. Does the design permit free flowing and prevent back-siphonage? Are location and number planned adequate?

7. Equipment attachments. Are they suitably sturdy, fully cleanable, and is storage provided for convenience and adequate protection?

8. Equipment bumpers. Do they provide adequate protection of walls and equipment?

9. Detergent dispensers. Can they be supplied easily? Do they give indication when supplies are needed? Do they function well?

10. Draperies, furniture, and decorative objects. Are they attractive, cleanable, and suitable?

11. Electrical cords, outlets, and switches. Are they in keeping with safety codes, properly placed, in sufficient number, and in good condition?

12. Exposed pipes. Can they be placed in an inconspicuous location and covered for protection and a good appearance?

13. Flatware. Is it smooth, shapely, and attractive? Does it require burnishing to retain a bright appearance? Will the weight withstand normal wear? Are plans adequate for cleaning, storing, and dispensing?

14. Floors, ramps, platforms, and stairs. Are they of material that will withstand expected wear? Can the material be fully cleaned for good sanitation? Are they nonskid and designed for safety?

15. Floor mats or coverings. Does the floor design permit their use without hazard of tripping? Are they well placed, safely flat, and readily cleanable?

16. Hoods. Are they effective in removing smoke and fumes without causing a draft that is uncomfortable for workers? Can hoods and filters be fully and easily cleaned?

17. Ladders. Are they sturdy, safe, and of appropriate size to meet needs? Are they conveniently stored?

18. Linen supplies. Are uniforms, table linens, aprons, and towels to be owned by the establishments or supplied by a laundry? What number is adequate? What provision will be needed for storage, collection of soiled laundry, and issuing of supplies?

19. Lighting. Has provision been made for the amount of illumination needed in areas according to work done or display requirements? Are lighting fixtures and equipment well placed and readily cleanable and serviceable?

20. Safety valves on urns and steam equipment. Will the functioning provide adequate safety? Can adjustments be made with minimum hazard?

21. Scales. Do they retain accuracy? Are they placed for convenient use? Are they easily cleanable? Is there a sufficient number for good work?

22. Shelving. Is it sturdy, cleanable, well placed, suitably sized, and adequate?

23. Small equipment. Is it sufficiently sturdy for expected use, adequate in amount, and stored for convenience and cleanliness?

24. Sinks. Are they constructed of sturdy, easily cleanable, and bright material that will withstand expected wear? Does the design and location permit thorough cleaning and discourage lodging of insects? Will the supporting structure bear maximum weights likely to be in or on the sinks? Are sizes appropriate to uses? Are they well placed for convenience? Are they designed for complete drainage?

25. Storage equipment. Has suitable transportation equipment been supplied to meet expected need? Has adequate protection been supplied to prevent spoilage and theft and to preserve good sanitation? Is all equipment suitably sturdy and readily cleanable?

26. Ventilation fans, ducts, and grills. Will they function effectively in removing smoke and fumes? Can they be easily and adequately cleaned?

27. Walls and ceiling. Do they give adequate reflection of light? Are the surfaces cleanable and capable of withstanding repeated cleaning?

Are the colors attractive, furnishing an appealing background for food-service?

28. Water temperatures. Are appropriate temperatures supplied for dishwashing, kitchen use, drinking water, and steam cleaning?

29. Water. Is there an ample supply of safe water under suitable pressure that is good tasting for drinking and softened if necessary?

30. Wheels and casters on mobile equipment. Do they roll easily? Are they sufficiently sturdy to bear maximum loads required? Are they cleanable?

31. Windows and screens. Are they available where needed and clean?

32. Worktables, mobile and stationary. Are surfaces smooth and readily cleanable and constructed of noncorrosive, nontoxic materials? Are drawers removable for cleaning and shelving free of difficult-to-clean lodging spots for soil?

33. All areas of the food facility (work sections, dining rooms, lounge and toilet areas, office, storage rooms, garbage and trash areas). Are they well ventilated, properly lighted, orderly, adequately equipped, at suitable temperature, and clean?

DISHWASHING

Dishwashing has a high rating of importance in foodservice facilities because of its significance in protecting sanitation; utilization of labor time; saving on operational costs for power, hot water, and detergent; and for prevention of loss and breakage of tableware. The pleasure of clientele is readily affected by the appearance and cleanliness of tableware. The sparkle of well-washed and fully rinsed dishes and the bright appearance and feel of properly cleansed flatware invite diners to enjoy their food.

The dishwashing operation includes removal of soiled tableware from dining areas; receiving, scraping, and stacking ready for washing; washing and drying of cups, glasses, dishes, flatware, and utensils; removal of tableware from baskets or a conveyor and stacking; and transfer to facilities for storage and dispensing or use. It is desirable that dishes be routed from the dining area in a manner that will create the least noise, confusion, and unsightliness. Most persons dislike the sight and clatter of dish scraping and stacking in the dining area. The manner in which dishes are removed differs with the type of institution. In table-service restaurants they are usually cleared from tables by waitresses or bus boys to trays or baskets and carried to the dishroom. In schools and industrial

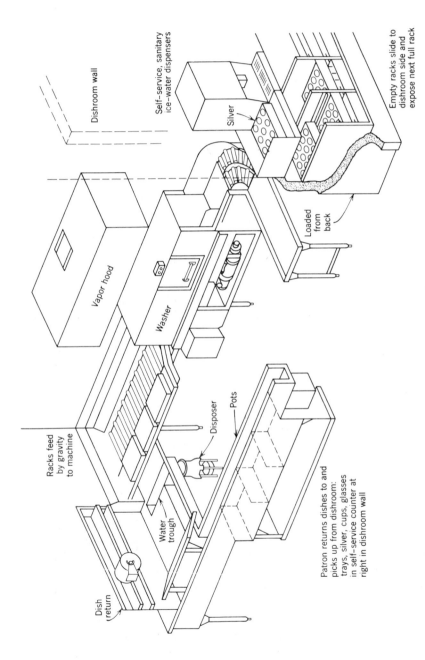

Figure 10.1 A dishroom designed for convenient deposit of soiled tableware and pick-up in the serving area of clean items that have been pushed through the wall from the dishroom. (*Courtesy Robert Whitney and Associates.*)

plants patrons frequently return dishes to collection points or a conveyor. Although the majority dislike returning trays to a central point after their meal, they will do it in industrial and school dining rooms if the custom is established as a part of maintaining minimal costs. If patrons are to bus their dishes, the placement port should be in line with the exit and where the path of exit will not cross that of patrons going to or from the serving area. Screen the port to lessen noise and improve the appearance of the room. This is sometimes done by means of a conveyor that carries the trays through a small port and out of sight. Patient trays in hospitals are generally collected on carts or trucks and moved by elevator or conveyor to a central dishwashing area.

Dishwashing Operation

Significant goals for the dishwashing section include thorough cleansing and protection of the sanitation of tableware and utensils, prevention of loss and breakage, and economical use of supplies and labor time. Good results in dishwashing are brought about through (1) completeness of scraping, washing, and rinsing actions; (2) water quality, quantity, and proper temperature; (3) effectiveness of detergent and rinsing agent; (4) type and quality of tableware; and (5) care in handling and proper procedures followed by the dishwashing personnel.

Thorough scraping lessens soil in the wash and directly influences bacterial count on the final result. A suitable force of water in the washing action must move soil from surfaces to be cleaned. The wash water and detergent are recycled, with a gradual flow of fresh water from the rinse section to refresh the wash solution as it picks up soil in the washing process. Detergent must be added gradually also, manually or by dispenser, in amounts sufficient to maintain an effective concentration. The dish is not clean nor fully sanitized until all of the washing solution has been removed by the higher-temperature flood of fresh rinse water.

It is important that the detergent attack fatty substances, loosen soil, and rinse free from surfaces to be cleaned. To obtain a bright, sparkling surface, tableware must be completely rinsed of soil residue and detergent. A rinsing solution that lowers the surface tension of water droplets will cause water to sheet away from surfaces in a manner that leaves the surfaces reasonably free from spots.

There are three water temperatures needed in the washing process. Prerinsing for the removal of coarse soil calls for a warm temperature 120° F (49° C) that will melt fat but not cook foods firmly onto the surfaces. The washing temperature should be 140° F (60° C) to be hot enough for effective cleansing action. Sanitizing calls for a rinse temperature of 180° F (82° C) for 10 seconds. Most bacteria are killed at 170° F (77° C) if held for 30 seconds or longer. At temperatures higher than 180° F (82° C) the water vaporizes sufficiently to interfere with the effectiveness of the rinsing action.

The type and quality of the tableware influences appearance gained through dishwashing. China surfaces from which the glaze has been removed through the hammering, rubbing action of wear will have a dull appearance that looks soiled. Plastic material does not absorb heat sufficiently during the washing process to quickly air dry and will remain wet unless some means such as a current of hot air or a good rinse solution is used to promote drying. Stained, tarnished, and worn flatware will require burnishing in addition to washing to produce a bright appearance.

Guard Sanitation.   Protection of sanitation calls for concerted effort on the part of both planners and operators. Regardless of equipment and detergent used, good results are dependent upon good judgment and good procedures regularly followed by dishwashing employees. Water temperatures are to be watched, detergent concentrations maintained, and sanitary handling practices faithfully followed. There are many examples in a one-man operation where the employee goes directly from scraping soiled dishes to handling clean dishes, taking them from baskets and stacking them, without benefit of hand washing. Some health authorities require that a wall close off the soiled dish area from the clean dish section to prevent possibilities for this method of contamination.

An organization of duties that provide separate workers for handling soiled and clean dishes is preferable for a one-man operation, but at times may not be practical. It is wise to take special precautions by placing a hand-washing sink in a convenient location so that employees will handle clean dishes with clean hands. Avoid hard-to-reach and difficult-to-clean areas and materials. Use special care in installing a conveyor so that all parts can be opened up for adequate cleaning. Select a dishwasher that can be opened up and dismantled where necessary for thorough cleaning. Choose a dishwasher, detergent dispensers, and other equipment for this section that meet National Sanitation Foundation standards.

Items important to good sanitation include adequate light, proper plumbing, good ventilation, and surfaces that are smooth, cleanable, and impervious to absorption of grease and moisture. The light should be well placed to avoid glare or shadow and be of 30 to 45 footcandles. The floor should have a hard, nonslip surface. Floor mats, if used, should be removable, lie flat, and be of a type that can be thoroughly scrubbed or steam cleaned. Coved corners are recommended for hard-surfaced walls and floor. Acoustical material or noise control devices are needed to lessen noise and should be cleanable. Good ventilation is essential to remove steam and provide a good circulation of air.

Hose attachments should be provided on the soiled dish table for flushing the table and cleaning the machine, and for use in flushing and cleaning the floor. Drains should be provided at points where spillage is most likely to occur, and the floor given a slight slope toward the drains. A hot water supply adequate in temperature and amount and at 20 to 25 lb pressure should be provided. Sewers and drains should be adequate to handle the large volume of water used in the section. Provide grease traps as needed and install these to prevent sewage from backing up into the dish machine. Have one large central trap, if possible. Install clean-out fittings in drain lines wherever they are needed. Plumbing, electrical, and other lines should be brought up through the legs of equipment or from overhead in a manner to minimize collection areas for grease and soil. Electrical wiring should be in concealed conduit.

Dish-handling Equipment. Conveyors provide quiet, inconspicuous help in moving dishes from dining areas to the dish room. When dishes are transported by hand, it is necessary for the dish room to be close to the dining room for step-saving. A conveyor can move the dishes to a remote area before scraping and stacking occur to avoid unpleasant noise. The speed of the conveyor belt should (1) be one with which customers feel comfortable in placing trays, (2) meet requirements for the number of trays arriving at a time, and (3) enable clearance with sufficient speed in the dish room. The length of belt exposed to receive trays, plus speed of movement, should be determined in terms of the number of trays that will arrive at a time. Breakage occurs and clearing of trays is more difficult when space is inadequate and customers stack one tray on top of another.

If service personnel move the soiled dishes to the dish room, routing should permit a smooth flow of traffic and eliminate worker delay, noise and expensive collisions. "In" and "out" doors should be provided, and the doors should be wide enough to permit passage of workers with wide trays. Automatic opening doors are helpful; usually right to left flow is desirable.

Loss and breakage of tableware may be lessened by workers separating silver and glasses from soiled dishes when clearing tables. Those who are clearing cafeteria or patient trays should remove these items and any paper waste before sending the tray to the soiled dish table for scraping. Plans for public schools should make it convenient for children to sepa-

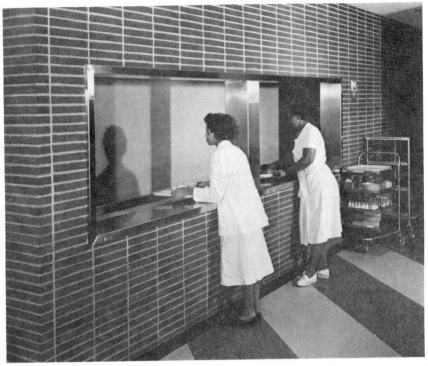

Figure 10.2 Conveyor belts should be located for convenient self-busing and sized to accommodate the number of dishes likely to arrive at one time.

rate these items before placing the trays in the soiled dish port. A wall opening next to the soiled dish port, equipped with a slide on the dish room side that reaches to a sink of water, is a good plan for soaking flatware. Paper waste may be placed in a swing top container or through another port that is significantly different from the flatware port to discourage confusion.

Keep in mind when selecting equipment the twelve steps usually followed in the dishwashing process, the first three of which may have been performed as indicated in the dining area. The procedures include:

1. Removal of paper, cloth, or other items that are not to be included in the dish-washing process.

2. Removal of flatware to a soak bath.

3. Sorting of cups and glasses into their respective racks.

4. Diverting milk glasses or other glasses that require soaking or brushing.

5. Scraping, sorting, and stacking dishes and trays.

6. Racking or placing items on a conveyor belt of the dish machine.

7. Placing racks of cups, glasses, and/or china in the machine.

8. Racking of silver and placing in the dish machine.

9. Removal and storage of tableware.

10. Inspection and burnishing of flatware.

11. Sorting and placing flatware in dispensers.

12. Drying and stacking of plastic trays.

Breakdown of the operation tends to happen when there is overloading of facilities, awkward motion, loss of work rhythm, interruptions, and lack of attention. These tend to happen when plans have not provided for sufficient space in relation to work load and a convenient area in which workers can work with normal rhythm, without unnecessary interruptions and according to proper sequence of operations. The point in the dishwashing procedure at which smooth flow is most likely to break down is in the receiving area of the soiled dish table. Plans to prevent this must provide for a suitable balance between maximum soiled dish arrival and space and labor to handle it.

Careful calculation of the probable load of dishes and their arrival schedule needs to be made to make plans to handle peak loads adequately. This should be based on the number served, the style of service, and the method of removal of dishes from dining areas. In establishments serving full-course dinners, approximately fifteen to twenty pieces of china, glassware, and silver will be used per person served within a 45- to 60-minute turnover period. In a cafeteria, the quantity drops to about three to ten pieces plus the tray, and the turnover period may average 30 minutes. Special service as well as regular service needs to be considered. In table service dining rooms and commercial cafeterias the tableware is cleared into trays or bus boxes for delivery to the soiled dish tables. In hospitals, patient trays may be sent to the dish room by conveyor, dumb waiter, or on carts, each requiring its particular handling technique. The following are some of the questions to be answered in making a calculation of requirements:

1. What kind and how many items will arrive on the soiled dish table per minute normally? As a maximum?

2. How many pieces can a worker, at normal pace, handle per minute?

Figure 10.3 Crowded dish tables mean excessive breakage, which can be avoided by adequate space and proper organization and flow of work.

3. How much space will be required for items on the soiled dish table during peak periods?

4. How will dishes arrive—as unsorted items in waiters' bus boxes; as unsorted trays on dumb waiters; as unsorted trays or bus boxes wheeled to the dishroom on tray carts, on which they can stand until time and space permits processing; or as a flood of self-bussed patron trays on a conveyor?

5. Can extra workers be available for peak period handling of dishes?

6. What size and type of dishwasher will be needed to wash the required load within desired time periods?

7. What dish table space, machine capacity, and number of workers will be required for satisfactory balance of capacity in proportion to needs.

Careful planning preventing dishroom pileups saves much expense and difficulty. A pileup on the soiled dish table may result in loss and breakage, plus greater difficulty in scraping, sorting, and stacking. It may cause delay in dining room clearing that results in a slowdown in service. Peak period pileups can sometimes be solved by better separation at bussing stations or at dining room collection points. Even the removal of flatware and glasses from trays can save time and loss. This may be done either by patrons returning trays or by foodservice employees. Having dish carts on which extra loads, such as those from catering areas, may remain during peak periods can help to relieve congestion.

Soiled dish tables should be adequate in size and support for the maximum number of dishes likely to arrive at one time. The gauge of the metal and the support must be sufficient to prevent sagging. Situations characterized by sudden and fluctuating masses of dishes require care in planning to prevent the temporary need from upsetting efficiency of normal operation. Providing extra workers for short periods is not always possible or practical. Excess dish table space may be expensive to install and difficult for few workers to cover in normal operation. Racks or tray trucks may be used to handle a temporary overload.

Space and facility needs to be provided for removal of coarse refuse and the sorting and stacking of dishes ready for filling baskets or placing these on the traveling belt of the dishwasher. How many dish baskets will be on the table at one time? Allow approximately 8 to 12 sq ft (.74 to 1.12 m^2) for two or three racks. More space is needed if dishes are allowed to accumulate before going through the machine. The smallest amount of space is required when dishes arrive in a steady flow and a rackless machine is used. Allow space for scraped, sorted, and stacked dishes. Determine the plan of work and the largest number of items likely to be stacked before feeding the machine.

Preflushing of dishes may be done in several ways. One is a continuous flow of water pumped over dishes as they are being scraped. In large facilities where several workers are required for this, the water may flow in a trough along the front of the table where flushing is done. Small units may use a single flood of water or flush by hose over a sink. The latter method is done by placing dishes in racks over a sink located in the soiled dish table in front of the dishwasher. The hose used is equipped with a trigger-operated nozzle. The sink dimensions are slightly larger than those of the dish baskets (20 in. × 20 in. or 51 cm × 51 cm). The sink has slides across the top to assure easy movement of the rack into the machine. Separate machines or a prerinse section of a large machine are commonly used for prerinsing.

The soiled dish table should have drainage that will prevent water from the table going into the dishwasher. A slight pitch away from the machine, possibly toward the prerinse sink, or a drain approximately

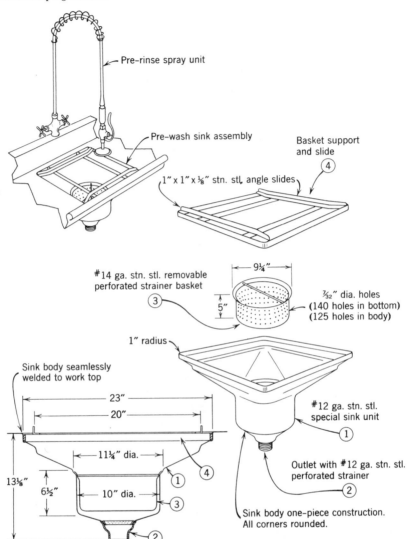

SANITARY TYPE PRE-WASH SINK ASSEMBLY

Figure 10.4 Sanitary-type prewash sink assembly. (*Courtesy S. Blickman, Inc., Weehawken, N. J.*)

3 in. (8 cm) wide extending the full width of the table near the entrance of the machine is desirable. The tables should be designed with a curb high enough to prevent overflow or spillage of water on the floor during the progress of work or cleaning. A height of 3 in. (8 cm) is recommended. If a conveyor belt moves onto the table, it should be con-

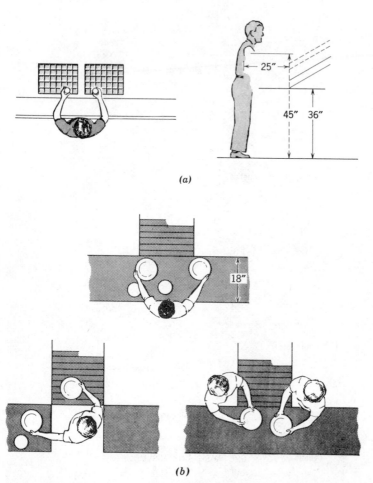

(a)

(b)

Figure 10.5 Arrangement of soiled dish area. (*a*) Placement of shelf for dish racks. Position racks at height and distance convenient in terms of average human measurement. (*b*) Position of soiled dish table in relation to feeding a continuous-belt-type dishwasher. Working beside or immediately in front of a machine is better than reaching across an expanse of table. (*Courtesy Robert Whitney and Associates.*)

structed for easy cleaning around and under it. It should be on a slightly raised area to prevent seepage of moisture under it. Scraping blocks, placed in convenient locations for workers, should be on raised coves to prevent liquids from running into garbage cans. Where disposal units are used, the block may be flush with the table or disposal cone.

The selection of size and type of dishwasher needs to be based on load requirements, space for handling, time limitations, and economical use of labor and supplies. A large flood of dishes may come to the table at peak periods and require immediate handling to supply needs because space limitations prohibit gradual handling. Where gradual handling is possible, fewer workers and a smaller capacity machine may be adequate. Calculation of machine size needed and labor requirements necessitates knowing time required for loading, movement time in the machine, drying time outside the machine before stacking and removal, and the speed of workers performing at normal rate. It is necessary to seek a balance between probable load, performance rate, and machine capacity. It is wise to provide for 25 percent more capacity than normally necessary.

Figure 10.6 A dishroom organized for a one-man operation during slack periods, with conveniently placed rack and bus box shelving. Sea Tac dish and pot room—Dishes enter on conveyor. (*Courtesy Robert Whitney and Associates.*)

Question whether the load is of right size and so distributed that labor is well utilized in using a manually operated machine. Determine if the load and distribution are such that assembly line methods and a larger machine gives better satisfaction.

The economics of dishwasher selection involves not only the initial cost of the machine installed, but also the comparative costs of labor, power, hot water, detergent, and racks or other supplies required in the operation. An automatic feature that reduces labor time one hour per day may amount to a sizable sum per year. The time saved, for example, through elimination of rack handling with rackless machines has added to their economic popularity.

Small facilities using hand methods of dishwashing will follow a cleaning routine similar to that in machine washing but they will use sinks and not machines. The dishes are preflushed with a spray, washed, rinsed, and sanitized. The preflushing keeps much soil from the wash water and makes washing easier. The wash water should be at 120° F to 160° F (49°C to 71° C). Most workers cannot wash in 160° F (71° C) water. The water in the second sink should be hotter and may be delivered against the dishes from a shower head spray with a trigger nozzle. If the dishes have been placed in a long-handled basket, they can be moved so they can be taken out without the hands going into the water into a third tank or sink that contains 170° F (77° C) water or 160° F (71° C) water plus a sterilizing solution. Allow 30 seconds in this water to sanitize. Space should be sufficient on the clean dish table for the baskets of dishes to set and air dry. Proper sanitizing and enough heat for air-drying depend upon maintaining 170° to 180° F (77° to 82° C) temperature in the third sink. This may be done by using a steady flow of water from a booster heater or by supplying a heating device such as steam in or a gas burner under the third sink.

Mobile storage units to move clean dishes from the dish room to service areas save labor in handling and help to protect sanitation. Mobile storage units that accommodate specific items only require more floor space than carts used for transport of a variety of items to fixed storage. Plans should provide space for transport equipment to be drawn close to the clean dish area for filling. If clean dishes are to be returned to serving pantries by conveyor or dumbwaiter, this relationship should be kept in mind.

Glasses and Flatware Washing. The glasses and flatware may be diverted for washing in separate machines than those used for dishes. This division is especially favored in large establishments. These items constitute the most intimate pieces of tableware. It is important not only that they be sanitary, but also that they be agreeable to touch. A roughness or greasiness is distasteful. Constant care should be exercised in sorting, cleansing, and sanitary handling of these items.

Procedures in dish rooms call for immediate removal of flatware to a soak sink and glasses and cups to racks. Provision should be made near the beginning of the dish washing line for this. Flatware may be washed in flat baskets or preferably held upright in wire baskets, or in perforated round containers of metal or plastic. These are then set in carrier baskets which are then put through the dishwasher. The flatware when taken from the soak bath before washing should not be sorted before placing in racks for washing. The irregular shapes and sizes of knives, forks, and spoons hold the pieces apart for more thorough cleansing. When washing in the upright position, the handles should be placed down to permit the full force of the wash to strike tines, blades, and bowls. When washed, these containers are dumped into clean containers so the handles only are lifted out by customers.

Following removal from the machine, silver may be dipped in a hot bath containing a solution to promote destaining and fast drying. A controlled method is needed for retaining sanitizing temperature for the dip. Another method for destaining and polishing is by machine, which tumbles it while going through an automatic cycle of washing, rinsing, and air drying. Toweling should never be done. Flatware may be spread on clean terrycloth or other pads for sorting. Burnishers are desirable in facilities that use silver flatware and large quantities of hollowware, such as beverage pots, sugars and creamers, casserole cradles, trays, and punch bowls. Plan lockable storage for silver hollowware in convenient relationship to place of use, with suitable provision for heating or chilling. Mobile storage should be considered for items used in different locations.

Glasses used for milk drinks or other foods that adhere may be cleaned by brushing before placing in racks. Brush machines are available that brush one or two glasses at a time. Brush-type glass washers that provide approved sanitation in cleaning with cold water and a germicidal detergent solution are available for counter use. Due to possibilities for neglect in using the germicidal solution, this procedure is not generally approved. When racks of glasses come from the dishwasher, they should be placed on carts or dollies for movement to the dispensing area. Glass and flatware washing are a normal part of dishwashing operations and should be kept in close relationship with it. Where separate machines are provided, allow at least 5 ft (1.52 m) for aisles between. In planning the equipment arrangement remember that the silver will be washed before burnishing. Soak sinks, dip sinks, and sorting tables must be placed where they will not interfere with the heavy flow of dishes.

Dishwashing Layout. Fact-finding and analysis of many aspects are needed before planning the layout of the dishwashing section. Necessary information includes:

1. Type of tableware to be washed and treatments required.

2. Volume of tableware to be processed within specified time limits.

3. Mode for travel and speed of delivery to the dishwashing area.

4. Methods used for scraping, washing, polishing, or other treatment.

5. Normal time requirements for various stages of processing or handling.

6. Space requirements equated to loads and processing methods.

7. Equipment needs.

8. Methods of transfer and types of storage

9. Sanitation standards and protection methods.

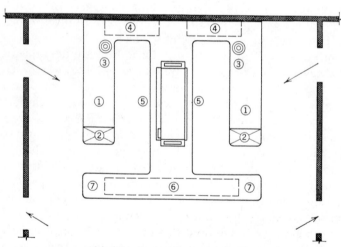

(*a*) Clearing tables at each side of the machine

1. Landing table.
2. General purpose sinks.
3. Power disposals.
4. Rack loading tables with inclined shelves over.

5. Rack returns.
6. Clean dish tables with storage shelves.
7. Silver sort areas.

Figure 10.7 Sample dishwashing layouts (*Courtesy G. S. Blakeslee & Co., Chicago, Ill.*)

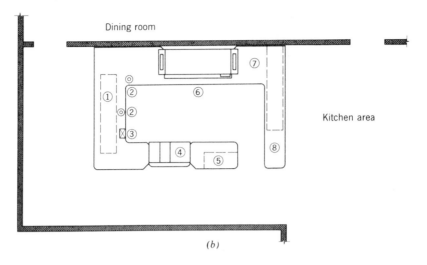

(*b*)

(*b*) Wall location in hollow-square layout

1. Landing table with inclined shelf over (for glass racks).
2. Scrap blocks.
3. Dump sink for glass contents.
4. Glasswasher. (Brush type.)

5. Clean glass table with storage shelves over and under.
6. Rack return.
7. Clean dish table with storage shelves over and under.
8. Silver sort area.

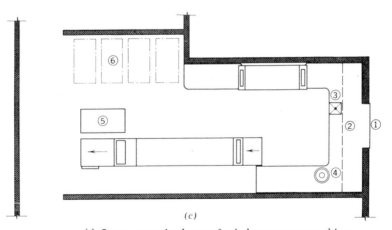

(*c*)

(*c*) Large capacity layout for belt-conveyor machines

1. Pass-through window.
2. Sorting and acraping talbe with cup and glass rack shelf over port.
3. Glassware dump sink with strainer.

4. Disposal
5. Clean dish cart.
6. Cart storage area.

Figure 10.7 (*continued*)

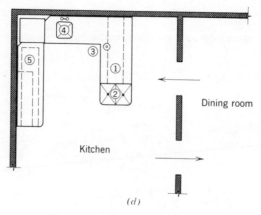

(d)

(*d*) Machine in a corner location

1. Landing table with inclined shelf above.
2. General purpose sinks.
3. Scrap block.

4. 18″ × 18″ flush sink with overhead spray.
5. Clean dish table with inclined shelf over flat shelf under.

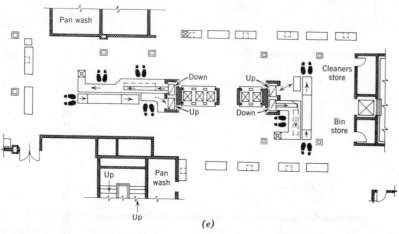

(e)

The type of tableware may vary from partitioned trays and stainless steel flatware in school foodservice to the silver and china of fine restaurants. Volume may require a one-man operation or a sizable crew performing assembly line duties. There is more repetition of motion in the dishwashing operation than in any section of a food facility. Study should be made of typical motions and those made most easily in order to utilize effort to greatest advantage. Conditions that simplify dishwashing motions are (1) having materials delivered within easy reach, (2) having materials of similar character, and (3) having loads and treatment that are repetitive and uniform. The height and width of work levels and rack shelving are important to convenient reach. The principles governing motion and work center planning should be applied. (See Chapter 3, Layout Analysis.)

The layout of tables and machine should be adapted to the character of the operation in terms of load, flow, organization of work and personnel, and in a manner to minimize motion. Load refers to the maximum volume of dishes handled by the section in a given period of time. Flow is the path that the dishes follow and the rate at which they appear on the soiled dish table—in even or in irregular quantities, fast or slow. If the work is organized like an assembly line where one worker does a specific task or where one or two workers perform a variety of functions, planning will be affected. Some operators may wish to shut down the dish machine during peak periods of receiving loads and scrape, sort, and stack only, so as to keep the soiled dish area cleared for incoming dishes. If so, the size of the soiled dish table and inventories of tableware must be planned for this.

The use of a conveyor serves to bring materials within reach and has the added advantage of promoting rhythm and stimulating continuous effort through the steady flow of material. Where a conveyor is not used, table size and worker location should be spaced so as to assure easy reach. Motion economy is better in large units where workers do classified tasks, such as racking glasses and cups only, scraping and stacking only, and feeding the machine only, than in cases where one person changes frequently from one function to another. Where one worker works alone doing several functions, motion economy is best if the flow of work permits performing one set of functions for a reasonable period, utilizing repetition of motion, and then shifting to another set of activities.

Plan of work and adequacy of space and supplies need to correspond. Specify a sufficient number of racks of different kinds (cup, glass, silver, and plate) to meet requirements if a rack-type dishwater is used. Plan a rack return from the clean dish table to the soiled dish area. It may be located across the face of the machine or along the back of the table behind the machine. Be sure that the reach of the worker will not be excessive in placing and taking the rack from the return, and that it is not in the way of operating the machine.

Tier or vertical use of space is important. Each worker should be allowed at least 2½ ft (0.76 m) linear space for working. Tables at which workers work at both sides may be 4 to 4½ ft (1.22 to 1.37 m) wide; those where one worker works on one side only may be 3 ft (0.91 m) wide. In early planning, from 9 to 11 sq ft (0.84 to 1.02 m²) may be used for estimating for each worker. The placement of overhead slanted shelves for glass and cup racks should be such as to permit free rhythmical motion to all parts of the racks with freedom from projections or posts that will interfere with the motion. It is better, if possible, to suspend them from overhead than from legs on the table. Motion should be minimized and not require excessive reaching up, stepping back, or stretching by the worker in the regular performance of the job. Plans for the work area should promote two-handed motion and reach and allow for a minimum of lifting of heavy racks loaded with dishes.

The layout of the dishwashing complex needs to provide for maximum loads and the largest number of workers required at peak periods, and it also must be convenient for one worker during slack periods. The hollow-square or U-shaped plan answers this need better than an L-shaped or straight-line plan, or one that requires the worker to go around the machine or table to attend to part of the functions. One employee working alone will scrape, sort, and stack dishes, load three or four baskets, and place them in the machine or feed the belt with a comparable number. Hand washing should follow, and then removal of the clean dishes, stacking, and placing them in storage carts. The worker will then return to scraping and basket filling. A manually operated machine will call for repeated placing and removing baskets in the machine and repeated operation of the machine. A fully automatic machine will require shoving baskets to the opening of the machine. The rackless machine eliminates the necessity of rack handling as the dishes are fed directly onto the belt.

It is desirable to have dishwashers located away from the wall far enough to permit cleaning and care. In large work sections where workers operate from both sides of the tables and mobile equipment will be used, it is desirable to have the dishwasher located centrally. In small operations where space is limited and few workers are employed, wall and corner locations may be used. Machines are available that can be operated from right or left. Designate in the specifications which direction is to be followed and where openings are to be for straight line or corner location.

POT AND PAN WASHING

The pot and pan washing section should be located near areas of the food facility (1) where the largest number of soiled pots and pans originate and (2) where it will be convenient for users to have the general storage of pots and pans. Distribution by cart of many equipment items to specific production and serving sections provides time-saving convenience. The heaviest flow of soiled items comes from the cooking and baking sections in the kitchen and from the serving section. The largest number of pots from the production section arrives shortly before and during meal service as production is completed; those from serving areas will come during and immediately following meal service. Proper location of this work area can do much to minimize cross traffic, backtracking, and travel in the kitchen. Mobile collection carts in various work sections can reduce travel and promote one-motion storage.

Plan for adequate space for the number of carts, mixer bowls, roasting pans, and other large equipment, both soiled and clean, that will be in the section at one time. Traffic jams can be caused and accidents result when space is inadequate, and items brought to the area spill into traffic lanes. The space allowance and arrangement should promote satisfactory work flow. The process of cleaning includes scraping, soaking, washing, rinsing, sanitizing, and drying. Scraping is a hand process usually done in conjunction with the soaking process. Disposal of the soft refuse may be done by screening, draining, and emptying it into the garbage can or by

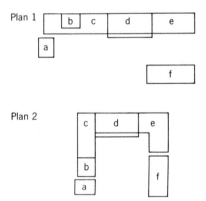

Figure 10.8 Suggested layouts in straight line and U-shape for pot washing, using a machine. Layouts may be reversed for flow from right to left. Carts may be drawn up to soak sink or to clean pot table during progress of work. Approximate equipment measurements:

 a. cart, 24 × 36 in (.60 × .92 m)
 b. soak sink, 24 × 30 in (.60 × .76 m)
 c. soiled pot table, 30 × 60 in (.76 × 1.52 m)
 d. machine, 36 × 60 in (.92 × 1.52 m)
 e. clean pot table, 30 × 66 in (.76 × 1.68 m)
 f. storage rack, 30 × 60 in (.76 × 1.52 m).

putting it through a disposal unit. Where screening and draining are done, it is well to have a removable drain basket of sufficient capacity for normal loads extending across the soiled pot table in front of the first sink. This will be convenient for handling swill garbage and will keep excess liquid from going into the garbage can.

The washing, rinsing, and sanitizing may be done by hand or by machine. In kitchens where there is a wide-belt conveyor-type dishwasher many of the kitchen trays, serving pans, and similar equipment may be washed in the dishwasher. Where pot-washing machines are used, the pots and pans move through compartments where they are subjected to a strong force of hot water pumped through high-pressure pumps. After their removal from the machines, it is necessary to have sufficient space where the pots may remain for air drying. Mechanical pot washers that operate in sinks are available also. Power-driven brushes may be used. In small kitchens the pot and pan sinks may be used for other purposes as well.

Equipment for the hand washing of pots consists of three-compartment sinks with a drainboard on one side for soiled pots and on the other for clean pots. Size of the drainboard for soiled pots will depend upon the collection method and whether a cart is used or pots are brought by hand, and also the number and size of pots that will be in the area at one time. The clean pots drainboard will be governed by size and number of pots to be dried by standing and the nearness of storage. The size of the sink compartments should permit handling of the largest pots to be washed in the sink and allow convenient reach and comfortable working position of workers. The size of roast pans, baking sheets, and mixer bowls may help guide sizing, except for very large mixer bowls on dollies that require washing without placing in the sink. A convenient floor drain is needed for the wash water from these extra-large objects.

The height of drainboards and sink top should be considered in relation to comfortable working height and in relationship to adjoining table surfaces. It is important for working comfort and for saving on hot water and detergent that sink compartments be no wider or deeper than required. Figure 10.9 illustrates posture positions of a worker 71 in. (1.80 m) tall working at a sink 38 in. (0.96 m) high and 28 in. (0.71 m) wide. The depth of pot sinks ranges from 12 to 16 in. (30 to 40 cm). A depth of 12 in. (30 cm) is usually adequate, and the worker can work with a more comfortable posture than at the deeper sink.

Work progresses best from left to right. The worker who is right-handed will hold the pot with the left hand and scrape or wash with the right. It is desirable to have an overhead spray centrally located and with sufficient extension to permit its use for flushing refuse from scraped

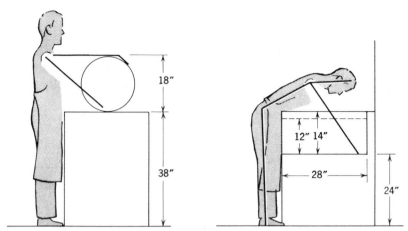

Figure 10.9   Posture positions of worker at pot sink.

pots as well as rinsing those that have been washed. In large departments where many heavy pots are handled a movable holding rack facilitates work. A track on which the rack can move can be formed by the front edge of the sink and the rim of a gutter extending along the back of the three compartments between the drainboards. The gutter and drainboards should have sufficient pitch for good drainage. The drains from the sinks and gutter areas should come together and flow to the grease trap and sewer.

Pot sinks may be wall mounted, leg mounted against the wall, or leg mounted and standing free in the open. It is sometimes desirable to have the sink in the open without splashbacks and with faucets centrally located so that workers may work from either side. Where the output of

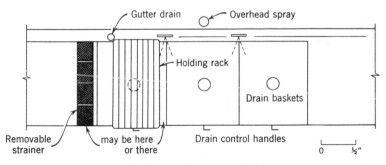

Figure 10.10   Suggested design for a pot sink.

a section is large enough to require two sets of sinks, they may be mounted back to back as a single unit. When placed next to a wall or other equipment, they should be installed to prevent vermin from lodging between the equipment and the wall or other equipment. This will require sealing in or setting away from another object. Mixing faucets preferably should be of the swinging type. Sanitation codes for the pot and pan washing section should be carefully followed.

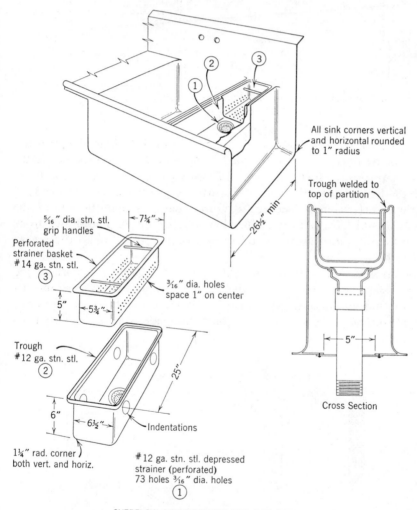

All sink corners vertical and horizontal rounded to 1" radius

Trough welded to top of partition

Cross Section

$\frac{5}{16}$" dia. stn. stl. grip handles

|←7¼"→|

Perforated strainer basket #14 ga. stn. stl.

③

5"

|←5¾"→|

$\frac{3}{16}$" dia. holes space 1" on center

Trough #12 ga. stn. stl.

②

6"

|←6½"→|

25"

26½" min

Indentations

1¼" rad. corner both vert. and horiz.

#12 ga. stn. stl. depressed strainer (perforated) 73 holes $\frac{3}{16}$" dia. holes

①

5"

OVERFLOW COMPARTMENT FOR POT SINKS

Figure 10.11 Detail of overflow compartment for pot sinks. (*Courtesy S. Blickman, Inc., Weehawken, N. J.*)

Plans for the pot and pan section include facilities for storage. They may consist of one large rack adjacent to the sinks, plus work section storage of small tools and equipment, or an adjacent rack for storage of less-used items and work section storage carts for the majority of utensils. Space allowance will need to be made appropriate to the system used. Mobile slatted or pipe constructed racks or carts are preferred to overhead or fixed shelves. Where hanging racks are used, such as those over the cook's tables, position them so that the point of grasp is approximately 6 ft (1.83 m) above the floor. Store utensils so that items can be readily seen and selected without having to move a stack in order to get an item required. Store in relation to use, such as roasting pans near the cook's table and ovens, serving equipment handy to the dish-up area, and the pie pans, baking sheets, and cake pans where they are most likely to be filled.

GENERAL KITCHEN HOUSEKEEPING

Essential care and cleaning of major equipment and surfaces in the kitchen can be facilitated through careful selection of design and materials. High, black, overhead hoods supply an example. One may be selected that is fairly self-cleaning or has filters that can be easily removed and put through the dishwasher. Adequate light is important to display surfaces for cleaning. Ease of dismantling equipment for cleaning can promote equipment use as well as good sanitation practice. Workers avoid using equipment that does not save time and effort in proportion to that required for cleaning after using. Grinders, choppers, and peelers often fall into this category.

The following are typical points relating to material and structural features that will influence housekeeping care:

1. Durable, easy to clean, smooth surfaces, rounded corners or junctures, free from pits and crevices or other lodging spots for soil

2. Adjustable, pear-shaped, round, or ball feet that permit leveling of equipment and will not catch mop cords.

3. Removable drawers and bins that may be cleaned in the dishwasher or sink.

4. Coved bases to eliminate legs and to enclose pipes for easier floor care.

5. Floor and wall materials or finishes that are durable and non-absorbent.

6. Drains in sufficient number and located in areas where most needed, such as in dishwashing, pot washing, cooking, refrigerator, and vegetable preparation areas. Spillage is most likely in such areas.

7. Mop sink and hose connection located for convenient flushing or filling.

8. General storage and refrigerator shelving that is sturdy, cleanable, and removable.

9. Equipment that can be easily dismantled and reassembled for thorough cleaning, such as
    a. Meat saws and slicers.
    b. Food grinders and cutters.
    c. Oven and steam cooker shelves.
    d. Range and broiler burners, grease pans, and shelves.
    e. Potato peeler plate and peeling trap
    f. Milk shake equipment.

10. Floor drain covers and catch basins that can be opened up for cleaning.

11. Cutting boards and equipment handles that are nonabsorbent and can be sanitized with water at a high temperature.

12. Shelving and condiment containers must be easy to reach and easy to clean. This is frequently a neglected, heterogenous, unsightly area. Small, removable buns with smooth, rounded surfaces located in high-shelf position are desirable.

TRUCK WASHING

Kitchen carts, dish storage units, and other mobile food handling equipment should be regularly washed to ensure satisfactory sanitation. The cleaning of such items is easiest if special provision is made for scrubbing and rinsing with a strong spray in an area where the water will be confined. This means having an area where there is space enough to work around the equipment. Hot and cold water with a hose connection that has a squeeze valve will be needed. A long -handled or irrigated brush is desirable. The area should have good floor drainage and splashproof walls. It is well to locate the section near that of dishwashing or pot washing, if possible. Carts used for soiled items are frequently used for return of clean ones and should be washed between uses.

GARBAGE DISPOSAL AND CAN WASHING

Food service refuse consists of swill garbage, paper, glass jars, wood crates, and tin cans. The bulk for disposal can be greatly reduced by mechanical means, such as disposal units, incinerators, and compacters. Incinerator installation should closely follow fire codes and be based on professional advice. The largest quantities of swill garbage usually originate in dishwashing, vegetable preparation, pot washing, and cooking in normal order from greatest to least. The largest amount of paper waste comes from the serving section and the bake shop. Certain egg, fruit, and vegetable crates, glass jars, and metal drums are salable or returnable to vendors. Storage space is required until they are picked up.

Cans can be washed by hand or by mechanical means. In hand washing the refuse adhering to the can is hosed off with cold water; the can is then scrubbed with a brush and hosed with hot water that is a mixture of cold water and steam. The hose should be equipped with a vacuum-breaker steam hose mounted 54 in. (1.37 m) above the floor and should have a squeeze valve. Cans may be laid in a trough, longer and deeper than the can, during cleaning. Cans cleaned mechanically may be inverted over a shallow bowllike support 16 in. (41 cm) high and subjected first to the cold water flushing and then to hot water, steam wash, and sterilizing. The outside of the can should be manually washed and rinsed. Another type of washer is a cabinet into which the cans are placed, completely enclosed, and washed inside and outside with water and steam. Doorjams to can washing areas should be of steel and the doors and walls bumpered.

Figure 10.12 Can washer and can storage rack. (*Courtesy* Institutions Magazine, *Chicago, Ill.*)

Excellent floor drainage in this area is essential. The walls and floor should be of tile or concrete and constructed for easy, thorough cleaning. A metal pipe rack should be provided on which cans may be inverted for drainage and airing. The rack should be of sufficient size to permit storage of cans until they are needed.

Volume and type of refuse, frequency of pickup, and climatic conditions will influence decisions relating to the best way of handling garbage. Included in considerations will be various means of reducing volume, refrigeration, and prevention of rodent attraction. Food garbage may be ground and flushed into the sewer by means of disposal units that are available in varying capacity and horsepower for grinding. The manufacturer's instructions for plumbing should be carefully followed. Difficulty may result if the drainage lines have insufficient drop and if machines are heavily fed with material that has a tendency to mat, such as paper and potato peelings.

Where a refrigerated room is provided, the temperature should be kept at approximately 50° F (10° C). Garbage readily attracts rodents and vermin. Not only must it be kept tightly closed and in a carefully screened or enclosed area, but the surrounding building and landscape should be such as to prevent vermin lodging. Garbage odors will attract them to the area. Loose piles of wood or rockeries provide rats and mice with nesting spots from which they can slip into food areas whenever doors are opened.

JANITOR AREA

The janitor's area will include space for (1) storage of replacement supplies, (2) storage of cleaning equipment, and (3) a place for filling and emptying the mop truck, with (4) a place nearby where mops may be hung for airing. This area must have (5) a sink for washing mops and cloths or sponges used in cleaning. The size required for the storage areas will depend upon the equipment needed for care of the facility and the policy concerning amount of supplies carried in stock and/or issued at one time. The janitor may or may not be responsible for replacement supplies of tableware, utensils, and similar items. Cleaning supplies commonly stored include cleaning agents, brushes, brooms, mops, light bulbs, vacuum cleaner, waxer and polisher, and stepladder.

The most suitable place for filling, emptying, and cleaning the mop truck is in the can washing area, which is well equipped for this need. Provision for storage nearby would be desirable. Mops will require good air circulation of dry air, and should be hung elsewhere than in the humid can washing room. The location of the storage room should be adjacent to the kitchen or dining room, where it will be most convenient for repeated trips to get replacement supplies or equipment.

The mop sink may be an 8 in. (20 cm) deep, coved 18 to 24 in. (46 to 61 cm) square part of the tile door. The floor is usually sloped slightly to it. A good drain with removable strainer is necessary, and a mixing faucet that will permit hose attachment should be provided.

Suggested Student Assignment

Observe and note the following in three food facilities, and state the housekeeping care given to each:

1. Floor material. Is a covering used? If so, state kind.

2. Material of wall finish.

3. Is an acoustical treatment used? If so state kind.

4. Dishes and flatware.

5. Material and finish of chairs and tables and other furnishings (state kind).

6. Ventilation type and material.

7. Are floor mats used? If so, state location.

8. Kind and amount of mobile equipment used.

9. Number and kind of scales used. State section where located.

10. Dishwashing and pot washing equipment.

11. Floor drains—number and location.

12. Shelving for utensils, refrigerators, dry stores—material, measurements, adequacy.

13. Sinks and worktables—material, design, and measurements. Give size and depth of sink compartments.

14. Facilities for garbage removal and can washing.

15. Kind and location of housekeeping equipment and cleaning materials. Evaluate the condition of each of the above items on the basis of

    1. Condition of wear.
    2. Appearance.
    3. Adequacy and convenience.
    4. Sanitation and safety.
    5. Appropriateness to use.

Make recommendations that you believe would improve conditions, with reasons for the recommendations.

Chapter 11

management office and facilities for employees and guests

Management of a food facility involves planning; maintaining records of many aspects of operation; interviewing personnel, tradesmen, and the public; performing such business operations as placing orders, keeping records, calculating payrolls, handling cash, and paying accounts; training, supervising, and instructing staff; and observing and directing operations. Performance of these management functions calls for an office area that is suitably located and adequately equipped. In a small facility the functions may be simplified so that one individual can cope with them. In a large operation each of the aspects of the operation may have sufficient magnitude to require separation into departments. Regardless of size, omission of a suitable place for the functions of management may ultimately be very expensive for the organization. The office is an important work section that should be planned in relationship to the food operation, even if it includes little more than a shelf and a desk.

Criteria based on functions to be performed, which may serve as a guide, include the following:

1. *Proximity* for continual awareness and ease of supervision in specific areas of responsibility. Convenient location can promote better control and utilization of management time and effort. Just as in driving on the highway, the person at the wheel must know direction, observe obstacles, and guide action. A manager needs to know what is happening and give timely instructions. Lack of awareness tends to result when a manager becomes absorbed with office activities in a remotely located office.

2. Ready *visibility* of areas to be supervised can save many steps in keeping aware of work progress. There are many times when office functions can be performed if things are able to be seen as progressing well in the various work sections.

3. *Accessibility,* through location of the office, is valuable for business contacts with personnel, tradesmen, patrons, and person seeking information or service. Where reasonably possible the office should have direct entry from public areas as well as close relationship with food sections. The public should not have to go through the kitchen to reach the office.

4. *Privacy* should be sufficient for carrying on business operations or counseling that are of a confidential nature.

5. *Adequacy.* The office should have enough space, be comfortable, and be equipped for efficient work. Many of the office activities require concentration for doing accurate work with reasonable speed. Freedom from needless distractions helps to save time and assure good results. Good light is essential. Proper ventilation and heat are necessary for health and comfort. Best economy calls for providing those items of equipment needed in performing essential functions with accuracy, speed, and convenience.

Food operations are characterized by variety. Many significant differences are true of management in terms of training background, standards and method of operation, relationship to ownership or those in authority, extent of responsibility, and specific preparation for the duties to be performed. Where there is one office for the food department, it is not unusual to find it next to a superintendent's office, representing a business operation or as a part of an accounting office for ease in recording, approving, and paying accounts or tucked away in a storeroom where the manager can stand guard on supplies, instead of being close to the most significant area of action, that of production and service of food. The choice of the office site should be at that point that gives the most effective control over responsibilities for which the specific office personnel are responsible.

Where it is not possible to select a location that affords a view of all areas for which management may be responsible, it is wise to choose nearness to those having major significance. The basis for choosing needs should be in terms of major values to be protected, such as quality of products, cost of labor and materials, service quality, patron satisfaction, and counseling services. Supervisory observation can often supply the "stitch in time" that guards utilization of labor and materials and ensures the use of approved techniques that may spell the difference between success and failure of the operation. "Merchandise for sale" calls for protection from the time that supplies enter the facility and are processed until the time that patrons' needs are served.

A peak period calling for close supervision is the time when food is being served. The tempo of activities increases, more personnel are actively supplying orders, distractions are numerous, and the food qualities that have been carefully created are during service at their highest and most fragile point. Supplying qualities of gracious service and regulating portions may mean gain or loss for the food operation. Alert supervision may prevent accidents that injure persons, waste food, destroy serving equipment, and impair the quality of service or food.

Food managers commonly carry numerous and varied responsibilities, some of which call for desk work and others observation or checking of work progress. It is well for a kitchen supervisor to know throughout the day what is happening. A view of the area where workers check in or out aids control and adds convenience in getting records for calculation of payroll. Entrances for receiving and storing within office view may promote receipt of goods by the authorized agent and instruction of

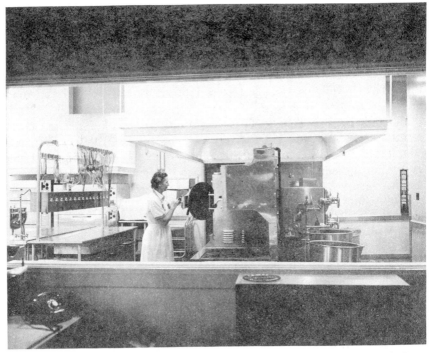

Figure 11.1 Production areas are readily viewed from this office window. (*Courtesy University of Washington, Seattle.*)

delivery men as to the location where material is to be placed. This can prevent error and save time and effort. A view of production sections may help to ensure proper procedures being followed and give assurance that foods are being prepared on schedule. The view of the various areas may be through a window or an open door.

There are numerous occasions in the operation of a food business when it is desirable to have private conferences. Typical of these situations are hiring, correcting, or counseling employees; discussing purchases with salesmen; discussing food or catering plans with patrons; and conferring about problems or complaints that may have arisen. Information overheard and half understood may be broadcast so as to be harmful. If conversations are within the hearing of workers who stop to listen, they may cause work delays.

The office, like other work sections, should be equipped for quick, easy, efficient performance of necessary functions. Work requiring mental concentration is usually done most efficiently when there is reasonable

freedom from distractions. An office for the routine checking of performance can be in the midst of activity, but where planning and mathe-
matical calculations are done the office workers should be protected
from needless disturbance. The size of the facility and the type of activities required will govern whether a table and shelf of books and records
will suffice or whether the office should be separately enclosed and more
fully equipped.

Management functions in large organizations are likely to be depart-
mentalized. The buyer will hold buying conferences, receive and check
samples, place orders, and send copies of orders to a receiving clerk and
an accounting department. Suitable space is needed for conferences and
for salesmen to sit while waiting. Equipment should be available for
cutting and testing samples. This may be done in a kitchenette adjacent
to the office or in the main kitchen.

The receiving clerk or storekeeper will need a desk or office area for
instructions and records near the receiving dock or storage area. Supplies
will be checked in and approved on the basis of the orders placed. The
order lists when received and the delivery slips or invoices will then be
sent to the accounting department with acknowledgement for payment.

The accounting department may be responsible for record keeping
and accounting. This activity will involve training and supervision of
cashiers; receiving, counting, and depositing cash; preparation of payrolls; and drawing checks for payment of payrolls and accounts. Suitable
computing equipment will promote accuracy and time saving. A safe
should be provided for cash and costly items requiring protection. It
should be heavy enough or so placed that it cannot be easily removed.

The employment officer, like the buyer, will have numerous conferences. If offices are adjacent, a common room may be used by those
waiting for an interview. The equipment can be simple. If training is a
responsibility of this department, an area for group meetings may be
needed.

Functions covered by many foodservice operations vary widely, and
special office facilities may be needed in terms of the specialized responsibilities. In hospitals, it is desirable that the chief dietitian's and the
therapeutic dietitians' offices be located near other administrative offices
for convenient consultation with the medical staff and exchange of information with other administrative departments. The office of the production dietitian should be adjacent to the production and service departments. An outpatient dietitian consults with and instructs patients
who are not in the hospital, and the office should be easily accessible
from the street. A close relationship with other members of the dietary
department is usually not necessary. Equipment will be needed for sim-

ple food demonstrations. Floor and ward dietitians who are responsible for individual needs of hospital patients may need an office in their respective areas. An efficient communication system is needed between offices and the main production and serving area.

The dietary department staff is frequently responsible for instruction in nutrition and diet therapy for dietetic interns, medical interns, nurses, and patients. The size and nature of the group will govern needs for space and equipment. It is a time-saving convenience for the classroom to be near the office.

The manager of catering and room service in hotels requires an office that is easily accessible to patrons and that is frequently near the main lobby. Good communication between patrons and this office and between the office and the kitchen is essential. The office should be equipped for planning, interviewing, recording, filing, and billing. It is desirable, where possible, for the office to be close to the special service areas.

All offices should have sufficient electrical outlets for attaching computers, lights, fans, typewriters, and other equipment likely to be used. The footcandles of light supplied should be appropriate for the amount of detailed work to be done (20 to 50 footcandles). Temperature controls and good ventilation are important for comfort and well-being and should be given special attention for small or crowded office areas. Acoustical treatment should be provided to muffle excess noise. Where several persons occupy one office, the noise of business machines, phones, and voices in conference may cause distractions that interfere with work. Valuable records and miscellaneous office supplies require appropriate storage. The office, like a well-designed tool, should satisfy significant functions and be a pleasure to use.

GUEST FACILITIES

The entrance to a dining room, the waiting area, and the facilities provided for guests create a lasting impression. The adequacy, cleanliness, and attractiveness that patrons view upon entering has an influence on their enjoyment of food served. The entrance should be easy to find and inviting in appearance. The doors for entrance and exit should be placed so as to prevent accidents between those entering and leaving. A waiting area should be provided that will accommodate the number who will be likely to arrive ahead of time, during a peak period when the dining room is filled, or who may wish to wait for a friend. The area should be comfortable and attractive and make patrons feel that they are in line for service. Coat, parcel, and umbrella storage should be provided where it can be readily seen and supervised either by management or the patrons. In college food units, students are likely to arrive for meals with books, supplies, and coats for which cloakroom storage will be required. The dining room entrance in residence halls should be from a hall or vestibule rather than from the lounge to lessen excess wear through the lounge.

Use of a telephone is frequently requested by patrons, and a paging system may be needed also. It is better to have a conveniently placed public telephone for patron use than to have business phones tied up by patron calls. A booth or location that will provide reasonable privacy for calls will be desirable. The location should be where it is convenient for the patron and where the calls will not disturb office workers or the cashier.

Toilet rooms should be provided for women and men. Locate these, if possible, adjacent or convenient to the waiting area. Attractive housekeeping and good sanitation is important for patron comfort and for creating a favorable impression of the food establishment.

EMPLOYEE FACILITIES

The type of locker room, toilet, lounge, and dining facility provided for employees tends to express management's respect for personnel standards and the dignity of workers. Good standards can do much to create goodwill and promote good health and sanitation practices. Toilet, locker, and dressing rooms that are bright, clean, and cheerful help to set the right note with workers who are instructed to create good standards in food production and service. It is to be remembered that the personal habits of personnel handling food is one of the strongest single factors in food safety and sanitation.

The employee entrance to dressing rooms should be convenient from the street and, if possible, observable from the office. Workers should not have to go through the kitchen work areas or the dining room in order to reach their dressing room. The time clock and instruction board should be located on the path that workers take from dressing room to work sections. Supervision of workers as they come on duty is desirable, and the time clock should be near and within view of the office.

When toilets are remote from work areas, busy workers tend to neglect good health practice and lazy workers use remoteness as an excuse for not being at work. Location adjacent to work areas is desirable and permits easy supervision. Toilets should be separated from all food areas by a hall or double entrance. Building codes often specify type and amount of fixtures to be furnished. Usually one toilet stool is provided for each twelve to fifteen employees and a lavatory for every eight to ten persons. In men's toilets a urinal is provided for each twelve to fifteen men. Toilet stalls should be enclosed by doors. Knee or foot-action flushing controls are recommended. The double entry doors to toilet rooms should be self-closing.

Suitable safety should be provided for employees' personal possessions while they are at work. It is an unsanitary practice for purses or other personal possessions to be carried and stored in work sections, and worry over their safety can interfere with work. Lockers may be large enough for clothing on hangers or of a small size appropriate for purses and and packages. The place where clothing is hung, whether for individuals or a group, should be long, deep, and wide enough for the clothing to hang without crowding. Proper sanitation requires that street clothing and uniforms be hung in separate compartments.

The appearance of the locker section is attractive when sealed in as a part of the wall. Where this is not possible, the lockers should have a slanted top that prevents unsightly clutter and dust collection. An enclosed base improves appearance and makes cleaning easier.

Allow ample dressing space and benches or chairs on which workers may sit when changing clothing. A cot or day bed should be furnished for women workers. Unless there are broken shifts, lounge facilities may be restricted to the dining area. Loafing and congregation in the dressing and toilet areas should be discouraged. Promote good grooming by having adequate light and good mirrors. A full-length mirror will be an effective reminder if placed where the employees can note personal appearance before leaving the dressing rooms. A mirror and cosmetic shelf can be used by more people if placed at one side of the lavatories where it can be used by individuals while others are washing their hands.

Shower equipment may not be practical on the basis of amount of use. Specific working conditions, kind of work, and the class of employees will influence the extent of use. Where ventilation is poor and the temperature and humidity high in work areas, showers will be especially appreciated. Employees from poor residence areas may not have convenient access to bath facilities. Some managers require employees to take a shower before dressing in uniforms. Showers in dressing rooms can help to ensure good standards of personal cleanliness of food workers.

Clean hands are essential in sanitary food handling. Production and service employees must often handle unsanitary objects as well as food in the normal course of their work. The objects may be as common as a food crate or parcel, a door knob, or a personal handkerchief. Therefore, lavatories need to be located in sufficient number and in convenient relationship to all food handling areas in order to promote sanitary food handling. The need is especially acute where there are large numbers of temporary employees (as in college food units) who arrive for work in street jackets which they quickly shed for waiters' coats and tend to go on duty without washing their hands. Hand washing over sinks used for food should not be permitted.

A work section in which there is strong likelihood of inadequate hand washing is dishwashing. Employees often scrape dirty dishes, fill baskets, then go directly to the clean dish table and handle clean dishes without washing their hands. This tends to happen most often where the unit is too small to employ separate individuals for the different activities. Prevention of this kind of contamination calls for a conveniently placed hand washing facility. Time loss and ignoring of proper practice result when the lavatory is inconveniently or remotely located.

Encourage the use of soap through supplying a suitable dispenser and a mild odorless soap. In addition to a paper towel dispenser, also provide a paper cup dispenser so that workers may get a drink of water when they wish. A bubbler fountain may be used if preferred.

It is valuable to foster friendly relationships in an employee group. Pride in belonging to the group, cooperation with each other on the job, understanding and liking that discourage turnover, and many other values may grow out of pleasantly dining together. An appropriate dining area can be one of the very important facilities for employees. It should promote rest, relaxation, and enjoyment during meals and coffee breaks. It may be a special room or a section of the main dining area. Although the furnishings in a special room may be simple, the room should be bright, cheerful, and homelike. Where space is limited, crowding may be prevented through the scheduling of meal periods. Good morale and restful dining are not likely to result when workers are required to dine alone or in a public dining room wearing uniforms that bear traces of their activities.

Employee instruction boards may vary in size, shape, use, and placement. The "general interest" bulletin board is often a framed cork board. Boards with removable letters or sections, as for menu boards, may be used effectively in production and serving sections for stating portion sizes. Permanent instructions, such as those for operating major equipment, may be framed under glass or glued to the wall and lacquered for waterproofing. These should be located near the equipment and in a position where they are easy to read. Avoid a clutter of material on bulletin boards or walls. Items that are too numerous in number or remain too long in one position tend to be ignored. Therefore they are worthless and create an unattractive appearance. If only recent and significant information is supplied in this way, the workers will give it more careful attention. Instructions supplied in this manner should be brief, adequate, clear, readily seen, up-to-date, and meaningful.

Suggested Student Assignments

1. Observe office facilities in three different types of food operations, such as a school, commercial, hospital, or industrial food department, and enumerate the specific management activities performed.

2. List all of the office equipment in each, and state the location of the office in relation to the food department.

3. List all staff members, areas of responsibility, hours on duty, time spent in the office, and duty-time spent elsewhere (state where spent).

4. Indicate how much of the office space and equipment are utilized during parts of the day by more than one staff member (state approximately how long).

5. Evaluate adequacy and suitability of space, location, and equipment. Recommend changes that you believe would be advantageous. (Find out probable cost.)

6. Describe guest facilities in three public eating places, and give your evaluation of them on the basis of convenient location, adequacy, and appeal.

7. What employee facilities are provided in the food facilities that you chose for analysis (under point 3)?

8. Plan a layout for an office and for employee facilities, and describe their location in relation to work sections.

9. Prepare specifications for the equipment shown in the office and employee facility plans.

Section 3

supporting factors and physical conditions

Chapter 12

energy

Well-made equipment of excellent value can be useless until it is properly "hooked up" to the correct energy source. The important connection may be power, water, steam, or proper surroundings. The factors involved may require a knowledge of engineering which some members of a planning team may lack, although they have essential information relating to needs. Engineers and others competent to work in these areas must be given statements of requirements so they can provide the necessary information. Team members who know operational or other requirements must work with the engineers to see that adequate standards are met.

It is not necessary for team members who lack engineering or mechanical backgrounds to become expert in this knowledge, but they should know how to communicate needs in a language that will be understood and not misinterpreted by the engineers and specialists. An engineer told to provide a minimum of 50 foot-candles of light on a work surface will understand the exact requirement. If told to provide enough light to see well, the amount of light provided may depend upon his sight and his judgment. Team members, lacking engineering knowledge, can better appreciate why engineers or specialists set up specific requirements if they know some of the technicalities involved. These team members should make themselves competent enough to work well with engineers and architects in securing the best possible plans.

The energy shortage has aroused awareness of utilizing energy more fully and preventing its waste. It has often been used carelessly in the past due to its low cost. It has been cheap compared with human effort. A kilowatt of electricity does the same work as thirty men in climbing the stairs of the Washington Monument. Many times heat, light, power, ventilation, air conditioning, heating, and humidity control have been over-provided just to be sure of there being enough. Prevention of such costly waste in the future may be forced by high cost or government regulation. A more satisfactory method of control can result through an accurate definition of needs with suitable provision for meeting them.

A knowledge of what energy is and how it works can help toward its conservation and the maximizing of its use. It is well for planners to know (1) types of available energy, (2) which one is most suited for a particular need, (3) how much is required to achieve desired results, (4) alternative ways of achieving the same results, (5) cost, and (6) when proper standards in energy use are met. To supplement or review information about energy some of the significant aspects are presented here in this section.

Energy and Its Sources

Energy is a force capable of exerting power. Some call it "power in action." Aristotle coined the word "energy" from two Greek words: *en* meaning at and *ergon* meaning work. Energy comes in many forms, and one form can be converted to another. Energy is like matter. It is indestructible, but it can be lost by becoming energy that is not used. Only about 60 percent of the energy used may result in power in an electrical motor. The rest is wasted heat or other energy form.

The main source of the earth's energy came from the sun many millions of years ago, but not directly as energy. Through a process of photosynthesis, the sun's energy was fixed in living earth substances containing carbon, hydrogen, and oxygen. This was then stored largely as coal, oil, and gas. This captured energy can today be released from these fuels by a process called "combustion." It is estimated that enough fossil fuels remain, at present usage rates, to last about 1000 years. Other forms of energy must be used then, or we will go without. Critical shortages in some fuels are now appearing. Gas reserves in this country, for instance, are said to be sufficient for only 40 years.

Direct solar energy may in the future be more fully used in meeting energy needs. Ways still need to be devised for storing massive daytime amounts to last until the next sunrise. Present technology is not capable of creating small, efficient photoelectric plants. Provision of all the electricity required in this country would call for plants covering an area greater than Massachusetts and Vermont. Energy from the warmth of the sun carried in sea water may in the future be concentrated to operate electrical plants. Or the energy in the waves of the wind, sea or tides may be harnessed and turned into electricty.

Energy from atomic fission or fusion presently appears probable but this is limited to nuclear substances stored in the earth. At the present time almost as much energy is used as an atomic plant creates. Until ways are found to produce ore and utilize its radiating power more efficiently, atomic energy will be extremely costly to produce. Water power still has potential, but even if all available were used, it would be insufficient. Time will be required to solve the energy problem, and it is important that planners and users call for minimum amounts needed and make the maximum utilization of the amount employed.

What energy is puzzles scientists. When the atom was shattered, a whole new science of physics opened up and a new science called "quantum physics" had to be developed to explain what had happened. The old Newtonian physics that explained matter, power, and energy in a more gross sense was no longer adequate to explain what happened to the very tiny fragments now being discovered. At this point, it seems that energy and matter are much the same thing, except that energy is matter on the move. Electrons are matter, but when moving they are electricity. Recently scientists froze electricity! Einstein's formula $E = mc^2$ (energy equals matter times the speed of light squared) means that a very tiny piece of matter contains a tremendous amount of power—the speed of light is 186,300 miles per second, which squared is over 353 billion.

The sun is constantly creating energy by a process of atomic fusion in which hydrogen is merging into helium. This is largely the source of the energy it sends out. Every day the sun radiates out tons of its mass as energy. At the rate it does this, it will do it for over a billion years. Although only one part in 120 million of the sun's energy reaches its planets, the amount received by the earth alone in 5 hours is more energy than is locked in the earth in its fossil fuels. The problem, as was noted, is in capturing this energy. Today, the earth probably uses only 3 to 5 percent of all it receives. The remainder radiates back into outer space. Our national problem of energy is not a small one and raises a challenge to every person to use it wisely.

ELECTRICITY

Electrons are tiny particles of matter. They are substances that form the outer shell around the nucleus of an atom. There also are tremendous numbers of free electrons in the air and in the earth. They move about pretty much in a random fashion, but if they can be gathered together in countless billions and directed along a path, they can exert tremendous power. Moving as a mass, they become an electrical current.

The flow of electrons as an electrical current can be compared to the flow of a stream of water. It can exert force. The larger the stream the more force is exerted. The greater the pressure behind the stream, the greater the force. Thus a stream of water flowing down rapids or over a waterfall has more power than the same quantity of water moving through a meadow. Resistance against the flow of electricity creates energy such as heat. A stream rushing over rocks creates heat even though one may not realize this. Unlike a stream of water, electricity has magnetic power, and this can be utilized to run a motor or do other useful things.

Electrical Measurement

The amount of electricity or water in a current can be measured. Water flowing through a pipe can be measured by the gallons (or liters) per minute that flow from the pipe. Electricity can be quantified by measuring the number of electrons that flow by a given point per second. If 6,242,800,000,000,000,000 electrons go by in a second, this is one ampere (amp or I) of electricity.

Water force is measured in pounds per square inch (psi) while the force behind electricity is measured in volts (v). A volt is the force required to push 1 amp of electricity by a given point in a second. The amount of power in electricity is stated in watts (w). The number of watts is equal to the force behind the flow (v) times the amount flowing (I) or $w = v \times I$. It follows that if $w = v \times I$, $I = w/v$ and $v = w/I$. Such formulas are helpful in establishing data for planning electrical requirements. Thus if it is found that 1,500 w of electricity will be used by one electric light circuit and the voltage is 120 v, the amperage carried will be 12½ I, which would mean the circuit should be fused for at least 15 amps and perhaps more since a circuit should have a 25 percent safety factor. It should be noted that if the voltage increases, the amperage decreases. For instance, if the 1,500-w requirement were on a 208-v line, the amperage required would be $1,500/208 = 7.2$. Often in planning circuits, electricity is carried in main lines at higher voltages, and then the voltage is reduced for the branch circuits or at the using point. This saves on wire size, amperage, and also on a loss of power in transmitting the electricity to the using area.

The price of electricity is often calculated on the amount used per hour. A watt-hour (wh) is a watt flowing steadily for an hour. A kilowatt-hour (kwh) is 1,000 w flowing steadily for an hour. In 1970 the Edison Electric Institute indicated electricity cost large industrial users an average of 1.66¢/kwh, small commercial users 2.12/kwh, and residential users 2.13¢/kwh.

For some industrial users the price of electricity is based on the amount used plus a maximum demand charge or in some cases on just a maximum demand charge. The maximum demand is based on the highest quantity of electricity used at any one specific point of time. This is usually in the daytime for foodservices. If maximum demand can be reduced, electrical costs can be reduced. Therefore some attention should be given in planning heating water, baking items, and so forth when the use of electricity is lighter. This may reduce the maximum demand.

Grounding Equipment and Systems

Electrons in electricity carry a negative charge. A positive charge has a terrific attraction to them, and they will be pulled toward it. When the negative electrons arrive at a positive body, they are neutralized and they become at rest locked to the positive charge. In other words, they are "grounded." However, as long as there are negative electrons and a positive force exists to attract them, they will flow toward this positive body. A battery has a body with a large number of negative electrons in it and another with a large number of positive charges in it. When a wire connection is made between the two bodies, the negative electrons flow to the positive side. This flow has power to do work such as light a globe or start an automobile. When a battery is "dead," there are no more positive charges or negative electrons to create the electrical flow. To recharge a battery, the current flow is reversed so it can start all over again.

An electrical current can flow in a direction not desired. This may be called a "short" because the flow path is shortened. An exposed wire can be touched causing a short which gives an individual a heavy shock; even death can result from shorts. Sometimes in equipment, electricity becomes free and does not flow where it should. Again there is danger of shock. Or the equipment may be damaged. For these reasons, electrical systems and equipment are frequently "grounded." To do this, a wire leading to a ground is set up. It conducts a charge only when electricity is free. The ground may be a water pipe, a copper rod buried deep in the ground, or some other device that will attract the free electricity. Grounding reduces the danger of shock and other hazards from electricity. Some systems may be given a ground wire that is colored green and runs to a secure ground. Three-pronged plugs usually indicate that one is a ground.

Conductors and Nonconductors

Silver, gold, platinum, copper, aluminum, and some other metals conduct electricity. Some conduct it more readily than others. Silver is the best conductor, whereas aluminum is about half as good a conductor as silver. The others are closer to silver than to aluminum in conductivity. Because of cost, the best conductors are not used except for special purposes. Copper is a good conductor and less expensive and is extensively used. Because aluminum is light and low in cost compared with the others, it is often used, especially in heavy wires. By using an aluminum No. 4 wire (0.2 in. in diameter), the same amount of electricity can be carried with the same amount of resistance as carried in a No. 6-size copper wire (0.16 in. in diameter).[1] (The lower the number of the wire, the larger the size in American Wire Gauge sizes). The

---

[1] Aluminum wiring has been known to cause 2 million home fires because of undersized wiring and installation. The federal commission for Consumer Product Safety has voted to develop mandatory safety standards for aluminum wiring and electrical devices. (*Seattle Post-Intelligencer*, August 9, 1975.)

greater the resistance of the conductor, the larger it must be to carry the same quantity of electricity with no increase in resistance to the flow.

Some substances will carry almost no electrical current. These are called nonconductors or insulators. Thus plastic or rubber may be wrapped around electrical wire to keep the flow of electricity where it should be. Glass, wood, and a wide number of other substances are used as insulators.

Resistance and Ohms

When resistance (R) is set up against the flow of electricity, heat is formed. Nickle, chromium, and their alloys resist the flow of electricity but also can rise to considerable temperatures before they melt. For this reason they make good heating elements. Thus when a chromolux, nichrome, or other heating element is attached to a good electrical conductor and a current is run through both, the electricity flows readily through the conductor, but when it reaches the element it is blocked and the resistance creates a large quantity of heat that may become so great that the element has a red glow or almost white glow to it.

The development of heat may be desirable in an element, but in a motor or electric wire heat may become so intense that the motor "burns out" or the wire becomes so hot it starts a fire. R increases as temperature does and therefore as a motor or wire heats up, resistance becomes greater. It takes 10 to 15 times as much electricity to create in a cold tungsten filament as much light as it creates when it is hot. Wires that become warm when electricity flows through them are undersized and a loss of power results as well as the danger of overheating.

R is measured in ohms. One ohm equals 1 amperage at 1 volt and R (ohms) = v/I. An element drawing 8.7 amps on a 115-v circuit has an R of 13.2 ohms (115/8.7 = 13.2). It follows that I = v/R and v = IR. This information is also of value in planning electrical requirements, and those concerned with planning should know what they mean and how they are used.[2] The amount of power or electrical energy used also can be ascertained if I and R are known because $w = I^2R$. Thus an element using 115 v at 8.7 I would require 1000 wh (115 × 8.7 = 1000.5). The same result may be obtained using $(8.7)^2$ × 13.2 (75.7 × 13.2 = 999.1).

Planners may sometimes hear the term "impedance" used instead of "resistance." Impedance is used to indicate resistance when AC (alternating current) is used.

[2] For example, if in checking a plan a circuit using 2000 w at 120 v was set for fusing at 15 amperes, an error in calculating requirements could quickly be shown by using the formula I = w/v, which would show 2000/120 = 16½ amperes + 25 percent safety factor or about 20 amperes required.

Circuits

When electricity starts out from an electric panel to give power, heat, or light to equipment, the wiring returns to the panel, completing what is called a "circuit." When a circuit is "open" no current flows because the connection at some point in the circuit is "broken." When a circuit is "closed," electricity is free to flow. A "short circuit" occurs when the circuit planned is shortened by a break in the wire or for some other reason. Short circuits can result in fires or do other damage or harm.

A panel box receives electricity from the *main* circuit and distributes it over *branch* circuits. The branches carry the electricity to the point where it is used. Panel boxes are equipped with *fuses* or *circuit breakers* that stop an overload of electricity from flowing into a circuit. Such an overload could cause a fire, or do damage to the equipment. A fuse is a device that has a wire thread that melts when a current over a specified amount flows through it. A circuit breaker trips open if an excessive quantity of electricity flows through it either because of the development of heat or because magnetic forces act to trip it.

The voltages and the number of circuits needed will dictate the size of the panel box. Sometimes supplemental panel boxes are installed after the main panel. In this case, higher voltages are run from the main panel to the supplemental panel where the voltages are broken down to those desired. The maximum temperature around a panel should be 90°F (32.2° C). Higher temperatures may cause malfunctioning or even cause breakers to trip. It is recommended panels have disconnect switches on the power side so electricity can be cut off in the panel in case of emergency. It may be desirable also to have disconnect switches that turn off special circuits in an emergency, leaving others on. Panels should be located where they can be quickly and easily reached. If locked, keys should be available in a secure place nearby. An electric meter is usually installed just before the main panel that measures the electrical flow from the company's lines. The reading on such a meter is usually in kwh and is the basis for charges for current used, as noted, the charge may be based on peak consumption or a combination of both.

Electrical Currents

Electricity may flow as a direct current (DC) or as an alternating current (AC). When the current flows evenly in one direction, it is DC. AC flows with an alternating pulse between a positive and negative flow which causes the current to alternate in its direction. It pulses back and forth. DC can be transmitted only about 20 to 30 miles. After this, the

R or friction from conductors drops the voltage force (potential) to a point at which the current is too weak to be very useful. Because AC can be stepped up to extremely high voltage by *transformers*, it can be given terrific force for transmission so AC current can be transferred easily up to 300 or more miles. If the voltage should drop, it can be run again through a transformer and the voltage increased for further transmission. When AC reaches its destination, transformers can then step down the voltage to the levels desired.

A *generator* of electricity called an "alternator" creates AC. A generator works by sweeping up masses of electrons out of a magnetic field, sending them on their way as an electric current. Most alternators revolve 3600 times per minute. This sets up 60 alternating pulses per second called "cycles" (c) or hertz (hz). A cycle in AC is a complete pulse from positive to negative back to positive. The number of cycles per second is called a "frequency." Most equipment in this country uses 60-cycle power, except for such equipment as microwave ovens, X-ray machines, and television, which use much higher frequencies. Equipment must be operated on the proper cycle. Name plates on equipment, information on the electrical units, and so forth will indicate the cycle required.

AC flowing only as one cycle or pulse has an uneven up and down flow since the current is pulsing between a negative and positive flow. Such single-cycle flow is suitable for most heating and lighting needs, but for power equipment a more steady current is needed. This can be obtained by using three- phase AC. This is three single-phases flowing one closely after the other. However, for motors operating elevators and some other equipment a more even flow than this is required. A *commutator* may then have to be used to change AC to DC so that a steady flow of electricity is obtained. Some operators may have DC and in this case the changeover would not be required.

The alternator making three-phase AC has three poles in a cycle so in one revolution three separate AC pulses are created. Usually each pulse is 120 v. Having three pulses in a cycle results in one pulse being close to maximum when another of the three is dropping and another is at low ebb. This gives a steadier current flow. Either a delta (Δ) or wye (Y) arrangement is used for locating the three poles on the alternator, the outer points of either being the pole location. Figure 12.1 shows graphically how these arrangements are made and the 120-v lines that run from each of the three-pole connections. The delta arrangement is more commonly used. A ground or neutral wire is always provided for either a wye or delta setup.

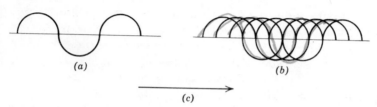

(a)   (b)

(c)

Figure 12.1 (a) AC, single-phase, with top of line positive and below the line negative surges. (b) AC, 3-phase; note how positive and negative variations level off when three surges occur in a cycle rather than one. (c) DC current flowing constantly in one direction from negative to positive.

Different voltages can be obtained from an alternator depending upon how electricity from the various poles is combined. If current is taken from any two poles or "hot" or "live" wires, the voltage is 120 v + 120 v or 240 v (which actually comes out as 208 v). If only one pole plus the neutral wire is used, the voltage is 120 v. If different voltages are required, transformers must change these voltages. (Although a transformer changes voltages, it will not change the phase.)

Most electrical companies transmit AC for short distances at 480/277 v. At the using point a transformer steps it back to 208/120 v. At the panel box, different combinations of wires then give either 208-v or 120-v circuits. If two hot wires are combined either with or without a neutral as a third wire, 208 v is obtained. If only one live wire is combined with the neutral, a 120-v circuit results. Heavy-duty equipment such as ranges, heavy motors, and heating units usually takes 208 v, whereas lighter loads such as light circuits and normal wall plugs will use 120 v. There may be good reason also for using heavier voltages than 208 v and if so, 480 v or other circuits may be set up. If these heavier voltages are not available, transformers in the facility can be set up to give them. All circuits should have a ground system to pull off any hazard electricity.

Using higher voltage permits use of smaller wiring, smaller conduits, and so forth, thus saving on cost. Smaller wire and other units are possible because as voltage increases amperage drops for the same amount of wattage. Thus a 15-kw load on a three-phase 208-v unit pulls 42 amps, which requires a No. 8-size copper wire, while the same load on a 480-v line pulls only 18 amps and requires a No. 12 copper wire, which is smaller. It is sometimes more economical to operate some equipment on higher rather than lower voltage, providing it is built for the higher voltage. Fluorescent lighting works better on higher voltages such as 277 v and also on higher frequencies than 60 cycles. While voltage is not a problem, the cycle may be because cycles cannot be changed. If 277 v

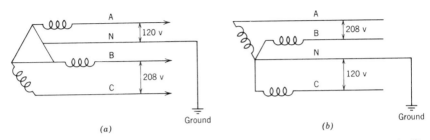

Figure 12.2 (*a*) The delta arrangement of poles on an alternator and (*b*) a wye arrangement. Note in (*a*) joining "hot" or "live" line A with neutral line N gives a 120-v current, while joining two "hot" or "live" lines B and C gives a 208-v current. Also, when two "hot" or "live" lines A and B are joined on the wye (*b*) arrangement a 208-v current is obtained, while joining neutral line N with the "hot" or "live" line C gives a 120-v current. A 2-wire, single-phase 120-v AC circuit results when one "hot" line is joined with N line, while a single-phase 2-wire 208-v AC circuit results when two "hot" lines are jointed. A 3-wire 120-volt single phase is obtained by joining A, B, or C with N, while 3-wire 208-v is obtained in this manner by N to joining two "hot" lines. Such a 3-wire circuit is suitable for light loads and small motors, the latter on 208-v. A 3-phase, 4-wire 120/208-v circuit is the same as the 3-wire, but the N is used. A 120-v circuit can yet be obtained by using any one of the three "hot" lines. A 3-phase, 4-wire arrangement of this kind is suitable for heavy or light load circuits and is usually the most flexible. Sometimes an additional N line is used which is grounded. In this case, the wire used is green and this gives rise to the term "green grounding system."

is run through the circuits, small 3- to 25-kva (kilowatt-volt-ampere) dry-type closet transformers can be installed at strategic spots to lower the voltage for other voltage needs.

Equipment specifications should require electrical equipment to meet *exact* electrical voltages. Slight undervoltage or overvoltage may be harmful to equipment or lead to an energy waste. Although manufacturers will indicate that motors or other equipment operate at either a 10 percent plus or minus voltage without harm, a motor on a 10 percent undervoltage will have a 20 percent loss in efficiency, hotter operation, and a shorter life and lower torque (twisting force). Similar undesirable results can come with overvoltage. Ovens and heating elements also do not function properly. An underload of 10 percent may cause a 30 percent drop in light power on a light globe. A 30 percent drop in voltage for an oven or range top may cause a 20 percent drop in its efficiency, while an overload of 10 percent may cause overheating and a much shorter operating life. Similarly, phasing and cycles should agree with the facility requirements, and these should be clearly stated in the specifications for equipment.

Motors, radios, televisions, and some other electrical equipment may be very susceptible to changes in current loads or voltages. Damage can easily result, and it is advisable in setting up equipment specifications to specify that the equipment carry a small fuse in the housing through which the electric current going into the equipment must pass. Thus if an oversurge occurs in the line, the equipment will not be burned out. A 30-amp breaker or fuse may let 30 amps through a circuit, which might be too much for a small or delicate piece of equipment. Fusing should be set to carry enough to operate the equipment but not much more. If equipment companies will not do this, installation specifications can require it on site.

Electrical Heat

Heat develops in an element due to friction created by resistance to electrical flow. If all flow stops no heat develops. Some electricity must be allowed to reach the end of the element and flow back to the source. When an element has a reddish glow infrared heat waves are produced. When the color becomes an almost white-red glow, greater radiation of heat is occurring. Infrared heat is suitable for many purposes, but for toasting or broiling heat radiation is required.

The forms of radiant energy have been grouped by scientists into a electromagnetic spectrum. The forms are characterized by wavelength and frequency of vibration (number of complete cycles per second). They are grouped in the spectrum from the shortest to the longest wavelength. Their length varies from miles to small thousandths of an inch. These, grouped from the shortest to the longest, are: cosmic rays, gamma rays, X-rays, ultraviolet, visible light, infrared (heat) waves, radar waves, microwaves, FM, TV, short (wireless) waves, radio, and sound. Light waves are measured in nanometers (nm) or billionths of a meter. The light band waves run from 400 to over 700 nm in length. Radio and some of the other larger waves are measured in centimeters or meters and are about 1000 cm or 10 m (3 yd) long or longer.

The shorter the waves the higher the frequency of vibration. Microwaves are not hot but create heat in material that is capable of absorbing them by agitating molecules that try to line up in the electrical field, thus developing friction that creates heat. The depth of penetration of microwaves varies from 1.5 in. (3.7 cm) to 3 in. (7.8 cm) as influenced by the nature of the material and the wave frequency. There are two microwave frequencies allocated by the Federal Communications Commission

(FCC) for industrial, scientific, and medical use. These are 2,450 MHz (megahertz or millions of cycles per second) with a wavelength of 5 in. (12 cm) and 915 MHz with a wavelength of 12.5 in. (32 cm).

Three characteristics of materials are of special interest in utilizing microwave-created heat. These are ability to reflect, absorb, and transmit the microwaves. Metals reflect the waves and do not absorb or transmit them. Metal in an oven lining reflects the waves into the food and keeps them from escaping into the room. Glass, china, paper, and plastics transmit microwaves but do not absorb them and therefore are suitable for cooking containers. Food or other materials containing moisture absorb microwaves, and the molecules are agitated to a degree that the friction creates heat.

Microwave ovens consist of certain basic parts: a low voltage line connects to a power supply that converts the low voltage to high voltage required by the microwave energy generator, an electronic vacuum tube called a "magnitron." Microwaves issuing from the magnitron flow through a waveguide and are stirred by a rotating paddle so as to disperse them more evenly throughout the oven cavity. The switch or lock that activates the microwave operation is in or connected with the door closure. A federal ruling calls for two safety interlocks or switches, either of which will prevent open-door operation. It requires that one of the locks or switches be hidden so it cannot be activated by any part of the body or by inserting a 4-in. (10-cm) rod.

Radiation leakage from microwave ovens presents certain health hazards. The Department of Health, Education, and Welfare has set standards for manufacturers of ovens to follow. The allowable emission

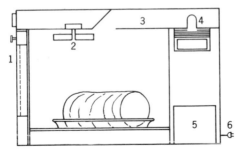

Figure 12.3 Basic parts of a microwave oven include (1) door with window, (2) stirrer that distributes microwaves more evenly as they are reflected back from metal sides of the oven, (3) wave guide that channels microwaves from the magnitron tube, (4) magnitron tube, (5) power supply, (6) and electric connection.

is 1 mw/cm^2, measured about 2 in. (5 cm) from the oven surface. Although specifications may be carefully written and regulations well followed, safety depends upon proper care and use of the oven. If it is improperly cleaned and has food particles clinging to edges of the door closure, or if a paper towel is caught in the door so that the door does not close securely, there can be leakage of microwaves. There is sometimes leakage around the window and as eyes are particularly susceptible to damage, users are cautioned not to peer into the window closely while the oven is operating.

Designing Circuits and Circuit Loads

When electricity flows through a circut operating a motor or other equipment, some voltage or power potential is lost. To design circuits correctly, this loss must be known in order that correct voltage, amperage, and wattage can be planned. The calculation is somewhat complex but is derived basically from a calculation of the loss potential in the conductor and various pieces of equipment. It is necessary at times to ascertain if additional loads can be put onto a circuit and again a calculation based on amount of R such addition will add to that already on the circuit must be made to know if the circuit will be overloaded.

Almost all equipment on circuits will be connected in what is termed "parallel." In doing this every unit drawing electricity receives its energy from the main conductor line and not through any other piece of equipment. In this way, no other piece of equipment is dependent upon its energy coming through another piece and all pieces on the circuit are guaranteed the same uniform amount and voltage of electricity. If the connection were in what is termed "connected in series," which means the electrical current flows from one piece of equipment to another, the voltage and amount of electricity received would decrease from the beginning to end of the series. When small Christmas tree lights are connected in series, the first light is usually brighter than the last one, especially if several strings are put together. Also, if one light burns out, no current goes through because the burned out light will not conduct electricity through it.

Almost every piece of electrical equipment will have a plate on it telling the cycle, phase, voltage, and wattage it requires. A circuit should have on it items that require the same first three, but the wattage can vary. For instance, a 120-v, single-phase, 60-c circuit could carry three 100-w light globes, a wall plug to which might be attached a small 840-w blender, and a clock and radio pulling 40 w. All require single-phase,

60 c, 120 v. The total wattage would be 1180, which would be about 10 amp (1180/120 = 9.83). Since all circuits should be fused 25 percent above maximum demand, a 15-amp circuit breaker or fuse would be ample for this circuit. However, it would not be suitable to add a 1½-hp electrical motor onto such a circuit. Such a motor requires three-phase power and would do better on 208 v rather than 120 v. Also, a hp is equal to 746 w and so about another 1100 w (1½ hp × 746 w = 1119) would be required on this circuit, which would mean that the amperage needed would be 19 (2280/120 = 19), which would considerably exceed the 15-amp breaker. Some heavy-duty equipment requires that it be the only unit on a circuit. Branch circuits should not run over 100 ft, and this may mean in a large facility that supplemental panels be placed distant from the main panel.

Most electrical companies deliver three-phase, 120/208-v, 4-wire service but larger foodservices may ask for three-phase, 277/480-v, 4-wire service. This can be obtained by stepping up the voltage using a transformer. Normally, 120 v is about a third of the total load used in foodservice; however, this varies.

Preliminary load requirements for foodservices can be taken from architectural tables that indicate broadly what is needed. Normally, a facility under 5000 sq ft takes a total of 200 amp or less at the main panel and a facility under 10,000 sq ft takes 400 amp or less. Total requirements will, of course, depend upon whether heating, air conditioning, and other high demand units are used. It is usual to estimate kitchen requirements on the basis of individual demand and not from general tables since the requirements can vary so much depending upon whether gas or other energy sources are used instead of electricity. The lighting load is usually estimated on the basis of 2 to 3 w/sq ft and storage and other low demand areas at 0.5 w/sq ft.

The National Electrical Council and the National Fire Protective Association have established standards for circuit loads and these should be followed. For instance, outlets for floor plugs are usually calculated as requiring 1.5 amp each (180 w) and a circuit on which they are placed should not carry over 60 percent of its total rated capacity. Thus a 15-amp circuit should not have more than 6 outlets of this type (15 × 60%/1.5 = 6). However, this is for small equipment. If heavy equipment is used, this does not follow. Reference to these codes can provide other helpful information also in planning circuits.

Circuits should carry the proper size wire. Wire sizes go either by the American Wire Gauge (AWG) or by the MCM (Thousand Circular Mils) standards. Small wires go by the AWG sizes. For instance, No. 10 and No. 12, 0.102 and 0.081 in. in diameter respectively, are usually used for electric light circuits and light-duty load circuits. A No. 0 AWG wire is 0.325 in. in diameter and a No. 0000 AWG wire, the largest size in this standard, is 0.460 in. in diameter. Wires that are ½ in. or over are in MCM sizes. Normally, MCM wires carry heavy loads in electrical transmission lines, whereas AWG wires transport loads in buildings. A 250 MCM is 0.500 in. in diameter and a 600 MCM is 0.775 in. in diameter. A range top pulling 12,000 w at 208 v will use 57.7 amp and require a 70-amp or larger breaker and a 3-wire No. 6 AWG line not including grounding wires. A small deep fryer pulls 1,300 w on a 120-v line and needs a 20-amp breaker and 2 No. 10 wires. Standard tables in architectural materials indicate desirable wire sizes for different electrical equipment and loads. These are based on the standards of the National Electrical Counsel, 80 Batterymarch St., Boston 02110 and the National Fire Protective Association, 60 Batterymarch St., Boston 02110.

The Electrical Plan

It is usual to have an electrical plan for lighting separate from that for equipment and other units. This allows presentation of each without confusing detail. After electrical equipment has been located properly and the circuits planned, it is possible then to set up the plan. Recently programs have been developed for computers that take much of the detail work out of such planning. All electrical units, switches, receptacles, motors, and other electrical details should be properly identified on the plan. Symbols are often used and reference to an architectural handbook can be helpful in identifying these for those who do not know what they mean. An electrical schedule may be set up which resembles an equipment schedule for a regular plan. After this, panel loads can be calculated and the location established. Panels usually carry about 75 percent or their maximum load, so should additional circuits be needed the addition is not a problem. It is important to check plans to see that space for panels, feeder lines, conduit lines, and so forth is provided.

Suggested Student Assignments

1. Read a recent article on energy and report its message to the class.

2. Form a panel with two or three other members of the class and discuss ways in which foodservices may reduce energy consumption. (Review National Restaurant Association reports and materials for information on the subject.)

3. Visit an electrical plant to observe how electricity is generated, transformed, and transmitted.

4. Visit a production kitchen and note the information on the equipment as to phase, cycle, voltage, and wattage.

5. Add wattage on various circuits and calculate amperage, checking to see that it is within limits established by the breakers or fuses on the circuit.

6. Using a delta or wye arrangement, set up a 2-wire, 120-v circuit, 3-wire 120/208 v-circuit, 3-wire 208-v circuit, and a 4-wire 120/208-v circuit.

7. Study an electrical plan for a facility and identify the various symbols and interpret the details of the plan.

8. Draw a simplified electrical plan for a circuit that carries a light load and another that carries a heavy load.

9. Answer problems utilizing various formulas such as $I \times v = w$, $w/v = I$, $I = v/R$ and $w = I^2R$. What is the wattage if the amperage is 1.5 and the voltage on the line is 120 v? If a circuit for a range pulls 12.5 kw on a 208-v line, what is the amperage and what should the breaker be in the panel?

(Answer to first question is $1.5 \times 120 = 180$ w, and to the second $12,500/208 = 60$ amps pulled $\times 1.25 = 75$-amp breaker in the panel to provide 25 percent over actual demand.)

Chapter 13
lighting

Lighting, through the utilization of electrical energy, serves both utilitarian and aesthetic needs in a food facility. Definition of requirements will involve amount, direction, and such qualities as color, steadiness, and diffusion. It should be sufficient to provide clear vision in a manner and to a degree that will not cause eye discomfort. Needs differ in given areas and artistic requirements also vary. Economic aspects are numerous, involving not only electrical power to create light and the utilization of natural light and effect of reflective surfaces but also the influence of light on work accomplishment and patron reactions. Work proceeds best when workers can see clearly and comprehend quickly. There tends to be less fatigue if they are free from eye strain and feel buoyant. The amount and quality of light tends to affect individuals psychologically in terms of lightness of spirit, calmness, or despondency.

It is desirable for the members of the planning team to carefully analyze lighting requirements for the various areas of the food facility and to set up standards to be met. Adequacy in lighting cannot be achieved by merely inserting extra lights to give the required candlepower. Light quantity will vary from 100 foot-candles (fc) in offices and kitchen work areas to the subdued light in dining and cocktail areas. Light must have quality as well as quantity. Achievement of desirable lighting patterns, variations, and contrasts is an art requiring considerable knowledge about light. Standards that have been set up by the Illuminating Engineering Society are helpful in establishing many of the requirements.

Characteristics of Light

Visible light is one part of the electromagnetic spectrum of radiant energy (see Chapter 12). It moves in undulating waves. The light waves energize the optic nerve, causing us to see. They strike an object and then bounce from it to the eye. Whatever light waves are reflected by the object is what is seen. Thus a leaf of a tree will have white light strike it. It absorbs all of the various waves except green. These green light waves will then be reflected and only green color will be seen. The various lengths of light waves excite the optic nerves differently, causing the eye to see different colors. Thus light waves in the 400 nanometer (nm) range are indigo; those in the 700 nm range are red. Combining different wave lengths gives different shades. White light is light of all lengths. However, if white light is filtered through a glass prism, a rainbow, or a mist, it is broken up into various colors. If an object reflects white light, such as white paper, no light waves are being absorbed by it. If colors are reflected the various bands making up the color are being reflected, while the others are being absorbed by the object. Black is the complete absence of light.

Light is energy and creates heat when it strikes an object. A white object reflects almost all of the energy striking it, but a black object absorbs most of it. The white object becomes less warm in the sunlight than a dark one. If a white and a black cloth of the same kind and weight are laid over snow in the sunlight, the snow under the black cloth will melt much faster than the snow under the white cloth because of the difference in the amount of energy absorbed.

Some artificial light appears white but actually is not white. It may lack certain red waves or others. Objects under such lights will not appear natural. For instance, some types of fluorescent lights do not give off waves in the red band. Thus a woman's lipstick under such light may appear purple or almost black. A cherry pie will have an unappetizing color. It is important, therefore, to have the right type of light where color reflection is important.

Sources of Light

A common source of light is daylight from the sun. A small quantity comes at night from celestial bodies and is merely a reflection of the sun's light waves striking the body. The main source of artificial light is from electricity. Electricity passing through certain substances, such as tungsten, will meet considerable resistance. This creates heat that quickly rises from red to white light. The maximum theoretical efficacy in a good tungsten (incandescent) light is 20 lumen (lm)/watt of electricity used. However, they will produce from 14 to 18 lm/w usually, or have 70 to 90 percent efficiency. Higher wattages are more efficient than lower wattages: a 100-w 120-v light will produce an average of 17.5 lm/w and a 50-w 120-v light will produce 12.8 lm/w.

Heat is the remainder of the energy produced and where a great number of incandescent lights are used, a large quantity of heat will be produced. In fact, so much heat can be produced in some types of operations that the heat can be captured and utilized to heat the building. In warm weather the heat created by the lights becomes a problem, but there are ways of utilizing this energy to produce cold air in a heat-absorbing type of refrigerating system (described in Chapter 22). Light can be produced by causing energy to strike a substance that fluoresces, such as mercury. Sometimes fluorescent and mercury lights are put into different categories because the substance fluorescing is different, although the theory for each is the same.

Lighting Principles

Light quantity is measured in lumens. The lumen is something like the footcandle, which is the amount of light concentrated on a specified surface area. If 1 lm is concentrated on a sq ft, the light value is 1 fc. If a lamp gives off 100 lm, 60 percent of which strikes a 10-sq ft surface (60 lm), the footcandles per square foot equals 6 fc. Normally, the footcandle value is understood to be square feet. Light meters are used to measure the footcandles. By holding a light meter up to the light at a specified spot, the amount of light in footcandles is measured by the device.

Light flows from its source, and we are only aware of it because surfaces reflect it. A mirror gives a high amount of reflection, but other substances may give very little. The fc or quantity of light striking a surface times the amount of reflectance gives a brightness value of an object measured in foot-Lamberts (f^L). If 9 lm strike a surface and 50 percent is the reflectance value, the f^Ls are $4\frac{1}{2}$ f^L. The equation could be written fc × reflectance factor = f^L, or lm striking a surface × reflectance factor = f^L.

Light intensity is measured in candlepower (cp), which is comparable to the voltage (pressure) in an electrical current or the psi in a water system. Candlepower is slightly different than lm because it indicates the strength or force of the light going in any direction from a luminaire (light source). Light decreases in intensity or amount as it travels. One reason is that it spreads out into thinner and thinner layers as it moves out into a wider circumference. If the cp is known, dividing this by the square of the distance traveled gives the fc. The equation is written cp/D^2 = fc. It follows that cp also equals fc × D^2. Thus if the cp is 20 and it travels 5 ft, the fc at that point is 0.8 ($20/5^2 = 0.8$). Or, if the light source is 8 ft away from the surface and the fc is 10, the cp at the luminaire is 640 ($10 \times 8^2 = 640$). Calculations for f^L, cp, lm, fc, or other units in light science are made to obtain proper lighting results. To understand what a good lighting engineer is doing and is talking about, team planners should know how these calculations are derived and what they mean.

Incandescent Light

If electricity is conducted through tungsten in the air, the tungsten quickly oxidizes in the air and the filament burns up. If this occurs where oxygen is not present, such oxidation does not occur and the light will last a long time. The modern incandescent light globe has a tung-

sten filament set within a glass globe (quartz is used for globes to withstand high heat). An inert gas, such as a mixture of argon and nitrogen,
fills the globe. The standard life of a good globe is 1000 hr. Tungsten
lights decline in efficiency due to heat gradually evaporating the tungsten.
This then deposits on the globe, darkening it, causing some of the light
to be absorbed. Finally, so much of the tungsten evaporates that the
filament ruptures and the current is stopped.

Some operations have a program of planned light replacement because
of loss of efficiency. It is a system in which *all* globes are replaced at a
specified time regardless of whether they are functioning or not. This is
done to maintain a high light level and to reduce cost. The labor to
replace a burned out individual light can cost more than the new light.
Replacing all at one time considerably reduces such labor cost. This is
especially true when an area has lights that are difficult to reach. A
stadium, for instance, may replace lights once a year on such a system.
To obtain the necessary operating life, which may be over 1000 hr, it
may use lights of a higher wattage than required but operate them on a
lower voltage. The lower voltage will give about the right amount of
light or wattage but, because the lights are being operated on a lower
voltage, they will have a longer life, thus achieving the desired time and
amount of light. Such lights burned 3 hr per night, 365 days a year will
perform satisfactorily.

Special incandescent lights are available. The tungsten-halogen lamp
is filled with iodine in combination with other inert gases. The iodine
will vaporize when the lamp becomes hot, and the hot iodine has the
ability to pick up the vaporized tungsten and return it to the filament
when it cools. This light avoids having a lowered light output due to
tungsten darkening and also has a longer life. It is more expensive than
regular tungsten lights because of the manner in which it must be made
and also because it is made of quartz and not glass. It has an expected
life of about 2000 hr.

There are rough service or vibration lights that can be placed in areas
where movement might quickly destroy other types of lights. Also special
lights are made that carry away the heat developed. These can be used
in refrigerated display cases and other areas where the heat build-up
would be undesirable. Krypton gas or other rare gases may be used to
give lights longer operating life.

Fluorescent Light

Energy can be saved by using fluorescent lighting rather than incandescent. Nearly 5 times as much light is given off by fluorescent lights

per watt than by incandescent lights. The lumens produced per watt by different lights usually average as follows: tungsten-halogen light 16 to 20 lm, fluorescent light 50 to 85 lm, mercury lamp 40 to 70 lm, metal-halide 60 to 80 lm, and high-pressure sodium 90 to 100 lm.

The operating life of a fluorescent light is also longer. Because the life of a fluorescent light is shortened by turning it off and on, some operations never turn off the lamp. The energy required to start a fluorescent light is considerable also and so energy can be saved if the light is left on in areas where it might be turned on and off many times during a day. Life spans of fluorescent are calculated on the basis of a 3-hr continuous burning time before being turned off. Light production declines considerably in fluorescents in the first 100-hr of burning and so light production is calculated on the basis of 80-hr of burning and not from the start. After 100 hr the light production is fairly steady.

Fluorescent lights operate with two cathodes inside on either end of the tube. When electricity flows into one, it becomes excited and starts a flow of electrons to the other cathode. These electrons in passing down the tube develop ultraviolet light which in turn activates phosphors on the inside lining of the tube. Light is the energy then produced. This is cool light and is the same kind of light that is present in glowworms or fireflies.

Fluorescent lights operate better on higher voltages, and some systems may require special devices, such as ballast devices, in the lights. A slow start and flickering are undesirable factors in such lights which may be corrected by using such special devices. Normally, the cost of installation and the lights is more than for incandescent lights but the cost of operation is less. Replacement cost should be considered in making cost comparisons. Operating the system on a frequency higher than 60 cycles may increase lighting efficiency, and decrease light size, weight, and heat output. Maintenance may be less and other benefits may occur. An outside frost may cause a 20 percent loss of light, whereas an inside one may cause only a 2 or 3 percent loss. Incandescent lights also have a higher efficiency if given an inside, rather than outside, frost. Clear lights have the lowest light loss but may contribute to glare.

Some fluorescent lights do not give off light equal to daylight in light colors. They frequently lack waves in the red color range and give off a light in the blue-green area. As noted red objects under such light do not have a natural color. By adding substances to the phosphors, red light waves can be produced to correct the deficiency. Generally, fluorescent or mercury lights are rated as follows in comparison with sunlight rated at 100: warm white 50, white 60, cool white 66, deluxe warm white 73, daylight 79, sign white 86, and deluxe cool white 89. Thus deluxe cool white would give 89 percent of the kind of light that sunlight gives. (Light from an incandescent light approximates daylight but gives off more waves in the yellow-orange range than found in daylight, probably due to the heat produced.)

Mercury Lights

When electricity flows through mercury, ultraviolet light waves are produced. This may be desirable in lamps used to produce sun tan. Mercury lamps filled with high-pressure mercury gas have a long operating life and high efficiency. The light has a large quantity of blue-green waves and, unless corrected, lacks red waves. They are used at times in refrigerators and other areas to destroy bacteria. The ultraviolet light is lethal to many micro-organisms. The light is not effective against bacteria over great distances and so such lights may be worthless if they are not close enough to the items requiring protection.

A special sodium-mercury lamp is used where a long operating life is desired. This light has a high lumen output.

Fluorescent and mercury lights may create noise in operating, especially if incorrect installation methods are used or the proper electrical current is not used. They may interfere with radio and other communication signals. Some mercury lights may require 5 to 10 minutes cooling period before they will go on again and this may present a problem. Sometimes a few incandescent lights are installed to maintain a light level when this happens. Fluorescent and mercury lights should be specified as the instant-start type unless there is some reason against this.

Light Quality

Light quality is made up of many factors. Manipulating these gives many interesting and useful effects. The quantity of light, its color, brightness, amount of diffusion, source, shadows, reflection, absorption, and a number of other factors may play a part in giving quality to light.

A large quantity of footcandles may be required in certain work areas, while in others a much more subdued lighting effect is desired. Table 13.1 summarizes some of the recommended footcandles for various areas in a facility.

The quantity of light on a surface is a very important factor in determining light quality. The quantity depends upon (1) lm emitted by the lamp, (2) the number of lamps per fixture, and (3) the number of fixtures. Not all of the light from a luminaire or source reaches the surface being considered. The percentage produced to that reaching the

Table 13.1 Minimum Footcandles of Light for Various Areas

Type area	Minimum fc	Type area	Minimum fc
Cashier	50	Auditorium	15–30
Fast service unit	50–100	Auditorium exhibits	30–50
Intimate dining, cocktail lounge		Dancing area	5
Light environment	10	Bathrooms, general	10
Subdued environment	5	Bathrooms, at mirror	30
Luxury foodservice		Bedroom, general	10–15
Light environment	30	Corridors, elevators, stairs	10
Subdued environment	15	Hotel or motel entrance	20
Food counters and displays	50	Reading or work areas	30
Food checker	70	Linen room, general	10
Detail work area	70–100	Linen room, sewing, etc.	100
Other kitchen areas	30	Hotel or motel lobby, general	10
Storerooms	10	Offices, accounting, etc.	100–150
Baking mixing room	50	Offices, general	100
Oven area	30	Mechanical rooms, general	10
Decorator's bench	100	Mechanical rooms, work-	
Fillings and other prepara-		table	50–100
tions	30–50	Parking lot, self parking	5
Loading platform	20	Parking lot, attendant	2
Storage area, active	20	Laundry, washing area	30
Storage area, inactive	1–5	Laundry, pressing, etc.	50–70
Building entrances	5–20	Outdoor signs, light surfaces	20–50
Building surroundings	1–5	Outdoor signs, dark surfaces	50–100

surface is called by a lighting engineer the "coefficient of utilization" (CU). This is never 100 percent because of blackening from soil on lamp globes, tungsten destruction, distance of travel, reflective value, and so forth. The two most important factors, soil on the lamp globes and blackening, are often called the "maintenance factor" (MF). This is usually considered to be 70 percent. The total CU contains the MF factor plus the other light-destroying factors. This may be calculated, but engineers frequently use tables for different fixtures and different work area levels. CU factors can vary anywhere from 15 to 90 percent. Much depends upon the light-destroying factors involved, the fixture, the quantity of light produced, the amount reflected from the ceiling and other surfaces, whether the light is direct, semidirect, or indirect, and whether or not the light is diffused or not.

The amount of light required is dictated by the area and the activity that occurs there. The number of luminaires, the amount of light each produces, the amount of area to be lighted, and the CU factor dictate how much light must come from the source. The formula used to determine the number of units that must be installed is as follows:

$$\text{No. of lamps or fixtures} = \frac{\text{fc needed} \times \text{area or sq ft}}{\text{lamps in the fixture} \times \text{lm/lamp} \times \text{CU} \times \text{MF}}$$

To discover the area each fixture must cover the formula is:

$$\text{Area/luminaires} = \frac{\text{lamps in fixture} \times \text{lm/lamp} \times \text{CU} \times \text{MF}}{\text{fc}}$$

Thus if 70 fc is desired on the work surface 36 in. above the floor in a room 45 × 75 ft and a fixture with 4 lamps, each of which produces 3,000 lm with a CU of 0.675 and the standard MF of .7 is used, the number of fixtures will be:

$$\frac{70 \times 45 \times 75}{4 \times 3{,}000 \times 0.675 \times 0.7} = \frac{236{,}250}{5628} = 42$$

The spacing for these fixtures must be obtained as follows:

$$\frac{4 \times 3{,}000 \times 0.675 \times 0.7}{70} = 80.4 \text{ sq ft}$$

for each fixture to cover. The engineer would then draw a grid for the area showing approximately 9-ft squares (9 × 9 = 81).

Light quality is affected by the direction of the light and how it is reflected. In certain places, shadows are desired to give pattern and variety. A hotel lobby lighted by a considerable quantity of diffused light appears stark and has a sort of "bled" appearance. If shadows are made on wall surfaces and other areas, the lobby becomes a much more interesting place. In work areas where close inspection occurs, especially on surfaces, shadows are helpful in delineating defects, edges, and so on. If the light strikes from all angles (is diffused), the worker has more difficulty in seeing varied levels on the objects and in seeing other surface variations.

Direct lighting gives the most shadows and the highest efficiency from the light produced. If used, shielding may be needed to prevent glare at certain angles. If undesirable features, such as pipes or ducts, must be hidden or if ceiling height should be made to appear lower, the ceiling can be painted a dark color so it will not reflect light and show the undesirable objects or indicate the ceiling height. The light then can be focused down only so the nonlighted area above is hidden in darkness. If direct light is spread out so that it is diffused well by the walls and floor, the attention of viewers will move toward furniture and other features in the room rather than to the walls since the walls darken slightly. If light concentration is desired, direct light is the best way to obtain it. Concentrating too much direct light on a work area gives an uncomfortable feeling to those working there.

Semidirect lighting is obtained when 60 to 90 percent of the light produced is directed downward and the remainder goes to the ceiling where reflection occurs. It is desirable that the ceiling have a good reflective value since the direct light can create a glare unless sufficient additional light comes from above. If done well, good diffusion occurs while at the same time some shadowing is possible. It is fairly efficient in energy use also.

If from 60 to 90 percent of the light is sent up and then reflected downward from the ceiling, a semi-indirect system results. The ceiling must have a fairly high reflectance. Paints and colors with satisfactory reflectance values may be used for this. The lights themselves are apt to stand out in such lighting because of the brightness of the ceiling. This may or may not be desirable. If the lights are shielded, the ceiling may appear higher than it is. Semi-indirect and indirect lighting create a monotony in light tone unless care is taken to see that variations in light brightness and contrast occur.

Indirect lighting results when 90 to 100 percent of the light goes to the ceiling and upper walls. It cannot be used in a ceiling lower than 9 ft since the lights must be at least 12 in. from the ceiling to give proper light spread. If cove lighting is used, the ceiling can be lower and has a sort of skylight quality to it. Local lighting from tables or other lamps down lower can give some texture. Otherwise, the high amount of diffusion leaves little variety in light pattern and considerable monotony. Indirect lighting gives the lowest efficiency in light use. It creates the least amount of glare. Lighting over 75 fc is usually not possible with indirect lighting since a ceiling brightness of over 400 f^L is required for this. An extremely bright ceiling itself can contribute a high amount of glare.

Color contributes to light quality. A green wall makes red foods appear more attractive, since the eye sees the opposite complementary color when the eye shifts from the wall color to the food. Thus the eye sees the food as redder than it really is. After looking at a blue wall one is likely to see more yellow in a yellow object. Pink, pale blue, ivory, and other light colors have the highest amount of reflectance with white the highest. Red, orange, brown, gray, and other dark colors reflect about one-fourth of the light that white and light colors do.

Glare is a disproportionate amount of light coming into the eye. It may come directly from the source or it may be reflected from some surface.

A bright stainless steel surface or a high sheen in a white tile wall may contribute glare to a person in the area. Glare is much more apt to occur if the flow of light is more than a 45° angle from the light source, although such light can fall upon a desk, table, or other object and be reflected back to create glare. Glare is annoying and can cause workers to lose productive capacity. It also can create blind spots that may lead to accidents.

The positioning of a light should receive attention to prevent its contributing to glare. Lamps giving a high amount of diffusion usually require less attention in preventing glare than those with little diffusion. Ceilings, walls, and other objects assisting in diffusion can reduce the potential also. Direct glare can be reduced by increasing the brightness behind the light. The lights of a car in daylight are less blinding than at night because of background light.

To achieve desirable light quality, the use of general and localized lighting calls for attention. General lighting is that which flows over the whole area. Localized lighting is that which comes from a set fixture in a given area. A room may need only a limited quantity of general lighting with special lighting required at different areas. A lounge appears much more interesting if the general light is sufficient for ordinary movement and concentrated light appears from table lamps and other units, Different kinds of light add interest also. In addition, light variation may be used to call attention to certain features and not to others in a room.

Normally, the recommended reflectance of room surfaces are:

Ceilings	80 to 90% (best reflectance is usually about 80%)
Walls	40 to 60% (best reflectance is usually about 50%)
Floors	21 to 39% (best reflectance is usually about 30%)
Furniture and equipment	26 to 44% (best reflectance is usually about 35%)

These reflectance values should be used only as broad guides, as they may not be advisable in every instance nor give the best lighting guality.

Contrast is an important factor in obtaining adequate light quality. It is easier to discern items if there is some contrast of light on them and on their backgrounds. Too much contrast between an object and its background, however, may be distasteful, and if the background is too bright, glare may result. The Illuminating Engineering Society (IES) says to achieve a desirable balance of contrast at a work place, the maximum contrast desired usually is a 1 to $\frac{1}{3}$ contrast between the work and adjacent surroundings, a 1 to $\frac{1}{10}$ contrast between the work and more remote darker surfaces, and a 1 to 10 contrast between the work and more remote lighter surfaces.

A lighting engineer or specialist, if given adequate instruction on the quantity of light and light quality, can develop a satisfactory lighting system and a very good lighting pattern. Team planners need to establish lists indicating the amount of light desired in the various areas. Reference to illuminating standards can be helpful, but remember that light tends to be overprovided. Where numerous lights that can be turned off are provided, in hall and special areas, energy can be conserved without loss of lighting efficiency. There needs to be thorough discussions between team planners and the person responsible for desired lighting effects in the various areas. Pictures showing desired effects can be useful. Construction factors and other features of the facility should be studied in terms of what should be emphasized by lighting and what should be hidden. Care taken in developing a suitable lighting plan will be well worth the time and effort required.

Suggested Student Assignments

1. Use a prism to discover how white light can be broken into different wavelengths resulting in different colors.

2. Examine an incandescent and a fluorescent light and make a drawing to show major components and how they work.

3. Locate for observation as many different types of light as possible, such as mercury, sodium-mercury, tungsten-halogen lamp, and others. Note the color qualities of these and also those of fluorescent lights that lack reds and others that have them. State where each of the lights is used, and evaluate the degree of satisfaction with color in the situation.

4. Select a given area to be lighted and secure the square footage covered; then calculate the number of lamps or fixtures required to light it.

5. Choose a facility plan and indicate the quantity of light to be given in the various areas.

6. Calculate the number of fixtures required if each fixture has 4 100-w light globes producing 1400 lm/globe if the CU is 65 percent and the MF is 70 percent and 50 fc are desired per square foot in a room having 700 sq ft. How many square feet of space will each fixture need to cover?

(Answer: 14 fixtures needed. 51 sq ft or a space 7.1 × 7.1 ft or 2.1 × 2. m)

Chapter 14

water, steam, and plumbing

WATER

The amount and quality of water available for use is of immediate concern for those planning a food facility. The water must be drinkable (potable). The public water supply in the United States normally is safe to consume due to Public Health regulations and inspections. Chlorination systems are widely used to destroy harmful pathogens. Water supplies in some areas have to be treated to remove sediment or coloring matter. Algunates, gelatinous compounds, or filters are used for this. Frequently, water coming from lakes or streams where there are decomposing organic materials, such as leaves, may be dark and need to be decolored. Iron is seldom found in sufficient quantity to cause problems. However, water flowing through rusty pipes may pick up enough iron to require removal. Water from lakes and streams may be acid enough to attack metal. This water must be treated to bring it above a p^H of 7.0. If the p^H is not corrected, copper piping must be used that will be resistant to attack from such water. Plastic piping may be used if codes permit.

Most food facilities will obtain water supply from municipal sources. This water will have been treated, except perhaps for softening, if the water is hard. Where such supply is not available, a facility may have to install its own water system. In addition to a chlorination system and any other necessary treatment, the planners must consider pump capacities, storage tanks, potability, and other aspects.

Hard water contains a quantity of alkaline salts that may interfere with its ability to clean items well or that may not give good results in cooking. Such water must be softened. The hardness of water is judged either on the basis of parts per million (ppm) of calcium carbonate in the water or on the basis of grains of hardness. One grain of hardness is equivalent to 17.1 ppm. If water contains over 65 ppm or 4 grains hardness, it usually must be softened. Hot water over 5 grains hardness will deposit hard water salts called "scale" in pipes and equipment. This can finally clog pipes or cause equipment to malfunction. Hard water salts will combine with detergents or soaps making an insoluble precipitate that spots glassware, dishes, and flatware. It also makes it necessary to use more detergent or soap since this bonding with the hard water salts removes detergent or soap as a cleaning agent.

One of the simplest and most economical methods of softening water is with the sodium-exchange system. This is a process in which sodium chloride (ordinary table salt but usually unrefined) is exchanged by a zeolite process for the magnesium, calcium, and other hard water substances. Thus water high in calcium carbonate will come out of the zeolite softener high in sodium bicarbonate, which is not hard water.

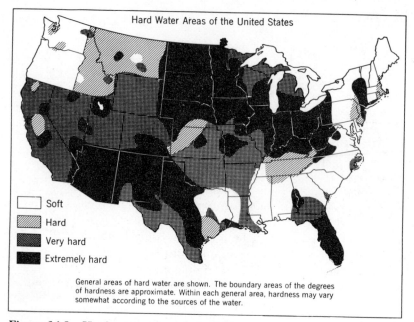

Figure 14.1 Hard water areas of the United States (*Courtesy Volume Feeding Management, New York.*)

The calcium carbonate is captured in the softener and from time to time the exchanger must be serviced and the supply of sodium chloride renewed. In some hospitals, an additional supply of water other than that softened by sodium must be available for patients who are on low-sodium diets. Water can be softened also by phosphates, which is a more expensive process. Water high in sodium bicarbonates makes poor coffee, therefore the water used for coffee making may be softened by phosphates. Many detergents and soaps contain phosphates that have been added to help soften the water and prevent the hard water salts from reducing the effectiveness of the cleaning compounds.

A quantity of water used in a facility may be substantial. A hotel may use 40 gal or more per guest per day, 40 to 60 percent of which is hot water at 160°F (71°C). A foodservice may use 5 gal or more per person served. A dishwasher uses an average of 1.8 gal per person served and this may vary from 2.1 gal per person for large banquets to 1.3 for light lunches. Hand washing of dishes requires less water than by machine. The demand for water may vary considerably. A hotel may find that 75 percent of its room demand for hot water comes at from 7 to 10 A.M. Adequate capacity for heating and storage of water must be planned to meet such demands. The need for hot water for a kitchen needs also to be carefully calculated.

The water pressure at a facility for water coming from large municipal mains is usually 50 to 80 psi. The most usual water pressure in a facility will be around 20 to 30 psi and at equipment such as lavatories, toilets, and dishwashers at from 10 to 15 psi. Open tap pressure is usually specified as 4 to 5 psi. For every psi, water can be lifted 2.3 ft. Thus if water is in the main at ground level at 50 psi, there is enough pressure to raise the water 115 ft (2.3 × 50 = 115). If the facility is 200 ft high, a supplemental tank and pumping system must be installed to get it up to the 200-ft level. In addition to lifting the water, additional pressure must be added so open tap pressure will be at 4 to 5 psi. Some systems pump water to tanks on top of the facility and then let it feed by gravity to lower levels. Usually enough pressure is built by the drop to provide the pressure required.

If a vacuum is made in a tube with one of its ends in water, water flows up into the tube. This is due to atmospheric pressure on the water surface pushing the water up into the tube where vacuum existed. Often the statement is made that "water is pulled up" by suction from a pump, but this is not true. The water is pushed up by the atmospheric pressure. The normal pressure of the atmosphere at sea level is 14.7 psi, which gives it a theoretical lift with a perfect vacuum of 34 ft (14.7 × 2.3). It is not possible, however, to have 100 percent efficient equipment, and so the limit a suction pump can "pull" water is about 25 ft. If the distance of the lift is greater than 25 ft, additional suction pumps must be put at higher levels. Frequently pumps that force the water up are used. This permits forcing the water a longer distance with only one pump. Air pressure can also force water up. The size of the pump and the quantity of pressure required must be calculated carefully.

Water may be heated in various ways. The efficiencies of fuels listed in Chapter 15 can be used to calculate the cost of heating water. Only about 60 percent of the Btus produced by burning gas or other fuels is utilized. Electricity may have a 90 percent or more efficiency, especially if the elements are buried in the water so that all of the heat produced goes into the water.

There is a heat loss in transporting water. Water may have to be heated to 160°F (71°C) or higher to reach a guest room in a hotel at 130°F (55°C). When water higher than 160°F (71°C) is needed at a using point, booster heaters are usually installed to raise the temperature there to that required. Water for guest use should not be much over 130°F (55°C). Some facilities heat water to 180°F (82°C) and then lower it to the temperatures required by means of mixing valves at the using point. About

40 percent of the total hot water load in foodservices is at 180°F (82°C) and 60 percent at 140°F (60°C). Approximately 55 percent of the total hot water use comes at peak periods of relatively short duration, closely coinciding with serving periods. About 28 percent of the remaining total comes before service and about 17 percent later. Hotels may need a 20 percent head start with a heating capacity of 15 to 20 percent per hour of the total need. Thus, if a hotel needs for guests 8000 gal per day of 130°F water, it should start with 2000 gal (25%) and be able each hour thereafter to heat an additional 1600 gal (20%) to meet needs. Better hotels have a lower peak demand than commercial hotels but have a higher total hot water requirement per guest.

Heaters and tanks should be sized to give sufficient lead in hot water to cover peak demands and recovery needs. Usually the quantity stored ahead is 15 to 25 percent of peak requirements. Improved instant-type heating units may lessen lead requirements. Circulators should be installed so water is instantly at the required temperature instead of being run until proper temperature of water is obtained. Tanks and lines should be insulated.

Steam[1]

Steam may be generated in a central boiler and then distributed, it may be produced in the equipment using it, or it may be produced by an outside supplier in the local area. Equipment in which the steam is generated for its own operation is called "self-contained." The amount of steam generated in the individual piece may be sufficient for its operation only, or sufficient for the operation of an additional item of equipment.

Steam generated in a boiler is measured in boiler horsepower (Bhp). One Bhp equals the production of 34.5 lb of steam per hour. Thus a boiler rated at 5 Bhp produces 172.5 lb of steam per hour. Ratings are controlled and must meet certain standard approved IBR ratings for cast iron boilers, the SBI steel boiler ratings, or other ratings by electric and gas associations. Chimney sizes must meet specified standards also.

Steam may be measured by psi. A steamer cooking food may be said to operate on 5 or 6 psi of steam. Another measure used for steam is the amount of steam flow/hr. This is the quantity of steam in pounds used or flowing to a piece of equipment in an hour. Calculation of the quantity of steam required for a kitchen is done by totaling the quantity of steam flow required by the individual items of equipment. Thus if 6

[1] A translation of values into metric values is not made here for the values used in the British system. Eventually, psi will probably be translated into g per cm, Bhp into kg of pressure, Btu's into calories, etc. When the change to the metric system occurs, these translation values will be established and then can be used.

pieces of equipment use a total of 163.9 lb of steam per hour, a 5 Bhp is required to supply it (163.9/34.5 = 4+). However, the boiler must have a greater generating capacity since there is always a loss of steam from the boiler to the equipment. In making quick calculations, engineers use rounded values to calculate heat needs for boiler production; a Bhp on this basis is considered to require 10 kwh of electricity or 34,000 Btus (British Thermal Units)[2] of heat. The efficiency rating of a boiler also governs the quantity of heat that must be furnished to supply the required steam. Thus a boiler that requires 136,000 Btus/hr with a 50 percent efficiency will deliver 68,000 Btus of heat into the water to make steam. This means that it will produce 2 Bhp/hr (68,000/34,000 = 2).

Boilers in which coils are installed are used most frequently to produce steam for kitchens and to heat water. This provides steam that can come in contact with food. Descaling compounds are sometimes used in boilers that may be toxic and steam produced in such boilers cannot be used on food. When water changes to steam, all of the solids in the water remain in the boiler. When water is hard, this means a large quantity of residue will be left and is often a problem. It is frequently necessary to replace coils because of this. Food frequently comes in contact with steam that is delivered into compartments. Reducers, regulators, or other units are often required to bring steam for the equipment in at the proper psi. Where steam does not flow freely but is contained as in coils or in the jacket of a steam kettle or other equipment, such equipment is not required.

The quantity of steam required *at the equipment* and the pounds of steam flow per hour is indicated in Table 14.1.

Table 14.1 Steam Flow per Hour for Equipment Needs

	Delivered Bhp	Steam flow, lb/hr
Large steamer (per compartment)	3/4	25.90
Steam-jacketed kettle (per 20 gal)	1	34.50
Direct-connected steamers*	1/2	17.25
Direct-connected Jet-cookers*	2-1/2	86.25
Coffee urn (per 10 gal)	1/10	3.45
Steam table (per sq ft)	1/20	1.72
Bain marie (per sq ft)	1/10	3.45
Warming oven (per sq ft)	1/20	1.72

* Requirements abstracted from Market Forge catalog for the manufacturer's specific equipment. Check requirements on equipment selected from other manufacturers.

[2] See definition in Chapter 15.

The quantity of steam delivered depends upon the psi and the pipe size. Table 14.2 summarizes pipe sizes required to deliver specific quantities of steam. The figures under each pipe size indicate the quantity of steam flow/hr that can be delivered at the different steam line pressures (psi). Engineers will use such data to calculate pipe sizes.

Table 14.2   Pipe Sizes for Steam Flow Requirements

Steam Line Pressure (psi)	Size of Pipe in Inches					
	½	¾	1	1¼	1½	2
5	60	110	200	390	550	970
10	70	125	220	430	610	1075
15	75	135	240	470	665	1170
20	80	145	255	505	715	1255
25	85	155	270	530	740	1300
30	90	165	285	565	800	1400
40	100	185	320	615	885	1550
50	108	200	345	680	965	1680
60	114	214	368	730	1030	1800
70	120	226	390	770	1095	1910

Thus if a kitchen required 240 lb of steam flow per hour at 15 psi, a 1 = in. pipe would be the minimum size that should be installed. Steam lines should be insulated.

In general at steam flow per hour rates of 200 lb or more, pressures in pipes drop 2 psi for every 240 times the pipe diameter that the pine line runs. Thus if a 1-in. (2.5 cm) pipe is installed and it runs 10 ft (300 cm) there will be 1 psi drop between the start of the pipe and the end. The calculation is 10 ft × 12 in. = 120 in., length of the run of the pipe divided by 1 in. (pipe diameter) × 240. The result is then multiplied by the 2 psi loss (10 × 12/1 × 240 = ½ × 2 = 1 psi loss or 300 cm/2.5 cm × 240 = ½ × 2 = 1 psi loss). Of if a pipe were 2 in. (5 cm) in diameter and ran for 60 ft (1800 cm) there would be a drop of 3 psi (60 × 12/2 × 240 = 1½ × 2 = 3 psi loss or 1800 cm/5 × 24D = 1½ × 2 = 3 psi loss). If this 2-in. (5 cm) line started with 10 psi of steam, at the other end of 60 ft (1800 cm) the psi would be 7 psi.

A psi loss also occurs because of the resistance of fittings, such as elbows and valves. This psi drop is called the "equivalent length of run drop" and must be added in with the psi line loss discussed in the pre-

Table 14.3 Equivalent Length Values of Some Fittings in Feet

Fittings	Pipe Size in Inches*					
	½	¾	1	1¼	1½	2
Standard elbow	1.3	1.8	2.2	3.0	3.5	4.8
Side outlet tee	3.0	4.0	5.0	6.0	7.0	8.0
Gate valve	0.3	0.4	0.5	0.6	0.8	1.1
Globe valve	14.0	18.0	23.0	29.0	34.0	46.0
Angle valve	7.0	10.0	12.0	15.0	18.0	22.0

* To get centimeter values in this table, multiply the inch values by 2.5.

vious paragraph. The final size of the pipe installed will be dictated by the combined valves of the psi loss from the line run plus the equivalent length of the run drop. As an example: If a 1-in. (2.5 cm) pipe ran 20 ft (600 cm) and in this run had two elbows, an angle valve, and a side outlet tee, an equivalent length of run of 21.4 ft (642 cm) would have to be added to the actual run of 20 ft (600 cm) making a total of 41.4 ft (1242 cm). The data in Table 14.3 would be used to calculate the various units of equivalent length for different fittings in the line. For instance, in this line each elbow adds 2.2 ft (66 cm) or a total of 4.4 ft (132 cm) for two, the angle vlave adds 12 ft (360 cm) and the side outlet tee 5 ft (150 cm) a total of 21.4 ft (642 cm) (2 × 2.2 + 12 + 5 = 21.4 or 642 cm).

Manufacturers provide instructions for connecting their equipment to steam lines and these should be closely followed. Normally, a globe valve to turn steam on or off, a ball float trap with a connection to drain, the pressure gauge, and pressure-reducing valve follow in that order into the equipment. The size of these units varies with the pipe size and steam requirements. Floor drains are usually 1½ or 2 in. (3.75 to 5.0 cm) IPS (inside pipe size). Solid equipment joints to drains should not be made.

Due to a large temperature difference between steam pipes when they are hot and cold, elongation may be a problem. In most facilities, an elongation device is added for every 100 ft (30 m) of pipeline run. Proper sloping must occur also. The slope usually given for every 10 ft (3 m) of line is ⅛ to ½ in. (0.3 to 1.3 cm). Good strapping is required also. Steam traps, reducing valves, return condensate lines, and other specialized equipment must be installed at proper locations. A capable heating engineer should be consulted on all requirements.

Good workmanship is essential to proper installation of plumbing. Joints should be tight fitting. Soldering is becoming more and more com-

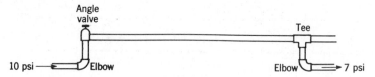

Figure 14.2 The fittings that make up the equivalent length of run drop described above. The actual run of the pipe and fittings is 20 ft, but due to fittings an additional 21.4 ft or run must be considered in the psi drop.

mon and solder points should be strong, neat, and wiped clean. Avoid excessive plumbing coming through the floor and place instead through the wall. Strap overhead plumbing. Faucets and fittings should be of high quality and of heavy weight to withstand the wear given them.

Underground sewer pipes may be glazed vitrified clay, plastic, or cast iron. Sewage pipes within buildings should be copper, plastic, or extra-heavy cast iron. Plastic may be allowed. Drain pipes should quickly run into larger pipe sizes. As soon as possible sewer lines should be 6 in. (15 cm) ID (inside dimension) pipe. If the volume of flow is heavy, a larger size may be needed. Sewer pipe sizes run up to 15 in. ID. Joints should be made perfectly tight by calking. Horizontal line slope should be ⅛ to ¼ in. (0.3 to 0.6 cm) ft (30 cm). Inside sewer lines should have cleanouts every 50 ft (15 m). All drains and sewage lines should be trapped.

Venting is required in plumbing systems. A vent is a waste stack that is connected to a sewer line and then extends through the roof to permit the sewer gas that rises to escape into the atmosphere instead of forcing its way through a trap. Traps provide resistance for the flow of such gas and also for the passage of vermin. Venting also prevents the downrush of water in drain and sewer lines from creating a suction that draws the water from the traps. The free flow of air allows pressures inside such lines to quickly adjust. Most codes allow for loop venting, which permits one venting system for a group of equipment instead of requiring that each piece of equipment be separately vented. The number of pieces and their size that can be loop-vented is regulated by local codes. The National Plumbing Code also provides standards. In some areas, devices that remove the need for venting are permitted.

A facility may have a need to remove storm or other outside water. A check should be made that the drainage provided is adequate. Pumps may have to be installed to remove water from drainage into basements or other low areas.

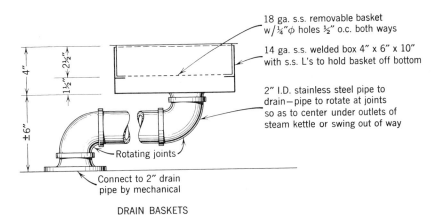

18 ga. s.s. removable basket
w/¼"φ holes ½" o.c. both ways

14 ga. s.s. welded box 4" x 6" x 10"
with s.s. L's to hold basket off bottom

2" I.D. stainless steel pipe to
drain—pipe to rotate at joints
so as to center under outlets of
steam kettle or swing out of way

Rotating joints

Connect to 2" drain
pipe by mechanical

DRAIN BASKETS

Figure 14.3 Swivel faucets and box type drains provide convenience at stock kettles. The drain box is high enough to prevent splashing and rotates so that it can be pushed aside for a container to be placed under the faucet. The box and strainer can be removed for washing at the pot sink. (*Courtesy University of Washington, Seattle.*)

Most municipalities have sewage disposal systems and a facility that will connect to sewer lines leading to these for sewage disposal. Most communities must now have systems that completely digest sewage and reduce it to harmless material. About 0.2 per cent of the sewage is solid material. This can be digested by bacteria except for a small quantity of sludge that must be removed from the system from time to time. Most systems use a preliminary settling tank in which excess liquid is drawn off. The remaining sewage is put through aeration tanks for about a 3-hr trip during which time bacteria digest the sewage to a point where it is 95 percent pure. Chlorination may be used to purify the remaining 5 percent before it is allowed to flow into drainage systems.

In some instances a facility may not be able to connect to a municipal sewage system and may have to build one to take care of the facility's needs. Local codes and U. S. Public Health Service authorities should be consulted and their requirements carefully followed. Usually a septic tank large enough to hold a day's sewage is required. Tees and baffles in the tank force the sewage to circulate and improve bacterial digestion. A seepage pit or drain field receives the digested sewage and allows it to flow into the soil. Soil requirements are strict as well as to the manner in which the drainage field is installed. A septic tank usually eliminates about 70 percent of the solid waste and the remaining 30 percent is digested in the drainage field.

Suggested Student Assignments

1. Visit a local municipal water and sewage department and inquire of officials what problems are encountered and how they are solved.

2. Compare the amount of detergent required to create comparable suds in 1 qt of hard water and 1 qt of softened water. (Use a carefully measured amount of common liquid household detergent for the test.)

3. Select a foodservice unit for study and calculate the amount of water and the temperatures required by the operation.

4. Calculate the amount of pressure required to supply water at 20 psi at a 250 ft level if the water is at 35 psi at the main line on the ground level.

5. Total the steam flow for a steam table measuring 2 ft × 10 ft (.61 × 3.0 m), a three-compartment steam cooker, and a direct-connected Jet-cooker. State the right pipe size.

6. Calculate the amount of steam required at the boiler to have 15 psi at the equipment if the line extends 40 ft and has a globe valve, three standard elbows, two side outlet tees, and an angle valve. What Bhp is required?

7. Study the plumbing plan for a building. Read the different specifications for equipment to be connected to the plumbing established by the plan.

Answers:

4. $35 \times 2.3 = 80.5$ $\dfrac{250 - 80.5}{2.3} = 86.5 \times 20 = 106.5 \ \text{lb}$

5. 198.4   1-in. pipe

6. 6 Bhp

Chapter 15

environmental planning

The comfort and well-being of people call for an environment in which the air is clean, maintained at suitable temperature and humidity, and kept free of obnoxious odors and other objectionable or injurious elements. Achieving this in foodservice and housing, where heat, odors, and excess air moisture are commonly created, presents special problems. The continual change in the level of objectionable factors, such as high and low temperatures, strong odors and air drafts, calls for a flexible environmental system of control. Planning members who are aware of problems need to participate actively in planning with heating and other specialists to achieve desirable results.

The goal is to obtain precisely controlled conditions that are highly flexible, quickly responsive, automatically controlled, and will operate at a minimum cost. Rule-of-thumb guides are likely to lead to serious errors and much higher costs. Exact definition of requirements is needed to produce the right conditions. It is desirable that the system be as maintenance-free as possible and contribute far less to pollution of the air and environment than those of the past. Standards that will provide helpful guidance in planning have been set up by (1) the National Warm Air Heating and Air Conditioning Association, 640 Engineers Building, Cleveland, Ohio 44114, and (2) the American Society of Heating, Refrigerating, and Air Conditioning Engineers, 205 Tuohy Avenue, Park Ridge, Illinois 60068.

AIR CONDITIONING

Air conditioning involves temperature, humidity, and air movement. Moisture-ladened air, though cool, may not feel comfortable because it has little drying effect. Drying of the air to a relative humidity of approximately 50 percent is desirable. If air must be cooled and moisture extracted, the cost is greater than if air is merely cooled. A common complaint against air conditioning in public areas is that the air is too cool. Usually air at 75° to 80°F (18.3 to 26.6°C) on a warm day is comfortable, providing the humidity is satisfactory.

Proper air velocities need to be maintained. Wide fluctuation is undesirable, and on- and off-cycles of air conditioning equipment need to be set to give small variation. Temperature rises as rooms fill with people because every human body gives off approximately 300 Btu[1] per hour or heat equivalent to that of a 100-watt incandescent light globe. About $\frac{1}{10}$ of a pound of moisture is expired by one room-occupant in an

---

[1] Btu = British thermal units; Btuh = British thermal units per hour. A Btu is the heat needed to raise a pound of water 1°F.

Figure 15.1a A removal of excess steam and fat fumes arising from cooking equipment may require a variety of ventilating equipment. (*Courtesy, George Bundy & Associates, Seattle, Wash.*)

hour. Air conditioning has the task of providing for changing conditions and changing load requirements.

Buildings can be sealed so tightly that the loss of heat from the inside to outside or the flow of air from the outside to inside is reduced considerably. When a building is properly constructed, the amount of air change resulting from seepage or infiltration from the outside is reduced from 1 to 2 air changes an hour to $\frac{1}{2}$ to $\frac{3}{4}$. This means a considerable saving in heating and air conditioning cost and, often, more than pays for the extra cost in constructing a tighter building. Vapor build-up is also reduced, that can blemish, cause rot, paint peeling, or create other undesirable conditions within the building. When tightly sealed, the building's environment is much more easy to control. Special problems occur when a large number of people go in and out of a building or when there must be a large number of doors, windows, and other openings. Much can be done, however, to reduce the influx of air one way or another. Just putting an air-flow vapor barrier on a revolving door or other entrance may save considerable heat loss or gain.

Figure 15.1b Equipment located back-to-back with equipment shown in Fig. 15.1a showing adjustment of hoods to height of equipment and area requiring ventilation. (*Courtesy George Bundy & Associates, Seattle, Wash.*)

Ventilation requirements should be based on the quantity of vapor and hot air to be exhausted. Heat and vapor build-up can be reduced by proper equipment selection and operation. Good insulation on ovens, bainmaries, steam tables, and other equipment will prevent heat loss. Selecting equipment designed to give maximum input of heat into products and minimum heat loss will reduce heat build-up. It has been estimated that from 30 to 50 percent of the heat generated for cooking foods is lost.

Structural features can be used to help prevent an undesirable spread of heat and vapors. Walls and partitions are useful, as around the dishwashing area. Partial partitions or structural components dropping from ceilings capture undesirable air and hold it until it can be eliminated. Double doors for pass-through areas or halls retard air speed. Lights dropping from ceilings can contribute to heat build-up. If lights are placed into ceilings so that the warmed air flows up into dead air spaces, heat will be reduced.

Air input must be balanced against air exhaust. If this is not done, negative or positive pressures will develop. The intake air for kitchens can frequently be taken from other areas; if brought from air conditioned spaces, this lessens requirements. Local codes usually provide regulations covering recirculated air in buildings. If air is taken from the dining area, only about 50 percent of total requirements should be drawn from there to prevent too heavy drain from the dining area. In planning input and output locations, avoid having them so close together that fresh air coming in instead of hot or vapor-laden air is pulled out.

Air ducts should be properly sized to allow free air passage. If ducts are not properly sized or have many turns, static pressure that increases fan requirements is built up. Air should be moved 1,500 to 2,100 (average 1,800 fpm); air at 2,000 fpm will carry away most of the dirt and grease so that they do not settle in the ducts. If it moves faster than 2,100 fpm, a rumbling noise is created. It is frequently desirable to insulate ducts that run through areas where they can lose their heat into working spaces. Ducts should be air tight and, where there is vapor condensation, ducts should be water tight and equipped with drains and lead backs to sewer lines to carry away condensate. Weather caps may be required over ducts where they come out of buildings. Filters and baffles should be used to change air flow and collect grease and dirt. Filters of steel mesh or shredded steel should be selected. Air velocities through filters about 300 to 400 fpm are recommended. Close-offs in case of fire and dampers equipped with fusible links that melt from 360 to 400° F are desirable. Ready access to switches is also desirable to reduce draft in case of fire. Certified performance ratings established by the National Association of Fan Manufacturers should be required for all fans or blowers selected. A single-entry-type fan with reversed blades will move grease and dirt through without allowing them to collect on the fan. Select the centrifugal type with forward or backward curved blades and either belt or direct drive. Some authorities recommend squirrel cage blowers because they have more power and capacity to expel air. Propeller fans are considered undesirable because they do not operate well against duct resistances.

About 15 cfm per person fresh air input is a good standard for a dining room. This air should be clean, fresh, and move at a velocity that is not noticeable but gives no feeling of stagnation. Local codes usually specify ventilating requirements for dining areas. An even distribution should be obtained to prevent noticeable air currents; usually 40 to 50 fpm air velocity is sufficient to give satisfactory air movement.

Once an installation is properly balanced in input and output air requirements, it is not advisable to deduct or add to ventilating requirements without changing the ventilating equipment. It is frequently desirable to have fans equipped to run at two speeds so that high speeds can be used at peak loads or summer operation and low speeds at non-peak loads or winter operation.

HEAT

Heat is energy produced by molecular action or vibration, or from chemical or atomic changes in matter. Regardless of how it is formed, it is the same thing and results in a feeling of warmth. Some scientists define heat as kinetic action or molecular disturbance. When molecules are in motion, heat develops. Because all substances have some molecular action going on in them, all possess some heat. When no molecular action is occurring, there is no heat. This is what is called "absolute zero."

Heat has some parallels with electricity. The random movement of electrons causes heat, while the smooth flow of a mass of electrons along a conductor causes electricity. When this smooth flow is blocked and the electrons are forced to pile up in a somewhat random fashion, as will occur in an electrical heating element, heat develops. A heated body releases an energy called "radiation" plus other forces that, if captured, can create an electrical force. Negative electrons and positive ions have been found to flow out of hot substances in proportion to the heat in the substance. A study of such flow is called "thermionics," and many electrical principles are involved.

When molecules vibrate or move, they develop a movement called "kinetic action." As a substance warms up, there is more kinetic action; as it cools, the kinetic action subsides. When there is a complete absence of kinetic action, there is a complete absence of heat. This absence of kinetic action and heat is the theoretical absolute zero ($-459°$ F or $-273°$ C). At absolute zero, gas no longer has pressure because its molecules have stopped moving. As movement occurs and speeds up, the temperature of a substance rises. Thus as we feel warmth, we are receiving an energy that helps to speed up the movement of molecules in our bodies.

Friction causes heat by moving the molecules. Microwaves moving in and out of matter bounce the molecules around, causing heat to rise in a substance. A fire can be started by rubbing two pieces of wood together; steel and quartz striking together makes the spark in a cigarette lighter. Copper or other good conductors of electricity allow a free flow of electricity with little blockage. But when the electricity tries to move through nichrome elements the blockage of electrons is so great that the molecules in the elements move rapidly and heat develops.

All substances will radiate energy from them. As their temperature increases, the amount of radiated energy increases. A glowing element sends out a large quantity of heat energy. As it moves from red to white heat, the type of energy (actually the wave length of the energy) changes. Red heat is largely infrared waves, while white heat is largely radiation. Radiated particles move with the speed of light; as they impinge upon an object, they release a considerable quantity of energy in the form of heat because the impact causes the molecules to move. As gas is compressed, it releases heat because its molecules become more and more crowded together, bumping each other more often and causing them to vibrate.

In chemical reactions, a release or absorption of electrons occurs from one substance to another. This may result in the release of heat. Such heat is called the "heat of reaction" or "heat of diffusion." When fuel burns, oxygen is chemically combining largely with hydrogen and carbon. The amount of heat released is so great that a flame results. When this happens, combustion is occurring, this can become a spontaneous reaction as long as the supply of oxygen, hydrogen, and carbon lasts and as long as the temperature that supports combustion is maintained. When many common fuels burn in air, the temperature rise may go as high as 3,600° F (about 2,000° C). A battery warms up when discharging because a chemical reaction is going on, indicating the release of electrons. A chemical change freeing heat is called "exothermic" (outgoing), and a chemical change absorbing heat is called "endothermic" (ingoing).

When atomic fusion or fission occurs, a tremendous amount of energy is released, much of which is in the form of heat energy. It is estimated that the temperature in the center of an atomic blast may be as high as 12,000° F (6,700° C). The terrific heat developed by the fusion of hydrogen into helium in the sun may cause the interior of the sun to be as high as 37,000° C. The outside temperature of the sun is much less, probably being about 6000° C as we observe from its color. An element that is so hot it has a red glow is not as hot as when it has a white glow. Sometimes the color of heat is used to judge the temperature. Thus a white tip on a gas flame indicates a high heat level. As the flame moves to yellow, the temperature is lower. The blue core in a gas flame is not blue heat, but gas and oxygen combining and rising to a combustible temperature.

Heat Measurement

Heat is measured in two ways: by degree (level or intensity) and by amount. The degree or level is indicated by temperature, while the amount is indicated by British thermal units (Btu) or calories. A Btu is the quantity of heat required to raise a pound of water 1° F, while a calorie is the amount of heat required to raise a gram of water 1° C. In the biosciences the "large calorie," which is equal to 1000 calories, is used. The "small calorie," defined here, is used in the physical sciences (e.g., chemistry, thermodynamics, and physics). The small calorie may be indicated by the abbreviation *cal*, while the large calorie may be indicated by *Cal* or Kcal. The calorie value of food is indicated by the large calorie, while the caloric value of a fuel is indicated by the small calorie. A small calorie equals 3.968 Btu, and a Btu equals 252 large calories. The amount of Btus released in burning specific fuels varies. For instance, crude petroleum has a Btu/lb value of 20,000; the best coals, 17,000 to 18,000; poor coal, 10,000; dried wood, 10,000; and straw, 8,000.

Three scales are used to measure the temperature or intensity (level) of heat: Fahrenheit (F), Celsius (C) and the Kelvin, or Absolute (K or A). The Fahrenheit scale was developed in 1724 by a German instrument worker, Gabriel Fahrenheit. On it, the melting point of ice is 32° and the boiling point of water is 212°. A Swedish professor of astronomy, Anders Celsius, developed a more logical scale in 1742. He made zero the melting point of ice, 100° the boiling point of water, and divided the interval into 100 equal degrees. This Celsius scale, sometimes referred to as the "centigrade" scale, is universally used in scientific work. The Absolute, or Kelvin, scale, named for Lord Kelvin for his share in its development, places 0° at the total absence of heat. The points between the freezing and boiling of water are divided into 100 degrees, and all other units of temperature are based on one of these. Thus absolute zero is 0° K, the melting point of ice is 273° K, and the boiling point of water is 373° K. If water in a scientific laboratory is at 50° C, it is 323° K (50 + 273 = 323). The K scale is used when extremely high or low temperatures are used. Thus the temperature of the northern lights is said to be around 8000° K.

In the Celsius scale there are 100 degrees between the melting point of ice and the boiling point of water, while in the Fahrenheit scale there are 180 degrees (212 − 32). Each Celsius degree equals 180/100, or 9/5 Fahrenheit degrees. To convert Celsius to Fahrenheit, the Celsius temperature is multiplied by 9/5 or 1.8 and then 32 is added. Thus, if the temperature is 50° C, the equation is (50 × 1.8) + 32 = 112, or 112° F. To convert Fahrenheit to Celsius, 32 degrees is deducted from the Fahrenheit temperature and the remainder is multiplied by 5/9 or 0.555.

For instance, 212° F (which is 100° C) in the equation reduces to (212 − 32) × 0.555 = 99.9° C. To change temperatures to the A or K scale, a Celsius temperature merely needs the addition of 273 to it. Thus, 58° C becomes 331° A; −25° C becomes 248° K. The easiest way to convert Fahrenheit to A or K would be to convert to Celsius and then to the A (K) scale. To convert the A (K) scale to either Celsius or Fahrenheit would be the inverse of converting the A (K) scale to Celsius and then to Fahrenheit.

Many liquids or solids expand or contract at a constant rate when heated or cooled. By using a liquid such as mercury or alcohol, Celsius and Fahrenheit were able to make a thermometer that would show the temperature as the liquid climbed or fell in a column on which the temperature scale was marked. Metals can also be used to measure the intensity of heat because they expand or contract similarly at a constant rate. A thermostat or meat thermometer operates on this principle. A thermostat can start a current of electricity to flow when metal cools to a point that a contact is made. As the temperature increases, the metal expands, breaking the contact and stopping the electrical current. A meat thermometer has a tiny spring inside the part inserted into the meat. This expands or twists as it warms up, turning a needle that is set in the head.

A thermocouple is an accurate thermometer used in science. If two different metal wires are joined in a wire one part being all nickle and the rest copper, and the copper end is heated, an electrical current will flow from the copper into the nickle wire. The amount of electricity flowing from one metal to another is always in exact ratio to the amount of heat in the substance. By measuring the quantity of this electrical flow, the temperature can be ascertained; instruments on a thermocouple do this automatically, so the reading comes in either Fahrenheit or Celsius, depending on the scale. It is of interest that while one end of a metal wire such as this receives heat, the other end of different metal gets cold. By reversing the metals, the end that got cold now gets hot while the other now gets cold. (That heat and electricity are closely related, as formerly indicated, is again emphasized.)

Temperature indicates the heat intensity of a substance and only indirectly the amount of heat in it. Heat quantity is measured in Btus or calories and not by degrees of K, C, or F. This difference between temperature and the amount of heat in a substance may be compared to water in a well. If the water level is 20 ft in the well, one knows only how high the water is, not the amount. Likewise, knowing that the temperature of water is 41° F (50° C) does not tell one how much heat is in the water. However, if the radius of the well is known in addition to its depth, the amount of water there can be calculated. Similarly, the amount of heat in this water can be ascertained if the amount of water and the temperature are known.[2]

Specific Heat

The quantity of heat in a substance can also be calculated if the substance, its mass, temperature, and specific heat are known. Specific heat is the quantity of heat in calories required to raise a gram of the substance 1° F. All substances do not have the ability to hold the same quantity of heat at the same temperature. A gram of water at 100° F (38° C) holds more heat in it than a gram of iron at 100° F (38° C). If 100 cal are put into 100 g of water, the temperature rises 100° C. But only about 9 cal need to be put into 100 g of iron to raise it to the same temperature; this is because water can hold more heat than iron without rising in temperature.

Water, compared with many substances (especially metals), holds a fairly substantial amount of heat before rising in temperature. For this reason, the amount it could hold before a gram rose 1° C was given a value of 1, and all other substances were given values in relation to this. In comparison with the specific heat of water at 1, that of other substances is, (steam) 0.444; ice, 0.493; air, 0.241; aluminum, 0.214; iron, 0.107, and copper and zinc, 0.09. Hydrogen, with a specific heat of 2.41, holds more heat per gram than any other substance. For this reason, hydrogen is sealed in electrical turbines to absorb heat and carry it away so the turbine does not get too hot. Note that ice and steam are about one-half the specific heat of the parent water. Iron, having $\frac{1}{11}$ the specific heat of water, rises 11° C for every 1° C water rises. (Moist food is considered to have the specific heat of water, or 1).

To raise the temperature of a 15-lb (6.8 Kg) aluminum kettle plus 50 lb (22.7 Kg) of water and potatoes from 40° F (4.4° C) to 212° F (100° C) takes 9152 Btus or 2,309,442 cal without considering heat loss in the process. The calculation will be 50 × 1 (specific heat of water and potatoes) + 15 lb of aluminum × 0.214 (specific heat of aluminum) = 53.21 and 53.21 × (212-40) = 9152 Btu. The calories needed are

[2] If the radius of a well is 2 ft, the volume of water will equal radius times height: 2 × 3.1416 (2 × 20), or 251 cu ft. One cu ft is about 7½ gal; therefore, there are about 1882 gal in the well. One gal weighs about 8.3 lb and one lb equals 454 g. The weight of the water is 8.3 × 454 × 1,882 = 7,091,752 g. Each gram of water contains 1 cal for every degree C, or a total of 7,091,752 cal. At 50°C there would be 50 × 7,091,752 cal in the water. Total quantity of heat would be calculated from absolute zero. 50°C equals 323°K (273 + 50) and 323 × 7,091,752 = 2,290,635,868 cal of heat in the total volume of the well water.

50 × 454 × 1 × (100 − 4.4) = 2,170,120 cal to heat the water and potatoes + 15 × 454 × 0.214 × (100 − 4.4) = 139,322 cal to heat the pot only, which, together with the food and water, equals 2,309,442 cal.

These calculations may seem obtuse, involved, complex, and not relative to planning and operating a food facility. They have been included with the hope that a fuller understanding will sharpen awareness of energy uses and utilization. Although the essential cooking may require only 2 million calories in a specific situation, through the use of inappropriate methods or carelessness, 6 million may be wasted. It is well to challenge plans and methods with such question as: Is there a better way? Can acceptable values be secured by means that reduce required heat input? Do some of the modern techniques increase or reduce energy and labor requirements?

Change of State from Heat

Most matter at low temperatures is a solid. The molecules are bound close together, and their movement is limited. As heat increases, molecules move away from each other and expansion results. A pot full of water spills over when heated because the cold water expands when warmed. At a fixed temperature, molecules in a substance such as ice or iron free themselves from their fixed state and move about freely. This signals the change from a solid state to a liquid. As the temperature of the liquid rises, the molecules move more rapidly and become farther apart. At another fixed temperature point, they break away from each other, changing from a liquid to a gas or vapor. This change of matter from a solid to a liquid to a gaseous state is called a "change of state." Heat is responsible for this because it generates a kinetic action which creates molecular movement causing a change of state in the matter.

The quantity of heat required to induce a change of state varies. The change of a pound of ice at 32° F (0° C) to water at 32° F (0° C) takes 144 Btu. To change a pound of water at 212° F or (100° C) takes 970 Btu. (The energy requirement to do this per gram would be calculated by multipling the Btus by 252.) The amount of heat required to change a solid to a liquid is called the "heat of fusion," and the heat required to change liquid to a vapor is called the "heat of vaporization." Different quantities of heat are required to do each of these things for different substances.

When vapor changes to a liquid and when a liquid changes to a solid, both changes give *off* heat, but, when a liquid changes to a vapor or a solid to a liquid, heat is *absorbed*. The phenomenon of requiring heat or giving off heat in making a change of state is important in calculating humidity, refrigeration, and other needs in a facility. Planners need to understand the basic principles and how to do some of the rudimentary calculations to contribute adequately to planning.

Water heated to 212° F (100° C) absorbs a certain quantity of heat, and considerably more when changing to steam; therefore steam is much hotter than water for cooking purposes. One pound of steam at 240° F (115.5° C) has 1040 additional Btus in it from the time it was boiling water at 212° F, because of the extra heat it took to get it to 240° F.

Heat and Color

When a flame is white or a bluish white, it is about 6,000° F (3,333° C). A yellow or orange flame will have a lower temperature. Bright red to a deep, dark, or cherry red is heat around 2,000° F (1110° C). However, even below the point where matter takes on a change of color due to heat, the hotter substance will radiate heat to a cooler one.

Heat Movement

Heat moves through (1) conduction, (2) convection, and (3) radiation. Each works in a different manner to transport heat, and some of the heat transported may differ from others. Radiated heat is different from heat transported by conduction and convection.

Conduction is the transfer of heat from one piece of matter to another. When heat is developed under a griddle, it is conducted through the griddle plate into material placed on top of it. The heat may be conducted through a pan, through fat or water medium, and into food to be cooked. The food is cooked as the temperatures rises from the heat conducted into the food. Conduction probably works because one particle of matter picks up heat, passing it on to another particle through kinetic action. Thus particles must be in contact with each other. Some substances transfer heat better than others. Silver, gold, platinum, copper, aluminum, and iron, in that order, are good heat conductors. These are good electrical conductors also. Stainless steel conducts heat poorly. Food in a stainless steel pan over direct heat scorches easily because the metal fails to spread the heat evenly and quickly. The use of metals that conduct heat quickly and evenly (e.g., copper, aluminum, or iron) as the bottom of a pot or as a core between layers of stainless steel helps in spreading and transferring the heat more evenly through the bright stainless steel.

Convection is the movement of heat transported by air, liquid, or some other medium of flow. A convection oven causes heat to flow by using a fan to push the air around. Rooms are heated by the natural convection of air. Warm air tends to rise and cooler air descend. This results in air movement from a heated surface upward over a cooler area, and as it loses its heat the air descends. It moves back into the heated area and again rises as it warms, and the cycle is repeated. Because of this, it is best to put a heating unit under a cooling surface such as a window. The cool air then drops down into the heater, where it is warmed. It moves out and up and back down so that a complete circle is made. Air that does not move, called "dead air," conducts heat poorly. Air must move, or convect, to transfer heat. The conduction value of air is 0.00005 compared with 0.001 for water and 0.210 for iron. Thus dead air space is a good insulator.

Radiation is energy that moves with the speed of light. It is matter, just like light. When radiated particles strike matter, they collide with a tremendous force even though the radiated particle is small. This causes vibration that develops heat. Any warmer body radiates heat to a cooler one. Heat flows in radiation because bodies have different temperatures. The hotter the one body and the colder the other, the faster and greater the radiation. A glowing substance with white heat emits a considerable quantity of radiated material. Broilers and toasters cook largely by radiated heat.

Dark surfaces absorb more radiation than light ones. Aluminum containers in which frozen food is to be baked in ovens may be painted with a dull, black paint on the outside. This improves heat absorption, thus shortening cooking time. If heat is to be kept inside an aluminum foil, the bright side should be inside and the dull side out. If bright foil faces an air space, it radiates heat back and will let only a small quantity pass. Thus reflective surfaces in buildings can send back much heat that otherwise would escape to the outside. The reflective surface should be on the side facing the area in which the heat is to be returned.

Radiated particles, like light, move in a straight line. They do not go around corners but, like light, can be reflected around them. "Heat shadows" are thus possible. Radiation passes through transparent objects just as light does. No heat is created in its passage. Heat is produced only when the radiated particle is stopped. However, when radiated particles and light go through a window and strike opaque or solid matter inside, heat is developed usually in the form of infrared waves. These waves cannot be transferred through transparent substances, but are stopped by them. Thus, in a room into which solar energy flows, a rapid build-up of heat can occur from the trapped infrared waves inside.

Heat and Humidity

Warm air can hold more heat and moisture than cold air. When moist air becomes cooler, it frequently not only loses heat but will also lose some of its moisture because it cannot hold as much moisture as warm air. When moist air rises into the upper atmosphere and cools, clouds form and it rains. Warm air striking a glass filled with ice water loses moisture on the glass, and gradually small beads of moisture gather on the glass. Refrigeration coils ice up because of moisture condensing on them as moisture-ladened air strikes them. The daytime air picks up moisture and loses it as dew on the cool ground as the air cools at night. When the sun rises and warms the atmosphere, the dew is picked up and redistributed as moisture in the air.

Moisture in air is often called "humidity.[3] Relative humidity (RH) is the amount of moisture in air as compared to the maximum amount it *could* hold at that temperature. Air at 50 percent RH holds only 50 percent of what it could hold at that temperature before it reaches the dew point. Air at 100 percent RH has reached a saturation point, and any more moisture picked up by it would cause condensation at that temperature. A slight cooling of the air would mean that it would lose some of the moisture because it no longer could hold the same quantity at the lower temperature. Air that has reached 100 percent RH, or dew point, can pick up more moisture if its temperature rises (which explains the drying effect in a refrigerator with the opening and closing of doors). One pound of air at 70° F (21° C) and 50 percent RH contains 0.008 lb of moisture, while a pound of air at 80° F (27° C) holding 0.008 lb of moisture will be 35 percent RH. At 60° F (16° C) the RH is nearly 70 percent. At about 50° F (10° C), this air reaches dew point or 100 percent RH.

Air that is dry will feel cooler than air of the same temperature carrying more moisture because dry air evaporates moisture from the skin and such evaporation requires some heat, which it takes from the body. When air is quite moist, such evaporation is much slower, therefore one feels warmer, even though the two air samples may be at the same tem-

---

[3] Absolute humidity (AH) is the percent or quantity of moisture in a given volume of air, usually per cubic foot. If AH is 2 percent, the air contains 2 percent moisture. AH in air can vary; the air volume is dependent on its temperature because warm air expands and cooler air contracts. The cubic feet of warm air with a 2 percent AH will have a higher AH per cubic foot if it cools. Mixing ratio humidity (MRH) and specific humidity (SH) do not vary because they are based on the mass of weight of water vapor per pound of air, as noted above for the 0.008-lb value. Both MRH and SH are usually the same, so they are frequently used interchangeably by heating and air conditioning engineers.

perature. Normally, a desirable RH in a room is 50 percent, but a range of 35–60 percent RH may be acceptable.

The quantity of humidity in air may be measured in several ways. Normally, the RH can be measured by taking the temperature of a dry and the temperature of a wet bulb. The moistened bulb will show a lower temperature depending on how much moisture is in the air because, when the moisture evaporates, heat is needed for the evaporation—which it draws from the bulb. If the air is saturated with moisture, little difference in temperature occurs between the dry and wet bulb. If the air is very dry, a considerable temperature difference is found. By referring to tables, the RH can be found based on the temperature difference. Thus, a 90° F (32° C) dry bulb temperature and a 76° F (25° C) wet bulb temperature indicate a RH of 54 percent.

Latent and Sensible Heat

For moisture to evaporate, heat is required. If no heat is present, it cannot turn to gas. Under 212° F (100° C), the amount of heat needed to evaporate a pound of water is greater than the 970 Btu needed at boiling. Usually a standard of 1061 Btu is used for calculating the heat needed to evaporate moisture around 70° F (21° C). This heat absorbed by moisture is not felt by individuals in a room unless the moisture is being evaporated from their bodies. In that case, as noted, they feel cooler. However, when moisture condenses in a room, it gives up its "latent" (hidden) heat, which is felt as a temperature rise in the room, a pound of moisture condensing in a room contributes 1061 Btu of heat. Heat felt in a room is called "sensible" heat. Latent heat can become sensible heat upon being lost from moisture. Because latent heat can become sensible heat when moisture is removed from the air, as it oftentimes must be in air conditioning, it is calculated as heat to be removed in cooling; but a heating engineer will not calculate it as heat when he plans the heating system of a building. In fact, a heating engineer may add moisture to the air that is warmed because cool air that is warmed becomes moisture hungry due to its low RH; it will then cause people to feel cooler than the air temperature really is.

Air at 72° F (22° C) and 35 percent RH holds about 0.0004 lb of moisture per pound of air. If this moisture is condensed and its heat goes into the air, the temperature of the air rises $4\frac{1}{4}$° F ($2\frac{1}{2}$° C). The air then becomes 76° F (24° C). If air is 87° F (31° C) and the RH is 50 percent, the air holds per lb 0.014 lb of moisture. If all this moisture condenses, a temperature rise of 15° F (8.3° C) occurs; the air temperature then goes to 102° F (39° C), which is quite warm. Thus latent heat can be a problem in cooling. A fairly high latent factor is desired in winter because moist air feels warmer.

Environmental engineers normally use a value of 2/3 sensible and 1/3 latent heat in estimating the total heat potential of air in calculating the quantity of sensible heat resulting from the latent heat in air. This total heat potential is called "enthalpy." This is, however, for living spaces holding only a normal number of people. If a dining room is filled with diners and a lot of personnel are working there also, the ratio of latent heat to sensible heat will rise considerably. Also, the amount of latent heat rises to sensible heat if human activity increases. An individual doing light work or being moderately active loses about 255 Btuh of sensible heat and 145 Btuh of latent heat. However, when dancing, the same individual will lose 305 Btuh of sensible heat and 545 Btuh of latent heat. The moisture build up and latent heat potential in a room, either because a large number of people are in a room or because of greater activity, can be a problem in air conditioning. Additional moisture build-up can occur because of moisture coming from steam, cleaning, or other reasons. For instance, an individual showering can put $\frac{1}{2}$ lb of very warm moisture into the air. Cooking three meals for one person in a day can add almost 5 lb of moisture. Washing dishes for these meals adds another pound. One house plant will put a pound of moisture in the air in a day. Mopping an 8×10 ft area adds nearly $2\frac{1}{2}$ lb of moisture to the air.

Heat from lights is mostly sensible heat and must be calculated in air conditioning. If lights use more than 5 w/sq ft of floor space, enough heat is generated to heat the building. Cooking equipment in commercial kitchens is considered to give off 65 percent of its heat in sensible heat and 35 percent in latent heat. If an efficient hood with good ventilation is placed over the equipment, most of the latent heat is removed. When such a hood is installed, the environmental engineer will eliminate latent heat from consideration and merely increase sensible heat by 10 percent to make up for the omission. Thus a 200 sq in. griddle rated at 6 kw and developing 20,400 Btuh produces about 6600 Btuh of sensible heat and 3600 Btuh of latent heat, or a total of over 10,000 Btuh. However, under a good hood, the total would be 7260 Btuh (6600 + 660 = 7260). Most manufacturers give information on the Btuh output both in sensible and latent heat. If they do not, an environmental engineer will take the total Btuh output as rated by the manufacturer and divide this by half and then consider it $\frac{2}{3}$ sensible heat and $\frac{1}{3}$ latent heat, except when under a good hood with good air draft, in the latter case, the sensible $\frac{2}{3}$ value is multiplied by 10 percent, and this is added as sensible heat and no value is added for latent heat.

Heating of Spaces

The inside environment must be defined to calculate the heating needs of a building. Normally, living spaces should be around 70° F (21° C) in winter and not higher than 78° F (26° C) in summer with a RH of around 50 percent. This can vary. Active workers prefer a slightly cooler atmosphere. The temperature outside in summer can affect the temperature needed inside.

Local codes may vary on the quantity of air that must be brought from the outside in ratio to air that is reused in the building. In very cold weather, a lot of cold air brought in and warmed increases the cost of heating considerably. Air at −30° F (−34° C) to be raised to 70° F (21° C) will have to be heated to over 100° F (67° C). Most codes require from 10–25 percent outside air, with the remainder being reused air. In addition to this air intake, additional air flows into the building from doors, windows, and other infiltration. Normally, the cubic feet per minute (cfm) of air intake per person is between 10 and 40 in food and housing facilities.

In preliminary planning, the building should be studied to see if its basic design is one that can be efficiently heated and cooled. Some buildings that are beautiful in design are impractical to heat or cool at low cost. The type of central well in a building as seen in the Brown Palace Hotel in Denver or in the Student Union Building at the University of Montana, or seen in moving stairs and other openings between floors, complicates the problem of heat control.

Heating engineers in setting up a heating system carefully calculate the amount of heat a building will lose through walls, ceilings, and floors. Most building materials have known heat transfer values. Engineers will speak of U, k, or R values. The U-value indicates the number of Btuh that go through a square foot of space of building material when there is a 1° F difference between the outside and inside temperature of the building. If there is a 40° F (22° C) difference, the U-coefficient must be multiplied by 40. A k-value is the amount of heat conducted through a square foot of homogeneous material 1 in. (2.5 cm) thick when there is a 1° F temperature difference between the inside and outside. Thus the only difference between U-value and k-value is that the U material may be more or less than 1 in. (2.5 cm) thick, and may be on a mixture of materials, but the k-value is always based on a 1 in. (2.5 cm) thickness and on one kind of material. If the surface with the k-value is more than 1 in. (2.5 cm) thick, the amount of heat lost through the surface must be multiplied by the true width. This then gives the U-value. Engineers may speak of a U-value or k-value as conductance values, written "C."

An R-value is the reciprocal of a U-value, or 1/U. It indicates the number of hours it takes a Btu to go through the material. If, for instance, an 8-in. (20 cm) concrete block wall has a U-value of 2 (2 Btuh going through when only a 1° F temperature difference exists between the inside and outside), the R-value is $\frac{1}{2}$, meaning that it takes a Btu a half hour to go through the material. The K-value of this wall is 0.25 (2.00/8.00) or $\frac{1}{4}$.

A heating engineer will calculate the total R, or thermal resistance (written R_T), of walls, ceilings, floors, roofs, and so on. This is helpful in indicating how much heat will be lost from the building at the desired temperature since he has now a total heat loss per hour. If too small a heating unit is added, the building will be too cold in the coldest weather. If a unit is too large, excess cost and perhaps poor heating results will occur.

For 550 sq ft (49.5 m²) of wall made of 4 in. (10 cm) brick, 6 in. (15 cm) concrete block, $\frac{3}{4}$ in. (1.8 cm) air space, and $\frac{3}{4}$ in. (1.8 cm) plaster, the engineer—by consulting tables and making necessary calculations— will find that the R_T is 3.33 (the U-value is 0.3). This may be too high and he may then ascertain what effect 3 in. (7.5 cm) of installation with a U-value of 0.087 would have. He will now find that the R_T value is 14.9, with a U-value of 0.067, which he considers one Btu being lost every 14.9 hours sufficiently low to give satisfactory results. This is shown by the fact that the wall, with a 60° F (16° C) temperature difference in midwinter, would have a heat transfer of 3,900 Btuh (0.3 U-value × 550 sq ft × 60° F temperature difference = 3,900) and, in the second wall, would have a 2211 Btuh transfer, over a third less, (0.067 × 550 × 60 = 2,211). Over a period of years, this additional cost of the insulation may be returned many times and may yield a building with more even heat.

Heat Loss and Insulation

Glass has high heat loss. A single pane has an R of 0.9; a double panel, 0.6; and a triple pane, 2.5. The U-values are 1.13, 0.61, and 0.41, respectively. Thus a 550 sq ft (49.5 m), surface of single pane glass with a temperature difference of 60° F (16° C) would have a heat loss of 40,230 Btuh (1.13 × 550 × 60).

A dead air space is a good insulator. If reflective paper, such as bright aluminum foil, is put on the inside of a dead air space pointing toward the space from which heat will come, a much more effective heat barrier is achieved. Thus, to prevent heat loss from inside a building, the reflective material should be on the outside wall of the dead air space. If it is to prevent entry of heat into the building, it would be on the opposite or inside wall. Putting reflective paper where there is no dead air space does little to insulate. Much heat can be lost where slabs or floors are on or near grade level. Having insulation below, dead air space, reflective material, and a warm basement underneath can do much to reduce heat loss. Much heat is lost where floors and ceilings join outer walls. If insulation is provided at this point, much heat loss can be reduced. The heat loss of a floor at this point can be around 30 Btuh/linear ft.

Calculating Heating Needs

The heat loss of a building will also be influenced by the outside design. Architects design buildings to meet a specific outside winter temperature. This may go as low as $-30°$ F ($-34°$ C) or lower and up to 20° F ($-7°$ C) or more. The lowest temperature is not used for this; an average of the coldest days in the area is used. Special tables give information on what the outside design requirements are. For instance, St. Paul, Minnesota, will have an outside design requirement of $-30°$ F ($-34°$ C); Portland, Oregon, a $+10°$ F ($-12°$ C), and Denver, Colorado, $-10°$ F ($-23°$ C). Normally, a winter wind of 15 mph is used, which gives an R of 0.17 for outside surface loss. Walls below grade are usually considered to lose 4 Btuh (R = 0.25), and basement floors, 2 Btuh (R = 0.5).

A heating engineer might present a planning team with the following calculations of heat loss from a motel that has 89,600 sq ft (8054 m²) of space or 1,075,000 cuft (32,500 m³) designed for 2° F ($-17°$ C) outside and 72° F (22° C) inside.[4] The building will be well constructed and have a calculated half air change per hour from seepage, transfer, and so forth. Local codes require that 20 percent of the air provided per hour be from the outside and that this must be based on the total capacity of the building. Extra outside air providing from 10 to 30 cfm must be provided for meeting rooms, dining areas, and other areas where smoke and other factors would require a greater input and output of air. This increases the total air requirements by 34,270 cfm.

---

[4] This is the simplest type of calculation made. If the Degree Day Method is used, based on number of degree days in cold weather, the calculation is more complex.

Total Btuh Loss for Motel

Btuh to provide heat loss from building surfaces	2,268,700 Btuh
$\frac{1}{2}$ air change/hr (1,075,000 cu ft/2 gives a cfh flow of 503,760 $\times$ 0.018* $\times$ 72-2° F	638,000 Btuh
20% (outside air) $\times$ 1,075,000 cu ft $\times$ 0.018 $\times$ 72-2° F	270,900 Btuh
34,270 cfm extra air $\times$ 1.08 $\times$ 72-2° F	2,590,812 Btuh
Total Btuh heat loss	5,764,412

Based on this requirement, the engineer would have to provide a heating plant that would produce around 6 million Btuh.

Different fuels might be available and the engineer might be requested to give the planning team information on costs plus recommendations. Normally, gas and oil have about 70 to 75 percent efficiency, which means the quantity of heat available from heating from the total Btuhs obtained by burning the particular fuel. Coal has about 70 percent, electricity, when elements are immersed in water, will have 95 to 100 percent efficiency. The following indicates the cost of different fuels based on a 5,700,000 Btuh requirement at a cost of $0.004/cu ft for gas, $0.10/gal for fuel oil, $10.00/ton for coal, and $0.017/kwh for electricity. The Btus from the various fuels are based on standard values. The Btu per unit for gas is for natural gas, for No. 1 or No. 2 fuel oil, and for anthracite (high heat value coal).

Type Fuel	Btu per Unit	Percent Efficiency	Net Btu per Unit	Total Units Needed per Hour	Dollar Cost per Unit	Total Cost per Hour
Gas	1,052/cu ft	75	789	7,224	0.004/cu ft	$2.89
Oil	141,000/gal	75	105,750	5.39	0.100/gal	5.38
Coal	29,200,000/ton	70	20,440,000	0.278	10.000/ton	2.73
Electricity	3,412/kwh	95	3,241.4	1,758.5	0.017/kwh	2.99

The engineer will show that all fuels are competitive except for oil. That oil and coal have to be stored, that coal is dirty, and that the area is in a good electrical-producing area cause the engineer to recommend electrical heat. Gas could be used but, because of a threatened shortage,

---

* This is a factor used by heating engineers to indicate the number of Btus required to heat 1 lb of air 1°F. This if obtained as follows: 0.241 (specific heat of air) $\times$ 0.075 (weight of a cubic foot of air) = 0.018. If cfm is used for air flow and not cfh, the factor 0.018 is multiplied by 60 min to get a factor of 1.08.

the planning team agree with his recommendation; but they refer the final decision to the owners because coal might also be a desirable fuel.

The team planners may recommend also that the heating engineer and other experts investigate the advisability of a total energy system which utilizes waste heat to heat spaces, provide heat for absorptive refrigeration or meet other energy needs.

Planners should inspect the heating system after installation and prior to acceptance. The inspection should cover the Btuh capacity of the system, adequacy of distribution, and efficiency of fuel use. Fossil fuels must have their waste products exhausted. The system should provide for maximum combustion of these fuels, which allows all the air needed to do this plus that needed to move away combustion products, but no more. An excess of air would mean that warm air is exhausted. A check can be made of flue gases to ascertain if efficient combustion is occurring and air flow is correct. For instance, if No. 2 fuel oil is used, the carbon dioxide content of the flue gas should not be over 12.3 percent of total bases if the excess air introduced is 20 percent. Engineers can make these calculations and refer to tables that give desirable levels. For such fuels, the stack temperature should not be over 600° F (316° C). If it is, a loss of heat is occurring. The smoke readings should not be greater than the standards established by the Institute of Boiler and Radiator Manufacturers, 393 Seventh Avenue, New York, New York 10001. All boilers of the system should meet the standards of the agencies previously mentioned.[5] If systems are checked in this manner and also checked frequently during subsequent operation, much air pollution from combustion products will be eliminated and savings on energy and cost will be made. Too frequently in the past, the planning for heating has been on a loose, haphazard basis. Buildings having a high heat loss, with just a bit more insulation or construction or design treatment, could have been built to save much energy. Heating systems that overprovide heat or distribute it poorly have been built. Planning-team members who acquaint themselves with basic needs in heating and how calculations are made for providing adequately can be effective in seeing that the best job is done and a minimum of energy used.

COOLING

Cooling an inside environment of a building may be needed every day of the year in some climates, while in others it may be required for a

---

[5] At the time of publication of this book, the standards used for heating, ventilating, and cooling were under scrutiny to determine whether they can be modified to reduce energy requirements. It is recommended, therefore, that those planning new buildings or remodeling old ones check standards for changes that may have been made.

short time only. Cooling may be needed for the entire day or only a part of a day. The East requires air conditioning 24 hr/day for 15 to 21 weeks of the year; the South, for 4 to 8 weeks longer. Other areas may require it for summer months only. Even in cold weather, cooling may be needed. A dining room with a large sun exposure on the west may build up enough heat in the afteroon to need cooling, even though the temperature outside is cold. Lights and heat from occupants may be sufficient to create cooling needs in a building center even though the outside rooms require heating.

Cooling requirements are calculated on the basis of the hottest part of the day, while heating needs are calculated for night when the weather is coldest. While heat given off by lights, individuals, latent heat, and equipment is not considered in heating, they are in cooling. U-values and others may be used, but most often heat-transfer values (HTM) are used to calculate cooling needs. The quantity of latent to sensible heat, as pointed out, is important also.

In many areas, a 15° F (8° C) temperature difference between the high outside temperature and the desired inside temperature is planned. Individuals coming into a 70° F (21° C) room when the temperature is 90° F (32° C) outside may find the temperature cold. The federal government recommends that 78° F (25° C) be a standard for living space in the summer. The humidity of the air should also be considered. Thus, in areas of high humidity, the temperature may be lower, but in very dry areas, such as Las Vegas, Nevada, the temperature can be higher because of the cooling effect of very dry air. Engineers calculate the effect of wind velocities in the summer to be lower than in the winter, so a smaller correction is made for this factor.

Building design is important. A roof overhang allows the sun to enter through glass in some areas in winter when the sun is low in the horizon, but the overhang stops heat in summer when the sun is high. The use of louvres or other items outside the building can also help provide shade in summer and allow solar heat to enter in winter, if adjustable. Trees and plants can do the same. Deciduous trees lose leaves in winter that shade a building from heat build-up in summer. Full outdoor shade reduces heat build-up by 80 percent. Shading from inside is far less efficient.

Engineers must vary the HTM values according to the type of climate —which may be classified as cool, medium, or hot. The hottest usual outside temperature is used instead of an average of the coldest days, as used in heating. Heat transfer values will depend on the type of climate, material, and wind velocities, in some instances. In normal living spaces, individuals are calculated as giving off 300 Btuh, but in foodservices, 400 Btuh are used, 255 being considered sensible heat and 145 being con-

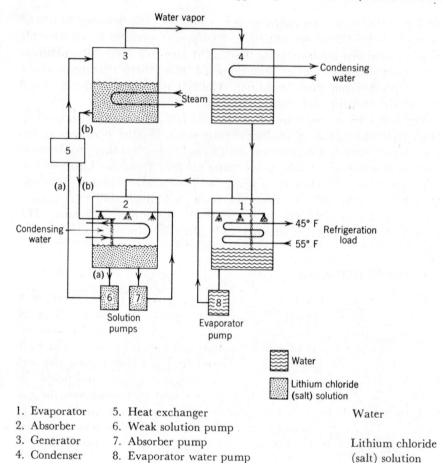

Figure 15.1 An absorptive system. Water pumped by the evaporator pump (8) is forced through sprays and as it falls it evaporates, cooling the interior of the evaporator (1). Water for cooling the building comes into coils in (1) at 55°F, is cooled and leaves at 45°F (7°C). Water vapor in (1) is conducted over to (2), the absorber. Salt (lithium chloride) solution pumped up and sprayed out picks up water vapor, drying the air, which is exhausted. The absorption of water vapor in the absorber (2) creates warmth which is carried away by condensing water flowing through coils. Moisture absorbed by the salt solution is carried down to the salt solution at the bottom where it weakens the solution. A continuous pick-up of the weakened solution occurs with pump (6); the weak solution (a) travels up through the heat exchanger (5) that warms the weak solution as it goes through. The weak solution (a) now moves up to (3) the generator. Here steam warms the solution to boiling, causing water vapor to be driven off and causing the salt solution to become concentrated again. Hot con-

sidered latent heat. An engineer may calculate only sensible heat and multiply it by 1.3 to get enthalpy. Equipment giving off considerable heat is calculated separately for the heat it gives off. Normally, planners can expect that the cooling Btuh required in northern climates is about half of the heating Btuh in winter. (Consult standards of the National Warm Air, Heating and Air Conditioning Association.)

The humidity or moisture in the air is a factor to consider in cooling. High RH values push up cooling requirements. Seattle, Washington, has a moderate outside temperature design and a low cooling requirement because it receives a steady, moderating air flow from the Japanese current that warms the climate in winter and cools it in summer. Spokane, Washington, 200 miles in from the coast, has much different requirements because it does not have the same moderating influence. The climate there is hotter in summer and colder in winter than in Seattle.

Cooling Systems

Cooling systems operate either by a process called "refrigeration" or a process called "absorption." Both operate on the basis of a change of state of a liquid to a gas, which requires heat and the condensation of the gas back to a liquid in which the absorbed heat is given off. The heat required to permit the liquid to expand to a gas comes from the surrounding areas, such as air or food in a refrigerator or air and people in a room. The gas carries the heat back to a unit that condenses the gas back to a liquid. In such condensation of the gas to a liquid, heat is given off. Figure 22.1 shows how a refrigeration system works. Compression helps to force the gas back to a liquid. In the process heat is given off.

In refrigeration, gas that has expanded in what is called the "expansion coils" which causes the cooling by pulling in heat is then carried to a compressor. This is a pump that puts pressure on the gas, causing the gas to lose the heat it picked up and, in doing so, it returns to a liquid.

---

centrated solution (b) now flows down through the heat exchanger where it gives up heat to warm the weak solution (a) flowing upward. The concentrated solution (b) then flows back into the absorber (2) where it is ready once more to pick up water vapor. The steam from the generator (3) now is carried over into the condensor (4). Here coils of cool water condense the steam back into water and this water flows back into (1) the evaporator where it can be evaporated and once more be sent through its cycle. (*Source. Mechanical and Electrical Equipment for Buildings*, William J. McGuinness and Benjamin Stein, 5th ed., John Wiley, p. 235. Reprinted by permission.)

It is ready to recirculate and pick up more heat when it expands in the coils.

Absorptive cooling is growing in use. It uses a liquid that turns into a gas in an evaporator. Again, this expansion or change of state requires heat, and it is taken from the surrounding area—the cooling area. The warmed gas is then carried to an absorber that reconverts the gas into a liquid releasing the heat. To do this, the absorber usually contains a liquid that has a high affinity for the gas. When this is sprayed in the chamber, the gas is absorbed. Many use saturated lithium chloride solutions that pull the gas back into the solution. When the solution absorbs as much gas as it can, it is taken to another area where it is heated to concentrate it back to a saturated solution. This prepares it so it can absorb gas again. Figure 15.1 shows the process commonly used.

The heat developed in a refrigeration compressor or an absorber can become a problem. It may cause heat build-up in machine or evaporating rooms, thus lessening the efficiency of the system and of motors and requiring it to be moved out at some cost. Engineers today often design systems in which such heat is captured and concentrated in a heat exchanger that gets hot enough to manufacture steam, hot water, or other hot substances.

In many modern buildings, air conditioning units and heating units are now the same machine. These are through-the-wall cabinets that cool in the summer and heat in the winter. In the summer, the compressor coil is vented to the outside so the heat from the compressor is dissipated outside and does not warm the room. In the winter, the compressor heat is turned inside. It is also possible to have large heat pumps in hotels or other buildings. The heat pump extracts heat from the refrigeration compressors and uses this to heat water, warm water for bathing pools, create steam, or even heat spaces.

Whenever possible, planners should be alert to utilize wasted heat. Too frequently in the past, heat from refrigeration compressors built up in the machine rooms, where it reduced motor efficiency and created extra cost by having to be moved away. Water flowing around such compressors could be heated or warmed and then carried to booster heaters, where additional warming could occur, or could be used for creating steam if required. The Kahala Hilton Hotel in Honolulu uses the heat from the compressors on its air conditioning units to warm water for bathing pools and also to warm water for other hotel needs. Such water flowing through heat exchangers can pick up heat carried to the exchangers from the compressors. These heat exchangers are inexpensive and are not difficult to operate. They pay for their installation in a short time.

Cooling Requirements

The hypothetical motel used previously as an example of heating requirements can also be used to illustrate the calculation of cooling requirements. An engineer would probably use the HTM method of calculation. By this method he might find out how much heat transferred into the building when the temperature was 90° F (32° C) outside and was 75° F (24° C) inside, these parameters being set by local summer conditions. His figures would be as follows:

Total Cooling Needs for Motel in Btus

Infiltration through building (by HTM method)		490,000 Btuh
Outside air drawn in for ventilation, air conditioning, and so on:		
$\frac{1}{2}$ air change/hr	503,760 cfh	
20% outside air	215,040 cfh	
34,270 cfm × 60	2,056,200 cfh	
	2,775,000 cfh × 0.018 × 1.3 × 15*	946,275 Btuh
Heat from lighting (89,600 sq ft × 2 w/sq ft × 3.41 Btuh**)		780,000 Btuh
Heat from people (2,000 individuals × 400 Btuh/person × 1.3)		1,040,000 Btuh
Heat from appliances, machinery, and so on		200,000 Btuh
		3,456,276 Btuh

---

* There will be 2,775,000 cfh of air from the outside coming into the building; 503,760 cfh from infiltration, doors, windows, etc.; 215,040 cfh because of a local requirement that 20 percent of the air used must come from the outside and 34,270 cfm (multiplied by 60 to make it cfh) that must be brought into meeting rooms, etc. The factor 0.018 is the number of Btus that must be extracted from 1 cu ft of air to lower it 1°F, which was explained earlier under heating. The 1.3 factor is the correction factor for latent heat in this air, and the factor of 15 is the temperature difference between 90°F (32°C) and 75°F (24°C).

** The lighting engineer states that the average amount of light in the building will be 2 w for every square foot of space. This is about normal for a hotel or motel. For each watt of electricity used for lighting, 3.41 Btuh are produced, so this factor is used to get the total Btuh from lights.

(Note that in heat from people the 400 Btu given off by one person is multiplied by 1.3, which corrects for the latent heat in the Btus.)

Normally, cooling needs are never quite as great as environmental engineers might calculate using this method because buildings do not heat up as fast as the outside. Thus, while it may be 86° F (30° C) outside, the building is only about 75° F (24° C) inside. Later, however, when the atmosphere begins to cool off, the building, having absorbed heat, will warm up inside. The total amount absorbed, however, even with such a temperature swing, is not as great as the temperature rise of the outside. Therefore, an engineer will often use a "swing correction factor" of 71 percent of total needs to arrive at the final cooling needs. Thus, in this motel, the total 3,456,275 Btuh for cooling needs times 71 percent ends as a final requirement of 2,453,955, which the engineer would probably round off to 2,500,000 Btuh.[6] He would then have to calculate the quantity of ice melt or cooling power in equipment required to give the amount of cooling. It should be noted that the total load would seldom be required, thus he will perhaps introduce several cooling units, so only those required to give the cooling desired would need to be operated.

Most cooling systems are planned to meet a cooling requirement of a specific number of Btuh. However, some engineers and others may still speak of the requirement measured by "ice melt." One ton of ice melt is equal to 12,000 Btuh, which is the quantity of heat required to melt a ton of ice at 32° F (0° C) to water at 32° F (0° C). If an environmental engineer established the cooling requirement in ice melt, the system under discussion would require slightly over 200 tons of cooling.

When air is used as a cooling medium, it is usually delivered in the room at 60° F (16° C). If air is at 90° F (32° C) and is cooled to 60° F (16° C), the difference is 30° F (17° C), which would require 0.54 of a Btuh for every cfh of air used ($30 \times 0.018 = 0.54$). If water is used, it is usually cooled to 45° F (7° C) from 55° F (13° C) and then piped to various areas, where this cooled water in coils reduces the air temperature of the area. If the room air is partially used, say 80 percent, and only 20 percent is brought from the outside, the Btuh requirement is less because much of the air is at 75° F (24° C) in the room, instead of 90° F (32° C) on the outside. The cooling of a local area therefore depends on the quantity of outside air brought in. It is usually considered preferable to cool with water than with air because the duct work alone for air flow can be a problem.

Conditioned air can be expensive for a kitchen. Many codes require 20 air changes per hour. An area 20 × 40 × 10 ft (6.15 × 12.30 × 3.07 m) with an air change of 20 times per hour will require 160,000 cu ft of air per hour. Many installations using conditioned air bring in 75 percent from the outside and the other 25 percent from cooled air from dining

[6] The statement was made previously that cooling Btuh are often half of the Btu's needed in northern climates for heating in winter. Without previously adjusting figures this indeed is the case in this example.

rooms or other adjacent areas. It is best for incoming air to be at ceiling height and as far as possible from the exhaust area.

Suggested Student Assignments

Arrange to have as class speakers:

(1) A construction engineer to discuss building construction that prevents heat loss and infiltration and permits successful climate control.

(2) An environmental engineer to discuss the problems in heating and cooling large buildings.

Arrange demonstrations:

(1) Strike quartz and steel together, noting spark that can start a fire. Examine action in a cigarette lighter.

(2) Using a Bunsen burner in which air input can be regulated, demonstrate the temperature differences of different color flames—white tip, yellow flame, and blue core—noting the speed with which each will ignite a piece of wood and, also, the difference in soot deposited on a pan bottom.

(3) Combine chemicals, the reaction of which will generate heat.

1. Prepare a table showing temperatures from freezing to boiling, converting Fahrenheit to Celsius, at 10-deg intervals. Continue the table by converting Celsius temperatures to Fahrenheit to 232°C.

2. Calculate the quantity of heat required to bring to 212°F 5 lb of presoaked beans in 10 gal of water if both are at 72°F. They are cooked in an 8-lb iron pot. How much heat is needed to bring 2 lb of noodles in 1½ gal of water in a 4-lb aluminum pot from 72°F to 212°F?

3. Calculate the quantity of heat, in Btu and calories, required to raise the following 50°F: (a) 1 lb of water, (b) 1 lb of ice, and (c) 1 lb of steam.

4. Draw a diagram illustrating how a refrigeration system and an absorptive cooling system works.

5. Explain the atmospheric condition that exists when it rains, and how it developed. How is it possible for a person to feel the latent heat in moist air?

6. If the RH is 35 percent and holds about 0.0004 when the air is 72°F (22°C), what is the AH? A cu ft of air at this temperature weighs 0.075 lb.

6. 0.5% AH (0.0004 ÷ 0.075 = 0.5%).
3. (a) 50 Btu, (b) 24.65 Btu, (c) 22.20 Btu.
2. 12,020 Btu for the beans and 2,080 Btu for the noodles.

Chapter 16
sound control

The type of materials, the amount of activity, and the specific conditions normally found in foodservice facilities result in noise conditions that call for control. The clanging of hard metal equipment, the bell-like ring of vitrified tableware, the reverberations from hard slick surfaces, an occasional crash against a resistant floor, the sound of many voices, plus the hustle and flutter of activity are characteristic and commonly create a noise level of 60 to 75 decibels. (Decibels are a measure of sound intensity.

Reverberation of sound waves tends to jumble speech so that words are not clearly understood. Hard surfaces reverberate (transfer) sound. Repetition of words in louder tones usually results in understanding. Persons in a food facility need to hear clearly as well as see. They need to be able to be understood when speaking at normal voice levels. Good acoustics can help prevent the irritations resulting from having to repeat orders and from having orders misunderstood. As stated in Chapter 4, noise can interfere with employee efficiency and increase fatigue. It can affect the pleasure and comfort of both workers and clientele.

PRINCIPLES OF SOUND

Sound waves are among the larger waves in the energy spectrum. They may measure from $1/2$ in. to 50 ft. Sound travels at the speed of 1,100 ft/sec. The energy in sound can be changed into other energy forms, such as heat or electricity. When sound is absorbed by an object, it can vibrate from the energy imparted.

Sound has different qualities, depending on a number of factors. One of the qualities is frequency of vibrations, or the number of times per second the sound vibrations occur. A vibration is called a "cycle," or "Hertz" (Hz), and is measured by vibrations per second. The human ear hears vibrations from 20/sec to 20,000/sec. Sound intensity in speech occurs from 600 to 4000 Hz. High-frequency sound travels by short waves, whereas low-frequency sound travels by longer waves. High-frequency sound tends to be more objectionable than low-frequency sound. Therefore, in establishing noise control, the frequency of the sound needs to be considered because the different frequency levels call for different treatment.

Another factor in sound measurement and treatment is the magnitude of the sound. Magnitude is the energy or power behind the sound. It is measured in watts per square centimeters. Because there are 929,034 sq cm in a square foot, the measurement of magnitude would be w/929. If an instrument measured a magnitude of 1860, the magnitude would be 2 ($1860 \div 929 = 2$).

Sound intensity and loudness are not the same. Intensity relates to the amount of sound and depends on the sound produced at the source divided by the square feet of area the sound covers. In this respect, the intensity is like a Btu or calorie. It indicates the quantity and not the level. As a parallel of the example of the well used in Chapter 15, it is like the measure that indicates how high the water level is in the well times the radius squared times 2 pi. Loudness is the level of intensity. It is to sound as temperature is to heat. It does not state the amount, but only how high the sound level is. It indicates how deep the water level is, and from this one can find how much water is in the well.

Loudness is measured in decibels (db). Sound ranges from 0 db, which is the lowest detectable by the human ear, to about 130 db. The sounds of ordinary office activity register at about 50 db; normal speech, about 60 to 70 db at 3 ft; shouting about 90 db at 5 ft; and a large orchestra in a crescendo, about 130 db. Sound at 130 db is painful to the human ear. In industrial areas, 90 db has been set as a maximum sound level; but Congress recently tried to get this dropped to 85 db because 90 db has been found to be detrimental to hearing when continued over a long time period. Many people have suffered ear damage from noise without realizing that the damage was occurring.

Some sounds may not register in high decibels, but may still be objectionable and even do harm to individuals. The high frequency of the sound created by a jet engine of an airplane can be so annoying and painful as to make one ill. It is necessary for those who are around this sound a great deal to wear ear protectors. Decibels are not additive. They combine to give a lower decibel rating. Thus 40 db added to 50 db gives 50.5 db and not 90; 50 db plus 50 db gives 54 db. The reason is that some of the sound waves combine so that they become the same thing.

Sound waves can be reflected just as heat or light waves are reflected. When too much is reflected, objectionable sound can be projected into an area. Reverberation is a mixture of reflected sound. In some instances it is desirable, and in others it is highly objectionable and interferes with hearing distinctly. Echoes are reflected sound that is delayed in travel to the reflector and back to the spot where it originally occurred.

Sound waves resemble light waves in that they can be diffused and also absorbed. The different building materials vary in their ability to reflect, diffuse, or absorb sound. They also display a variation in ability to reflect or absorb different frequencies of sound. Sound engineers use a factor called the "coefficient of absorption" in calculating the quantities of sound absorbed and reflected. This is the ratio of sound absorbed to the total quantity of sound striking a substance. Table 16.1 shows some of the absorption factors of some substances; the amount reflected for both high- and low-frequency sounds are also given.

Table 16.1   Sound Adsorption Qualities of Some Materials

Material	Coefficient of Absorption		Percent Sound Reflected	
	High Fre-quency	Low Fre-quency	High Fre-quency	Low Fre-quency
Glass	0.35	0.04	65	96
Carpet or foam rubber	0.08	0.63	92	37
Heavy drapery	0.14	0.65	86	35
Marble, glazed tile, concrete, terrazzo, and painted brick	0.01	0.03	99	97

These data indicate that glass has a high transmission of sound at high frequencies and that hard surfaces, such as marble, will transfer both high and low frequencies with little absorption. Heavy textiles and carpets do a better job of absorbing high frequencies than they do low ones. A sound engineer looks at these records of sound-absorbing qualities of materials in using them to absorb or reflect sound as required.

METHODS OF CONTROL

Sound control is needed in almost every space in a food facility. In meeting rooms and auditoriums, it may be important to move or project sound, direct it to certain areas, and prevent or encourage its absorption. In other areas, sound may have to be stopped or deadened. There are techniques for doing this.

Sound can be concentrated and then directed to a specific area by using a hard concave surface. The original sound comes into the concave surface, where it concentrates, and then the hard surface sends it back in the desired direction. Thus a speaker can be on a stage and his voice lifted to a concave surface somewhat ahead of and above him, and then the voice sounds can be transferred down to an audience. In a dining room, a concave ceiling might cause sound concentration problems because sounds might be directed down to areas where a high noise value would occur.

Sound can be diffused by using a convex soft surface. This is just opposite of using a concave hard surface to concentrate and direct sound. A convex soft surface makes a good sound deadener.

Reverberations and echoes may be stopped by shortening the sound paths. Hollow drop ceilings, objects, and other units may be used to do this. Sound may also be captured in space and prevented from echoing or reverberating.

Sound can transfer itself by a process called "creep." This happens when sound travels along a wall or some other object. It may not be heard a short distance from the wall or object, but can be heard by anyone standing close to the wall or object. Thus, among an audience listening to a singer on the stage, those in the center of the auditorium will hear the singing well while those seated along the aisle near the wall will hear both the singing directly and hear it transferred later from the wall. Soft, absorbing materials can prevent creep.

The best way to reduce sound is to stop it at its source. This can be done by quieting equipment and by instructing personnel to speak in moderate tones. Some equipment is noisy because it is poorly mounted or fastened. Some equipment makes noise because it is not maintained properly. A fan in a room can emit low-frequency sounds that may not be too undesirable, but the resulting air flow rushing out from the vent can give off medium-frequency sound plus high-frequency sounds that come from the air diffuser and damper which give objectionable noise. This could be stopped by proper insulation of the inside of the duct before noise from the fan gets out of the duct. It might be stopped also by better mounting of the fan and duct.

Sound deadening may occur by using soft absorptive materials. Sound will enter these and be captured in the air spaces so that the waves are not reflected. The effectiveness of such absorptive materials depends on the porosity and kind of material. Thickness is also a factor (see Table 16.2). It is desirable to have some air space behind absorbing materials. Thus a ceiling of absorptive materials is more effective if it does not adhere directly to the ceiling surface but is affixed at a level somewhat below it. Sound can be deadened also by using a panel resonator, a thin membrane of material such as thin plywood placed before an air space. Sound strikes it and it vibrates slowly, capturing sound.

Sound can be deadened by a series isolator. This type holds and absorbs sound. For example, an inverted box can be built, lined with sound-absorbing material, and attached to the ceiling over a machine. The machine noise rises, goes into the hollow area, and dies there. Such a device over a dish machine should have moisture-proof absorptive materials and a vent installed so moist hot air is pulled out. Sound barriers around noisy areas can be effective. A lattice of wood will sop up sound. A waffle-type lattice with 3-in. (7.5 cm) squares will stop most sound waves over 3 in. (7.5 cm). Height barriers up to 4 or 5 ft (1.2 to 1.5 m) can lower sound levels from 8 to 10 db.

Sealing buildings to prevent sound from getting through walls can help. A hole one inch square can let more sound through than 100 sq ft of wall space. Sound can travel along pipes, ducts, and other connectors between spaces, especially if the connectors are metal. Carpeting, draperies, furniture, and people absorb sound. Footsteps across a bare floor of a room that has nothing in it gives striking sound comparison with that in the same room carpeted and furnished.

If sound is dropped below that of a noise level, it is not heard. Thus an individual in an office next to a busy street may not hear sounds from the next office; but those in the next office on the other side where the noise level is much less will hear the sounds in spite of the traffic. Sound-deadening materials should be used between walls in such cases. Noise levels can vary. During the day the noise may be high, but at night it can drop so sounds not heard during the day now become audible.

MAINTENANCE CONSIDERATIONS IN TREATMENT SELECTION

SELECTION OF ACOUSTICAL TREATMENT

When selecting an acoustical material for a food unit, not only its sound-absorbing quality, but also its maintenance, fire rating, and appearance need to be considered as a part of a decorative scheme. Kitchen areas, where acoustical material is likely to be used, are usually humid. It is well to select a material that is moisture resistant. Codes should be checked in determining the acceptability of a specific material in relation to fire resistance. Many materials are fire resistant; others that may be combustible are slow burning. Maintenance may require frequent washing or repainting for sanitation and a good appearance. All of the materials may be cleaned by vacuuming. Many may be washed with a damp cloth. A few may be scrubbed with a brush. None of the porous or fibrous tiles should be subjected to a large amount of water because it will cause discoloration and buckling. Most of the materials can be painted by brush or spray, using a thin paint that will not clog the holes or crevices. Sealing the surface will greatly lessen or destroy the acoustical efficiency.

Most of the noise-control materials are in the form of tiles or panels. Some of these are perforated in straight-row design and others in random

Table 16.2 Relative Noise Reduction Percentages of Acoustical Materials*

Product	Noise Reduction	Cost	Fire Rating	Maintenance
Regularly perforated cellulose fiber tile	55–85	Low initial cost. Installation cost low to medium, depending on method.	Combustible. Slow-burning when ordered with special paint finish.	Repaintable without appreciable loss of efficiency. Easily cleaned.
Random perforated cellulose fiber tile	50–80			
Slotted perforated cellulose fiber tile	60–75			
Fissured or textured cellulose tile (wood fiber)	50–75			
Fissured or textured cellulose tile (cork)	35–55	Medium initial cost. Medium installation cost.	Slow-burning.	Easily cleaned with vacuum cleaner. Careful painting will not materially affect efficiency. Cork easily cleaned with damp cloth.

Material		Cost		
Perforated mineral fiber tile	50–90	Moderate initial cost. Medium installation cost.		Easily cleaned. Repaintable without appreciable loss of efficiency.
Fissured mineral fiber tile	55–85	Moderate initial cost. Medium installation cost.	Fire-resistant.	Easily cleaned with damp cloth or vacuum cleaner. Careful repainting will not materially affect efficiency.
Textured or smooth mineral fiber tile	40–95	Low to moderate initial cost. Medium installation cost.	Fire-resistant.	Easily cleaned with vacuum cleaner. Extremely careful repainting necessary in some cases.
Membrane-faced mineral fiber tile or board	60–80	Moderate initial cost. Medium installation cost.	Fire-resistant.	Plastic membrane easily cleaned with damp cloth. May be repainted.
Perforated metal pans with mineral fiber pads	55–95	High initial cost. High installation cost.	Fire-resistant.	Repaintable and washable.
Perforated asbestos board panels with mineral fiber pads	65–90	Medium initial cost. Medium installation cost.	Fire-resistant.	Easily cleaned. May be repainted without appreciable loss of efficiency.

*"Sound Advice," *Institutions Magazine*, Chicago, Illinois, October 1957.

pattern. They may be textured, fissured, or slotted. Sprayed-on and troweled-on cellulose fiber, mineral fiber, and plastic plaster are also available. The wide variety facilitates the selection of a material to harmonize with a specific plan of decoration.

Suggested Student Assignments

Arrange for a sound engineer to discuss current techniques used to increase, direct, and deaden sound, and the problems commonly encountered.

Arrange for students to experience sound at different levels: 30, 60, 70, 90 and 130 db. (The physics department or an engineer may have measuring equipment and records or tapes that might be borrowed for this purpose.)

1. Note and evaluate sound conditions in various sections of a food facility from the standpoints of (a) interference with understanding words uttered at normal speaking levels, (b) a pleasant noise level, (c) a distracting noise level, (d) the source of sounds, and (e) the quality of sounds heard.

2. Analyze the sounds heard from the standpoints of (a) acceptability, (b) likelihood of repetition, and (c) need for correction.

3. Recommend a method for the correction of objectionable sounds in a facility.

4. Locate and identify the sound-control methods used in five modern buildings. Evaluate them from the standpoints of (a) effectiveness, (b) appearance, (c) maintenance, and (d) fire safety.

Chapter 17

floors and walls

The factors on which the selection of floors and walls should be based include (1) sanitation and safety, (2) durability and cost, (3) comfort and quietness, and (4) attractiveness. The needs of specific areas of a food facility should be kept in mind when making a selection. Differences may be found in relation to wear, maintenance that will be required and likely to be given, length of time the installation will be used, and plans for decoration.

SANITATION AND SAFETY

Floors and walls should have easily cleanable surfaces and be reasonably impervious to the absorption of grease and moisture. They should be free from cracks or crevices, where soil may lodge, and from irregularities that might cause accidents. The surfaces should be resistant to attack or damage from hot water, cleaning agents normally used, and the repeated scrubbing necessary to keep them in good condition.

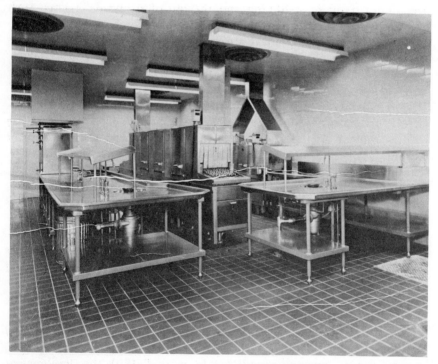

Figure 17.1 A well-lighted, easy-to-clean dishwashing area that has a quarry tile floor, glazed tile walls, and good ventilation treatment.

An important safety factor in relation to floors is the degree to which they provide sure footing. Slippery surfaces are a common cause of falls, which result in physical injury and the breakage of equipment. Tests show that among the most slippery are waxed maple, cement, and pressed wood. The least slippery include rubber, cork, and asphalt tile. Linoleum, linotile, ceramic tile, quarry tile, and magnesite are one and a half times less slippery than maple.

DURABILITY AND COST

Expected use should be equated to durability and cost. Where there is likely to be heavy wear, the most economical floor in terms of total investment plus maintenance will be one, like quarry tile, that will withstand hard wear and require a minimum of maintenance. The same degree of sturdiness is rarely required throughout a food facility. Conditions calling for durable and resistant flooring are heavy traffic, especially that involving the movement of mobile equipment; excess moisture and grease that may soften or erode; and rapid accumulation of soil that necessitates frequent scrubbing and the use of strong detergents. Such conditions are characteristic of receiving, preparation, dishwashing, potwashing, and garbage removal areas. Dining rooms usually require less vigorous wear or cleaning and may be covered with less costly, lighter, and more decorative materials. Walls and ceilings should also differ according to requirements.

Workmanship in laying floors will influence their durability and satisfactory use. Smooth junctures and close abutment are required. The binding cement or mortar should be water and grease proof and resist erosion. The type or nature of the subfloor may determine the life, appearance, and cost. Alkaline and moisture resistant floorings should be used on concrete below grade. Special treatment is necessary, depending on the subfloor used, and architects should carefully consider all factors when setting up specifications.

The installation cost of wood floors is usually high in relation to material cost. Quarry tile, mosaic floors, and other types of hard materials laid in cement or mastics have a high installation cost. Ceramics should be laid so that there is not more than $3/16$ in. between joints. Mosaics are usually shipped premounted on paper, which helps somewhat to reduce installation cost.

Floor thickness will also affect durability. All floorings selected should have color and design throughout the thickness of the material so that, as wear occurs, appearance will not be marred. With the development of the tough plastics, the use of battleship linoleum about $1/4$ in. thick

Figure 17.2 Well-laid ceramic tile makes an attractive, easy-to-clean floor.

and $10\frac{1}{2}$ lb per sq yd has declined. The recommended gauge for plastics is $\frac{3}{16}$ in.; rubber and cork, $\frac{3}{8}$ in. (especially for heavy traffic, such as on stairs); terrazzo topping, $\frac{1}{2}$ to $\frac{3}{4}$ in. thick on top a 2 to 3 in. bed of cement; quarry, $1\frac{1}{4}$ to $1\frac{1}{2}$ in.; ceramic tiles, a minimum of $\frac{1}{4}$ in. Wood floors should normally be of maximum thickness because of the frequent need in facilities for resanding, plus traffic wear. Concrete floors should be poured 3 to 4 in. on or below grade and slightly less above grade. If an oxychloride floor is poured over a base of concrete, the concrete base should be from 2 to 3 in. thick with the oxychloride topping about 1 in. thick.

Wall surfaces in work areas should be hard and smooth. Decorative effects and the desire to cushion noise may make it desirable to use other surfaces in dining areas. Glazed tiles are popular as a wall surface for kitchens and serving areas because of their ease of cleaning and durability. They may be used as a covering for the entire wall or for only the lower section to a height of 6 to 8 ft. The remainder of the wall may be plaster and painted. Smooth, hard, plastic-coated plywood may be used

Figure 17.3 Good floors, good light, hard-surfaced walls, and acoustical ceilings provide fine supporting facilities. (*Michael Reese Hospital, Chicago.*)

in both the serving and dining areas. Textured plastic coverings in colored patterns give decoration as well as good durability. Hard wood molding or metal guards can be used to protect walls. Metal corners may also be required.

Different paints are used for low-cost walls. Acrylic paints have a moisture base. They will not peel and are used in areas having a high humidity. Lacquer-based paints made of synthetic resins dissolved in an organic solvent other than turpentine or mineral spirits and pigments dry and harden quickly and may be used on concrete. They have a high resistance to the alkali of concrete. Paints containing chlorinated rubber of a styrene-butadiene resin may be used with success on concrete floors resting on subgrade. Vinyl-resin paints are used mostly on walls. These paints may be used in washrooms, laundries, or other highly humid areas. Paints with mold-resistant qualities are available for use in storage areas or fermentation rooms where mold is a problem.

COMFORT AND QUIETNESS

A resilient floor is quiet and reduces fatigue. Before installing floors, these factors should be checked but equated against durability and use requirements. The force of the blow of a leather heel was found to vary from 7 lb on high-density cork to 9.1 lb on quarry tile. Below 8½ lb were rubber tile, linoleum, linotile, beech wood, pressed wood, maple, and magnesite; above 8½ lb were asphalt tile, cement, ceramic tile, terrazzo, and quarry tile.[1]

Table 17.1 gives the loudness of various noises, expressed in decibels (20 to 40 for quiet conversation, 40 to 60 for average office noise, 100 to 120 for boiler factory), obtained in impacts with various floor types.

Table 17.1 Loudness Level (in Decibels) * Produced from Falling Plates and Impact of Heels†

	4½ Inch Plate Dropped 30 Inches to Floor	Impact of Leather Heel	Impact of Rubber Heel
Cork tile	62	38	37
Rubber tile	62	40	36
Linoleum	64	39	36
Linotile	66	40	37
Asphalt tile	68	43	37
Maple flooring	68	43	38
Magnesite	68	39	36
Cement	77	39	35
Ceramic tile	79	39	36
Terrazzo	79	39	35
Quarry tile	80	39	36

* Zero decibel is taken as the threshold of audibility.

† Dorothy Goodrich, *Floor Materials, Qualities Desirable for the Institution Food Service Unit*, master's thesis, University of Washington, 1940.

ATTRACTIVENESS

Decor, which is important, may vary widely. Floors and walls can be an important and harmonious part of the decorative scheme. Warmth

[1] Dorothy Goodrich, *Floor Materials, Qualities Desirable for the Institution Food Service Unit*, Master's thesis, University of Washington, 1940.

Figure 17.4 Washable carpeting furnishes a resilient, non-skid floor surface in a waiter pick-up area. (*Courtesy George Bundy & Associates, Seattle, Wash.*)

and good taste are essential for attractiveness and patron appeal. Creating a pleasant atmosphere for both patrons and workers is involved. Psychological reactions to color and physical eye comfort should be considered. The use of expert assistance in planning the decor may be money well spent in terms of resulting satisfactions.

The beauty and appeal of floors and wall finishes can be spoiled by soil, abrasion, or scarring. Selecting for attractiveness is, therefore, closely allied to those factors involving ease of cleaning and durability. Costly maintenance or replacement tends to increase unsightly neglect. The easiest floors and wall finishes to maintain are those that may be conditioned by simple cleaning and that do not require special treatment, such as waxing and polishing. Discoloration, staining, chipping, and rapid soil build-up spoil appearance. Fibrous or porous materials are more susceptible to staining than hard surfaces and hold soil, thus requiring more vigorous cleaning.

A trim, coved base along walls and equipment adds to good appearance. Rubber coves are available for use with resilient flooring, and ceramic tiles in cove form may be obtained. Use of rounded corners and edges and equipment bases that eliminate the need for cleaning under low equipment tends to increase sanitary and appearance factors. Appealing custom appearance in design can be created by using tiles of different colors. Patterns may be incorporated in floors to mark off areas, guide patrons, or indicate table and chair placement.

Table 17.2 indicates ratings of floors (excellent, good, fair, or poor) in relation to desirable qualities.

Some of the characteristic factors of the most commonly used floors are as follows:

Quarry Tile. Durable, cleanable, stain resistant, good footing. Procure in ceramic or dairy paver tile thickness. Initial expense high but gives long-time service; not resilient; tends to be noisy. Use for heavy wear and traffic.

Table 17.2*

	Comfort Underfoot	Quietness	Cleanability	Maintenance	Slipperiness with Grease or Wax	Resistance to: Abrasion	Dents or Cracks	Grease	Alkali Cleaners	Color Change
Resilient Floor Materials										
Asphalt tile, dark colors	F	F	G	F	F	F	P	P	G	G
Asphalt tile, light colors	F	F	G	F	F	F	P	F	G	G
Asphalt tile, grease-proof	F	F	G	F	G	F	P	E	G	G
Rubber tile	E	E	G	P	P	F	E	P	G	G
Linoleum tile	F	G	G	P	F	E	G	E	P	F
Cork tile	E	E	F-G	P	F-E	F-P	G-P	F	G-P	P
Vinyl plastic tile	G	G	G	E	E	P	E	E	E	E
Vinyl-asbestos tile	F	F	F	E	E	E	F	E	E	E
Linoleum sheet (inlaid)	G	G	G	P	F	G	G	E	P	F
Vinyl sheet	G	G	F	F	E	G	G	E	E	E
Hard Floor Materials										
Quarry tile	P	P	G	E	E	G	G-E	E	E	E
Oxychloride cement	F-G	F-G	G	E	G	G	G-E	E	P	E
Concrete	P	P	F	F	P	F	F	E	G	E
Terrazzo	P	P	E	G	P	E	G	E	P	E
Wood	F	P	F	F	F	P	G	P	F	P

* Adapted from *Volume Feeding Management,* March 1958, p. 54.

Ceramic Tile. Like quarry tile in durability and so forth. steam equipment basins and so forth, where close fit is desired ꓶꓳr-ing, specify 1 to 10 percent abrasive. Shows footprints and is not resilient.

Magnesite or Oxychloride. Easy to lay, reasonably inexpensive, somewhat resilient, nonslippery. Stains and erodes; easy to clean. Specify copper bearing and vermin-proof type. Place only on sturdy bases. Lay quickly and seal before dirt gets in. Add marble chips to form a terrazzo. These floorings are less costly, less durable, and more difficult to clean than ceramic or quarry tile.

Terrazzo. Marble chips in a cement binders; not impervious to attack from grease or other materials. Slick when wet. Has tendency to crack or separate along metal strips, creating cleaning problem. Not suitable for kitchens. Attractive and durable for entrance and dining areas.

Cement. Low cost. Use hardeners and sealers to produce hard finish. Not resilient and is slippery. Erodes easily. Best used for storage and restroom areas.

Asphalt Tile. Specify grease proof. Low resilience, nonslippery but brittleness makes it have low utility for heavy traffic. Good for below grade. Use only nonorganic cleaners and waxes.

Vinyl Tile. Resilient, nonslippery, easy to maintain, and water and grease resistant. Tough and durable. May dent. Has beauty, comfort, and quietness. Use vinyl asbestos below grade. Fairly high in cost.

Linoleum. Resilient flooring made from powdered cork, oxidized linseed oil, gums, fillers, and pigments on burlap backing. Dents easily. Attacked by fat solvents. Wears readily.

Hardwood. Attractive, resilient, wears easily and requires waxing and polishing. All grades give good wear but vary in appearance.

Suggested Student Assignments

1. Observe the flooring materials used in different sections of three foodservice establishments. Find out, if possible, how long they have been in use and evaluate them from the standpoints of appearance, kind of care required, degree of wear apparent, slipperiness, and suitability.

2. Visit flooring companies and observe the flooring materials available and comparative prices per square foot. Inquire where installation of the chosen flooring materials may be observed. Visit the location to study appearance amount of care required, and degree of wear.

3. Evaluate various types of wall coverings from the standpoint of cost, appearance, durability, cleanability, etc.

Section 4

equipment selection

Chapter 18

general principles
for equipment selection

Equipment values are based on the degree to which the equipment is needed and satisfactorily fulfills functions for which it is needed. A food facility's standards, volume, and financial success may be directly affected by its equipment. Needs will vary according to the specific operation; they will be influenced by menu, volume, peak loads, type of service, utilities and services available, layout, and many other factors. Many aspects are to be carefully weighed in making selections.

GENERAL TYPES

Food facility equipment may be (1) custom-built for a specific installation or (2) chosen from the standard stock of manufacturers. Stock equipment produced in large quantity from a standard pattern is lower in cost than a piece built to a specific design. Adjustment to a particular need, however, may give the custom-built equipment greater economic value. Detailed drawings and exact specifications are needed when buying custom-built equipment. A manufacturer's number or catalog description may be used when ordering stock equipment.

Many pieces of specialized equipment have been developed by manufacturers to improve operating efficiency. One need not depend on a range surface and a variety of pots and skillets today. It is now possible to obtain temperature-controlled grills or deep-fat fryers of a size or type to fit specific needs. Cooking may be done in a steam kettle, steam cooker, broiler, oven, or rotisserie. Specialized equipment can be had for the various sections of a food facility to improve quality, increase handling of volume, or provide operating efficiency.

SELECTION POINTS

The selection of equipment to yield the best values for a food operation will be based on (1) essentiality of need, (2) cost, (3) performance, (4) satisfaction of specific needs, (5) safety and sanitation, (6) appearance and design, and (7) general utility values.

Essentiality of Need

Need should be evaluated in terms of whether the equipment is required to improve quality, handle quantity, or reduce cost and time of operation. A range may not be needed in a school kitchen where the bulk of food is prepared in steam cookers and ovens. A dishwasher might be advisable in certain units in terms of labor saving. Needs should be listed in original planning as (a) essential or basic, (b) high utility, and (c) useful. Such listing will facilitate appropriate allocation of funds.

Where purchases are not all made at one time, this list will guide architects and others in planning for future additions.

Equipment may be regarded as essential that furnishes the most practical means of securing the quantity and quality of food or services required. On such a basis the purchase of expensive equipment may be challenged if the market affords a reliable supply of acceptable products that would eliminate need for the equipment. Analysis should be made as to whether market prices compare favorably with the costs to the facility of equipment plus labor plus raw materials to produce the equivalent supplies or services. Calculation should be made, for example, as to whether it is better to equip a meat shop or buy prefabricated meat, to have a vegetable peeler or use preprocessed vegetables, and to operate a bake shop or buy commercial pies and cakes. Where standards are high, quality may easily be the determining factor.

It is rarely wise to purchase more or larger equipment than required for immediate needs. One may be oversold and overequipped in certain areas and have an inadequate amount for satisfactory work in others. This often happens when plans are made by persons unfamiliar with kitchen production and specific service needs. Investment costs, loss through obsolescence, labor cost for cleaning and maintenance, plus changes that mean the equipment is no longer used, should discourage the purchase beyond requirements. Probable growth or change affecting future needs may cause certain service and utility installations to be listed as essential. This will include those installations that can be made in the original construction a great deal more cheaply and easily than at a later time. It may be difficult and expensive, for example, to put in electrical conduit or dig and install larger sewer lines later, when more or larger equipment is likely to be added.

Cost

There are many points to consider in evaluating the immediate and ultimate cost of equipment. Those of major significance are (a) initial price, (b) installation expense, (c) repair, depreciation, and insurance, (d) financing expense, (e) operating cost, and (f) values lost versus those created. A comparison of market prices and selection of specific makes is a beginning for such a study. Records of performance that will aid evaluation should be sought. Is the item durable and inexpensive to use or are frequent repairs needed? Is the manufacturer reliable and prompt in supplying repairs and parts?

Installation may add a sizable percentage to the cost of the equipment. Bid prices may or may not include installation. Question whether special conditions will have to be met, such as utility piping, wiring, hoods, ducts, or fire proofing, which will add expense.

Repair, depreciation, and insurance may be important factors in ultimate cost. Equipment that is too light or poorly constructed is likely to need frequent repair and adjustment. Difficulty in cleaning will increase operating cost. The accepted durability of equipment for accounting purposes is 10 years, or a depreciation of 10 percent. Well-constructed equipment, kept in suitable repair and not mistreated, will often last 15 to 20 years. Certain kitchen machines may be too complicated to be repaired or conditioned by local mechanics. If company service is not readily available, such equipment may be a bad investment. A breakdown of certain equipment can seriously impair quality of the operation and add to labor cost. Significant value is added to specific equipment in terms of a company's reliability, promptness in parts delivery and servicing, and gratuitous inspection and adjustment of equipment periodically.

Interest to be earned or paid can be considered as a part of cost evaluation. Will funds on hand yield more loaned for interest or invested in equipment? Will equipment yield values to offset the interest that must be paid for the money borrowed? Can satisfactory adjustment be made to reduce the amount of borrowed funds required? Where the equipment budget is severely limited it is well to study the various ways of reducing costs. Among these may be possibilities of buying good used equipment, renting equipment, or reducing the need for equipment through use of processed food or menu simplification. It is better not to purchase equipment than to spend money for that which will not perform satisfactorily.

An evaluation of operating cost will pertain to labor saved or required and supplies or power used. Some operators use the following formula in judging equipment needs:

$$\frac{A}{B + C + D} = E$$

where A = actual savings in labor during life of equipment.

B = cost of equipment installed, less resale value at the end of its life.

C = operation and maintenance costs during life of equipment.

D = interest on investment.

If E is 1.0 or more, the equipment should more than pay for itself in savings in labor. If E is 1.5 or more, the purchase is highly advisable. Situations exist where budgetary limitations forbid purchase even under circumstances where E is large. Overextension of capital for equipment is not advisable if it means the business must be severely hampered in operation because of it. Equipment that will require a minimum of labor should be selected.

Utilities to operate equipment may affect choice. A comparison between dishwashers, for example, may show a pronounced difference in the amount of water required, the fuel to heat the water, and the power to operate the motors. Its operation may mean an efficient or poor utilization of detergent and wetting agent. Gas and electricity are the most used fuels for heating water and cooking. The cost of comparable units differs in various areas. It is well to obtain estimates of local costs before deciding on equipment that uses a specific fuel. Select equipment that utilizes the fuel to a maximum degree. Ovens, for example, may have specific features that help to ensure maximum use of heat. These include insulation for heat retention, windows for visibility so that doors will not be opened to cause heat loss, thermostats and timers to control heat, and automatic shut-offs to save heat. Automatic recorders of temperature indicate when temperatures have been allowed to vary from desired standards. A rough estimate of fuel required per meal served on an average is .33 kw of electricity or 1800 Btu of gas. Small operations have been found to require more heat energy per meal. In the calculation of an energy ratio between electricity and gas the ratio of gas to electricity was found to average 1.6 to 1. In most operations where all electric units are used for cooking, 40 to 60 percent of the total electrical connected load is used for cooking.

Performance

Equipment is selected to fulfill specific functions. Comparisons of market offerings should be based on the degree of satisfaction afforded and how long it is likely to maintain the given record. If it is to slice or chop, will it make a clean cut or bruise and tear the food? If it is to transport, will it move easily and safely or break down under a normal load? Is the machine easy to operate or must one follow a complicated book of instructions? It should be easy to assemble and disassemble and to clean thoroughly. Workers will use a slow method of preparation rather than handle equipment that is complicated to clean.

Cost should be equated to performance. Several makes and models are usually available. Some may have special features that ensure better performance. Many times, for a small difference in cost, a considerable upgrading in performance can be obtained. It is well to base evaluations on performance records; for this, users are the best source. If possible, see the equipment in operation and inspect the quality and quantity of work done. Actual tests will also provide a good basis for judgment. Manufacturers and dealers are often willing to loan equipment for tests, if handling and installation costs are not prohibitive. Examine equipment at shows or showrooms and collect information from equipment companies.

How long is the equipment likely to serve reliably in its functioning? The value of its performance is closely related to its remaining in good working order. Equipment that gets out of adjustment easily may give poor service and be costly to maintain.

Satisfaction of Specific Needs

The selection of equipment for the various sections of a specific food facility calls for careful calculation if investment is to be wisely made and successful operation assured. A detailed analysis of needs is necessary. There are no short cuts in the form of equipment lists required by all operations. Being over- and underequipped for a specific operation is a common hazard resulting from blindly following someone else's plan. The experience of others may give valuable information, but it must be evaluated in the light of specific needs. Manufacturer's statements must also be considered in terms of normal use. A mixer, for example, can be operated under normal conditions at only 40 to 50 percent of total capacity. Only rarely at slow speed can 65 percent capacity be reached. Steam-jacketed kettles vary in working capacity by 65 to 75 percent, depending on the solidity of the food and the manipulation required. Capacities are often stated without recognition of operational requirements by those who manufacture rather than by those who use the equipment.

Three reliable methods are used by layout planners in estimating equipment needs: (a) A detailed analysis of work needs may be made through the use of industrial engineering techniques, as described in Chapter 3. (b) A production chart and a production summary can serve as a basis for judging equipment requirements. (c) Calculation of functional requirements in relation to equipment specifications, such as number and portion needs in relation to equipment capacity.

The production charts (b), which are used for estimating equipment needs, should list menu items, total quantities required, type and size of equipment needed, time required for batch preparation, and other pertinent factors. Serving periods for estimating adequacy of production in relation to serving demands should be indicated. From this chart a production summary is made indicating utilization of equipment and ability of equipment to meet production demands. Table 18.1 is a typical menu used in an institution serving 300 patrons three meals a day. The portion

Table 18.1   Menu, Portion, and Total Production Required To Serve 300
Patrons Three Meals A Day

Menu No. 1

Menu	Portion*	Total Quantity Required
Orange juice		
Farina	6 oz (¾ C)	13½ gal
Milk		
Fried eggs	2	50 doz
Hot biscuits	2 (¾ oz dough each)	32 lb
Butter		
Coffee or milk		
Fruit cup		
Grilled loin steaks	8 oz, ½″	150 lb
Mushroom gravy	2½ oz	6 gal
Hash brown potatoes	6 oz (1 c)	100 lb
Peas	4 oz (½ c)	9 gal (including liquid)
Bread, butter	ad lib	40 lb bread dough
Blueberry pie	⅙ pie	50 pies
Tea or milk		
Chicken casserole	8 oz (1 c)	6½ gal sauce, 35 lb net chicken
Boiled rice	4 oz (½ c)	9½ gal
String beans	4 oz (¾ c)	10½ gal (including liquid)
Tossed vegetable salad		
French dressing	1¼ T	6 qt
Bread, butter	ad lib	43½ lb bread dough
Butterscotch bars	2 (approx. 1 oz dough each)	34 lb

* Only portions and total production required, as shown on production chart, are
listed here.

sizes and total quantity required are given. Table 18.2 is a production
time chart showing how these foods proceed through equipment. Table
18.3 is the production summary based on the findings obtained in Table
18.2. The data required to estimate the adequacy of the equipment used
are listed. Percent utilization of capacity is the result of dividing *maximum useable capacity* into *maximum production at one time*. Any utili-

zation of capacity of 80 percent or over is considered satisfactory, but this factor considered alone may be misleading. Usage time is an important factor and the usage times listed here are not uncommon, although undesirable. More dual type equipment or more complete equipment usage is desirable in layout planning. *Average production rate per minute* is derived by dividing the *total production* into *usage time*.

A study of the data obtained in Table 18.3 indicates that one each of a 10- and 20-qt trunnion steam-jacketed kettle would reduce the demands for cooking in pots. The installation of a high-pressure steamer may be indicated.

The simplest method used to calculate the adequacy of equipment is (c). This determines the actual productive capacity of equipment and evaluates it in terms of production demands. The steps followed in making this study are:

Select a representative sample of typical foods to be processed through the equipment. For each food item list the following:

1. Anticipated number of portions required and portion size either in weight or volume, depending upon the method used for portioning.

2. Multiply the anticipated number of portions by portion size to obtain total quantity required. Translate if necessary into state in which food item is to be processed through equipment, that is, as purchased, ready-to-cook, and so forth.

3. Calculate in portions and in weight or volume demands from service for food, especially peak demands. Calculate maximum demand per minute.

4. Obtain accurate information on quantities and time required for processing the food item through equipment. Information on different models of equipment may be required. This information should give productive capacity per minute of the equipment in quantity produced per batch and number of portions.

5. From steps (3) and (4) calculate size or number of pieces of equipment required to produce the quantity of food per minute to meet maximum serving demands per minute. Take into consideration the following:

    a. Certain foods lose quality soon after they are prepared and batch times should be such that, during the required holding and serving, quality is retained.

    b. Quality of the product is oftentimes affected by the quantity processed. Quantities prepared should be limited to those yielding high-quality products.

Table 18.2 The Production Time Chart

Menu Items and Equipment Required	Total Production	A.M. 7:00	7:30	8:00	8:30	9:00	9:30	10:00	10:30	11:00	11:30	12:00	12:30	1:00	1:30	2:00	2:30	3:00
Steam-jacketed kettles 10 gal																		
Mushroom gravy	6 gal																	
Sauce (chicken casserole)	6½ gal																	
Peas	9 gal																	
String beans	10½ gal																	
20 gal																		
Blueberries	14 gal																	
Farina	13½ gal										▬							
Rice	9½ gal																	
30 gal																		
Chicken, eviscerated	70 lb or 23 gal																	
Potatoes, diced (parboiled)	19½ gal / 100 lb (EP)																	
Mixers 12 qt																		
French dressing	6 qt																	
60 qt																		
Bread dough	59 qt or 83½ lb																	
Pie dough	35½ qt							½ batch		▬		½ batch						
Butterscotch bar dough	36 qt											▬						
Biscuit dough	35 qt															▬		
Ovens Type 125—3 deck																		
Blueberry pies	50 to 10″														30 tins	▬		
Bread	40 pans (1# 14oz) 11″ × 3″																	
Butterscotch bars	6 pans 16″ × 25″																	
Biscuits	6 pans 16″ × 25″																	
Hash browns	6 pans 16″ × 26″																	
Chicken casserole	6 pans 16″ × 26″																	
Grills (2) 17″ × 33″																		
Eggs, fried	600																	
Steaks, grilled	300 (8 oz, ½″)																	

Hours of Preparation and Service

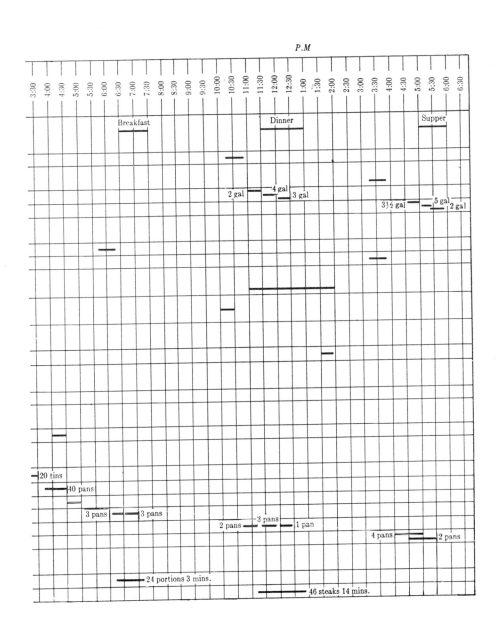

Table 18.3

Menu

Equipment and Item	No. Units of Equipment	Available Capacity	Usage Time hr. min.	Total Production
Steam kettles *				
10 gal	1	10 gal	2 30	32 gal
20 gal	1	20 gal	1 15	37 gal
30 gal	1	30 gal	3 30	42½ gal
Totals	3	60 gal	7 15	111½ gal
Mixers *				
12 qt	1	12 qt	15	6 qt
60 qt	1	60 qt	2 10	165½ qt
Totals	2	72 qt	2 25	171½ qt
Ovens				
Type 125				
Pies	3 deck	30 tins (105 lb)	1 30	50 tins
Bread	3 deck	45 pans (83½ lb)	35	40 pans (72 lb net)
Butterscotch bars	3 deck	6 pans (34½ lb)	30	6 pans (34½ lb)
Biscuits	1½ deck	6 pans (32 lb)	30	6 pans (32 lb)
Hash brown potatoes	1 deck	6 pans (106 lb)	1 30	6 pans (106 lb)
Chicken casserole	3 deck	6 pans (102 lb)	1 30	6 pans (102 lb)
Totals	1–3 deck	463½ lb	6 5	516 lb
Grills				
17″ × 33″	2			
Eggs		1122 sq in.	39	9000 sq in. (600 eggs)
Steaks		1122 sq in.	1 38	8415 sq in. (300 steaks)
Totals	2	2244 sq in.	2 17	17415 sq in.

* See Table 18.2 for items processed through steam kettles and mixers.

Production Summary

No. 1

Batches	Maximum Production at One Time	Maximum Usable Capacity	Average Production per Minute	Utilization of Working Capacity, %
8	6½ gal	6½ gal	0.36 gal	100
3	14 gal	15 gal	0.50 gal	93.3
2	23 gal	23 gal	0.50 gal	100
13	43½ gal	44½ gal	0.40 gal	97.8
1	6 qt	8 qt	0.40 qt	75
5	36 qt	40 qt	1.27 qt	90
6	42 qt	48 qt	1.11 qt	87.5
2	30 tins (105 lb)	30 tins (105 lb)	0.40 tins	100
1	40 pans (72 lb net)	45 pans (83½ lb)	1.11 pans (2 lb net)	90
1	6 pans (34½ lb)	6 pans (34½ lb)	0.2 pans (1.15 lb)	100
2	3 pans (16 lb)	6 pans (32 lb)	0.20 pans (1.07 lb)	50
3	2 pans (35 lb)	6 pans (106 lb)	0.07 pans (1.18 lb)	33
2	3 pans (51 lb)	6 pans (102 lb)	0.07 pans (1.13 lb)	50
11	352 lb	463½ lb	1.27 lb	82.5
12½	720 sq in. (48 eggs)	1122 sq in.	16 eggs	62
7½	1122 sq in. (46 steaks)	1122 sq in.	3.14 steaks	100
20	1842 sq in.	2244 sq in.	127 sq in.	81

   c. Ability of employees to handle and use equipment with ease and safety should be considered.

6. Make a table listing types of equipment and sizes or capacities required to meet production needs.[1]

Safety and Sanitation

When selecting equipment consideration should be given to its freedom from hazards to safety and sanitation and the extent to which it protects against injury or contamination. For equipment to be safe, it must be made of nontoxic materials that will withstand normal wear and be thoroughly cleanable. All sharp edges and moving parts that are hazardous should be guarded and be free from "surprise features" that may be the cause of injury.

Self-service equipment should be carefully checked. Gooseneck venting should be provided self-service coffee urns so that hot water overflows will not burn customers. Moving belts or conveyors on which customers deposit dishes should be safety proof. Fabricated equipment should be so constructed that there are no sharp or rough edges that can catch, tear, or cut. Safety-type pilot lights and adequate venting should be on all gas equipment. Overloads on electrical equipment should be avoided and all electrical, even 110 to 120 single phase, equipment should be grounded. Wiring should not be open or liable to wearing or fraying. Steam kettles should be equipped with side lift handles or with automatic condensation control devices to avert burns. Equipment requiring extended reach into dangerous areas should be avoided. Safety catches should be on

---

[1] These seven steps in evaluating the adequacy of a high-pressure steamer to produce 800 5-oz portions of steamed whole potatoes would be:

  a. steamed whole potatoes.

  b. portions: 800 5-oz portions.

  c. 800×5 oz = 250 lb pared potatoes; purchase pared potatoes 5 oz each.

  d. serving time $1\frac{1}{2}$ hr; demand loads are 500 portions (156 lb) first 45 min., next 20 min. 150 servings (46 lb), and next 25 min. 150 servings (46 lb). Peak demand is approximately 12 portions or $3\frac{1}{2}$ lb potatoes per min. Requirements of equipment are now known.

  e. a 30-lb pressure electric cooker is the only model available. Capacity is 20 lb whole potatoes or 64 portions every 12 min. or $1\frac{2}{3}$ lb per min.; this time includes load and unload time.

  f. two steamers will process 40 lb (128 portions) every 12 min. or $3\frac{1}{3}$ lb per min. ($10\frac{1}{2}$ portions). If at beginning of serving 40 lb (128 portions) are processed, peak demand can be met by producing 3 batches in the next 36 min. (120 lb or 384 portions). Since new batches will arrive at the counter every 12 min. and potatoes can be held 20 min. without loss of quality, the two steamers will satisfy production requirements and retain product quality.

steamer doors so that opening is not possible without exhausting of steam. Mobile equipment should be equipped with wheel locks where necessary.

Sanitary features of equipment will affect customer reaction as well as influence food quality and production costs. Keeping foods at proper temperatures to avoid bacterial growth is important. Equipment should help to eliminate chances of food contamination. Avoid having equipment with rough surfaces and inaccessible areas requiring cleaning. Wooden table tops have been replaced by metal surfaces and cutting boards that are impervious to absorption. Food cutters, slicers, and similar equipment requiring thorough cleaning should be easy to take apart and reassemble. Stainless, durable surfaces, coved corners, and filters that can be washed in the dish machine promote easy cleaning.

Appearance and Design

Equipment should be attractive in design and workmanship. It should be in harmony with the standards of the facility, the building, its purpose, and the other items of equipment. In many dining rooms it is not desirable that impressions of economy, speed, and mechanization be over-obvious even though use of the principles may be essential for the operation. Equipment that creates a spirit of quiet refinement, ease, and luxury may be selected for some rooms, and in others the frank display of practical operation is generally acceptable.

Design of foodservice equipment should stress function, simplicity, and maximum utilization of space. Smooth flowing lines permit ease of cleaning. Design that gives strength and utility as well as beauty should be sought. Designs that permit multiplicity of use are desirable. Color harmony and an attractive blending of materials can be attained. The mixing of equipment made of different metals may be satisfactory or unsatisfactory. Black iron may go well with some metals or enamel-covered equipment and poorly with others. It is not necessary for a kitchen to have all stainless steel equipment. Scale of equipment should be considered in its selection, and a similarity of design between pieces of equipment should be achieved.

Food facility planners add expense when they ask for equipment expensive to make and poor in design. Equipment manufacturers frequently complain that they are called upon to construct equipment designed by those who lack a knowledge of good equipment construction and design. More standardization in design and more emphasis on economy factors in designing equipment will reduce costs.

General Utility Values

Quietness of operation should not be forgotten in selecting mechanical equipment. At times space relationship may be important for labor saving and because only a given space exists. Space in such instances is a major consideration. Mobility may also be a factor. Distance relationship for certain installations and special features of a building may make it necessary to select one piece of equipment rather than another. Remote motors and condensers for refrigeration may have to be so far from the refrigerated area that self-contained units must be purchased for good efficiency. Specialized equipment will have advantages or disadvantages that are specific to the type of equipment selected. Usually these special utility factors will have special weight in the selection of equipment because of their intrinsic value.

The selection of equipment from reliable dealers and reliable equipment manufacturers is important. Equipment should bear the approval of associations that establish construction, performance, and sanitary standards. It is important that equipment meet local code requirements of the area in which it is installed.

CONSTRUCTION PRINCIPLES

Principles of construction of food facility equipment pertain to: (1) design, (2) material, and (3) construction standards. These are factors that influence satisfactory functioning and economical operation. Major goals are to produce simple, functional designs in equipment that will yield maximum utility and durability at reasonable cost and be in keeping with high sanitation and safety standards. The design of equipment should be aimed toward quality production and convenient use.

Much progress has been made in adapting equipment to meet modern needs, but there are many areas where further development is greatly needed. Thermostats permit too wide a variation in temperature. More precision is needed. Grills tend to heat unevenly and ovens to have "dead" spots. More automation is needed, plus duality, flexibility, and mobility. Better use of space and better functioning to lower production costs are also needed.

Construction costs should be minimized when it is possible to do so without lowering standards. Labor and material costs can sometimes be saved by using materials that are less expensive and easier to fabricate. Labor in providing certain forms and finishes should be evaluated. Examples of this include the use of aluminum or chrome-plated steel instead of stainless steel for legs, galvaneal (galvanized iron) on interiors and nonfacing exteriors, No. 2 or 100 grit finish for stainless steel instead of No. 4, angle edges instead of curved edges, plastic drawers instead of stainless steel drawers or brake bent or pressed sinks instead of all-welded sinks. More economical methods of construction need to be devised and more standardized equipment used. It is difficult to justify the price of a custom-built sink or a simple roast beef cart that is as high in price as a moderate-priced automobile.

Equipment should be built sufficiently durable to give good service during its operational life. Balance of durability is oftentimes neglected. Frames are built to last forever, while the functional parts last only a short time. Easy replacement of the worn 'parts should be designed into equipment. Why should it be necessary to discard good frames on ovens and stoves and purchase new ones because linings and insulation cannot be easily replaced? Why should good stainless steel equipment built for a

Table 18.4 U. S. Standard Gauges for Sheet and Plate Metal and Their Thickness

U.S. Standard Gage Number	Decimal	Fractions of an Inch Sheet Steel	Stainless Steel and Monel
		Plate	
000	0.3750″	$\frac{3}{8}$	$\frac{3}{8}$
0	0.3125″	$\frac{5}{16}$	$\frac{5}{16}$
1	0.2812″	$\frac{9}{32}$	$\frac{9}{32}$
2	0.2656″	$\frac{17}{64}$	$\frac{17}{64}$
3		$\frac{15}{64}$	$\frac{1}{4}$
4		$\frac{7}{32}$	$\frac{15}{64}$
5		$\frac{13}{64}$	$\frac{7}{32}$
6		$\frac{3}{16}$	$\frac{13}{64}$
7		$\frac{11}{64}$	$\frac{3}{16}$
		Sheet	
8	0.1644″	$\frac{11}{64}$	$\frac{11}{64}$
10	0.1345″	$\frac{9}{64}$	$\frac{9}{64}$
12	0.1046″	$\frac{7}{64}$	$\frac{7}{64}$
14	0.0747″	$\frac{5}{64}$	$\frac{5}{64}$
16	0.0598″	$\frac{1}{16}$	$\frac{1}{16}$
18	0.0478″	$\frac{3}{64}$	$\frac{3}{64}$
20	0.0359″	$\frac{1}{32}$*	$\frac{1}{32}$*
24	0.0239″	$\frac{1}{40}$	$\frac{1}{40}$

* This thickness is usually slightly over $\frac{1}{32}$ in.

20-year life span have to be discarded because of a failure of elements or other functional parts? Excess durability built into equipment may be undesirable. New or improved models may make it desirable to replace equipment at established time intervals. The junkyards or storerooms of food facilities are filled with the mistakes of equipment manufacturers who have not properly assessed durability factors in their equipment.

MATERIALS

The cost of labor represents a significant part of equipment cost, and the labor cost for making a piece of equipment from either less desirable or better materials is approximately the same. Proper selection of materials used in equipment should be made consistent with expected life, use, and budgetary limitations. Additional strength may be achieved by proper use of angle construction or channeling. The recommendations of the National Sanitation Foundation should be followed for materials.[1]

Wood

Wood has the advantage of being light in weight and economical, but its permeability to bacteria and moisture, absorption of food odors and stains, and its low resistance to wear make it a material with low utility and sanitation value. Its use in kitchens is usually restricted to cabinets and shelving unless economy is a major factor or construction is temporary. Because it cushions noise, has beauty, and can furnish variety in color and texture, it is used for dining room equipment. Moisture-proof plywood, pressed wood, or plywood covered or impregnated with plastics have been satisfactorily used as facing materials or for surfaces that receive only light wear.

Metal

Metal sheets and plates are usually specified according to a standard gauge indicating the weight of the material per square foot. A 20-gauge stainless steel sheet weighs 1.5 lb per sq ft. Fabricated equipment is seldom made of plates thicker than $\frac{3}{8}$ in. Cast materials may be heavier.

The type finish or polish given metals is frequently referred to in equipment construction. Table 18.5 indicates some of the finishes used.

High finishes require more labor and add cost to the equipment, and should be used only when there is a distinct advantage. Where the sur-

---

[1] *Standard No. 2*, "Standards—Food Service Equipment," National Sanitation Foundation, University of Michigan, Ann Arbor, Michigan, 1952, p. 7.

Table 18.5 Standard Finishes on Stainless Steel

Finish	Description
No. 1	Hot-rolled, annealed and pickled; a dull rough finish
No. 2B	Full finish—bright, smooth—cold-rolled
No. 2D	Full finish—dull and smooth—cold-rolled
No. 4	Standard finish for foodservice equipment; may be obtained on one or both sides of a sheet—bright satin finish produced with abrasives.
No. 6	High tampico-brushed finish with soft, velvety luster used primarily as a finish for tableware, etc. This finish highly buffed in 2B.
No. 7	High glossy polish with mirror or highly reflective finish from fine grinding and high buffing.
No. 100 grit	A polish that is more durable and cheaper for foodservice use than No. 4. It does not have as high a polish and this gives it more durability since under heavy wear No. 4 finish dulls. Obtained by first grinding down with No. 60 grit paper and then with No. 100 grit.

face is not seen, dull finishes are adequate and save money. An inexpensive brilliant mirror finish for stainless steel can be obtained by electropolishing, but this finish has not been too successful when used for foodservice equipment.

Covered Metals. Plated metals are usually specified according to the weight per square foot of the metal. A 32-oz sheet is called heavy, while a 24-oz one is called medium. Electroplating is the most common method used for plating and the most satisfactory. The thickness of the plating is specified as so many ounces of plating material per square foot. Preparation of the base metal for plating is called "pickling," which is usually treatment with acid. Plating metals are chromium, nickel, and tin over base metals of steel, copper, or brass. Chromium over steel gives a beautiful, easily cleanable, silvery, high-luster finish and is frequently used for toasters, waffle irons, trim, and areas where high luster is desired. Copper is usually plated to make it corrosion resistant. Nickel or chromium-plated copper is used where high heat conductivity is desired. A bright, high quality corrosion resistant plate is obtained over copper if three coats of nickel plate are covered by a final chrome plating. Brass plated with chrome or nickel is used extensively for fittings; tinned brass or whitened brass fittings are not as acceptable.

Wrought iron covered with two coats of lacquer is sometimes used in kitchen fabrication but aluminum alloys are replacing it in many instances. These metals are used primarily for legs, supporting materials, wall brackets, and such equipment as racks, hoods or baffles.

Cold-rolled steel may be covered with vitreous enamel and used for wall linings of equipment. It may be known either as vitreous enamel steel or porcelainized steel. The steel is first bonderized, a pickling process used to give adherence and anticorrosion qualities to the base metal. It is then coated with a silicon or glasslike type material and baked at temperatures of 1,400 to 1,600°F. The first or ground coat is generally blueblack in color and provides the bond to the metal. Additional coats are applied and fired to obtain white or colored surfaces. The specifications for this material should state that not less than three coats will be accepted without runs, checks, or other imperfections. Vitreous enamel steel is used on refrigerators, ovens, and other large pieces of equipment where surfaces are large, and economy, as well as a hard, durable, easily cleanable, noncorrosive type surface, is desired. It has the disadvantage of chipping or crazing. Cast iron is sometimes covered with a heavy coating of vitreous enamel and used for plumbing fixtures.

Full pickled sheet steel is frequently covered with zinc and used for making sinks, tables, and other equipment. It is called "galvaneal" or "galvanized" iron. Electrogalvanizing is preferred, but some pieces may be dipped in two coats of hot galvanizing compounds. The compound should be approximately 98 percent zinc, but a small quantity of copper may be added to retard the rusting through of the iron base. A total coating of about 2 oz compound to the sq ft is usually satisfactory. All surfaces should be completely covered with the coating. Sheets of galvanized material may be used for equipment fabrication, but this is not as satisfactory as equipment made from full pickled steel and then galvanized. If sheet galvaneal is used, it should be open-hearth, copper bearing, heavy hot galvanized material, and the welds should be brushed and recoated with two coats of zinc or aluminum bronze lacquer.

Although galvaneal steel is not as workable as stainless steel, it can be rolled and will take a good weld that can be ground down. The coating is subject to wear, exposing the steel, which will rust, pit, and corrode. Galvanized sinks have a life expectancy of 5 to 7 years, while tables will last longer and shelving a long time. China and crockery are given black markings from the zinc, and wooden platforms are usually made to cover areas where dishes come in contact with the galvanized material. Gauges slightly heavier than those used for stainless steel are usually specified for galvaneal equipment.

Aluminized steel is now being used for baffles, linings, flues, combustion chambers, reflector plates, and element retainers in electric and gas equipment. It has the ability to return about 80 percent of the heat as radiant heat. Used as reflector material it is as adequate as stainless steel and less expensive. It is also being used as a heat reflector where heat must be turned away. It has high heat resistance and structural strength.

Plain or Mixed Metals. Stainless steel is an alloy with good appearance, easy cleanability, and high resistance to corrosion. It is inert chemically, stainproof, nonmagnetic, ductile, strong, and durable. Stainless steel recommended for foodservice equipment is No. 302 and contains 18 percent chromium, 8 percent nickel, and no more than 0.08 percent carbon, 2 percent manganese, 0.04 percent phosphorous, 0.03 percent sulfur, and 1 percent silicon. Because of its 18 percent chromium and 8 percent nickel content it is called "18-8" stainless steel. It is more expensive than some other metals, but its durability and other service factors make it desirable in spite of cost. The chromium forms a tightly adhering chromium oxide film over the surface of the steel, giving anticorrosive qualities and a white silvery sheen. If the film is broken and oxygen is present, the oxide forms instantly.

Stainless steel takes special skill and powerful equipment to fashion because its strength is twice that of mild steel. Its high ductility or bendability allows it, however, to shape well in fabrication. It will take strong welds, but because of its poor heat conductivity it will warp, bend, or discolor unless a skilled operator makes the weld. Trace of welds should be removed by grinding and polishing. Oxyacetylene welding may be used for 20 gauge or lighter stainless steels but for heavier gauges the arc-type weld is recommended. Acetylene welding also has the disadvantge, if not properly done, of causing carburization, giving a weld of poor strength and low corrosion resistance. Arc welding may cause holes in metal lighter than 20 gauge. Heliarc (also called "heliweld" or "inert arc") welds are made with a torch that dispenses helium or argon gas around a single tungsten electrode eliminating oxygen and thus carburization. This weld has only a small bead that saves labor in grinding down. Tack or spot welding or riveting straps under seams and filling with solder should not be permitted. Welds should be free from pitting, cracking, or other mechanical imperfections. Riveting may be permitted, if necessary, to join equipment by "field joints," a joint made at the point of installation. It is sometimes possible to do heliarc welds on the job and thus avoid field joints.

Monel metal is composed of ⅔ nickel and ⅓ copper and has the appearance and sheen of stainless steel, although, when stainless steel is placed side by side, the monel is readily distinguishable from its coppery color. A small amount of iron may be used to give the monel more strength and durability. Monel takes a high polish like stainless steel. Monel is more susceptible to attack from foods than stainless steel but less so than aluminum.

Aluminum is an inexpensive metal receiving increasing use in food-service equipment. Its light weight and strength make it desirable for mobile equipment. It conducts heat well and may be used for griddles, pots and pans, and other cooking equipment. It can be given a dull, plain, or highly polished finish. Cold-rolling gives a hard, durable finish. Anodized aluminum is especially treated by heat to give the surface extra hardness. Aluminum sheet is seldom used for table tops or sinks because it abrades easily. It cleans easily, but it may be attacked by mild alkalis and strong acids and may color, especially if iron is present. An aluminum oxide forms a protective coating over the aluminum, and this is responsible for the whitish silvery color. Aluminum alloys that give greater durability and less corrosion are being developed. Aluminum castings are sometimes used for equipment in place of cast iron castings.

Special treatement is sometimes used to give color to aluminum surfaces. Penetration, however, is only slight, and scratching will show the original aluminum color underneath. The gauge for aluminum and other nonferrous sheet and plate metals are not United States gauges given in Table 18.4 but are listed according to the Brown and Sharpe gauge.

Copper is used when high heat conductivity is desired. At one time it was much used for utensils, but because of its cost, weight, frequent need for retinning, and its reaction with foods, it is less used. Copper also destroys ascorbic acid. Some copper is still used for sugar cooking kettles or where it is desirable that heat be captured and spread quickly through the utensil to the food. Copper is sometimes used for linings for urns and steam table pans. Its thickness is specified by ounces per square foot in the same manner as plated metals. A 32-oz copper sheet is 0.0403 in. thick.

Cold-rolled polished steel is a highly durable metal used for table tops and other equipment. It is not as workable as stainless steel but edges can be rolled down to a 2 in. radius. It rusts and must be oiled or greased when not in use. It is used in inexpensive or temporary equipment. It may be used for supports or areas not subject to friction and covered with two coats of aluminum paint. Steel channels and angles are placed under much stainless steel equipment to give additional support and to reduce the gauge of the stainless steel required.

Black iron is used in some equipment for facings and linings but is mostly used for baking sheets and roasting pans. It may be treated to be rust resistant. It has good heat absorption qualities.

Cast iron is frequently used for bracings and for supporting stands for heavy equipment. Castings are also used for heavy-duty range tops and griddles. Cast iron is made by pouring the molten metal into molds. It is more porous, less ductile, and breaks more easily than rolled iron. At one time it was widely used for cast iron skillets, Dutch ovens, griddles, and other cooking or baking utensils but more recently is meeting strong competition from aluminum.

Nonmetallic Compounds

Glass or ceramic equipment is used for food containers especially where metals may give off-flavors because of electrolytic action. Glass or ceramic equipment is highly resistant to acids and alkalies. Plate glass is used for doors in equipment. Its primary utility is its smooth, impervious surface, low-cost, easy cleanability, and visibility. It shatters easily. Specify chip-proof plate and edges protected to prevent chipping, and state that exposed edges should be ground smooth.

Plastics are being used more and more in foodservice equipment. Heavy, tough molded drawers have been found satisfactory for some equipment. It is durable and inexpensive and increasing use will undoubtedly be made of plastics in future equipment construction.

DESIGN AND CONSTRUCTION STANDARDS

The equipment construction will influence good sanitation in the facility. The design and construction should permit easy operation, cleaning, and maintenance. There should be smooth flowing lines, and no protruding parts, crevices, rivets, bolts, open pipes, or open service lines. All areas apt to harbor vermin or act as dirt catchers should be sealed off or made easily cleanable. Removable panels can be installed on sealed off interiors to permit entry, and the panels fitted tightly so that vermin and soil cannot enter. Steps, bases, and other substructures should be sealed off against penetration of soil and vermin.

Where moisture or condensation is apt to accumulate, care must be taken that drip pans are properly placed to catch this. The pans should be easily removable and cleanable. All drainage devices should be

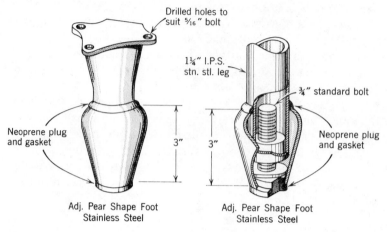

Drilled holes to
suit ⁵⁄₁₆″ bolt

1¼″ I.P.S.
stn. stl. leg

¾″ standard bolt

Neoprene plug
and gasket

3″   3″

Neoprene plug
and gasket

Adj. Pear Shape Foot   Adj. Pear Shape Foot
Stainless Steel   Stainless Steel

Figure 18.1   Adjustable pear shape foot. (*Courtesy S. Blickman, Inc., Weehawken, N. J.*)

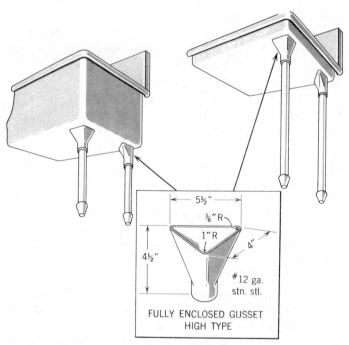

← 5½″ →

⅜″ R

1″ R

4½″   4″

#12 ga.
stn. stl.

FULLY ENCLOSED GUSSET
HIGH TYPE

Figure 18.2   Fully enclosed gusset. (*Courtesy S. Blickman, Inc., Weehawken, N. J.*)

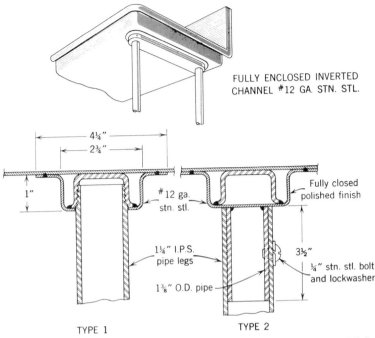

FULLY ENCLOSED INVERTED
CHANNEL #12 GA. STN. STL.

Figure 18.3 Fully enclosed inverted channel. (*Courtesy S. Blickman, Inc.,*
Weehawken, N. J.)

pitched to give good run off. Strainers should be removable. Where
needed, gutters should be installed to carry off grease and moisture. The
gutters should be easily cleanable.

Standards of workmanship are an important part of good construction
and can only be done by manufacturers who possess good standards,
have well-equipped plants, and skilled workmen. Good construction
standards have been enunciated by the National Sanitation Foundation.
These should be closely followed in establishing standards for equipment
construction.[2] Equipment brochures and catalogs published by reputable
equipment manufacturers may also be used in establishing reliable
standards.

Equipment buyers should see that all internal angles on equipment are
rounded, specifying minimum angles recommended by the National Sani-

[2] See, especially, *Standard No. 2*, "Standards—Food Service Equipment," National
Sanitation Foundation, University of Michigan, Ann Arbor, Michigan, Figs. e.0113-3.361,
3.37-3.401, 3.41 (Ruling No. 1), 3.054.

tation Foundation; however, better equipment manufacturers will usually exceed these recommendations. Square corners should be avoided and external corners should be rounded, closed, and smooth.[3] Raised edges of $3/16$ in. or more are used where drip or seepage might occur. Other edges are used to give utility, finish, or strength to equipment. Exposed edges and nosing should be rounded on a $3/4$ in. diameter with the bottom edge of the rounded edge not less than $3/4$ in. from the edge of the body to make cleaning beneath easy and to discourage vermin. Where edges are turned down they should be tightly fitted to the body. Edges turned down away from the body should be at least $3/4$ in. away at their nearest point. Rounded edges should be not less than $1\frac{1}{2}$ in. in diameter. Where openings are made in tops the edge should be turned down and if seepage may occur the edge should be raised. Usually edges of sink drainboards and other tables where splash occurs are raised 3 in. and then turned down on a rounded edge. Splash backs that fit against a wall are tightly scribed to the wall about 10 or 12 in. up.[4]

Channeling or bracing used to give added strength are usually made of iron or steel if not exposed. Body frames may be constructed of angles, pipe, or tubing and then covered with sheet materials. When good channel or bracing is provided, lighter covering materials may be used. Shelving, turned down edges, pipe supports, and so forth, will give added strength to equipment. Strong welds and sufficient bracing to hold heavy loads are required. Channeling or open angles that offer places for harboring of vermin should be avoided.[5] All tubing should be welded or seamless type and easily cleanable, with no crevices at welds. Concealed bolt construction and proper treatment of such bolts where iron bolts are solidly welded into stainless steel should be specified. Avoid, if possible, bolts and screws on fixtures, specifying, if they must be used, acorn nut type with round heads. Countersink bolt or screw heads, if they must be used, fill and solder grinding down to a smooth finish. Avoid trim for doors, bodies, and cabinet corners. Use heavier gauge metals instead. Reduce inside framework if possible by using heavier gauge metals.

The strength of the material will depend upon the loads the equipment must bear. In general the heavier the gauge, the greater the flatness of the equipment and the better the finish. Table 18.6 gives some gauges generally recommended for standard pieces of equipment.

Doors, except for heavy ones, should be removable and, if sliding, should be hung from the top and roll on either ball bearing or nylon

---

[3] *Ibid*, see Fig. 3.02.

[4] *Ibid.*, see Fig. 3.054.

[5] *Ibid.*, see Fig. 3.06.

Table 18.6 Gauges Commonly Recommended for Equipment

Item	Recommended Gauge for Top*	Framework or Bracing if Required†
Bain marie	14	$1\frac{1}{4}'' \times 1\frac{1}{4}'' \times \frac{1}{8}''$
Canopies or hoods	20	$2'' \times 2'' \times$ 10–14 gauge
Drainboards	12–14	12 gage angle, 3″ wide
Sinks	12–14	
Steam tables and counters	12–14	$1\frac{1}{2}'' \times 1\frac{1}{2}'' \times \frac{1}{8}''-\frac{3}{16}''$
Tables	12–14	$.1\frac{1}{2}'' \times 1\frac{1}{2}'' \times \frac{1}{8}''-\frac{3}{16}''$
Urn stand	14	$1\frac{1}{2}'' \times 1\frac{1}{2}'' \times \frac{1}{8}''-\frac{3}{16}''$
Wall backings	20–22	
Trucks	16 (shelving)	$1\frac{1}{2}'' \times 1\frac{1}{2}'' \times \frac{1}{8}''$
Bodies	20	
Bottoms	18	
Doors	18–20	(may require some)
Shelving	16–18	
Sides	16–18–20	
Legs	10–12 ($1\frac{5}{8}''$ OD) or $2'' \times 2'' \times \frac{1}{8}''$ or $1\frac{1}{2}'' \times 1\frac{1}{2}'' \times \frac{1}{8}''$	

* These gauges listed are recommended for stainless steel. Galvanized steel or steel might take one gauge heavier, that is, if 12 gauge stainless steel is recommended, 10 gauge would be required for the other metals.

† Framework or bracing may vary according to size of the equipment. Thus for small hoods or canopies no bracing is required and the trim is made slightly heavier than the remainder of the structure, giving sufficient strength. Wall or ceiling supports would also tend to reduce the need for angle support. Sometimes a lighter gauge top is used on equipment with a heavier galvanized metal underneath, such as 20-gauge stainless steel might be put over a 14-gauge galvanized top for an urn stand. Shelving, trim, edging turndowns, and so forth, all affect required amount of support. Integral costruction also adds strength. Metal cross bars beween the legs of equipment, and so forth give strength. All these factors should be considered in an estimate of required supports.

glides. Vibration or jar should be eliminated. Bottom guides should be open, shallow, and wide for ease of cleaning and should be open-slotted so soil will drop through. The bottom shelf should be designed so that soil can be easily swept out. All gaskets should be cleanable and removable. Protective channels for glass doors should fit tightly and the glass should be at least $\frac{1}{4}$ in. plate fitted into strong channel frames. Single

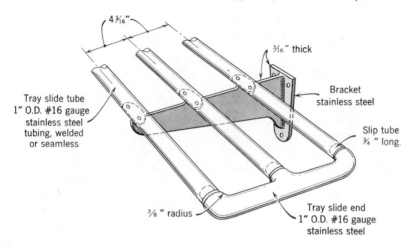

4 3/16"

3/16" thick

Tray slide tube
1" O.D. #16 gauge
stainless steel
tubing, welded
or seamless

Bracket
stainless steel

Slip tube
3/4" long.

3/8" radius

Tray slide end
1" O.D. #16 gauge
stainless steel

Figure 18.4 Specify for tray slide assembly: (1) 16 gauge or better stainless steel tubing, not nickel silver tubing, and (2) 30 percent nickel silver or stainless steel brackets, ground and highly polished. (*Courtesy S. Blickman, Inc., Weehawken, N. J.*)

panel doors have only one thickness of metal and usually need additional brace support. Better construction occurs when double panel doors are framed into channel shaped sections, reinforced and the corners welded so that the door is tightly sealed. Avoid trim on doors to make for easier cleaning. If necessary, doors can be insulated against heat loss or heat penetration. Metal doors should usually be 16 gauge, with inside doors braced full length with channel shaped sections for stiffening and for fastening recessed handles. Limit stops should be provided. Dust proof racks overhead should be fastened in such a way as to prevent vibration or jarring. Depressed openings in place of handles on doors should be easily cleanable. Swinging doors should be mounted on hinges sufficiently strong to carry the weight of the door and the use it will receive. If possible, doors should be eliminated since their opening and closing is a work motion that contributes little to production time. Doors are usually desirable to provide protection. The National Sanitation Foundation's recommendations for door construction should be closely followed.

Drawers and bins should be removable and so constructed as to be easily cleanable. They should be made of galvaneal, plastics, or better. Limit stops or safety-catches, roller bearing glides or nylon glides, and self-closing drawers are desirable. Bins should be balanced properly so that they are not hazards when closed too quickly. The fronts of drawers

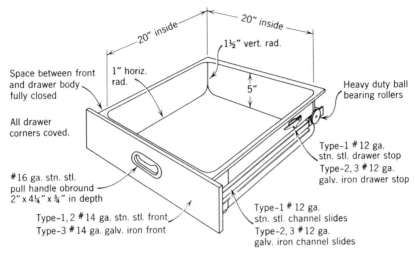

20″ inside

20″ inside

1½″ vert. rad.

Space between front and drawer body fully closed

1″ horiz. rad.

5″

Heavy duty ball bearing rollers

All drawer corners coved.

Type-1 #12 ga. stn. stl. drawer stop
Type-2, 3 #12 ga. galv. iron drawer stop

#16 ga. stn. stl. pull handle obround 2″ x 4¼″ x ¾″ in depth

Type-1, 2 #14 ga. stn. stl. front
Type-3 #14 ga. galv. iron front

Type-1 #12 ga. stn. stl. channel slides
Type-2, 3 #12 ga. galv. iron channel slides

Type-1 All stn. stl. construction, #18 ga. stn. stl. body
Type-2 Galv. iron, with stn. stl. front only #18 ga. galv. iron body
Type-3 All galv. iron construction #18 ga. galv. iron body

ROUNDED CORNER WORK DRAWERS

Figure 18.5 Rounded corner work drawers. (*Courtesy S. Blickman, Inc., Weehawken, N. J.*)

and bins are usually 16 gauge or better, with 20-gauge bodies. They should be flanged back approximately ½ in. Standard depths are usually 5 in., but this may not always be proper. Specify depth to suit the storage required. In some cases have removable bottoms so that they can be hung during work hours where workers can quickly select tools hanging from them. Good construction for bins calls for rounded fronts and fully rounded bottoms. Bodies should be 18 gauge, with 14 to 16 gauge fronts. Tops should be removable.

Wherever possible shelving should be removable and frequently adjustable. Shelving can be made so that it rests upon frame construction. It should exclude vermin. Size of the shelving should be such that in closed interiors it can be easily removed and handled. Where shelving must bear heavy loads, bracing, with turned down edging, is recommended. Under shelves should be 14 to 16 gauge and edges should be turned down 1 to 1½ in. If the shelving is slatted, slats should not be more than 1½ in. apart.

Wall shelving is becoming less and less used; more mobile shelving is taking its place. Where wall shelving is used, white metal streamlined

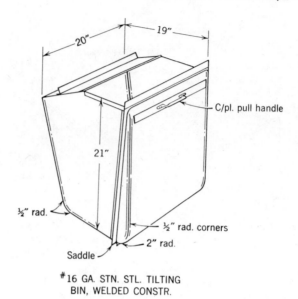

Figure 18.6   Titling bin. (*Courtesy S. Blickman, Inc., Weehawken, N. J.*)

brackets with single slottless head tie-in bolts have been found satisfactory. Provide clearance between rear of shelf and back of fixture or wall. Slatted type shelving is usually constructed of 12 gauge metal with lateral bands at least 1½ in. wide and not more than 1½ in. apart. Additional strength is gained if longitudinal bands are used. It is recommended that in tables 30 in. wide, at least two longitudinal angle braces be welded in. Pipe frame shelving would be of 1 in. OD, 12 gauge. It should be all welded construction with welds ground smooth and rounded so that all corners are coved. Flanged corners should be closed tightly to prevent soil accumulation. Diverting shelves placed to catch seepage should be turned up a minimum of 2 in. and made with closed angles and corners. The angles or cleats holding shelving should be removable and easily cleaned.

Heating strips in enclosed interiors or in equipment should be baffled and guarded against spillage of food. Immersion electric heaters in bain maries and steam tables should be protected. Electrical equipment put into water for cleaning should be tightly sealed so that water penetration does not cause harm. Insulated areas should be sealed and guarded against moisture damage. Equipment that must be dipped into water should be able to stand high water temperatures.

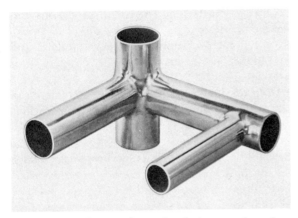

Figure 18.7 Intersections of tubular members have generous fillets, polished smooth, free of pits or crevices and easy to clean. (*Courtesy S. Blickman, Inc., Weehawken, N. J.*)

Figure 18.8 Well-formed edge and corner construction. (*Courtesy S. Blickman, Inc., Weehawken, N. J.*)

SPECIFICATION STANDARDS[6]

Equipment specifications should define exactly what is desired and the condition for its purchase. Written specifications become an established record, prevent misunderstandings and dissatisfaction, and make it possible upon delivery to determine performance. Precise, clear, and tightly written specifications are desirable. They leave little doubt as to what is desired and contractors can precisely calculate costs and often give lower prices. Disagreements will be avoided because both parties know what is expected. The terms and language used should be common in the trade.

[6] See Appendix for one example of equipment specifications.

Specifications usually have a section devoted to general provisions and another delineating specific factors desired in individual pieces of equipment. General conditions or general provisions are fairly standard and the American Institute of Architects has forms that usually cover most of the provisions needed.

Specifications may vary from one or two simply written statements to extensively written documents, depending upon conditions. Specifications should be written simply and concisely, and give only those details necessary to assure delivery of the equipment desired. They should represent the minimum quality acceptable and set up exact performance. Under competitive conditions the specifications will represent a close approximation to the maximum performance contractors will deliver, for few can afford to deliver more than specified. Assistance in writing specifications can be obtained from reliable equipment firms, but care should be taken in using such sources to leave bidding free and open and not restricted to one or a few bidders.

General conditions are general instructions to bidders, which apply to all the equipment purchased and usually set forth the conditions under which bids will be received. They should establish the form of the proposal for a bid, which is usually an itemized schedule of equipment listing the unit price of each item, identifying the item by name and number as given on the plan and specifications. If provision is made in the general conditions to accept individual bid items, aggregate bids, or a total bid for all the equipment, it should be so stated. Proposals should be delivered, sealed on or before a specified date and addressed to the individual or agency as given in the general conditions. Each proposal should be accompanied by a bid bond or certified check; this may be from 5 to 10 percent of the total bid. Conditions vary and practices and policies common to the area should be ascertained. After the contract is awarded the successful bidder is required to furnish a satisfactory surety bond to guarantee fulfillment of conditions. The bond is then returned when satisfactory delivery occurs.

General conditions should also clarify the relationship of the owner, architect, contractor, sub-contractors, and material men to each other. Responsibility should be clarified in regard to the owner's authority, architect's supervision, the obtaining and returning of drawings and specifications, schedule for commencement of work and completion of it, when and how payments will be made as work progresses, working conditions at site, storage limits, removal of rubbish, insurance that must be held by the successful bidder (fire, liability, and property damage), general information, and final approval and acceptance. The scope of the work should be established. Contractors usually furnish the utilities used to install equipment. Some public institutions do not pay taxes and this should be stated if applicable. Installation may or may not be separate. If it is a part of the contract, then installation standards should be specified and the type of workmanship acceptable described. Connection to utilities should be specified if such installation is required.

Delivery and shipment conditions should be specified. Dates for arrival, method of shipping, and other conditions should be stated. Bid prices should include shipping charges. Exact destination should be stated. Shipment to a central freight depot in a locality may mean additional shipping costs.

Alternate bid acceptability should be defined. The final decision of what is or is not a satisfactory alternate should rest largely with those using and operating the equipment—the operation members of the planning team.

Under some conditions policy prevents the use of proprietary or trade names. Under others, a proprietary or trade name can be used, provided the clause "or equal" is used. The burden of proof of what is equal shall be upon the bidder and the operating member of the team shall have the final decision. It is recommended that, instead of the clause "or equal" being used, a list of acceptable products be named and allowance made also for "base bid alternates." It is difficult to keep up with all the equipment changes occurring and frequently manufacturers or others are aware of new equipment superior to that named in the specifications. Allowing for base bid alternates gives an opportunity to offer other items that may be satisfactory as the equipment named.

Bids for equipment are frequently separated from the general building contract. General conditions should cover only provisions required to obtain and perhaps install the equipment and should not repeat or cover other contingencies. Provision should be made to eliminate from consideration bidders who do not have the potentiality to perform adequately on the contract and a statement should be in the general conditions that price alone will not be the sole criteria for awarding bids.

Specific factors for individual items make up the second section of specifications. They may be for custom built or for standard stock items. They will differ somewhat in the amount of detail required. Specifications for standard stock items are usually quite simple but since nothing is preestablished for custom-built equipment, all factors must be covered and the need for accuracy and detail make the specifications for this equipment longer and more difficult to write.

Specifications for equipment are frequently accompanied by a blueprint of the layout ($\frac{1}{4}$ in. to 1 ft). Usually included are electrical and plumbing plans. These drawings should locate each item specified and

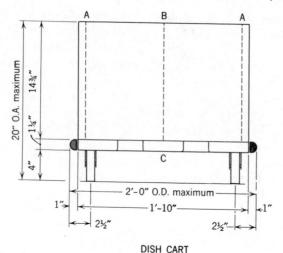

DISH CART

Figure 18.9   Rough sketch of mobile dish cart.

Suggested features:

A—1″ × ⅛″ SS angle support at corners #4

B—14 g SS center panel #4

Sides and Bottom, 14 g #4

Lift up doors on either end 16 or 18 g SS, #4

Note Colson 6914 bumpers with Colson 6906 corners

Swivel rubber tires

Maximum height 20″, Maximum width 2′0″, Maximum length 2′0″.

C—suggested only 16 g galv bottom with angle supports below 14 g SS #4 bottom.

identify it by a corresponding item number in the specifications and the proposal for bid. The name or identiy of both standard stock and custom-built items should be clearly established. The use of federal specifications and standards as published by the General Services Administration Federal Supply Service, may be helpful in establishing identity and details required. The quantities of equipment required should be clearly stated.

If custom-built equipment is purchased, quality of workmanship, standards of construction, materials, fittings, and fastenings should be covered in the general conditions. Samples of work to be done should be required from successful bidders and held for comparison when equipment is delivered. Shop drawings (¾ in. to 1 ft) should be submitted within a specified time after the bid is awarded. These should be approved by the members of the planning team with desired changes noted in red pencil and one copy approved as changed and returned to the bidder. These drawings establish final construction details and should be given careful scrutiny before return.

When specifications for custom-built equipment are submitted, it may also be desirable to submit clear, accurate, two-dimensional perspective drawings of all such equipment. Rough drawings giving essential construction and design characteristics should be made by operation members of the planning team. If necessary, this rough drawing can be smoothed up by a professional draftsman. Good drawings tighten specifications and correct omissions and errors. Experience has shown that if sharp, accurate drawings accompany precisely, tightly written specifications, better equipment is obtained at a lower cost. See Figures 18.9, 18.10, 18.11, and 18.12.

Standard stock items are usually in storage awaiting demand. Manufacturers publish brochures or catalogs listing essential details of the construction, performance, and so forth, of such equipment, reducing the need to repeat this in specifications. Usually the name of the item and some other designation such as model number is sufficient to establish the identity of the item desired.

Specifications for standard stock equipment should specify, if applicable, the correct name of the equipment, catalog number, model number, the type of heating or power source to be used (if steam, psi; if gas, type and approximate Btu per cu ft; if electricity, voltage, phase, AC or DC and cycles if AC and wattage), plus other required details so that the equipment will satisfy requirements upon delivery. All points affording choice or variation must be covered. Precision is sometimes attempted by using proprietary or trade names. The specifications for standard stock equipment should contain a request for at least three operating manuals and a spare parts list of the equipment delivered. One of each of these should be kept respectively in the files of the foodservice office, in the maintenance and repair manual where foodservice employees and others may refer to it, and in the maintenance engineer's department or others responsible for the upkeep and maintenance of the equipment.

EQUIPMENT AND UTILITY SUMMARY

Equipment that has been wisely chosen and well constructed has an additional requirement to function satisfactorily. It must be properly installed and supplied with the essential utilities. In order to avoid costly omissions it is well to list each item of equipment and indicate the utility needs and/or any other supply or condition essential to its functioning satisfactorily. The manufacturers of equipment supply this in-

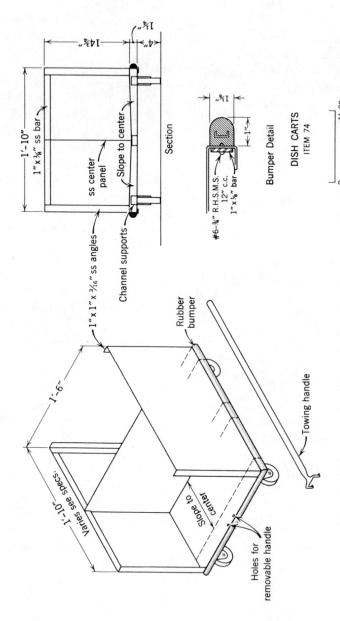

Figure 18.10 Smooth drawing of dish cart presented with specifications for bidding. Made from rough drawing shown in Figure 18.9.

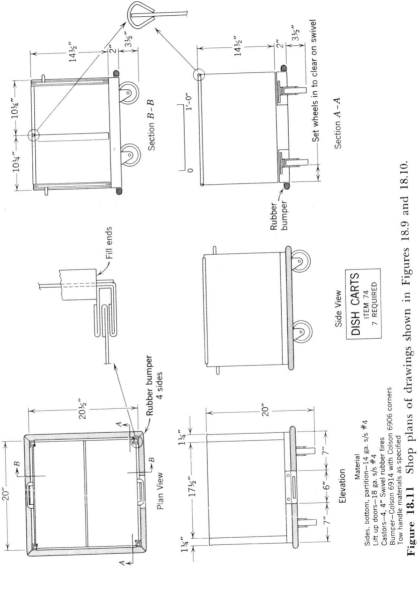

Section B-B

Set wheels in to clear on swivel

Section A-A

Rubber bumper

Fill ends

Side View

DISH CARTS
ITEM 74
7 REQUIRED

Rubber bumper
4 sides

Plan View

Elevation

Material

Sides, bottom, partition—14 ga. s/s #4
Lift up doors—18 ga. s/s #4
Castors—4, 4″ Swivel rubber tires
Bumper—Colson 6914 with Colson 6906 corners
Tow handle materials as specified

Figure 18.11 Shop plans of drawings shown in Figures 18.9 and 18.10.

Figure 18.12   Actual dish cart from drawings in Figures 18.9, 18.10, and 18.11.
Note that the cart was designed to roll into under-counter heated area.

formation as it pertains to items that they supply. The summary chart
when completed will give an overall view of utility requirements and
will pinpoint any special needs or conditions to be met.

Suggested Student Assignment

Select a foodservice facility for study and analyze each of the aspects pertaining
to equipment selection for each item of the equipment from the standpoints
presented in Chapter 18.

REFERENCES

Dana, Arthur W., *Kitchen Planning for Quantity Food Service*, Harper and
Brothers, New York, 1949.
Fabrication of U.S.S. Stainless and Heat Resisting Steels, United States Steel,
Pittsburgh, Pa., 1948.

National Sanitation Foundation Testing Laboratories, *Descriptive Details for the Guidance of Technical and Supervisory Personnel.*

Ramsey, Charles George and Harold R. Sleeper, *Architectural Graphic Standards*, 6th ed., John Wiley and Sons, New York, 1956.

Segeler, C. George and J. Stanford Setchell, *Commercial Kitchens*, American Gas Association, New York, 1948.

West, Bessie B. and LeVelle Wood, *Food Service in Institutions*, 4th ed., John Wiley and Sons, New York, 1955.

Chapter 19

mechanical equipment

FOOD PREPARATION MACHINES

Mixers

Mixers are among the most important of the bake shop machines. Their performance is judged in terms of smooth blending of materials and satisfactory incorporation of air. Specifications for purchasing should be stated as to make, model, size, type material, and finish of machine and parts, and an itemized list of the attachments required.

The mixer model may refer to a specific manufacturer's design or a bench or floor type. Mixers may also be upright or horizontal. The bench models are usually sized from 5 to 20 qt, with the smaller sizes used on a work table and the larger models placed so the top of the mixer bowl is about the same height as the work table. Floor models in upright mixers range from 30 to 400 qt capacity. The capacity selected should be the one best adapted to volume needs, quality in production, and handling convenience. The size should be in keeping with the capacity of related equipment.

The upright mixer may be a floor or bench type having an overhead motor mounted on a stand. The motor drives a mixing arm and a shaft for operating special attachments, such as a juice extractor, a slicer, or a grinder. A variety of whips, beaters, and dough hook attachments may be obtained to provide varying strength and mixing action. Large capacity mixers, such as 120-qt, may be adapted for use of smaller bowls, such as a 40-qt bowl, by means of an adapter ring and proper attachments. Most mixers have three or four speeds but some have nine or more. Automatic timers can be specified. Large mixers may have mechanical lifts that raise and lower bowls and even dump them.

The mixing arm of the upright mixer moves in a circle while rotating the beater. This is called "planetary action." Some main arms and beaters turn in the same direction while others turn in opposite directions. Large mixers should be purchased with bowl dollies, adapters, and, if possible, with an electric bowl raiser and timer. Bowl raisers are available on 30- to 80-qt machines. Other useful attachments include an oil dropper, bowl splash cover extension rim, pouring shute, soup strainer, and colander. Important selection points are ease of cleaning and sanitary use, satisfactory performance, durability, compactness of space requirements, appearance, and ease of operation and maintenance.

Large horizontal mixers are used in bakeshops having high volume, as in large central kitchens. A heavy duty motor rotates a shaft in a horizontal cylinder giving the mixing action desired. High and low speed mixers are used. There are variable speeds possible also in individual mixers.

A third type of mixer resembles the horizontal one and has open top tanks with a mixing shaft entering the tank from one end and rotating mixing paddles. It may have only one or two speeds.

It is well for all types to have sealed-in motors. Consideratios should be given to available servicing and speed of parts replacement. Mixers should be installed so they are level. Large mixers should be fastened to

Table 19.1 Capacities of Food Mixers*

Size Mixer Motor	15 qt ⅓ HP	20 qt ⅓ HP	30 qt ¾ HP	60 qt 1 HP	80 qt 1½ HP	80 or 110 qt 2 HP
Kitchen Materials						
Eggwhites	1½ pt	1 qt	1½ qt	2 qt	2½ qt	2½ qt
Mashed potatoes	12 lb	15 lb	23 lb	42 lb	55 lb	60 lb
Mayonnaise (qt of oil)	6 qt	10 qt	12 qt	18 qt	24 qt	30 qt
Meringue (pt of water)	1 pt	1½ pt	2 pt	3 pt	6 pt	6 pt
Waffle or hot cake batter	6 qt	8 qt	12 qt	24 qt	32 qt	32 qt
Whipped cream	3 qt	4 qt	6 qt	12 qt	16 qt	16 qt
Bake shop materials						
Angel Food (8–10 oz cake)	10	15	22	45	60	60
Box or slab cake	15 lb	21 lb	30 lb	52 lb	80 lb	90 lb
Cup cakes	16 doz	22 doz	33 doz	65 doz	90 doz	110 doz
Layer cakes	15 lb	20 lb	30 lb	60 lb	82 lb	82 lb
Pound cake	15 lb	21 lb	30 lb	52 lb	80 lb	90 lb
Short sponge cake	10 lb	15 lb	23 lb	45 lb	70 lb	70 lb
Sponge cake batter	8 lb	12 lb	18 lb	36 lb	54 lb	54 lb
Sugar cookies	26 doz	35 doz	50 doz	100 doz	115 doz	125 doz
Bread or roll dough	16 lb	25 lb	45 lb	70 lb	105 lb	150 lb
Heavy bread dough	—	15 lb	30 lb	60 lb	90 lb	125 lb
Noodle dough	7 lb	8 lb	10 lb	15 lb	35 lb	35 lb
Pie dough	12 lb	17 lb	27 lb	50 lb	62 lb	75 lb
Pizza dough	10 lb	14 lb	21 lb	42 lb	56 lb	56 lb
Raised doughnut dough	—	9 lb	15 lb	30 lb	45 lb	60 lb
Eggs and sugar (for sponge cake)	6 lb	8 lb	12 lb	24 lb	36 lb	36 lb
Fondant icing	9 lb	12 lb	18 lb	36 lb	52 lb	63 lb
Marshmallow icing	1½ lb	2 lb	3 lb	5 lb	7 lb	10 lb
Shortening and sugar creamed	12 lb	16 lb	24 lb	48 lb	60 lb	63 lb

* *Volume Feeding Management,* Conover-Mast Publications, 205 East 42nd Street, New York 17, N.Y.

the floor. Beaters and accessories should be of noncorrosive metal. The bowls for upright mixers may be tinned steel or stainless steel.

Mixers are used in the cooking section and preparation areas for whipping potatoes and blending various mixtures. They may be used for cutting, shredding, and grinding through use of special attachments. Small kitchens may have only one mixer, which is used by all work sections. Mobility is frequently desirable for small mixers. When estimating required size, allow for mixing action, increase of volume in mixing, and prevention of splashing in use of the mixer.

Food Cutters and Choppers

The food cutter having a rotating bowl with a plow formation on the lid to guide the food under two power-driven knives has been on the market for some time. For safety it is important that guards prevent operation when the knives are uncovered. Choose models that can be taken apart for thorough cleaning. Attachments may be obtained for use on a shaft from the motor. These cutters may be procured in bench or pedestal models.

Food choppers or grinders may operate as an attachment on another motor driven piece of equipment but for heavy work, independent equipment is preferred. Models are available with grinding capacity through a $\frac{1}{8}$ in. plate as follows:

Horsepower	$\frac{1}{4}$	$\frac{1}{3}$	$\frac{1}{2}$	$\frac{3}{4}$	$1\frac{1}{2}$	2	3	5	$7\frac{1}{2}$
Capacity (lb/min)	4–5	6–8	12–14	14–20	24–25	25–30	37	60	70–75

Important selection points are the manner in which the chopper cuts, safety, and sanitary factors. Plates from $\frac{1}{8}$ to $\frac{1}{2}$ in. are available and usually a feed pan and wooden stomper are furnished with the machine. The cylinder may be horizontal or at a slant to provide gravity flow.

Slicers

Slicers may be completely hand-operated, semiautomatic, fully automatic, or completely automatic. Hand-operated units are used where the volume is small. The knife of a semiautomatic rotates mechanically by a motor while the carriage is pushed back and forth by hand. Normally they can produce 50 to 70 slices/min. Electric power drives both the knife and the carriage in the fully automatic model. The speed can be specified to be from 30 to 50 strokes/min. Variable speed machines can be regulated to 1 to 55 slices/min. Some items are better sliced at slower speeds while others may be sliced at faster ones. Slower speeds are used for hot, crumbly foods and the faster ones for firm, solid foods that do not break up easily. Knife diameters are from 7 to 16 in. (17½ to 40 cm) for most institutional sizes. Larger bladed machines have more versatility but also take up more space.

Most slicers are gravity fed with the carriage on an angle pointing down toward the knife. A weighted plate pushes the food against the rotating blade. A horizontal type slicer is available which is good for

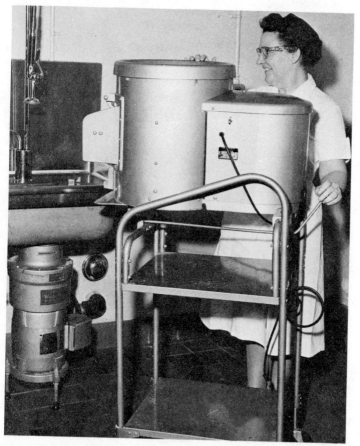

Figure 19.1 Mobile peeler models may be moved away from the sink when not in use so that sink may be used more conveniently for other purposes. Note disposal installed in shallow sink for vegetable refuse. (*Courtesy University of Washington, Seattle.*)

slicing juicy items such as rare roast beef. This slicer makes it possible to retain juices that may be as much as 2 percent of the product.

Ease of maintenance and cleaning are factors deserving strong consideration when selecting a slicer. Check ease of disassembly and exposure for cleaning of all parts. Standards prescribed by NSF should be required. The machine should be as safety-proof as possible. Check guards. Some machines cannot be operated when guards are not in place. The machine should be electrically grounded and installed on a firm, level surface. A sharpener should come with the machine.

Slicers giving variations in slice thickness can be obtained in most slicers from 10 slices per inch to slices ¾ in. thick. The vertical blade type is less desirable for slicing foods that crumble or fold as they are sliced. The angle blade type is preferred. The diameter of the knife limits the size or diameter of the material sliced to approximately one-half its diameter.

Knives should be of high-quality steel, taking a keen edge and holding it. The slicer blade should be easily sharpened. The knives should be well guarded. Some slicers have self-contained portion scales to weigh portions as they are sliced, and others have counters that count the portions as they are sliced.

Vegetable Peeler

Vegetable peelers are sized from 7 to 60 lb capacity. The smallest are table or bench models, while the larger are floor types. If desired, they may be mobile so that they may be moved away from the production line when not in use. Automatic timers and adjustable discharge chutes are available. Motors vary from ¼ hp on the 7-lb model to 1 hp for the largest. Height should be specified so the peeler discharges properly on an inspection table or into a sink. The discharge height is normally 37 in. (92.5 cm). State whether right-hand or left-hand operation is needed. The production capacity of different sizes operating from 1 to 3 min is as follows:

Food Item	Bench Model		Floor Model		
	7–lb (¼ hp)	15–20 lb (⅓ hp)	15–20 lb (⅓ hp)	30–33 lb (¾ hp))	50–60 lb (1 hp)
Potatoes	7 lb	15–20 lb	15–20 lb	30–33 lb	50–60 lb
Beets	4–5 lb	10–25 lb	10–15 lb	15–25 lb	25–30 lb
Carrots	4–5 lb	8–12 lb	8–12 lb	15–25 lb	30–45 lb

Note: To obtain Kilograms divide pounds by 2.2.

CLEANING OR HOUSEKEEPING SECTIONS

Dishwashers

When specifying dishwashers indicate (1) manufacturer and model number—the model number will refer chiefly to design, size, and capacity; (2) body material—galvanized or stainless steel; (3) direction of travel—in and out as in a counter model, at right angles for corner installation and right to left or left to right; (4) electric current—voltage, current cycles and phase; (5) method of heating—manual or thermostatic control of gas, electricity or steam; (6) booster heater for rinse water—to be mounted or unmounted and to use gas, electricity, or steam; (7) racks required in excess of standard equipment listing type—plate, cup, or glass, cutlery—and number; (8) approval—NSF and UL; (9) special accessories, such as ventilating cowls, locked selector switch, and time control; and (10) date and place of delivery.

Rack and conveyor belt (flight type) machines are available. Tableware is placed in racks for the rack type and are manually placed in or automatically carried through the machine. A moving belt or ratchets are available to move racks through in 2-tank and 3-tank machines. A single-tank machine must have the rack placed manually inside the machine, the door closed, the wash cycle started either manually or automatically which then goes into the rinse cycle. After completion of the rinse cycle, the door must be opened and the rack manually moved out of the machine. On automatic machines, after the rack has been moved onto the belt or where the ratchets can catch it the other operations are automatic.

The conveyor-belt or flight type machines do not require racks. Dishes are placed directly on the conveyor, which is a continuous belt that carries the dishes through the machine. Operations are activated at specified points to prerinse, wash, rinse, and finally rinse the dishes. Conveyor speeds may vary 5 to 15 ft (1.5 to 4.5 m) per minute. Eight feet (214 m) per minute equals approximately 40 spaces on the conveyor belt or forty cafeteria trays and would yield an hourly capacity of 2400 trays. The time of wash and rinse are regulated by the conveyor speed and this speed in turn is regulated by the quantity of water or force that can be directed at the dishes to get proper cleansing and sanitizing action. When specifying these machines a statement should be made of desired belt width, if there is intention to put wide baking sheets or similarly wide equipment through the machine.

A dish machine cleans by water pressure at from 15 to 20 psi. Moving or nonmoving spray manifolds above and nonmoving usually below drive water against the units and remove soil. In the wash area, a detergent added promotes removal of soil but about 70 percent of the cleaning is due to force of the water. Open end machines require splash curtains at each end. It is desirable to have curtains inside between wash and rinse sections. It is important to note that all objects on the belt do not hold the curtain in such manner as to prevent the water from a specific section from striking the items to be cleaned. This is likely to occur where a section is very short and items such as cafeteria trays are washed.

Research has shown that low bacterial count on washed dishes is promoted by adequate prerinsing that reduces soil from being carried into the wash solution. Preflush or prerinse machines are used with dish machines often to remove a large part of the food and grease from items. The machines are usually connected to the water system with a mixing valve that yields the proper water temperature. The valve should be capable of adjustment. Manual prerinsing may be done on individual items when scraping under a spray or on a rack of dishes placed over a sink located near the opening of the machine, by spraying the dishes from an overhead spray equipped with a trigger valve. Some items and certain soil require a presoak.

A single-tank machine has a cycle of washing and rinsing that starts when the machine is turned on. On some, the final rinse has to be activated by the operator. A rinse that operates only when required rather than continuously saves energy. Single-tank machines may be obtained with a prewash cycle. A 2-tank machine will usually have a wash, rinse, and final rinse. Water from the final rinse flows into the rinse section and an overflow from the rinse into the wash section refreshes it. A standing overflow in the wash section permits grease, soil, and scum to flow into the drain. The dilution of the wash water with the fresh water calls for gradual addition of detergent in the concentration required for cleaning. A 3-tank machine has a prerinse, wash, rinse, and final rinse and operates much the same as a 2-tank machine in other respects.

The temperatures maintaining in each of the compartments are important to soil removal and sanitizing. A water temperature warm enough to soften fats but not hot enough to cook food onto objects, 125 to 140° F (47 to 57° C), is desirable for the prerinse. The wash solution should be 150 to 165° F (66 to 74° C), rinse temperature 160° F (71° C), and the final rinse should be 180° F (81° C) for 10 seconds or 170° F (77° C) for 30 seconds to sanitize. The highest temperature used on machines for the final rinse is 195° F. It is important to note, however, that at temperatures above 180° F (81° C) there is vaporization of the water which interferes with the force of the rinsing action. Booster heaters are likely to be needed to ensure proper temperatures. While water delivered to the machine should be from 15 to 20 psi, the psi at

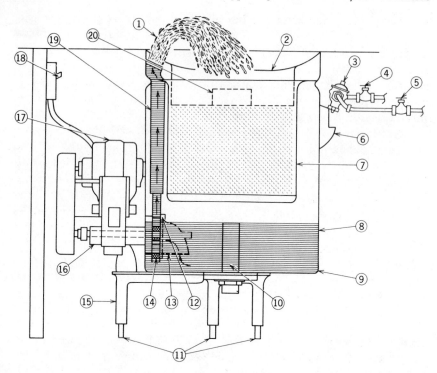

Figure 19.2 Diagram of a preflushing machine. The soil drops through (2) the scraping plate discharge opening and is caught there while water seeps through where it is picked up at the bottom and recirculated. (*U. S. Department of Defense Drawing.*)

the open wash manifold will be from 4 to 6 psi and at the rinse manifold about the same or slightly higher. The final rinse usually flows at 20 psi, but this may vary.

Detergents are fed into the machine either manually or by a dispenser. Detergent concentration indicators are available to indicate the detergent concentration in the machine. Some control this concentration automatically, while others do not. Most machines have a needle that when in the green area in the middle of a dial indicates a concentration of 0.20 to 0.25 percent by weight or about 8 to 10 lb (3.5 to 4.5 Kg) per 1,000 meals. Concentrations of 0.15 to 0.40 percent are capable of automatic control. Most machines have an "on" and "off" switch and white light indicating that the concentration and dispenser are proper. A red light goes on when malfunctioning occurs, such as lack of detergent sup-

Figure 19.3 Dishwasher and prerinse machine in a a wall location with good access to the working parts. Scraping table with disposer and overhead shelf for baskets. Note mechanized preflush, basket return behind machine, good lighting, well-placed floor drain, and well-built equipment. (*Courtesy The Salvajar Co., Kansas City, Mo.*)

ply. Some have a buzzer that sounds. Dispensers should be placed within full view of the dish machine operators as they work.

Some dishes do not dry well, especially plastics. Rinse aids can be added by injectors into the final rinse to promote water run-off and thus aid drying. From 75 to 200 ppm are needed for proper run-off. The rinse should flow at a rate of 4 to 15 gpm at from 15 to 30 psi. Injectors should be capable of adjustment and dispense from 6 to 8 oz (170 to 227 gr) of rinse aid fluid for every 1,000 meals. Specifications should state all the requirements desired as detailed here. Some units to promote drying use a fan or special velocity blower that dries dishes by air-flow as they move out of the clean end of the machine.

The dish machine area should be complete with adequate soiled and clean dish tables, sorting tables for silver, and other required units. The allowed bacterial counts on utensils after coming from the machine are from $30/cm^2$ (American Hospital Association) to $100/cm^2$ (Mallman and

USPH). A properly equipped unit, well planned and operated, should be able to give the lower count. Silverware will usually yield higher counts than other tableware.

Freshwater and Steckler[1] indicate the following standards are used to size machines to operations: When the number of pieces is 1400/hr install a single-tank machine, 3000 to 5200 install either a 180 rack per hour carousel or a 2-tank rack machine, 7000 to 9000 pieces a large carousel or a 3-tank conveyor or flight type machine. Cafeterias may be able to manage a slightly larger load than this. Carousel–type machines are efficient but have a serious defect in that workers frequently handle soiled and clean dishes without hand washing in between since the two areas are together.

Many factors influence the size requirements of dishmachines for operations. The quantity of dishes is the most significant factor but the speed at which dishes are returned for service may also influence sizing. Some operations may demand excess sizing to obtain rapid return of dishes. Others may have an inventory sufficient to satisfy the complete requirements for a meal and dishes can accumulate and be washed during lull periods. This gives a more even use of full shift dishwashing labor. Glass machines, silver washing machines, and other units reduce requirements. Adding pots and pans to the dishwashing load increases the total load. Using paper goods reduces the load. A careful analysis of specific conditions in each installation is necessary to establish dishwashing requirements.

High standards of construction that conform to NSF recommendations are needed. Galvaneal bodies will last 7 to 10 years or longer and s/s will have double this life expectancy. Frames should be made of durable, rigid angle construction and bodies should be no lighter than 16-gage metal on smaller machines and no lighter than 14 gauge on larger ones. Bodies of galvaneal should be no lighter than 12 gauge on any type machine. All interiors (spray arms, and so forth) should be constructed of ni-resit metal or stainless steel. All welded construction should be specified. Motors should be splash-proof type and installed so as to be away from steam and moisture. The motors should be sealed-in type and protected from overloads. Conveyor type machines should be equipped with an adjustable friction clutch that will release in case of a jam. Plumbing should conform to local codes and necessary vacuum breakers should be provided. Machines that meet the standards of the Plumbing Engineers Testing Laboratories usually meet local requirements. Tanks

[1] John Freshwater and David M. Steckler, *Evaluation of Dishwashing Systems in Food Service Establishments*, Marketing Research Report, No. 1003, USDA, October, 1973.

should be provided with adequate size drains protected against plugging by perforated overflow caps or similar devices. Well-pitched drainage from the tank bottoms should be provided. All other areas should have no standing water after drains have been opened. Tanks should be suitably baffled to prevent undesirable overrun occurring from one tank to the other. Separation of tanks by air space should be provided so that there will be no heat transfer from one tank to the other. The number of standard items furnished and the number of extras should be ascertained. If the extra equipment required is written into the specifications, the cost is usually less than when it is purchased separately. All washing and rinse operations should have accurate temperature indicators and automatic thermostats for controlling temperatures. Automatic cycle machines should have signal lights indicating *on* and *off* operation. Scrap trays should be provided and basket type machines should come with three or more standard sized baskets. The necessary booster-heaters with thermostats, line strainers, relief valves, steam traps, solenoid steam valves, hot water pressure regulators and pressure gages should be specified. Exhaust ducts should be provided and hoods should be added, if

Figure 19.4 Sanitary dish handling is promoted by having a wall that separates soiled dish section from the clean dish end of the machine.

necessary, to prevent the escape of steam and heat. Pumps should be guaranteed against leakage. Sanitary type feet should be provided.

Dish machines are made for corner, wall, or center installation and specifications should state location so that doors and panels can be properly located. Machines installed against a wall should have easy access to all machinery and other equipment from the open side. Conveyors should be made of stainless steel and peg type conveyor belts may have nylon links and pegs. Doors should be counterbalanced, easily opened, and non-leaking. The machine should clean easily inside and out. Spray arms should be easily detached and cleaned. Hose attachments should be provided. If gas heaters are used, flues should be provided. Service, spare parts, and easy maintenance should be checked. The type heaters to be used for boosters and tanks, type electrical current, water pressure, and other factors necessary for proper regulation of the machine in the installation should be stated. Shipment should be specified in sections if the machine is so large it cannot be brought into the building for installation as one unit. Detergent and wetting agent dispensers are usually added after installation and are a separate purchase.

Dishmachines usually operate at only 70 percent of maximum capacity and some manufacturers may state 100 or 70 percent capacity for their machines. The average seated service operation will have five to seven dishes per customer for breakfast and seven to ten dishes per customer for lunch and dinner. Cafeteria operations will have 20 percent less than this. Normally, three partial meals can be counted as one meal. In addition to these dishes, flatware and other items that are not used for individual service must be added to the dishwashing load. On the average, about twenty-five pieces can be loaded into a basket. In a $19\frac{3}{4} \times 19\frac{3}{4}$ in. basket 14 dinner plates, 28 pie plates or saucers, 20 cups, 10 soup bowls, 36 glasses, or 50 pieces of flatware can be loaded.

Pot and Pan Washing

Most pots and pans are manually washed. In some operations a mechanical brush driven by a motor is used. Pot and pan machines should have as high construction standards as dish machines. They should be provided with proper controls and auxiliary equipment to make operation automatic and adequate. Continuous or batch type machines are available. The continuous type machine usually rotates during the wash and rinse cycle and an operator does not have to move to load or unload pots and pans. Pot machines are available for operations serving 3,500 to 12,000 meals per day. The largest machines operate on load, wash, rewash, rinse, and drain cycles. Wash temperature is

140° F and final rinse is 180° F. Strainer baskets to catch food soil should be provided.

Glass Washers

Separating glass washing from dish washing is recommended for many operations. It may be satisfactorily combined with dishwashing if the water is fairly soft, the dishes are well prewashed, the dish load is not too heavy, and a good detergent is used. Glasses are frequently washed in a single tank, spray rinse dish machine located in the dishwashing area but separate from the main dishwashing operation.

Manual washing is still done in many operations, especially in counter units, fountains, and bars. Most local public health codes require washing and sanitizing conditions for manual dishwashing. Small manually operated brush units that can be placed in a sink for washing the glasses are available. A new mechanically driven brush machine using cold water has recently been announced. It can be attached near fountains or counter units as well as in dish sections.

Silver Washers

Flatware may be washed in dishmachines by standing in perforated cans, "business end" up and going through the dish machine later, dipped in a 180°F rinse with a wetting agent that retains polish and prevents spotting. One machanical washer on the market is a tumble type completing an automatic cycle of wash, rinse, and dry (200°F air) in $3\frac{1}{2}$ minutes. From 150 to 300 pieces of flatware are washed in a cycle. Water usage is three gallons per cycle. A 30-ampere, 115-v, 60-cycle current is required.

Silver burnishers of the barrel type using shot are frequently required in operations having a large quantity of silver. Models are made that burnish 75 to 500 pieces of silver flatware at a time.

Can Washers

The time used to wash, scrub, and hose a large number of garbage cans manually can be significant. Can washers can be substantial labor savers in cleaning and sanitizing cans. A can washer that operates with hot water 20 to 35 psi and low steam pressure is available. It will wash cans up to $21\frac{3}{4}$ in. in diameter. The dimensions are $21\frac{3}{4}$ in. for the bowl and overall height of $25\frac{1}{2}$ in. It should be installed in an area where there is a watertight floor with good drainage and where it will not be in the line of traffic.

Disposals

The use of different types of disposal machines has increased in the last 20 years. Basically they are of two types, the revolving turntable that grinds or minces refuse and flushes it into the sewage system and the compactor that places pressure on waste, including paper, plastics, bones, glass and metal containers, and packs it into a solid mass. This is then placed in containers and taken away. The latter type largely extracts moisture. There are new devices on the market that combine the preflush with a compactor and much soil formerly left in dish machines is now removed. A ¾-hp revolving turntable disposal can dispose of 300 to 600 lb of waste per hour and a 2 hp can double this. Compactors usually handle large quantities and are suitable where there is a central disposal area. Most operate on the hammermill principle. Some preflush-disposal units have been found to increase bacteria on utensils. Others have been found to have a high water requirement that may not be desirable in areas where water is not plentiful. Careful consideration needs to be made on many factors before final selection is made.

The use of disposal units eliminates the labor required in handling garbage. Most disposals operate by using running water to carry food into spinning gears that shred it into small pieces. As the size grows smaller, it is forced down into smaller and smaller orifices until it is about ⅛ in. in size, and then is flushed into the sewer. Some large disposals have screw type shafts that force the waste into grinders. Disposals should not be connected to grease traps, and drains should have a pitch of at least ¼ in. per foot. Two to 3-inch drains are required. The power required to operate the disposal may vary ⅓ to 5 hp. Water consumption for the smaller units is 2 to 3 gpm; the larger sizes require 8 to 10 gpm.

Small disposals are frequently installed at origin points of garbage, such as soiled dish tables, pot and pan sinks, vegetable preparation units, butcher shops, diet kitchens, and soda fountains. Small disposals will have difficulty in grinding bones, milk cartons, asparagus, celery and artichoke leaves, but the larger models have little difficulty with most food and paper wastes. Although ⅓ to ½ hp models may be adequate to handle light wastes, nothing less than 1½ hp models should be installed in areas where the quantity of waste is sizable.

Disposals installed in soiled dish tables and other areas should be provided with a stainless steel cone, rubber garbage block, overhead spray, and a built-in silver guard. A compact model is desirable. Quietness of operation is also an important selection factor. Controls should be easy

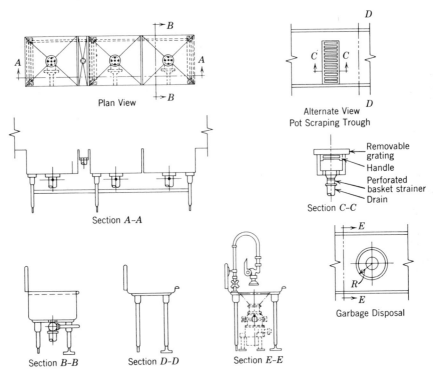

Plan View

Alternate View
Pot Scraping Trough

Section A-A

Removable grating
Handle
Perforated basket strainer
Drain
Section C-C

Garbage Disposal

Section B-B   Section D-D   Section E-E

Figure 19.5 Sinks for hand washing dishes or pots and pans. Maximum water temperature for hand washing, in first sink, is 120° F (49° C), second sink temperature is 120° to 140° F (49° to 60° C) and for rinsing in third sink 180° F (82° C) for 30 sec. Immersion baskets are used for second and third sinks. A thermometer should be available to record temperatures. An alternative to having a third sink is to have a final rinse cabinet with a nozzle spray delivering 10 gpm at 180°F (82°C) at the manifold for 5 sec or 5 gpm for 10 sec. (*U.S. Dept. of Defense, Military Hankbook 740.*)

to operate and should be installed in a place convenient to the operator. Central installations might be on tables where waste is dumped and then fed into the disposal.

Before selecting a disposal, check local codes, the type waste to be handled, capacities of available machines, repair and spare part service, protection against accidental entry of flatware, balance and freedom from vibration, anti-splash guards, noise control, accessories, and maintenance cost.

Figure 19.6 A mobile scrubber allows the night janitor to increase cleaning productivity greatly.

Mechanical Sanitation Equipment

There are many new appliances being developed in sanitation equipment that save man hours and perform jobs more efficiently. Planners should investigate the market for available equipment in this area and utilize wherever possible to reduce labor costs.

MISCELLANEOUS BAKE SHOP EQUIPMENT

Many operators find specialized equipment, such as dough dividers, rounders, and pie rollers, to have sound economic value in labor saving, portion uniformity, and improved quality. A medium size divider and rounder can shape 1,000 rolls per hour. A motor-driven pie roller rolls pie crust or cookie dough to desired thickness in two operations and in one third the time required for hand rolling by a skilled worker. The capacity is 200 to 300 per hour. When quantities of sweet breads are produced, a dough roller or sheeter may be used to roll the doughs for final make-up. It may also be used for pizzas. Large power sifters for bakeries will sift a barrel of flour in 4 to 6 minutes and small ones have a capacity of 50 lb per minute.

Accurate scales are required in preparing large quantity formulas. Although a wide variety of sizes are available, one has not been designed to fit the particular needs in institution kitchens. In kitchens using 60- or 80-qt mixers, it is desirable to have a formula scale that will weigh quickly and accurately from ½ oz to 50 lb. Needed also are tare adjustment and platform size that are adapted for standard containers used when measuring ingredients and scaling mixtures for baking. Significant selection points for a scale are accuracy, speed and ease in using, durability, compactness, and a design and finish that will be attractive and easy to clean. Beams and counter weights requiring adjustment tend to be time consuming. Light weight spring scales quickly lose accuracy.

Large bake shops in some food facilities may require many of the pieces of equipment found desirable by commercial bakers, such as large horizontal mixers, cookie droppers, conveyors, dough chutes, dough hoppers, dividers, molders, panners, pan greasers, automatic depanners, tunnel ovens, and other highly specialized equipment. Consultation with bakery planning specialists is recommended when such installation is being considered.

Suggested Student Assignments

Observe and list mechanical equipment used in three different food operations, such as college food units, commercial restaurant, hospital, and school lunchroom.

1. Mixers, food cutters, and slicers—Are there more than one of each of these items used in one facility, and in what work section is each located? Do the workers from more than one work section use any one item of equipment? State kind of preparation for which the equipment is used and state which workers use which items of equipment. State mixer size and the largest volume required in preparing for normal operation. Are attachments conveniently stored? Describe the cleaning and sanitizing aspects required for each item.

2. Describe the equipment used in dish handling:
   a. Removal from dining area.
   b. Scraping, stacking, and prerinsing.
   c. Type and size of dishwasher used.
   d. Method of detergent dispensing.
   e. Rinsing agent used and how applied.
   f. Water temperatures maintained, as taken from thermometer reading on the machine.

g. Possibility of contamination due to handling methods, explain where and how it may be corrected.

h. Time allowed for air drying.

i. Drying problems due to type of tableware, and how corrected.

j. Methods used for transportation and storage.

3. Describe and evaluate the pot washing procedure followed in each unit.

4. Are disposals used? If so, where are they located, what sizes are used, and for what purpose? Are compactors used? What hp is used for each disposal?

Chapter 20

cooking equipment

Specialization on foods in menus and changes in systems of operation has brought about changes in the cooking equipment selected for food operations. Just as there are many types of food preparation there are specific pieces of equipment best suited to its preparation. A list of value priorities should be carefully examined in relation to its selection. The list should include such points as particular adaptation to specific use, speed of heating, control of temperature and humidity, sturdy construction, ease of operation, safety, economy, insulation, possibility for ease and thoroughness in cleaning, and suitable capacity for volume required.

DRY HEAT COOKING EQUIPMENT

Ovens

Deck ovens are sized from one bun pan to over seventy bun pans per oven. They may be roasting or baking, with the former deck 12 to 15 in. high and the latter having decks 4 to 8 in. high. Height of deck is of special significance where used in stacks of three or four. Too many roasting decks will make the top deck too high and the bottom deck too low for convenience. Base-fired gas ovens containing several decks will have the hottest temperature at the bottom and coolest at the top. Separately fired decks give best control. Multiple heat conduits for base-fired ovens have made it possible to secure more even heating. New types of gas-fired ovens have stainless steel interiors, better precision thermostats, and a device that, working as a thermocouple, will turn off the gas automatically when the interior of a roast or other item reaches an established temperature.

Conventional electric ovens are usually heated from underneath the deck and the heat indirectly circulated.

Oven decks may be stationary or moving. Stationary decks are especially satisfactory for small ovens. Depth of decks is important, If a peel is required, extra labor and space are necessary. Moving decks may rotate like a merry-go-round, move on a traveling belt, or revolve on a reel like a ferris wheel. The latter is most commonly used. Some reel ovens will hold six to seventy bun pans 18 × 26 in. in size. Some of the smaller ovens are quite compact and reel ovens save space over deck ovens. The traveling belt ovens are usually used only in large operations.

Ovens should permit easy and thorough cleaning. Oven decks of ceramic material should be non-absorbent and sufficiently hard so they will not be injured in cleaning. Some oven decks are removable for easy cleaning. Spillage should not be allowed to seep down. Wiring or manifolds should be concealed. Easy access to all parts is desirable.

Figure 20.1 The deck oven has been and will continue to be widely used for conventional baking. The convection oven offers compactness and more rapid baking and finds much favor where these qualities are most desirable. (*Courtesy General Electric Co., Chicago Heights, Ill.*)

Ovens should be all-welded construction of structural steel to give durable, rigid frames. Outside bodies should be 16 to 18 gauge metal attached to solid frame support with durable finishes. Inner linings should be 18 gauge rustproof sheet metal, reinforced to prevent bucking. Aluminized reflective linings or stainless steel reduce fuel costs. Fronts should be all one piece construction. Forced air ovens that may provide more even heat and more rapid cooking at lower temperatures are now on the market.

The type and quantity of insulating materials used are important for economy of operation and heat reduction. At least four inches of non-sagging, rodent-proof, spun fiberglass, or other material equally as efficient, should be found on all sides. Larger ovens may have thicker insulation. The outside surface of any oven, even after extended use, should be easily touched. Walls surrounding insulation should be tightly sealed so moisture cannot enter. Heat loss around doors should be minimized and break strips should prevent heat from flowing out. Handles should be cool to the touch. Doors should be sturdy and contain windows giving view of contents, without requiring the opening of the door. Doors should easily hold 150 lb in weight and be counterbalanced for easy opening and closing and to prevent slamming. Hinges should be heavy duty type. Doors should open level with the bottom of the oven or deck.

Heating units should be durable and made of warp-proof alloys. Separate controls to individual elements or burners may be required. Thermostatic control should be precise between 150 and 550° F. Signal lights to indicate when the oven is on, timers, and outside indicating thermometers should be on the ovens. Chambers should be vented, dampered, and baffling as required, to direct heat present. Controls should be in front, easily accessible to workers. Vapor should be conducted out and not allowed to flow back as condensate.

Oven decks over 36 in. wide should have 10 to 12 gauge sheet steel bottoms and those less than that, 14-gauge. Tile or ceramic materials may be mounted on the steel to provide more even heat. Steam pressure of 5 to 7 lb may be required and a separate steam generator is available for this purpose at boiler horsepowers of 3, 6, 8½, 10, 12, and 13½, respectively, for 12, 20, 30, 42, or 48 pan (18 × 26 in.) oven. Each deck should be distributed evenly. Traps and drains should be provided so water will not be blown into the oven.

A good oven should come to 450° F in 20 minutes and should have good recovery ability. Proper heat circulation is important. Ovens should be able to cool quickly as dropping temperatures are required.

Gas deck ovens having 3.3 to 14 sq ft of space per deck and holding 1 to 4 baking sheets (18 × 26 in.) may be obtained. Btu input per hour may vary between 20,000 for the two-pan size to 58,000 for a separately fired three-deck oven, 14 sq ft per deck, holding 2 baking sheets per

Table 20.1 Productive Capacities and Energy Demands of Electrical Ovens*

Type Oven	Single Oven Size, in Inches			Approx. Square Feet of Space	Capacity 18" × 26" Pans	Kilowatt Energy Demand
	Width	Depth	Height			
Range	36	38¼	12–15	4.3	2 (if middle shelf used)	6.0
Deck	22¾	27½	8–12	4.0	1	6.0
Deck	37¼	28½	8–12	7.2	2	6.2
Deck	37¼	57	8–12	14.5	4	7.5
Deck	56¼	57	8–12	22.0	6	11.0

* Data taken from Hotpoint brochures.

deck. A three-deck base fired oven containing 2 baking sheets will require approximately 42,000 Btu input per hour.

Convection ovens have high productive capacity for the cubic area which they occupy. Large roll-in types are available that will take a rack of 22 shelves loaded with food. Small counter models are also available. Some are divided into compartments to permit different types of baking at one time. Convection ovens have a fan to move the hot air, and this circulation of the air makes it possible for the shelves to be closer together than in the conventional oven and to process a larger load in a given space. The fan is usually in the back and distributes the air directly over the food or through mufflers or ducts. Some have baffles to direct the heat. When the fan is turned off the oven functions in the same manner as a conventional oven, and food cannot be placed close together.

A damper and venting are desirable and the oven should be checked to see if it is airtight and does not have a high heat loss. The unit should have tightly sealed walls that do not permit moisture seepage. Good insulation is a requirement, usually of spun fiberglass, rodent-proof, so set that it does not pack. Some ovens have been found to have uneven baking spots when heavily loaded. It is well to check this.

Easy cleaning is an important factor. Concealed wiring and manifolds should be present. Inner linings should be 16 to 18 gauge rust-proof sheet metal reinforced to avoid buckling. Shelf racks and shelving should be checked for strength. The outside covering should be of 16 to 18 gauge metal which is durable and easily cleaned. This should be attached to a solid frame of angle iron.

Doors should be equipped with moisture free windows and have sturdy hinges and handles. Some have counterbalancing doors. Ovens that have separate compartments for simultaneous baking at different temperatures may have a Dutch-door-type arrangement so that one compartment can be opened without disturbing the others. Check thermostats for variation, which should not be more than 20° F (11° C) variance over that desired. The thermostat should be capable of setting on calibrations from 150° F to 500° F (71° to 260° C). The oven should be equipped with a timer and have signal lights to indicate when the unit is on or off. Glass in doors is sometimes available. This permits seeing inside without opening the door.

The heating elements should warp-proof of nichrome or some other suitable and durable alloy. The entire unit should have easy access to the mechanical parts and be easy serviceable. Check convenient availability of spare parts and servicing.

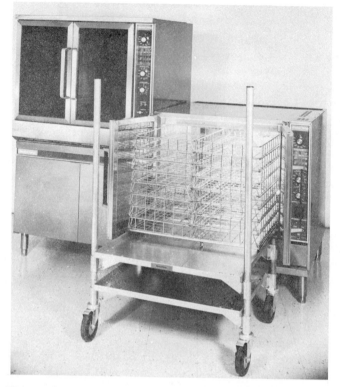

Figure 20.2 A convection oven with a roll-in unit for use in satellite food service. (*Market Forge, Everett, Mass.*)

Ranges and Griddles

A range consists of a frame used as a mounting for the cooking top and oven. Angle frame, as required, should be incorporated for sturdy support and all-welded bodies of at least 16 to 17 gauge should be on all heavy-duty ranges with surface areas of the frame of heavier metal. Heating units should be made of heavy cast iron alloys or other durable material. They may be solid, open, or grills. Each fuel has a special type desirable under specified conditions. Baffling, fins, and venting may be required. Care should be taken in sizing. Best work height may vary, depending on the type of cooking done. Body materials may be chrome plated, stainless steel, sheet steel, porcelain, or black iron.

Full surface or rectangular solid heating plates are used for continuous heavy cookery production. Round or open units are used for speedy, intermittent cookery. Individual types of tops may be combined with

Figure 20.3 A compact unit combining three types of cooking. Note shelf-type hood with removable filters. (*Courtesy Wells Commercial Sales Co., San Francisco.*)

units, such as broilers, ovens, fryers, and plate warmers, to meet production needs. Spacer plates are used to eliminate unsanitary areas. Round type units and grills are placed in service lines of cafeterias or behind counter production areas in short-order restaurants. Counter type units may be used.

Heavy duty ranges should usually be selected for normal use. Medium duty units or restaurant type units are used where operational demands are not heavy. Medium duty ranges are frequently combined with other cooking units for short-order work; these may be from 2 to 8½ ft long. Smaller units may be used for counter or fountain work. Some specific types of operations require rapid individual type cookery, and ranges called "chop suey" ranges are used for this purpose. Mobility in ranges or grills may be desirable.

Gas and electricity are the most common fuels used. Solid type electrical heating units have heating coils imbedded in the cast iron or steel plate, and rectangle plates 12 × 24 × 1¼ in. thick, using 5 to 6 kw, are common. They are frequently mounted three to a range section or in combination with other types of electrical heating units. Solid round units, about 10 to 11 in. in diameter (called French plates), with resistance coils imbedded in cast metal about ⅜ in. thick require about 2.5 kw. High speed, open, enclosed tubular type heating units about 8½ in. in diameter using 3.5 kw are used for some purposes. Heavy pots break them down, however.

Grills are usually ½ in. thick and made of cast iron, steel, or aluminum. They may vary in size depending upon production demands but normal sizes are 220 to 960 sq in. Electrical units require 3 to 16 kw and may be wired for voltages of 115, 208, 230, or 450. Thermostatic heat control may be obtained between 250 to 850° F.[1]

Easy cleaning drip pans to catch spillage, back splashes to make clean-up easier, grease guards, grease troughs, grease receptacles, and other factors should be checked for purchase. Manganese-nickel asbestos covered wiring should lead to all elements and switch boxes. Gas equipment should have safety pilots and automatic lighters, concealed piping, and manifolds, and thermostatic control.

Calculate size and amount of range or grill top required in terms of menu, volume and other specialized equipment, such as broilers, fryers, and steam equipment used. Labor and cooking times are reduced if stocks, soups, and similar items are processed in steam equipment rather than in stock pots on a range top.

Tilting pans give desirable flexibility in food processing as they may be used as griddles, deep fryers, stew pots, and range tops. They operate on electricity, gas, or steam. Some of the higher temperatures are not available if heated by steam. They should be equipped with a lip and a cover. They should be mounted for easy cleaning around and underneath. Most of these units are 7 in. (17½ cm) deep and may vary in other dimensions from 16 in. (40 cm) square to 22 to 39 in. (55 to 97½ cm).

Labor-saving tools are available for use at the griddle to reduce time to load and unload items, thus increasing production capacity. For instance, egg droppers are available that will drop a large number at one time. Hotcake dispensers help also. Multiple flippers are available. Pro-

---

[1] A good gas or electrical unit should, in 8 minutes from turning on, bring 1 qt water at 50°F to a rolling boil.

duction capacities as stated by manufacturers are usually reduced by 40 percent to allow for time factors which they have not considered. Table 20.2 shows some of the data used by manufacturers that should be decreased 40 percent when calculating actual production capacities:

Table 20.2   Griddle Capacities for Different Foods

Menu Items	Griddle Sizes and Units Per Hour		
	24 × 36 in. (60 × 87½ cm)	32 × 36 in. (80 × 90 cm)	32 × 72 in. (80 × 180 cm)
Hamburger (4 oz or 3½ in. dia. or 114 g and 9 cm dia.)	48	60	90
Tenderloin steak (5 oz or 125 g)	36	45	90
Minute steak (4 oz or 114 g)	18	22	44
Bacon (22 to 32 sli/lb or 454 g)	6 lb (2.72 kg)	7½ lb (3.4 kg)	16 lb (7.3 kg)
Pork sausage portions (1½ oz or 40 g)	45	56	112
Fish cake portions (2 oz or 57 g)	45	56	112
Fried egg portions (2 eggs)	45	56	112
Griddle cakes (4 in or 10 cm dia.)	32	40	80
Fried potatoes (4 oz or 114 g portions)	15–18	20–25	40–50
Ham steaks (5 oz or 142 g)	54	66	132
Liver (3 oz or 85 g portion)	27	35	70
Fried onions (2 oz or 85 g portion)	60	75	150

Broilers

Broilers cook largely by radiant or infrared heat. The most rapid cooking is by radiant heat or when the heating element glows with a white heat (from 1500° to 2000° F or 850 to 1100° C). Some broilers have ceramic or metal alloy units that reach a glowing temperature quickly thus giving off considerable quantities of radiant heat energy. Other broilers utilize infrared waves that increase cooking time but nevertheless are quite effective. Temperatures will range from 1000° to 1500° F (550° to 850° C). Regular charcoal, gas, or electric units are less efficient but still will produce good results, and they have a long history of use.

Figure 20.4 A tilting fry-pan or skillet may be used for a variety of cooking. A water connection beside it adds greatly to convenience. (*Courtesy Market Forge, Everett, Mass.*)

Broilers can be wasteful of heat. Therefore selection should be based on maximum utilization of heat. Some broilers are on the market which will come to temperature in 3 to 5 min. An infrared broiler can come to broiling temperature in 1½ min. The regular types should be expected to come to broiling temperature in 10 min. Charcoal broilers will take longer than this. Flexibility in heating is desirable. For instance, zone heating will save heating the entire broiler for a few items. Similar saving might be gained through having two smaller broilers instead of one large one, so that one only need be operated when loads are light. Proper concentration and direction of heat is necessary. Reflective linings assist in directing radiant heat. Insulation may reduce heat loss and save energy. A new broiler on the market broils from underneath on a 1-in. wavy grid and has a quartz broiler hood that can be lowered over the items to broil from the top. Utilization of heat that moves upward can do much to assist in maximizing heat use. For example, a small salamander or griddle may be placed above the broiler on which foods may be cooked or toasted. Some locate ovens above for baking or as a warming foods ready for service. Variable temperature controls and separate switches should be provided. Air drafts should not affect flames or cool foods.

Broiler bodies should be made of 16 gauge or better sheet steel rigidly reinforced with sturdy angle support. Construction should be simple and all welded construction should be specified. Finishes can be those used on ranges. Grids should be rugged, sturdy, and easy to adjust to proper levels from 1½ to 8 in. (3.8 to 20.3 cm) from the heat source. Grids should pull in and out easily and safety stop locks should be provided. All areas should be easily accessible for cleaning and repair. A sloping grease trough under the grid should catch grease and drippings and conduct them to a grease receptacle. Charcoal broiler beds should be of heavy construction.

All heating units and parts should be warpproof. Some broiler units have lift-out sides for wiping down and cleaning. Wide spaces between grids make it difficult to hold small items and also permit flare up of flames if grease catches fire. Baffling should prevent heat blast and overly heated sides. The fewer mechanical parts, the less maintenance required usually.

Broilers are available with 475 to 850 sq in. (1.2 to 2.2 sq m) of grid and may be single or stacked. A salamander is a small over-range broiler, usually used for toasting items, making au gratin dishes and broiling a few items. They are sometimes called backshelf-broilers. These may be obtained with 230 to 530 sq in. (0.6 to 1.3 sq m) of grid. Counter broilers are available with grids that are 20 × 20 in. (50 × 50 cm) using 74000 Btu/hr to those with grids 30 × 30 in. (75 × 75 cm) using 145,000 Btu/hr. Some are portable.

Manufacturers' statements need to be evaluated in terms of specific use. For instance, one claims that a broiler holding 9 steaks will broil 90/hr. If so, the steaks must be very thin or are served extremely rare. Another claims that each sq ft (0.3 sq m) will produce 20 to 25 lb (9 to 11 kg) of broiled fish, poultry, or steak/hr. Another advertises that on a 600 sq in. (3750 cm²) grid holding 24 hamburger patties, 420 can be broiled in an hour. This allows slightly less than 3 min cooking time. Many manufacturers use the surface capacity and cooking time to calculate the quantity that can be prepared, forgetting that there is a load and unload time loss to consider. This is an error frequently made in calculating equipment load capacity.

Good flues are needed to remove smoke, odors, and combustion products. The exhaust blower should be planned to remove a minimum of 500 cu ft (14.2 m³)/min. for every sq ft (0.3 m²) of grid space. Thus a grid 24 × 26 in or 4.3 sq ft 60 × 65 cm or 0.4 m²) will require 2150 cfm of exhaust. Exhausts should be covered with filters. Some may be within 4 in (10 cm) of the grid and represent considerable fire hazard unless properly maintained and equipped with ducts that have automatic turn-offs or other devices to reduce fire hazards. Filters should be removable for frequent washing.

Fryers

Temperature control, fast recovery time, economical utilization of fat, flavor protection, ease and safety of use, and good cleaning, as well as sturdiness, design, and size, are desirable factors in selecting deep fat fryers. Larger models or counter models as narrow as 12 in. are available. Also available are some that are flush with the counter top for cooking to order. Rapid recovery makes it possible to decrease batch times and increase quantity produced. Automatic fryers are available with timers. Frying may be done under pressure and this reduces cooking time. A bell signals the end of the cooking time.

Gas-fired models using fin type or tube-fired heaters and electric models using hinged elements are available for heavy duty use. Some of these gas and electric models are equipped with a recessed zone in the frying container to catch food particles and hold them at 100 to 200° F. Improved filtering devices are obtainable. When positioning fryers, allow working and storage space around them.

Table 20.3 Productive Capacities of Deep-Fat Fryers

	Fat Capacity of Fryer		
Item	10 to 15 lb	30 to 40 lb	45 to 60 lb
French-fried potatoes ⅛″ thick	21 lb	61 lb	90 lb
Fish fillets 5″ × ½″	8–10 fillets	8.8 lb	17 lb
Shrimp	2 lb	5.6 lb	7.75 lb
Chicken, 8 oz portion	4 portions	7 portions	14 portions
1 lb portion	2 portions	3½ portions	7 portions
Croquettes	2 lb	8.8 lb	14.6 lb
Doughnuts 2½″ diameter	16	30	64

Figure 20.5 A conveyor-fryer regulates time and eliminates guesswork. Time of frying is controlled by placement of foods in conveyor. (*Courtesy* Food Service Magazine, *Madison, Wis.*)

Fryers should fry from 1½ to 2 times their weight of fat per hour. Fryer requirements for some short-order operations are sometimes based on a load of ½ lb of fried potatoes per seat per hour.

Operational techniques, such as preblanching of fried potatoes or purchasing them preblanched, and partial cooking of chickens or other items, will increase productive capacity, and these must be evaluated in sizing.

Fryers that fry under pressure cook by heat in the fat and by steam under pressure. The steam may come from moisture in the food or be added in the cooking process. A lid seals the fryer tightly after food is added to the hot fat. Cooking is more rapid and the food is tenderized somewhat by the action of the steam under pressure. Chicken normally cooking in 20 minutes cooks in such a fryer in 7 to 9 min. One manufacturer claims that his 15-lb (7.3 kg) capacity unit produces from 90 to 100 lbs (41 to 56 kg)/hr. Under actual working conditions with delays, loading and unloading time, the capacity is likely to be closer to 50 to 60 lb (25 to 27 kg). Some operators find using two smaller pressure fryers preferable to installing one large one, for flexibility in handling low peaks of production. This also permits staggered production for while one is being unloaded another can be loaded, resulting in fresher products and better utilization of labor. One user found using a 6-lb and a 15-lb fat capacity fryer met its needs. The capacity of most units is from one lb of food to every 3 lb of fat to a pound of food to every 4 lb of fat. In regular fryers this is 1.5 for potatoes and 1.7 for other foods.

Another fryer is the doughnut fryer. The capacity required should be based on sufficient doughnuts produced to meet peak demands without doughnuts becoming 3 hours old before sale. Automatic, semi-automatic or manual machines are on the market. If volume is available and labor can be reduced, the higher cost automatic machine is likely to be worth the price. The machine selected should have good appearance and be an interest-arouser if placed where customers see it operate. Ventilation to remove frying odors and cleanability of the machine are important.

A hood may be required over the machine to remove unpleasing odors of fat and the volatile fat that saturates surroundings and becomes stale. Most doughnut fryers come equipped with a doughnut dropper. The dropper should be capable of being adjusted to control size. It should make different shapes also, such as French crullers, Bismarcks, Long Johns, etc. Fryers equipped with frying screens should have them between 2 and 3 (5 to 7.5 cm) below doughnuts moving over the frying fat. If closer, the doughnuts may stick, crack or break up. If too deep, the doughnuts may turn over before they should or distort in shape.

Most units are complex machines, especially the automated ones. The cost of maintenance should be evaluated, therefore, before purchase. The NSF standards for deep-frying equipment should be observed.

Sediment and other material can destroy the efficiency of fat for frying and reduce the quality of the products fried. More attention is being given, therefore to collection and removal of sediment. Some have deep well indentations that allow the material to settle to the bottom in a "cool zone" which removes it from temperatures that char it. Frying kettles should be removable so that they can be taken to sinks for cleaning. Ease of removing and filtering fat from the kettle is important. Frequent filtering may save from 25 to 50 percent of the fat used as well as improving the products. If the volume used is large a filtering machine may be warranted. If the volume is small, simple straining equipment will suffice for removing undesirable materials, such as a wire strainer on which a cloth is placed. One of the most efficient filters has a cone of soft absorbent cotton placed inside a stainless steel strainer. The fat is either siphoned from the fryer or lifted manually and poured into the cone. More complex filters using power pumps that force the fat through filters are available. Some may be potential hazards. Certain toxic metals such as copper or brass help breakdown fat. Metals exposure should be examined on equipment. Stainless steel is highly satisfactory.

Microwave Ovens

The high speed of heating possible with microwave has great utility for some special purposes. It is necessary to use different techniques than those required for conventional preparation. The depth of penetration is from 1½ to 3 in. (3.7 to 7.5 cm) and foods having greater depth or diameter such as large roasts, require the use of standby time for heat to be conducted to the full depth. Browning does not occur with microwaves alone. It may be achieved by using infrared lights in the chamber or by post or prebrowning to achieve a desired appearance and flavor.

A microwave oven can be highly useful if it is well integrated into certain production systems. A hospital, for example, that utilizes it on a floor to heat hot foods immediately before service may find it very satis-

Figure 20.6 Microwave cooking is dramatic in speed. (*Courtesy Raytheon Manufacturing Co., Waltham, Mass.*)

factory. It has been used for quick treatment of foods in fast food and other operations. In such operations, many foods are prepared ahead of service and held frozen or chilled in portion sizes and then quickly heated for service in a microwave oven. Some use it for quick thawing of frozen foods. Unless it is integrated into a system according to need and through preplanning it is likely to become a novelty expenditure to gather dust.

Large models are available that will accommodate a large turkey or roast. There is evidence, however, that shrinkage is greater with microwave cooking than with conventional cooking. For hospitals or other facilities where it would be convenient to heat foods on a served tray, it is possible to obtain a shield that covers the cold food to prevent its heating while the other foods are quickly heated. The unit is equipped with a thermostat that allows a short bit of heat to build up in the chamber to warm the food as desired and then shut off. In a few moments the heat is on again and then off. This pulsing of the heat cycle gives a more uniformly heated product without some of the excessive heat treatment likely to occur with foods treated in a microwave oven. Another experimental unit under test utilizes steam under pressure along with infrared lights to cook food. It is thought that the steam would help cook the food while the infrared lights would brown it so as to enhance the cooking action of the microwave energy.

Recent data indicates that some microwave ovens have a high enough leakage of energy as to be hazardous for personnel working near them. Therefore the seal of units should be carefully checked before purchase. It is wise also to investigate the availability of servicing and spare parts before purchase. Ease of maintenance, cleanability, safety, and ease of repair should be strong selection factors.

STEAM EQUIPMENT

When selecting steam equipment consider (1) the source and character of the steam and (2) the type and capacity of equipment best suited to specific needs. The pressure requirement may be important. Usually 5 psi is necessary, but for fast cooking, as in "jet" cookers, 15 psi is required. The steam should be reasonably dry. The condensate may be drained off by having a trap installed close to the reducing valve. Where adequate steam is not available from a central plant, provision may be made for equipment to generate its own steam; or install a boiler near the kitchen. The latter is preferred if the amount used is great.

Steam Cookers

When selecting steam cookers consider size in relation to cooking time and speed of service. Many items, particularly steamed vegetables, should be cooked on a rotation to supply the items freshly cooked every 15 or 20 minutes during the serving period. How many persons are to be served per minute? If 5 portions were served per minute per line of service 75 orders would be required every 15 min. Both cooking time and handling time to drain, season, pan and deliver are to be counted. Units are available that accommodate three full size 12 × 20 in. (30.5 × 50.8 cm) steam table plans (about 72 portions) to those having an 18 pan capacity (approximately 432 portions). The cookers that utilize 15 psi are often in one or two pan capacity and cook in much less time. Few, if any, free venting type steamers are used in any but small quantity cooking units.

Steam cookers vary in (1) number of compartments and size, (2) source of steam, (3) type base, and (4) design. Widths vary from those in which a 12 × 20 in. (30.5 × 50.8 cm) pan will fit to those taking 18 × 26 in. (45.7 × 66 cm) pans, and compartments may be single or in stacks of two or three. Occasionally four stacks may be used, but inconvenient heights of bottom and top compartments result. Mounting may be on legs, enclosed base, pedestal, or wall mounted. One, two, or three shelves may be in each compartment; they may be stationary or operate to pull out

Figure 20.7 A compartment steam cooker with adjustable shelves wide enough for two standard steam table pans placed side by side. (*Courtesy Market Forge, Everett, Mass.*)

when the door is opened. Those with three shelves are usually designed for 2½ in. deep pans or less.

Select steamers with heavy duty gaskets. When selecting cooking containers, choose those suitable for the material to be cooked, that will minimize handling, and will permit suitable load size for workers to lift. The use of serving pans may often minimize transfer. Baskets that are tall or flat, requiring only one or two to fit the compartment height, wide or narrow for one or two in the compartment width, and perforated or solid for products with or without liquid, are available. Pans of serving size 2½ to 4 in. (7.6 to 10 cm) in depth, either solid or porforated, may be obtained.

Steam cookers should be equipped with timers, safety valves and pressure gages. They also need an automatic exhaust and a solenoid cut-off. The condensate in compartments should flow to a drain which is trapped near the reducing valve.

The production capacity of steam-cookers as stated by manufacturers should be evaluated in relation to needs and cooking times. A broad guide in their selection might be based as follows:

Table 20.4   Meals per Hour Cooked in Low-Pressure Steam Cookers

Number of Meals	Number of Compartments		
200 to 500	1 to 2 compartments	or	1 to 3 compartments
500 to 750	1 to 3 compartments	or	3 to 4 compartments
750 to 1000	1 to 3 compartments or 2 2-compartments	or	4 to 6 compartments
1000 up	1 to 2 compartments/ 500 mls/hr served	or	1 compartment/200 to 300 mls/hr

Steam Kettles

Steam kettle sizes are from 10 to 150 gal for stationary types and from 1 qt to 80 gal for tilt type. Choice of sizes should be made in terms of specific foods, volume and speed of turnover. Tender foods are crushed by mass and movement. Unless power stirrers are used, 40-gal kettles should be considered maximum size for the preparation of entrees or other foods requiring stirring. Even this represents a heavy mass of food to tax the average woman worker. Kettles ranging from 5 to 20 gal are satisfactory for the rotation cooking of vegetables. Kettles larger than 40

Figure 20.8 A tilting 40-gal kettle with pan holder (*Market Forge, Everett, Mass.*)

gal may be used for products having a high liquid content, such as for simmering stock.

Models of steam kettles differ in relation to (1) depth, which may be deep or shallow; (2) steam-jacketing, which may be full or ⅔; (3) mounting, which may be on legs, a pedestal, or wall mounted; (4) type, such as tilting or stationary; and (5) source of steam, which may be direct or self-generated. The materials commonly used are aluminum and stainless steel; the finish may be dull or polished. Available are certain models that may be connected to cold water, which, when turned into the jacket after the steam is turned off, gives faster cooling of mixtures.

The cooking capacity of kettles should be based on a maximum load to fill the kettle to about ⅔ to ¾ full. More than this makes manipulation of food difficult without spillage occurring. Planners use a rough guide that for every 4 lb (1¾ kg) of poultry or 8 lb (3¾ kg) of meat or vegetables, a gal of kettle is required. Thus, if a kettle capacity is to simmer 80 lb (37 kg) of meat, a 10-gal kettle would be needed which, if ⅔ full, would require a 15-gal (54 l) kettle. If kettles are to be used also to make stock or soups, basing size on the volume to be prepared is preferable. It takes 6¼ gal (22½ l) to serve 100 8-oz portions (237 ml or 227 g) of soup or stew. If 500 portions are served, 32 gal (117 l) will be required and a 40-gal (144 l) kettle would be the size to specify for this quantity. It may be preferable to install smaller kettles rather than one large one to give more flexibility. It is preferable, however, if large quantities of stock, soup, stews, and similar foods are prepared frequently to choose an adequate size for them rather than to divide batches.

When planning for kettles easy facilities for emptying contents is important. The type of food to be prepared in the kettles and whether it can be drawn off or must be poured may influence whether a tilt kettle or stationary kettle is selected. Give attention to such safety factors as control of degree of tilt on tilt kettles and prevention of splash of hot

Figure 20.9 Wall-mounted steam equipment presents good appearance and facilitates cleaning. Convenient water supply, adequate drainage, plus good light and ventilation are needed. Note small kettles mounted to empty over sink. (*Courtesy B. H. Hubbert and Sons, Baltimore, Md.*)

liquid in draining stationary kettles. Drain boxes can be made available commercially or by having them constructed, to keep fluids from pouring from sufficient distance to splash. (See design shown in Figure 14.3.)

Cleanability of kettles and convenient water supply should be remembered. A swivel faucet beside the kettles can save many steps in water for cooking and for cleaning. Steam guard handles should be specified. Work heights and widths in terms of normal reach should be considered. Kettles that are so high that workers must stand on ladders to work in them are hazardous. Steam equipment may need a hood over it, and if gas fired will need an exhaust to eliminate fumes. If the gas burner is attached by direct flue, a draft diverter should be installed. Kettles that are wall-suspended are preferable to floor mounting unless they are very large units. The equipment plus contents have sufficient weight to require sturdy bridge-work for their support. (See Fig. 20-9 below.) An automatic water-gauge that stops the flow of water at a preset amount is available for installation.

Table model steam-kettles are available in sizes 1, 4, 5, 6, 8, 10, and 20 qt (947 ml and 3.8, 4.7, 5.7, 7.6, 9.5, and 18.9 l). Some sizes may be obtained in tilting type. Floor models vary from 10 qt (9.5 l) to 200 or more gal (1135 l). Some used in central commissaries may hold 4,000 gal. (15,142 l).

Figure 20.10 Steel structure that supports wall-mounted equipment shown in Figure 20.9. Cabrini Hospital, Seattle. (*Courtesy B. H. Hubbert and Sons, Baltimore, Md.*)

Miscellaneous Small Equipment

Toasters

Two types of toasters are used, the slot and the conveyor type. The first, with either two or four slots, may be made up into batteries with fully automatic or with hand operation. A variable timer adjusts the length of the toasting period. The units require from 1.3 to 9.8 kw. The slots may be sized for either bread or bun toasting. A gas heated slot toaster operates by a gravity feed system. Bread is dropped into the toaster and timed by a variable timer. The first slice takes one minute to toast and succeeding ones 20 seconds. When toasted they fall by gravity from the bottom of the toaster.

Where requirements are heavy and continuous, conveyor models best used are either gas or electric. The gas model uses .003 kw electricity for driving the motor, and a 4 in. flue is needed. Two ceramic radiants direct heat to the bread as it travels on a small chain-driven platform.

Conveyor toasters produce from 360 to 900 slices of toast per hour and production rate for a popup slot may be as high as 60 to 75/hr. Required voltages may vary from 120 v to 440 v or higher. All large units should be equipped with overload cutoffs so toast will not burn when the machine jams. Sanitary and cleaning factors are important. The crumb tray should be easily removable for cleaning and be accessible. A wide variety of settings should be available from very light to quite dark. All electric models should meet the UL requirements and gas models those of the AGA. NSF standards should be met also. Special toasters have been developed for toasting rolls, bagels, buns, waffles or pancakes. Some have special baskets with retainer bars which prevent bread or buns from curling. The bars should swing out of the way as the bread unloads.

Data on a common gas and electric toaster are as follows:

Size in Inches			Capacity per Minute		Energy Requirements	
Width	Depth	Height	Toast	Burns*	Elect. kw	Gas—Btu input per hr.
18⅜	18⅝	29⅜	6	6–9	2.6	12,000
23⅛	16⅝	29⅜	9–12	12–15	3.6	20,000

* Including wiener buns.

SIDE VIEW

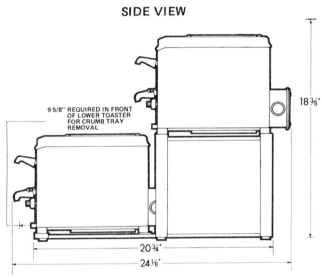

9-5/8" REQUIRED IN FRONT
OF LOWER TOASTER
FOR CRUMB TRAY
REMOVAL

18⅜"

20¾"

24⅛"

Figure 20.11 Tandem placement of toasters promotes flexibility in meeting demands, and maintains ability to produce a large quantity of toast within a short time. Units may be set up also in sets of 6 or more in this manner to give an almost continuous production of fresh product. Such units are sometimes placed in dormitory dining halls and other residence institutions, beside the bread and butter, to permit residents to prepare their own fresh toast. (*Drawings from McGraw-Edison Co., Algonquin, Ill.*)

Toasting may also be done on a griddle, in a broiler, or in a hot oven. A heavy duty broiler can produce 1200 slices of bread or half buns toasted per hour.

Waffle Bakers

Waffle bakers may be obtained in single units and in batteries up to 6. The shape may be rectangular or round. The baking grids should be made of a non-stick type metal that conducts heat rapidly and evenly. Lipped grids are best, for they prevent over-flow. A flexible or floating type hinge allows the waffle to expand during baking. Average baking time per iron is 6 minutes. Bell timers and signal lights that indicate heating and baking time are desirable. Preheat switches and automatic temperature controls on individual waffle irons will permit them to be turned off when not required. Removable drip pans to catch spillage aid cleanup.

Each baker requires approximately 750 to 825 watts.

Egg Cookers

Automatically timed egg cookers may be heated by steam, gas, or electricity. An electrically heated one in common use has small buckets that will hold three or four eggs each. The eggs are submerged in hot water for cooking and a timer-controlled release allows them to rise out of the water at the end of the cooking period.

Suggested Student Assignments

1. Observe food operations using (a) a conventional oven, (b) convection oven, and (c) microwave oven and describe how each is used in terms of schedule of use, time periods for specific products prepared, procedures of operation, problems that commonly arise connected with use, and quality of products as affected by baking.

2. Note range surface in three different food operations and state fuel used, arrangement of top (such as open burner or plates, number and how divided), amount of time range is normally used in food preparation and for what purposes and suitability of size in relation to amount used.

3. Observe griddles in there different food operations and note size, source of heat, amount and type of heat control, for what used and amount of use.

4. Observe broiling where gas, electric, charcoal, and char-broilers are used. State size, amount and type of use, method and ease of control, and care required.

5. Observe fryers both gas fired and electric. Note amount and type of use, amount of fat required, care and handling of fat, ease of operation and cleaning.

6. Observe use of a microwave oven and state how used, kind and quantity of food prepared in a peak hour of service, and quality of food.

7. Observe use of steam cookers and kettles in three different food operations. Note steam pressure used, kind of food prepared, length of cooking time, appearance and quality of products, and safety precautions in operating. Describe operating procedure and type of care required in cleaning.

Chapter 21

serving equipment

Characteristics in the service of food vary from a simple presentation of food to the hands of consumers at a window to the meticulous presentation of meals in fine restaurants. The commodities dispensed in each instance are fragile in quality. The consumers' enjoyment of the food is usually tempered by the general appearance and manner in which it is presented. Equipment is needed for the serving of food that will help to (1) preserve food palatability, (2) promote speed of service, (3) ensure sanitation, (4) present a good appearance, (5) provide comfort, safety, and convenience for workers and consumers, (6) give flexibility for adjustment to changes, and (7) fit satisfactorily into the specific economic program.

Tables and Chairs

Dining areas can be enhanced in appearance and comfort by the attractiveness of the tables and chairs selected. Flexibility is desirable that will give variety to total number seated and to seating arrangement. Storage may be an important consideration if removal from the room is likely to occur for periodic cleaning of the floor or for use of the room for other purposes. It is well to consider whether chairs will need to be moved or stacked regularly for floor cleaning. Proper initial provision may help to reduce scarring that will spoil appearance.

Tables vary in height, size, and shape. The height may be as low as 17 in. ($42\frac{1}{2}$ cm) for a coffee or cocktail table or as high as 30 in. (75 cm). Tables from 26 to 30 in. (65 to 75 cm) are considered standard depending upon patron size and need. Table surface size is gauged in terms of individual place-setting which varies from 20 to 30 in. (51 to 75 cm). The smaller allowance is made for children and for crowded banquet space. Normal place-setting allowance is 24 in. (61 cm) linear space. Tables over 42 in. (107 cm) long should have at least six legs, unless they are sturdy, banquet, folding tables. The bearing weight of food, dishes, and individuals leaning on the tables should be considered in specifying the number of legs and top strength. The table legs should be equipped with levelers and also have nonfriction type glides or plastic boots on the bottom of the legs to prevent marring floors.

A strong, mar-resistant surface is desirable for table tops. Plastic impregnated wood is attractive and acceptably durable. Plastic makes a good cover and gives softness. It reduces the need for tablecloths or doilies for informal type service. If the top is plastic over plywood, specify that the plastic be not less than $\frac{1}{16}$ in. (1.6 cm) of high-pressure thermosetting, chip and stain resistant laminated plastic. The plywood should be an inch (2.5 cm) thick, 5 to 9 ply. Waterproof cement should be used. Plywood can be covered also with a hardwood such as Luan mahogany or other similarly beautifully grained wood and finished with a durable, nonstain finish. Counter tops should be fairly resistant to scratching, alcohol, or water damage, as well as resistant to burns from cigarettes or cigars. Folding tables need to be specified to have suitable tops with a strong, welded-steel base.

Chairs may be made of wood, plywood, plastic impregnated wood, plastic, or metal. Strength of material and workmanship are important to durability. A number of hardwoods are suitable for chairs, the best being birch, hard maple, walnut, and oak. Walnut may have reduced life because it can dry out and split. Birch can be strengthened by impregnating with plastic. This gives a highly serviceable chair. Bentwood chairs are best made of hard elm. The more wood that is exposed on chairs, the higher the cost. Molded plywood, 7 ply $\frac{5}{8}$ in. (16 mm) gives a strong chair. The crossing of the grains of wood in plywood increase strength. Molded rigid urethane is the strongest plastic used for chairs. A high impact polystyrene can be used also for legs and backs. Fiberglass has good durability. Plastics can be combined with wood or metal effectively.

Metal chairs may be made from cast aluminum, tube aluminum either square or round, chrome, baked enamel on steel or wrought iron. Aluminum can be anodized to take different colors but scratches will show through the color to the silver color of aluminum. Tubular chairs should have stainless steel or other glides to reduce marring of floors. Metal pins are satisfactory on wooden chairs. Some glides may be cushioned with a rubber gasket between the glide and chair foot. Metal legs should be provided with proper glides also. Leg bottoms should be broad enough to give secure footing and not pierce or dent the flooring. Ball feet may be put onto some chairs. These are good for use over a rug, especially the long fiber shag rugs. Luxury chairs may be of the swivel type.

Durability and appearance is influenced by the workmanship on chairs. Metal chairs should be welded with strong, smooth welds. Seats may be fastened to metal frames with screws or bolts. Wooden chairs may be glued, with screws used at points of stress. All chairs should be examined to determine strength at points of stress, such as where the back joins the seat and where the legs join the seat. Legs should be reinforced by spreaders below the seat. Strong bracing will be required to stand stress given chairs by occupants tipping back. Turn chairs over, note junctures, and test strength by placing one leg on the floor at a time and pressing down as hard as possible. Note any give or yielding. Note how the legs are joined to the seat. They should fit tightly, be well in-forced and securely fastened. In armchairs, note how arms are fastened to the chair and whether they are strong enough to take stress. Both concave and straight backs give satisfactory use if properly made and fastened to the chair. Concave backs tend to be more comfortable than straight backs.

Durability and appearance are influenced by the chair's finish. Poorly finished wood tends to splinter and wear quickly, and shows mars more readily. It is likely to cause snagging of hose. Spray finish on wood is less expensive than rubbed or glazed finish but not as beautiful. If chairs are of the stacking type, check to see that they will not experience excessive wear at corners or points of contact. Note the amount of play possible when several chairs are stacked together. They should fit securely so that they will not topple or rub when moved or handled. It is advisable to select dollies or other mobile equipment on which they fit well and are suitable for moving chairs and tables.

The best weight for a chair if from 10 to 12 lb ($4\frac{1}{2}$ to $5\frac{1}{2}$ kg), unless heavier or lighter ones are needed for special purposes. Armchairs usually weigh between 15 to 22 lb (6.8 to 10 kg). Folding chairs should fold easily and stack well.

Chairs should be easily cleaned and dusted. Coverings should be durable, burnproof, soft, and hold their shape when stretched. Padding should have good resilience. It is usually specified as from $1\frac{1}{2}$ to 2 in. (3.75 to 5 cm) thick, with some as thick as 4 in. (10 cm). Cotton is durable and has good resilience. It may be combined with foam rubber under it. Leather as a covering is attractive in appearance and gives good wear, but is costly. Fabrics are durable and less expensive, but care needs to be taken in their selection for suitable pattern and color that will harmonize and not show stain readily. The fabric should be treated to be stain resistant, and should be easily cleanable. Many plastics have a soft, beautiful sheen and are easily cleaned. Some will stretch. Vinyl that has been perforated fits well to padding and permits good transfer of air upon impact. If seats have springs under them, barbed nails should be used for fastening so that they will not fall out.

Tables and chairs should be selected together. Sizing should be suitable for need. Small children need lower tables and lower chairs. Large individuals do not like either undersized or oversized units. Flexibility should be sought. An 18 in. (45 cm) high chair should be selected for a 30 in. (75 cm) high table and a 17 in. (43 cm) chair for a 29 in. (73 cm) table. Regularly chairs are from 16 to 18 in. (40 to 45 cm) high at the seat. Legs at the base should be a minimum of 14 in. (35 cm) apart. The seat should be 14 in. (35 cm) deep and 16 in. (40 cm) wide. The height of the back from the seat should be 16 to 17 in. (40 to 43 cm). The overall height of the chair is from 29 to 34 in. (73 to 75 cm). Sizes will vary if arm chairs or other types are selected.

Tables and chairs selected for meeting and board rooms may vary from those used in dining rooms. They need to be appropriate to the area. A luxurious board room of a corporation, where meals may be served occasionally, will have a substantial table and comfortable chairs. Those used in a fast turnover restaurant are likely to be lighter and less sumptious.

The size chosen for table tops need to be determined in relation to the type of meals served, the manner of service and the type, size, and number of pieces of tableware that will be on the table during the meal. In cafeterias the table top dimensions will be influenced by the size and shape of the trays used and the number of individuals to be seated at a table. Tables 42 to 48 in. (106 to 122 cm) long and 30 in. (75 cm) wide give good flexibility for institutional use.

Round tables may be desirable for banquet use. These usually seat 8 but they are available for 6 and 12 also. The cabaret tables usually stand on a center base which eliminates legs. To prevent tippiness, a 30 to 36 in. (75 to 90 cm) top is placed on a 19½ to 22 in. (48½ to 55 cm) dia. base at the bottom. They should weigh from 50 to 60 lb (23 to 27 kg) for best stability. They should have both levelers and glides. Folding tables may be 30 in. (75) square or 30 in. (75 cm) wide and from 36 to 96 in. (90 to 240 cm) long for banquet service. They should be equipped with lock legs. Some tables used for banquets are as narrow as 18 in. (45 cm). This width permits them to be used as writing tables during meetings and then put together to form a 36 in. width (90 cm), and when covered with silence cloths and tablecloths serve both purposes very well. In rare instances these tables may be as narrow as 15 in. (38 cm).

In selecting equipment for dining areas, the use of platforms should be considered. These can be purchased in different sizes and heights. Some may stack so tiered arrangements can be made. They should be strong and durable and able to take the bearing weights. If equipped with legs, check to be sure that they are strong and will support the stress given them.

COUNTERS

Counters may be required as work areas or for food display. They may provide a base for certain pieces of equipment or may be combined with steam tables, cold pans, fountain, urn stands, or other serving equipment.

Cafeteria counters are usually 34 to 36 in. high and 24 to 30 in. wide, with about a 12-in. wide tray slide. If a work ledge or cutting board is on the working side, the overall width will be approximately 44 in. For strength, most counters should be mounted on frames of $1\frac{1}{2} \times 1\frac{1}{2} \times \frac{3}{16}$ in. galvaneal angle finished with two coats of silvertone lacquer or aluminum paint. For heavy wear, 14-gauge stainless steel tops are specified and lighter gauge or other materials where wear will be lighter. Metal tops should have edges turned down $1\frac{1}{2}$ to 2 in., bull-nosed and designed for good sanitation. If field joints are necessary, hairline joining with metal cover should be specified. No bead or rivet heads should show. Panels enclosing the counter may be of 18 to 20 gauge stainless steel, $1\frac{1}{4}$ in. formica or vitreous enamel. The counter may be mounted on 6 to 8 in. legs, either stainless steel, white metal or vitreous enamel, on a 14-gauge stainless steel front platform or a solid masonry base. Cantilever mounting is recommended, or the counter may be suspended between columns. Openings should be planned as required, such as ice cream cabinet, cold pans, and so forth, and utilities or services should be provided as needed. A tray slide, 3-bar, 1 in. OD, 12 to 16 gauge, should be mounted on white metal brackets that are spaced on centers not to exceed 42 in. if trays are to be moved in front of the counter.

Open food displays must be shielded by vertical or slanted sneeze-guards; these may be hinged for ease in cleaning. The guards should be supported on brackets on 42 in. centers and should be vented to prevent steaming. There is usually a landing shelf over the guard. Shelving, if provided under the counter, should be 18-gauge stainless steel or 16-gauge galvaneal and removable; however, consideration should be given to use of mobile, undercounter storage instead of fixed shelving.

If the cashier station is a part of the counter, a space at least 30 in. wide should be provided. An electrical outlet will be needed for an electric cash register. A drawer approximately 20×20 in. should be provided. A foot rest may be installed if desired.

There is a variety of cash registers to fit specific needs. Some speed calculation and minimize error by indicating correct change. Some permit itemizing so that number and kind of items can be tallied. The machine selected should be simple to operate, especially if a number of different personnel are to use it. It should provide a tape for record in counting cash and for bookkeeping. Separate drawers may be required also for persons using the machine.

Cash registers are available that can be reset for specific items at different prices and a different number of units sold. Thus a drive-in may have a plain hamburger and one that is "deluxe." Each can be priced into the machine. The price for one to five of each on an order may be totaled so that if a certain number are sold, only one ring up is needed. For the hamburger selling at 40 cents, the machine may be set so if three are sold, only a 3 multiplier button need be pushed down along with the plain hamburger key to print cost of sale as $1.20.

It may be desirable to specify a reset counter. This moves ahead each time a total is cleared. Such a device makes it difficult for employees to manipulate cash and furnishes management a record of operations which they have been unable to supervise. Customer counters are available and as in the cash reset counter, move ahead each time a customer count is taken, making a traffic tally. An instant loading of tape saves time during busy periods over one that must be rethreaded while customers wait.

Check tallies can provide useful information for management pertaining to popularity of menu items, volume served from day to day, and income. Consideration should be given to speeding the tallying of checks. The availability of an adding machine may help employees to more quickly tally checks without error. A quick food tallying register that prints out the item, prices and totals it with an identifying number and date is available. Time stamping may be included also. The slip or a duplicate may be given to the guest. The tallying register dollar total should coincide with the cash register total. The machine may be connected also to an ordering system so orders are immediately transferred to the kitchen or production area. A variation of this system is to have customers able to pushbutton their orders. The machine notifies production of the order, prints out the check, totals it, and may give other information if desired. A memory storage unit can be added so management may have retrievable information on items sold, numbers served, peak periods, and other information.

Stools may or may not be required at coffee shop counters where patrons eat. Seats that are cantilevered make for ease in cleaning. Counters are frequently built of wood with a masonry base and a counter top of vinyl, linoleum, or hard plastic. A very satisfactory top is made of high pressure sealed laminate. Stools for the counters 42 in. (107 cm) high may be raised on a pedestal from the floor level and a foot rest provided or they may be set on a masonry base, 8 in. (20 cm) high. The first is considered best from the standpoint of safety.

Display cases on cafeteria counters vary from 9 to 18 in. (23 to 46 cm) wide and are mounted on stainless steel upright angle, square or tubular frames. They may be cantilevered to promote good appearance and ease of cleaning. Plate glass ¼ in. (6 mm) thick, protected by nickel-silver channels, may be used for sides and shelving. If for self-service, they should be equipped with sneeze-guards.

Figure 21.1 Cantilever display shelves provide an attractive appearance and freedom from obstruction by uprights on counters. Note seamless counter top and welded stainless steel tray slide. (*Courtesy S. Blickman, Inc., Weehawken, N. J.*)

HOT FOOD EQUIPMENT

Warming Equipment

Food warmers are required to keep quantities of prepared food hot for service, to have foods available for immediate service, and to take peak loads off the kitchen. Plates and dish warmers for serving hot food are required. Soups, gravies, stews, many entree dishes, and some sauces require serving temperatures of about 180°F. Others, such as sliced meat, roasts, and vegetables, require lower temperatures. Moist or dry heat may be required, according to type food stored. Length of time foods can be held will affect the size of containers most suitable and the space needed in a warming area. Heat used for warming equipment may be electricity, gas, or steam. Non-glow strip heaters baffled for protection and heat circulation are frequently used to provide heat for under areas, in addition to the heat used for spaces above. Insulation of doors and sides with asbestos sheets or rock wool should be provided. Dish warming equipment opposite the service counter on the waiters' side may also be provided. Access doors into such areas should be provided so waiters can reach the heated dishes.

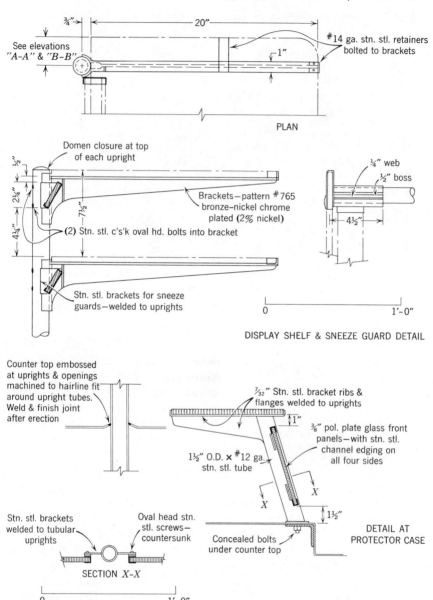

Figure 21.2 Detail of display shelf, sneeze-guard and protector case. (*Courtesy S. Blickman, Inc., Weehawken, N. J.*)

Food warming equipment used in cafeterias is usually combined with service counters. In such equipment showmanship in displaying hot foods should be remembered. Rectangular or square hot table containers will give more food holding capacity than round containers and will present a more attractive food display. Flexibility in serving counters is needed. Menu variations should be considered in planning the hot table. Proper placement of foods and dishes should be considered to enable workers to work to the best advantage with their right and left hands. Evaluate carefully the desirability of placing dish leveling equipment in the counter. Time may be saved by having dishes in containers at right angles to the serving counter.

Steam tables can be selected from many offerings in standard stock and need not be custom-built. Steam tables are 24 to 32 in. wide and frequently come equipped with an 8 in. wide, 2 in. thick laminated maple cutting board or stainless steel shelf used as a plate-rest. Openings in the steam table should be supported by channeling or angle support as necessary, and adequate frame support and strong legs should give under support.

A bain marie is an open hot water bath having a perforated false bottom on which containers of food may be set. It usually is near or a part of the cooks' section. Rotation cooking yielding a continuous supply of freshly cooked food has reduced the use of bain maries. Where they are employed, the use will be heavy, and they should be constructed of 14-gauge stainless steel tops with supporting channeling and frame work sufficient to support weights given during use. Water-bath types are most desirable. Width are usually between 24 and 30 in. The depth of water chamber is usually 10 in. The length is sized according to needs as indicated by process through equipment studies.

Heated pass-through compartments are convenient for use in cafeteria and other operations where service is from a counter. Pass-throughs should be well insulated and some may be equipped with blower fans to spread the heat throughout. Humidity controls are also installed. Pass-throughs may be sized to hold mobile carts of food or individual pans of food. Good door insulation and seals should be provided. If doors are hinged and open from the bottom, construction of the door should be rugged to hold weights and wear given when it is open.

Mobile food warming equipment is finding rapid acceptance. These can be set for thermostatic control and humidities can be regulated. They can be operated on electricity and bottled gas or canned heat can be used if electricity is not available or too expensive. Mobile warming equipment is usually heated by electrical units with blower fans installed.

The growth of central commissaries and satellite units has lead to increased attention being given to means of transporting food that will help in maintaining quality and reduce sanitation hazards. Different systems and items of equipment have evolved. The number in the form of food carts, insulated tote boxes, and thermal retention trays is too great to permit the description of each type. Some require input of electricity to hold foods either warm or cold. Others require insulation that will maintain temperature.

Important selection points for this equipment in addition to temperature retention is ease of thorough cleaning and sanitizing plus durability that will withstand the hurried, oftrepeated and sometimes rough handling it is likely to receive in the transporting of food. Mobile units should have a protective molding or rubber bumpers that will protect walls and doors from marring. Some plastic covered units should be made of high impact thermo-formed cycolac at least $\frac{3}{16}$ in. thick in one piece construction with no seams. Interiors should have coved corners and no rough edges, seams or places where soil collect and be difficult to remove. Insulation should be foamed urethane with an 8.7 R factor and a 0.11 K factor; usually this requires insulation of $1\frac{1}{2}$ in. (3.8 cm) thickness or more. Capacities should be checked to make sure that they will be suited to standard-size units. The food units should be such that they can be cleaned with standard detergents and water temperature of 180° F (81° C). If units are not mobile, they should be easily portable or combined with suitable mobile equipment for ease of movement without excessive lifting and/or carrying. The equipment should be tested for its ability to maintain the desired temperature for the required period of time. The following are temperature maintenance standards established by a manufacturer of this type of equipment (see Table 21.1).

Many small specialized types of food warmers are being used. Roll warmers are popular for holding hot breads and many other foods.

Table 21.1 Recommended Food Temperatures at Loading and After Holding

At Loading	1 hr	2 hr	3 hr	4 hr	5 hr
Hot 170°F (76°C)	163°F (72°C)	162.2°F (71.6°C)	161.2°F (71°C)	160.5°F (70.7°C)	160°F (70.4°C)
Cold 38°F (3.3°C)	38.5°F (3.5°C)	39°F (3.8°C)	40.2°F (4.5°C)	41°F (4.9°C)	42°F (5.5°C)
Frozen −10°F (23.1°C)	−9.6°F (−22.9°C)	−8.2°F (−22.1°C)	−7.1°F (−21.5°C)	−6.0°F (−20.0°C)	−5.4°F (118.7°C)

Those of 12 to 32 doz capacity require 0.8 to 1.2 kw. They may be used in food operations for hot pies, premade hot sandwiches and other hot foods in addition to breads. The drawer type containers are convenient when located near the grill or hot table in the serving area.

Infrared tube or bulb units can be used to keep food warm. These use quartz or metal filaments that give off infrared heat waves. About 90 percent of the electricity used in turned into heat. Most are designed, not for cooking, but to keep food warm, although they also can be designed to give out enough heat for cooking. They are thought to reduce loss of moisture in holding meats over conventional heating units.

The bulbs are usually 8 to 10 in. (20 to 25 cm) high and require more overhead space than tube heaters which are from 3 to 4 in. high (7½ to 10 cm) high. The minimum linear space used by the tube type is 2½ in. (6.3 cm). The bulbs give a circular heat and so units must overlap in coverage, a requirement not necessary with the tubular units. Flexibility is gained if the height above the food is adjustable. Some bulb units are mounted on swivel bases that slant the heat waves so that they cover a larger area than if placed facing directly down. Tube heaters are usually less attractive than bulb arrangements but they can be hooked together to give considerable heating diversity. Stainless steel shelving is best used infrared heat. Wood, some plastics, and other fusible materials may be harmed by the heat. The heating device should be checked for ease of cleaning and maintenance. Some units are guaranteed for a longer operating life than others.

Heated dishes for serving are a problem where plans require repeated handling. Care should be taken in planning for their placement, heating, and use in order to minimize handling. If dishes are loaded into mobile equipment at the dish machine and moved into heated chambers at service areas, much handling is eliminated. Sturdy construction is needed in mobile carts to bear the heavy weight of dishes. Dish warming equipment should be well insulated and have proper placement planned for ease of use and labor saving.

Coffee Urns

Coffee urns of 2 to 125 gal (7.6 to 473 l) capacity are available; a boiler may be as large as 250 gal (946 l). The outer shell is usually of chromium plated metal, stainless steel, or, in economy models, from 18-gauge cold rolled steel covered with vitreous enamel. At times 14-gauge stainless steel trim is provided on the latter. The inner shell or the container in which the coffee is made must be of highly durable material that is non-toxic and will not react with the coffee brew to give off-flavors. Inner

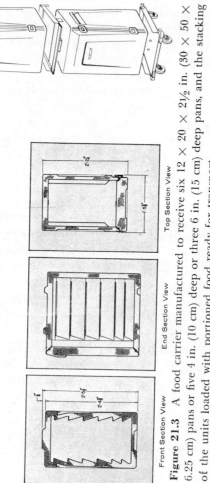

Front Section View   End Section View   Top Section View

Figure 21.3 A food carrier manufactured to receive six 12 × 20 × 2½ in. (30 × 50 × 6.25 cm) pans or five 4 in. (10 cm) deep or three 6 in. (15 cm) deep pans, and the stacking of the units loaded with portioned food ready for transport.

shells may be made of stainless steel (20 gauge from 2 to 5 gal capacity and 18 gauge over that size), heat resisting glass, china, or earthenware, vitrified stone or copper plated material. Stainless steel is the most frequently used because it can be drawn. Drawing gives no seam construction, although new welding techniques now provide almost indestructible type welds. Furthermore, stainless steel is a highly durable, noncorrosive type material that will not react with a coffee brew to create an undesirable flavor. Glass, earthenware, and vitrified stone are excellent for coffee containers. However, they are somewhat fragile and spare containers should be carried when they are used. They can only be made up to certain sizes. Earthenware crazes and off flavors can result from captured oxidized essences in the crazing. Specify metal urns for shipboard use or for export. Complete drainage of inner shells should be specified.

Urn capacities should be stated in several ways. Actual gallon capacity of brew contained should be named. In addition, the capacity of the boiler surrounding the inner shell should be given. In the best urns the lining between the inner shell and the boiler prevents cooling of coffee when the boiler is filled with cold water. This liner is frequently made of 24- to 32-oz heavily plated copper or 20-gauge stainless steel. Corrugation of sides and bottoms of the boiler gives added strength.

All urns should be specified with gauges to indicate capacity. Faucets and fittings should be of top quality and nonslip, nonleak type. Wooden or plastic parts should be provided where necessary to prevent hands from touching hot areas. Faucets should permit thorough cleaning.

Automatic urns are designed so that when the water has reached the proper temperature it flows over the coffee, and in so doing saves labor and insures proper temperatures being used. Accurate measurements of coffee and water leads to a uniform product. Time to brew the coffee is minimized. Manually operated pressure urns require more worker time and attention, but they have good production capacity and are reliable. They do not require the handling of boiling water. Both the automatic and the manually operated urns will not function until water has reached brewing temperature. Manual pour-over urns require that personnel handle boiling brew and allow more chance for brew variation than the automatic or manually operated urns. However, they cost less and are adequate for a meticulous coffee maker and low demand for coffee.

Single, twin, or three-battery urns are on the market. Large, remote coffee making equipment may also be purchased. These may be purchased with pressure or siphon type units or nonsiphon type units. The former uses steam pressure to force boiling water as a spray over the grounds. In nonsiphoning types the brew must be made by manually pouring hot water over the grounds. Repouring pumps are available for large urns. A ¼-hp splash proof motor to pump 2½ gal per min is adequate for the largest urns.

Leachers or containers to hold coffee grounds during coffee making are available as rings to hold muslin bags, stainless steel filters using filter paper bottoms, or stainless steel units that have a series of perforated stainless steel sheets placed one over another to give an effective low process leach action.

A three-urn battery is composed of two coffee urns of a given size and a boiler equal in capacity to the total capacity of the two coffee urns. For example, a battery with two 3-gal urns would have a 6-gal capacity boiler.

Thorough cleaning is essential if a good coffee brew is to be made and all areas on urns should be easily accessible and made of good materials for proper cleaning. Piping or repouring urns or coffee service from distant points should be easily demountable and in easy lenghts for cleaning. Volume gauges and all inner areas should be accessible.

Specifications for coffee urns should state the type heat to be used, thermostatic control, and service cut-outs required. Steam heat usually requires coils in the boiler of the urn. Electrical heaters should be of the threaded immersion type, and specifications should require safety cut-offs if the boiler becomes empty. State that draw-offs should not leave immersion heaters exposed. If gas is used, standard speed burners should be specified. If urns are to be self-service, specifications should state that the urn be equipped with a goose-neck overflow to prevent hot water and steam spillage on patrons while at the urn. If urns are to be used for double service, the specifications should also state that both sides are to have draw-off faucets.

Many operators find that coffee brewers that make an 8-cup or 12-cup pot of coffee are more satisfactory in many situations than urns. The coffee is fresher usually and quantities can be more easily adjusted to the needs of service. Urns are likely to require a large batch in order to obtain a good brew. Automatic units for making 8-cup or 12-cups may have pushbutton control which relieves the maker after the coffee has been scaled into the extractor. Hot water, built up in a reserve tank or from an instantaneous heating element, then flows through the coffee grounds into the pot. The unit automatically closes off the water flow when the proper quantity has poured through. These units can be installed in counters or near service areas reducing travel. They are comparatively inexpensive, but if a large number must be placed in a unit an urn may provide greater volume in less space. Urns are likely to be faster and quicker for handling a large number in a cafeteria line.

Urn stands are usually enclosed and supplies or cups and saucers are kept in the heated enclosure on mobile equipment. A 4 in. wide 2 in. deep drain is usually provided across the top under the urn faucets. This area should be pitched to a drain. A nonsplash louvred drain plate (removable) should be specified to keep the level of this drain area flush with the table top. Usually a marine edge is specified for the top. Service openings should be raised integrally to provide seamless eschutcheons, through which the service lines can be brought and leakage avoided. Specify 14-gauge tops for heavy duty units. Bracing and frame support are required.

COLD FOOD EQUIPMENT

Cold pans may be mechanically cooled or cooled by ice beds. Drains should be provided. The pan should be 16 gauge and where chipped ice is used, a removable, perforated false bottom, 16 gauge, should be used. Pans should be 6 to 8 in. deep and 24 in. wide. They should be insulated under with 2 in. corkboard, housed in 18-gauge galvaneal. Pans should be pitched $\frac{1}{8}$ in. to the foot for drainage. Counter tops should be turned down $1\frac{1}{4}$ in. into the pan and welded. Composition breaker strips should be installed under the counter top turn downs on all sides. In mechanical units dehydrated seamless copper cooling evaporator coils should be installed and encased in hydrolene.

Fountains

Most fountains are best purchased from standard stock. Compact units for small operations are available with a set of sirup jars fitting one standard opening of an ice cream cabinet. Small counter dispensers, having mix faucets for three refrigerated carbonated beverages and four sirup pumps, fit into a space 21 in. high by 28 in. wide and $20\frac{1}{2}$ in. deep. They contain three 1-gal sirup containers. The carbonic gas is remotely stored. Water and drain connections and an electrical outlet are required. These small models are useful for step-saving distribution in a large operation or if volume is not great.

Standard fountain equipment may contain sirup wells, pumps, carbonator, drinking water, sink, dipper well, ice cream cabinets, and a refrigerated storage area. The equipment is also designed for use with separate ice cream storage. Sanitation is highly important. Dipper wells with running water should be provided and should be 4 in. in diameter, with interior angles of $\frac{1}{16}$ in. radius.

Tips on how to buy and use faucets for coffee urns.

The coffee urn faucet is one of the few moving parts of the urn and beyond question the hardest working part—it may operate up to 288 times to only one time for another part. As such, it is truly the heart of the urn and should be a prime consideration when buying new equipment or modernizing old.

Faucets vary in style and material. Brass, stainless steel and nylon are the most common materials. Popular styles are:

Self-closing (with either flexible seals or "O" ring seals) (Fig. 1)

Key-cock (with either ground metal plugs or metal plugs or metal to rubber seals) (Fig. 2 & 3)

Push-pull (with metal to rubber seals) (Fig. 4)

Here is your check list guide to purchasing or specifying the proper faucet for your application. When in doubt as to which faucet to buy, be sure to consult with your urn or faucet supplier.

1. Style or type of faucet best suited to YOUR purpose.
2. Service life of faucet.
3. Construction of faucet with regard to sanitation.
4. Ease with which faucet may be maintained in proper operating condition.
5. Availability of replacement parts.
6. Initial cost and cost of maintenance.
7. Reputation and guarantee of manufacturer.
8. Design and appearance.

Once you have obtained the proper faucets, the quality of your coffee is governed in large part by your standards of cleanliness. Good coffee cannot be made in unclean equipment—when you brew a "bad" batch of coffee, do not be too hasty in condemning the roast or the urn manufacturer. Check the condition of the urn, and in particular, look to see whether your faucets have been cleaned properly. Set forth below are the salient points in caring for and cleaning the faucets and fittings on your urn equipment.

1. Rinse with clear water after each batch of coffee. (Fig. 6)

2. EACH DAY remove faucet from shank. Clean through shank into urn, brushing out all coffee deposits. Scrub inside of faucet with hot water and urn cleaner. Rinse in clear hot water. Assemble faucet to shank and partially fill urn with clear water. (Fig. 5 & 7)

3. EACH WEEK remove faucet from shank and disassemble as recommended by manufacturer. Scrub all parts in hot water with urn cleaner. Scrub shank clean with urn brush. Assemble faucet to shank and rinse by passing hot water through entire unit. Place few gallons of clear water in urn. (Fig. 8)

4. When in doubt as to how to clean your faucet, write direct to the faucet manufacturers, or to the urn manufacturer, for explicit instructions.

Addresses of major coffee urn faucet manufacturers:

Economy Faucet Company, 11 New York Avenue, Newark, New Jersey.

Tomlinson No-Drip Faucet Co., 1601 St. Clair Avenue, Cleveland 14, Ohio.

Wyott Manufacturing Company, P.O. Box 898, Cheyenne, Wyoming.

Figure 21.4 Faucets play major role in coffee quality. (Courtesy Food Service Magazine, Madison, Wis.)

Suggested Student Assignments

1. Note type of seating and material used in three different dining areas. Evaluate seating from standpoint of (a) comfort, (b) amount of care required, (c) ease of handling by customer and janitor, (d) ease of cleaning, (e) appearance, and (f) durability.

2. What is the table height and dimensions in three dining areas? What is the material of the tables and how finished? Do the tables have glides? What housekeeping care is required for tables? Are tables attractive?

3. Observe two cafeteria counters and two coffee shop counters and state: (a) height, (b) width, (c) arrangement of top, (d) storage areas for food, serving tools and dishes, (e) work space, (f) sanitary protection, (g) appearance, (h) convenience features, and (i) care required.

4. Locate five examples of equipment used for retaining desired temperature in food and state how used in a (a) commercial restaurant, (b) hospital, (c) school foodservice, and (d) for transporting food. Evaluate each in terms of (a) effectiveness, (b) convenience, (c) sanitation aspects, and (d) appearance.

5. Note beverage equipment used in three different dining areas, and state (a) brewing method, (b) amount brewed at one time, (c) greatest length of holding period, (d) total time required (worker time spent each brewing period times the number of times brewing is done), (e) adequacy of volume and serving speed, (f) location convenience of brewing equipment (for brewing and for service), and (g) coffee quality.

6. Observe fountain service in a coffee shop. What items are served? How are they prepared? State volume of each item served and equipment required for its preparation. Analyze adequacy, convenience, sanitation factors, and appearance.

Chapter 22

refrigeration and low-temperature storage equipment

Suitable refrigerated storage is highly significant for preserving materials and ensuring good sanitation. Because of the many advantages, the use of refrigeration and low-temperature storage has greatly increased. The amount needed will vary with the type of food offered in different facilities. Amounts must be calculated in relation to the nature and volume of the materials required by the individual facility. An allowance should be made as a margin of safety and for flexibility. Current use of frozen foods has increased the need for more low-temperature storage than formerly required. The manner in which it is used influences its location in the layout.

REFRIGERATION SYSTEM

The equipment required to lower temperatures is a motor, a compressor, a condenser, an evaporator, controls, valves and other subsidiary equipment, and an insulated enclosed area. Temperatures are lowered by taking advantage of the thermodynamic property of liquids that require

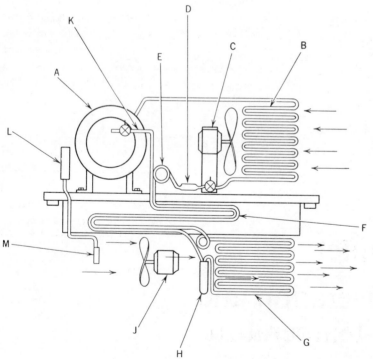

Figure 22.1 General Schematic of Refrigeration Assembly.

heat to expand or contract. The heat absorbed in the refrigerated area is given off at the condenser in the compression type units, and these condensers for cooling require either air or water. Large machines are usually water cooled while self-contained units are air cooled. Machine rooms where motors and condensers are located should have water piped to them, have drains, and be well ventilated if air-cooled equipment is placed there. Diagrams showing the basic components of both a refrigeration and absorption cooling system will be found in Figures 22.1 and 15.2.

Special refrigerated and low-temperature areas may be required to avoid flavor absorption of different foods and to give required variable temperatures and humidity. Table 22.1 indicates recommended temperatures and relative humidity levels. To freeze foods rapidly a shelf at −15° to −30°F may be used. Some planners of food services are recommending −10°F common storage for frozen items with a much lower temperature area behind this area, separated by an inner door.

Large refrigerator- and low-temperature units are usually operated with motor and condenser in a remote area. If more than 20 to 30 ft away, the pipes carrying refrigerant should be adequately insulated. In addition, the areas themselves will require electrical current for light and blower fans; drainage must be provided for moisture run-off. Drainage lines for condensate should not be connected directly to sewers but should be broken to prevent contaminants from returning up from the sewer lines into the refrigerated area. Check drain location and the need for an electric condensate evaporator.

Table 22.1 Recommended Conditions for Refrigerated and Low Temperature Areas

Foods	Temporary Storage	Holding Storage	Recommended Relative Humidity, %
Vegetables and fruits	36–42° F	32–36° F	95
Meats	34–38	32–36	85
Fish	30–40	30–40	85
Eggs	36–42	31–45	95
Butter and cheese	38–45	35–40	85
Bottled beverages	35–45	40–45	—
Frozen foods	10–30	0−−10	—
Ice cream	6–12 (for dishing)	0−−10	—

Full air-duct controlled air flow usually gives best temperature control, especially if a dual fan and coil system is installed. Freezers should hold a steady −10° to −12° F (−23° to 24° C). In humid climates, it is desirable to have anti-sweat heaters around door openings, to prevent them from freezing shut and being difficult to open. A vent system should be installed in walk-ins where odor or humidity may be a problem. The amount of coil installed should be calculated to give 80 percent relative humidity. Consider the need for a positive dial thermometer, a pilot light door mounted or in the face of the cooler to indicate when power is on or off. Some sound system may be installed to notify when temperatures go too high inside. A safety latch for inside openings should be installed in walk-ins to prevent individuals from being locked in. Refrigeration coils and condensing units should carry a 5-year minimum guarantee.

Air-cooled units are used for smaller requirements, while the larger condensers are usually water cooled. In quite large installations the heat from condensers may be used for other purposes such as heating water. Top-mounted installations for reach-ins give better utilization of space than either bottom or side-mounted. Adjustable shelving is desirable, and half an inch spacing is most versatile. The convenience of roll-in compartments should be considered in relation to preparation and service sections. Pan slides into which standard pans will fit, and files that can be moved from cart to storage, help to reduce handling of material. There is likely to be some need for standard adjustable shelving. Door gaskets should be grease-proof vinyl and easy to clean and change. Check space for door opening, and if too limited sliding doors may be preferable. Doors should be self-closing. Glass doors or windows in doors may reduce door opening in search of items. Weigh whether locks are needed. Choose a finish that is durable and easy to clean, and will retain good appearance in spite of repeated cleaning. Stainless steel, although costly, is durable and retains a bright appearance. Some of the high-baked acrylics give good service. Units chosen should be fully NSF approved.

TYPES OF REFRIGERATION EQUIPMENT

Types of refrigerating or low-temperature units may be (1) mobile or fixed reach-ins, (2) specialized units, (3) walk-ins, and (4) ice-making equipment.

Reach-ins

Reach-ins may furnish all the storage required in a small operation but in large ones they are used for storage needs within the work center.

They may be refrigerated or low temperature. Standard stock items are available in the former from 20 to 90 cu ft and in the latter from 12 to 20 cu ft but some as large as 30 cu ft have been used. Proper sizing of reach-ins to meet specific needs is important. Check net capacities carefully. Slide doors or windows may be required. Right or left door openings should be indicated. Specify inside lights. Insulation for refrigerators and low-temperature units should be 3 in. and 3 to 6 in. respectively, and the moisture resistant, non-settling type. Outside and inside seams should be welded. Coving on interiors and exteriors should be ⅝ in. Sturdy construction of doors, hardware, and fixtures is a requirement. Doors may be full or half length. Specify strong catches. Shelving should be adjustable. Door gaskets should provide reasonable wear and be replaceable. Locking devices and adjustable strikes should be specified. Stainless steel or heavy chrome plated brass or bronze should be the metal used for hardware. Rust-proof drains with bell-type drain traps should be provided.

Bake shop refrigerators should be designed to take slide-in equipment in addition to stored supplies. Refrigerators sized for mobile equipment may be desired. Under the counter or backbar refrigeration frequently is required close to points of use. Drawer-type units are useful near broilers

Figure 22.2 A mobile, refrigerated cabinet dispenses cold milk for school children. (*Courtesy American Machine & Foundry Co., New York.*)

and other preparation areas and in service counters. Waitress units frequently are provided with small units for cream, butter, cocktails, salads, fountain supplies, and other items. Low-temperature storage may be needed with this for ice cream. Bottled beverage containers are also placed where service is required.

Low-temperature, reach-in equipment is finding increasing use in food-services. Predished frozen foods or frozen foods cooked to order are stored at points of use for rapid service. Where quantities of frozen cooked foods, meats, vegetables, fruits and other foods are used, it is practical to locate the unit in the work center. Usually just below freezing temperatures are desirable.

Low-temperature reach-ins may be upright or chest type. The upright units cost slightly more and will lose more refrigerated air than the chest type, but they have the advantage of being easier to defrost, take less floor space, and are easier to use for storage and removal of items. The upright must have space provided for open doors. The chest type may provide additional counter space if mobile and located under a counter where it can be pulled out, or drawers may be provided.

Pass-through units open from both sides. If they cannot be located adjacent to both production and service areas, they should be designed to hold mobile carts that can be loaded in the production area and rolled to the pass-through. Tight seals of doors to the floor should be made if mobile units are rolled in.

Specialized Equipment

Specialized equipment, such as fountains, may be very similar to reach-ins. A fountain, however, must provide for different refrigeration needs and, for that reason, two or more condensing units may be required. Drinking and carbonated water must be provided at about 38 to 40°F. Refrigerated space of about 40°F for whipped cream and other food must also be provided. Syrup racks must be kept refrigerated. Ice cream must be 6 to 10°F for dishing.

Salad pans or cold pans may be required in cafeteria counters for displays of salads, juices, sliced fruits, desserts, or other chilled foods. Some cold pans are designed to be flooded with water that freezes and then foods are placed upon this ice. These units should be provided with drainage. Display refrigerators or cases frequently are used for foods to be held at temperatures of 50°F or below. Wall-type refrigerators are now on the market. Glass walls and doors should be made of double or triple glass to provide insulation and prevent clouding. Provide insulating circuit breakers between cold pans and table support units.

Beverage Units

Refrigerated fruit juice dispensers that hold 2½ to 5 gal (9.46 and 18.92 l) are available. They are usually equipped with small self-contained refrigerating units. Carbonated beverage dispensers come in various sizes and vary in the number of drinks of different kinds they will deliver. Most dispensers will dispense from one to six kinds, and a few may dispense more. Some require two-handed operation where the operator holds the glass in one hand and pulls the lever down to fill it. Some operate by pushing the glass against the flow release permitting a one-hand operation. Where paper cups are to be used it is important that the push release operates easily enough not to crush the cup. One type operates from a hose. By pushing a button at the nozzle end of the hose, the operator can get the kind of beverage desired. The machine should be guaranteed to dispense a given number of drinks per hour and that all drinks will be at a specified temperature. Machines may dispense drinks from containers that are premixed or they may mix the syrup and the carbonation liquid as the drink is made. Both should carbonization adjusters on them so the drink is properly carbonated. The syrup is mixed in the drink at the time of delivery (called post dispensing as contrasted to premix dispensing), the amount of syrup delivered per drink should be capable of adjustment.

The size of the machine purchased should be equated to demand. For large volume operations machines are available that produce initially 600 drinks per hour and then have a recovery of 300 drinks per hour. Most models dispense two to six drinks per minute. Counter top units are available, and where space is limited models may be obtained to fit under the counter. Mobile units are available also. Counter models have an advantage in promoting impulse sales. Locating a dispenser over a sink eliminates need for a drip tray, and container to hold drip.

Stainless steel construction or high-temperature baked acrylic finishes present a good appearance and are easy to clean. Drip trays should be easily removable for cleaning. Cleaning nozzles can be purchased as additional equipment. A carbonation tester should be purchased if the machine does not have one.

Bulk milk dispensers may be used. These units are self-contained refrigerated units that hold from 2½ to 5 gal (9.5 to 18.9 l). They are usually designed to take milk containers as delivered from the dairy. They should possess many of the features mentioned for carbonated beverage dispensers. They should hold the milk at a steady 35° to 37° F (1.7° to 2.7° C). The milk for milk shakes and malts should be colder than this if a thick drink is desired, since the colder the milk the thicker the drink. (Malted milk mixers may be attached to the front of the dispenser in some models.) It is desirable to have the dispenser automatically refrigerated, except for special needs where the serving period is short and insulated units are needed that will hold the milk at a safe temperature for several hours. Usually these are stainless steel with solid fiberglass or similar good insulating material. Some may have an ice chamber which acts to keep the beverage cold.

Cream dispensers are usually insulated units holding from a quart to three quarts of cream. Many are operated by hand pump that delivers a set amount of cream. They are usually placed at coffee dispensing units so delivery can be made at the same time that coffee is drawn. Some operations use separate containers for the cream and others deliver the cream into the cup along with the coffee. If individual containers are prepoured, a central station may be set up for this and a larger dispenser purchased which is refrigerated.

Sanitation is important with all types of beverage dispensers. Interiors should be easily cleaned and also the outside. All areas coming in contact with the beverage should be opened up or disassembled for thorough cleaning. Ease in disassembling and reassembling for cleaning should be checked. All spigots, spouts, and faucets should be the nondrip type. They should meet standards of U.S. Dept. of Public Health and those of the NSF.

The use of large amounts of drinking water at about 40°F places heavy demands upon refrigeration equipment; careful sizing is required to meet demands adequately. Tank or storage coolers, instantaneous coolers, or a combination of the two are used. These can usually be provided from standard stock equipment for either bubbler drinking type fountain or glass filler type. Water stations may be placed at islands for self-dispensing in cafeterias or at strategic spots for waiter or waitress use in others. Mobile carts may be used for this in place of shelving. Provide waste chutes for paper cups.

Ice is frequently required in addition to chilled water for the latter and storage in this case must be provided close to the water source. Storage for pitchers, carafes, and glasses should be provided. The estimated quantity of chilled water required per person served is 10 to 12 oz. Peak demands should be ascertained and equipment sized to meet this need. The peak average quantity of chilled water used per hour per stool at a counter or fountain lunch is $\frac{1}{3}$ to $\frac{1}{2}$ gal per stool. In addition, carbonated water at approximately $\frac{1}{3}$ the amount of chilled water must be provided. Instantaneous types of water coolers can be obtained in packaged units.

Figure 22.3a A walk-in refrigerator with adjustable wire shelving and a quarry tile floor. (*Courtesy George Bunby & Associates, Seattle, Wash.*)

Specifications should state mechanical requirements, such as voltage, phase, cycle, and current. Louvred panels should be used to provide air for self-contained units. Check carefully sanitary features and cleaning under the units. To cool 25 gal per hour requires a 14-gal tank and a ½-hp motor and compressor. This will give 624 8-oz glasses in the first hour and 400 after that, or approximately 1000 in a 2-hour period.

Walk-ins

Walk-ins are usually designed to carry large quantities of food and are usually used for storage in central areas, although some local storage may be provided if the requirements are high. Location of walk-ins should be such as to make delivery of foods from receiving to production and to service units as short and easy as possible. They should be located where they can be easily supervised. They may be an integral part of the building and as such are often constructed of concrete or they may be knockdown or prefabricated rooms put up in sections. Temperature and humidity conditions should be carefully planned. The usual number of walk-ins used by a large food service is three—one for fruits and vegetables, one for meats, poultry and fish, and one for dairy products, although more may be added if specialized requirements make this desirable. Frequently a salad walk-in or garbage refrigerated rooms are provided. Baker's walk-ins are sometimes located close to the bake shop. Small operations find one walk-in sufficient but optimum storage conditions do not prevail for all types of foods.

Low-temperature walk-ins are used in large operations. A small low-temperature unit may be provided for small operations. Over-supplied foods in many foodservice operations are frozen until needed. Utilization of labor during low production peaks is improved by having pre-preparation occur during these times. Some food services provide carry-over food spaces. One award winning operation serving approximately 5500 meals per week installed low-temperature walk-in space 7 × 10 × 8 ft high for holding prepared foods.

Refrigerated walk-ins should have good insulation at least 3 in. wide or more, and low-temperature walk-ins at least 5 to 8 in. thick. Vaporproof, easily cleanable, durable walls, ceilings, and floors should be installed. The floor should be on a level plane with the outside floor and insulation should be installed below floor level. Outside floors are sometimes laid with a gradual incline to offset different levels, if this cannot be done. Quarry tile for floors and good quality corkboard blocks covered with an asphalt finish and painted with three coats of good quality aluminum paint for walls and ceilings have given satisfaction. Care must be taken to seal over insulation materials completely so moisture cannot penetrate. Sturdy, well-insulated doors with heavy duty, corrosion-resistant, lock-type hardware should be used. Inside emergency opening devices should be provided. Meat rails, shelving, and other equipment used to hang foods or shelving on which foods are placed should be adjustable, durable, sturdy, and made of non-corrosion type materials. Outside temperature dials should be provided.

A number of prefabricated walk-ins can be purchased, some of which are as large as refrigerated buildings. They should be specified for standard heights. Units are available as low as 6½ ft (2 m) and as high as 10½ ft (3¼ m). The systems may require from ⅓ to 10 hp motors. Rigid

Figure 22.3b A reach-in compartment that is a part of walk-in refrigerator shown in 22.3a. (*Courtesy George Bunby & Associates, Seattle, Wash.*)

urethane 4 in. (10 cm) thick insulation with a 0.029 U[1] factor and a UL 25 low flame spread nonburning rating should be specified. Walls should be rigid and of light reflective material tightly joined to allow no moisture penetration. Standard finishes for interiors and exteriors are 24 gauge bright galvanized steel or white painted steel, 0.040 embossed patterned aluminum, 22 gauge type 304, No. 2B finish, stainless steel or anodized aluminum. In many instances these same requirements can be applied to other refrigeration put into the facility.

Walk-ins of the knock-down or fabricated type are used when walk-in space is required and cannot be furnished by integral construction. Standards should be equivalent to that required for integral walk-ins. They should be designed to handle mobile equipment. Modular planning for equipment use and portion sizes will greatly assist in achieving better utilization of expensive space.

[1] This would be a 0.116 (4 in × 0.029 = 0.116) k factor which compares with a urethane slab (0.139 k), styrofoam slab (0.25 k), or corkboard (0.270 k) which would give U-values respectively of 0.056, 0.100 and 0.108.

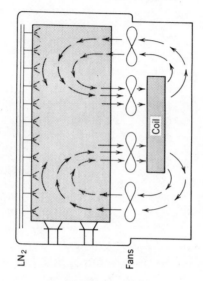

Winder

LN₂   Fans

Figure 22.4 Rapid freezing may be accomplished by circulating air temperature as low as −20°F and also by injecting liquid nitrogen into the compartment at a temperature of −320°F.

Ice Makers

Many foodservices have ice making equipment. In large hotels, restaurants, or cafeterias, huge equipment is required; the plant is located outside the foodservice area and delivery of ice is made as required. Purity is essential. Sanitary and well-insulated facilities should be provided for ice storage.

Ice makers to make ice in block or bulk form that can be broken up in sizes desired for use by chippers or crushers are available. Capacities run from 40 to 4000 lb per day. Cube makers may be purchased and some may be adjustable to freeze cubes as small as ¼ in. or as large as 1 in. Crushed or flaked ice machines may be obtained also. Self-contained units freezing 20 to 600 lb (18 to 272 kg) of ice per day may be obtained. Electricity, cold water, and drainage must be provided. Insulated mobile carts having thermostatic controls to turn off the automatic when the cart is full are also on the market.

Cube ice lasts longer in drinks, which makes this form desirable for take-out drinks or drinks to be held before consumption. Flake ice cools the drink faster but melts faster also. Small cubes or flakes make a drink appear larger in the glass than large cubes. Flake machines usually produce more ice per day than cube machines. Machines should carry a guarantee of performance including the amount they make in an hour or day.

Large machines are usually water-cooled, but some are air-cooled. Combination air-water-cooled units are available also. Cost of water and adequate drainage are required on water-cooled units. Suit the unit to the available space. Installation at point of use is desirable and, if possible, sufficient bin capacity so ice can be achieved to these areas. One machine on the market manufacturers ice and delivers it via pipes to other areas. Bins should be well insulated and be able to hold ice in a refrigerated area for almost a week. It may be less expensive to purchase a smaller machine and let it run for longer periods and purchase more bins for storage. Capacities stated by manufacturers are usually for a 24-hr period at 70° F (21° C) room temperature and 60° F (15½° C) incoming water temperature.

Ice delivered in one cost study was $1.75 to $2.00/100 lb (45.4 kg). The cost of the same amount of ice made in an $1,800 machine, amortized in 5 years, was 55¢/100 lb (45.4 kg). An added advantage with the machine was that it gave greater flexibility than depending upon delivered ice. The ice may be more sanitary also. A nonfunctioning ice machine, on the other hand, can be a real problem when ice is needed in a facility.

Suggested Student Assignments

1. Observe the refrigeration equipment in two large food operations and list items of refrigeration equipment with specifications for size, capacity, type, temperature maintained, and how used. Where is each located?

2. Write the specifications for the refrigeration equipment for a specified food operation.

Chapter 23

auxiliary equipment

The auxiliary or helping out equipment in food facilities supports the essential activities in conjunction with other items in work sections. Size, design, and structure that meet specific needs are important for satisfactory use.

Hoods

Hoods are used for the removal of heat, grease, moisture, and steam. The removal of odors and pollution products from air exhausted from kitchens has received increased emphasis. Pollution control devices are available that can be placed into ventilators and hoods. These operate both with hot water spray from nozzles and electrostatic precipator cell units. In some cases, activated charcoal units can be added. In addition, some of the units contain fire control devices that have automatic closing dampers and a fine spray of water to put out fires. Figure 23.1 shows a drawing of a ventilator with the pollution and fire control units installed. Pollution control units are available also that can be installed in the duct system on the roof. Water requirements tend to be high and this may present a problem in some areas. For instance, a device exhausting 180,000 cfh will require 34½ gpm at 60 psi for both pollution and fire control, if both are operating.

The size and placement of the hood in relation to heat and pollutants to be removed are important. As with a vacuum sweeper, the closer the suction is to the object to be removed the more effective it is likely to be. For this reason, low hoods over griddles and fryers are favored. Canopies should usually have about a 2 in. (5 cm) overhang for each foot above the equipment. The usual clearance of high canopies is 5 ft (1.5 m) above equipment and a minimum of 6 ft 3 in. (1.60 m) where workers pass under it. To work properly, canopies should be at least 2 ft (61 cm) from the bottom edge to the top and one outlet should be provided for every 6 to 18 linear ft (1.83 to 2.44 m) of canopy. Low canopies of the back-shelf type sit about 18 to 22 in. (45 to 55 cm) above the equipment and give the strongest pull of air where it is most needed. They may vary from 200 cfm to a high of 350 cfm per lineal food of appliance. The National Fire Protective Association recommends that all hoods be equipped with grease filters or be provided with a fire extinguishing system that meets their No. 96 Standard. Filters should not be installed less than 3½ ft (1.05 m) above an open flame and not less than 4½ ft (1.35 m) above charcoal flames. Filters should be easily removable and of a size easily sent through the dishwasher.

Canopy hoods should be integrally constructed with smooth surfaces, free of crevices, trim, or other projections. Suitable drains should be pro-

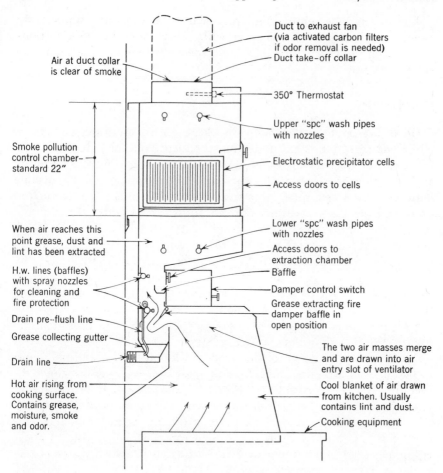

Air at duct collar
is clear of smoke

Smoke pollution
control chamber–
standard 22"

When air reaches this
point grease, dust and
lint has been extracted

H.w. lines (baffles)
with spray nozzles
for cleaning and
fire protection

Drain pre-flush line

Grease collecting gutter

Drain line

Hot air rising from
cooking surface.
Contains grease,
moisture, smoke
and odor.

Duct to exhaust fan
(via activated carbon filters
if odor removal is needed)
Duct take-off collar

350° Thermostat

Upper "spc" wash pipes
with nozzles

Electrostatic precipitator cells

Access doors to cells

Lower "spc" wash pipes
with nozzles

Access doors to
extraction chamber

Baffle

Damper control switch

Grease extracting fire
damper baffle in
open position

The two air masses merge
and are drawn into air
entry slot of ventilator

Cool blanket of air drawn
from kitchen. Usually
contains lint and dust.

Cooking equipment

Figure 23.1 A ventilator equipped with a fire and pollution control unit. Air drawn into the fire damper baffle is made to move in a circuitous route which throws grease and lint into the baffle, collecting it there. The 350° F (75° C) sensing thermostat at the top triggers the damper-closing unit and the fine water spray in case of fire. As the air moves up it passes through the electrostatic precipitator cells and washing sprays which removes smoke and other pollution products. (*Courtesy Gaylord Industries, Inc.*)

vided for condensate and grease troughs not less than 1¼ × 1¼ in. should permit easy cleaning. Baffles, dampers, turning vanes, and so forth, should be easily removable and cleanable. An automatic device should close dampers and vents when temperatures go over 360 to 400° F. Hoods should be rigidly supported to equipment, wall, or ceiling. Marine

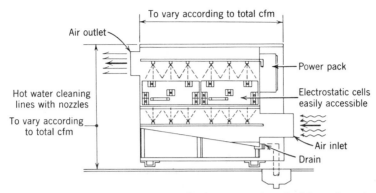

Figure 23.2 A roof-mounted pollution control unit. Note that the air enters from below on the duct system and passes through a water and electrostatic precipitator cell cleaning unit and then out where it is exhausted into the atmosphere. This unit unlike the one shown in Figure 23.1, does not contain the fire control device. (*Courtesy Gaylord Industries, Inc.*)

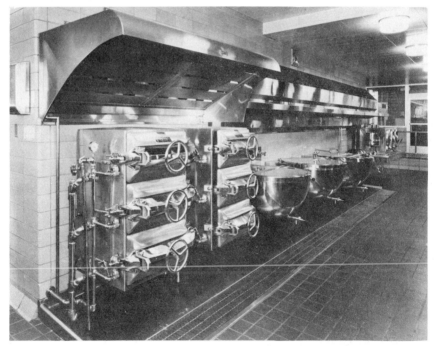

Figure 23.3 Hoods designed for steam equipment. (*Courtesy Cleveland Range Co., Cleveland.*)

type or sealed-in vapor proof lights should be installed as required for proper illumination.[2]

POT RACKS

Pot racks may be overhead bar type or shelf type. The overhead racks may have 1, 2, or 3 bars formed in a straight line, oval, half-oval, or revolving round forms. Where three bars are used, two form an oval and a third is centered for support at a distance approximately 12 in. below the level of the others. Stainless steel 2 × $\frac{1}{4}$ in. thick, seamlessly welded, ground, and polished is recommended. Drop-forged pot hooks of stainless steel are riveted on 6 in. centers on each side of all three bars. The stainless steel ceiling hangers are flanged over and bolted to the pot rack. Where ceiling hangers are more than 48 in. long, they are cross-braced. Less durable and expensive models may be made of iron painted with two coats of aluminum paint or steel lacquered black.

Mounting may also be by means of a pipe support that passes through the table with the rack firmly attached to the table structure. Revolving racks are sometimes used where space and reach are limited. Heavy, bulky items should be stored on shelves that minimize lifting and do not overload hung pot racks. Spacing should be planned for large equipment, such as mixer bowls. Some items may be hung from hooks.

Adjustable, portable shelving of perforated sheet metal, metal bands, or pipe is suitable for pot and pan storage units. Solid metal shelving will not permit as good circulation of air. These racks should be mobile in most instances. To support the weights required, the structure should be sturdy. Smooth, easily cleanable surfaces are desirable. The height and balance should be such as to permit easy reach to pots and should not be top-heavy.

SHELVING

Shelving may come in many forms and be for a variety of storage materials. Wood in plain, compressed, or plywood forms may be used for linen cabinets and paper supplies or where there is little likelihood of heavy wear, moisture, or grease from materials. Most shelving should be adjustable and removable. Surfaces should be smooth. The framework may be angle or pipe, sectional or completely detachable for removal from the storage area for complete scrubbing and cleaning. Materials commonly used are aluminum alloys, galvanized and stainless steels. Shelving may be mobile.

[2] For further discussion, see "Commercial Kitchen Ventilation" by E. A. Jahn, American Gas Association, 420 Lexington Ave., New York, N.Y.

CABINETS

Enclosed units may be constructed as separate units or incorporated as a part of other equipment, such as serving counters or work tables. Doors may need to open out to expose the full width of a shelf area or they may slide in opposite directions only or in either direction. Shelves should be removable for easy and thorough cleaning. If food is to be stored and good ventilation is required, louvres or openings should be placed for proper air circulation. Material may be wood, aluminum alloys, galvanized or stainless steel. The required gage will depend on the size of the cabinet, condition of wear, and material used.

Proof boxes are a special type cabinet used in the bake shop. Gas, steam, or electricity is required to maintain a temperature of 90 to 100° F. and to operate an evaporator to maintain a relative humidity of 80 to 85 percent. Because of the high humidity, non-rusting metals should be used. Mobility is desirable to enable the baker to fill at the bench, move away while proofing, and thence to the oven for baking. Size to accommodate pans.

SINKS

Sinks as individual pieces of equipment are available as standard stock equipment with or without drainboards. They are frequently incorporated into work tables for work centers. Pot and pan and vegetable sinks may be sized larger than normal, while counter, fountain, and other utility sinks may be smaller. In a pot sink, three or four compartments may be required. Compartments of $24 \times 28 \times 14$ in. deep are large enough for standard baking sheets, roasting pans, and similar large equipment. Depth of the sink should be studied; 16 in. may be too deep for some purposes and 12 or 14 in. better. The distance of the bottom of the sink to the floor, plus the overall height, will dictate whether or not the sink is at a convenient work level. Where tall workers are employed sinks of 38 in. are used and the sink bottoms are 22 in. off the floor. More study needs to be given to sink heights.

Good construction is required for sinks. A 3 in. raised edge is frequently used above the drainboard where spillage may occur. Compartment walls should be one piece double construction. Splash-backs should be integral with tops of sufficient height and sealed tightly to the wall or 4 in. away from the wall for easy cleaning.

Strong bracing should be given drainboards. The minimum pitch should be $1/8$ in. per foot. Corrguated drainboards are used for fountains, bars, and other areas where inverted glasses are allowed to drain. Corrugations should be not less than $3/32$ in. deep and sufficiently wide

Figure 23.4   A well-constructed general purpose sink. (*Courtesy S. Blickman, Inc., Weehawken, N. J.*)

for ease of cleaning. Drainboards for clean and soiled items should be separate; if they are parallel the clean utensil section should be at least ½ in. above the dirty utensil section. Sliding drainboards should be constructed to prevent seepage or overflow and should be easily cleanable.

Specifications for sinks should state type outlet, drain, overflow, and drilling to be made for hot and cold water. The drilling is usually done on 8 in. centers for each compartment unless swinging faucets are used. Faucets are usually not furnished and should be specified if desired. Drains are usually 2 in. They should have removable strainers with or without remote control. Overflows between two sink compartments should be 6 in. wide. Overflows should be fitted with removable strainer plates or baskets. Drains should have cleanouts before drainage pipes enter inaccessible areas. Frequently a brass tailpiece is used as a plug for the sink. This allows the overflow of accumulated refuse to drain off while holding the water in the sink. Waste and water fittings should be of corrosion resisting materials. The National Sanitation Foundation's recommendations for sink construction should be closely followed.

Sinks for manual washing of dishes should be of three units—one for washing, one for sanitizing, and one for rinsing. Sanitizing may be done

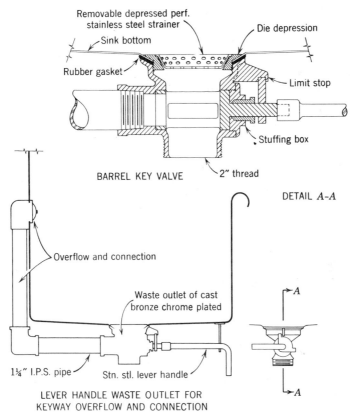

Removable depressed perf.
stainless steel strainer

Die depression

Sink bottom

Rubber gasket

Limit stop

Stuffing box

BARREL KEY VALVE

2" thread

DETAIL A-A

Overflow and connection

Waste outlet of cast
bronze chrome plated

A

1¼" I.P.S. pipe   Stn. stl. lever handle

LEVER HANDLE WASTE OUTLET FOR
KEYWAY OVERFLOW AND CONNECTION

A

Figure 23.5 Lever handle waste outlet for keyway overflow and connection. (*Courtesy S. Blickman, Inc., Weehawken, N. J.*)

by holding dishes 2 minutes in 170° F water, boiling for ½ minute, or holding in a solution of free chlorine of 50 ppm.

removable drainer baskets. Floor sinks are rapidly displacing slop or

Dump sinks for disposal of liquids and debris should be fitted with janitor's sinks. Floor sinks should be recessed 6 to 8 in. and be easily cleanable.

TABLES

Working surfaces should be carefully planned in relation to work center needs, height, available space, surface material, and storage facilities. Although certain large, sturdily built tables in fixed locations may be required, smaller mobile units add greatly to flexibility and convenience.

Finish of edges is important. Some of the edges recommended for tables, sinks and curbs are:

1. Fully rounded with bullnosed corner. Edges are rolled 1½ in. in diameter so all radii are equal horizontally and vertically and corners are fully rounded and integral with top and side rolls.

2. Raised rolled edge. Similar to above, except edges are raised ⅜ in. before forming edge rolls. This is useful as a curb against spillage.

3. Inverted "V" edge. The edges are integrally raised ½ in. and then bent down 2 in. to form a straight sided edge and then straight back ½ in. The corners are mitred, welded, ground, and polished to be in harmony with the top. This edge furnishes a curb against spillage, such as might occur on an urn stand.

4. Recessed curb. The edge may be formed similarly to 3 except it is not raised and the 2 in. apron is recessed through the center ½ in.

5. Curbs and vertical corners. The edges of dish table curbs and sink edges may be rounded in a manner similar to that described for table edge 1, and the vertical edges or corners may be coved on a 1 in. radii or formed into a square corner. The coved edges are preferred for ease of cleaning.

Large tables that receive heavy usage should be constructed of 12 to 14-gauge stainless steel, with channeling and bracing used as required for sturdiness. The stainless steel top may be satisfactorily used for all types of cooking and pastry work. Some prefer wood surfaces, however, for some of the tables in the baking section and the pantry. The latter should be made of 3 in. sectional hard maple, glued and bolted, with concealed metal tie rods. Flush dowels should conceal the head and burr of the tie rods.

Table widths vary from 15 in. for a mobile unit to 30, 36, and 42 in. for large tables. The length varies widely. They should be amply supported with legs to provide sturdiness and prevent sagging. If over 7 ft long, six legs are recommended or strong channeling must be provided. Heights of tables should be adjusted to job requirements. Small tables that may be pulled over the lap are convenient for vegetable or pantry workers who may sit down while working. Even heights of 40 in. are desirable for certain tasks. Tables may be constructed to stand on a platform 14 to 18 in. high. The durable floor material may form the bottom shelf. Plans should be made for toe space and for coving at the floor.

Ingredient tables for bakers and cooks should have spice drawers located in a high shelf position, with equipment drawers and either tilting or rolling bins under the top. A hanging pot rack should be sus-

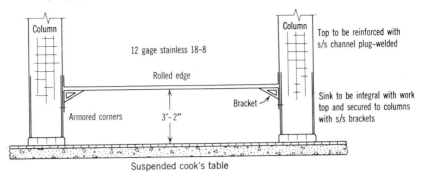

Suspended cook's table

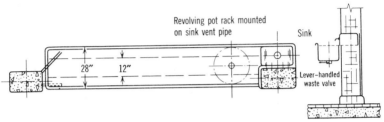

Figure 23.6 Cook's table suspended from structural columns permits parking of various mobile units underneath. (*Courtesy Volume Feeding Management, New York.*)

pended above it. Space for the scales may be allowed at the end of the table next to the mixer or a separate, small, portable table planned to fit between the ingredient table and the mixer. For large facilities, which are likely to measure sizable quantities into the mixer, mobile bins are preferred. Where small amounts are used, as flour for thickening by a cook, the tilt bins permitting a one-handed operation for opening may be better. Where rolling bins are used, the spacing for small drawers should harmonize with the width of the bins. A stretcher should be so spaced under the table where rolling bins are used, which will serve as a stop that will position the front of the bin flush with the face of the table.

Tables should permit complete cleaning and be so built as to have smooth, cleanable surfaces free from crevices where soil may lodge. Wall mounting facilitates cleaning. Drawers should be vermin and dust proof. Work tables need to be equipped with drawers, shelves, or open space that will best fit the needs in the work center.

Dish tables receive rugged use in most operations. They should be strongly built of 12 to 14 gauge stainless steel and braced laterally with 3 in. wide channeling. Legs should be 1⅝ OD, 10-gauge metal. Shelf

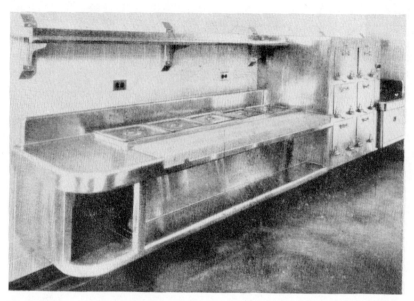

Figure 23.7 A wall-mounted sandwich table in a back counter, designed for convenience and easy cleaning. (*Courtesy S. Blickman, Inc., Weehawken, N. J.*)

Figure 23.8 A salad work center with shelves for equipment. (*Courtesy Southern Equipment Co., St. Louis, Mo.*)

bracing underneath should be kept at a minimum to give ease of cleaning under and allow use of mobile equipment. Catch-all space should be avoided. Edges are usually turned up 3 in. and rolled on a 1½ in. diameter with bull-nose corners but may be left open and flashed into dishmachines of the basket type. Back splashes of 10 in. are sometimes used when the tables are placed against the wall. If necessary, tray rests for unloading soiled dishes should be provided for dish delivery. Good bracing should be provided these rests. Overhead shelves should be provided for glasses and small dishes. A slightly turned edge on the opposite side will prevent items being pushed off in loading. Overhead shelves should be 14 gauge and edges should be rolled. The quantity of shelving required should be calculated. If glasses and other small dishes can be directly loaded into baskets standing on shelves or table space, labor is saved but slightly more time will be required of waiters if they have to do it.

It is desirable to construct conveyor tops integral with the rest of the table but space must be left open for passage of the belt. A hole for garbage and waste or garbage disposal is usually provided near the dish machine where stacking or loading will occur. Scrap blocks should be made of grease-resistant, solid prime rubber, not synthetic, and should be

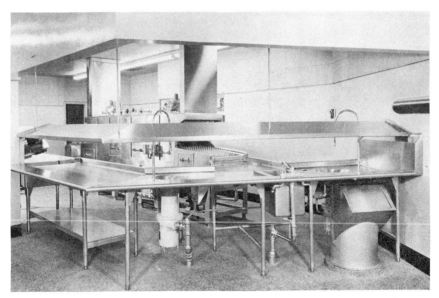

Figure 23.9 Soiled dish table with rack shelf hung from the ceiling. Note silver soak sink. (*Courtesy G. S. Blakeslee and Co., Chicago.*)

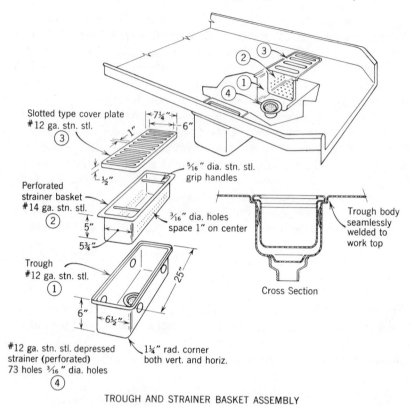

Slotted type cover plate
#12 ga. stn. stl.
③

Perforated
strainer basket
#14 ga. stn. stl.
②

Trough
#12 ga. stn. stl.
①

#12 ga. stn. stl. depressed
strainer (perforated)
73 holes ³⁄₁₆ " dia. holes
④

⁵⁄₁₆ " dia. stn. stl.
grip handles

³⁄₁₆ " dia. holes
space 1" on center

1¼" rad. corner
both vert. and horiz.

Trough body
seamlessly
welded to
work top

Cross Section

TROUGH AND STRAINER BASKET ASSEMBLY

Figure 23.10 Detail of trough and strainer basket assembly for draining soiled dish table. (*Courtesy S. Blickman, Inc., Weehawken, N. J.*)

removable. The hole should be constructed to prevent refuse from falling outside the garbage receptacle and the edge should be integrally raised ½ in. to prevent leakage.

Drainage should be provided near the machine and the table should be sloped to the drainage. Sometimes a depression 4 in. deep and 6 in. wide is placed across the entrance of the table into the machine. A removable perforated basket is placed over this level with the table top. Drainage may go into disposals. Other drainage areas may have to be provided on large tables. Preflush sinks may be required and these should be at least 8 in. deep and sized properly for the baskets used. Strainer basket and overhead spray assembly may need to be provided. Soaking sinks may also have to be provided; the size required will depend upon the estimated number of dishes encrusted with egg or other materials that will have to be soaked. Soaking sinks are also used for bleaching coffee cups, and so forth. It may be desirable to have table flush covers for the sinks. Removable strainers should be installed in drains and sinks.

The clean dish table on basket type machines should be adequate to hold the dishes until they are dry. It is usually calculated that 60 percent of the table space of this type should be for clean dishes and 40 percent for soiled. Mobile tables should be provided, along with other mobile storage equipment at the clean dish ends of basketless machines. The sizing of the table and shelves to be used for working space and dish storage will depend upon the way the work is to be done in the unit and the amount of dishes that will arrive in specified periods. If dishes are to be stacked only during peak periods and then washed during lulls, more soiled dish space will be required. Provide for sound-deadening under all table tops where noise may be a problem.

Suggested Student Assignments

1. Observe hoods in five food operations, and describe the following:
   a. Location, giving height above source of heat or pollution.
   b. Size in relation to area to be ventilated.
   c. Type of filter and how cleaned.
   d. Effectiveness in removing heat and pollutants.
   e. Comfort for workers in terms of location and draft.

2. Observe the pot and utensil storage in the five food operations and describe
   a. Location in relation to work sections.
   b. Convenience in finding items required for work.
   c. Adequacy in terms of number of items handled and sanitation protection.

3. Write specifications for a custom-built pot sink, cook's table, and storeroom shelving.

Chapter 24

transportation
and mobile equipment

Transportation devices to carry loads, save steps, lessen fatigue, and reduce labor can do much to reduce labor costs and speed accomplishment. The bringing of materials and equipment to workers and the flexible movement of equipment for forming good work centers can greatly improve productivity. Rehandling of stored equipment and supplies can be lessened through the use of mobile units. Careful evaluation of means for increasing mobility is important. In the planning, care should be taken to see that storage space for mobile equipment is available and aisles and work areas are sufficiently large to allow their entry and use in the work center.

CONVEYORS AND ELEVATORS

Vertical conveyors, elevators, or dumb waiters for movement of materials are frequently required and unless planned to suit the need can be the cause of much delay and confusion in the movement of supplies and meals. Subveyors may make it possible to utilize space that otherwise would not be available. The location of dishwashing sections or food production areas, such as bake shops, on another floor than the serving area becomes feasible when good vertical transportation is available. The location of banquet rooms or other special dining spaces above or below production areas become possible when good vertical transportation is available. Systems may be devised with pushbutton control for sending foods or supplies to the location where desired. Elevators, dumb-waiters, or trayveyors should be installed according to need and as a part of an operational plan. Motorized conveyors may operate as belts or tracks horizontally undercounter, at working level or overhead, and as vertical carriers. Raising, lowering, or moving at horizontal level motions may be combined in the movement of items.

A reliable firm or specialist should be consulted before designing a conveyor or elevator system. Specific information will be required, such as number of people or items to be transported, the time limitations, speed, size of trays, tote boxes, number of floors to be served and floor heights (floor to floor), length of take-off or feeder belts (if any are required), type of service wanted (up, down reversible), electric current available, and a sketch or plan of operation. A durable, easily maintained, easily cleaned, smooth functioning system is desired. All areas should be easily accessible for cleaning and maintenance. Entry and exits areas should be of stainless steel. Rigid frame support should be provided for subveyor and conveyor housings and belt chassis.

The most popular uses for which these conveyors have been employed include the assembling of meals, such as hospital trays and school

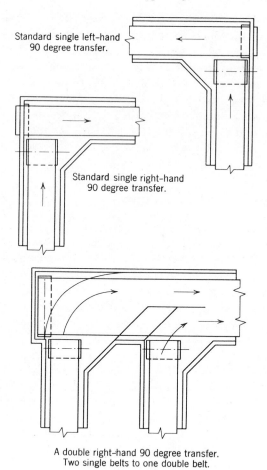

Standard single left–hand
90 degree transfer.

Standard single right–hand
90 degree transfer.

A double right–hand 90 degree transfer.
Two single belts to one double belt.

Figure 24.1   Horizontal 90-degree transfer on conveyors. *(Courtesy Samuel Olson Manufacturing Co., Chicago.)*

lunches, the removal of soiled dishes from dining areas, the delivery of supplies and equipment to serving stations, and the distribution of hospital trays to patient floors. The movement of soiled dishes by these means not only saves steps but also speeds work, lessens noise and unsightliness in dining areas, and may reduce breakage. The speed of the conveyor can be controlled to permit proper handling. A speed of 15 ft per minute will space trays and dishes from a cafeteria or hospital service so that workers can work at a normal rate in scrapping, sorting, and stacking. Subveyor and conveyor systems are usually planned to deliver approximately sixty to seventy-five dishes per minute or approximately

Figure 24.2 An example of vertical and horizontal movement in movement of hospital trays.

ten 14 × 18 in. trays onto a soiled dish table per minute. Pile-up and excess speed will increase breakage. Important values of conveyors in connection with soiled dish handling is the keeping of waiters and other outside personnel out of this work section, the reduction of noise, and the utilization of space to the best advantage.

BELT CONVEYORS

Care should be taken, in selecting belt material, installation, and general design, to guard good sanitation. The belt should be a sturdy material that is resistant to grease and animal fats. It should be installed in such a way as to permit washing above and underneath. Limit switches to stop a vertical conveyor should be installed to prevent pile-up when trays are not removed from a belt that is being supplied by a vertical conveyor. Spillage sometimes occurs inside vertical shafts and provision should be made for regular cleaning of the shafts. Care should be taken with ventilation to prevent possibilities of chilling drafts where food is to be transported.

Specifications for belt conveyors should indicate: (1) width of belt; (2) length of belt; (3) belt material; (4) directional movement and

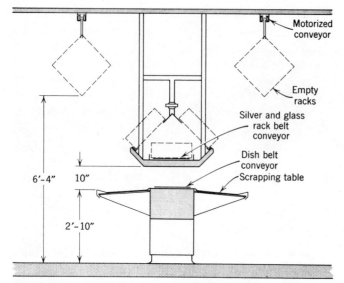

Figure 24.3 Conveyors save time and labor in a large dishwashing operation. Houston Club, Houston. (*Courtesy* Institutions Magazine, *Chicago.*)

This cross-section view gives a good picture of how three separate conveyors are incorporated into the solid dish table at the Houston Club, Houston. The belt running through the center of the table at table height brings incoming trays of soiled dishes. Glasses and cups are sorted out and placed in racks held at an angle on second level; a conveyor through the center of this section carries filled racks to the machine. The overhead unit carries a supply of empty racks. In addition, an overhead gravity unit is connected to the end of the dish machine to move large silver pieces.

whether one way or reversible; (5) location of head; and (6) placement and completeness of access of machinery. Vertical conveyors may be ascending, descending, and reversible. The widths may vary to accommodate standard-sized cafeteria and hospital trays, bus boxes, and oval trays. Movement may be controlled by means of a floor selector that stops the conveyor at the desired location or it may be continuous. Indication should be made by specification on all points affording choice.

Track Conveyors

The overhead, track type conveyor may be motorized or manually operated. The track may be straight or curved.

Roller Conveyors

Roller conveyors may move by gravity or be activated through friction from a motor-driven belt. The amount of friction may be controlled so that action can be held up when desired by light pressure of the hand or load pile-up. Gravity conveyors may be the roller or skate-wheel type. The rollers may be made of hardwood, plastic, or light metal. They may also be rubber covered. The diameter of the rollers range from 3/4 to 6 in. and lengths according to need. They may have precision ball bearings or bronze bearings inside or use external bearings. Gravity rollers are considered to be the most economical of all conveyors for handling of supplies, and are widely used. They may be straight, curved, or spiral and at varying degrees of pitch.

Gravity Slides or Chutes

This equipment requires pitch for ease of movement. The pitch should be at least 2½ to 3 in. per foot. Spiral chutes may be fully enclosed or open, and used between floors for handling bags, boxes, and other wrapped materials. Open containers, those that are too light or fragile and those that are wire wrapped, may not slide well or safely. Gravity rollers are better for these items and have more general use than the slides, but they are more expensive to construct.

Elevators and Dumb-waiters

The movement of food carts or trucks and other sizable objects from one floor to another frequently requires the use of an elevator or dumbwaiter. Models of widely differing sizes, speed of movement, and degrees of refinement are available. Elevator doors of a double leaf flush type, equipped with automatic opening and closing device, are desirable for food operations. Dumb-waiters are often used in hospitals for sending food to service kitchens from the main kitchen and for movement of small tray carts to patient floors. It is important to consider load capacity, space requirements, draft protection, sanitary features and desired operating speed when choosing this equipment. If banquet areas are used for exhibits or trade shows, a heavy duty elevator, sized to meet the space and load demands, must be installed. These elevators are usually slow moving and if they are used for food transport, the food should be placed in mobile insulated units. Chilling drafts or air currents through shafts of vertical transport equipment should be avoided. Food should not be transported in guest elevators. If mobile equipment is transported in elevators or dumb-waiters, self-leveling equipment should be installed. High speed dumb-waiters may be used for transfer of bulk foods or trays on small carts. Proper sizing with tray slides or shelf space for pans is desirable.

Planners may have to indicate to elevator or conveyor consultants the basic needs of the facility for transport and therefore should know what some of the requirements are in such planning. Adequate service must be obtained at a minimum cost. Costs of transport can be high and maximum efficiency is needed. The cost of installing an elevator system in a 30-story building may be 10 percent of the total construction cost.

The number of individuals or units to be moved in an hour is usually taken as the basis for calculating elevator needs. Normally in hotels 12 to 15 percent of the hotel capacity is considered moved to the destination in 5 minutes of elevator operation. In a normal hotel, the number of rooms times 1.3 is often used to calculate the number of people to be moved. In a hotel catering to conventions 1.7 is usually used. If carts plus individuals are moved as in foodservices the number of units and space required for both must be calculated. For restaurants and other facilities transporting people only, the capacity of the dining areas and the turnover rate plus flow of traffic may be used to establish numbers to be carried. In office buildings, estimates are frequently based on the footage of space. Normally one individual is considered as the occupant of every 90 to 110 sq ft of space, but if the occupants are largely stenographers and clerks, 50 sq ft is used. Thus, a floor having a large number of clerks and stenographers with 7,500 sq ft would be considered to have 150 people to be moved.

The elevator wait of 40 to 70 sec is considered normal. Elevator travel time for people in a building should not be more than 1 to $1\frac{1}{4}$ min. If over this, the longer the time, the greater the annoyance. Speeds of cars must be varied according to the distance traveled. The type of clientele may also dictate elevator speed—or the type of food, if food is the main product transported. Some facilities cater to people who are in a hurry and have only a limited amount of time for a lunch period, others may specialize on a more leisurely service.

Floor heights are usually calculated as being from 9 to 12 ft (2.7 to 3.7 m) high. A car going 10 floors would travel 90 to 108 ft (27 to 33 m). Normally cars will travel from 400 to 600 fpm but systems are installed in which cars travel from 250 to 1,400 fpm.

The number of individuals to be transported must be indicated. If a 200-room convention hotel is being planned and 15 percent of the occupants are to be moved in 5 min (300 sec) with a 50-sec wait, the number to be moved would be $1.7 \times 200 \times 0.15$ or 51, which probably would be rounded off to 50 moved every 5 min. If the hotel is 10 stories high with 12 ft for each floor the distance of travel is 120 ft. An expert is likely to recommend on this basis cars of 2500 or 3000-lb weight capacity that carry respectively 17 or 20 people. It is usual to calculate car capacity as only 80 percent of maximum and thus each car would be considered to hold 14 or 16 respectively. The engineer now checks standard tables and finds that a 2500-lb car will take 120 sec for a round trip at a speed of 400 fpm and 110 sec at 600 fpm, while a 3000-lb car will require respectively 135 sec and 124 sec. Thus the 2500-lb car in 5 minutes can make $2\frac{1}{2}$ trips at 400 fpm and $2\frac{3}{4}$ trips at 600 fpm and the 3,000-lb car will make respectively $2\frac{1}{4}$ and 2.4 trips. The following summary is therefore made:

Number of people transported in 5 min

	400 fpm	600 fpm
2500-lb car	35*	38
3000-lb car	36	38

* $2\frac{1}{2}$ trips in a 2500-lb car holding 14 people equals 35 people transported in 5 min.

However, a 50-sec wait has been specified and since the fastest round trip is $2\frac{3}{4}$ trips every 300 sec or over 100 sec per trip, the engineer may recommend a compromise of a slightly longer wait using two 2500-lb cars which would move 70 people in the time allowed. He could present information using larger cars at higher speeds using only one car. Based on cost, this might be shown to be the most favorable system except that with only one system and a breakdown the whole hotel would be immobilized except for the stairways. This might cause the planners to choose the two 2500-lb cars.

Similar calculation would be followed if the transport required was for food or other items on service elevators. Engineers use rather complex formulas for making calculations but basically the calculations made will be based on the type of information given here.

Space needs for elevators at entrances must be well planned. The location also of the elevators in relationship to rooms or spaces they are to serve must be cosidered. Elevators may be banked in a row or opposite each other. The minimum distance between elevators across from each other should be 6 ft (1.83 m) but for a normal lobby, hall or other waiting area the minimum set if 10 ft (3 m). Good visibility is to be provided around doors so people moving in or out of the elevators have a view of the area. There are some elevator systems which are computer controlled so that they may be changed in circuit to meet service demands.

Escalators are used when distance of travel is not great, such as several floors. Department stores use them so that patrons can see merchandise on the floors and also to provide good transportation between floors. They have the advantage of providing instant and independent travel, unless a line forms at the boarding area.

Dumb-waiter requirements will be based on the quantity and type of items to be transported, and time requirements. Normally, speeds from 50 to 300 fpm are used. If the quantity is large and the distance for transport is not great a geared elevator or an elevator operated by hydraulic lift may be used. Freight elevators must be considered also on the basis of the weight per sq ft they must carry.

MOBILE EQUIPMENT

Casters for Mobile Equipment

Much of the durability and satisfaction in use of mobile equipment will depend on the quality of casters on which it moves. They should be (1) easy rolling, (2) durable, (3) moisture, chemical and grease resistant, (4) quiet, and (5) adequately sturdy to support required weight. When specifying, state (1) wheel diameter, which should be as large as practical; (2) type of tread, such as rubber or hard tread; (3) ball bearing; (4) finish, such as cadmium plated or other; (5) type adapter, such as stem, plate, or other fitting; and (6) swivel or rigid. Also indicate if wheel locks are desired.

The larger the wheel diameter the easier the movement of a load. Casters, 5 in. in diameter, are popular for carts and other mobile equipment. The rubber tires may be solid, pneumatic, or semipneumatic and the hard treads may be of steel, aluminum, or plastic. The finish may be enameled or cadmium plated, which is preferable for rust proofing. All swivel casters are selected when it is desirable to maneuver a piece of equipment into a space, using sideways as well as forward and back motion. Two rigid casters at one end assist in guiding equipment in a direct line. Wheel locks on two wheels help to fix position of portable equipment. It is important to note appropriate sturdiness in fork and axle. If these are too light for trucks transporting heavy loads, they are likely to become bent or give way.

Bumpers

Bumpers on equipment, walls, and doors where needed, will be essential in preventing scarring if a great deal of mobile equipment is used, particularly if equipment is heavy and difficult to maneuver. Equipment bumpers are made of rubber molded to the desired forms. They may be corner bumpers to cover the vertical edges or placed at baseboard height to hold equipment from hitting the wall or other objects. Doughnut-shaped bumpers may be placed on the shaft above the casters and on cart or truck handles. They may be made of 1 in. OD encirculing rubber doughnut set in $1\frac{1}{4} \times \frac{1}{2} \times \frac{1}{8}$ in. seamless channel from the same metal as the uprights. The channels should be connected to the chassis by $2 \times \frac{3}{16}$ in screws. They will add approximately 5 in. in length and 4 in. in width to the overall dimensions where used on the caster shaft.

Continuous rubber bumpers around the bottom of equipment are an effective protection. These bumpers may be procured in widths varying from $\frac{5}{8}$ to $1\frac{1}{4}$ in. and in depth from $\frac{1}{2}$ to $1\frac{1}{8}$ in. They are molded on a steel strap or bar and may or may not be set in a channel. The size and weight chosen must be adequate for bumpering the size and weight of the mobile equipment.

Doors to garbage rooms, receiving, and storage need protection from the movement of heavy mobile loads. Steel either galvanized or stainless in 1 in. pipe or sheet form may be used. Stainless steel of 16 or 18 gauge fitted tightly over a 1×3 in. board makes an effective wall protection. It is to be positioned at a height to give maximum protection.

Construction Standards

Flexibility of many pieces of equipment can be increased by placing them on casters. Large equipment may be mounted directly on casters and lesser pieces on a mobile base or table. Attention should be paid to securing proper working height. Food cutters, slicers, and small mixers are usually satisfactory on tables that are 18 to 24 in. high. One under-shelf in such tables, 8 to 10 in. above the floor, will be convenient for use and add rigidity and strength to the frame. A drawer 4 to 5 in. deep may be hung under the top for storage of small equipment.

Carts may be factory or custom built in a wide variety of sizes and designs. They may be made of aluminum, galvanized iron, or stainless steel in various gauges. The supports or frames may be continuous tubing, tubing used for uprights only, and angle frame. Materials are sometimes combined. For example, a frame of aluminum tubing and stainless shelves may be satisfactory as a light weight cart. Heavy use requires sturdy, durable materials and gauge. Sixteen gauge should be used for galvanized steel and 18 gauge for stainless steel, and 1 in. OD $\times$ 16-gauge wall tubing. Utility carts may have two or three shelves and may be approximately 36 in. high. To lessen delivery costs these models are de-

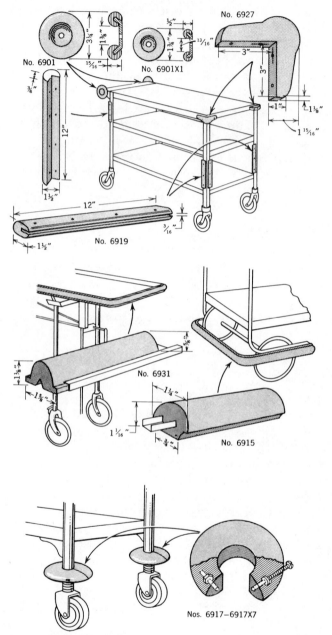

Figure 24.4 Examples of equipment bumper. (*Courtesy The Colson Corp., Elyria, Ohio.*)

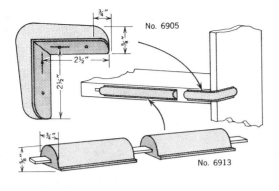

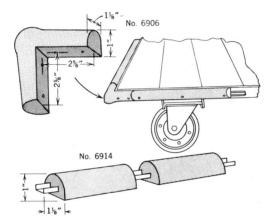

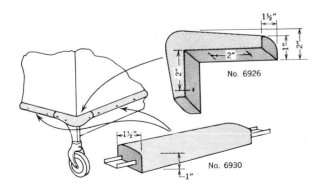

Figure 24.4 *(continued)*

signed for compact shipment and local assembly. The length and width should be sized in terms of use. If it is to be used for bussing dishes, care should be taken to select bus boxes, so that one or two boxes will fit well on a shelf. Tray carts may have four to eight shelves each to hold one tray, and from four to six shelves each to hold from three to five trays. Ease of maneuvering should be considered when selecting them.

The sturdiness of construction should be in proportion to the load that a cart will be required to carry. A cart 5 to 6 ft × 30 in. wide carrying a moderate load should have an angle frame of $1\frac{1}{2} \times 1\frac{1}{2} \times \frac{1}{8}$ in. Shelving should be not less than 16 gauge and should be turned down 1 to $1\frac{1}{2}$ in. on the edges with edges sealed. Angle support may be necessary under the shelving for support if very heavy loads are to be handled. A cart such as this with five shelves will be about $5\frac{1}{2}$ ft high with shelves on 8 in. centers and is suitable for dish transport but may have to have 12 gauge shelves.

Figure 24.5 Dollies provide convenient transportation for many items, such as milk cases or cup and glass racks.

Dollies and Platform Trucks

The dolly consists of a metal frame with casters, of a size to fit garbage cans, one or more milk cases, or cup and glass racks. It may or may not have a handle. They are usually constructed of steel.

The platform truck is almost synonymous with the dolly and the names may, in certain instances, be used interchangeably. Generally the platform truck is considered to be one of greater size, sturdier build, and equipped with handles. The platform may be of aluminum, wood or steel and the fittings of aluminum, steel, or stainless steel. Size and sturdiness of build should be governed in terms of intended use, and the size and weight governed in terms of whether a man or woman will be using the equipment. The platform truck generally used by the receiving and storage clerk is 4 to 5 ft long and 2 ft 3 in. wide. The casters may be equal in size and located at the four corners. All may be swivel, or the two front ones swivel and the back ones stationary. For easy maneuverability, the casters may be in a diamond formation with two large stationary ones on the two sides of the truck and smaller swivel casters in the center at the ends.

Figure 24.6 Mobile equipment facilitates one motion storage.

Lift Trucks

A hydraulic lift may be used as a part of a hand cart that may be used conveniently by women workers, or as a lifting device for the movement of pallets on which heavy loads of food supplies are stored. Lift trucks are available in varying sizes and selection should be made in terms of specific use.

Mobile Racks and Cabinets

A framework or rack designed to fit modular containers of a specified size that are supported on ledges in the framework may be mounted on casters. The framework is usually of angle construction of aluminum, galvanized steel, or stainless steel, with ledges formed by angles or corregations of like metal. The racks may be open or closed and heated or unheated. For flexible use it is important that they be planned for modular pans, such as the standard hot table pans, baking sheets, and trays. Avoid excess height impossible to see over and that may be upset. Choose for cabinet or under counter use. These racks are very useful for

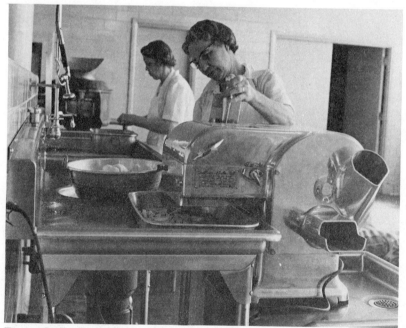

Figure 24.7 A mobile cutter provides quick change for preparation needs in the vegetable preparation unit.

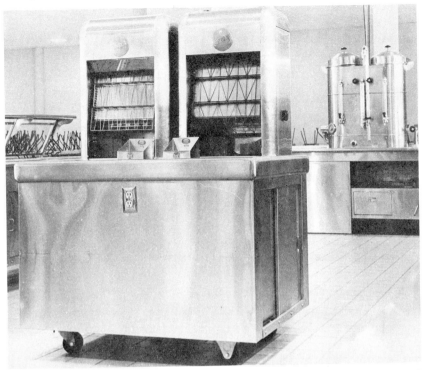

Figure 24.8 Mobility of toasters makes it possible to obtain variation in service needs behind a service counter.

storage, for holding materials during preparation to reduce space required in work centers, and for predishing of portions for service.

Trucks

The terms cart and truck are often used interchangeably and are frequently applied to mobile racks also. The term truck, as it is used here, refers to heavier, more complicated structures, designed for specific purposes, such as mop trucks, food trucks for hot or cold foodservice and dispensing units. A wide variety of trucks that are equipped for hot and cold food and beverage service are offered for hospital and industrial foodservice.

Hot or cold food trucks should be well insulated and where electrically heated should have signal light to indicate when electricity is on or off. Food trucks should have 14 to 16-gauge tops and 18-gauge bodies with angle frame inside where necessary for rigid support. Shelves may be

Figure 24.9 Unheated enclosed cabinet that can be rolled into a refrigerator are suitable for salad storage. (*Courtesy Cresent Metal Products Inc., Cleveland.*)

included underneath top. Mobile canteens should be built of 3-in. ship channel chassis reinforced with angle iron of 18 gauge for the super-structure. The design should be based on the food items to be offered, such as hot and cold beverages, hot rolls, doughnuts, sandwiches, candy, and cigarettes with cup dispensers. The units may be open or enclosed.

Self-leveling units may be stationary or portable, and unheated, heated, or refrigerated. They are used for cup, glass, tray, bowl, bread, and plate dispensing. One-motion storage of items from the dishwashing is possible when such units are mobile. Space requirements will depend on the measurements of the item dispensed, whether the truck is open or en-closed, and whether heated, refrigerated, or neither. Space should be allowed in work centers and in relation to other equipment according to desired use.

Facilities in which mobile equipment is used should be planned for its use. Automatically opening doors, sufficiently wide aisles, adequate space in work areas, flush floor walk-ins, and protected corners are essential. Storage areas for the mobile equipment must be planned but if mobile equipment takes the place of fixed shelving, then space may be found along walls.

Figure 24.10 Attractive mobile counters used for service in a multipurpose room.

Portable Carriers

The term portable has frequently been applied to any piece of equipment that may be moved. It is used here to signify those items that may be carried, and the term mobile is applied to those that are moved on wheels or casters.

Many times amounts to be transported are small enough to be moved quickly and easily by hand or on a mobile base. Cases, cabinets, and round thermos containers have been designed for such use. They may be shaped in such a manner as to permit stacking on dollies or special carts. The cabinets may be equipped for electric or canned heat and designed for the standard hot table pans or baking sheets. Pie cases may have shelves or slides to fit eight or ten pie pans of standard size. These have a handle in the top and the cabinets a handle at each end for carrying. Insulated cabinets are used in hotels for room service meals, and may be transported by cart or under a drop-leaf table. It is important that items carried be light as practical in weight. Aluminum or a light gauge of stainless steel is often used for that reason.

Vacuum-insulated containers made of 18-8 stainless steel are available in groups of two to four food pan assemblies varying in size from 1½ to 5 gal, and in one only unit of 11 gal capacity. Thermos jugs equipped with faucet for beverages vary in size from 2 to 10 gal capacity. Accessories are available to use in connection with them, for moving by hand cart, heating by means of a rod, for filling, pumping, and cup dispensing.

Chapter 25

utensils and tableware

Small equipment and tableware may claim 20 to 30 percent of the budget for food facility equipment. Although the amount spent for individual items may appear negligible, the large quantity required makes an impressive total. Careful selection is significant to work efficiency, initial cost, and operation expense. The items are numerous and differ widely in character and use. There are certain selection points that are generally applicable.

SELECTION POINTS

The important selection points for this equipment are:

1. Satisfaction for specific use—Is it convenient, safe, and sanitary to use? Will it enhance quality or quantity in production or service? Will it save labor or make work easier? Is it essential?

2. Appearance—Is it attractive in itself and harmonious with the other equipment?

3. Durability—Is it satisfactorily durable in relation to functional needs for specific use and volume of work? Will operating expenses be appropriate in terms of repair, renewal, and replacement?

4. Cost—Selection should be evaluated in terms of appropriate expenditure as initial investment and probable operation cost. Can its purchase be justified economically?

Small equipment and tableware are usually made according to factory specifications. Manufacturers furnish brochures giving description and pictures of the majority of items. Actual selection can often be made from displays in dealer's showrooms. Valuable records of use may be gained from those who are using specific equipment. Even with items that are small and "expendable," the initial selection will be important in establishing a pattern to be followed for many years. A change of make, material, or design may result in a heterogeneity that is unattractive and inconvenient. Changing an entire set of tableware or serving equipment, for example, may add greatly to expense.

MATERIALS

The material of which utensils and tableware is made will strongly influence durability, utility, beauty, and cost. Normally this ware is subjected to fairly vigorous hammering through repeated use and rapid handling. Massive utensils, on the other hand, are heavy to handle and may be a serious fatigue factor. Each of the materials in popular use has specific advantages and disadvantages in relation to its intended use.

Aluminum

Aluminum utensils are relatively inexpensive, light in weight, and conduct heat rapidly. The metal is soft and can be damaged through rough treatment. With suitable care it will withstand many years of active use. It may be damaged by cleaning with coarse abrasives and alkalis. Light weight ware dents easily and may be bent out of shape through heavy use. Aluminum has a bright appearance that may last through the use of mild cleaning methods. It has high thermal conductivity and distributes heat evenly. It is sometimes used as a core or covering of other metals that conduct heat less well.

Many utensils are made from sheets of fairly pure aluminum and from spun, drawn, and punched pressed aluminum. Certain heavy pots and pans are cast. Alloys are used with aluminum to develop greater hardness and corrosion resistance. Anodized or surface hardened material is used extensively. The cast utensils should be made from aluminum that conforms to TS-4021 Standards of the United States Bureau of Standards. This type will resist staining and corrosion under normal use.

Copper

The satisfactory heat conduction of copper has caused it to be used as a core or covering of metals that are less efficient in heat conduction. It stains and discolors readily, requiring extra effort in maintenance. The green rust on copper known as verdigris is poisonous. Copper is a soft metal that may be scratched or dented. It has a beautiful warm color when polished. When used where it will not be subjected to friction, it may be lacquered to preserve its bright appearance.

Cast-iron

Cast-iron utensils are made from molten gray iron poured into a mold. It is a close grained metal that may be machined to produce a smooth finish. The exteriors are black. The cost is comparatively low. Utensils of this material may be broken or cracked if dropped on a hard surface. A suitably heavy weight is an important factor for even heat distribution and for sufficient sturdiness to withstand commercial use. The cast-iron will rust unless protected by a thin film of salt-free oil, especially where it is allowed to stand without use for considerable period of time.

Sheet Steel

Many pieces of kitchen utensils are made of sheet steel, such as roasting pans, bread pans, pie tins, baking sheets, muffin pans, and light skillets. They are relatively inexpensive. The steel rusts readily and certain protective covering is required. Lacquer finish is frequently used as a protection when it is manufactured. This is usually burned off before the item is used. The steel that is not otherwise covered should be given a thin film of oil to prevent rusting if the item is to stand for a long period without being used.

Tin

Tin coating is used on many pieces of steel utensils. This supplies a bright finish and one that is resistant to rust. Tin is soft and a thin coating will wear off in a fairly short period of use. It is more desirable to discard light inexpensive pieces, such as pie tins, rather than to have them retinned. Large bowls, such as those used for mixing machines, colanders, and similar utensils may be retinned. Small utensils, such as pie tins and muffin pans, are usually made of tinned sheet steel. Hot dipped tinware should be specified for commercial use.

Porcelain-enamel

Porcelain-enamel utensils are made from sheet steel covered with one or more layers of porcelain enamel. They have very limited use and acceptance in commercial establishments because of their tendency to chip, heat craze, or crack. This ware is inexpensive, highly resistant to food acids, and easy to clean. Commercial standards for porcelain-enamel equipment may be found in National Bureau of Standards publication, TS-4482.

Stainless Steel

The bright, durable, easy to clean, rust-free stainless steel holds a popular place as a material for both kitchen utensils and tableware. It has many good features and some less favorable ones. Its major drawbacks are in terms of weight, cost, and slow, spotty heat conduction. It reflects radiant heat away and so is seldom used for baking utensils. "Hot spots" develop in stainless steel cooking utensils. It distributes heat poorly and those surfaces in contact with the heating surface carry heat directly into the food. Better heat distribution is secured by laminating layers of stainless steel with a core of a metal such as copper or sheet steel that conducts heat well. Copper or aluminum may also be used to cover the bottom of cooking pots. This laminated metal is known as "cladded" metal. Sometimes stainless steel utensils are covered on the outside with a layer of copper by means of electroplating.

Its durable, attractive appearance is an important asset of stainless steel. It is tough in withstanding rugged use and vigorous cleaning methods. The gauge of metal should be suitable in relation to size of the item and the intended use. Many of the pans, for example, should not be less than 16 gauge. Most of these utensils are drawn.

Stainless steel flatware for table use is usually made of a high grade alloy of chromium, steel, and nickel. Nickel gives it a whitish, silvery luster. Cheaper grades, which lack nickel, have a blue metallic color. The lower quality of flatware is made by punch pressing the shapes from sheets of stainless steel. The thickness is the same throughout. It can be detected readily by the somewhat rough appearing edges and the pebbly appearance where the press cut through the metal around handle edges and between fork tines. This ware is usually poorly balanced.

The more expensive stainless steel flatware is fashioned or graded. Handles, spoon bowls, and fork tines are tapered and the finish is smooth and even. This flatware is usually reinforced at stress points. Graded ware usually has simple smooth flowing lines and is quite attractive. Patterns of all stainless steel are usually simple and pressed ware may have slight embossed designs. The finishes are bright, semi-dull, and satin.

The strength of stainless steel is greater than that of similar weight silverplate. Strength can be tested by bending the spoon bowl where it joins the handle or by placing one of the outside tines on a hard surface and pushing. Good ware can be bent only with great difficulty. Flatware knives should be in one piece. Stainless steel blades with silverplated handles are sometimes found in knives. The blade should be set into the handle with solder, not cement, for the knife to give adequate wear.

Silver Plate

The character of the base metal is important to the durability of silver plated ware. The most rugged treatment given this ware is during collection in the dining room and washing. The silver plating is soft and contributes little to sturdiness. Nickel silver is the standard metal for the base and the alloy should contain as much as 18 percent nickel for satisfactory rigidity and toughness. Silver-plated pieces on bases having 12 percent nickel bend and dent easily. The silver peels from the steel as soon as the steel has attracted moisture under the plating.

The nickel silver blanks pressed from sheet metal are rolled and formed to have proper shape, size, and balance. They are trimmed and polished to have smooth edges and polished surfaces free from roughness or pebbles that would be unpleasant in use and be points where extra wear might occur. Plating methods used by the leading silver manufacturers differ, but approximate specifications for quality are as follows:

A 1 or Standard Plate has 5 oz of silver used for plating one gross of teaspoons and in like proportions for other items.

Half Standard Plate has approximately one half of Standard Plate or 2½ oz of silver used for plating one gross of teaspoons.

Triple Plate has 6 oz of silver used for plating one gross of teaspoons.

Extra heavy Hotel Plate has 8 or more ounces of silver used for plating one gross of teaspoons. This ware goes through more preparation and finishing processes to toughen it and give it a hard finish than used in lower grades.

Banquet Plate has one half the quantity of silver used as that for extra heavy hotel plate. It is produced in a few items only. The weight of the blank and finish are identical.

Hotel Plate may be reinforced at points where the greatest wear is likely to occur, such as the bottom of the spoon or fork bowl. The reinforcing may be by means of an inlay of silver or by spot plating before applying the general plating.

Pieces of table flatware are "intimate" pieces that directly influence dining pleasure. The items are handled and carried to the lips. Attractiveness, smooth clean surface, and comfortable balance are important. A gritty or greasy feel and tip heaviness create a poor impression and spoil enjoyment of the food. The design may be plain, semi-ornate, or ornate and the finish may be bright, butler or satin finish to meet varied tastes and fit into a specific decorative plan.

China

The term china has sometimes been used to include all of the clay or ceramic materials found in food facilities. There are four distinct types of clayware. (1) Earthenware is an unvitrified, soft porous product that may or may not have a glaze. (2) Pottery has a glaze and the clay from which the body is made of slightly better quality than earthenware. These two types of clayware are not suitable for use in food establishments except for decorative purposes. (3) Stoneware is vitrified and has a glazed surface. The clay is coarser than that used for porcelain. Its use is most suitable for heavy serving dishes, beverage containers, and kitchen crockery. (4) Vitrified china and porcelain are synonymous. The body of the ware is made of a fine quality of clay, which is fired to vitrification in the bisque. It has a glaze applied that upon refiring forms a transparent glassy surface. The number of times china is fired will be influenced by the colors used for decoration. The number of colors, the intricacy of the pattern, and the amount of handling required have a strong influence on price. The quality of the body and the glaze and the strictness of the grading also affect price.

The life of china depends on several factors. The body of the ware must be strong enough to withstand the repeated hammering of normal use and the glaze must be tough in resisting friction from the weight of other dishes stacked on it or sliding over it. The edge of coffee cups that are repeatedly stacked often become etched so that they are unpleasant to use even when they are not chipped or broken. Unless a sturdy glaze is used the centers of plates will wear from repeated cutting of food and from stacking, and will be dull and unsightly. It is important that dishes stack evenly to reduce the danger of stacks tipping or sliding, resulting in breakage.

The weight of the china and the shape of the edge will influence the strength of dishes. Light weight used in homes is practical only where it can be given gentle care. The appeal of its beauty and delicacy is sufficient to promote its use in exclusive establishments. The semi-heavy with a slight rolled edge and the institution weight have correspondingly greater sturdiness. Certain of the scalloped edges appear to have more strength than the plain circle.

The grading of china is of concern to the extent that it influences appearance, sanitation, roughness that may cause scarring of surfaces on which it is placed, and irregularities that cause poor stacking quality. Common defects include: (1) crookedness caused by warping or uneven shrinkage; (2) crazing, which refers to cracks in the glaze; (3) denting, which refers to cracks in the body under the glaze; (4) pin holes are tiny depressions or holes in the glaze; (5) spots and stains may be caused by a particle of iron in the clay or other discoloration of the slip; (6) white patches may be caused by accidental splashes of slip or poor mixing of the glaze; (7) unevenness in color; and (8) scars caused by marks of the stilts on which dishes rest during firing of the glaze.

The Bureau of Standards has established tests for satisfactory strength on the basis of various temperature, shock and impact tests. Manufacturers vary in "judging degrees of perfection." Buyers should specify carefully and examine the wares purchased. The grades based on strict selection include: (1) *selects,* which appear perfect to a careful grader; (2) *firsts,* which are almost perfect; (3) *seconds,* which have minor defects that are not conspicuous; (4) *third grade* possesses obvious blemishes of a type that do not weaken or eliminate the ware for possible use; and (5) culls or lumps, which are badly warped, chipped or scarred. Run of the kiln may include the two top grades and the best of the seconds.

Manufacturers of vitrified china identify their products with backstamps. Terms used to designate pieces commonly used commercially

This   Not this
Figure 25.1 To get the size of dishes, measure the overall diameter.

differ in certain instances from those used for home ware. Specification for items should indicate item name, size, weight, pattern, shape, and such other qualities that may identify choice as body color or rim style.

Dealers often select patterns they have found or believe will be popular and carry them in "open stock." Large quantity shipments of this ware usually yield a price advantage over patterns used exclusively by one establishment in a local area. The length of time that the ware will be carried in "open stock" will largely depend on continued popularity. Designation of size should be given by exact measurement in terms of overall diameter or weight of contents. Using the old method of measuring bowl of plates, inside the rim may lead to error. Slight measurement changes on reordering of dishes may interfere with use of leveling equipment and with satisfactory stacking.

Glass

In the past the use of glass was largely limited to bowls and beverage service. Today complete sets of dinnerware are available. The cost, use, and durability of it compare well with that of china. The designation of size and shape is made in a similar manner to china for both table and oven ware. The formula for certain items designed for cooking combines glass and plastic in such a manner as to develop outstanding toughness and resistance to rapid, extreme temperature changes. The glass used for glass cooking utensils contains metal and other compounds that give them resistance against heat, shock, and makes them better heat conductors. Glass utensils are easy to clean, are extremely resistant to corrosion, but are fragile.

The glass commonly used for water or beverage glasses and salad or dessert plates may be classified by composition as lead or lime glass and rock crystal, and by shaping as blown or pressed glass. Rock crystal, a potassium and lead silicate, is beautifully clear and shining. It is of top quality and price and is used only in a few food establishments. Lead glass, which is widely used, is less brittle than lime glass and may be shaped into desired form by blowing molten glass into a mold. Molten lime glass is deposited in a mold, pressed, polished and tempered.

Judgment of quality in glassware may be based on five points. (1) Good glassware has a lustrous appearance and clarity that give it a clean sparkling look free from cloudiness or discoloration. (2) The edges should be smooth and regular. (3) The shape should be well balanced and symmetrical. (4) Defects such as waviness, specks, and bubbles should be at a minimum. (5) Where pattern is used, it should show skillful cratsmanship.

Breakage and surface wear of glassware and cups are minimized by washing, handling, and storage in racks. Metal racks with plastisol covering of areas that come in contact with the dish are desirable.

Table 25.1 lists items in quantities commonly needed and the number of racks required for handling them.

Plastics

The development of plastics has brought many valuable qualities to ware used for small equipment and table service in institutions. Its use has yielded sanitary and heat proof handles for tools and utensils, plus light weight, attractive durable trays, buckets, bowls, garbage cans, and numerous other kitchen items. Its low heat conductivity makes it an effective insulator. This quality, on the other hand, means that it does not absorb enough heat to dry quickly when coming from the dishwasher. It tends to muffle sound and is therefore quiet to use. It does not break easily. It is frequently combined with other material, such as wood, metal, or textiles, to improve its strength. A tray having an excellent service record is composed of synthetic resin and tough wood fiber.

Melamine alpha-cellulose-filled tableware is made from plastic, paper pulp, and color pigments. It should be of the heavy-duty type and should comply with Commercial Standards CS173-50 as published by the Department of Commerce. Melamine ware is made by subjecting the raw plastic mixture to high pressure and temperatures. Decorations may now be implanted in the ware and such decorations should be an integral part of the ware and as durable as the undecorated portion. Plastic ware should be resistant to cracking at dry heat when placed in 170° F for 8 hrs and against corrosion from boiling sulfuric solutions.

Plastic trays and tableware from the various manufacturers vary in toughness of surface, imperviousness to absorption, buckling, and cracking. Examination of specific makes that have been in use for some time is recommended before making a selection. If this dinnerware is contem-

Table 25.1 Glasses, Cups and Racks Required for Washing and Storage [a] *

	Coffee Shop		Dining Room			Banquet Room			Cafeteria			Fountain	
Number of Seats	100	200	100	200	300	100	200	300	100	200	300	25/50	75/100
5 oz juice	144	252	144	252	350	144	256	360	108	216	329	72	144
36/rack	4	7	4	7	10	4	7	10	3	6	9	2	4
10 oz water	300	500	300	500	700	200	300	450	300	600	900	100	200
25/rack	12	20	12	20	28	8	12	18	12	24	36	4	8
12 oz iced tea	200	300	200	300	400	150	250	400	200	400	600	100	200
25/rack	8	12	8	12	16	6	10	16	8	16	24	4	8
7 oz beverage												108	216
36/rack												3	6
12 oz malted												75	150
25/rack												3	6
10 oz goblet	300	500	300	500	700	200	300	450					
25/rack	12	20	12	20	28	8	12	18					
5½ oz sherbet	150	250	150	250	350	150	250	350				75	150
25/rack	6	10	6	10	14	6	10	14				3	6
4½ oz fruit cocktail	150	250	150	250	350	150	250	350	100	200	300	75	150
25/rack	6	10	6	10	14	6	10	14	4	8	12	3	6
4½ oz parfait	144	252	144	252	360	144	252	360	108	216	324	72	144
36/rack	4	7	4	7	10	4	7	10	3	6	9	2	4
5½ oz champagne						150	250	350					
25/rack						6	10	14					
cups	300	500	300	500	700	160	280	400	300	600	900	100	200
20/rack	15	25	15	25	35	8	14	20	15	30	45	5	10

[a] Courtesy of Seco Company, St. Louis, Mo.
* Rack size is approximately 19¾ by 19¾ in.

plated, note how well the ware withstands cutting of food on the dish and friction characteristic of normal use. Minimum standards have been worked out by leading manufacturers and the United States Bureau of Standards for thickness, finish, and resistance to acid, boiling water, and dry heat.

The use of color in plastics offers opportunity for color coding that reduces *search* by workers for specific equipment. Handles of different color that identify size of scoops or dishes, for example, is a convenience. This is a feature that could be exploited more fully and with greater standardization by equipment manufacturers. An award winning drive-in identifies different carhop orders by using a separate colored tray for each carhop.

SELECTION OF TABLEWARE

The quantity of flatware and dishes required will depend upon:

1. The number of customers served.
2. Type service.
3. Menu items.
4. Length of serving period.

Figure 25.2 Plastic tote boxes should be light in weight, sturdy, and chosen to fit the transportation equipment.

5. Duration of peak serving period.

6. Speed of service or turnover.

7. Speed of wash and sanitizing and return to service.

8. Allowance for loss and breakage.

Some operations carry one and one-half times their seating capacity in flatware and dishes. Other operations find they must carry four or five times the seating capacity to have adequate supplies. This is especially true in fast service operations. One industrial cafeteria chain has found that carrying an inventory to satisfy the full needs for a meal period reduces breakage and replacement costs more than 25 percent. The inventory carried will depend upon the item. The ordinary operation would not carry two times its seating capacity in oyster forks, ice teaspoons, creamers, or relish trays. Again, it might find it advisable, if it catered to heavy coffee breaks, to carry four times the seating capacity in cups, saucers, and teaspoons. Each facility should base its inventory on the specific conditions of operation found in that establishment.

Many types of dishware are used in food services. Appearance is important. Design and color must be satisfying to the customers and blend with the design and decor of the facility and other table appointments. Durability and sanitation should receive consideration, along with weight and size. Heavy dishes make heavy loads for workers. Size is important in properly presenting food portions and in giving food an attractive appearance. Weight and size must be remembered in relation to dispensing equipment. Price may be a governing factor in purchasing.

SELECTION OF UTENSILS

Good pots and pans should be designed to suit their intended use. They should be heavy enough gage to be durable, yet light enough to be handled easily. Cooking utensils should be made of materials that conduct heat rapidly and give good heat distribution. Bottoms should be flat rather than round if used for cooking so that they conduct heat well from the heating surface. They should resist bending or denting. Covers should fit; spouts should have non-drip edges and pour well; and rims should be smoothly turned and finished. There should be no rough or sharp edges. Handles should be firmly attached, heat resisting, be fitted to the hand, and in such a position as to give good leverage in lifting. Extra strength should be given handles by riveting where necessary. They should be easy to clean, with no cracks or crevices. The material from which they are made should be of non-corrosive material.

Quantities and sizes required should be selected after analysis of requirements. Capacities of pots and pans are most usually stated in liquid quarts filled to the brim with a 5 percent plus or minus tolerance measured to the point of first overflow. Capacity of much coffee equipment is usually stated in terms of 5-oz cups.

Dish tote boxes should be water tight and made either of heavy plastic or 20-gauge metal bent over $5/16$ in. diameter brass wire at the top. All boxes should possess good grip handles or rims. They should be chip and warp proof and sufficiently sturdy to support probable loads. Reinforcing with a center metal band of $1\frac{1}{2}$ in., 12-gage metal gives added strength.

Knives are of such importance to a production worker that many cooks and chefs own their own. Even the lowly paring knife offers variety for selection, and one should be chosen that has (1) a good blade that will receive and hold a sharp edge, (2) a shape of blade that will be effective for intended use, and (3) a handle that is comfortable to hold and sanitary. Vegetable workers grip that handle tightly for long periods of time. The handle needs to be large enough so that hands will not become cramped. For the salad worker, the blade must be sharp and also stainless. A salad knife needs a sharp, slender, stainless blade long enough to cut through a head of lettuce or cabbage. A blade $7\frac{1}{2}$ to 8 in. is satisfactory, and the cutting edge should be straight, curving slightly toward the tip for slicing or making julienne strips.

The French knife has many uses in institution kitchens. It is especially good for dicing and chopping. It should be selected with (1) a good quality carbon steel blade that will receive and hold a sharp edge, (2) a weight and balance in the knife for easy handling, (3) proper length of blade for intended use, and (4) well made, sanitary handle. The volume and kind of materials to be cut will influence the weight and length of blade desirable. Sanitary, easy-to-clean construction is important for all knives.

The choice of modular pans appropriate for a variety of uses and that will fit special equipment in which they are to be used in recommended. It adds greatly to convenience to have the 12 × 20 in. serving pan fit not only the serving table but also a mobile rack, steam table and oven compartment, and the storage area. The choice of major equipment should be tied in with this plan in order for it to be fully effective.

CHECK LIST OF SMALL EQUIPMENT

Items of small equipment for consideration when preparing lists for initial estimates include the following:

For the delivery and storage area

Box opener
Box cutter
Crowbar
Hammer
Pliers
Screw driver

Scales
Scoops, grocer type, aluminum
Spindle or clip board
Storage containers, such as cans or bins
Step ladder

Vegetable preparation area

Boards for cutting 15 × 20 × 1¾ in., maple
Bowls, mixing
Colander
Cutter and grater (may be machine attachments)
Knife, French 10 or 12 in. blade
Knives, paring

Knives, utility, 6 in. blade
Hand parer with swivel-action blade
Potato ball cutter
Potato eyer knife
Pots, stock, aluminum, 15 qt, shallow
Mobile storage units with removable pans or lugs
Vegetable brushes

Meat preparation

Brush, steel, block
Cleaver, 7 or 8 in. blade
Knives, boning, light
Knife, French, 10 or 12 in. blade
Knife, slicing
Knife, steak or butcher

Pans, s/s, 12 × 20 × 1 in., 2 or 2½ in.
Saw, butchers, 24 in.
Sharpener, knife, electric
Steel, butchers, 12–14 in.
Trays or baking sheets for portion-ready meat

Cooking Section

Board, cutting, 12 × 20 × 1¾ in.
Boiler, double aluminum
Bowls, mixing, s/s, 1½ qt, 3 qt, 5 qt, 8 qt, 13 qt
Cannister set
Casseroles, individual 5, 6, or 8 oz
Colander, large aluminum or s/s
Counter pans, s/s to fit No. 200
Cutter, biscuit, 2 or 2½ in.
Dredges, aluminum

Fork, cooks, 12 and 20 in.
Knife, carving
Knife, French, 10 and 12 in. blade
Knives, paring
Knife, slicing
Knife, utility, 6 in.
Ladles, s/s, 2, 4, and 8 oz
Measures, aluminum with pouring lip, cup, pt, qt, and gal
Paddles for stirring in stock kettles (24, 36, 48 in.)

Cooking Section

Pans, bake, aluminum, 12 × 20 × 4 in.

Pans, roasting, 16 × 20 × 5 in. with lugs

Pans, dish, aluminum, 14 qt or 20 qt

Pans, frying, cast iron or aluminum approx. (8, 10 and 12 × 2 in.)

Pans, sauce, aluminum or s/s, in 1 qt, 2 qt, 6 qt, and 8 qt

Pot, stock, aluminum or retinned steel or s/s

Scales, utility

Scoops, s/s, Nos. 12, 16, 20

Skimmer, s/s 5 in.

Spatulas, 6, 8, 10 in blade

Spatula, offset

Spoons, measuring, s/s or aluminum

Spoons, serving, s/s perforated or slotted

Spoons, serving, s/s, solid

Stool

Steamer baskets, tall, narrow, or wide; solid or perforated

Strainers, Chinese, s/s

Thermometer, meat

Trucks, kitchen, 3 deck

Turner, utility, s/s

Whip, wire, 8, 12, 16, 24, 36 in., sanitary handle

Bakery Section

Beaters, egg rotary

Bowl, mixing, s/s, 12 qt, 25 qt, and mobile stand

Brushes, pastry

Corer, apple

Cups, custard, 4 or 5 oz

Cutters, biscuit, 2 or 2½ in.

Cutters, cookie, assorted

Divider, dough (chopping knife)

Knife, French, 10 or 12 in. blade

Knife, paring

Knife, utility, 6 in. blade

Measures, aluminum, pouring lip, cup, pt, qt, and gallon

Muffin pans, aluminum or retinned steel, 2¼ in. diameter

Pans, aluminum or retinned steel 18 × 26 × 1 in., 12 × 20 × 2½ in., 12 × 20 × 1 in., 8 × 8 × 2 in., 10 × 4 × 4 in.

Pans, pie, aluminum or retinned steel, 9 in. diameter × 1¼ in.

Pans, tube, aluminum, 3½ in.

Pastry bags

Pastry tips, set

Peel, if needed

Rolling pin, revolving handles, 15 in. × 3½ in. diameter

Scales

Scoops, grocer, aluminum, 1 lb

Scoops, ice cream, s/s with plastic handle, Nos. 20, 30, and 40

Scraper, dough

Scraper, rubber, large

Sieve, flour, aluminum, 14 in diameter

Spatulas, s/s, 6 and 10 in.

Spoons, measuring, s/s or aluminum

Spoons, serving, solid, s/s

Spoons, mixing, wooden

Stools, kitchen

Whips, wire with sanitary handle, 8, 12, 16, 24 in.

Spice cans

Salad and Sandwich Preparation

Board, cutting, 15 × 20 × 1¾ in.
Can opener, heavy duty table model
Colander, large, s/s or aluminum
Cutter, melon ball
Egg slicer
Knife, chopping, 2 curved blades
Bowl, hard wood, 15 or 17 in.
Knife, French, 12 in. blade
Knife, salad or utility type, 6 or 7 in. blade
Knife, paring
Ladle, 8 oz
Measures, aluminum with pouring lip, cup, pt, qt, and gal

Molds, individual, aluminum
Pans, dish, s/s, 14 qt
Pans, steam table or pudding
Pans, round bottom mixing, s/s, 15 in. diameter
Scoops, Nos. 12, 16, 20 and 30
Spoons, measuring, s/s or aluminum
Spoons, serving, perforated, s/s
Spoons, serving, solid, s/s
Spatulas, wide blade, s/s, 6 and 10 in.
Spatula, sandwich spreader
Tongs, s/s, 6 and 8 in.
Trays

Serving Section

Board, menu
Board, cutting, 13 × 16 × 1½ in.
Bottle opener
Can opener, table or wall type
Container, butter
Container, eggs
Cooker, egg, electric
Clock, electric
Cream dispenser
Fork, serving, s/s, 2-tine, 12 in.
Knife, salad or utility
Ladles, s/s, 2, 6, or 8 oz
Counter pans, s/s
Pitchers, 3¾ or 4 qt, s/s
Scoops or dishers, Nos. 12, 16, 20, 30
Pie server, offset, s/s
Spoons, serving, perforated, s/s 13 in.
Paper napkin dispenser
Silver dispenser

Bus boxes
Bus carts
Dish storage carts
Spoons, serving, solid, s/s, 13 in.
Trays, plastic 14 × 18 in.
Turner, utility, s/s
Tongs, Pom, 6 and 9 in.
Drip-cut servers, 16 oz, 32 oz
Dish racks for storage and dollies
Ash trays, glass
Dishes
Glassware
Coffee decanters
Utility forks
Utility knives
Dessert spoons
Teaspoons
Bouillon spoons
Sugar dispensers
Salt and pepper shakers

Housekeeping Section

Broom, corn
Brushes, assorted clean-up
Brush, floor
Cans, garbage and trash with dollies
Dish racks
Containers for detergents, s/s
Mops, dry
Mops, wet
Mop truck or pails on dolly
Pan, dust
Scraper, plate, rubber

Wastebasket
Aprons, Indian head, twill or duck
  bib and butchers
Uniforms
Hot pads
Kitchen towels
Counter towels
Table cloths
Table pads
Waiters coats

Office Section

Cash box
Chair, posture type
Book case
Calculator
Files, recipe, inventory, letter
Filing cabinets

Typewriter
Lamps
Wastebaskets
Phone
Typewriter table or desk

Table 25.2 Suggested Inventory of Flatware and Dishes, in Dozens

Dining Room Capacity	50	100	200
Plates, dinner	8	12	24
Plates, salad, dessert, and liner	12	24	45
Plates, bread and butter	8	12	24
Bouillon cups	5	10	18
Grapefruit or oatmeal nappies	5	8	12
Cups	9	20	35
Saucers	8	16	32
Fruits	7	12	24
Utility knives	6	12	20
Utility forks	8	16	30
Teaspoons	10	20	40
Dessert spoons	3	5	10
Bouillon spoons	3	8	12

Suggested Student Assignments

1. Prepare a list of utensils for a specified food operation with sufficient specifications for purchase.

2. Obtain prices for the equipment.

3. List tableware required for the food operation in quantities required for an initial purchase in relation to the anticipated number to be served.

4. Indicate the type and amount of storage space required for the quantity of tableware listed.

5. Visit tableware showrooms and compare prices of different patterns. On what are the price differences based?

appendix

ABBREVIATIONS

AC   alternating current
AGA   American Gas Company
AH   absolute humidity
AHA   Americal Hospital Association
ASHRAE   American Society of Heating, Refrigerating, and Air Conditioning Engineers
AWG   American Wire Gauge
amp   ampere or I
Bhp   boiler horsepower
Btu   British thermal unit
Btuh   British thermal units per hour
c   cycle
cfh   cubic feet per hour
cfm   cubic feet per minute
cm   centimeter
cp   candlepower
CU   coefficient of utilization
cu ft   cubic foot of feet
°C   degree Celsius
D²   square of distance
db   decibel
DC   direct current
dia   diameter
fc   foot candles
fpm   feet per minute
fL   foot Lambert
FM   frequency modulation
ft   foot or feet
°F   degree Fahrenheit
g   gram
gal   gallon
gpm   gallons per minute
hp   horsepower
hr   hour
HTM   heat transfer value
Hz   Hertz (sound vibration)
I   ampere
ID   inside dimension
IES   Illuminating Engineering Society

in.   inch
IPS   inside pipe size
°K   degree Kelvin
kg   kilogram
kl   kiloliter
kw   kilowatt
kwh   killowatt hour
l   liter
lb   pound
lm   lumin
m   meter
m²   square meter
m³   cubic meter
MCM   thousand circular Mils (wire)
MF   maintenance factor
ml   milliliter
min   minute
mm   millimeter
MRH   mixing ratio humidity
nm   nanometer (light waves)
NSF   National Science Foundation
oz   ounce
ppm   parts per million
psi   pressure per square inch
qt   quart
R   resistance (electricity)
RH   relative humidity
sec   second
SH   specific humidity
sq cm   square centimeter
sq ft   square foot or feet
TV   television
UL   Underwriters Laboratory
USPH   U. S. Public Health
v   volt
vol   volume
w   watt
wh   watt hour
wt   weight
yd   yard

FEASIBILITY STUDY

FEASIBILITY STUDY

1. Country and State
   a. Economics
   b. Trends
   c. Travel
   d. National promotional agencies

2. Community
   a. Economics
   b. Trend of population
   c. Transient traffic statistics
   d. Transportation facilities
   e. Local attractions
   f. Civic promotional agencies
   g. Zoning and building regulations
   h. Real estate tax races and assessment bases
   i. Alcoholic beverage and other monopolies
   j. Social usage of hotels
   k. Availability of materials and supplies (operating)
   l. Labor
      (1) Supply
         (a) Supervisory
         (b) Technical
         (c) Common
      (2) Wage trends
      (3) Labor legislation in effect and pending
   m. Earthquake history of area and other disaster hazard

3. Local Hotel, Club and Restaurant Factors
   a. Existing facilities
      (1) Names and locations
      (2) Capacities
      (3) Present demand for their services and facilities

   (4) Prevailing room rates and food rates
   (5) Hotel associations
   (6) Hotel trade schools
   (7) Development of regional resort areas
   b. Future competition
      (1) Contemplated plans for hotels, clubs
      (2) Contemplated plans for enlargement of present facilities
      (3) Current competitive economics

LOCAL EQUITY GROUP

1. Identity
2. Responsibility
3. Associations and Connections
4. Experience in Hotels
5. Availability of Bank Guarantee or Government Guarantee

PHYSICAL ASPECTS

1. Site
   a. Advantages
      (1) Size and shape of lot
      (2) Location in relation to business, amusement and social life of city
      (3) Accessibility: public carrier availability
      (4) Traffic and circulation habits of local inhabitants in that area
      (5) Character of neighbourhood
      (6) Physical contours of site

PHYSICAL ASPECTS (Cont.)

    (7) Ground characteristics which have direct bearing on cost of building foundation and on building maintenance (necessity for pump, etc.)

    (8) Shop rental possibilities

    (9) Direction of expansion of city

    (10) Parking facilities

    (11) Zoning

    (12) Building restrictions

    (13) Information on disturbing noises from nearby installations such as railroads, airports, factories, churchbells, street traffic etc.

    (14) Include map of city showing location of proposed hotel, RR station, American Embassy, churches, airport, beaches, bus stations, other hotels, business center, etc. (Map published by City Planning Commission or similar group)

    (15) Photographs of competitive hotels.

    (16) Aerial photograph of site and/or adjacent areas

b. Disadvantages

    (1) Related to items (1) to (12) of a above.

    (2) Other

c. Alternates

    (1) Location

    (2) Advantages-see a (1) to

    (3) Disadvantages-see b (1) to (2)

    (4) Other

2. Building

a. Type

    (1) Transient, semi-residential, resort

    (2) Materials

        (a) Kind

        (b) Availability

        (c) Building to be earthquake proof and fireproof

    (3) Style: Colonial, contemporary, etc.

    (4) Heat, ventilation & air conditioning

        (a) Climate, seasons-extremes and average temperatures and humidities

        (b) Local demands and habits

        (c) Extent of air-conditioning and ventilation of rooms, public spaces, work spaces, including barber and beauty shops, etc.

        (d) Extent of heat insulation

b. Size

    (1) Number of rooms by types and size

    (2) Height of building

    (3) Number of stores and concessions

    (4) Number, type and size of public rooms

        (a) Restaurants

        (b) Ballroom and private dining rooms

        (c) Bars and cocktail lounges

        (d) Lobby and similar space

    (5) Ratio of public room to guest room space

PHYSICAL ASPECTS (Cont.)

  (6) Other facilities
    (a) Grounds-tennis
      courts, golf course,
      etc.
    (b) Garage
    (c) Swimming pool
    (d) Turkish baths
    (e) Health features in
      connection with
      climate, mineral
      springs, etc.
    (f) Barber shop
    (g) Beauty parlor
 c. Hotel services and facilities
  requirements
  (1) Laundry
    (a) Guest laundry
    (b) House laundry
  (2) Valet
  (3) Dry cleaning
  (4) Electrician's shop
  (5) Carpenter's shop
  (6) Upholstery shop
  (7) Paint shop
    (a) Legal or insurance
      restrictions
  (8) Radio
  (5) Circulating iced water
  (10) Bakery
  (11) Plumber's shop
  (12) Mechanics shop
  (13) Silverware cleaning and
    polishing
  (14) Locksmith
 d. Utilities and sanitation
  (1) Power
    (a) Availability
    (b) Rates
    (c) Type current-power-
      light
  (2) Water
    (a) Availability

    (b) Rates
    (c) Potability and suit-
      ability for laundry
      boilers (treatment
      necessary?)
    (d) Permit and taxes on
      artesian wells
    (e) Pressure and tem-
      perature extremes
 (3) Heat
    (a) Type: steam, hot wa-
      ter, radiant, air,
      etc.
    (b) Fuel-its availability
      and cost
    (c) Process steam for kit-
      chens, laundry, etc.
    (d) Fuel for kitchens &
      bakery
 (4) Telephones
    (a) Availability
    (b) Rates
    (c) Bi-lingual operators
      on city exchange?
      hotel exchange?
    (d) Other communica-
      tion or signal sys-
      tems, such as pneu-
      matic tubes, telau-
      tographs, hall sig-
      nals for maids, etc.
 (5) Sanitation
    (a) Code
    (b) Prevailing standards
      and requirements
    (c) Existing and planned
      waste disposal
      methods
    (d) Refrigeration
    (a) Types for food
    (b) Types for garbage
    (c) Ice cream manufact-
      urer storage
 (7) Fire alarms, fighting equipment & escapes

PHYSICAL ASPECTS (Cont.)

   e. Estimated construction time
      (schedule)
     (1) Demolition
     (2) Foundation
     (3) Building
     (4) Equipping
3. Furniture & Furnishings (by classes)
   a. Availability
4. Accoustical Treatment of Public
    Rooms and Guest Rooms

FINANCIAL ASPECTS

1. Estimate of Capital Required
   a. Land
   b. Building
   c. Furniture and furnishings
   d. Working capital and other (incl.
      organisation, financing and
      pre-opening expenses)
2. Operational Estimates
   a. Estimate of capacity utilisation
   b. Estimate of percentage of per-
      manent guests
   c. Proposed average room rate by
      seasons
     (1) Proposed allowances and
        discounts, if any
   d. Food and beverages
     (1) Costs
     (2) Proposed sales prices
     (3) Estimated volume of sales
   e. Estimated net income from
      sources other than rooms and
      food and beverages
     (1) Cigarstand
     (2) Newsstand
     (3) Candy and soda shop
     (4) Telephone
     (5) Valet
     (6) Check rooms and wash-
        rooms
     (7) Porters

     (8) Barber shop
     (9) Beauty parlor
   (10) Baths
   (11) Florist
   (12) Guests' Laundry
   (13) Store rentals
   (14) Other (detail)
   f. Salary and wage rates
   g. Pre-opening and other organi-
      sational expenses
   h. Real estate taxes
   i. Income taxes
   j. Management fees
3. Proposal for Financing
   a. Estimated amount of equity
      capital required
   b. Estimated amount of Export-
      Import bank loan required
   c. Estimated time schedule for
      capital outlay
   d. Estimated money to be spent in
      the United States
   e. Estimated money to be spent
      in other countries

MARKET ANALYSIS

1. Determination of visitors by cate-
    gories
   a. Tourists
   b. Vacationers
   c. Business travellers
2. Sources for gaining such information.

MISCELLANEOUS

1. Import Duties
2. Excise Taxes
3. Labor Laws
4. Trade Agreements and Treaties
5. Government Regulations and Ex-
    emptions Affecting Hotel Impor-
    tations, etc.

CONCLUSIONS

1. Opinions and Recommendations

INSTRUCTIONS TO BIDDERS

Proposals, to be entitled to consideration, must be made in accordance with the following general instructions:

1. Examination of Site and Documents

    Before submitting a proposal, the bidder shall:
    (a) carefully examine the drawings and specifications,
    (b) fully inform himself of existing conditions and limitations,
    (c) include in his bid sums sufficent to cover all items required by contract, and shall rely entirely upon his own examinations in making his proposal.

2. Interpretations

    Should a bidder find discrepancies in, or omissions from, the drawings or specifications, or be in doubt as to their meaning, he should at once notify _____ hereinafter referred to as _____, who will send written instructions or addenda to all bidders. _____ will not be responsbile for oral interpretations. Questions received less than 48 hour before bids close cannot be answered. All addenda issued during the time of bidding will be incorporated into contract. Address all communications to _____

    _____.

3. Form of Bid

    The proposal shall not contain any recapitulation of the work to be done. Numbers shall be stated both in writing and in figures.
    The completed proposal shall be without interlineation, alteration or erasure.
    Bidder shall present bid by item. Bidder may also give a total bid for all items or for any group if the total price is less than the sum of item bids. If a bid for a group or all items is given it should be clearly indicated what items are included in such a bid. No bidder may bid on a part of an item. _____ reserves the right to accept or reject any item, group or total bid.

4. Alternates

    Alternate bids, other than those called for in the specifications and listed in the bid form will not be considered.

5. Signature

    Each bid must be signed in longhand by the bidder with his usual signature. Bids by partnerships must be signed with the partnership name by one of the partners, followed by the signature and designation of the partner signing; bids by corporation, followed by the name of the state of incorporation and by the signature of the president, secretary or other

person authorized to bind it in the matter. The name of each person sign-
ing shall be typed or printed below the signature.

6. Bid Guarantee

As a guarantee that if awaraded the contract the bidder will execute same
and furnish bond required by the specifications, each bid shall be accompanied by:
(a) a certified check, or
(b) a bank cashier's check
made in the name of _____.

7. Modifications

No oral, telephone, or telegraphic bids or modifications will be considered.

8. Disposition of Bid Guarantees

The successful bidder's check will be retained until he has entered into contract and furnished the required bond. The owner reserves the right to hold
the bid guarantees of the two next lowest or preferred bidders until he has
done so, or for a period of thirty (30) days, whichever is the shorter time.
Checks of all other bidders will be returned as soon as practicable after bids
are opened. Should a bidder fail to enter into contract and furnish bond
within ten days after his proposal has been accepted, his bid guarantee shall
be forfeited to the owner as liquidated damages, not as a penalty.

9. Evidence of Qualification

Upon request of the owner, a bidder whose proposal is under consideration
for the award of the contract shall submit promptly satisafctory evidence
of his financial resources, his experience, and the organization and equipment he has available for the performance of the contract.

10. Withdrawal of Bids

Any bidder may withdraw his bid, either personally or by written request,
at any time prior to the time set for the bid opening. No bid may be with-
drawn or modified after the time set for the opening thereof, unless and
until the award of the contract is delayed for a period exceeding thirty
(30) days.

11. Division of Responsibility

Attention of bidders is called to parts 1–09 and 1–10 of the specifications,
for kitchen fixtures and equipment, Section I, General.

12. General Provisions

*Provisions of the General Condition for the Construction of Buildings, 6th
ed. AIA Form A2 revised 9-1-51 (hereinafter called General Conditions)*

shall apply to this contract, except that articles 28 and 31 shall be omitted. The word architect in these general conditions shall be interpreted to mean the _____.

SPECIAL PROVISIONS

1. General Statement

   The following paragraphs refer especially to this particular project. They are a part of the standard *General Instructions* immediately preceding, and shall supersede same whenever they are in conflict.

2. Number of Specified Items Required

   Whenever, in these specifictions an article, device or piece of equipment is referred to in the regular number, such reference shall apply to any such articles as are shown on drawings or required to complete the installation.

3. Abbeviations

   The work "approved," as used herein, means "approved by _____" and "for approval" means "approval of the _____ at _____."
   "ASTM Specifications" means Standard Specifications for the American Society for Testing Materials, 1916 Race Street, Philadelphia 3, Pennsylvania.
   "Selected" means "selected by _____."
   Where the words "or equal" are used, _____ is the sole judge of the quality and suitability of the proposed substitutions.

4. Approval of Substitutions

   Requests for approval of a different material or articles other than that specified shall be accompanied by samples, record of performance, certified copies of tests by impartial and recognized laboratories, and such additional information as _____ may reasonably request. Such samples and data shall be furnished sufficiently in advance to allow time for investigation before a decision must be made. When _____ approves a substitution, it is with the understanding that the contractor guarantees the substituted article to be equal or better than the one specified.
   If the supplier or bidder submits a proposal on items that are not in exact accordance with the specification—such alternate bid must include the manufacturer's name and model number of the particular item submitted. In addition to this, all such bids are to be fully explained, supported by, and accompanied with complete detailed information drawings and descriptive literature that may be applicable, and provided further that such explanatory information, drawings, and literature shall set forth and fully describe in every respect and detail, any proposed deviations or departures from the applicable manufacturer's specifications or numbers noted herein. All

equipment furnished as equal to the items specified must be equal in quality, finish, operating features, etc., to the items specified and approved by owner.

5. Sub-Contracts

Divisions in these specifications conform roughly to customary trade practice. They are used for convenience only. _____ is not bound to define the limits of any sub-contract.

6. Checking of Drawings

Contractors shall carefully study and compare all drawings, specifications, etc., furnished to them by _____ and shall check dimensions, materials and methods of construction, bringing into play the skill and experience for which they are compensated under this contract. They shall report to _____ for rectification of any errors, inconsistencies or omissions they may thus discover, and shall do no work in connection therewith until directed by _____ as to how to proceed. Contractors may inspect building at_____ .

7. Prior Use of Occupancy

The owner reserves the right to use or occupy the building or any portion thereof, or to use equipment installed under the contract, prior to final acceptance. Such use or occupancy shall not constitute acceptance of the work or any part thereof.

8. Fire Insurance

The owner assumes no risk for loss by fire to any portion of the building or equipment thereof, whether completed, in process of construction or installation, or stored on the premises, during the life of any contract for any portion of the construction. The making of partial payments to the contractors shall not be construed as creating an insurable interest by or for the owner, or as relieving the various contractors of their sureties of responsibility for loss by fire or other casualty occurring prior to final acceptance of the building. This paragraph supersedes Article 29 or the *General Conditions.*

9. Payment for Drawings and Specifications

For construction purposes, two sets of drawings and specifications covering his own work and one set each of other prime contractor's work will be furnished to the contractor without charge. Additional copies will be furnished by _____ upon payment to him of the cost of reproduction. This paragraph supersedes Article 4 of the *General Conditions, AIA 2, revised* 9-1-51.

10. Delivery must be made 60 days after date of letting contract.

11. Limit of Operations

Construction operations and parking of cars shall be confined to areas designated by owner. Routing of trucks shall be as directed. This paragraph amplifies Article 42 of the *General Conditions. AIA Form 2*, revised 9-1-51.

12. Bond

Secure and pay for surety bond issued by State-Licensed Bonding Company, in form bound herewith, in the following penal sums:

Performance clause . . . . 100% of Contract Sum.
Payment clause . . . . 100% of Contract Sum.
Maintenance clause . . . . 100% of Contract Sum.

13. Test Samples

Furnish samples of materials for testing if and when requested.

14. Itemized Schedule of Costs

Successful bidder shall prepare a complete detailed breakdown of costs. Sum of all items shall be equal to contract price. This shall be furnished to _____ within 15 days of notification of award. Minor additions or deductions will be based upon this breakdown. Example of such a breakdown required would be on standard equipment and fabrication required for fabrication and installation of service counter.

15. Shop Drawings

Supplementing Article 5 of the *General Conditions, AIA Form 2*, revised 9-1-51, the words "such other copies as may be needed" at the end of the second sentence shall mean "three other copies" making a total of five corrected copies required, two of which will be returned to the contractor.

16. Equipment Lists

Successful bidder shall prepare complete lists of all equipment to be installed, giving maker's name and catalogue numbers and obtain the approval of _____ before ordering. See also paragraphs 3 and 4 of Special Provisions regarding substitutions, (4) *Approval of Substitutions*.

17. Time for Completion

The work under this contract shall be commenced on a date to be specified in a written order to the contractor to proceed, and shall be delivered within 75 consecutive calendar days from and after said date stated in the contractor's bid for the work, or as hereinafter to be agreed upon: the agreement to govern in case of discrepancy.

18. Liquidated Damages

For each calendar day after the date above fixed for completion that the work remains uncompleted, the contractor shall pay the owner the sum of $50.00 as fixed, agreed, liquidated damages, and this sum is not to be construed as in any sense a penalty. Should an extension of time be granted to the contractor, he shall indemnify and save the owner harmless from any other contractor caused by such extension.

19. Use of Premises

The owner will provide adequate space for uncrating and assembling equipment within the building. This contractor shall confine his materials to spaces allotted and shall not unreasonably encumber the building premises.

20. Progress Schedule

Prepare, on form satisfactory to _____, a construction progress schedule. Show proposed dates of submission of shop drawings, resubmission of shop drawings, fabrication period, shipping period, installaton period. This shall be furnished to _____ within 15 days of award of contract.

21. Work Not Included in This Contract

The following work will be performed under separate contracts operating concurrently with the work of this contract, and is not included in this contract:
    (a) Plumbing, heating and ventilating
    (b) Electrical work
    (c) General construction work
    (d) Furnishing
    (e) Casework

22. Damage

If the owner should suffer damage in any manner because of any wrongful act or neglect of the contractor or of anyone employed by him, he shall be reimbursed for such damage.

Claims under this clause shall be made in writing within a reasonable time at the first observance of such damage, except as expressly stipulated otherwise in the case of faulty work or materials, and shall be adjusted by agreement or arbitration.

23. Signs

No signs shall be placed on the property.

24. Available Materials

_____ has attempted to avoid use of unavailable materials; it will therefore consider that the contract sum is based on furnishing all materials exactly as specified. Should it develop that any material specified is unobtainable and a substitution necessary, an equitable adjustment of the contract sum will be made.

25. Overhead and Profit on Changes

The value of extra work authorized pursuant to Article 15 of *General Conditions* shall be the actual cost of the additional direct labor, materials and subcontract work involved, plus an allowance for overhead and profit as follows:

1. When the total cost of an authorized extra, including overhead and profit, is less than $500.00 the allowance for overhead and profit shall not exceed 25% of the actual cost.
2. When the total cost of an authorized extra, including overhead and profit, exceeds $500.00, the allowance for overhead and profit shall not exceed 20% of the actual cost.
3. When an authorized extra excludes the furnishing and delivery only of an equipment item costing the contractor more than $300.00, the additional allowance to the contractor for purchasing and handling such an item shall not exceed 10% of his purchase price.

26. Guaranty

All equipment covered by this specification and accompanying drawings shall be guaranteed, for purposes intended, in writing, for one year from date of final acceptance. Any defect in material or workmanship shall be promptly rectified by this contractor without cost to the owner during this period.

27. Instructions for Use of Equipment

This contractor shall furnish complete printed instructions for the proper use of all equipment furnished under this contract and in addition he shall furnish a duly qualified instructor for a period of one week, to instruct persons designated by the owner, in the proper operation of all equipment furnished.

28. Architectural Supervision

Architectural supervision of this kitchen contract for equipment shall be performed by ————————.

SPECIFICATIONS FOR KITCHEN FIXTURES AND EQUIPMENT

Section I—General

1-01 Scope of Work

The contractor shall furnish all fixtures and equipment as listed in the acceptance of bid according to specifications and as shown on the drawings. Shipment shall be to ———— Address. Delivery must be made within 60 days of letting of the contract.

1-02 Work by Others

A. The mechanical contractor of the _____

_____ will provide all waste, vent, gas, steam and condensate return services. Piping by mechanical contractor will be complete to floor level or above so that connection can be conveniently made by equipment contractor. All plumbing lines and fittings shall be stainless steel, chrome or nickel covered from floor connection to equipment. No lead or iron pipe fittings shall be visible unless authorized by _____.

B. The electrical contractor will furnish necessary wiring, conduit connections to floor level or slightly above so that convenient connection can be made to all kitchen equipment or fixtures.

1-03 Samples Required

Where applicable the successful bidder shall deliver and set up at the place designated by _____ samples of the following:

A sectional portion of a stainless steel sink and drain board with splash back showing all pertinent construction features such as:

Welding

Forming

Finishes—exposed and unexposed

The sample is to be typical of the type of work the bidder intends to use for all stainless steel construction.

The successful bidder shall furnish samples as requested by _____.

Samples will be retained until acceptance of his work.

1-04 Inspection

Equipment will be inspected by the _____.

Any equipment or fixtures not in accordance wtih specifications and drawings shall be promptly replaced at no cost to the owner.

1-05 Materials

A. Stainless Steel:

1. All sheets to be commercial 18-8 stainless steel, U.S. Standard gauges as noted herein or called for on drawings.

2. Unexposed reinforcing is to be 12 gauge galvanized iron or heavier with 1 coat zinc chromate painted over with 2 coats silver-tone or aluminum lacquer. Reinforcing and lateral bracing on tops and drains easily visible shall be 12 gauge 18-8 stainless steel and approximately 3″ wide. This is to be integrally welded to tops and drains with evidence of weld removed.

3. Finishes: #2B on shelving or where concealed. Elsewhere, #4.

4. Sheets to be stretcher leveled, non-magnetic, free of buckles, warps, scratches and other surface imperfections.

B. Galvanized Steel: To be copper bearing steel, "Armco," "Toncan," or equal, U.S. Standard gauges as called for, sheets free from buckles, warps, scratches and other imperfections. All galvanized steel parts to be finished with two (2) coats of silver-tone lacquer.

C. Plywood: Douglas Fir, Waterproof Grade.

D. Hardwood Top: Kiln dried northern hard maple. Selected edge grain.

E. Formica: To be bonded to ¾" waterproof plywood with proper waterproof adhesive and under even and proper pressure in a press. Panels as manufactured by the Colotyle Corp., or equal.

1-06 Workmanship

A. All jointing and connections to adjacent surfaces shall be done in such a manner as to render all parts easily cleaned, dust and vermin tight, and to present a neat finished appearance. Splash backs and other surfaces adjoining walls shall be *tightly* fastened to wall. Fastening shall be by stainless steel screws, flathead counter sunk to be flush with surface. Screws to be 6" o.c. around edges of equipment. General contractor shall furnish at proper location within wall strongly wooden backing for the attachment of these screws. Gaps ⅛" or smaller at bases and walls are to be sealed with caulking, A. C. Horn Co.'s "Vulcatex" or approved equal. Fixtures shall be solidly braced and reinforced where necessary.

B. Welds to be Heli-arc type and shall be homogenous with parts welded, free from imperfections of any kind. Welding rods used are to be of same material as parts welded, and filler pieces of filling with solder will not be acceptable. Excess metal shall be ground off and joints finished smooth to match adjoining surfaces. Field joists will not be accepted except as noted. All equipment is to be all-welded seamless construction with all joints, crevices etc., eliminated and all traces of welding removed.

C. Brake folds shall be free of textured appearance or other imperfections.

D. Sheared edges shall be free of burs, slivers, etc., and shall be smooth to touch.

1-07 Standard Materials and Construction: Shall be as listed below unless otherwise noted.

A. Stainless Steel Drains, Table, and Counter Tops: Shall be of the gauge specified except where noted, with edges 180° to ¾" outside radius, and corners bull nosed to same radius, mitred, welded and ground smooth. Backs shall be made integral and of same gauge metal as tops, with intersections rolled to ¾" radius. Where insets are to be made into countertops, and are not to be welded, the seal shall be made with latex gaskets. All tops, drains, or table tops where specified shall be reinforced or braced with 12 gauge black iron with zinc chromated painted with aluminum 8" × 2" channel welded to underside. Channels shall run full length of center right angle to braces running from front to back. 1" OD stainless steel tubing shall be welded to channels on approximately 4' centers. Such reinforcing or bracing is to be provided wherever in specifications substantial support is specified for extra heavy loads such equipment shall bear.

B. Stainless Steel Sinks: Sinks shall be gauge specified with edges rolled 180° to ¾" radius. Backs and drainboards are to be made integral and of the same metal, with all intersections rolled to ¾" radius. Drains are to be Blickman LHO-50-C or approved equal. Supply fixtures to be American Standard San. B900 swing spout faucet or approved equal, except where noted otherwise. Each sink compartment to be provided with overflow consisting of 1¼" whitened brass piping leading from overflow aperture at rear of compartment in bronze fittings. Aperture shall be covered with stainless steel strainer.

C. Legs: To be 1¼" OD stainless steel tubing, No. 12 gauge. At top they are to be threaded into white metal flanges and braced where shown with 16 gauge stainless steel gussets which are welded to fixture. At bottom, legs are to be fitted to adjustable white sanitary feet. Legs are not to be threaded. Legs are to be seamless.

D. Bodies: Bodies shall be made of 20 gauge stainless steel #4 finish unless otherwise stated. Bodies shall be formed in angles at top not less than 1½" wide. Bottom shall be formed into channel not less than 4" wide and wider to suit base overhand and 1¼ turned up web. All bodies unless otherwise stated shall be supported on base provided by others. All pilasters, center and ends, shall be turned 1½" with ¾" web; shelves and bottom shall butt turned in edge to form uniform construction. Bodies shall have channel supports of 14 gauge black iron approximately 3" wide as required, primed and painted with zinc chromate painted with 2 coats of aluminum. Where bodies are specified to be made with formica, bracing shall be adequate to bear weights to which equipment will be subjected. No rough edges must show. Workmanship must be top grade.

E. Pipe Braces: Where shown use 1" OD seamless stainless steel tubing, 14 gauge.

F. Pipe Shelves: Shall be 1" OD seamless stainless steel tubing, 14 gauge spaced not over 4" outside center. Entire pipe understructure shall be seamlessly welded, ground smooth, and polished.

G. Intermediate Shelves: 18 gauge stainless steel or galvanized steel or formica as noted. Where marked adjustable, use stainless steel adjustable clip brackets and slotted holes ½" outside center through divider panels. All shelves shall butt turned in edge of body.

H. Sliding Doors: 18 gauge stainless steel front face, 20 gauge galvanized steel back face, filled with approved sound deadening material or, where specified, with insulating material or formica as stated. Doors are to be removable for cleaning. Hardware is to be as follows:

1. Track: Overhead type formed in body; provide stop to keep doors closed.
2. Door sheaves: Ball bearing 1¼ diameter, case hardened wheel. Sheaves to be dipped in hard oil and track to be filled with same.
3. Bottom guides: Brass roller pins at center of door (neoprene or nylon acceptable), fitting into groove at bottom of door, except where detailed differently. Groove to be open to permit dirt to drop through.
4. Rubber bumpers: as specified.
5. Handles: Die-pressed stainless steel recesses in door face, Blickman type or equal.

I. Hinged Doors: Door construction to be same as sliding doors above. Hardware is to be as follows:
   1. Hinges—stainless steel continuous piano hinges ¾" leaf.
   2. Catches—heavy duty "Snuggler."
   3. Locks—Corbin #0666. Polished chrome finish.
   4. Pulls—white metal of approved design.

J. Exposed Panels: Including access panels—16 gauge stainless steel or formica.

K. Backs and Dividers: 18 gage stainless steel or galvanized steel or formica or plywood as noted.

L. Electric Outlets and Switches: Indicated to be of adequate capacity with plates and housings of satin finish stainless steel or heavy chrome plate.

M. Plumbing and Electrical Conduit: All plumbing pipe and fittings, refrigeration tubing, electrical conduit, etc. furnished by kitchen equipment contractor shall be stainless steel, chrome or nickel covered except where brass or other type fittings are specified.

1-08 Utilites

Electric—110-208 volt 60 cycle; 3 phase motors ½ hp or over to be 208 volt 3 phase. Smaller than ½ hp to be 110 volt, single phase.

1-09 Kitchen Equipment Contractor

To co-operate to the fullest extent with other crafts involved. It will be his responsibility to cut all holes necessary for piping, conduit, traps, etc., location of valves, controls and switches for convenient operation and to provide proper space for piping, etc., in fixtures so that piping will not interfere with the function of the fixtures.

1-10 Filed Joints

Only where specified.

Table A.1 Estimated Space Requirements for Paper Supplies

Item	No. to Case	Case Dimensions (Length-Width-Height)	Cubic Feet (Per Case)
Hot food containers			
8 oz squat	1000	$20\frac{3}{16} \times 16\frac{1}{4} \times 29\frac{9}{16}$	5.4
10 oz squat	500	$21\frac{15}{16} \times 9\frac{1}{16} \times 39\frac{5}{16}$	3.4
12 oz squat	500	$22\frac{1}{4} \times 9\frac{3}{16} \times 29\frac{3}{4}$	3.5
Freezing containers			
16 oz squat	500	$24\frac{1}{8} \times 9\frac{15}{16} \times 30$	4.2
16 oz squat lids	2000	$22\frac{1}{4} \times 11\frac{5}{8} \times 9\frac{1}{4}$	1.4
32 oz squat	500	$25\frac{1}{2} \times 20\frac{1}{2} \times 18\frac{15}{16}$	5.7
32 oz squat lids	2000	$23\frac{13}{16} \times 13\frac{1}{8} \times 9\frac{7}{8}$	1.8
Cold cups			
6 oz—2 piece	2500	$11\frac{1}{4} \times 14\frac{1}{4} \times 23\frac{1}{2}$	2.8
6 oz—Cone	5000	$17\frac{1}{4} \times 13\frac{7}{8} \times 20\frac{7}{8}$	2.9
5 oz—2 piece	2500	$13\frac{13}{16} \times 13\frac{13}{16} \times 15$	1.7
5 oz—Button Bottom	2500	$13\frac{13}{16} \times 13\frac{13}{16} \times 15$	1.7
5 oz—Cone	5000	$16\frac{5}{16} \times 13\frac{1}{8} \times 20\frac{5}{8}$	2.6
5 oz—Pleated	2500	$13\frac{13}{16} \times 13\frac{13}{16} \times 15\frac{5}{8}$	1.7
10 oz—2 piece	2500	$16\frac{7}{16} \times 16\frac{7}{16} \times 24\frac{1}{4}$	3.8
9 oz—2 piece	2500	$15\frac{13}{16} \times 15\frac{13}{16} \times 23\frac{15}{16}$	3.5
10 oz—Round Bottom	3000	$15\frac{7}{8} \times 12 \times 21\frac{3}{8}$	2.4
10 oz—Cone	3000	$15\frac{7}{8} \times 12 \times 21\frac{3}{8}$	2.4
Dessert dishes			
4 oz—Pleated	3000	$20\frac{1}{16} \times 16\frac{1}{8} \times 15\frac{7}{8}$	3.0
6 oz—Pleated	5000	$20\frac{1}{16} \times 20\frac{1}{16} \times 19\frac{5}{8}$	4.6
5 oz—2 piece	2500	$20\frac{1}{16} \times 16\frac{1}{16} \times 13\frac{1}{8}$	2.45
7 oz—2 piece	2500	$21\frac{1}{16} \times 16\frac{13}{16} \times 13\frac{7}{8}$	2.84
Portion cups			
No.			
050 ($\frac{1}{2}$ oz)	5000	$13\frac{5}{8} \times 7\frac{9}{16} \times 11\frac{3}{4}$	0.7
050S ($\frac{1}{2}$ oz) Squat	5000	$13\frac{5}{8} \times 9\frac{3}{4} \times 15\frac{1}{4}$	1.2
075S ($\frac{3}{4}$ oz) Squat	5000	$13\frac{5}{8} \times 11 \times 17\frac{1}{4}$	1.5
075 ($\frac{3}{4}$ oz)	5000	$13\frac{3}{4} \times 8\frac{1}{2} \times 13\frac{1}{4}$	0.9
100 (1 oz)	5000	$14 \times 9\frac{7}{16} \times 14\frac{3}{4}$	1.1
125 ($1\frac{1}{4}$ oz)	5000	$13\frac{7}{8} \times 10\frac{1}{4} \times 16$	1.3
200 (2 oz)	5000	$14 \times 11\frac{5}{16} \times 17\frac{3}{4}$	1.6
250 ($2\frac{1}{2}$ oz)	5000	$14\frac{1}{8} \times 11\frac{1}{4} \times 19\frac{1}{4}$	1.8
325 ($3\frac{1}{4}$ oz)	5000	$14\frac{1}{4} \times 13\frac{1}{2} \times 21$	2.3
400 (4 oz)	5000	$14\frac{3}{4} \times 14\frac{1}{4} \times 23$	2.8
550 ($5\frac{1}{2}$ oz)	5000	$16\frac{15}{16} \times 14\frac{3}{8} \times 26\frac{3}{4}$	3.8
Plates			
9 inch	1000	$20\frac{7}{8} \times 18\frac{3}{8} \times 9\frac{7}{8}$	2.2
8 inch	1000	$22\frac{3}{8} \times 16\frac{3}{8} \times 8\frac{7}{8}$	1.9
7 inch	1000	$22\frac{3}{8} \times 14\frac{5}{8} \times 8$	1.5
6 inch	1000	$19 \times 12 \times 6$	1.0

Appendix

References

1. Gilbert, Thomas and Marilyn B. Gilbert, *Thinking Metric*, John Wiley and Sons, Inc. New York, 1973.
   Chisholm, J. L., *Units of Weight and Measure, International (metric) and U.S. Customary*, National Bureau of Standards, U.S. Government Printing Office, Washington, D. C. 20402.
2. Institutions/Volume Feeding, 5 South Wabash Avenue, Chicago, July 15, 1974.
3. State of Washington Department of Health, *Directory of Licensed Nursing Homes*, Olympia, Wash., 1969.
4. Pederson, R. B., A. C. Avery, R. D. Richard, J. D. Osenton and H. H. Pope, *Increasing Productivity in Foodservice*, Cahners Books, Inc, Boston, 1973.
   McGuinness, W. J. and Stein, B., *Mechanical Equipment for Buildings*, 5th ed., John Wiley and Sons, New York, 1971.
5. Mundel, Marvin E., *Systematic Motion and Time Study*, Prentice-Hall, Englewood Cliffs, N. J., 1965.
6. Thomas, Orpha Mae Huffman, *A Scientific Basis of the Design of Institution of Institution Kitchens*, 1947. Doctoral thesis on file at Purdue University Library.
7. Williamson, B. J., "Tomorrows System—the Food Factory—Today," *Journal of The American Dietetic Association*, May 1975.
8. Knight, Gladys, Tourist and Resort Section, School of Hotel, Restaurant and Institution Management Michigan State University.
9. *Ordinance and Code Regulating Eating and Drinking Establishments*, Public Health Bulletin No. 280, U. S. Department Public Health Service, Washington, D. C.
10. Morehouse, Ward III, *The Christian Science Monitor*, July 16, 1975.
11. R_X Plan in Minimal Food Handling," *Institutions Magazine*, July 1972.
12. AP, P-I Staff, "Aluminum Wiring Hazard," *Seattle Post-Intelligencer*, August 9, 1975.

Bibliography

Advanced Learning Systems, Inc., "A New Approach to Management's Role in Back Safety," 25 E. Salem St., Hackensack, N.J.

American Gas Association, *Commercial Kitchens*, 605 3rd Ave., New York, 1962.

American Hospital Association and American Dietetic Association, *Hospital Food Service Manual*, American Hospital Association, Chicago, 1972.

American Institute of Baking, "Guidelines for Selecting a Consultant in Food Service Equipment and Layout," "Frozen Bread Dough" and "Freezing Unbaked Fruit Pies," 400 E. Ontario St., Chicago, n.d.

American Machine and Foundry Co., 261 Madison Ave., New York.

Anetsberger Brothers, Inc., "Proofing Manual," Northbrook, Ill., n.d.

Avery, A., "Simplified Food Service Layout," *Cornell Quarterly*, Ithaca, N.Y., May 1968.

Bangs, O. Ernest, "The New Food Service Operation" and "Ideas are Food for Thought in Food Service Planning," Duke Manufacturing Co., 2305 N. Broadway, St. Louis, 1966 and 1967.

Blaker, G., and Donaldson, B. "Systems Analysis, a Tool for Management," *American Dietetics Association Journal*, August 1969, p. 121.

Blickman, Bruce, "Good Kitchen Design Aids Efficient Service," *Club Operations*, March 1964.

Cleveland Range Co., Division of Alco Foodservice Equipment Co., 1331 E. 179 St., Cleveland.

Colbourne Manufacturing Co., "Bench Dough Roller," 157 W. Division St., Chicago, n.d.

Committee on Food Equipment Standards, National Science Foundation, various publications and manuals, Ann Arbor, Mich., various dates.

Cooking for Profit, Gas Magazine, Inc., 1202 S. Park St., Madison, Wis.: "Now One-Pan Cooking Saves Labor," June 1975; "The New Breed of Grease Filters," June 1975; "Ice Machines and You," April 1975; "Steam Cooking," February 1975; "Pressure Fryers," September 1975 and October 1974; "Proper Care of Fats and Fry Kettles," December 1974 and September 1975; "A Griddle Designed for High Productivity," August 1974; "Trash Compactors," July 1974; and "Equipment Checklist for Energy Conservation," April 1974.

Crescent Metal Products/Crown X, 12711 Taft Ave., Cleveland.

Dana, Arthur W., *Kitchen Planning for Quantity Food Service*, Harper & Bros., New York, 1949.

Detecto Scales, Inc., Catalog No. 556 and Series 1100, Brooklyn, N.Y., n.d.

Donovan, A. C., "Developing, Testing and Evaluating a Dishwashing Facility," *Hospitals*, June 16, 1968.

Dover Corporation/Groen Division, instruction manuals and booklets on steamjacketed kettles, 1900 Pratt Blvd., Elk Grove Village, Ill.

Dreyfuss, Henry, *Designing for People*, Simon & Schuster, New York, 1970.

Drive-In Management, Choosing Equipment Series, 1968–71, New York.

Duke Manufacturing Co., 2305 Broadway, St. Louis.

Eberhart-Mussay Import C., "Bun and Roll Divider and Moulder," West Chester, Pa., n.d.

Flambert, Richard, "Programming the Design of School Lunch Facilities," Duke Manufacturing Co., 2305 N. Broadway, St. Louis.

Flambert, Richard, and Neibert, W. D., "Engineering Requirements in Foodservice Planning," *Cornell Quarterly*, Ithaca, N.Y., May 1968.

Fletcher, Richard E., "Creative Ideas for Kitchen Planning," *Inplant Food Management*, 1964.

FMC Corporation/Food Processing Machinery Division, 103 E. Maple St., Hoopeston, Ill.

Folsom, Leroi A., *How To Master The Tools of Your Trade*, Dimensions Press, Gilford, Conn., 1965.

Fowler, S. F., West, B. B., and Shugart, G. S., *Food for Fifty*, John Wiley & Sons, New York, 1961.

French, T. E., and Vierck, C. J., *Engineering Drawing*, McGraw-Hill Book Co., New York, 1960.

Gardner, Jerry A., *Contract Foodservice/Vending*, Cahner Books, Boston, 1973.

General Electric Company, Owners Manuals, Commercial Equipment Department, Chicago Heights, Ill., n.d.

Globe Slicing Machine Co., "Specifications and Service Manual," Stamford, Conn., n.d.

Hall, Carl W., Farrall, A. W., and Rippen, G. L., *Encyclopedia of Food Engineering*, AVI Publishing Co., 250 E. State St., Westport, Conn., 1971.

Heinemeyer, J. M., and Ostenso, G. L., "Food Production Materials Handling," *American Dietetics Association Journal*, June 1968, p. 490.

Heldman, Dennis R., *Food Process Engineering*, AVI Publishing Co., 250 E. State St., Westport, Conn., 1975.

Hobart Co., instruction manuals for cutters, mixers, dishwashers, disposals, refrigerators, and scales, Troy, Ohio, n.d.

Holman, J. H., "Steam: Combating the Energy/Food Crunch," *School Food Service Journal*, Denver, January 1975.

Institutions/Volume Feeding, Cahners Publishing Co., 5 South Wabash Ave., Chicago, July 15, 1974.

Jopke, R. and J. Hass, "Contamination in Dishwashing Facilities," *Hospitals*, March 1970.

Jopke, R., J. Hass, and Ann Donovan, "Food Waste Disposers and Contamination," *Hospital Progress*, October 1969.

Jopke, R., B. Sorenson, J. Hass, and Ann Donovan, "Microbiological Contamination on Hospital Tableware," *Hospital Progress*, June 1970.

Kapala, C., and M. Merritt, "Methods of Removing Hard Water Scale," U.S. Dept. of Agriculture, Agr. Res. Service Technical Report 67-83-CM, Washington, D.C., 1967.

Kazarian, Edward A., *Food Service Facilities Planning*, AVI Publishing Co., Westport, Conn., 1975.

Kleinfeld, E., "Handling Kitchen Cleanup Problems," *Cornell Quarterly*, Ithaca, N.Y., May 1968.

Kotschevar, Lendal H., *Quantity Food Production*, 4th ed., Cahners Books, Boston, 1974; *Foodservice in Extended Care Facilities*, chap. 10, Cahners Books, Boston, 1973; *Management by Menu*, National Institute for the Foodservice Industry, 120 S. Riverside Plaza, Chicago, 1975; "Basic Factors in Foodservice Planning," *Cornell Quarterly*, Ithaca, N.Y., May 1968; "Principles for Selecting Food Service Equipment," Duke Manufacturing Co., 2305 N. Broadway, St. Louis, 1968.

Lincoln Manufacturing Co., 1111 N. Hadley Rd., Fort Wayne, Ind.

Litton Industries, 400 Shelard Plaza South, Minneapolis.

Longre, Karla, *Quantity Food Sanitation*, John Wiley & Sons, New York, 1968.

Market Forge, 35 Garvey St., Everett, Mass.

McClain, D. R., and Son, "Instruction and Suggestions for Care and Use of Rol-Sheeter," 4730 Durfee Ave., Pico Rivers, Calif., n.d.

McGraw Edison Co./Food Equipment Division, Washington St., Algonquin, Ill.

Merkel, James A., Basic Engineering Principles, AVI Publishing Co., 250 E. State St., Westport, Conn., 1974.

Michigan State University, "Improve Your Kitchen Storage," Extension Bulletin 365, East Lansing, 1966.

Modern Schools, Electrical Information Publications, 2132 Fordem Ave., Madison, Wis., "The Electric Convection Oven." November 1972; "Water Heating for the Food Service Kitchen," November 1973; "The Energy Misers," December 1973; "System Intelligence in the Food Service Kitchen," January 1974; "Summer Shutdown of The Foodservice Facilities," May 1974; and "Energy Watch" and "Energy Conservation Dictates Electric Heat," December 1975.

Montag, G. M., and Tamashunas, V. M., "Engineered Kitchen Layout Planning Design," American Dietetic Association Journal, August 1969.

Mundel, Marvin E., Motion and Time Study, 3rd ed., Prentice-Hall, Englewood Cliffs, N.J. 1960.

National Restaurant Association, "Energy Requirements for Meal Preparation," MRI Report 3889-D (R), Chicago, 1975.

National Restaurant Association, "OSHA Affects You—Disregard Will Bring Penalties," NRA News reprint, n.d.

Pinchard, C. P., "Automated Dishwashing," Cornell Quarterly, Ithaca, N.Y., May 1968.

Potter, Norman N., Food Service, AVI Publishing Co., Westport, Conn.

Richardson, Treva M., Sanitation for Foodservice Workers, Cahners Books, 89 Franklin St., Boston, 1974.

Sanstadt, Helen, "Wheels for Foodservice Systems," Cooking for Profit, 1202 S. Park St., Madison, Wis., March 1974.

School Food Service Journal, Denver.

Seco Co., "Seco Food Preparation and Service Equipment, St. Louis, P.O. Box 7116, n.d.

Seelye, Elwyn E., Design, 3rd ed., John Wiley & Sons, New York, 1960.

Sleeper, Harold R., Building Planning and Design Standards, John Wiley & Sons, New York, 1955.

Terrell, Margaret E., Large Quantity Recipes, J. B. Lippincott Co., Philadelphia, 1975.

Terrell, Margaret E., Professional Food Preparation, John Wiley & Sons, New York, 1971.

Thorner, M. E., Convenience and Fast Food Handbook, AVI Publishing Co., 250 E. State St., Westport, Conn., 1973.

Thorner, M. E. and Manning, P. B., Quality Control in Food Service, AVI Publishing Co., 250 E. State St., Westport, Conn., 1976.

Tresslar, Donald K., et al., Refrigeration and Refrigeration Equipment, Vol. 1, and *Freezing of Precooked and Prepared Foods,* Vol. 4, AVI Publishing Co., 250 E. State St., Westport, Conn., 1968.

Triplett, Earl D., "New Directions in Inplant Feeding," *Cornell Quarterly,* Ithaca, N.Y., May 1968.

Tucker, Gina, *The Science of Housekeeping,* 2nd ed., Cahners Books, Boston, 1973.

U.S. Dept. of Agriculture, "Evaluation of Dishwashing Systems," Agr. Res. Service Report No. 1003, Washington, D.C., 1973.

U.S. Dept. of Commerce, Small Business Administration, "Use of Templets and Scale Models in Plant Layouts," Washington, D.C., 1954.

U.S. Small Business Administration and Federal Energy Administration, "An Energy Handbook," U.S. Government Printing Office, Washington, D.C., 1975 (Stock No. 041-018-00052).

Van Egmond, Dorothy, *School Foodservice,* AVI Publishing Co., 250 E. State St., Westport, Conn., 1974.

Washington State Dept. of Health, Division of Public Health Engineering, "Food and Beverage Service Worker's Manual," Olympia, Wash., n.d.

Wells Commercial Sales Co., "How to Use and Care for Wells Electric Fry Kettles," South San Francisco, n.d.

West, B. B., Wood, Levelle, and Harger, Virginia, Food Service in Institutions, 4th ed., John Wiley & Sons, New York, 1968.

Wilkinson, Jule, *The Complete Book of Cooking Equipment, The Preparation Kitchen, The Components of Communication,* and *The Three C's of Atmosphere,* Cahners Books, Boston, 1972.

Williamson, Betty Jane, "Tomorrow's System, the Food Factory, Today," *American Dietetic Association Journal,* Chicago, 1974.

Wolf Range Co., "Owners Manual," 19600 S. Alameda St., Compton, Calif., n.d.

Index